THE LAW OF WAR

In 2015, the United States Department of Defense published its long-awaited *Law of War Manual*, making a significant statement on the position of the DoD on important military matters. While readers recognise the *Manual*'s legal and strategic importance, they may question whether particular statements of law are legally accurate or complete. This book offers a unique in-depth review of the complete *Manual*, including revisions, on a paragraph-by-paragraph, line-by-line and word-by-word basis. The authors offer their personal assessment of the DoD's declared view as to the law that regulates the conduct of warfare, a subject of unparalleled current importance. William H. Boothby and Wolff Heintschel von Heinegg offer a balanced, articulate and authoritative critique for readers perusing the *Manual* in whatever capacity.

William H. Boothby is an associate fellow at the Geneva Centre for Security Policy. A former Air Commodore, he retired as Deputy Director of Legal Services for the RAF in 2011.

Wolff Heintschel von Heinegg is the Chair of Public Law, in particular Public International Law, European Law and Foreign Constitutional Law, at the Europa-Universität Viadrina in Germany.

The Law of War

A DETAILED ASSESSMENT OF THE US DEPARTMENT OF DEFENSE LAW OF WAR MANUAL

WILLIAM H. BOOTHBY

WOLFF HEINTSCHEL VON HEINEGG

CAMBRIDGE
UNIVERSITY PRESS

CAMBRIDGE
UNIVERSITY PRESS

University Printing House, Cambridge CB2 8BS, United Kingdom

One Liberty Plaza, 20th Floor, New York, NY 10006, USA

477 Williamstown Road, Port Melbourne, VIC 3207, Australia

314–321, 3rd Floor, Plot 3, Splendor Forum, Jasola District Centre, New Delhi - 110025, India

79 Anson Road, #06–04/06, Singapore 079906

Cambridge University Press is part of the University of Cambridge.

It furthers the University's mission by disseminating knowledge in the pursuit of education, learning, and research at the highest international levels of excellence.

www.cambridge.org
Information on this title: www.cambridge.org/9781108427586
DOI: 10.1017/9781108639422

First published 2018

Printed in the United States of America by Sheridan Books, Inc.

A catalogue record for this publication is available from the British Library

Library of Congress Cataloging-in-Publication data
Names: Boothby, William H., author. | Heintschel von Heinegg, Wolff, author.
Title: The law of war : a detailed assessment of the US Department of Defense law of war manual / William H. Boothby, Wolff Heintschel von Heinegg.
Description: Cambridge, United Kingdom ; New York, NY, USA : Cambridge University Press, 2018. | Includes bibliographical references.
Identifiers: LCCN 2017058259 | ISBN 9781108427586 (hardback)
Subjects: LCSH: United States. Department of Defense. Office of General Counsel. Department of Defense law of war manual. | War (International law). | Military law – United States. | International and municipal law – United States.
Classification: LCC KZ6385 .B664 2018 | DDC 343.73/01 – DC23
LC record available at https://lccn.loc.gov/2017058259

ISBN 978-1-108-42758-6 Hardback

To Monika and Katja

Contents

Preface *page* xix
List of Abbreviations xxi

Introduction 1
The Readership 4

1 **General Background** 6
Purpose and Scope of the *Manual* 6
Use of Footnotes, Sources, Cross-References and Signals in the *Manual* 7
Definition of the Law of War 10
Object and Nature of War 13
War as a Legal Concept 14
Law of War Distinguished from Certain Topics 16
Treaties 19
Customary International Law 21
Subsidiary Means of Determining International Law 23
Legal Force of the Law of War 24
Jus ad Bellum 26

2 **Principles** 30
Military Necessity 31
Humanity 34
Proportionality 36
Distinction 37
Honor 39

3 **Application of the Law of War** 42

Situations to Which the Law of War Applies 45
Status of the Parties and the Law of War 45
When *Jus in Bello* Rules Apply 48
Relationship between *Jus in Bello* and *Jus ad Bellum* 53
Reciprocity and Law of War Rules 55
Applying Rules by Analogy 57
End of Hostilities and the Application of the Law of War 58
Law of War Duties also Applicable in Peace 59

4 **Classes of Persons** 60

The Armed Forces and the Civilian Population 61
Lawful Combatants and Unprivileged Belligerents 63
Rights, Duties and Liabilities of Combatants 65
Armed Forces of a State 68
Other Militia and Volunteer Corps 71
Levee en Masse 76
Rights, Duties and Liabilities of Civilians 77
Military Medical and Religious Personnel 78
Rights, Duties and Liabilities of Military Medical and Religious Personnel 80
Authorized Staff of Voluntary Aid Societies 81
Staff of a Recognized Aid Society of a Neutral Country 81
Auxiliary Medical Personnel 82
Personnel Engaged in Duties Relating to the Protection of Cultural Property 83
Persons Authorized to Accompany the Armed Forces 85
Crews of Merchant Marine Vessels or Civil Aircraft 89
Spies, Saboteurs and Other Persons Engaged in Similar Acts Behind Enemy Lines 90
Private Persons Who Engage in Hostilities 93
Rights, Duties and Liabilities of Unprivileged Belligerents 96
Children 98
Mercenaries 100
API Provisions on Civil Defense Personnel 101
Law Enforcement Officers 101
Journalists 102
Delegates or Representatives of the Protecting Powers 103

ICRC and Other Impartial Humanitarian Organizations 104
Determining the Status of Detainees in Cases of Doubt 105

5 **The Conduct of Hostilities** 107

Overview of the Rules for the Protection of Civilians 108
Assessing Information under the Law of War 112
Rules on Conducting Assaults, Bombardments and Other Attacks 113
Discrimination in Conducting Attacks and Military Objectives 118
Combatants 123
Civilians Taking a Direct Part in Hostilities 127
Persons Placed *Hors de Combat* 129
Feasible Precautions in Conducting Attacks to Reduce the Risk of Harm to Protected Persons and Objects 131
Proportionality in Conducting Attacks 134
Attacks on Works, Facilities or Installations Containing Dangerous Forces 138
Feasible Precautions to Reduce the Risk of Harm to Protected Persons and Objects by the Party Subject to Attack 139
Undefended Cities, Towns and Villages 140
Prohibition on Using Protected Persons and Objects to Shield, Favor or Impede Military Operations 142
Seizure and Destruction of Enemy Property 143
Protection of Cultural Property during Hostilities 146
Sieges and Encircled Areas 149
Starvation 151
Overview of Good Faith, Perfidy and Ruses 152
Treachery or Perfidy Used to Kill or Wound 152
Use of Enemy Flags, Insignia and Military Uniforms 153
Improper Use of Certain Signs 154
Ruses of War and Other Lawful Deceptions 154
Non-Forcible Means and Methods of Warfare 155
Prohibition Against Compelling Enemy Nationals to Take Part in the Operations of War Directed Against Their Own Country 156

6 **Weapons** 157

Introduction 157
DoD Policy of Reviewing the Legality of Weapons 158

Prohibited Weapons and Lawful Weapons 159
Weapons Calculated to Cause Superfluous Injury 164
Inherently Indiscriminate Weapons 165
Poison, Poisoned Weapons, Poisonous Gases and Other Chemical Weapons 166
Biological Weapons 168
Certain Environmental Modification Techniques 168
Weapons Injuring by Fragments Not Detectable by X-Rays 169
Landmines, Booby-Traps and Other Devices 169
Cluster Munitions 173
Incendiary Weapons 174
Laser Weapons 176
Riot Control Agents 177
Herbicides 178
Nuclear Weapons 178
Explosive Ordnance 179
Explosive Remnants of War 179

7 **Wounded, Sick, Shipwrecked, Dead and the Medical Services** 181

Introduction 181
Application of the Protections 182
Respect for and Protection of Wounded, Sick and Shipwrecked 183
Search, Collection and Affirmative Protection 185
Humane Treatment and Care of Enemy Military Wounded, Sick and Shipwrecked in the Power of a Party to the Conflict 186
Accountability Information from Enemy Wounded, Sick, Shipwrecked and Dead 188
Treatment and Handling of Enemy Military Dead 188
Respect and Protection of Categories of Medical and Religious Personnel 189
Captured Medical and Religious Personnel 190
Military Medical Units and Facilities 192
Ground Transports of the Wounded and Sick, or of Medical Equipment 194
Hospital Ships, Sick Bays in Warships and Coastal Rescue Craft 194
Military Medical Aircraft 196
Display of the Distinctive Emblem to Facilitate Identification 197

Protection of Civilians Who Are Wounded, Sick, Infirm or Expectant Mothers 198
Civilian Hospitals and Their Personnel 199
Land and Sea Civilian Hospital Convoys 199
Civilian Medical Aircraft 199
API Provisions on the Wounded, Sick and Shipwrecked 200

8 **Detention – Overview and Baseline Rules** 201

Introduction 201
Humane Treatment of Detainees 204
Security Measures 205
Interrogation 206
Medical Care 207
Criminal Procedure and Punishment 211
Concluding Remarks 212

9 **Prisoners of War** 213

Introduction 213
General Principles Applicable to the Treatment of PWs 213
Entitlement to PW Status 214
National-Level GPW Implementation 216
Humane Treatment and Basic Protections for PWs 216
Security Measures with Respect to PWs 218
Interrogation of PWs 219
Evacuation from Combat Areas 220
Transit or Screening Facilities 221
General Conditions in PW Camps – Location, Safety, Hygiene and Living Conditions 221
Segregation of PWs 223
Food, Water, Tobacco and Clothing for PWs 223
Medical Attention for Interned PWs 224
Intellectual, Physical and Recreational Activities 225
Canteens for PWs 226
Financial Resources of PWs 226
PW Labor 227
PW Correspondence 229
Private Legal Matters of PWs 230
Internal Discipline of PW Camps 231
PW Requests, Complaints and Reports about Conditions of Captivity 232

PW Representatives 233
PW Escapes 234
General Principles Applicable to PW Discipline 235
Disciplinary Proceedings and Punishment 236
Judicial Proceedings and Punishment 237
Transfer of PWs from the PW Camp 239
Transfer of PWs to the Custody of Another Detaining Power 239
National Accounting of the Detention of PWs 239
Role of the Protecting Power in GPW 240
Access to PWs by the Protecting Powers, ICRC and Relief Organizations 240
Death of PWs 241
Exchanges and Other Release and Repatriation of PWs during Hostilities 242
Direct Repatriation and Accommodation in Neutral Countries during Hostilities 242
Release and Repatriation after Hostilities 243
PWs Whom the Detaining Power Is Not Required to Repatriate 244
Procedure on Release and Repatriation after Hostilities 245
Concluding Remarks 245

10 **Civilians in the Hands of a Party to the Conflict** 247

Introduction 247
National-Level GC Implementation Measures 248
Protected Person Status 248
Derogation for Security Reasons 250
Humane Treatment and Other Basic Protections for Protected Persons 251
Measures of Control and Security 252
General Treatment of Protected Persons in a Belligerent's Own Territory 254
Expulsion from Areas within a Belligerent's Home Territory and Departure and Transfers of Protected Persons from a Belligerent's Home Territory 255
Internment 256
Segregation of Internees 258
Safety, Hygiene and Living Conditions in Places of Internment 258
Canteens for Internees 259
Food, Water, Tobacco and Clothing for Internees 259

Medical Attention for Internees 260
Religious Exercise by Internees 261
Intellectual, Physical and Recreational Activities 261
Internee Labor 262
Internees' Articles of Personal Use 262
Financial Resources of Internees 262
Administration of Places of Internment and Discipline 263
Internee Petitions, Complaints and Reports about Conditions of Internment 264
Internee Committees 265
Internee Correspondence and Relief Shipments 265
Private Legal Matters of Internees 267
Internees and Visits of Families and Friends 268
Internee Escapes 268
General Provisions Applicable to Both Judicial and Disciplinary Sanctions Regarding Internees 268
Disciplinary Proceedings and Punishment 269
Judicial Proceedings Regarding Protected Persons in Occupied Territory or Internees in a Belligerent's Home Territory 270
Transfers of Internees from the Place of Internment 271
National Accounting for Protected Persons in Its Power 272
Role of the Protecting Power in GC 274
Access to Internees by Protecting Powers, ICRC and Other Relief Organizations 274
Death of Internees 275
Release, Return, Repatriation of Internees after the Close of Hostilities 276
Concluding Remarks 276

11 **Military Occupation** 278
Introduction 278
When Military Occupation Law Applies 282
End of Occupation and Duration of GC Obligations 284
Legal Position of the Occupying Power 285
Duty of the Occupying Power to Ensure Public Order and Safety 285
Protection of the Population of an Occupied Territory 286
Authority of the Occupying Power over Inhabitants 287
Administration of Occupied Territory 288

Local Law and Legislation 288
Ordinary Courts in Occupied Territory 289
Criminal Law in Occupied Territory 290
Movement of Persons in Occupied Territory 292
Protection of Children in Occupied Territory 293
Food and Medical Supplies for the Civilian Population 294
Public Health and Hygiene 294
Spiritual Assistance 295
Relief Efforts and Consignments 295
Enemy Property during Occupation 297
Protection of Cultural Property during Occupation 300
Labor of Protected Persons in Occupied Territory 301
Judges and Other Public Officials 303
Public Finances and Taxes 303
Other Economic Regulation of Occupied Territory 305
Concluding Remarks 306

12 Non-Hostile Relations between Belligerents 308

Introduction 308
Principle of Good Faith in Non-Hostile Relations 309
Methods of Communication between Belligerents 309
The White Flag of Truce to Initiate Negotiations 310
Rules for Parlementaires 311
Military Passports, Safe-Conducts and Safeguards 313
Cartels 314
Capitulations – Negotiated Instruments of Surrender 314
Capitulations – Subjects Usually Addressed 316
Capitulations – Violations and Denunciation 317
Armistices and Other Cease-Fire Agreements 318
Armistices – Subjects Usually Addressed 319
Armistices – Violations and Denunciation 321
UN Security Council Cease-Fires 322

13 Naval Warfare 323

Law of the Sea 324
Overview of Rules for Naval Engagements 326
Fundamentals of the Law of Naval Warfare 326
Other Aspects Dealt With in Section 13.3 328
Enemy Warships 331
Enemy Merchant Vessels 332

Enemy Vessels Exempt from Capture or Destruction 336
Submarine Warfare 338
Belligerent Control of the Immediate Area of Naval Operations 339
Maritime and Airspace Zones – Exclusion, War, Operational, Warning and Safety 341
Blockade 345
Naval Mines 347
Torpedoes 350
Deception by Naval Forces, Including the Use of Enemy or Neutral Flags 350
Concluding Remarks 351

14 **Air and Space Warfare** 352
Introduction 352
Legal Boundaries of Airspace 354
Aircraft Status 357
Status of Aircrew on Military Aircraft 359
Measures Short of Attack – Interception, Diversion and Capture 361
Belligerent Control of Aviation in the Immediate Vicinity of Hostilities 362
Airspace Zones 363
Attacks Against Military Objectives in the Air 363
Air Attacks Against Military Objectives on the Ground 366
International Law and Warfare in Outer Space 368
Concluding Remarks 370

15 **The Law of Neutrality** 371
Introduction 373
Application of the Law of Neutrality 375
Overview of the Law of Neutrality's Framework of Reciprocal Rights and Duties 377
Remedies for Violations of Neutrality Law 377
Prohibition on the Use of Neutral Territory as a Base of Operations 378
Neutral Persons 379
Neutral Waters 380
Passage of Belligerent Vessels and Aircraft through International Straits and Archipelagic Sea Lanes 382
Sections 15.9 and 15.10 382

Right of Angary 383
Neutral Commerce and Carriage of Contraband 383
Belligerent Right of Visit and Search of Merchant Vessels and Civil Aircraft 386
Acquisition of Enemy Character by Neutral-Flagged Merchant Vessels and Neutral-Marked Civil Aircraft 387
Capture of Neutral Vessels and Aircraft 388
Sections 15.16, 15.17 and 15.18 388
Concluding Remarks 389

16 **Cyber Operations** 390
Introduction 390
Application of the Law of War to Cyber Operations 391
Cyber Operations and the *Jus ad Bellum* 393
Cyber Operations and the Law of Neutrality 395
Cyber Operations and *Jus in Bello* 396
Legal Review of Weapons That Employ Cyber Capabilities 400
Concluding Remarks 400

17 **Non-International Armed Conflict** 401
Introduction 402
Application of International Law to Non-International Armed Conflicts 404
Sections 17.3 and 17.4 406
Principle of Distinction 407
Respect and Humane Treatment of Persons Taking no Active Part in Hostilities in Non-International Armed Conflict 409
Rules on Conducting Attacks in Non-International Armed Conflict 410
Sections 17.8 and 17.9 410
Protection of Children in Non-International Armed Conflict 412
Protection of Cultural Property in Non-International Armed Conflict 412
Use of Captured or Surrendered Enemy Personnel in Non-International Armed Conflict 412
Weapons in Non-International Armed Conflict 413
Protection of the Wounded, Sick, Shipwrecked and Dead 413
Medical and Religious Personnel and Medical Transports 414
Display of the Distinctive Emblem 415
Detention in Non-International Armed Conflict 415

Non-Intervention and Neutral Duties in Non-International Armed Conflict 416
Concluding Remarks 418

18 **Implementation and Enforcement of the Law of War** 419
Introduction 419
Prudential Reasons Supporting the Implementation and Enforcement of the Law of War 421
Duties of Individual Members of the Armed Forces 421
Sections 18.4 to 18.8 421
States' Obligations with Respect to Violations of the Law of War 422
State Responses to Violations of the Law of War by the Enemy 422
War Crimes 425
Concluding Remarks 426

19 **Documentary Appendix – Notes on Treaties and Other Relevant Documents** 428
Lists of Treaties and Other Documents 428
The Lieber Code 430
1856 Paris Declaration Respecting Maritime Law 430
1864 GWS 431
1868 St Petersburg Declaration 431
1899 and 1907 Hague Declarations on Weapons 431
1899 Hague Convention II and 1907 Hague Convention IV and Their Annexed Regulations 432
1923 Hague Air and Radio Rules 433
1925 Geneva Gas and Bacteriological Protocol 434
1929 Geneva Conventions 434
1930 London Treaty for the Limitation and Reduction of Naval Armament and 1936 London Protocol 434
1935 Roerich Pact 435
1949 Geneva Conventions 435
1954 Hague Cultural Property Convention 437
Vienna Convention on the Law of Treaties 437
Biological Weapons Convention 437
Additional Protocols to the 1949 Geneva Conventions 438
CCW, CCW Amended Article 1 and CCW Protocols 440

Chemical Weapons Convention 442
Rome Statute 443
1999 UN Secretary General's Bulletin for UN Forces 443
2005 ICRC Study on Customary International Humanitarian Law 444

20 **Post-Publication Amendments** 445

May 2016 Amendments 445
December 2016 Amendments 449

Preface

The preparation of a commentary on a national military manual is a somewhat unique undertaking. That very aspect would cause most observers to ask why indeed would one wish to do it. When the *Manual* in question extends to approximately 1200 pages and addresses the law of war in very considerable detail, the question takes on added poignancy. Part at least of the answer lies in the fact that this is a military manual issued by no lesser an authority than the United States Department of Defense (US DoD). And yet the document does not describe itself as expressing the US national position on law of war matters. Indeed, the document makes it abundantly clear that the views expressed are those of the Department and may not necessarily be those of the US Government as a whole.

So, the reader starts to wonder what the legal status of the text is, and this very legal ambiguity was another factor that caused the present authors to contemplate writing this book. As we started to look at the different chapters, we noticed that there was much to praise but, also, elements that merited criticism. The idea started to form that a systematic, paragraph-by-paragraph commentary addressing all of the substantive provisions of the *Law of War Manual* and of the amendment documents should be prepared. There was never any doubt that this would be a considerable task.

It would be tempting to divide such a task among a significant number of authors, each of them taking on the review of a substantial but not overburdensome number of pages of text. That would not, however, have led to what the present authors were trying to produce, namely a text that reflects the kind of consistency of approach only normally to be achieved by means of very limited authorship. At the same time, what we wanted to write was an accessible, well-written commentary with which we both agreed, i.e. essentially a joint view. In short, there could be no shortcut. Both of us had to go through the whole text in some detail, and the pages that follow are the result of that significant endeavour.

The aim throughout has been to give a balanced appraisal of what the *Manual* has to say. While criticism is offered where it is considered to be merited, praise is also forthcoming. Indeed, the most praiseworthy aspect of all is the very decision to publish a manual on this most complex, politically sensitive and controversial subject at all. That the Defense Department of a State of the military stature and global significance of the United States has been prepared to do so does much to take international understanding of the law of war forwards, and is thus to be regarded as an inherently good thing.

Undoubtedly there are improvements that could be made to the current text, and we have made suggestions throughout the book of where we consider such improvements might profitably be considered. The issuing of the two amendment sheets discussed at Chapter 20 indicates that the DoD is not averse to making such amendments where they are thought to be appropriate. It is to be hoped that such amendments will continue to appear from time to time and that the *Manual*'s legal accuracy will accordingly be further enhanced as the months and years go by.

More particularly, we hope that this book will be of assistance to users of the *Manual*, whether they be military lawyers, policy staffs, academics, military thinkers or others with an interest in the Law of War in its many contexts. Those users, whoever they may be, should understand that in the following pages we have put forward our joint personal views on the matters discussed. We do not seek to persuade as to the correctness of our view. Indeed, we positively invite readers to form their own opinions on the various points that we make. We do not speak for any government or institution, and we explicitly recognise that the purpose of the *Manual* is to set forth the Department's position, not that of commenting academics.

Nevertheless, we hope that what we have written will be found useful.

Finally, we would like to thank our wives for their patient understanding during the very many hours of study while the book was being written. We also thank Cambridge University Press for agreeing to publish, and all at CUP who have handled the publication process with such efficiency. Finally, we thank you, the reader, for taking the time to consider our thoughts on these matters.

Bill Boothby
Wolff Heintschel von Heinegg

Abbreviations

Amended Mines Protocol – Amended Protocol on Prohibitions or Restrictions on the Use of Mines, Booby-Traps and Other Devices (1996)

AMW *Manual* – *HPCR Manual on International Law Applicable to Air and Missile Warfare*, Program on Humanitarian Policy and Conflict Research at Harvard University (2010)

API – Protocol Additional to the Geneva Conventions of 12 August 1949 and Relating to the Protection of Victims of International Armed Conflicts, Geneva (8 June 1977)

API Commentary – Y Sandoz, C Swinarski and B Zimmermann (eds), *Commentary on the Protocol Additional to the Geneva Conventions of 12 August 1949, and Relating to the Protection of Victims of International Armed Conflicts*, International Committee of the Red Cross (1987)

APII – Protocol Additional to the Geneva Conventions of 12 August 1949 and Relating to the Protection of Victims of Non-International Armed Conflicts, Geneva (8 June 1977)

APIII – Protocol Additional to the Geneva Conventions of 12 August 1949, and Relating to the Adoption of an Additional Distinctive Emblem (Protocol III) (8 December 2005)

CCW – Convention on Prohibitions or Restrictions on the Use of Certain Conventional Weapons which May be Deemed to be Excessively Injurious or to Have Indiscriminate Effects (1980)

CWC – Convention on the Prohibition of the Development, Production, Stockpiling and Use of Chemical Weapons, and on their Destruction, Paris (13 January 1993)

DoD Manual – *United States Department of Defense Law of War Manual*, United States Department of Defense (June 2015)

FM 27–10 (Change No. 1 1976) – *US Department of the Army Field Manual: The Law of Land Warfare*, United States Department of the Army (1956), as amended by Change No. 1, dated 15 July 1976
GC – Geneva Convention Relative to the Protection of Civilian Persons in Time of War of August 12, 1949
German Manual – Bundesministerium der Verteidigung Joint Service Regulation (ZDv) 15/2, *Law of Armed Conflict Manual* (May 2013)
GPW – Geneva Convention Relative to the Treatment of Prisoners of War of August 12, 1949
GPW Commentary – J S Pictet (ed.), *Commentary III on Geneva Convention Relative to the Treatment of Prisoners of War*, International Committee of the Red Cross (1960)
GWS – Geneva Convention for the Amelioration of the Condition of the Wounded and Sick in Armed Forces in the Field of August 12, 1949
GWS Commentary – J S Pictet (ed.), *Commentary I on Geneva Convention for the Amelioration of the Condition of the Wounded and Sick in Armed Forces in the Field*, International Committee of the Red Cross (1952)
GWS-Sea – Geneva Convention for the Amelioration of the Condition of Wounded, Sick and Shipwrecked Members of Armed Forces at Sea of August 12, 1949
GWS-Sea Commentary – J S Pictet (ed.), *Commentary II on Geneva Convention for the Amelioration of the Condition of Wounded, Sick and Shipwrecked Members of Armed Forces at Sea*, International Committee of the Red Cross (1960)
Hague Regulations – Regulations Respecting the Laws and Customs of War on Land Annexed to Hague Convention IV (18 October 1907)
ICJ – International Court of Justice
ICRC – International Committee of the Red Cross
ICRC Customary Law Study – J-M Henckaerts and L Doswald-Beck, *Customary International Humanitarian Law, vol. 1: Rules*, International Committee of the Red Cross (2005)
ICRC Commentary GCI – ICRC, *Commentary on the First Geneva Convention*. Cambridge: Cambridge University Press (2016)
ILC – International Law Commission
Lieber Code – Instructions for the Government of Armies of the United States in the Field, US Army General Order No. 100 (24 April 1863)
NWP 1–14M – *The US Commander's Handbook on the Law of Naval Operations*, NWP 1–14M, Department of the Navy, Department of Homeland Security (July 2007)

PW – prisoner of war

San Remo Manual – Louise Doswald-Beck (ed.), *San Remo Manual on International Law Applicable to Armed Conflicts at Sea*, Cambridge: Cambridge University Press (1995)

Tallinn Manual – *Tallinn Manual on the International Law Applicable to Cyber Warfare* (2013)

Tallinn Manual 2.0 – M N Schmitt (ed.), *Tallinn Manual 2.0 on the International Law Applicable to Cyber Operations*, Cambridge: Cambridge University Press (2017)

UK Manual – *The Manual of the Law of Armed Conflict*, UK Ministry of Defence (2004)

1958 *UK Manual* – *The Law of War on Land*, being Part III of the *Manual of Military Law* (1958)

United States Air Force Publication – Department of the Air Force, *Air Force Operations and The Law*, 85, 3rd edn. The Judge Advocate General's School (2014)

UNCLOS – 1982 UN Convention on the Law of the Sea, UN Doc. A/CONF.62/121 of 10 December 1982, 1833 UNTS 396

Introduction

In July 2015, the United States Department of Defense (US DoD) published its long-awaited *Law of War Manual*[1] ('the *Manual*' or '*DoD Manual*'). It is well known that there had been earlier drafts of this publication, on which the present authors had been invited to comment. Indeed, one of the present authors was a peer reviewer of that earlier text and attended a meeting in Charlottesville, Virginia at a time when its publication appeared to be imminent. There followed, however, a period in which that text was the subject of reassessment and amendment, and it is a revised text that has now been published under the authority of the US DoD.

The United States is to be congratulated on its decision to publish a manual on this topic, a decision that cannot have been easy. There is always the fear that by publishing an authoritative text on such a subject, the State may be tying itself to legal interpretations that may prove inconvenient or damaging in light of future, unpredictable circumstances. It must also always be borne in mind that the legal interpretations offered by a State of the stature of the United States are likely to be employed by its adversaries and potential adversaries at times of their choosing and to potentially adverse effect. The operational and rhetorical flexibility that silence may appear to afford may for some officials be an attractive argument against publication. That a country like the United States is prepared to set forth its appreciation of what the law requires, as well as its basis for reaching those conclusions, advances the law itself and gives the US a departmentally approved benchmark against which personnel can be trained in this most important body of law.

On any reckoning, the publication of a military manual on the law of war by the United States is an event of the most considerable significance. Such

[1] *United States Department of Defense Law of War Manual*, Office of the General Counsel, Department of Defense (12 June 2015).

a document would normally be regarded as having the status of State practice – or at least of *opinio juris* – and as representing the United States' official interpretation of the vitally important matters of law therein addressed. The *Manual* does, however, state that the collective view of all departments of the US Government is not necessarily reflected in its pages, and the reader is therefore somewhat left to speculate as to its actual status and claimed authority in international law.

While there has already been discussion of elements of the *Manual*, particularly among United States commentators, there has not yet been a comprehensive published assessment of its contents by commentators from outside the US. This volume is intended to provide that assessment. The present authors have addressed all 1200 pages of the *Manual*, including the two amendments published in 2016, on a paragraph-by-paragraph, line-by-line and sometimes word-by-word basis in order to set forth their personal appreciations. It must be stressed that those personal appreciations are based exclusively on the published *Manual* text and do not draw in any sense on versions of the proposed *Manual* previously seen by them.

In order to achieve this detailed assessment of the *Manual*'s provisions, sufficient of the propositions given in the *Manual* have been reported in the book's text in order that the specific comments will make sense to the reader. Where statements in the *Manual* are considered to be legally correct, this is made clear. By the same token, where criticism seems to be merited, the present authors do not shy away from offering that critique. Throughout, the aim is to offer a fair and balanced assessment with the purpose of assisting the reader to form his or her own view as to the various propositions of law that are being addressed.

In order to assist the reader as far as possible, the *Manual*'s chapter numbering system is replicated in this volume, with the *Manual*'s roman numeral chapter numbers having their equivalents in this volume in Arabic numerals. The *Manual*'s system of section headings is also replicated, and all comments are made referring to the relevant paragraph numbers in the *Manual*, with the specific text that is considered to merit comment being quoted where doing so is considered necessary to ensure clarity of understanding. As the intended purpose of this book is to achieve a detailed assessment of the *Manual* that reflects the personal views of the present authors, the reader will find the present text generally to be lightly footnoted.

When considering the criticisms offered in this book, it should be appreciated, as the present authors do, that to prepare and publish a military manual on the present scale is a very considerable task involving much scholarship. The present authors congratulate the United States for its decision to publish and hope that their comments will be accepted in the spirit in which they are offered, namely as constructive suggestions.

As even the most casual observer of the *Manual* will note, it is a very lengthy document in which there is extensive reference to authorities in the very numerous footnotes accompanying its formal text. The present authors largely focus their comments on the main text, but refer where necessary to specific footnotes in order to develop relevant points of critique. A couple of comments should, however, be made here about the footnotes in the *Manual*. They often cite internal memoranda, academic articles, speeches of officials, documents transmitting treaties for consideration of ratification and similar items. It is often unclear whether these texts are being cited as purported legal justification for the proposition of law being advanced in the *Manual*'s main text, or whether they are intended merely to explain the US view of a particular matter.

It should therefore be recalled that it is the general practice of States supported by *opinio juris*, not the practice of an individual State, that must be demonstrated to establish a customary law rule. Moreover, and as a matter of international law, if the United States has become a party to a particular treaty, its obligations under that treaty fall to be determined by reference to the normal rules of treaty interpretation, taking into account any relevant statements of interpretation or reservations that the United States may have submitted, and that have not been rejected by the other States party. If the interpretation argued in the *Manual* is not supportable by applying these rules of interpretation, then the interpretation becomes legally incorrect and no amount of correspondence between or from senior US Government officials will alter the obligations binding on the United States at the level of international law.

Another point of a general nature concerns the importance of identifying which rules are customary in nature, being something that the *Manual* all too frequently avoids doing. A reader of the *Manual* will be concerned to know which rules are recognised by the US as customary not just because they will be the rules by which the US considers itself bound under customary law. That reader will also wish to know by which rules the US considers an adverse party, or for that matter some other State or armed group operating with the United States, to be bound, as this will identify the behaviours to be expected from that State or group, and will be the basis for arguing that there has, or has not, been a legal breach. While the *Manual* occasionally identifies certain rules that are considered to be customary, it does not address the matter consistently. The present authors consider that this is a matter that requires rectification.

Comment may be made in the following chapters because the relevant passage is of particular legal value, because it raises issues of legal interest, because it contains assertions that can be questioned or for some other reason. It should not be assumed that the present authors necessarily agree with all of the statements to which no reference is made in the present text. Indeed, the challenge in preparing a book of this nature is to limit sufficiently the scope of the paragraphs that are considered and of the comments that are made with a view to achieving an overall text that is of manageable length, that discusses the issues with the required clarity and that, it is hoped, adds value. That is what is being attempted here. When considering any words of criticism, however, the reader should bear in mind, as the present authors have done, the difficult task that the writing of a manual of this sort represents, and should appreciate the scholarship and hard work that it represents accordingly.

It is appreciated that two sets of amendments have been published by the DoD since the appearance of the original *Manual* text. There were two possible approaches to that situation. The first would have been to prepare the present volume on the basis of the *Manual* text as most recently amended. However, the present authors could not know when further amendments might appear. Moreover, the *Manual* did originally appear and was published in its June 2015 version, on which it is therefore legitimate to comment. Chapters 1 to 19 of this book therefore address the corresponding chapters of the *Manual* in their original, June 2015 form, and Chapter 20 considers the amendment lists that have appeared as at the date of publication. The present authors plan to publish comment on any amendment lists that appear after the publication of the present book by electronic means to be agreed with the publishers.

The present authors stress that this book reflects their personal views on the various topics addressed. They do not seek to represent the view of any Government, State or institution, and they absolutely accept that other observers may well have differing views. Their purpose in publishing the present text is not necessarily to seek to persuade the reader of the correctness of their own view as such, but rather, where appropriate, to place before the reader their own appreciation based on their own collective experience.

THE READERSHIP

The target audience for this book consists, essentially, of the users of the *DoD Manual* itself. Military lawyers, commanders, specialists in military doctrine, military staff colleges, ministry and military policy staffs, academics and all those with an interest and/or professional involvement in the conduct of military and other operations associated with conflict will all benefit from this book. The book has, however, also been carefully written as a self-standing text so that its readers will gain a thorough view of the law of war as a whole. The title has therefore been carefully chosen in order to reflect this.

1

General Background

PURPOSE AND SCOPE OF THE MANUAL

It is logical that the *Manual* should start with an explanation of the purpose that it is designed to fulfil and of the matters that it is designed to address. That purpose is stated to be to provide information as to the law of war to DoD personnel responsible for implementing that law and for executing military operations.[1] There then follows an explanation that the *Manual* represents the views of the DoD of the United States but that that department reserves the right to alter its interpretation of the law. Moreover, the *Manual* does not necessarily reflect the views of other departments of State, nor of the United States as such. This is significant because military manuals of this kind are frequently regarded as having the status of State practice, and thus as contributing to the development of customary law.[2] As this paragraph makes it clear that the relevant text lacks cross-departmental and national endorsement, its provisions cannot necessarily be regarded as reflecting the official US view, which is unfortunate. The best that it seems one can say is that the positions expressed in the *Manual* may reflect the position of the United States and will reflect the position of its DoD subject to any amendment of the text that may be published.

There follows a paragraph that explains that the *Manual* is not intended to create any right or benefit enforceable at law. While that may be the case, the statements in the *Manual* may provide valuable evidence as to what the DoD considers the correct legal position to be, which might of course be a relevant factor in legal proceedings.

[1] *DoD Manual*, paragraph 1.1.1.

[2] Consider I Brownlie, *Principles of International Law*, 7th edn. Oxford: Oxford University Press (2008), 6; see also Y Dinstein, Customary International Law and Treaties, 322 *Hague Recueil des Cours* 272 (2006).

Paragraph 1.1.2 notes that the *Manual* does not definitively explain all law of war issues, its focus being on the *jus in bello*, which it describes as 'law relating to the conduct of hostilities and the protection of war victims'. It would have been better had it been made clear that the subject of the *Manual* goes rather wider than this, covering that part of international law that applies to situations of armed conflict. The paragraph makes the point that the *Manual* seeks to address the law that applies to the US, including treaties to which the US is party and applicable customary international law. The reader of the *Manual* will find that sometimes an assertion is made as to the customary status of a particular rule or of a treaty provision, but that frequently no such assertion is made. The effect is that the reader is often left in doubt as to whether the DoD does or does not consider a particular rule to be customary. Quite properly, the paragraph makes the point that although the views of other States may be referenced in the *Manual*, it is no purpose of the *Manual* to describe other States' views.

It is on balance useful that at this early stage in the text, the *Manual* reminds legal practitioners of the need to consider appropriate primary legal and policy sources, e.g. treaties, judicial decisions, regulations etc., and to apply the law to the facts. The *Manual* does of course state the law as at the date of publication, i.e. June 2015, so self-evidently any statement in it must be understood in the light of any relevant subsequent legal developments.

USE OF FOOTNOTES, SOURCES, CROSS-REFERENCES AND SIGNALS IN THE MANUAL

Paragraph 1.2.1 explains that footnotes are used in the *Manual* to provide sources, to cross-refer to other sections of the *Manual* and to clarify, elaborate on and support the main text. The paragraph then states that an effort has been made to avoid discussion in the footnotes of propositions that differ from those in the main text because of the understandable preference that the main text should contain as much information as possible, e.g. as to exceptions to the application of a general rule, and because such tangential discussion in the footnotes would have made the maintenance of consistency across the *Manual* more difficult. Hence, the paragraph explains that tangential discussion has been avoided in favour of cross-references to sections in which a topic is dealt with in greater detail.

The present authors consider this to be a worthy methodology, although there are points of criticism that can legitimately be levelled at the footnoting of some chapters. To take an example, Chapters VII, IX and X quote verbatim, or virtually verbatim, extracts from e.g. relevant Geneva Conventions in the main text and then repeat those verbatim quotes in each footnote. Such a practice expands an already very lengthy text with little or no evident added value.

Distributed throughout the *Manual*, there are also numerous footnotes which arguably do not constitute sources of the relevant proposition of law, but which consist e.g. of internal US administrative documents, extracts from articles written by US officials, extracts from training course materials and extracts from what appears to the reader to be private or at best semi-official correspondence. While such references may serve to demonstrate that the cited individuals have in the past expressed a view that matches that taken in the *Manual* text, they are unlikely to contribute significantly to demonstrating the provenance of the stated position as a matter of international law. There are occasions when these domestic, US-based extracts are cited in evident preference to an obvious, authoritative source of international law, sometimes but not always contained in Additional Protocol I.[3] Moreover, Additional Protocol II, to which the US is not a party,[4] is frequently quoted without any explanation of why it is considered to reflect the US position on the law relating to non-international armed conflicts. Perhaps these are aspects that would benefit from further reflection if additional amendments to the text are considered.

In general, the authors of the present book have focused their attention on the main *Manual* text. While footnotes are referred to in this book on numerous occasions, it is the main *Manual* text that is regarded as setting forth the DoD's position on the relevant matters. Paragraph 1.2.2 comments sensibly on the use to which the footnotes should be put, and in paragraph 1.2.2.1 the basis on which a number of the sources cited in the *Manual* were selected is explained. There can be no doubt that the *Manual*'s footnotes contain an invaluable wealth of information which does indeed serve to explain the propositions in the *Manual* and to deepen the understanding of its readers. The eminence of the authors of many of those sources speaks for itself.

In the closing section of the paragraph, the understandable point is made that citation of a source should not be taken to mean that the source represents the DoD position, nor as endorsement of the source. Some parts of the cited source may represent the DoD position while other parts may not, which is

3 Protocol Additional to the Geneva Conventions of 12 August 1949 and Relating to the Protection of Victims of International Armed Conflicts, Geneva (8 June 1977) (API).

4 Protocol Additional to the Geneva Conventions of 12 August 1949 and Relating to the Protection of Victims of Non-International Armed Conflicts, Geneva (8 June 1977) (APII) and source www.icrc.org, reviewed on 5 September 2017.

one reason why the discussion in this book focuses on the main *Manual* text, which incontrovertibly represents the DoD's stated view.

One particularly pleasing feature of the *Manual* is its citation of what paragraph 1.2.2.2 refers to as 'older sources'. The paragraph indicates that these older sources are used because they are particularly influential, or to show the origin of a legal proposition or to show that a rule or formulation has a long history. This does not of course mean, as the paragraph acknowledges, that every aspect of older sources such as the Lieber Code[5] remains current law. In this context, the paragraph notes by way of example that the 1958 *UK Manual*[6] was highly influential and had eminent authorship, but that more recent UK manuals more accurately reflect the UK's current position on the law of war, particularly in light of its 1998 ratification of API.

Paragraph 1.2.2.4 explains that US Government and DoD policies and regulations are sometimes cited as evidence of past practice but notes that the prime focus of the *Manual* is on the law. Moreover, the evident point is made that the fact that certain policies etc. are mentioned should not blind the reader to the fact that other policies etc. on that or related matters likely exist, while sometimes superseded policies etc. may be cited to demonstrate past practice.

The paragraph then argues that policies etc. often exceed the requirements of applicable law and that the mere citation of a policy etc. in the *Manual* 'should not be understood to reflect the view that the policy or regulation's requirements have been promulgated out of a sense of legal obligation for the purposes of assessing customary international law or otherwise intending to reflect legal requirements'. This is a rather wordy caveat which might leave the reader wondering what indeed the purpose in citing such policies or regulations might be in a manual designed to explain the law of war. The answer would seem to be to demonstrate the approach to a topic independently of the law on the matter and on the basis that the relevant legal position is to be found in the main *Manual* text. The authors of the present book find this to be another good reason for focusing the present commentary on that main *Manual* text.

Citation forms, the use of cross-references and the use of signals are respectively explained in paragraphs 1.2.2.5, 1.2.3 and 1.2.4 and do not require discussion here.

5 Instructions for the Government of Armies of the United States in the Field, US Army General Order No. 100 (24 April 1863).

6 *The Law of War on Land, being Part III of the Manual of Military Law* (1958).

DEFINITION OF THE LAW OF WAR

Section 1.3 describes the law of war for the purposes of the *Manual* as 'that part of international law that regulates the resort to armed force; the conduct of hostilities and the protection of war victims in both international and non-international armed conflict; belligerent occupation; and the relationships between belligerent, neutral and non-belligerent States'. This approach rather masks an important difference between the *jus in bello* and the *jus ad bellum*, namely that the former applies equally both to aggressors and to victims of aggression. The section explains that for the purposes of the *Manual*, the law of war comprises treaties and customary law applicable to the United States. The only other issue that one would take with all this relates to the title. It is, one would suggest, no exaggeration to state that most of the rest of the world refers to the 'law of armed conflict'. Ever since the adoption of the Geneva Conventions of 1949, with their Common Article 2, it is the existence of a situation of armed conflict that triggers the application of this body of law. However, the name by which the topic is known is, one would suggest, the least important of matters, and it is the substantive rules and adherence to them that should have and retain the greatest attention.

Paragraph 1.3.1.1 notes that other interpretations of the law of war omit the law on the resort to the use of force, but the adopted definition has the merit of being comprehensive. Paragraph 1.3.1.2 sensibly seems to suggest that the law of war and the law of armed conflict are synonymous and notes that while international humanitarian law is often used to convey the same meaning, in some usages it has a narrower meaning, e.g. omitting the law of neutrality.

In discussing the law of war's relationship with other bodies of law, paragraph 1.3.2 notes that such issues are often resolved by regarding the law of war as the *lex specialis* governing armed conflict, but comments that much may depend on the specific legal rule in question. The *Manual* then considers in specific paragraphs, discussed later, particular approaches to determining how the law of war relates to other bodies of law. Overall, the position is taken that although there are these different approaches and although the ultimate outcome may depend on the specific rule and context, 'the law of war, as the *lex specialis* of armed conflict, is the controlling body of law with regard to the conduct of hostilities and the protection of war victims'. This assertion would have been unproblematic had a narrower concept than 'the law of war' been employed. It is, however, somewhat difficult to appreciate how the *lex specialis* rule can properly be applied to the *Manual*'s notion of the law of war, comprising as it does both *jus in bello* and *jus ad bellum*.

Paragraph 1.3.2.1 looks further at the law of war as *lex specialis*, noting correctly that the *lex specialis* principle generally means that the special rule overrides the general law because it takes better account of the particular features of the relevant context bringing about a more equitable result more in line with the intent of those who made the law. The paragraph reinforces the *lex specialis* approach by noting that the law of war has been developed with special consideration of the circumstances of war, that it constitutes the only authoritative rules of action between hostile armies and that law of war treaties have been seen as *lex specialis* in relation to treaties providing peacetime norms on the same subjects.

Addressing the second aspect of this relationship, paragraph 1.3.2.2 suggests that other laws should be so construed as to avoid conflict with the law of war. Underlying this approach, as the paragraph correctly observes, is the appreciation that the law of war is established and distinct from the principles of law that generally apply in peacetime and that new international law is not interpreted as amending it absent a clear indication to the contrary. An interesting example in reverse is cited, namely the provisions of GC[7] that exclude certain classes of individual from the notion of 'protected person' and that thus avoid conflict between GC and the law relating to diplomatic representation.[8] Noting the provision of the Chicago Convention 1944 that explicitly specifies that it does not affect the freedom of action of States during armed conflict,[9] the paragraph states the position that 'infringements on the law of war through international agreements that primarily address situations other than armed conflict are not to be presumed', a proposition with which the present authors agree.

In the final element of the paragraph, the relationship between international law and potentially conflicting provisions of US domestic law is discussed, a matter upon which the present authors are content not to comment.

The third aspect of the relationship between the law of war and other bodies of law, namely using the law of war to interpret general standards in their application to armed conflict, is discussed in paragraph 1.3.2.3. The *Manual* cites the use of the law of war to inform domestic law authorisations for the conduct of military operations and the use of the law of war to interpret during periods of armed conflict due regard obligations in Article 3(d) of the Chicago Convention 1944 (for military aircraft regulations to have due regard to the

7 Geneva Convention Relative to the Protection of Civilian Persons in Time of War of August 12, 1949.

8 GC, Article 4(2) is the relevant provision.

9 Convention on International Civil Aviation (Chicago Convention) 1944, Article 89.

safety of civil aircraft) and in the law of the sea. The fourth and final aspect of the relationship between the law of war and other bodies of law concerns the incorporation into the law of war of concepts from other bodies of law. Cited examples include the incorporation of the civil law notion of usufruct into occupation law and the inclusion by reference within Common Article 3 of fundamental judicial guarantees.[10]

Paragraph 1.3.3 explains, again correctly, that the law of war is in some respects prohibitive and in other respects permissive. The law on the conduct of hostilities is rightly given as an example of law that is essentially prohibitive rather than permissive, in the sense that it prohibits certain actions when conducting hostilities. The paragraph suggests a philosophical basis for this approach, namely that States are independent entities with freedom to act and that treaty provisions and customary rules reflect restrictions on that freedom that they have accepted. The next sentence then suggests, '[t]hus, the authority to take actions under the law of war would be viewed as emanating from the State's rights as a sovereign entity rather than from any particular instrument of international law'. Perhaps the words 'under the law of war' could usefully be deleted from this sentence, as neither the authority nor the action derives from the law of war. Subject to that relatively minor adjustment, the sentiments underlying the paragraph are to be welcomed, particularly given recent rather misguided jurisprudence suggesting that absent specific treaty-based provision, States lack legal authority to, for example, detain during non-international armed conflicts.[11]

An interesting additional aspect to the prohibitive nature of the law on the conduct of hostilities arises from the next part of the paragraph, where it is observed that this prohibitive approach is consistent with the equal application of the *jus in bello* to, as the *Manual* puts it, defenders and aggressors alike, or, as it might more accurately be put, to those representing States that have and have not breached the *jus ad bellum* alike. However, while the one may be consistent with the other, there is no legal association between them. Specifically, the principle of equal application is neither evidence of, nor the basis for, the prohibitive terms in which much of the law of war is expressed, and it would have been helpful had this been made clear when the relationship between the *jus ad bellum* and the *jus in bello* was discussed. As the

[10] Article 3(1)(d) common to the Geneva Conventions, 1949.

[11] See proceedings before the UK Court of Appeal in *Mohammed* v. *Secretary of State for Defence, Rahmatullah and others* v. *MOD and FCO [2015] EWCA Civ* 843, but see the UK Supreme Court Judgments, *Abd Ali Hameed Al-Waheed (Appellant)* v. *Ministry of Defence (Respondent)* and *Serdar Mohammed (Respondent)* v. *Ministry of Defence (Appellant)* [2017] UKSC 2, pp. 56–7, paragraph 111.

paragraph points out in its concluding sentence, however, in the absence of any explicit rule of the law of war dealing with a matter that does not necessarily mean that an action will be lawful, the general principles of the law of war will still need to be adhered to.

Paragraph 1.3.3.2 draws attention to a few permissive aspects of the law of war, examples being action justified by military necessity and the exercise of authority over occupied territory by the Occupying Power.

Paragraph 1.3.4 then lists some purposes of the law of war. The first of these is 'protecting combatants, non-combatants and civilians from unnecessary suffering', a formulation which is not entirely accurate. Non-combatants consist of medical and religious personnel, who are entitled to special protection from attack, and to whom the unnecessary suffering principle should therefore be irrelevant.[12] Likewise, civilians must not be made the object of attack, and the incidental injury of civilians must, to the extent feasible, be minimised. The unnecessary suffering principle is of greatest relevance to combatants and to civilians taking a direct part in the hostilities, and these are the two classes of individual who should, it is felt, be referred to in the cited piece of text.

The remaining stated purposes of the law of war are: to provide certain fundamental protections for persons who fall into enemy hands, including PWs, civilians, military wounded, sick and shipwrecked; to facilitate the restoration of peace; to assist military commanders to ensure the disciplined and efficient use of military force; and to preserve the professionalism and humanity of combatants. At a practical level, one might add as purposes: the protection of the civilian population from the worst effects of war; and limiting the scope of the conflict e.g. by application of the law of neutrality.

OBJECT AND NATURE OF WAR

One can only agree with section 1.4 that understanding the object and nature of war is important to understanding and applying the law of war. Paragraph 1.4.1 explains the object of war in terms of securing the submission of the enemy as quickly and efficiently as possible. Importantly, military defeat of the enemy is intended to advance political objectives, and as paragraph 1.4.1 rightly points out, even where the political objectives are limited, the object of the war remains to achieve the submission of the enemy as quickly and efficiently as possible. One way of looking at the matter, therefore, which is not specifically discussed in the *Manual*'s main text, is that war is resorted to after political and diplomatic processes have been found to be, or are assessed to

12 The protection of medical and religious personnel from attack is discussed in Chapter 7.

be, unsuitable, and is essentially an indirect way of achieving, as a last resort, political goals through the employment and expenditure of military methods and resources.

Paragraph 1.4.1 states that '[t]he object of war informs the principle of military necessity', from which the reader will deduce that military necessity is directly linked to achieving the military defeat of the enemy. The nature of war, on the other hand, is described in paragraph 1.4.2 as a violent clash of interests characterised by the use of force. The paragraph emphasises violence as an essential ingredient which renders suffering as the unfortunate, tragic but unavoidable consequence of war. The paragraph then identifies Hague and Geneva law and the principle of humanity as seeking to reduce consequent but unnecessary suffering and destruction.

The limited and uncertain nature of the information available during warfare, the chaotic nature of combat and the attempts by each side to deceive the other, often lawfully, add a vital additional aspect to the picture of contemporary conflict.[13]

The section as a whole is therefore setting out some essentially incontrovertible propositions which give a useful conceptual background to the discussion in the rest of the *Manual* of the substantive principles and rules of the law of war. It is against the realities of the character of modern conflict, after all, that any assessment of the practicability of particular law of war rules must of necessity be based.

WAR AS A LEGAL CONCEPT

The decision of the authors of the *Manual* to adopt the term 'Law of War' renders it vitally important that the reader understands what is, and respectively is not, to be included in the notion of 'war'. For clarification of that matter, the reader should turn to section 1.5. Noting that the word is sometimes used as a legal concept and that its precise meaning is likely to be context-dependent, the section refers to war as 'a condition in which a State is prosecuting its rights by military force, usually against another State'. Perhaps it would be better to refer to 'policy objectives' rather than 'rights', given that the concept of war needs to be understood as also encompassing activities in which a State has no belief in the legal rectitude of what it is doing. So, when paragraph 1.5.1 talks about war as the use of force to vindicate a State's rights under international law, the same objections of under-inclusivity arise.

The paragraph does, however, make the important and valid point that the legal concept of war applies more broadly than the mere employment of force

[13] *DoD Manual*, paragraph 1.4.2.2.

or commission of acts of violence. Perhaps the most authoritative definition of war, to which the *Manual* does not here refer, is that given by Oppenheim, namely that war is 'the contention between two or more States, through their armed forces, for the purpose of overpowering each other, and imposing such conditions of peace as the victor pleases'.[14] War was therefore a concept inextricably linked to the involvement of States on opposing sides to the conflict. The observation therefore, towards the end of paragraph 1.5.1, that 'certain law of war rules apply to non-international armed conflicts' may, in the context of the immediately preceding sentence, cause some readers to gain the mistaken impression that non-international armed conflicts are some subspecies of 'war'. That would be wrong. They are not, simply because at most one State is involved in non-international armed conflicts, whereas the concept of war has the involvement of two or more States on opposing sides at its core. The final sentence of paragraph 1.5.1 then adds, after the reference to non-international armed conflicts, '(such as intra-State conflicts or conflicts between a State and a non-State armed group)'. This is liable to cause the reader further confusion. Non-international armed conflicts are 'intra-State conflicts'. It is not that the latter is an example of the former; rather, it is that the two expressions are two ways of referring to the same thing. Second, conflicts between a State and a non-State armed group are not an alternative to intra-State conflicts, they are a form of intra-State conflict. Third, no mention is made here of conflicts between armed groups within a State, which constitute one of the two forms of non-international armed conflict.

Paragraph 1.5.2 refers again to the varying interpretations of the meaning of 'war', 'armed conflict' and 'hostilities' in both domestic and international law. In domestic US law, the differing interpretations are stated to depend on the context in which the terms are used. Noting that Congress has the constitutional power to declare war, the paragraph continues: 'Thus, "war" might be interpreted to determine whether a military operation constitutes "war" in this sense', a sentence whose meaning is at best somewhat opaque. Certain other contexts for the use of force in US domestic law are then cited.

In the context of international law, the paragraph argues that a state of 'war' can affect what obligations a State that is not involved has under the law of neutrality. Again, the precise intended meaning is not clear. If the sentence is intended to imply that different rules of neutrality arise depending on whether a conflict between States is termed a 'war', an 'armed conflict' or 'hostilities', no authority for this proposition is cited, and the present authors are not aware of such a justification. Of course, if the intended distinction is between 'war'

[14] L Oppenheim, *International Law: A Treatise, vol. II: Disputes, War and Neutrality*, 4th edn. Harlow: Longman Green Co. (1926), 115.

in the sense of a conflict between States and an armed conflict that is non-international in character, neutrality does not apply to the latter, but it is not clear that that is what is meant. However, and most importantly, the paragraph explains that the terms 'war' and 'armed conflict' are used to describe when the *jus in bello* applies. So, from the perspective of the application of *jus in bello*, the reader must remember that in the *Manual* the three terms are being used interchangeably.

LAW OF WAR DISTINGUISHED FROM CERTAIN TOPICS

The *Manual* at this point positions its notion of the 'law of war' in relation to other relevant bodies of law, and does this by considering each such related body of law in turn.

Paragraph 1.6.1 correctly recognises that the law of war is a substantial part, but not the totality, of operational law. Operational law comprises domestic foreign and international law relating to the activities of military forces across the conflict spectrum. As the paragraph rightly states, it involves various disciplines, including military justice, administrative and civil law, legal assistance, the handling of claims, procurement law, national security law, fiscal law and the law of war. The mix of required disciplines will inevitably vary as between States, but the list given in the *Manual* accurately represents the diverse skills required.

Paragraph 1.6.2 tackles the topic of arms control, which it interprets as comprising various efforts to reduce numbers, types, performance characteristics, proliferation, testing or other characteristics of certain categories of weapon. It takes the form of bilateral and multilateral treaties, non-binding political agreements and unilateral statements of intention or policy. The paragraph notes the link between arms control and non-proliferation, disarmament and associated confidence-building measures. The capacity for arms control to overlap with the law of war in certain treaties is noted, with Protocol IV to the Conventional Weapons Convention (CCW) and the Chemical Weapons Convention (CWC), both discussed in Chapter VI of the *Manual* and in Chapter 6 of the present book, being correctly cited as examples of such treaties.

Human rights treaties are referred to in paragraph 1.6.3 as addressing primarily the obligations of governments with respect to the rights of individuals, including their own nationals. By way of example, the paragraph cites the requirements to refrain from subjecting individuals to arbitrary detention, to arbitrary deprivation of life and to cruel, inhuman or degrading treatment or punishment. The paragraph notes that human rights treaties 'have been described as primarily applicable to the relationship between a state and individuals in peacetime', a formulation which leaves the reader unclear whether this is a description that the authors of the *Manual* embrace or reject. The present authors suggest that the description is accurate. The power to derogate from certain provisions contained in some human rights treaties is then mentioned. The paragraph closes by making the valid points that law of war treaties are chiefly concerned with the relationship with nationals of the enemy State and that they do not permit of derogation. The point could also have been made that human rights law treaties do not contemplate targeting on the basis of membership of a class, such as combatant, a concept that is critical to the effective conduct of hostilities and that is recognised in, indeed central to, the principle of distinction, that cardinal and intransgressible principle of the law of war.

Paragraph 1.6.3.1 acknowledges that the rules of the law of war and of human rights law may in some circumstances 'appear to' conflict, and that such conflicts may be resolved by the principle that the law of war is the *lex specialis* in periods of armed conflict 'and, as such, is the controlling body of law with regard to the conduct of hostilities and the protection of war victims'. It is good to see that position, and the principle, being expressed with clarity.

Citing as an example the right to challenge the lawfulness of an arrest under Article 9 of the International Covenant on Civil and Political Rights (ICCPR) and the apparent conflict with the authority under the law of war to detain persons without criminal charge or judicial process, the *Manual* notes the US position that Article 9 does not affect a State's authorities under the law of war; the paragraph specifies that these include 'a State's authority in both international and non-international armed conflicts to detain enemy combatants until the end of the hostilities'.[15] The paragraph should, however, have distinguished between international and non-international armed conflicts. In relation to the latter, there are no provisions corresponding to GPW,[16] and there is no explicit authority under the *lex scripta* of the law of war to detain persons. The paragraph then notes that some international courts or commissions have interpreted human rights provisions by reference to the law of war as *lex specialis* when assessing armed-conflict situations, and the associated footnote cites some useful examples.[17] The next element of the paragraph acknowledges, however, that human rights treaties would have a controlling

[15] *DoD Manual*, paragraph 1.6.3.1, second element. It is vitally important to recall the US understanding of the word 'combatant', as to which see section 5.8 of the *Manual* and the corresponding discussion in Chapter 5 of the present book.

[16] Geneva Convention Relative to the Treatment of Prisoners of War of August 12, 1949.

[17] *DoD Manual*, footnote 93 on page 23.

effect in relation to matters that are within their scope of application and that are not addressed by the law of war, and cites the example of voting rights at elections.

Paragraph 1.6.3.2 notes that other States, including potential coalition partners, may have different views as to the applicability of human rights treaties, either due to differing interpretations of the legal position or by virtue of participation in different human rights treaties. It is explicitly noted that the European Court of Human Rights and certain States have interpreted certain provisions of the European Convention on Human Rights as applicable to military forces operating abroad during occupation. The reader will appreciate that the jurisprudence of the European Court has recently taken matters rather further than this,[18] and it is suggested that this aspect of the paragraph may need updating. It is also worthy of note that there are arguments to be considered that decisions in one human rights forum, for example the European Court, may have the capacity to influence interpretations under other human rights instruments.

Noting that the US is a party to the ICCPR, paragraph 1.6.3.3 points to the obligations of a State under the Covenant with respect to persons within its territory and subject to its jurisdiction. The US position is then stated in terms: 'The United States has long interpreted the ICCPR not to apply abroad.' The paragraph explains that the reference in the ICCPR to 'within its territory' was proposed by the US delegate 'specifically to ensure that a State Party's obligations would not apply to persons outside its territory'.

Paragraph 1.6.3.4 addresses the Convention against Torture, to which the US is a State party. Noting that the Convention was not intended to supersede the prohibitions of torture in the Geneva Conventions, their Additional Protocols and in customary law, the paragraph nevertheless points out that the Convention against Torture continues to apply when a State is engaged in an armed conflict such that a state of war could not justify a State's torture of individuals. The paragraph also expresses the view that the obligations under the treaty that apply to a State party in any territory under its jurisdiction also extend to certain areas beyond the sovereign territory of the State party and specifically to all places that the State party controls as a governmental authority. In an associated footnote, a public acknowledgement made on 12 November 2014 by the acting legal adviser at the US Department of State to the effect that the US currently exercised such control at the US Naval Station at Guantanamo Bay, Cuba, is cited.

18 Consider, for example, the case of *Jaloud* v. *the Netherlands*, case 47708/08, ECtHR Grand Chamber, Judgment, 20 November 2014 and associated cases.

Paragraph 1.6.4 makes brief reference to the *just war tradition*, noting that this tradition describes customs, ethical teaching and moral codes developed over the centuries by military thinkers and philosophers to seek moral justifications of and limitations to war. Arguing that the just war tradition provides part of the philosophical foundation for the modern law of war, the paragraph suggests that the tradition remains relevant for the employment of US military forces and for war-fighting. There are however some aspects of the tradition which are fundamentally at odds with the whole approach embodied in the law of war. For example, the law of war principle that the *jus ad bellum* and the *jus in bello* are separate bodies of law and that the latter applies equally between the parties to the conflict irrespective of whether they breached or complied with the former is not necessarily consistent with aspects of the just war tradition.

Paragraph 1.6.5 cites the definition of *rules of engagement*[19] (ROE) as 'directives issued by competent military authority that delineate the circumstances and limitations under which United States forces will initiate and/or continue combat engagement with other forces encountered'. This would seem to be a rather narrow understanding of rules of engagement, which may, depending on the circumstances, regulate e.g. wider aspects of the use of force, military posture etc. Pointing out that ROE are used by States to tailor the rules for the use of military force to the circumstances of a military operation, the paragraph notes that the rules reflect legal, policy and operational considerations and are consistent with the international law and law of war obligations of the United States. The vital point made in the paragraph is that ROE may restrict action that would otherwise be lawful under international law but may not permit action that would breach international law.

Paragraph 1.6.6 then refers to the *Code of Conduct for US Armed Forces*, which constitutes a moral guide to govern the conduct of US armed forces in resisting capture and if they fall into enemy hands.

TREATIES

Section 1.7 gives the widely accepted definition of treaties as international agreements between States in written form and governed by international law, points out that treaties bind under international law the States that are parties to them, notes that the US publishes on an annual basis lists of the treaties and other international agreements that are in force for the US and points

[19] The quoted language is taken from Joint Publication 1–04, entitled Legal Support to Military Operations, GL-3, dated 17 August 2011.

out that various terms may be used in the titles to treaties. The constitutional requirement in the US as set forth in paragraph 1.7.1.1 is stated to be that the treaty must receive the advice and consent of the Senate before US ratification of or accession to the treaty can take place. Mention is then made of certain executive agreements that would not be classed as treaties for these purposes but that would constitute treaties under international law.

Paragraph 1.7.2 then mentions the essentials in relation to reservations to treaties, noting that a State may limit the application of a provision in a treaty by making reservations to it provided that the treaty text does not prohibit reservations and provided that the reservation(s) made is/are compatible with the object and purpose of the treaty. The CWC, discussed in Chapter VI of the *Manual* and in Chapter 6 of this book, is rightly cited as an example of a treaty that prohibits reservations. Interestingly, no mention is made here of statements of interpretation falling short of reservations and in which a State may set forth its understanding of the meanings that it gives to particular expressions or provisions in the treaty. Perhaps a suitably succinct mention of such statements is called for, not least because States participating in treaties that prohibit reservations may nevertheless clarify their interpretation of specific terms provided that the legal effect of the relevant provision is not thereby altered.

Paragraph 1.7.3 notes that States may under certain circumstances[20] withdraw from a treaty, that certain law of war and arms-control treaties specify the terms on which States may withdraw from the relevant treaty and that even if States do withdraw from a law of war treaty, they remain bound by customary international law principles and rules.

Curiously, paragraph 1.7.4 discusses when subsequent practice of States can be taken into account in interpreting a treaty but omits to provide the basic rule as to interpretation. For ease of reference, that basic rule is given in Article 31 of the Vienna Convention on the Law of Treaties as follows: 'A treaty shall be interpreted in good faith in accordance with the ordinary meaning to be given to the terms of the treaty in their context and in the light of its object and purpose.'[21] The elements that constitute the context for these purposes are specified in Article 31(2) as including the text, preamble (if any), annexes, certain related agreements among all the parties to the treaty and certain instruments made by one or more parties in connection with the conclusion of the treaty. Other matters that must be taken into account, in addition to the context, include the subsequent practice referred to in paragraph 1.7.4.

[20] See further Vienna Convention on the Law of Treaties, 1969, Article 54.

[21] Vienna Convention on the Law of Treaties, 1969, Article 31(1).

Perhaps this paragraph could usefully be expanded to deal with the matters discussed here. Certainly, the existing paragraph is right when it asserts that subsequent practice may be important when it amounts to objective evidence of the understanding of the parties as to the meaning of the treaty.[22] Self-evidently, and as paragraph 1.7.5 mentions, a State may pass domestic implementing legislation associated with its participation in a treaty, and the contents of that legislation may show the State's interpretation of the terms of a treaty.

CUSTOMARY INTERNATIONAL LAW

Customary international law is nicely defined by section 1.8 as resulting from a 'general and consistent practice of States that is followed by them from a sense of legal obligation (*opiniojuris*)'. The paragraph then, after accepting that customary international law is generally binding on all States, correctly asserts: 'States that have been persistent objectors to a customary international law rule during its development are not bound by that rule.'[23] The section could usefully add that States whose interests are specially affected may prevent the emergence of a rule of customary international law e.g. by their contrary practice. In such a circumstance, it would not be necessary for such a State to become a persistent objector. The *Manual* is right to express the view that assessing whether a customary rule of international law has developed may be a difficult task. It would not, however, be right to imply that such a conclusion is unachievable, and perhaps that is something that could usefully be said here also.

Paragraph 1.8.1 correctly takes the position that treaties may or may not reflect customary law, or may be based on customary law while not precisely reflecting it. The *Manual* suggests, probably fairly, the API rules as to combatant status as examples of treaty rules that are not customary in nature. The paragraph makes the important point that where a treaty reflects a customary rule, the respective treaty and customary rules have separate identities. The reader's understanding of that point might be assisted if the explanatory sentence were to state something along the lines of: 'When a treaty rule has customary law status, the treaty and customary law rules remain distinct, so if the treaty provision does not apply to the relevant circumstances, the distinct customary law rule is likely to be applicable.' This only arises, of course, if the

[22] The use of encrypted communications in hospital ships and the GWS-Sea's related provisions are discussed at paragraph 7.12.2.7 and constitute a useful example here.

[23] For a concurring, highly authoritative view, see I Brownlie, *Principles of Public International Law*, 7th edn. Oxford: Oxford University Press (2008), 11.

customary law and treaty rules accurately replicate one another, which as the paragraph observes, is not always the case.

Paragraph 1.8.2 looks at the requirement for a general and consistent practice of States to support a purported customary rule and correctly identifies four factors to consider when evaluating a purported customary rule. First, is State practice sufficiently dense and consistent to meet the requirement that it be 'extensive and virtually uniform'? Second, the analysis of State practice should include an assessment of actual operational practice of States during armed conflict. Acknowledging the importance of manuals and other official statements, the *Manual* emphasises that 'they cannot replace a meaningful assessment of operational State practice'. Third, paragraph 1.8.2.3 mentions that States that have a distinctive history of participation in the relevant matter, frequently referred to as 'specially affected States', must support the purported rule, citing as an example of a specially affected State the United Kingdom in relation to the law of the sea. A related, good point is made that States either with a wealth of experience or that have had the opportunity to develop well-considered military doctrine 'may be expected to have contributed a greater quantity and quality of State practice relevant to the law of war than States that have not'. All States, in this sense, do not rank equally.

Fourth, paragraph 1.8.2.4 points out, again correctly, that evidence of contrary practice must be considered in determining whether a rule of customary international law exists.

Paragraph 1.8.3 deals with the vital ingredient of *opinio juris*, drawing the distinction between conduct animated by a sense of legal obligation and conduct that merely reflects the policies or practical interests of States. *Opinio juris* cannot be inferred from conduct, nor can it be assumed to exist on the mere basis of a consistent absence of a particular activity. The *Manual* explains that the consistent absence of attacks using nuclear weapons does not imply *opinio juris* in favour of a prohibition. Paragraph 1.8.3.1 acknowledges that finding evidence of *opinio juris* may be difficult and cautions, justifiably, against inferring it from treaty provision, noting that references in military manuals may merely reflect treaty obligations or policy. Curiously, *opinio juris* may be found in the very official statements of States to which reference is made in paragraph 1.8.2.2.

It is interesting that in paragraph 1.8.4 there is the third explicit reference to the importance of the persistent objector rule as excluding the application of a customary rule to a State that has persistently objected to it during its development. Reading this section, one is struck by the considerable and evident importance that the United States attaches to the rules relating to specially affected States and to persistent objection.

SUBSIDIARY MEANS OF DETERMINING INTERNATIONAL LAW

Following the lead of Article 38(1)(d) of the Statute of the International Court of Justice (ICJ), section 1.9 notes judicial decisions and teachings of the most highly qualified publicists as being subsidiary means of determining the existence of rules of international law. The section continues: 'These means are subsidiary in the sense that they do not, in themselves, constitute sources of treaty or customary international law.' The sentence is seeking to express a correct thought, but somehow fails. It would be more accurate to say that the recognised sources of international law consist of its fundamental principles, treaties and customary principles and rules, and then to explain that while the judicial decisions and teachings referred to in Article 38(1)(d) may well be authoritative, they are at best indicative of the content of a rule, but cannot in themselves be treated as the formal basis for the rule itself.

The section is then at risk of confusing the reader further. In the second element, it suggests that discretion needs to be exercised in weighing sources, as sources vary significantly in their probative value, a statement which is plainly incorrect. A source of international law does not have probative value. It is the law. A treaty, for example, constitutes that part of international law on the relevant point, and anyone wanting to know what the law is consults that treaty. Likewise, customary law constitutes that part of the law as such, it is not probative of anything. The various elements of State practice and of *opinio juris* will be probative of the issue whether a rule of customary law has crystallised, but once the rule has crystallised, that rule is also the law, not probative of the law.

The section then cites as an example of this suggested variable probative value of sources of international law the US rejection of elements of the ICRC Customary Law Study[24] report. Technically, that Study report is not, in the opinion of the present authors, a source of customary law. It is – and the distinction in the present context is an important one – a publication of considerable length, scholarship and authority which seeks to describe customary law and which has been prepared by most highly qualified publicists. It therefore has the indicative status referred to in Article 38(1)(d) of the ICJ Statute but is not a source of international law.

Paragraph 1.9.1 refers to judicial decisions, noting that they are generally only consulted as persuasive authority, as the judgment of an international court usually only binds the parties to the litigation as to the issues of that case.

[24] J-M Henckaerts and L Doswald-Beck, *Customary International Humanitarian Law, vol. 1: Rules*, International Committee of the Red Cross (2005).

The *Manual* takes the position that the legal reasoning underlying decisions of the ICJ cannot bind States, meaning presumably States in general, and that the decisions of international tribunals such as the International Criminal Tribunal for the Former Yugoslavia and the International Criminal Tribunal for Rwanda cannot, in strict law, bind later casework of the same tribunal, nor can they bind other courts. However, and as the *Manual* correctly implies, this does not mean that prior decisions will necessarily be ignored, and courts may indeed adhere to their earlier legal positions in the absence of good reason to depart therefrom. This is all true, but perhaps the discussion should be balanced by noting that there are numerous examples that show the profound, and most positive, influence that the decisions of such tribunals can have on the development of the understanding of international law.

Paragraph 1.9.2 then addresses the writings of the most highly qualified publicists, citing as examples the writings of Hugo Grotius, Emmerich de Vattel, Francis Lieber and Hersch Lauterpacht. The paragraph suggests, rightly, that there is a high standard for determining which writings are included, and that the writings are only as authoritative as the evidence on which they are based. The point could be made, however, that such evidence may not necessarily be stated on the face of the relevant text. Ultimately, in the view of the present authors, it is the eminence of the relevant publicist, the learned and authoritative nature of his or her writings and the reputation for subject-matter depth, accuracy and excellence that he or she has that are the salient points. As the *Manual* points out, the writings should only be relied upon to the extent that they reflect existing law, as opposed to a view as to what future law should comprise.

LEGAL FORCE OF THE LAW OF WAR

Paragraph 1.10.1 suggests that '[t]he technical force of a law of war rule depends on whether it takes the form of a treaty or customary international law'. Although the precise intended meaning of 'technical force' in this sentence is unclear, the general apparent message of the sentence is incorrect. A rule of international law is equally binding on States that are in fact bound by it, irrespective of whether the rule is based on treaty provision or on customary international law. The only significant difference between the two sources of the law is that only States party are bound by a treaty whereas all States, subject to the persistent objector exclusion, are bound by rules of customary law. If this is what the sentence is intended to convey, perhaps some amendment should be considered.

Paragraph 1.10.1.1 briefly summarises the obligation of good-faith performance, the fact that treaties enter into force *inter alia* after a State deposits its consent to be bound and the expiry of and withdrawal from treaties. The *Manual* then states: 'In some cases, a reservation may also modify the obligations imposed by a treaty on that State.' If a reservation is entered when a State signifies its consent to be bound by a treaty, it will have the effect of changing the obligations imposed by the treaty on that State. If a statement made by a State when signifying its consent does not change the obligations imposed by the treaty, that statement does not amount to a reservation. The important point is then made that a treaty only creates law, meaning rights that may be invoked, as between the States that are party to it.

Paragraph 1.10.1.2 notes that customary law generally binds all States and then refers, this time for the fourth time, to the persistent objector rule. Paragraph 1.10.1.3 correctly notes that international law is primarily concerned with relations between States, such that States' international law obligations are to other States. While individuals may have obligations under international law, the paragraph correctly points out that the law of war does not provide individuals with a right to claim compensation for violations direct from a State. The claim must be on a State-to-State basis.[25]

Paragraph 1.10.1.4 describes the relationship between international law and domestic law obligations, noting correctly that domestic law requirements do not excuse non-compliance with obligations under international law. The long-standing DoD policy that DoD personnel must comply with the international law obligations of the United States is noted in paragraph 1.10.2, and paragraph 1.10.2.1 explains that treaties to which the US is party are part of US law, citing Article VI of the US Constitution. Paragraph 1.10.2.2 distinguishes between self-executing and non-self-executing treaties, in that the latter do not require legislation in order to become effective at domestic law, but fails to assist the reader by giving examples, particularly of the former, with the result that the discussion of this point remains arguably rather too theoretical for a military manual.

Paragraph 1.10.2.2 then suggests the following: 'The customary law of war is part of US law insofar as it is not inconsistent with any treaty to which the United States is a Party, or a controlling executive or legislative act.' This sits rather uncomfortably with the widely recognised position that customary law, subject to the persistent objector exclusion, binds all States. A customary law rule might be affected by the conclusion of a subsequent treaty, but this will

[25] See Hague Convention IV, 1907, Article 3; API, Article 91.

not be the case if the customary rule is *erga omnes*. The proposition that an executive or legislative act at domestic law can render customary international law inapplicable is simply incorrect.

JUS AD BELLUM

Acknowledging that *jus in bello* rules operate independently of whether a party to the conflict has complied with the *jus ad bellum* in resorting to the use of force, section 1.11 explains that parts of *jus ad bellum* are relevant to *jus in bello* and that the general focus of the *Manual* is on the latter. Paragraph 1.11.1 explains that certain *jus ad bellum* criteria are rooted in just war tradition principles, such as 'a competent authority to order the war for a public purpose; a just cause (such as self-defense); the means must be proportionate to the just cause; all peaceful alternatives must have been exhausted; and a right intention on the part of the just belligerent'. As the paragraph observes, these principles may be reflected in modern law of war rules, such as self-defence as reflected in the UN Charter and in the just cause principle.

The criterion that war must be ordered by a competent authority for a public purpose (i.e. right authority) renders the resort to military force the prerogative of the State. It is reflected in the limitation of combatant status to armed forces of the State, in the corresponding general denial of that status to private individuals and in the prohibition of certain private acts of hostility such as piracy and terrorism 'outside the context of patriotic resistance against an enemy State during international armed conflict'.[26] These observations are correct, but only insofar as they apply to international armed conflicts. While this would be implicit under the traditional understanding of the meaning of 'war', the fact that the *Manual* also discusses non-international armed conflicts suggests that this limitation should have been made explicitly clear.

Paragraph 1.11.1.2 explains the proportionality criterion as involving weighing the contemplated action against the justification for taking action. So, the proportionality of measures taken in self-defence must be judged against the nature – and, it is suggested, against the degree – of the threat being addressed. The paragraph then draws the parallel between these notions of proportionality and the necessity requirement in the law of self-defence and suggests, rightly, that assessing the proportionality of action taken in self-defence may involve considering whether an actual or imminent armed attack is part of a continuing pattern of attacks and what force is reasonably necessary to discourage future armed attacks or threats thereof. Importantly, the paragraph

[26] *DoD Manual*, paragraph 1.11.1.1.

distinguishes clearly between the *jus ad bellum* criterion of proportionality and the *jus in bello* proportionality rule.

Paragraph 1.11.1.3 concludes this part of the discussion by noting that the *jus ad bellum* condition of necessity requires that there be no reasonable alternative means of redress available and properly distinguishes this idea of necessity from the *jus in bello* concept of military necessity.

Paragraph 1.11.2 correctly identifies the UN Charter as providing the modern treaty framework for the *jus ad bellum*, and the primary responsibility of the UN Security Council for the maintenance of international peace and security. The paragraph states: 'The UN Security Council may determine the existence of any threat to the peace, breach of the peace or act of aggression . . . ' However, the associated footnote[27] accurately quotes the language of Article 39 of the Charter, which provides that the Security Council 'shall' determine the existence of these states of affairs. Using the verb 'may' in the main *Manual* text does not adequately reflect the prescriptive nature of the Charter provision. The paragraph then properly reflects that the Security Council has the discretion to make decisions as to the taking of action. Perhaps, and this is a minor point, the position would be more accurately and completely put if the sentence were to state: '. . . and may decide whether, and if so which, measures shall be taken under the Charter to maintain or restore international peace and security.' As the paragraph notes, the Security Council may choose to authorise the use of military force, as discussed later.

The obligations of UN Member States as provided in Articles 2(5), 25, 49 and 103 of the UN Charter are restated in paragraph 1.11.2.1. The obligations are to assist the UN in any action it takes under the Charter, to refrain from assisting any State against which the UN is taking preventive or enforcement action, to accept and carry out UN Security Council decisions in accordance with the Charter and to afford mutual assistance in carrying out measures decided on by the Security Council. If there is a conflict between the obligations of Members of the United Nations under the UN Charter and their obligations under any other international agreement, the obligations under the UN Charter prevail.

Paragraph 1.11.3 correctly quotes the Article 2(4) UN Charter prohibition of the use of force, noting that the resort to the use of force must have a legal basis in order not to violate the provision. The most serious and dangerous form of the illegal use of force is aggression, and initiating a war of aggression is, as paragraph 1.11.3.1 explains, a serious international crime. Whether

[27] *DoD Manual*, footnote 200 on page 42.

an act of aggression has been committed must be assessed in the light of the circumstances of the particular case. As the paragraph notes, General Assembly Resolution 3314 suggests matters for the Security Council to consider when determining whether an act of aggression has taken place. The paragraph then gives the US view that the definition of an act of aggression adopted at the first Review Conference of the Rome Statute of the International Criminal Court in Kampala does not reflect customary international law. No further explanation is given.

Paragraph 1.11.4 lists as rationales for the use of force: the inherent right to use force in self-defence; use of force authorised by the UN Security Council acting under Chapter VII of the Charter; and the use of force with the consent of the territorial State. Paragraph 1.11.4.4 suggests that violations of law of war treaties applicable to non-international armed conflicts have generally not been understood to provide an independent basis for intervening in a State. One might add that violations of customary law applicable in non-international armed conflict have also not generally been so understood. In this connection, the *Manual* notes that the US rejects the rationale put forward by the UK and some other States that intervention for humanitarian reasons may be a legal basis for the resort to force, noting that the Kosovo conflict was justified by the US on the basis of a number of other factors. Of course, the paragraph is right to note that military action for humanitarian reasons may be authorised by the UN Security Council.

Paragraph 1.11.5 addresses the right to use force in self-defence by quoting verbatim Article 51 of the UN Charter, making the useful point that Article 51 was not intended to supersede the inherent right of self-defence in customary international law. To be legitimate, the defending State's actions must be proportionate to the nature and, it is suggested, extent of the threat being faced. The defending State's actions must also be necessary, so reasonably available and suitable peaceful alternatives must have been exhausted. Under customary law, States continue to have the right to take measures in response to imminent attacks. The main *Manual* text might usefully explain that the measures referred to in the previous sentence may include forceful measures, subject to the proportionality and necessity requirements.

Paragraph 1.11.5.2 reports the US view that any use of unlawful force potentially gives rise to the right to use force in self-defence. The paragraph notes that 'others . . . would be inclined to draw more of a distinction' between armed attacks and uses of force that do not give rise to that right. While the relevant footnote[28] makes this clear, the main *Manual* text ought perhaps explicitly to

[28] *DoD Manual*, footnote 231 on page 48.

note that those 'others' include no lesser an authority than the ICJ[29] and, it is suggested, the overwhelming majority of other States.

Paragraph 1.11.5.3 expresses the view that the right to act in self-defence extends to a right to use force to protect a State's nationals abroad. The paragraph reports that the US has taken such action when the government of the relevant territory was unwilling or unable to protect those persons. It is not made clear, and arguably the paragraph should clarify, whether the US considers that such action is only permissible if the 'unwilling or unable' test is satisfied. It is however correct, as the paragraph states, that the State acting in defence of its nationals does not have to wait until actual violence is used against them if an attack against them is imminent. This legal basis for the use of force also applies to foreign nationals if the affected States of nationality have explicitly or implicitly consented, but action taken in self-defence in such circumstances must be constrained by that consent and by any conditions that the relevant State(s) placed upon it.

The related and difficult topic of the right to use force in self-defence against non-State actors is discussed in paragraph 1.11.5.4, where the point is made that the inherent right of self-defence applies in response to any armed attack, not just armed attacks by States, and that any force used must comply with international law. This is certainly consistent with the US view that any use of unlawful force potentially gives rise to the right to use force in self-defence. Paragraph 1.11.5.5 notes that the self-defence right under Article 51 of the UN Charter extends to collective self-defence, which must proceed with the affected State's consent but not necessarily pursuant to an explicit request. The obligation set forth in Article 51 of the UN Charter to report measures taken in self-defence to the UN Security Council is mentioned in paragraph 1.11.5.6. The paragraph should also have pointed out that the right may be exercised extra-territorially if the State from whose territory the non-State actors launched their attacks is unwilling or unable to terminate those attacks. This is an important point because in such circumstances a trans-border non-international armed conflict may come into existence.

[29] Military and Paramilitary Activities in and against Nicaragua (*Nicaragua* v. *United States*), Merits, Judgment, 1986 ICJ 14, 101 (paragraph 191).

2

Principles

Chapter II of the *Manual* addresses the fundamental principles on which the law of war is based. If one were to ask several experts in the law of war which principles they consider to be fundamental to it, they would likely produce lists that would not agree in all respects. However all experts would include military necessity and humanity as the two foundation stones on which much of the law of war is constructed, whether it be customary or treaty-based. It is the relationship between these apparently contradictory yet actually complementary notions that determines where the line must be drawn between the need to protect and the requirement to get the military job done. As we shall see, the *Manual* sees the principles of distinction and proportionality as expressions of these two great fundamental principles, but adds a third: honour, which some might prefer to call chivalry.

Paragraph 2.1.1 rightly mentions that general principles of law common to the major legal systems of the world are a recognised part and, the present authors would add, source of international law.[1] It is important to bear in mind that the 'general principles' referred to in the paragraph are rooted in national legal systems. These, as is made clear in footnote 3 to Chapter II, must be distinguished from principles of international law. Most of the latter seem to be derived from international rather than domestic law. Thus, the Martens Clause to which reference is made in the footnote specifically refers to the 'principles of the law of nations', which are not the same thing as 'general principles of law recognized by civilized nations'.

Paragraph 2.1.2, consistently with the opening remarks to the present chapter, explains that the law of war principles provide the foundation for the specific law of war rules. As the paragraph rightly notes, the principles are less

[1] The *Manual* references the Statute of the International Court of Justice, San Francisco, 26 June 1945, Article 38(1)(c).

specific than the particular rules, leaving more room for interpretation. Paragraph 2.1.2.1 rightly explains that the principles assist the interpretation and application of specific rules and that the military necessity principle has been incorporated into them. The humanity principle may, as the *Manual* suggests, 'assist in the proper interpretation and application of law of war rules that are based on humanitarian considerations'.

Paragraph 2.1.2.2 explains that when there is no specific law of war rule on a matter, the principles of the law of war provide guidance as to conduct in war. In this regard, attention is drawn to the Martens Clause,[2] although, as the paragraph notes, the considerable progress that has been made since the formulation of that clause in articulating the law of war reduces the number of occasions when reliance must be placed on the principles alone.

Paragraph 2.1.2.3 draws attention to the coherence of the law of war principles and leads to the discussion of each of them in turn. However, the paragraph includes brief definitions of military necessity, humanity and proportionality that are not correct.

MILITARY NECESSITY

Section 2.2 defines military necessity as 'the principle that justifies the use of all measures needed to defeat the enemy as quickly and efficiently as possible that are not prohibited by the law of war'. This definition omits the reference in the widely accepted definition of military necessity to achieving the defeat of the enemy 'with the minimum expenditure of life and resources'. The definition has, however, the merit of expressing the principle in permissive terms, which helps to demonstrate its status as the counterpoint to the other great principle: that of humanity.[3] The principle is, as paragraph 2.2.1 explains, a justification for action that may take the forms, for example, of destruction or seizure of persons or property and attack, and it has relevance for concepts such as 'taking a direct part in hostilities' and 'military objective'. The paragraph rightly observes that the principle may also justify alternative methods of subduing the enemy, such as capture of persons, propaganda and intelligence gathering. The final part of the paragraph notes, with care, that military

[2] 'Until a more complete code of the laws of war has been issued, the high contracting Parties deem it expedient to declare that, in cases not included in the Regulations adopted by them, the inhabitants and the belligerents remain under the protection and the rule of the principles of the law of nations, as they result from the usages established among civilized peoples, from the laws of humanity, and the dictates of the public conscience'; Hague Convention IV, 1907, paragraph 8 of the preamble.

[3] See, for example, the definition in *UK Manual*, paragraph 2.2 as amended.

necessity 'also justifies certain incidental harms that inevitably result from the actions it justifies'. The apparent circularity in this formulation is probably inevitable, but the underlying thought is correct. As the next sentence points out, it is the principle of proportionality that determines the extent to which military necessity justifies such harms. Therein lies the significance of the word 'certain' in the quoted extract.

Paragraph 2.2.2.1 makes the important point that military necessity does not justify action that is specifically prohibited by law of war rules.[4] So, military necessity 'cannot justify departures from the law of war because States have crafted the law of war specifically with the war's exigencies in mind'. It therefore follows that prohibitions in the law of war reflect 'States' determinations that such conduct is militarily unnecessary *per se*'.[5]

Tucked away in the final sentence of this paragraph, a most important point is made: namely, that the fact that law of war rules are formulated with military requirements in mind is an important aspect of the doctrine that the law of war is the *lex specialis* governing armed conflict. The *lex specialis* notion is discussed in Chapter I of the *Manual* and in Chapter 1 of the present book.

Paragraph 2.2.2.2 notes that some law of war rules expressly incorporate military necessity into the rule, for example by specifying that action that would otherwise be contrary to the rule may be justified by absolute or imperative military necessity. The important point is then made that, in these cases, military necessity must not be conflated with mere convenience. Rules to which these considerations apply are noted by the *Manual* to include: the limited circumstances in which the activities of the representatives or delegates of the Protecting Powers may lawfully be restricted; the internment or placing in assigned residence of protected persons by reference to the security of the Detaining Power; the decision by the Occupying Power to take safety measures in respect of protected persons; and the seizure or destruction of enemy property.[6]

Other law of war rules may only require compliance to the extent feasible or as far as is consistent with military necessity. The *Manual* lists as examples of such rules: the requirement to take feasible precautions to reduce the risk of harm to the civilian population, protected persons and objects; that military medical and religious personnel whose retention is not indispensable should

4 Contrary notions, often described as *Kriegsraison*, have therefore been authoritatively rejected; H Lauterpacht, *II Oppenheim's International Law*, 231–32, paragraph 69 is cited by the *Manual* in this regard; *DoD Manual*, footnote 24 on pages 53–4.

5 *DoD Manual*, paragraph 2.2.2.1.

6 These topics are respectively discussed in Chapters IV, X, V and XI of the *Manual* and in Chapters 4, 5, 10 and 11 of this book.

be returned to the party to which they belong *inter alia* as soon as military requirements permit; that prisoner of war (PW) camps shall be marked in the prescribed way whenever military considerations permit; and that military necessity may require the quantity of relief shipments to civilian internees to be limited.[7]

Paragraph 2.2.3 develops the idea that military necessity is difficult to define and apply, noting that the facts and circumstances of a situation are likely to determine what is necessary in war, that different people will assess military necessity differently and that evaluating what is necessary is impeded by the limited and unreliable nature of the available information. The *Manual* then offers suggestions as to the proper approach to evaluating military necessity.

The decision maker is not constrained to consider only the demands of the particular situation, but may keep in mind the broader imperatives of winning the war as quickly and efficiently as possible. Properly emphasising the importance of the speed and efficiency with which victory is secured, paragraph 2.2.3.1 suggests as an example that when assessing the military advantage of attacking an object, one may consider the entire war strategy rather than only the potential tactical gains from attacking that object: 'An interpretation of military necessity that only permitted consideration of the immediate situation could prolong the fighting and increase the overall suffering caused by the war.'[8]

Care is required. The UK and numerous other States have, in the context of the API proportionality rule, made the point that 'the military advantage anticipated from an attack is intended to refer to the advantage anticipated from the attack considered as a whole and not only from isolated or particular parts of the attack'.[9] Accordingly, while the States making that or similar statements acknowledge that the advantage to be considered relates to the attack as a whole, it remains the *military* advantage anticipated from the *attack* that falls to be assessed. The relevance of the campaign as a whole lies in determining whether there is any military advantage at all to be anticipated from the attack. If the attack is irrelevant to the military war strategy, it will yield no military advantage, with the result that the object in question will not be a military objective and an attack having it as its object will therefore be unlawful. In short, this argument must not be used as a basis for broadening the understanding of 'military objective' beyond what the applicable law will permit.

7 These topics are discussed more specifically in Chapters V, VII, IX and X of the *Manual* and in Chapters 5, 7, 9 and 10 of this book.

8 *DoD Manual*, paragraph 2.2.3.1.

9 Statement (i) made by the United Kingdom on ratification of API on 28 January 1998.

The paragraph then briefly addresses a topic of considerable controversy in the law of war. In its *Interpretive Guidance* document,[10] the ICRC included text in which it controversially[11] argued that in addition to restraints imposed by international law on specific means and methods of warfare, 'the kind and degree of force which is permissible against persons not entitled to protection against direct attack must not exceed what is actually necessary to accomplish a legitimate military purpose in the prevailing circumstances'.[12] In the final part of paragraph 3.3.2.1, the *Manual* rejects that approach as not reflecting customary law or treaty law applicable to DoD personnel. The paragraph explains that the law of war does not require that enemy combatants be warned or that they be given an opportunity to surrender before being made the object of attack. The paragraph concludes with the observation that the law of war may justify the use of overwhelming force against enemy military objectives. The general approach in these sentences is, in the view of the present authors, legally correct. The only amendment that the present authors would suggest concerns the last sentence, which might usefully be redrafted to state that the fact that overwhelming force is used in prosecuting a particular attack will not, *per se*, render that attack unlawful. Moreover, there is no law of war obligation to attempt to capture an enemy combatant or directly participating civilian rather than to attack him or her.

Paragraph 2.2.3.3 notes the recognition in the law of war that a person must assess the military necessity of an action based on the information available to him or her at the relevant time, and cannot be judged on the basis of information that comes to light later.[13]

HUMANITY

Section 2.3 defines humanity as the principle that forbids the infliction of suffering, injury or destruction unnecessary to accomplish a legitimate military purpose, which, as a footnote associated with section 2.3 demonstrates,

[10] N Melzer, *Interpretive Guidance on the Notion of Direct Participation in Hostilities*, ICRC, May 2009.

[11] See W Hays Parks, Part IX of the ICRC 'Direct Participation in Hostilities' Study: No Mandate, No Expertise, and Legally Incorrect, 42 *NYUJILP* 769 (2010).

[12] Melzer, *Interpretive Guidance*, 77.

[13] This rule was reflected by the UK and certain other countries in statements made when ratifying API, in the UK's case on 28 January 1998. The UK statement is: 'Military commanders and others responsible for planning, deciding upon, or executing attacks necessarily have to reach decisions on the basis of their assessment of the information from all sources which is reasonably available to them at the relevant time'; Statement (c) made by the UK on ratification of API on 28 January 1998.

closely follows the formulations in the *Canadian* and *UK Manuals*.[14] As paragraph 2.3.1 accurately points out, the military necessity principle does not justify actions such as cruelty or wanton violence that are not necessary to secure the defeat of the enemy as quickly and efficiently as possible, and once a military purpose has been achieved, the *Manual* states that inflicting additional suffering 'is unnecessary and should be avoided'. The paragraph therefore specifies, again correctly, as two expressions of the principle of humanity, that: once a combatant has been rendered *hors de combat*, he or she should not be made the object of attack; and the civilian population is immune from being made the object of attack, because 'their inoffensive and harmless character means that there is no military purpose served by attacking them'.

Paragraph 2.3.1.1 puts the position nicely when it explains that the principles of military necessity and of humanity are naturally complementary, with the latter being the logical inverse of the former, and it is indeed right that the principle of humanity shows how necessity can function as a limitation as well as a justification: essentially, one would comment, by justifying what is deemed to be justifiable and limiting what is considered to be unacceptable. The important point that the paragraph draws out well is that because humanity forbids unnecessary actions, it is not in tension with military effectiveness, which it actually reinforces.

Paragraph 2.3.2 suggests that humanity animates certain law of war rules, citing as examples: the fundamental safeguards of those who fall into enemy hands; the protection of the civilian population, civilian objects, medical personnel, units and transports; the prohibition of weapons calculated to cause superfluous injury; and the prohibition of weapons that are inherently indiscriminate. Numerous other examples could, of course, be cited. The paragraph then gives a good example of the application of the principle in the interpretation of the law of war rule requiring PWs to be interned only in facilities on land and the understanding that this does not prohibit detention on ships pending the establishment of suitable facilities on land.[15]

However, the section can be criticised in that it does not refer adequately to the clearly relevant obligations to respect and protect protected persons and objects. By referring to this explicitly, the important point could be made that humanity goes beyond prohibiting certain actions by obliging the parties to

[14] *DoD Manual*, footnote 53 on page 58 cites paragraph 2.4 of *The Manual of the Law of Armed Conflict*, UK Ministry of Defence (2004) (*UK Manual*) and paragraph 202(6) of Office of the Judge Advocate General (Canada), *Joint Doctrine Manual: Law of Armed Conflict at the Operational and Tactic Levels*, ch. 8 (2001) (*Canadian Manual*).

[15] GPW, Article 22(1); *DoD Manual*, paragraph 9.10.4.

the conflict to take positive measures, such as the search for and rescue of the wounded, sick and shipwrecked and actions in relation to the dead.

PROPORTIONALITY

Section 2.4 defines proportionality as the principle that 'even where one is justified in acting, one must not act in [a] way that is unreasonable or excessive', and notes that this might be viewed as a restatement of the military concept of economy of force. The *UK Manual* explains the principle of proportionality as requiring 'that the losses resulting from a military action should not be excessive in relation to the expected military advantage'. The two formulations of the principle do not actually conflict with one another, but the reference in the *DoD Manual* to the military concept of economy of force might cause some readers to mistakenly see the principle as focused on the expenditure of the resources of the force undertaking the action rather than on the degree and scope of the harm, damage and suffering that the action involves. Indeed, as has already been noted, the economy of force aspect ought to have been discussed more fully in the context of military necessity, and the discussion of it in the present section is somewhat misplaced.

Unfortunately repeating what the present authors consider to be an error of approach in paragraphs 2.6.1 and 2.6.3 of the *UK Manual*, paragraph 2.4.1.1 of the *DoD Manual* starts to discuss *jus in bello* proportionality considerations, thereby potentially eroding in the minds of its readers the important distinction between the two. This part of the *DoD Manual* discussion employs terms that are not entirely clear and may thus confuse the reader. Arguably, this paragraph should instead emphasise the difference between the fundamental *principle* of proportionality (and its requirement for a balance between the purpose of military operations and the harm to which they give rise) and the proportionality *rule* as set forth in API, Article 51(5)(b). The final sentence of the paragraph in particular is problematic. The more general criticisms as to content apply equally in relation to paragraph 2.4.1.2. The focus of this section should, it is suggested, be entirely upon the proportionality principle, and discussion of the targeting rule of proportionality should be left to Chapter V.

Paragraph 2.4.2 states that '[t]he principle of proportionality is reflected in many areas of the law of war'. It would arguably be more accurate to suggest that notions of proportionality are so reflected. The principle is limited to the idea that harm resulting from military action, including harm caused to the opposing armed forces and to military objectives, must not be excessive in relation to that which the military action is designed to achieve.

The discussion in paragraph 2.4.2 again seems to involve both the principle and the rule of proportionality. One danger of this approach at this early point in the *Manual* is to imply that *ad bellum* and *in bello* concepts should not be treated in the separate way the *Manual* itself rightly argues for earlier in the chapter. The *Manual* is perhaps rather stretching the point when it contends that proportionality considerations may be understood to apply to the requirement that the party subject to attack must take feasible precautions to reduce the risk of incidental harm. This rule is most clearly stated in Article 58 of API and is a rule of feasibility, not proportionality. If a precaution can feasibly be taken, there is a requirement to take it; proportionality does not enter into the matter.

The paragraph also correctly notes that reprisal action must be proportionate to the illegal acts giving rise to it.

As a general comment, the section should make a sharper distinction between notions of excessiveness, as reflected in the proportionality rule, and the fundamentally different concepts underlying the superfluous injury/unnecessary suffering principle. This rather illustrates the problem with this section: namely, its attempt to apply the concept of proportionality to all the issues that are addressed there.

DISTINCTION

Section 2.5 correctly explains the distinction principle as requiring 'parties to a conflict to distinguish principally between the armed forces and the civilian population, and between unprotected and protected objects'. While the discrimination principle, which prohibits indiscriminate attacks, is derived from the distinction principle, it is not right to suggest, as the section does, that the two are synonymous. The section does, however, make the important point that the distinction principle involves two duties: to distinguish in conducting attacks and to distinguish a party's own persons and objects.

As paragraph 2.5.1 rightly notes, it is the distinction principle that requires parties to the conflict to classify persons and objects, with differing rights, duties and liabilities applying to each class. While the main focus of distinction is indeed to separate (perhaps 'differentiate between' would be a better expression) the armed forces and the civilian population, the paragraph rightly notes that there are certain special cases. The paragraph implies that one such special case, namely military medical and religious personnel, are treated like combatants in the matter of detention. This is not entirely accurate, as such personnel, unlike combatants, have retained personnel status if detained by the opposing party to the conflict. This matter is discussed in Chapters VII and IX of the *Manual* and in Chapters 7 and 9 of this book. The paragraph rightly points out that a person cannot claim the distinct rights of combatant and civilian at the same time. In that sense, the classifications being discussed here are mutually exclusive.

Paragraph 2.5.2 makes the important and correct link between the distinction principle, the military necessity requirement only to make enemy combatants and military objectives the object of attack and the humanity requirement not to make the civilian population and other protected persons and objects the object of attack (while acting in good faith on the basis of the information available at the time).

Paragraph 2.5.3 correctly explains that distinguishing a party's own persons and objects involves using its best efforts to separate its military forces and war-making activities from the civilian population so that civilian casualties and damage to civilian objects incidental to attacks on military objectives can be minimised as far as possible. Paragraph 2.5.3.1 develops the point by noting that parties to the conflict must take measures in offence and defence to help ensure that military forces and civilians can be distinguished from one another, namely: the prohibition of the perfidious disguise of armed forces, discussed in paragraph 5.22 of the *Manual*; the requirement to mark protected persons and objects, discussed in paragraph 5.14.4; and the requirement to identify certain persons and objects as unprotected (e.g. by the use of fixed distinctive signs recognisable at a distance), discussed at paragraph 4.6.4.

Paragraph 2.5.3.2 rightly notes the link between distinction and the requirement for parties to the conflict to take feasible measures to separate physically their own military objectives from the civilian population, other protected persons and objects (e.g. by evacuating civilians from danger areas and, if feasible, by not placing military objectives in densely populated areas). On a related theme, paragraph 2.5.3.3 properly states the rule that parties to the conflict must refrain from misusing civilians and other protected persons and objects, e.g. by using hostages to shield their own military objectives or to deter enemy military operations. This is an activity which the paragraph rightly describes as breaching trust with the enemy, undermining respect for the law of war and, thus, as breaching honour (see next section).

Paragraph 2.5.4 makes the points that distinction does not prohibit the use of camouflage and that US forces have worn non-standard uniforms to blend with local forces. The former point is correct, so long as the camouflage is not designed to make the individual or object appear to be civilian in nature. The latter point is correct, so long as the uniforms that are being used are uniforms of friendly forces and are not enemy military uniforms. The *Manual* correctly mentions that the principle of distinction does not prohibit e.g.

the use of a hitherto civilian object for military purposes, thus rendering it a military objective. The paragraph then states that if such an object were to be seized from the enemy, such seizure would have to have been demanded by the imperative necessities of war. If 'such an object' is understood as meaning a civilian object that has not become a military objective by use, this statement in the *Manual* is only correct so long as it does not apply to the law of prize. The important point is then made that the principle of distinction does not prohibit the employment of persons with medical training as combatants by refraining from designating them as exclusively engaged in medical activities.

The complementary nature of the obligations to distinguish in conducting attacks and to distinguish a party's own persons and objects is properly stated in paragraph 2.5.5. The party undertaking attacks is not relieved of its obligations in this regard by the failure of the adverse party to distinguish its military objectives from civilian persons and objects, but if this adverse party fails to discharge this obligation, this has implications for the practical ability of the attacking party to distinguish, as is well noted in the paragraph. As the paragraph goes on to show, this reciprocity aspect works in the opposite direction too, in the sense that the extent to which the attacking force discriminates may affect whether the opposing party distinguishes its own military objectives from civilian persons and objects. The poignant example of the use of the Red Cross emblem is cited, the valid point being that the failure by an attacking party to respect the emblem will affect the willingness of the party receiving such attacks to continue to distinguish medical personnel and transports.

HONOR

Section 2.6 addresses the third fundamental principle, which the *Manual* terms 'honor', and which may also be described as 'chivalry'. These expressions are, subject to the discussion that follows, largely synonymous in practical terms. Honour, the *Manual* tells us, requires a certain amount of fairness in offence and defence, and a certain mutual respect between opposing forces.[16] Paragraph 2.6.1 notes the origins of the concept in warriors' codes of honour dating back to a variety of cultures and time periods, contrasting this with the rather more specific link between chivalry and the European knights of the Middle Ages. So, honour would forbid 'resort to means, expedients or conduct that would constitute a breach of trust with the enemy'.[17]

[16] Language that was evidently inspired by the 1958 *UK Manual*, paragraph 3.

[17] *DoD Manual*, paragraph 2.6.2.

Paragraph 2.6.2.1 then suggests that there is a link between honour (and what it argues is a requirement for a certain amount of fairness in offence and defence) and the rule that parties to the conflict must accept that their right to choose methods of injuring the enemy is not unlimited.[18] The proposition that the right of the parties to choose methods and means of warfare is not unlimited is an established and self-standing principle of the law of war, reflected in Article 35(1) of Additional Protocol I. It is not dependent on, nor does it derive from, a principle of honour. Similarly, the obligation to conduct hostilities in accordance with the law of war is based on established law and is neither based on nor reliant upon a principle of honour. Discussions of 'fairness' in the present context need to be approached with considerable caution, particularly if it is being suggested that there is some sort of obligation to go beyond the requirements imposed by law. Putting the subjective aspect of fairness to one side, there is no generally accepted requirement that warfare shall be fair, but there is a generally accepted requirement that the law shall be complied with.

Paragraph 2.6.2.2 contends that honour is the basis of the rule that prohibits 'means, expedients or conduct' that would constitute a breach of trust with the enemy, giving as a specific example the requirement to refrain from taking advantage of the opponent's adherence to the law by falsely claiming the law's protections. The present authors regard this as a somewhat artificial link. The requirement of good faith is essential to the effective application of the relevant rules of law, and it has been agreed and applied by States on that basis. The *Manual* cites as manifestations of the honour principle the provisions relating to perfidy and to treacherous killing and injuring, discussed in Chapter V of the *Manual* and in Chapter 5 of this book. The reasons given in the *Manual* as to why honour forbids such conduct are that it undermines the law's protections, impairs non-hostile relations and damages the basis for restoring peace, short of total annihilation of the adverse party. The *Manual* also sees a link between honour and certain other rules prohibiting the misuse of certain signs, fighting in enemy uniform, feigning non-hostile relations to seek a military advantage and compelling enemy nationals to take part in operations against their own country. Honour, the *Manual* suggests, does not prohibit ruses or other lawful deceptions. However, and as noted earlier, the claimed link between these substantive legal rules and honour seems rather artificial, even tenuous.

Paragraph 2.6.3 states that honour demands a degree of mutual respect between opposing forces, is a core basis for the humane treatment of PWs,

[18] Hague Regulations 1907, Article 22; API, Article 35(1).

is reflected in the requirement that PWs and their captors treat one another with mutual respect[19] and must be taken into account when capitulations are agreed between belligerents.[20]

The idea that combatants are a common class of professionals who have undertaken to act honourably is put forward in paragraph 2.6.3.2, along with the associated thought that private persons are generally deprived of the privileges of combatant status because they do not belong to this class of combatants. The suggestion is that this notion of a common class of combatants feeds into the preference for PWs to be tried by military rather than civilian courts.

19 See, for example, *DoD Manual*, paragraphs 9.5.1 and 9.22.3.

20 Discussed in *DoD Manual*, paragraph 12.8.3.

3

Application of the Law of War

Section 3.1 correctly notes that whether a particular law of war rule applies to a situation may depend on a variety of issues. It lists examples of those issues as follows: '(1) whether a state of "war", "hostilities" or "armed conflict" exists, (2) whether a party is recognised as a belligerent or as a State, and (3) whether an enemy State has accepted that law of war rule.' As to the second point, the reference to recognition as a State is problematic because recognition as a State is not constitutive. As to the third, one would comment that customary rules will apply irrespective of whether a State accepts them (subject to the limited persistent objector rule). If this third point were to be limited to treaty rules, its basis would be Common Article 2(3) of the Geneva Conventions, which can be interpreted as rendering the Conventions inapplicable between a State party and a non-party unless the latter has accepted and applies the Conventions. As to the first point, it is unclear what 'or' conveys. So, if 'war', 'hostilities' and 'armed conflict' are being used synonymously, such that the point being made is that the application of the rule will depend on the existence of a state of armed conflict, the reader will readily agree. If, by contrast, it is being implied that differing rules apply as between war, hostilities and armed conflict, this would only be the case if 'hostilities' is being used to suggest a state of affairs falling short of armed conflict, which does not appear to be the case.

Noting the sometimes rapid change in the character of military operations, the section explains that DoD practice has often been to apply law of war rules 'even in certain cases where these rules might not technically be applicable as a matter of law'. Such a policy is, of course, unobjectionable if it has the effect of enhancing the rights and protection of victims or of applying additional constraints to the conduct of military operations. If, by contrast, such a policy were to have the opposite effect, the particular application of the policy would be unlawful. So, if applying the policy were to have the effect, for example, of permitting the detention of persons whose detention in situations falling short of armed conflict were unlawful, the legality of the detention policy would have to be judged by reference to the situation as it existed.

The DoD policy that we have just discussed is then repeated twice in paragraph 3.1.1, referring on the second occasion to treaty law rules. In a fourth statement of the DoD practice, a justification for the policy is given as 'these standards in the law of war reflect legal standards that must be adhered to in all circumstances (i.e. whether there is a state of armed conflict or not)', an explanation that does not take the discussion very much further.

The fifth articulation of the policy comes in the first sentence in paragraph 3.1.1.1. The reader will inevitably wonder whether this unnecessary level of repetition reflects limited review of the text of Chapter III. In the next sentence, it is suggested that 'it may be appropriate to act consistently with the terms of a treaty (even as applied in dealings with a non-Party to a treaty) because the general principles of the treaty have been determined to be declaratory of customary international law'. If a rule has customary law status, it binds all States, including the United States, irrespective of their participation in a treaty reflecting – or that may have initiated – the customary rule. The 'it may be appropriate to act' is therefore incorrect and should be replaced by language to the effect that the customary rule(s) must be complied with. If the final sentence of the first part of paragraph 3.1.1.1 is intended to make the somewhat self-evident point that practice that is consistent with a treaty rule will be consistent with a customary rule that is making like provision, this is of course both obvious and correct.

The second part of paragraph 3.1.1.1 argues that it may also be important to act consistently with the terms of a treaty because the treaty represents modern international public opinion. The discussion to date has not made it clear to the reader whether we are talking here of a treaty to which the State in question, relevantly the US, is or is not a party. If the US is bound by a treaty, it is required by law to adhere to its terms, and that is an end to the matter. If the US is not a party to a treaty and if the terms of the treaty have not achieved customary status, the US may choose as a matter of policy to comply with all or some of the provisions of the treaty. Perhaps a simple, brief statement of the position along these lines would make matters rather clearer. The final sentence of paragraph 3.1.1.1 accurately notes that other policy considerations, including efficacious training standards and relations with coalition partners, may inspire a policy decision that DoD practice should be consistent with a particular law of war treaty rule even if that rule does not apply to US forces as a matter of law.

The final sentence of paragraph 3.1.1 is then repeated, almost verbatim, as the first sentence of paragraph 3.1.1.2. The argument is made that applying law of war standards in situations that do not comprise armed conflict 'provides assurance that the standards adhered to equal or exceed those required'. What exactly is meant by 'standards' is not at this point made clear. If the word is being used to mean 'rules', there are potential circumstances in which adhering to law of war rules in a situation that does not constitute armed conflict will result in less protection for certain individuals and greater latitude in the prosecution of military operations than the applicable law would permit.[1] The very generalised statements made in the early part of this chapter therefore need to be approached with some caution.

In a sense, the next part of the paragraph argues against the thesis that has so far been adopted, when it observes that elementary considerations of humanity, which apply in wartime and during peace, have been understood to apply in a more exacting way in the latter. It is not made clear whether this is the US understanding of the matter or whether this is simply reporting the views expressed in the *Corfu Channel* case to which reference is made in the relevant footnote.[2] The paragraph continues: '[t]hus, these legal standards, at a minimum, must be adhered to in all circumstances.' Perhaps it would be more accurate to state that the more exacting interpretation of a particular standard must be applied in the circumstances to which that more exacting interpretation has been found applicable. Simply applying the less exacting wartime interpretation during peacetime would not, it is suggested, be a satisfactory approach.

The argument in the paragraph, however, that the basic humanitarian principles reflected in Common Article 3 reflect minimum humane treatment standards for detainees in any military operation, including those not addressed by the law of war, is clearly correct. The word 'minimum' here reflects that other applicable rules must also be complied with. It is also noted that the US supports adherence to the guarantees in Article 75 of API in international armed conflicts. As is noted elsewhere, the present authors suggest that the US might usefully support the application of those guarantees in both

[1] Consider, for example, class-based targeting, detention operations and requisitioning.

[2] *DoD Manual*, footnote 11 on page 72 referring to the *Corfu Channel* case (*United Kingdom v. Albania*), Merits, Judgment, 1949 ICJ, 4, 22.

classes of armed conflict, and might express its view as to whether, as the present authors believe, they represent customary law.

SITUATIONS TO WHICH THE LAW OF WAR APPLIES

Section 3.2 lists the kinds of topic that are covered by the law of war, noting that it establishes: rules on the resort to the use of force; rules on the conduct of hostilities and the protection of war victims in international and non-international armed conflicts; 'rules between belligerents and neutrals', which presumably is intended to mean rules as to the relationship between belligerents and neutrals and as to the behaviour of each towards the other; rules for military occupation, a state of affairs which the *Manual* should explain should be treated as an international armed conflict; and peacetime duties that help to implement such rules. The paragraph then suggests that law of war rules can sometimes be applied by analogy to other contexts. While this is correct, when applied by analogy in a context other than that in which the rule applies as a matter of law, it will likely take the form of voluntary best practice or guidance rather than applicable law.

STATUS OF THE PARTIES AND THE LAW OF WAR

Paragraph 3.3.1 notes that when two or more States oppose one another, the result is an international armed conflict. The paragraph then contends that 'a state of war can exist when States are not on opposite sides of the conflict', basing this view on a US-decided case.[3] This statement would be unobjectionable if it were 'armed conflict' that was being so described. However, we have it on no lesser an authority than Oppenheim that war is 'the contention between two or more States, through their armed forces, for the purpose of overpowering each other, and imposing such conditions of peace as the victor pleases'.[4] War is therefore restricted to contentions between States.

The paragraph then describes these other kinds of conflict as non-international armed conflicts or conflicts not of an international character. That, of course, is incorrect, because of what has just been discussed. The paragraph, however, rightly acknowledges that non-international armed conflicts include two non-State armed groups fighting against one another and States fighting against non-State armed groups, even if international borders

[3] The Prizes Case, 67 U.S. 635, 666 (1863).

[4] Oppenheim, *International Law*, 115.

are crossed in the fighting. This aspect and the differences in the law as it applies to the two classes of conflict are addressed in Chapter XVII of the *Manual* and in Chapter 17 of this book.

Paragraph 3.3.1.1 explains that the application of *jus in bello* rules does not necessarily affect the status of the parties, pointing out that a person may be afforded PW protections but not status, and that the application of humanitarian rules towards enemy non-State armed groups does not affect their legal status, e.g. by recognising them as lawful belligerents. It might be better if this sentence were to refer to the application as a matter of policy of humanitarian protections that are reflected in rules of the *jus in bello*, as this is what it is assumed is in fact meant here.

Paragraph 3.3.1.2 then rightly addresses the complexities that frequently arise in practice by noting that it may be possible to characterise parts of a conflict as international in character and other parts as non-international.

Paragraph 3.3.2 addresses the situation where the government of one State is not recognised by the other State involved in the conflict. The paragraph suggests that in this situation, 'under certain circumstances, rules of international armed conflict may apply to a conflict between a State and a government it does not recognise'. There are two criticisms that can be made here. First, if as the first sentence of the paragraph indicates, the conflict is between two States, the fact that the first State does not recognise the government of the second is irrelevant to the characterisation of the conflict between them, not least because a government is merely an organ of an existing State. It remains a conflict between two States, and is therefore international in character. The second point is that it therefore follows that the 'under certain circumstances' language is misplaced, and it is the body of the law of international armed conflict that will apply, not just particular rules.[5] The paragraph requires correction in these respects.

Paragraph 3.3.3 notes that in certain conflicts, States have recognised armed groups as belligerents for certain legal purposes. The paragraph states: 'For the purpose of applying humanitarian rules, recognition of the armed group as having belligerent rights is neither a prerequisite for nor a result of applying humanitarian rules.' This is another statement in this chapter which it is difficult to accept in the terms in which it is written. Thus, as Yoram Dinstein explains, if insurgents in an internal armed conflict obtain from the central Government recognition of belligerency (as happened in the American Civil War of 1861–5), the conflict has to be treated as if it were an international

[5] Consider Y Dinstein, *The Conduct of Hostilities under the Law of International Armed Conflict*, 3rd edn. Cambridge: Cambridge University Press (2016), 37.

armed conflict and consequently all the norms of the law of international armed conflict become applicable.[6] It is therefore clear that recognition of belligerency is indeed a prerequisite to the application of certain protective rules of the law of international armed conflict to the members of the non-State armed group.

Paragraph 3.3.3.1 notes the practice of some States in recognising the belligerency of a rebel group involved in an armed conflict not involving the recognising State. The paragraph lists certain conditions that historically had to be met before an outside State could recognise a non-State armed group as a belligerent: 'a general state of armed conflict within a territory; the armed group occupies and administers a significant portion of national territory; the armed group acts under responsible chain of command and respects the laws of war; and circumstances exist that make it necessary for outside States to define their attitude toward the conflict.'[7] The paragraph should have made it clear whether the US accepts this notion of the recognition of belligerency by other States or not. The possibility that such a recognition might be interpreted as an unfriendly act is irrelevant to the acceptability or otherwise of the concept.

Paragraph 3.3.3.2 considers situations in which a State involved in hostilities against a non-State armed group takes action, such as the proclamation of a blockade, that recognises the belligerency of the non-State armed group, at least for certain purposes. Unfortunately, the paragraph limits itself to reporting historical events, notably President Lincoln's proclamation of a blockade during the American Civil War. As a result, the paragraph provides no guidance as to the US position on these matters. The paragraph should have made it clear whether recognition of belligerency by taking such action reflects current law in the US view.

Referencing important authorities dating from both World Wars, paragraph 3.3.3.3 addresses the situation in which a State recognises an armed group that fights alongside it as having belligerent status, perhaps in order to persuade the enemy to accord combatant status to the group's members. The paragraph suggests that an armed group so recognised may be regarded as analogous to an organised resistance movement belonging to a State that is party to the conflict. It is, however, clear that it is a recognition of belligerency by the State against which the armed group is fighting that would

[6] Dinstein, *Conduct of Hostilities*, n. 5, 37.

[7] The *Manual* cites as authority H Lauterpacht, *Recognition in International Law*. Cambridge: Cambridge University Press (1947), 175–6. The *Manual* notes that the doctrine has not been invoked often and would likely be regarded by the State engaged in hostilities against the group as an unfriendly act, which is clearly correct.

be necessary to achieve combatant status for the armed group's members, and the suggested analogy is, in the view of the present authors, doubtful at best.

Paragraph 3.3.4 refers to Article 1(4) of API, which treats armed conflicts in which peoples are fighting against colonial domination or alien occupation and against racist regimes in exercise of their right of self-determination as being international in character. As is well known, the US strongly objects to this provision 'as making the applicability of the rules of international armed conflict turn on subjective and politicized criteria that would eliminate the distinction' between the two classes of conflict. The *Manual* contends, correctly, that this provision of API is not customary in nature, which rather causes the reader to wonder why the US position as to the customary nature of other rules is so infrequently noted elsewhere in the *Manual*.

WHEN JUS IN BELLO RULES APPLY

Section 3.4 would be improved were it to deal with international and non-international armed conflicts in discrete subsections.

The section explains that *jus in bello* treaties 'often provide that they apply in cases of "declared war or any other armed conflict", even if the state of war is not recognised by them'. The reason why this sentence lacks clarity of meaning is because important words are missing. Parenthetically, it is particularly curious that the reader must wait until the fourth section of the chapter before this most critically important provision is given. One would rather have expected to see it early in the chapter as one of the key positions around which the rest of the chapter would be constructed. Be that as it may, the correct quote, taken from Article 2(1) common to the Geneva Conventions of 1949, would refer to 'all cases of declared war or of any other armed conflict which may arise between two or more of the High Contracting Parties, even if the state of war is not recognised by one of them'.

The paragraph then states that this standard has been understood to result in the application of the customary law of war. This is an odd way of putting the matter. The 'has been understood' language makes it unclear what the US view is, which may of course have been deliberate.

Section 3.4 usefully draws the distinction between the *jus ad bellum* and the *jus in bello*, and puts the matter in interesting terms by explaining that the fact that a State's actions comply with the latter is not determinative as to their lawfulness under the former. The *Manual* then asserts that the fact that *jus in bello* restrictions apply is not determinative of whether the permissions sometimes seen as inherent to that body of law may be relied upon by a State or non-State actor. The better view, in the opinion of the present authors, is that if *jus in bello* applies, the whole of that body of law applies in terms of its restrictions. To interpret the permissions implicit in the *jus in bello* as justifying action that is prohibited in *jus ad bellum* terms, for example as being an armed attack, is self-evidently wrong. Put simply, an armed attack that targets only military objectives does not, by virtue of doing so, cease to be an armed attack. Likewise, an act of aggression directed at lawful targets does not cease to breach the prohibition of aggressive war by virtue of being directed at military objectives or combatants.

Paragraph 3.4.1 starts with an ambiguous sentence, namely: '*Jus in bello* rules apply when a party intends to conduct hostilities.' It is true, as later parts of the paragraph note, that there are obligations that arise under the law of war before hostilities commence, and this interpretation of the quoted sentence would therefore be correct. It is not, however, correct to say that the law formally applies as soon as an intention to go to war forms. It is 'a resort to armed force between States or protracted armed violence between governmental authorities and organised armed groups within a State' that triggers the application of the *jus in bello*,[8] not the mere formation of an intent without more. So, if this alternative interpretation is what is meant by the statement in paragraph 3.4.1, then the statement is incorrect. The paragraph is right that if a party chooses to go to war or if a State finds it necessary to respond to attacks with military force, the military operations must comply with *jus in bello* rules. As the paragraph rightly points out, law of war considerations apply to the planning of the military operations; certain GPW and GC obligations are triggered by the onset of hostilities; and some action (e.g. to protect the civilian population against the effects of attacks) may be required before fighting begins.

Paragraph 3.4.1.1 cites the reference in Common Article 2 to cases of 'declared war' as an example of how *jus in bello* restrictions apply if a party intends to conduct hostilities. Certainly, if a State were to declare war in advance of the commencement of hostilities and with a view to those hostilities ensuing at some future time, the *jus in bello* would apply from the time of the declaration. To that extent, the *jus in bello* would apply when the declaring party intended to conduct hostilities, but its application would be attributable to the declaration, as opposed to the intent.

Accepting, as the *Manual* states, that formal declarations of war are rare in the modern era, the paragraph could usefully make the point that States do

[8] *Prosecutor* v. *Tadić a/k/a Dule*, Case No. IT-94-1-AR, Decision on the Defence Motion for Interlocutory Appeal on Jurisdiction (2 October 1995), paragraph 70.

sometimes issue an ultimatum in advance of an armed conflict, which may, depending on how it is expressed, amount to a conditional war declaration. The paragraph notes that officials may make similar public statements or may express the view that the State is involved in an armed conflict. The paragraph argues that these kinds of statements about *jus ad bellum* may be probative of the applicability of *jus in bello* restrictions. Much will inevitably depend on exactly what is said, and by whom. Generally speaking, however, the test as to the existence or otherwise of a state of armed conflict is factual, and based on events. The paragraph then, however, correctly explains that if a State makes a statement that it has suffered a wrongful attack under the *jus ad bellum*, this will indicate that the State regards the *jus in bello* as applying to that attack and to its own military operations against the adversary. This would, in the view of the present authors, be on the basis that the state of armed conflict arises from the moment when one State's armed forces use military force pursuant to a confrontation with the armed forces of another State.

Paragraph 3.4.1.2 asserts that non-State armed groups are bound by the restrictions in the law of war concerning the conduct of hostilities when they intend to conduct hostilities. While it is correct that they are bound by the *jus in bello* when participating in an armed conflict, the discussion in the preceding paragraphs has not entirely clarified exactly what is meant by the 'when they intend' language. The paragraph does, however, note that such groups lack what it describes as 'competent authority', with the result, according to the *Manual*, that 'there would not be a basis for non-State armed groups to claim the permissions that may be viewed as inherent in parts of the law of war'. As an example, it is noted that members of a non-State armed group may be subject to prosecution under domestic law for their participation in the hostilities. It should, however, be noted that the *jus in bello* does not prohibit non-State armed groups from participating in an armed conflict. So, while the members of the group lack immunity under applicable domestic law, the group itself certainly has the authority, in the sense of not being prohibited, to be a party to a non-international armed conflict.

Paragraph 3.4.2 accurately states the well-recognised position that *jus in bello* rules apply when parties are actually conducting hostilities, even if war has not been declared or a state of war is not recognised by them. It also correctly points out that the *de facto* existence of an armed conflict triggers what might be better described as the application of the *jus in bello*, with all its rights and obligations. It is interesting that, so far in the discussion, no mention has been made of the interpretation of armed conflict put forward in *Prosecutor* v. *Tadić*, where it was suggested, in relation to international armed conflicts, that 'an armed conflict exists whenever there is a resort to armed force between States'.[9] The US interpretation of international armed conflict is stated to be 'any situation in which there is hostile action between the armed forces of two parties, regardless of the duration, intensity or scope of the fighting'. The only aspect of this interpretation that one would question is the use of the word 'parties'. It would be more accurate to refer to States, as otherwise one is potentially including non-international armed conflicts within the definition, which is clearly not the intention. The word 'parties' was used in the original formulation to refer to 'parties to the Geneva Conventions', but the employment of that word in the paragraph may leave the reader with a somewhat different understanding.[10]

Paragraph 3.4.2.1 explains that 'States have specified that *jus in bello* rules apply even if a state of hostilities is not recognized by them because States have frequently denied that they are at "war"' and points out that this sometimes results in a refusal to comply with *jus in bello* obligations. Such denials may, as the paragraph observes, be motivated by various factors, including the wish to avoid escalation or to facilitate diplomatic resolution, domestic law considerations, economic costs and the wish to avoid acknowledging the effectiveness of an opposing force. The paragraph also notes the reluctance of States to acknowledge that military operations have triggered the application of Common Article 3. The motivation here, the *Manual* states, is often an unwillingness to do anything that enhances the perceived status of rebels or that would give any appearance of legitimacy to their actions. While the paragraph closes with the important legal point that the application of humanitarian rules does not affect the legal status of the parties to a conflict, it should really also have reemphasised that denial of, or failure to acknowledge, the existence of an armed conflict does not absolve the parties involved from their obligation to comply with the law.

Paragraph 3.4.2.2 puts forward the widely recognised interpretation that 'situations of internal disturbances and tensions, such as riots, isolated and sporadic acts of violence, and other acts of a similar nature do not amount to an armed conflict'.[11] This rather illustrates why it was a mistake in this section not to maintain a clear distinction between international and non-international armed conflicts, because it is somewhat self-evident that internal disturbances can never trigger the application of the law of international armed conflict.

9 *Prosecutor* v. *Tadić*, (1996) 105 ILR 419, 488. See paragraph 3.4.2.2 for a discussion of the *Tadić* interpretation of non-international armed conflict.

10 See *DoD Manual*, footnote 67 on page 82.

11 The associated footnote sensibly cites as authorities provisions to which the US is party, namely Article 1 of the Conventional Weapons Convention (CCW) as amended in 2001, and Article 1(2) of the Amended Mines Protocol to the CCW. It invites consideration of Article 1(2) of APII, 1977, to which the US is not a party; source www.icrc.org, consulted on 17 December 2017.

Furthermore, it would have been useful for the *Manual* to deal here with the important issue of distinguishing incidents in the air or at sea from situations of international armed conflict. Users of the *Manual* will wish to know which kinds of air or maritime incident will be regarded by the US as giving rise to an international armed conflict.

Noting that 'armed conflict not of an international character' was not defined in Common Article 3 of the Geneva Conventions 1949, the paragraph points out that numerous views have been expressed as to what constitutes non-international armed conflict. The intensity of the conflict and the organisation of the parties are mentioned as the criteria that have been assessed to distinguish between non-international armed conflicts and internal tensions and disturbances, and the *Tadić* case is referenced in support. In an important footnote, these criteria are explained in considerable and useful detail by reference to the jurisprudence of the ICTY.[12]

In its final sentence, the paragraph suggests a rule of thumb to the effect that when parties are in fact engaged in the sorts of activity that the law of war contemplates, such as detention of enemy military personnel without criminal charge or bombardment of military objectives, those activities are subject to the law of war. Some comments should be made. First is that it would not only be those activities that would be subject to the law of war: all activities associated with the conflict would be so subject. Second, there may be some activities that the law of war contemplates that would not trigger a state of armed conflict, particularly in the non-international context. Third, the involvement of at least one non-State organised armed group is an essential requirement, as, in the absence of the involvement of such a group, a non-international armed conflict cannot come into existence even if the protracted armed violence requirement is satisfied. The better approach, therefore, is to apply the *Tadić* criteria.

Paragraph 3.4.2.3 addresses the effect of what has been discussed by suggesting that 'States are not required to apply law of war rules when using domestic law enforcement tools to respond to ordinary crimes, including acts of terrorism'. It would be more accurate to put this the other way round, as States are required not, for example, to use class-based targeting of the sort permitted under the law of war when dealing with domestic law situations. Application of law of war targeting rules in domestic law enforcement situations would likely give rise to the prosecution and conviction of those using such targeting methods, e.g. on the basis of the use of force without lawful authority. The next sentence contends that States may apply their domestic law and

[12] See *DoD Manual*, footnote 76 on pages 84–5.

prosecute acts of terrorism by non-State armed groups. It is assumed that the sentence is intended to mean that they may use their domestic law to prosecute persons accused of committing acts of terrorism. Moreover, given that sporadic and isolated acts of violence do not, according to paragraph 3.4.2.2, amount to non-international armed conflict, the sentence under discussion would more appropriately indicate that States must act in accordance with domestic law in such circumstances.

In the next sentence, the *Manual* addresses what the present authors regard as a major contemporary issue. The sentence observes: 'States, however, have at times decided to resort to military force to counter a terrorist or similar threat that is beyond the capabilities of ordinary law enforcement to address.' There are, of course, numerous examples of situations in which States have decided to apply law enforcement rules and in which military forces are employed in aid of the civil power and are subject to domestic law constraints. The 'Troubles' in Northern Ireland from 1969 until the ratification of the Good Friday Agreement in May 1998 are a case in point. The potential legal difficulty arises not so much with these situations as with circumstances in which the military force to which States feel the need to resort is of a sort normally associated with armed conflict but where the situation being addressed does not, for whatever reason, amount to an armed conflict, e.g. because the relevant armed group does not satisfy the 'organisation' criterion. So, while it is true, as the *Manual* observes, that '[i]f States intend to conduct hostilities, then they are also bound by the applicable *jus in bello* restrictions', the more difficult question is whether States are entitled by the situation to conduct those hostilities at all. Moreover, and reflecting a point made earlier in this chapter, it is not the intent to conduct hostilities that triggers the application of the *jus in bello*: it is the factual situation that determines whether the law of armed conflict applies.

RELATIONSHIP BETWEEN JUS IN BELLO AND JUS AD BELLUM

Paragraph 3.5.1 rightly states that the *jus ad bellum* and *jus in bello* should not be conflated, as to do so risks misunderstanding and the misapplication of relevant concepts. The paragraph illustrates the point by reference to the differing *ad bellum* and *in bello* meanings of proportionality, but incorrectly uses the word 'disproportionate' when discussing the *in bello* meaning. When proportionality is used in the *in bello* context, the rule is concerned with excessiveness, as is explained in Chapter 5. Paragraph 3.5.2 observes that *jus ad bellum* and *jus in bello* generally operate independently of one another, such that compliance with *jus in bello* is required irrespective of whether a State may be regarded as the aggressor or of whether the original resort to the use of force was lawful under the *jus ad bellum*. Thus, as the paragraph correctly deduces, the obligation under Common Article 1 of the Geneva Conventions for States to respect and ensure respect for the Conventions in all circumstances applies regardless of whether a party to the Conventions is the aggressor or lawfully used force in self-defence. Equally, the law of occupation applies once an occupation is established, irrespective of whether the initial invasion was lawful.[13] Paragraph 3.5.2.2 rather develops the same point by explaining that a party that complies with the *jus in bello* rules may nevertheless commit aggression, a point that was noted earlier in the present chapter. The likely intended meaning would emerge more readily if the sentence were instead to refer to the party having committed aggression. The point here, again as noted earlier, is that the mere fact that a party's aggressive act and/or acts thereafter comply with *jus in bello* does not preclude that the party has breached *jus ad bellum*.

The paragraph adds that violations of law of war treaties applicable to non-international armed conflicts generally have not been understood to provide a legal basis for a non-belligerent State to intervene against the State in that conflict. This sentence is probably correct, although it raises a wealth of issues, including the extent of the suggested 'responsibility to protect' obligation and the possible arguments in favour of a right to intervene to prevent a humanitarian catastrophe. It is perhaps wise that the *Manual* does not explore those issues in the present section.

Paragraph 3.5.2.3 gives a convincing explanation based on sovereignty and humanity of why *jus in bello* rules operate independently of the *jus ad bellum*. As the paragraph comments, a law of war that only protected parties justly resorting to the use of force would leave both sides – believing the opponent's cause to be unjust – with the impression that they are free to depart from *jus in bello* rules, with the result that nobody would benefit from the law of war's humanitarian protections. The independence of the two bodies of law is also stated to be influenced by the fact that it would be unjust to punish soldiers on the basis of *jus ad bellum* considerations over which they have no influence.

Paragraph 3.5.3 identifies that the two bodies of law are sometimes related, with *jus ad bellum* sometimes influencing how *jus in bello* operates. The interesting example is the *jus ad bellum* principle of competent authority that lies at the root of the distinction between international and non-international armed conflicts: a principle that is also reflected in the *jus in bello* rules as to entitlement to the privileges of combatant status. This paragraph of the *Manual* should not, however, be misunderstood as implying that the *jus ad bellum* can modify the *jus in bello*. Perhaps this point could be added to the

[13] *DoD Manual*, paragraph 3.5.2.1.

paragraph's text. Moreover, one could debate the wisdom of referring to competent authority here at all, given its roots in just war doctrine, as opposed to UN Charter law.

Noting the centrality of the Charter of the United Nations to modern *jus ad bellum*, paragraph 3.5.4 points out that decisions of the UN Security Council when acting under Chapter VII of the Charter might create obligations that conflict with and prevail over customary or treaty-based law of war obligations, even though the Security Council frequently affirms the obligation to comply with the law of war. Nevertheless, the paragraph should have made the specific point that the Security Council may relieve a party to the conflict from certain limitations prescribed by the law, such as the requirement for a blockade to be effective and impartial. The paragraph also notes the potential for decisions of the Security Council to alter the obligations of Member States under the law of neutrality and to give additional authority to an Occupying Power to govern occupied territory.

RECIPROCITY AND LAW OF WAR RULES

Reciprocity is a difficult issue in the law of war, and the *Manual* wisely takes the position in section 3.6 that the requirement to comply with many law of war rules does not depend on whether the enemy complies with those rules. Of course, as paragraph 3.6.1 notes, reciprocity – or, at least, the level of confidence that an adversary will in fact abide by a treaty rule – may critically determine the willingness of States to enter into treaty obligations. This is, however, a somewhat meaningless and irrelevant element in the paragraph under discussion, because what really matters is that each party to the conflict complies with the law as it exists. The paragraph draws attention to general participation clauses, in which the relevant treaty is stated only to apply to armed conflicts in which all the parties to the conflict are also parties to the treaty. The *Manual* refers to treaties on neutrality in that regard, but there are numerous other early treaties dealing with weapons, as well as, most importantly, Hague Convention IV of 1907 and its annexed regulations, the application of which is similarly limited.[14]

The paragraph points out that other treaties provide that if some parties to an armed conflict are party to the treaty while others are not, then those that are party to the treaty are bound by it *inter se*, but not in relation to the States that are not so bound. Common Article 2 to the Geneva Conventions is rightly cited as an example of such a provision. However, the Geneva Conventions, in Common Article 2(3), provide that States are bound in relation to a State

[14] Consider, for example, Hague Convention IV, 1907, Article 2.

that is not party to the treaty but that accepts and applies the treaty's provisions. It follows from this that the Conventions do not apply as a matter of treaty law if a non-party State that does not accept and apply the provisions joins the conflict: a clear application of the notion of reciprocity.

If a treaty rule has achieved customary status, the customary rule will apply to all States (subject to the limited exclusion for persistently objecting States) irrespective of any general participation or similar clause that may be included in the treaty. The paragraph reflects this position correctly.

Paragraph 3.6.2 suggests that notions of reciprocity also influence enforcement of the law of war, citing the case of reprisals.[15] The strength of any argument to that effect is immediately diminished, however, when the paragraph acknowledges the prohibitions of particular reprisal actions under the law of war. The *Manual* is arguably on safer ground when it suggests that reciprocity may be a practical way of encouraging compliance by the adversary with the law of war.

Paragraphs 3.6.3 and 3.6.3.1 point to the inclusion of notions of reciprocity in the substance of particular law of war rules as a reflection of the idea of doing unto others what you would have them do to yourself. The paragraph suggests this inspires the idea of treating PWs as the Detaining Power would wish its own forces to be treated, if held by the enemy. Similarly, the paragraph proposes that it is proper to expect that each party's approach to the release and repatriation of PWs will be both reasonable and broadly commensurate with the conduct of the other.

Developing the theme a little further, the *Manual* points out the benefits and burdens aspect of some of the law of war's rules as another manifestation of the operation of reciprocity. Good examples that the *Manual* offers are the requirement for militia and volunteer corps members to accept certain conditions in order to achieve combatant status and the obligation that hospital ships and coastal rescue craft are not used for military purposes in order to have protection from capture and from being made the object of attack.[16]

Paragraph 3.6.3.3 rightly notes that the ability of a party to the conflict to comply with a particular duty may be affected by whether the opposing party has complied with a corresponding duty. An attacker's obligation to discriminate in attack and the duty of parties to the conflict to take precautions against the effects of attacks are cited as examples of this.

[15] Reprisals are defined and discussed in section 18.18.

[16] The requirement not to use cultural property for military purposes in order to retain its specially protected status and the respective rights and duties of belligerents and of neutrals are cited as other examples of the application of reciprocity notions in particular law of war rules.

APPLYING RULES BY ANALOGY

Paragraph 3.7.1 suggests that treaty provisions sometimes apply rules by analogy, citing the requirement under the Geneva Conventions for neutral or non-belligerent States to apply by analogy the rules relating to the protection of the wounded and sick to such persons when they are interned under the law of neutrality. Also cited is the application by analogy of the GC rules as to penal procedures for protected persons in occupied territory to proceedings against internees who are in the national territory of the Detaining Power. Strictly speaking, this does not consist of applying these rules by analogy. Rather, the treaty obligation designed for belligerents is being extended to neutrals. An analogy would involve an unintended lacuna and an identity of interests.

Paragraph 3.7.2 then most helpfully suggests certain other activities in which it may be appropriate to apply law of war rules by analogy even though there is no treaty requirement to do so. Whether such an analogy will be applied in any particular circumstance will presumably be a policy issue, although that is not made explicit. It will not, however, be appropriate to apply rules by analogy as a matter of policy if the effect of so doing is to diminish protections that other applicable rules may already afford to victims. This aspect should be considered when determining whether law of war rules should indeed be applied by analogy in the contexts suggested in paragraph 3.7.2, namely: the application of GWS[17] and GWS-Sea[18] rules for the respectful handling of enemy dead to all persons; the application of *jus in bello* rules in certain situations involving neutral or non-belligerent States; the application of humanitarian law of war rules in situations outside armed conflict;[19] the application of occupation law provisions for the protection of the civilian population to situations not amounting to belligerent occupation;[20] and the application of certain international armed conflict law rules in situations of non-international armed conflict.

17 This is the abbreviation used in the Manual, and thus here also, to denote the Geneva Convention for the Amelioration of the Condition of the Wounded and Sick in Armed Forces in the Field of August 12, 1949.

18 This is the abbreviation used in the Manual, and thus here also, to denote the Geneva Convention for the Amelioration of the Condition of Wounded, Sick and Shipwrecked Members of Armed Forces at Sea of August 12, 1949.

19 This is only likely to be acceptable if the protection afforded by the humanitarian law of war rule exceeds that offered by other applicable law.

20 Paragraph 3.7.2.3 suggests by way of example, again sensibly, that it may be appropriate for a State that liberates its ally's territory from enemy control to apply by analogy the rules of occupation law to the administration of such territory pending an agreement with the allied government.

Paragraph 3.7.2.1 sensibly suggests that some law of war rules may be applied by analogy e.g. to relations between a belligerent and a neutral or to relations between co-belligerents. So, a belligerent may take feasible precautions to protect the civilian population of a neutral or a co-belligerent from the effects of military operations. Similarly, although the GC excludes certain persons from the definition of 'protected persons' based on their nationality, 'it may be appropriate to afford such persons the standards of treatment for protected persons'. Paragraph 3.7.2.2 repeats the idea that it may be appropriate to apply to military operations occurring outside the context of armed conflict the elementary considerations of humanity reflected in law of war rules, which is of course right.

END OF HOSTILITIES AND THE APPLICATION OF THE LAW OF WAR

Having noted that, subject to certain exceptions, the law of war ceases to apply after hostilities have ended, paragraph 3.8.1 clarifies the idea of the end of hostilities as being when the opposing parties decide to end hostilities and actually do so. This is uncontroversial. The paragraph goes on to explain that hostilities may be ended by: an agreement, usually in the form of a peace treaty; a unilateral declaration of one party ending the war, if the other party does not continue the hostilities or reject the declaration; complete subjugation of the enemy State and its allies; or the simple ending of hostilities.

Paragraph 3.8.1.1 distinguishes peace agreements from armistices[21] and from ceasefires which suspend hostilities. All such agreements are discussed in more depth in Chapter XII of the *Manual* and in Chapter 12 of the present book. The role of the UN Security Council in the ending of hostilities is addressed in section 12.14. Paragraph 3.8.1.2 notes that hostilities may end without a written agreement, e.g. when one party is fully subjugated. Noting the difficulty sometimes in distinguishing between an end of an armed conflict and a lull in hostilities, the paragraph correctly suggests that hostilities would not generally be deemed to have ended without an agreement unless the circumstances show that they are not to be resumed or unless a lapse of time suggests that resumption is unlikely.

Paragraph 3.8.2 helpfully and rightly draws attention to some of the law of war duties that continue to apply after the hostilities have ended. PWs remain protected until their final release and repatriation. Protected persons remain

[21] While, according to the Hague Regulations, Article 36, an armistice only 'suspends' military operations, it can be argued that some armistices have had the effect of terminating the armed conflict.

protected by the GC until their release, repatriation or re-establishment. Duties under occupation law may continue beyond the end of the hostilities. Paragraph 3.8.3 points to certain law of war obligations that arise at the end of active hostilities, such as the marking of minefields, de-mining and clearance of explosive ordnance, and the release of PWs and of protected persons. All such matters are addressed more specifically later in the *Manual*.

It is a matter of some regret that this section of the *Manual* does not address the interpretation of the different terms used in the Conventions and in Additional Protocol I. Thus, the section should have drawn attention to the use of the phrase 'cessation of active hostilities' in Article 118(1) of GPW and of 'general close of military operations' in Article 3(b) of Additional Protocol I, and should have explained the significance of the words used. Furthermore, reference should have been made to the *Tadić* judgment, according to which the cessation of a non-international armed conflict requires not just a cessation of hostilities, but an agreement.[22]

LAW OF WAR DUTIES ALSO APPLICABLE IN PEACE

Section 3.9 draws attention to law of war duties that also apply when there is no armed conflict under way. These are stated to include: the dissemination of information regarding the law of war; law of war training of the armed forces; the issue of instructions and regulations to the armed forces in conformity with the law of war; the legal review of new weapons; the taking of appropriate measures to safeguard cultural property; and the taking of other measures to ensure the implementation and enforcement of law of war treaties. There are, of course, other important obligations that might have been mentioned, such as the obligation to take precautions against the effects of attacks (some of which may require action before the hostilities commence), the obligation to ensure that certain objects entitled to special protection are appropriately marked etc.

As the *Manual* rightly points out, neutrals, who by definition are not participants in the armed conflict, have obligations under the law of neutrality.

[22] *Prosecutor* v. *Tadić*, n. 8, paragraph 70.

4

Classes of Persons

Section 4.1 introduces the chapter with the idea that the system under the law of war of applying classifications to the persons participating in or affected by warfare has the purpose of confining the hostilities between opposing military forces and of protecting the civilian population from the effects of war. Paragraph 4.1.1 explains that the terms describing the different classes of person are often used in confusing and contradictory ways. The paragraph's observation that 'understanding the substantive standards that apply to a person in the applicable circumstances is more important than using a particular label or a particular system of classification' appears sensible until one recognises that the law of war's system of rights, permissions and prohibitions is largely based on classifications, so the achievement of clarity as to the application of each classification is a necessary precursor to the proper application of the system of law that we have.

Paragraph 4.1.1.1 correctly notes that particular terms may be given more than one meaning, citing the words 'combatant' and 'non-combatant' as examples. The issues arising from the US usage of the former term will be discussed later in relation to paragraph 4.3.2. As to non-combatants, after noting the various ways in which the word has been used in the literature, paragraph 4.1.1.1 indicates that '[i]n contemporary parlance, however, the term "noncombatant" should generally be used to mean military medical and religious personnel, but can also include those combatants placed *hors de combat*'. It would, arguably, have been more helpful to state in terms the exact meaning to be given to the term in the *Manual*, as, confronted with the quoted sentence, the reader is left in a certain amount of doubt as to how it is being used on any particular occasion. Paragraph 4.1.1.2 points out that more than one word may be used to describe a similar concept, citing 'combatant' and 'belligerent' – an aspect that will also be discussed in relation to paragraph 4.3.2.

Paragraph 4.1.2 is making an important point, namely that in analysing a person's rights, duties and liabilities under the law of war, the particular issue must be assessed by applying the legal rules pertinent to that issue to the relevant facts of the case, 'rather than deriving an answer based on a conclusory[1] labelling of a person'.

THE ARMED FORCES AND THE CIVILIAN POPULATION

Section 4.2 notes that the law of war has recognised that the population of an enemy State is divided into two classes: the armed forces and the civilian population. Unfortunately, the following words are then added to the sentence: 'also, respectively, sometimes called "combatants" and "civilians."' This sits uncomfortably with the discussion in paragraph 4.1.1.1 of 'non-combatants', which, that paragraph explained, should generally be used to mean military medical and religious personnel. Clarity could, of course, be achieved by adopting exactly this interpretation for non-combatants throughout the *Manual* and by then adjusting the discussion of particular legal issues accordingly. So, in the sentence currently under discussion, 'armed forces' would be noted as comprising combatants and non-combatants. The section then asserts: 'This division results from the principle of distinction.' It would be more accurate to say that the division is central to the principle of distinction: the division is certainly not the result of that principle. Rather, the principle seeks to achieve the protection of persons classed as civilians, so in a sense the principle of distinction is the result of the classifications, rather than the other way round.

A footnote to paragraph 4.2.1 cites Article 21 of the Lieber Code, to the effect that the 'citizen or native of a hostile country is thus an enemy, as one of the constituents of the hostile state or nation, and as such is subjected to the hardships of the war'. As a statement of observable fact, this is of course correct. The *Manual* text stipulates, however, that such citizens or nationals 'may be subjected to the hardships of war by an enemy State', which seems to imply that not only may they as a matter of fact suffer consequential hardships, but they may lawfully be made to do so by deliberate actions of their adversary that have such hardship as their purpose. Opinions will differ as to whether such an approach is consistent with the customary principle of distinction as articulated in Article 48 of API, or with the similarly customary constant

[1] 'Conclusory': 'consisting of or relating to a conclusion or assertion for which no supporting evidence is offered'; *Merriam-Webster Dictionary* at merriam-webster.com, consulted on 17 December 2017.

care obligation in Article 57(1) of the same treaty. The US understanding that limits both provisions to attacks would imply that it is indeed consistent with that understanding. Of course, this implies that in an armed conflict, the US population might also legitimately be made to suffer on similar grounds at the hands of a State that interprets its legal obligations similarly.

The final sentence of the paragraph suggests that the separation of the armed forces and the civilian population has greatly mitigated the evils of war. The present authors would rather suggest that the reverse is the case: that armed forces in many conflicts are increasingly intermingling themselves with the civilian population, that they are using that population as shields or otherwise to favour their own military operations and that casualties among civilians in armed conflicts thus continue to rise unacceptably, both in absolute terms and as a proportion of total casualties. It is perhaps significant that the authorities cited in support of this passage in the *Manual* date from 1908 and 1911.

Paragraph 4.2.2 correctly specifies that no person may claim the rights, duties and liabilities of combatants and civilians at the same time. That is an interesting and somewhat novel way of expressing the point. It would more usually be said that a person is either a civilian or a combatant, not both. Paragraph 4.2.3 then contends that certain classes of person do not fit neatly within the armed forces/civilians dichotomy, having attributes of both combatant and civilian status. The three groups concerned – personnel engaged in humanitarian duties, certain authorised supporters of the armed forces and unprivileged belligerents – are discussed in turn in the subsequent paragraphs.

Paragraph 4.2.3.1 considers certain types of personnel who, the *Manual* argues, have humanitarian duties that involve them in hostilities but entitle them to special protection. These personnel are stated to be military medical and religious personnel, authorised staff of voluntary aid societies, staff of a recognised aid society of a neutral country, auxiliary medical personnel and personnel engaged in the protection of cultural property. Each of these kinds of personnel is discussed in later paragraphs of the *Manual* and will be addressed later in the present chapter. For the time being, it suffices to note that none of the stated classes of individual, when undertaking their functions, would ordinarily take a part in hostilities, and that the classifications of combatant, non-combatant and civilian would adequately encompass all such individuals.

Paragraph 4.2.3.2 refers to categories of personnel who, again according to the *Manual*, are not members of the armed forces but are nevertheless authorised to support the armed forces in the fighting, namely persons authorised to accompany the armed forces but who are not members thereof and members of the crews of a belligerent's merchant marine vessels and civil aircraft. Again, there is a need for some caution. The persons authorised to accompany the armed forces are referred to in Article 4A(4) of GPW. They will indeed be civilians, and the significance of the reference to them in Article 4A(4) is that they are entitled to PW status if captured. Such persons will not necessarily take a direct part in, or give support linked to, the hostilities. If they were to take part in hostilities, they would have a similar legal position to any other civilian taking a direct part in hostilities. Likewise, members of the crews of a belligerent's merchant marine vessels and civil aircraft have PW status if captured (by virtue of Article 4A(5) of GPW), are likely to be civilians and may well not be supporting the armed forces in the fighting. If they were to do so, they also would be civilians taking a direct part in the hostilities, with the attendant consequences for their legal status. Accordingly, it is difficult to see the justification for a discrete classification here.

Paragraph 4.2.3.3 suggests that unprivileged belligerents, as the *Manual* calls them, are generally subject to the liabilities of both combatants and civilians. Which civilian liabilities are being referred to here is not made clear. Unprivileged belligerents are stated to include persons engaged in spying and sabotage behind enemy lines and private persons engaging in hostilities. Both classes of individual are discussed in later paragraphs of Chapter IV and will thus be addressed later in the present chapter. For the present, it suffices to observe that the discussion seems to be unnecessarily complex, and that greater simplicity and, arguably, legal accuracy would be achieved if simpler and clearer definitions for the terms used were to be applied from the outset.

LAWFUL COMBATANTS AND UNPRIVILEGED BELLIGERENTS

Section 4.3 gets to grips with the issues surrounding notions of unprivileged belligerents and lawful and unlawful combatants. For a State that is party to API, the term 'unlawful combatant' is a contradiction in terms, in that only combatants have the right to participate in hostilities and all combatants have that right. Illegal participation in a conflict therefore does not apply to persons fulfilling the combatant criteria. In the US view, as section 4.3 explains, the terms 'unlawful combatants' and 'unprivileged belligerents' refer to persons 'who, by engaging in hostilities, have incurred one or more of the corresponding liabilities of combatant status', such as being made the object of attack or being subjected to detention, 'but who are not entitled to any of the distinct privileges of combatant status', such as combatant immunity and PW status. Paragraph 4.3.1 notes that States have, in a few cases, recognised certain categories of unprivileged belligerents, mentioning in particular spies and saboteurs.[2] Reference could also, of course, usefully have been made to mercenaries and to API, Article 47. As the paragraph correctly observes, States have generally refrained from recognising unprivileged belligerents as a class in treaties in the way that classes of lawful combatant have been defined, and have been reluctant in treaties to afford them PW status or full civilian protections. So, the US position, as reflected in the *Manual,* is that the class of unprivileged belligerent is 'an implicit consequence of creating the classes of lawful combatants and peaceful civilians'. The reader may be tempted to respond 'it ain't necessarily so', as demonstrated by API's classes of combatant, civilian and directly participating civilian. However, the US view is that unprivileged belligerents will include members of the armed forces who have forfeited combatant status, e.g. by engaging in spying or sabotage, and private persons who have forfeited one or more protections of civilian status by engaging in hostilities.[3]

Paragraph 4.3.2.1 explains the various usages to which the words 'combatant' and 'belligerent' have been put in treaties and the literature, while paragraph 4.3.2.2 refers to the various usages of the words 'privileged', 'unprivileged', 'qualified' and 'unqualified' in relation to combatants and belligerents. Importantly, paragraph 4.3.2.4 explains that '[t]his *Manual* generally uses "combatant" to refer implicitly to lawful or privileged combatants'. The meaning is clear, although the point could perhaps be made more elegantly by stating that the term refers to persons who have the right to participate in the hostilities, but such a preference is perhaps to be expected from authors from API States party. The paragraph then explains that the *Manual* 'generally uses the term "unprivileged belligerent" . . . to refer to persons who are subject to one or more of the liabilities of combatant status, but are not entitled to receive its distinct privileges'. The only criticism here refers to the use of the word 'generally': the reader immediately wonders when, and why, the term is given some other meaning. It would, perhaps, be sensible for the paragraph to answer that question explicitly, as otherwise the reader will of necessity be unsure whether a particular use of the term conforms to the general rule or is one of the exceptions.

Paragraph 4.3.3 lists the three classes of person that, according to the US interpretation, constitute lawful or privileged combatants. Readers from States that are party to API will readily appreciate that combatant status is dealt with in Articles 43 and 44 of that treaty. The three classes identified in

[2] Footnote 31 on page 103 references the Hague Regulations 1907, Articles 29–31 and GC, Article 5.

[3] *DoD Manual*, paragraph 4.3.1.

paragraph 4.3.3 will be discussed later, in relation to sections 4.5, 4.6 and 4.7, respectively.

Paragraph 4.3.4 discusses two kinds of unprivileged belligerent. The first kind consists of persons who have initially qualified as combatants 'but who have acted so as to forfeit the privileges of combatant status by engaging in spying or sabotage'. The present authors would regard such persons, in accordance with API, as unprivileged combatants, because they retain combatant status but their activities preclude their enjoyment of the privileges of that status. The second kind of unprivileged belligerent identified in paragraph 4.3.4 consists of 'persons who never meet the qualifications to be entitled to the privileges of combatant status, but who have, by engaging in hostilities, incurred the corresponding liabilities of combatant status'. The very convoluted terms in which this is expressed belies the unnecessary nature of the legal complication involved. What we are usually talking about here is civilians who are taking a direct part in the hostilities. For a State party to API, such persons are and remain civilians who lose their protection as such if and for such time as they take that direct part. Be that as it may, these two classes will be discussed later in relation to sections 4.17 and 4.18. Paragraph 4.3.4 then makes the point that the difference between the two categories, namely that members of the former will revert to combatant status after the relevant activity ends while those of the latter category have no combatant status to return to, rather supports the present authors' point that the two classes of individual are in fact and law fundamentally different.

RIGHTS, DUTIES AND LIABILITIES OF COMBATANTS

The opening lines of section 4.4 summarise the rights and consequences associated with combatant status, and the ensuing paragraphs take these in turn and discuss them. Paragraph 4.4.1 correctly points out that combatants: may engage in hostilities and may, unless they have been placed *hors de combat*, be made the object of attack by enemy combatants; must conduct their operations in accordance with the law of war, e.g. they must distinguish themselves from the civilian population; may not kill or wound the enemy by resort to perfidy;[4] must only direct their attacks against military objectives; and must take feasible precautions in conducting attacks to reduce the risk of harm to the civilian population.[5]

[4] Note that for States party to API, the prohibition extends to capturing the enemy by resort to perfidy; API, Article 37(1).

[5] The obligation is actually to do everything feasible, that is practically possible in the circumstances, to avoid and in any event to minimise incidental civilian deaths and injuries and incidental damage to civilian objects.

Paragraph 4.4.2 rightly observes that combatants are liable to capture and detention by enemy combatants but are entitled to PW status when they fall into enemy hands during an international armed conflict. As the paragraph notes, Chapter IX of the *Manual* addresses the rights, privileges and duties of PWs, to a number of which brief reference is made in the present paragraph. The reader is referred to Chapter 9 for a discussion of what the *Manual* has to say about PWs.

As has already been noted, combatants captured while engaging in spying or sabotage forfeit their entitlement to PW status, and where there is doubt as to a detainee's entitlement to that status, the person should be afforded the protection of PW status until their actual status has been determined by a competent tribunal.[6]

Describing it as a special legal immunity from the domestic law of the enemy State, paragraph 4.4.3 explains that combatant immunity means that a combatant's killing, wounding or other warlike acts are not individual crimes or offences 'if they are done under military authority and are not prohibited by the law of war'. To be pedantic, and to avoid any potential ambiguity of meaning, it might be better to amend part of the quoted text to read 'and if they are not prohibited', in order to make it abundantly clear that compliance with the law of war is a condition of combatant immunity. Citing US precedent, the paragraph points out that combatant immunity also means that lawful acts of war undertaken with military authority do not attract civil legal liability. Perhaps in a footnote, reference might usefully have been made to the limited, State-based liability provisions in Article 3 of the Hague Regulations[7] and in Article 91 of API. The paragraph correctly points out that, subject to the requirement for a fair and regular trial, combatants do not have immunity from domestic law (1) for their warlike acts that are not in conformity with the law of war or (2) when engaging in spying or sabotage. For States that are party to API, 'while acting as a mercenary' should be added to this list.[8]

Paragraph 4.4.3.1 correctly distinguishes between combatant immunity, discussed in the previous paragraph, and entitlement to PW status when captured. In the latter part of the paragraph, the significant point is made that some persons listed in GPW Article 4 as being entitled if captured to PW status, such as persons authorised to accompany the armed forces, do not have combatant immunity.

6 *DoD Manual*, paragraph 4.4.2, final element.

7 Regulations Respecting the Laws and Customs of War on Land Annexed to Hague Convention IV (1907).

8 API, Article 47(1).

Paragraph 4.4.3.2 explains the view that combatant immunity is an application of the notion of sovereign immunity. Richard Baxter is quoted: 'the act of the soldier who conforms to the law of war and does not engage in private acts of warfare is an act of state depriving the enemy state of jurisdiction.'[9] The paragraph emphasises the requirement that combatants act under the commission of a belligerent State, reflecting the principle that only States may authorise the resort to force. The way the paragraph is written leaves the reader in doubt as to whether this reflects the US view. Perhaps that is deliberate.

Paragraph 4.4.4 notes that enemy armed forces may include nationals of neutral or other non-belligerent States, and makes the correct points that such persons should be treated like any other members of that State's armed forces and that they are entitled to PW status if captured during an international armed conflict. Paragraph 4.4.4.2 notes that combatant immunity does not apply as between a combatant and his or her State of nationality. Accordingly, international law does not prevent a State from punishing its nationals that it captures from among the ranks of enemy forces. Having noted in paragraph 4.4.3.1 the distinction between entitlement to PW status and combatant immunity, paragraph 4.4.4.2, in the midst of a discussion relating to combatant immunity, includes a sentence linked to GPW Article 87. While the point made in that sentence is correct, namely that certain provisions of GPW assume that the person affected is not a national of the Detaining Power, one wonders whether its inclusion in this particular paragraph is necessary or helpful.

Paragraph 4.4.4.2 closes with the observation that while combatants who join enemy forces may not be able to claim immunity from their State of nationality, they may be subject to what the *Manual* describes as 'the liabilities of combatant status', including that they may be made the object of attack or may be detained. While the notions of the privileges and liabilities of combatant status may lead to some arguably unnecessary complication, there is nothing legally incorrect in the notions as such. Similarly, nationals of an allied or co-belligerent State who are captured while serving with enemy forces may be handed over to their State of nationality. Curiously, the paragraph then notes correctly that such persons are not entitled to PW status in the hands of their State of nationality. Perhaps the point of greater relevance to the preceding discussion is that such persons also do not have immunity from the domestic law jurisdiction of their State of nationality.

[9] R Baxter, The Municipal and International Law Basis of Jurisdiction over War Crimes, 28 *British Yearbook of International Law* 382 (1951), 385. Note also the Lieber Code, Article 41.

There is an additional problem with this paragraph, arising from its reference to non-international armed conflicts: there is no legal status such as 'combatant' associated with such conflicts, so no status-linked privileges, such as combatant privileges, apply. It follows that a rebel may always be prosecuted for having engaged in hostilities, irrespective of whether the acts constituting that engagement complied with or breached the law of war.

Anyone from an API State party reading the present book should note that Article 43 of that treaty defines armed forces of a party to a conflict in terms of armed forces, groups and units under a command responsible to that party to the conflict, and grants all members of the armed forces, other than medical and religious personnel, combatant status. No reference is made to the nationality of the individuals concerned. If a particular individual who does not have enemy State nationality is nevertheless a member of the enemy State's armed forces, he or she will be a combatant,[10] and, as Article 44(1) provides, '[a]ny combatant . . . who falls into the power of an adverse Party shall be a prisoner of war'. If the capturing party is adverse to the party under the command of which the captured individuals' armed force, group or unit sits, Article 44(1) would seem to grant the individuals, including those who are nationals of the capturing State, PW status. It is interesting therefore to note in paragraph 4.4.4.3 that US practice has been to grant such individuals PW status 'if they claim such protection'. It being unlikely that the majority of affected individuals will be aware of the legal intricacies discussed in the present paragraphs, one wonders why the application of the policy is limited in this way.

ARMED FORCES OF A STATE

As a preliminary observation, it should be pointed out that this section fails to explain that, as reflected in Article 3 of the Hague Regulations 1907, the regular armed forces are an organ of the State and the members of the armed forces are appointed or commissioned by the State. This is an important point in view of the references in later paragraphs of the section to e.g. forces of a government in exile.

Paragraph 4.5.1 usefully starts with the basic proposition that the armed forces of a State may include a number of components, including militia and volunteer corps that form part of the armed forces. After describing the US armed forces as including the active-duty military, reserve forces, National Guard and Coast Guard, the paragraph also notes that members

[10] Subject to the stated exclusion of medical and religious personnel.

of certain other US organisations may also be classed as members of the US armed forces.[11] Paragraph 4.5.1.1 correctly observes that international law treats reserve forces personnel that are part of the armed forces in the same way as it treats other members of the armed forces. The United States' reserve armed forces are then listed.

Paragraph 4.5.2 looks at the different classes of members of the armed forces. Specifically, paragraph 4.5.2.1 describes special operations forces as 'military forces specially organized, trained, and equipped to achieve military, political, economic, and psychological objectives by unconventional military means in hostile, denied, or politically sensitive areas'. The paragraph makes the correct point that, as members of the armed forces, such personnel have the same rights, duties and liabilities as other members of the armed forces, citing the illegality of Adolf Hitler's order during World War II directing the summary execution of captured allied special operations forces.[12] The paragraph correctly notes that special operations forces may forfeit their protections temporarily if they engage in spying or sabotage. The paragraph then contends that military personnel who do not wear the standard uniform of their armed forces may nonetheless remain entitled to the privileges of combatant status 'because the wearing of such uniforms does not constitute the element of "acting clandestinely or under false pretenses"'. There are two criticisms here. First, it is assumed that the sentence should be referring to the failure to wear a uniform or fixed distinctive sign or emblem. Second, while the failure to wear a uniform may not *per se* be sufficient evidence of false pretence, it is certainly an indication of false pretence, to be considered alongside all of the other relevant circumstances. The paragraph then rightly emphasises that special operations forces personnel remain entitled to the privileges of combatant status even when operating detached and behind enemy lines.

Paragraph 4.5.2.2 correctly explains that members of the armed forces with medical training but who are not designated as military medical personnel are classed as combatants. However, if they fall into the power of the enemy during an international armed conflict, they may be required by the Detaining Power to exercise their medical functions by tending to fellow PWs.[13] Such individuals remain PWs but receive the same treatment as captured medical personnel and must be exempted from work under Article 49 GPW, as the *Manual* rightly states.

[11] The footnotes to the paragraph explain that in specified circumstances, the President may by Executive Order declare one named organisation to be a military service and may transfer officers of another named organisation to the service and jurisdiction of a military department.

[12] See *DoD Manual*, footnotes 102 and 103 on pages 113 and 114.

[13] The *Manual* correctly bases this observation on GPW, Article 32.

Paragraph 4.5.2.3 points out that similar arrangements apply in relation to ministers of religion who are not designated as military religious personnel. They, too, are combatants, but if they fall into enemy hands during an international armed conflict, they may minister to fellow PWs even though they have not officiated as chaplains to their own forces. For this purpose, they must receive the same treatment as chaplains retained by the Detaining Power and must not be obliged to do any other work.

Paragraph 4.5.2.4 observes that what it describes as 'draftees', perhaps known in other States as 'conscripts', i.e. persons compelled to join a State's armed forces, are treated the same as any other member of the armed forces. Rather than referring to how such persons are treated, perhaps it would be better simply to state that such persons are combatants and have the rights, duties and privileges associated with that status.

Paragraph 4.5.2.5 rightly explains that deserters who fall into enemy hands are PWs and that those who are interned by a neutral Power must be treated as PWs.[14] The paragraph goes on to make the legally accurate points that desertion is a matter for domestic law, not international law, and that deserters subsequently captured by their own armed forces are not PWs because they are no longer in the power of the enemy and because combatant immunity does not apply between the combatant and his or her State of nationality.

Paragraph 4.5.2.6 describes defectors as persons from one side's armed forces who voluntarily join the armed forces of the opposing side. The paragraph correctly explains that they would not be regarded as PWs in the hands of their adopted armed force because, as noted in Chapter IX of the *Manual*, they did not 'fall into' the hands of that party. If captured by the State to which they originally owed allegiance, they would not have PW status because combatant privileges do not apply as between a combatant and his or her State of nationality.

During international armed conflicts, members of regular armed forces who profess allegiance to a government or authority not recognised by the Detaining Power are, as paragraph 4.5.3 rightly notes, treated as members of the armed forces of a State, receive PW status if captured and should receive the rights, duties and privileges of combatants. The *Manual* cites the example from World War II of members of armed forces who continued fighting after their State had been occupied. Such forces might indeed continue to fight for a government in exile or for a government that has ceased to exist. The paragraph argues that such a government, presumably

[14] GPW, Article 4B(2).

if it continues to exist, will provide the right authority for its regular armed forces to continue to participate in the ongoing war and to have PW status if captured.

Paragraph 4.5.4 explains, with commendable clarity, the provision in GPW Article 4B(1). That provision relates to persons who belong, or have belonged, to the armed forces of an occupied State. If the Occupying Power considers it necessary to intern them by reason of their allegiance to the occupied State, it must accord them PW status if the following circumstances apply to them: that the Occupying Power has made the decision to intern even though the persons concerned were originally liberated while hostilities continued outside occupied territory; that such persons have made an unsuccessful attempt to rejoin the armed forces to which they belong and which are engaged in combat; or that such persons fail to comply with a summons made to them with a view to internment. As the paragraph explains, the effect of the provision is to apply to such persons the rules as to PWs, including the rules as to escape. As the *Manual* explains, 'a demobilized person who disobeyed an internment order and attempted to escape to rejoin his or her armed force would, like a POW, be subject, at most, to disciplinary punishment in respect of the act of escape'. This provision, as the *Manual* rightly notes, only applies so long as a state of international armed conflict continues, and will therefore not apply once all hostilities have ended.

OTHER MILITIA AND VOLUNTEER CORPS

Section 4.6 addresses the members of militia and of volunteer corps that are not part of the armed forces of a State but that have the rights, duties and privileges of combatant status. Surprisingly, it does this primarily by reference to Article 4A(2) of GPW. That provision, of course, is concerned with only one right, namely the right to PW status in the event of capture. It is Article 1 of the Hague Regulations that, for States not party to API, determines the applicability of '[t]he laws, rights, and duties of war', not just to armies but 'also to militia and volunteer corps', fulfilling the criteria specified in that article. Article 4A(2) is certainly relevant, but the Hague Regulations provision would seem to be of principle importance.

The text of Article 4A(2) is then accurately quoted, with its repetition of the four criteria from the Hague Regulations. Section 4.6 of the *Manual*, however, states that '[u]nder these conditions, . . . members of these armed groups may operate as combatants in or outside their own territory, even if this territory is occupied'. As has been noted, it is the reference to 'the laws, rights and duties of war' in the Hague Regulations that enables the members of such militia and volunteer corps to operate as combatants, not Article 4A(2). There is then a brief reference to *levee en masse*, which, at this stage in the discussion, is likely to raise more questions than it answers.

Paragraph 4.6.1 correctly notes the origins of the four criteria in the Hague Regulations of 1899 and 1907, that they reflect attributes commonly found in the armed forces of a State and that they help to protect the civilian population from the hardships of war while contributing to the military effectiveness of the force. Interestingly, the paragraph suggests that the criteria reflect a burdens–benefit principle, in that the receipt of certain benefits under the law of war requires the assumption of certain burdens.

Paragraph 4.6.1.1 correctly observes that the criteria apply to the militia or volunteer corps as a whole, as opposed to an individual member. Thus, if an individual member fails to satisfy the criteria, that does not deprive the militia as a whole of the application of the laws, rights and duties of war, so long as the militia as a whole does generally satisfy them. Likewise, if the militia as a whole generally does not satisfy the criteria, the fact that an individual member does satisfy them does not entitle that individual to combatant status under those criteria.

It is at this point that the *Manual* very briefly notes that API alters, for States that are party to that treaty, 'the conditions under which armed groups that are not part of a State's armed forces may qualify for combatant status'.[15] After the briefest footnote reference to the numbers of the relevant API articles, paragraph 4.6.1.2 notes: the US objection that the relevant API provisions relax the requirements for obtaining combatant status; that, in large part on this basis, the US declined to become party to API; that the changes reflected in the API provisions would undermine the protection of the civilian population; and that, in the US view, the relevant API provisions do not have customary law status.

Paragraph 4.6.1.3 has a side title: 'Application of GPW 4A(2) Conditions to the Armed Forces of a State.' As noted earlier, the reference here should be to Article 1 of the Hague Regulations, not to GPW. The paragraph correctly notes: 'The text of the GPW does not expressly apply the conditions in Article 4A(2) of the GPW to the armed forces of a State.' The same can also be said of Article 1 of the Hague Regulations. The paragraph then asserts, incorrectly, that 'under the GPW, members of the armed forces of a State receive combatant status (including its privileges and liabilities) by virtue of their membership in the armed forces of a State'. This sentence rather gets things the wrong way round. While it is true that members of the armed forces

[15] *DoD Manual*, paragraph 4.6.1.2.

of a State receive combatant status by virtue of that membership, they do not receive that status under GPW. It would be more accurate to state that Article 4A(1) of GPW, which grants PW status on capture to members of the armed forces of a party to the conflict, is the application in that context of the wider application, in Article 1 of the Hague Regulations, of the laws, rights and duties of war to armies.

Paragraph 4.6.1.3 contains the following sentence: 'If an armed force of a state systematically failed to distinguish itself from the civilian population and to conduct its operations in accordance with the law of war, its members should not expect to receive the privileges afforded lawful combatants.' There is no treaty basis for this position in Article 1 of the Hague Regulations, in Article 4A of GPW or in Articles 43 and 44 of API. Indeed, all of these provisions rather lead to the opposite conclusion. The assumption that the four criteria are implicit in the armed forces of States does not necessarily presuppose that all members of an army that does not exhibit one or more of them are deprived of combatant status. The present authors rather conclude that it is the individuals who have failed to comply with particular criteria who are liable for the offences that they commit, and that depriving the force as a whole of combatant status resembles prohibited collective punishment. The authorities cited in favour of the stated US position are an opinion of the assistant Attorney General and an extract from Bothe, Partsch and Solf that does not address the specific issue.[16] Yet again, in the final sentence of the paragraph, it is noted that persons engaged in spying or sabotage forfeit entitlement to the privileges of combatant status if they are captured while engaged in those activities, and, again, mercenaries could usefully be added in here – if, that is, this repetition is deemed necessary.

The chapter then starts to discuss these matters by reference to 'armed groups'. If this is the US position, then it is right that the chapter uses the language reflecting that position. However, the law, as set forth in Article 1 of the Hague Regulations, refers explicitly to militia and volunteer corps. While the language of the *Manual* will be adopted in the remaining discussion, this point should nevertheless be borne in mind.

After noting these preliminaries, the *Manual* starts to address the relevant criteria. Paragraph 4.6.2 discusses the notion of 'belonging to a party to the conflict', tying this notion of 'belonging' to the concept of right authority under the *jus ad bellum*. As noted earlier in this chapter, however, Article 3

[16] See J S Bybee, Assistant Attorney General, Status of Taliban Forces under Article 4 of the Third Geneva Convention of 1949, 7 February 2002, 26 Opinions of the Office of Legal Counsel, 1, 4 (2002) cited in *DoD Manual*, footnote 153 on page 121.

of the Hague Regulations reflects that the armed forces of a State are organs of that State. It is therefore clear that the armed forces, volunteer groups and militias discussed here are State organs, and that the associated requirement for authorisation or commissioning by the State derives from the *jus in bello*, of which these provisions of the Hague Regulations are a part, not from the *jus ad bellum*.

As the paragraph correctly points out, members of a non-State armed group are not entitled to combatant status even if they satisfy the four criteria (discussed later), but this is also reflective of the *jus in bello*. The paragraph notes that the authority may be oral or written; that a formal acknowledgement by the State that the armed group belongs to it is sufficient; that a mere claim by the members of the group that it is acting on behalf of a State is not sufficient; and that support and direction from the State may establish that the group belongs to the State.

Paragraph 4.6.3 addresses the first of the four criteria applicable to militias and volunteer corps, namely that of being commanded by a person responsible for his or her subordinates. The paragraph translates this, correctly, into a requirement that there be a commander with effective authority over the armed group, commenting that this helps to ensure that the armed group has sufficient discipline and organisation to conduct its operations in accordance with the law of war. The paragraph notes that the commander may derive his or her authority from a regular or temporary commission, or from some other position or authority, such as election by the members, and that the State may provide members of the group with certificates or military badges to show their responsibility to higher authority, thus distinguishing them from private persons acting on individual initiative. So, as the paragraph rightly explains, it is the commander's authority over his or her subordinates that gives rise to a corresponding duty to ensure that those subordinates conduct their operations in accordance with the law of war.

The second criterion, discussed in paragraph 4.6.4, is that of having a fixed distinctive sign recognisable at a distance. In parentheses, it should be noted that Article 1 of the Hague Regulations refers to an 'emblem', but this is probably a distinction without much of a difference. The first sentence of the paragraph suggests that members of the group 'should' display the sign or other device. It would seem that the wrong verb has been chosen here, and that this is an obligation that should be reflected in the word 'must'. The paragraph correctly observes that the essence of the requirement is to distinguish the members of the armed group from the civilian population, e.g. by protecting the civilian population from erroneously being made the object of attack. No particular sign or emblem is specified, and wearing a military uniform satisfies the condition. The issue, as the paragraph notes, is whether the sign or device enables the person to be distinguished from the civilian population: the use of a helmet or other head dress that makes the silhouette of the person readily distinguishable or the use of a partial uniform or of an armband may, as the paragraph suggests, meet the requirement. While there is no requirement to notify the enemy of the sign or device, it may facilitate claims to PW status by captured personnel to do so.[17]

Paragraph 4.6.4.2 starts by reporting the interpretation of the word 'fixed' in this criterion as indicating something that cannot easily be removed and disposed of at the first indication of danger, such as the wearing of a uniform or the sewing on of a badge. The next sentence, based on writings of Francis Lieber in relation to the American Civil War, suggests that it would be 'important to assess whether members of the armed group are functionally distinguishable from the civilian population, even if the distinctive sign that they wear is not permanent and could be removed'. But either the members of the group wear a fixed sign or they do not, and having stated that these are criteria that, in the US view, determine entitlement to combatant status, it seems strange to then interpret an individual criterion in a way that arguably erodes its meaning.

Paragraph 4.6.4.3, citing a wealth of reliable authority, concludes correctly that although the word 'distance' in 'visible at a distance' is not defined, it may be interpreted as requiring that the sign be easily distinguishable by the naked eye of an ordinary person at a distance at which the form of the individual can be determined.

Paragraph 4.6.5, referring to the third criterion that the members of the armed group must carry their arms openly, makes the obvious deduction that the requirement is not satisfied if the armed group makes a practice of carrying only concealed weapons or of hiding its weapons on the approach of enemy forces. The paragraph adds, 'to avoid identification as fighters'. However, the motive for such routine concealment of weapons is not relevant. It is the fact of such routine concealment that would deprive the members of the armed group of combatant status.

Paragraph 4.6.6 briefly addresses the final criterion, namely that of conducting operations in accordance with the laws and customs of war. The paragraph notes that this is an obligation of the armed group as a whole, and that evidence that the armed group enforces the law (e.g. by promulgating instructions as to law of war requirements and punishing violations) would help to establish that it meets the criterion.

[17] *DoD Manual*, paragraph 4.6.4.1.

LEVEE EN MASSE

Section 4.7 correctly describes a *levee en masse* as 'a spontaneous uprising of the inhabitants of non-occupied territory who, on the approach of the enemy in an international armed conflict, take up arms to resist the invading forces, without having time to form themselves into regular armed units. Participants in a *levee en masse* are entitled to the privileges of combatant status, provided that they carry their arms openly and respect the laws and customs of war.' This reflects the requirements of Article 2 of the Hague Regulations, which is cited in the associated footnote,[18] but only after reference to GPW, Article 4A(6). For the reasons already discussed, it is considered that these references in the footnote should be reversed; i.e. it is Article 2 of the Hague Regulations that grants such persons combatant status, whereas Article 4A(6) is only concerned with their PW status in the event of capture.

Paragraph 4.7.1.1 makes the point that the spontaneity of a *levee en masse* generally precludes wearing a distinctive sign or being organised under a responsible command, while paragraph 4.7.1.2 notes that a *levee en masse* reflects the right of inhabitants to resist approaching enemy forces, and that non-inhabitants who travel to a territory to resist invading forces are not entitled to participate in a *levee en masse*. Once occupation has been established or a territory has been invaded, a *levee en masse* no longer applies. The paragraph correctly contrasts members of an organised resistance movement, who may operate as combatants inside or outside their own territory even if the territory is occupied, and cites Article 4A(2) of GPW in support. It should be noted, however, that these individuals are included within the wider notion of members of militia and other volunteer corps, and that the combatant status of members of such bodies is established in Article 1 of the Hague Regulations, not in GPW.

As paragraph 4.7.2 suggests, where some inhabitants have formed a *levee en masse*, it may be justifiable for the invading force to detain all persons of military age in the area and treat them as PWs, while those who join a *levee en masse* may be treated as PWs even if they take no actual part in the fighting. The paragraph then correctly observes that persons who are only believed to have participated in a *levee en masse* and who are detained should be treated as PWs until their status has been determined by a competent tribunal. Persons who do not join a *levee en masse* but who commit private acts of hostility against enemy forces do not, as the paragraph correctly suggests, have combatant immunity.

[18] See *DoD Manual*, footnote 173 on page 125.

RIGHTS, DUTIES AND LIABILITIES OF CIVILIANS

Paragraph 4.8.1 explores the differing ways in which the word 'civilian' is used in the law of war. In contradistinction to the word 'military', paragraph 4.8.1.1 notes that 'civilian' describes persons who are not military personnel, such as those authorised to accompany the armed forces. The present authors would note that persons authorised to accompany armed forces are civilian in just the same sense that members of the population are civilian, so it is a somewhat artificial distinction that is being elaborated here. Paragraph 4.8.1.2 discuses the word 'civilian' in contradistinction to the word 'combatant', noting that 'civilian' is often used to describe persons who are not combatants. The paragraph then notes that civilians in this sense are sometimes being referred to as persons who lack the right to participate in hostilities and sometimes as persons who have not in fact so participated. As readers will appreciate, this is discussing the potential ambiguities arising from the US approach. For States that are party to API, the notion of combatant is clearly defined in Article 43(2), and all other persons are civilians. Of course, the word 'civilian' may be used informally in a variety of ways, but that does not and should not affect its interpretation in the law of war.

Paragraph 4.8.1.3 draws attention to the use of the word 'civilian' in the GC context, noting that the word, although used in GC, is not defined there. It then considers some of the types of individual who come within the GC notion of 'protected persons'. Paragraph 4.8.1.4 notes that the API definition of a civilian is anyone who is not a combatant, points out the US objection to the API definition of 'combatant' and observes that APII contains no definition of civilian. Paragraph 4.8.1.5 informs the reader that '[t]his *Manual* generally uses "civilian" to mean a member of the civilian population, i.e. a person who is neither part of nor associated with an armed force or group, nor otherwise engaged in hostilities'. First, and on a point of detail, it would have been better to insert 'when the word is used as a noun', as applying the stated meaning to the adjectival use of the word produces a nonsense. Second, the reader will also wonder what the word 'generally' indicates, and would probably welcome an indication of when the word is not being given the stated meaning. Third, there are many kinds of association that an individual might have with an armed force or group, and the present authors doubt that they would all deprive the person concerned of civilian status. Fourth, it will be noted that so far as the US is concerned, engagement in hostilities deprives an individual – who may not be a member of an armed group – of civilian status. For States that are party to API, the individual retains civilian status but loses protection from attack while so participating.

Paragraph 4.8.2 notes that civilians may not be made the object of attack unless they take a direct part in hostilities. The paragraph makes brief reference to the particular protection of the wounded, sick and of expectant mothers, to the proportionality rule and to the requirement to take precautions: all topics addressed in more detail elsewhere in the *Manual*. It then restates that civilians who engage in hostilities forfeit civilian protection 'and may be liable to treatment in one or more respects as unprivileged belligerents'.

Paragraph 4.8.3 correctly notes that civilians may, subject to military necessity, be the subject of non-violent measures such as searches or temporary detention, or, for imperative reasons of security, internment or assigned residence. As the paragraph notes, Chapter X considers these and related matters in depth, as does Chapter 10 of this book. The paragraph however, rightly notes the special consideration required during detention for special categories of civilian, such as children.

Paragraph 4.8.4 explains, accurately, that civilians lack the combatant's privilege in relation to the domestic law of the enemy State; these matters are also discussed later in the same paragraph. Again, one wonders why so much repetition is considered necessary. The paragraph does, however, usefully cross-refer to Chapter XI's discussion of the authority of the Occupying Power over inhabitants and to the special cases of participants in a *levee en masse*, persons who accompany armed forces and members of (the crews of) merchant marine vessels and civil aircraft. As a matter of detail, the bracketed words in the previous sentence should be inserted appropriately in the paragraph in the *Manual*.

MILITARY MEDICAL AND RELIGIOUS PERSONNEL

Adopting the language of GWS, Article 24, section 4.9 defines military medical and religious personnel as '[m]edical personnel exclusively engaged in the search for, or the collection, transport, or treatment of the wounded or sick, or in the prevention of disease, staff exclusively engaged in the administration of medical units and establishments, as well as chaplains attached to the armed forces'. The authorised staff of voluntary aid societies and the staff of a recognised aid society of a neutral country are discussed later in Chapter IV (and later in this chapter). For unclear reasons, paragraph 4.9.1 then essentially repeats the GWS, Article 24 definition given a few lines previously in the *Manual*, and the first lines of paragraph 4.9.1.1 inexplicably state the first part of the definition for the third time. The paragraph does, however, usefully list examples of such persons, namely 'military physicians, dentists, nurses, orderlies, stretcher-bearers, and other persons belonging to the armed forces who give direct care to the wounded and sick'. The paragraph correctly notes that, ordinarily, veterinary personnel would not qualify for military medical status as being part of the veterinary service, but that some such individuals would so qualify, e.g. if they were exclusively engaged in providing health services to military personnel, such as by performing food safety inspections.

Paragraph 4.9.1.2 emphasises that the staff engaged in the administration of medical units and establishments must be exclusively so engaged to be classed as medical personnel in accordance with the provision. Cooks, clerks, supply personnel and crews operating permanent medical aircraft are correctly stated to be examples. Paragraph 4.9.1.3 notes that chaplains attached to the armed forces include any cleric, regardless of faith, who is so attached and who is assigned duties of an exclusively spiritual or religious nature. Paragraph 4.9.2 correctly identifies three requirements for the acquisition and retention of military medical and religious personnel status: belonging to a force whose members qualify for PW status; being designated as exclusively medical or religious personnel by their armed force; and serving exclusively in a medical or religious capacity. The *Manual* rightly comments that underlying their protected status is the principle that the armed forces have committed to using these personnel exclusively in a humanitarian role. Citing the *GWS Commentary*,[19] the *Manual* suggests, perhaps unnecessarily, that these personnel have a supranational and quasi-neutral character. One would have thought it sufficient to point out that they do not take part in the hostilities and that their specially protected status reflects their humanitarian tasks, often undertaken in close proximity to the fighting.

Taking the three requirements in turn, paragraph 4.9.2.1 asserts that military medical and religious personnel must belong to the armed forces of a State, i.e. to an armed force whose members qualify for PW status if captured. This would exclude medical personnel belonging to non-State armed groups. Article 9 of APII should, however, be considered here. It identifies, in relation to the non-international armed conflicts covered by that treaty, medical and religious personnel as a class of persons to be respected and protected. This reflects, in the view of the present authors, a provision of customary law applicable to all classes of non-international armed conflict. The final sentence of the paragraph is correct, however, in stating that medical personnel of non-State armed groups do not have retained personnel status if captured, but it

[19] J S Pictet (ed.) *Commentary I on Geneva Convention for the Amelioration of the Condition of the Wounded and Sick in Armed Forces in the Field*. International Committee of the Red Cross (1952).

might mention that individuals may so qualify if they otherwise come within one of the classes of individual thereby entitled to such status.

The requirement to be designated by their armed forces is explained in paragraph 4.9.2.2 as involving designation as part of the official medical or religious service of the armed forces. As the paragraph notes, military medical or religious personnel status is not acquired merely by members of the armed forces having medical training or performing medical functions: those who combine a medical function with a combat function do not, as the paragraph correctly points out, have military medical or religious status, although if detained, such personnel may be required to perform medical duties.

As paragraph 4.9.2.3 emphasises, to qualify as military medical or religious personnel, individuals must exclusively serve in a humanitarian capacity, and that assignment must generally be permanent. The intended meaning of the next sentence is evident: namely, that military medical personnel who combine humanitarian duties with tasks involving acts that are harmful to the enemy do not have military medical or religious personnel status. There is, however, an error in the sentence, so that, read literally, it can be understood to convey a different meaning, and redrafting is recommended. Later in the paragraph, persons engaged in combat search and rescue missions are correctly described as not exclusively engaged in humanitarian duties. This is because preventing capture of combatants by the enemy constitutes an act harmful to the enemy – although, as the paragraph notes, such personnel may be treated as auxiliary medical personnel or as members of the armed forces with medical training but who are not members of the medical service. The paragraph argues that captured military medical personnel who refuse to perform their medical duties to care for fellow prisoners would not be entitled to retained personnel status. This is a development of the idea that there is an affirmative obligation for such persons to perform in a humanitarian capacity. The present authors consider this a somewhat obscure argument that should not be allowed to dilute the special protection afforded by GWS, Article 24.

RIGHTS, DUTIES AND LIABILITIES OF MILITARY MEDICAL AND RELIGIOUS PERSONNEL

Section 4.10 correctly notes that military medical and religious personnel must be respected and protected at all times. Paragraph 4.10.1 adds that they may not be made the object of attack but must accept the risk of incidental harm arising from military operations. It notes that they may not commit acts harmful to the enemy, such as resisting lawful capture, but may employ arms in self-defence or in defence of their patients against unlawful attacks. These matters are discussed in more detail in Chapter VII of the *Manual* and Chapter 7 of the present book.

As paragraph 4.10.2 observes, if military medical or religious personnel fall into the power of the adverse party during an international armed conflict, they have the status of retained personnel. Some of their rights and responsibilities are summarised in the paragraph, but they are dealt with in greater detail in Chapter VII of the *Manual* and Chapter 7 of the present book.

AUTHORIZED STAFF OF VOLUNTARY AID SOCIETIES

As section 4.11 explains, States may choose to employ staff of National Red Cross Societies and of voluntary aid societies in the same way as medical and religious personnel. GWS, Article 26(1) provides that if such staff 'are subject to military laws and regulations' they 'are placed on the same footing as' military medical and religious personnel. This is correctly reflected in the paragraph. Attention is also drawn in the paragraph to the notification requirement in Article 26(2). Paragraph 4.11.1 then explains that this rule applies to staff of the American National Red Cross, with those that support the US armed forces being subject to the Uniform Code of Military Justice (UCMJ).

STAFF OF A RECOGNIZED AID SOCIETY OF A NEUTRAL COUNTRY

Section 4.12 identifies staff of recognised aid societies of a neutral country provided to a party to the conflict in accordance with GWS, Article 27 as a discrete class of person for the purposes of the present chapter. Article 27 actually refers to a 'recognized Society', as opposed to 'aid societies', although the latter, as the *Manual* indicates, is what is meant. The section should specify, as Article 27(1) does, that it is specifically medical personnel and units that are covered by the provision, but the section notes correctly the obligations of the neutral government to notify the adversary of the State it is assisting of its consent to the provision of the relevant assistance and of the assisted party to notify its adversary before making use of the assistance.[20] As GWS, Article 27(3) and (4) notes, and as the section repeats, such assistance shall not be considered interference in the conflict, and the relevant personnel must be supplied with identity cards, provided for in GWS, Article 40, before leaving the neutral country.

The section then sets out accurately the particular rights enjoyed by such personnel under Article 32 of GWS. If they fall into the hands of the adverse

[20] GWS, Article 27(2).

party, they may not be detained.[21] Absent contrary agreement, they may return to their own country or, if that is not possible, to the territory of the party to the conflict in whose service they were as soon as a route for their return is open and military considerations permit. Pending release, they continue their work under the direction of the adverse party, preferably tending to the wounded and sick of the party to the conflict in whose service they were. They may take with them their effects, personal articles, valuables, instruments, arms and, if possible, means of transport. Both parties must secure to them the food, lodging, allowances and pay granted to corresponding personnel of their own armed forces; the food must be sufficient in quantity, quality and variety to keep the personnel in a normal state of health; and they may fly their national flag.[22]

AUXILIARY MEDICAL PERSONNEL

Section 4.13 defines auxiliary medical personnel in accordance with Article 25 of GWS as '[m]embers of the armed forces specially trained for employment, should the need arise, as hospital orderlies, nurses or auxiliary stretcher-bearers, in the search for or the collection, transport, or treatment of the wounded and sick' in international armed conflict. The section correctly states that such persons will generally be treated as combatants and that when carrying out their medical duties, they must wear the white armlet bearing the distinctive sign – better referred to, one would suggest, as the 'distinctive emblem'. The paragraph states that while performing their medical duties they shall not be made the object of attack. In fact, Article 25 requires that they 'be respected and protected if they are carrying out these [medical] duties at the time when they come into contact with the enemy or fall into his hands'. The 'respect and protect' obligation goes very much wider than not making them the object of attack, so it would seem that this paragraph requires amendment.

Paragraph 4.13.1 notes recent US practice as being not to employ auxiliary medical personnel. The paragraph notes, however, that other States may do so, and that 'certain members of the medical corps, who do not qualify as military medical personnel because they perform duties inconsistent with exclusive medical status, may be treated like auxiliary medical personnel'.

Paragraph 4.13.2 correctly points out that persons who perform medical duties or who have medical training do not thereby acquire auxiliary medical status. The paragraph states that the person concerned must receive appropriate training and must be designated as such by his or her armed

[21] GWS, Article 33(1). [22] GWS, Article 43(1).

forces. The former requirement is correct, and is reflected in Article 25. The latter requirement, designation, is not reflected in the cited authority, namely GWS *Commentary*, page 222, nor in Article 25. It would be more accurate to state that he or she must have been detailed or ordered to perform such auxiliary medical duties. Designation by the armed forces implies a more formal arrangement than the applicable law seems to contemplate. The paragraph states that the individual must be supplied with appropriate identification, including an armband and a special identity document. GWS *Commentary*, pages 223–4 constitutes the cited authority, but a passage three paragraphs earlier in the Commentary indicates, perhaps more accurately, that 'there is no need for them to have a special card. Their ordinary military identity documents must simply specify what special training they have received, the temporary character of their duties and their authority for wearing the armlet.'

Paragraph 4.13.3 repeats the understatement of the protection to be afforded to auxiliary medical personnel by indicating that they must not be made the object of attack, whereas Article 25 specifies that they must be respected and protected. The paragraph then repeats in summary form matters discussed in Chapter VII, and in Chapter 7 of the present book, as to the wearing by such personnel of the armlet and as to their obligation to refrain from acts harmful to the enemy while undertaking their medical duties.

The status of auxiliary medical personnel on capture during an international armed conflict as PWs is correctly observed in paragraph 4.13.4, although as the paragraph notes they may be required to perform their medical duties as necessary. Specifically, they do not benefit from the repatriation arrangements accorded to retained personnel.

PERSONNEL ENGAGED IN DUTIES RELATING TO THE PROTECTION OF CULTURAL PROPERTY

Paragraph 4.14.1 repeats almost verbatim Article 15 of the Hague Cultural Property Convention 1954, to the effect that, so far as is consistent with interests of security, personnel engaged in cultural property protection must be respected and, if they fall into the hands of the adverse party, must be allowed to continue to carry out their duties – if the relevant cultural property has also fallen into the hands of the opposing party. The paragraph notes the similarity of the arrangements for military medical and religious personnel continuing to perform their duties after capture and that no special agreement may diminish their protection.[23] Paragraph 4.14.1.2 notes that States may have within

[23] Hague Cultural Property Convention 1954, Article 24(2).

their armed forces personnel whose purpose is to secure respect for cultural property and to cooperate with the civilian authorities responsible for safeguarding it. Practice during World War II is mentioned, and the undertaking in Article 7(2) of the 1954 Convention is rightly cited. Paragraph 4.14.1.2 then explains that armed custodians specially empowered to protect cultural property may be used. Guarding cultural property subject to special protection in this way is not, however, deemed to be a use of it for military purposes, such as would deprive it of special protection.[24]

Paragraph 4.14.2 then identifies, and describes the respective roles of, persons responsible for the duties of control under the Regulations for the Execution of the 1954 Hague Cultural Property Convention, noting that they must not exceed their mandate and that they must take into account the security needs of the relevant party to the conflict, acting in accordance with the requirements of the military situation as communicated to them by that State. The relevant persons, whose roles and duties are noted in each case, are: the Director-General of UNESCO; the representative for cultural property situated in a State's territory, who must be appointed by a State that becomes involved in an international armed conflict; the special representative for cultural property in occupied territory, who must be appointed by a State that is in occupation of territory; delegates appointed by the Protecting Powers to perform certain functions in relation to cultural property protection;[25] the Commissioner-General for Cultural Property;[26] and inspectors and experts appointed by the Commissioner-General.

Paragraph 4.14.3 notes that the persons responsible for duties of control under the Hague Cultural Property Convention Regulations and those engaged in duties for the protection of cultural property must carry a special identity card bearing the distinctive emblem, displayed once,[27] and that they may wear an armlet bearing the distinctive emblem, displayed once, and issued and stamped by the competent authorities.[28]

[24] *DoD Manual*, paragraph 4.14.1.2.

[25] These functions include taking note of violations of the 1954 Convention, investigating (subject to approvals) such violations, making representations to secure their cessation and notifying the Commissioner-General of their occurrence; *DoD Manual*, paragraph 4.14.2.3.

[26] The *Manual* notes that the appointment of the Commissioner-General is subject to the approval of the party to which he is accredited; *DoD Manual*, paragraph 4.14.2.4.

[27] Regulations for the Execution of the 1954 Hague Cultural Property Convention (Hague Cultural Property Regulations), Article 21(2).

[28] Hague Cultural Property Regulations, Article 21(1). The *Manual* repeats Article 21(4) of the Regulations, to the effect that such persons may not without legitimate reason be deprived of their identity card or of the right to wear the armlet.

PERSONS AUTHORIZED TO ACCOMPANY THE ARMED FORCES

Section 4.15 argues that persons who are authorised to accompany the armed forces constitute a special category. The section acknowledges that such persons are often referred to as 'civilians'. Indeed, the present authors would point out that they are in fact civilians, so far as States that are party to API are concerned, as they are not combatants as defined in Article 43(2). The section, however, distinguishes such persons from the civilian population on the basis that they 'are authorized – in some cases, are ordered – to accompany military forces into a theatre of operations to support the force'. The section correctly notes that such persons may not be made the object of attack unless they take a direct part in hostilities. In that respect, the reader will appreciate, they are indistinguishable from civilians in general. The paragraph also correctly notes that like other civilians, they may, where military necessity so requires, be detained by enemy military forces, although by virtue of their listing under Article 4A(4) of GPW they will, unlike civilians in general, have PW status if captured. The section then asserts, without cited authority, that they will 'have legal immunity from the enemy's domestic law for providing authorized support services to the armed forces'. Subject to the possibility of a plea of 'act of state', this is plainly incorrect. Combatant immunity does not apply to such persons, because they do not have combatant status, and if captured by the enemy they are therefore liable to arrest, trial and punishment for their acts that constitute breaches of the enemy's domestic criminal law.

Paragraph 4.15.1 lists persons who come within the suggested category as including 'employees of the Department of Defense, employees of other government agencies sent to support the armed forces, and other authorized persons working on government contracts to support the armed forces'. The paragraph again makes the point that these persons are often referred to, and treated as, civilians, and one might comment that this is unsurprising as civilians is palpably what they usually are. Paragraph 4.15.2 acknowledges, as is the case, that the law as to the conduct of hostilities applies in relation to persons accompanying the armed forces similarly to the manner of its operation in relation to civilians. The paragraph suggests, however, that this similarity only applies in some respects. Certainly, like civilians, and as paragraph 4.15.2.1 again points out, such persons may not be made the object of attack unless they take a direct part in hostilities. Paragraph 4.15.2.2 notes that the law of war does not actually prohibit persons accompanying the armed forces from taking a direct part in hostilities, but neither does it prohibit civilians in general from doing so. If the support that persons accompanying the armed forces provide constitutes direct participation, that does not, as the paragraph correctly notes, deprive them of PW status if they are captured. The paragraph then suggests that, although the law of war does not prohibit using persons accompanying the armed forces to provide support that constitutes direct participation, commanders should exercise care when placing such persons in situations in which an attacking enemy might interpret their activities as constituting direct participation, 'as there may be legal and policy considerations against such use'. This is an eminently sensible way of addressing the matter for the purposes of the present *Manual*, and the reader assumes that it is left to other, not necessarily published documents to set forth the relevant legal and policy considerations.

The final sentence of the paragraph prohibits commanders from employing persons authorised to accompany the armed forces to perform duties and functions traditionally performed by a military person with the purpose of shielding a military objective from attack. There are, of course, other forms that such shielding might take, which might also involve persons authorised to accompany the armed forces and which would similarly breach the law of war.[29]

Paragraph 4.15.2.3 points out the increased risk of death or injury to which persons authorised to accompany the armed forces are exposed by virtue of their greater proximity to military objectives; for example, they might suffer incidental injury as a result of an attack against the force they accompany, the location where they serve might itself be a military objective or their presence at a military objective might lead to the false appreciation that they are combatants or directly participating civilians.

Paragraph 4.15.2.4 correctly states that persons authorised to accompany the armed forces have the right to use force in self-defence against unlawful attacks, citing attacks by bandits as an example. The paragraph explains, correctly in law, that they should not resist capture by an enemy force whom they expect to comply with the law of war, as such resistance may constitute direct participation in hostilities, rendering them liable to be attacked. The corollary is not spelt out in the *Manual*. The present authors suggest it is this: if the attack breaches the law of war, or if the past conduct of the attackers leads the persons authorised to accompany the armed forces reasonably to believe that the impending attack will be conducted unlawfully, then the use of force against the attackers in self-defence is likely to be lawful. The US policy of arming such authorised persons is then mentioned, and the US approach is stated: namely, that a State may decide to arm persons authorised to

[29] Consider API, Article 51(7) and GC, Article 28.

accompany the armed forces for personal security and self-defence purposes without incorporating them into the armed forces or otherwise authorising them to act as combatants. This would seem in general to be a sensible approach, but in the view of the present authors, any such decision to arm should be subject to considerations of necessity and appropriateness. There are likely to be circumstances in which arming such individuals would be unnecessary and perhaps counter-productive.

Paragraph 4.15.2.5 suggests that the law of war does not prohibit persons authorised to accompany the armed forces from wearing uniform, including the uniform of the armed forces they accompany. The present authors would sound a note of caution about this statement. If the uniform of such armed forces constitutes the 'fixed distinctive sign recognisable at a distance' that is an element of combatant status as that notion is applied by the US, large numbers of persons who are not members of the armed forces but who also wear that sign might cause it no longer to be distinctive. The present authors would therefore applaud the US's recent practice, as reported in the *Manual*, of making the two uniforms distinct.[30] While wearing a uniform may indeed increase the danger that a person will be attacked, the second part of the paragraph suggests that being authorised by a State to wear a military uniform does not necessarily authorise the person to act as a combatant. This is true as far as it goes, but it would arguably be better for the paragraph simply to note that the wearing of a uniform and the possession of combatant status are distinct matters, and that the former does not necessarily imply the latter.

Paragraph 4.15.2.6 draws the important and legally correct distinction between persons authorised to accompany the armed forces who provide security against criminal elements and such persons who directly participate in the hostilities. In principle, as the paragraph correctly suggests, the former do not lose their protection from attack by virtue of that activity, although it will sometimes be factually difficult to distinguish between protection from criminal elements and participation in the fight. While acknowledging that the associated footnote refers to examples of direct participation, the reader of this paragraph should not, of course, be left with the impression that defending against the armed forces of a State is the only activity that would deprive a person authorised to accompany the armed forces of his or her protection as a civilian. It is therefore suggested that the paragraph refer more generally to any action amounting to direct participation. The paragraph then usefully refers to DoD policy on the matter.

30 *DoD Manual*, paragraph 4.15.2.5, second sentence.

Paragraph 4.15.3 notes that persons authorised to accompany the armed forces may be lawfully detained and are entitled to PW status if detained during an international armed conflict. Requirements as to advances of pay and equivalence of rank for such PWs and as to identity cards are mentioned in this paragraph but discussed in Chapter IX of the *Manual* and Chapter 9 of the present volume.

Paragraph 4.15.4 gets to grips with the direct participation issue. It expresses the US view that 'persons authorised to accompany the armed forces may lawfully support armed forces in the conduct of hostilities', which, as an expression of the international law on the matter, is plainly correct. However, the issue here is really whether a capturing enemy State can lawfully convict and punish such persons for their support activities. The paragraph contends that '[s]uch persons should not be liable under an enemy State's domestic law for providing authorized support services'. The fact that the support service is authorised does not, however, protect the relevant individual under international law. If the authorised support does amount to direct participation, the relevant individual, on capture, is liable to be tried for the relevant crimes. If the support does not amount to direct participation, then the statement in the *Manual* is correct, and it would also be right to state that the individual should not be prosecuted for aiding the enemy in relation to acts that do not constitute direct participation in the hostilities, partly at least because no allegiance was owed at the relevant time to the prosecuting enemy State. Similarly, he or she should not be punished for acts that were undertaken in lawful self-defence; indeed, this is likely to be a defence, at any event, under the criminal law of the relevant State.

The paragraph suggests that such persons should not engage in unauthorised participation in the hostilities, matters which are discussed in sections 4.18 and 4.19, and cross-refers to the jurisdictional issues that may arise and to the potential command and individual responsibilities of commanders. It describes these, with implied and it is suggested inappropriate distaste, as 'theories' of responsibility and liability.

Having read this substantial section, the reader is rather left with the impression that persons authorised to accompany the armed forces are not a distinct class of individual as such. They are merely civilians who, essentially for practical reasons, are granted PW status in the event of capture, and who otherwise are allocated by international law the same rights, protections, restrictions and liabilities as other civilians. Their possible proximity to the scene of battle and their supporting role cause rules as to direct participation and as to protection from attack to have a sharper relevance, but those rules do not materially change in their application to the relevant individuals as against their application to civilians in general.

CREWS OF MERCHANT MARINE VESSELS OR CIVIL AIRCRAFT

The chapeau to section 4.16 points out that the crews of merchant marine vessels or civil aircraft of a belligerent fall into a special category and are in many respects treated like persons authorised to accompany the armed forces. The chapeau continues: 'Under certain circumstances, crews of merchant marine vessels or civil aircraft of a neutral that engage in hostilities may be treated like the crews of belligerent vessels or aircraft.' This is problematic, as the crews of neutral merchant vessels or civil aircraft are not listed in Article 4A(5) of GPW. It follows from this that such crews do not enjoy PW status under the Convention, although the vessels or aircraft may be lawfully targeted if they contribute to the enemy's military action by use. The cross-reference in footnote 323 of Chapter IV to paragraph 15.14 is unhelpful, because that paragraph says nothing about the status of crews of neutral merchant vessels or civil aircraft that have become lawful targets. Nevertheless, the assertion that they may be treated like the crews of belligerent merchant vessels or civil aircraft ignores the fact that under GPW, it is only the crews of belligerent merchant vessels or civil aircraft that have PW status on capture. Moreover, neutral merchant vessel and civil aircraft crews are not entitled to actively resist or disobey lawful belligerent orders. Indeed, such action may be considered to amount to direct participation.

After noting in paragraph 4.16.1 the activities that are, and respectively are not, permitted for merchant vessels and civil aircraft, paragraph 4.16.2 correctly observes that members of the crews of merchant marine vessels and of civil aircraft of a belligerent are entitled to PW status if captured during an international armed conflict, if they do not benefit from more favourable treatment under international law. The paragraph then draws attention to particular provisions of Hague Convention XI of 1907 under which 'the captain, officers and members of the crew [of captured enemy merchant ships] when nationals of the enemy State, are not made prisoners of war, on condition that they make a formal promise in writing, not to undertake, while hostilities last, any service connected with the operations of the war'.[31] As the *Manual* implies, whether these provisions still constitute good law or are now regarded

[31] Hague Convention XI, Article 6. As the *Manual* correctly reflects, Article 8 states that this does not apply to ships taking part in the hostilities.

as moribund is unclear. It is therefore unclear whether Convention IX offers the 'more favourable treatment' referred to earlier in this paragraph.

SPIES, SABOTEURS AND OTHER PERSONS ENGAGED IN SIMILAR ACTS BEHIND ENEMY LINES

The introductory paragraphs of section 4.17 make the basic and correct point that States may lawfully employ spies, saboteurs and other persons to engage in activities behind enemy lines. It then makes the less satisfactory suggestion that 'these activities are punishable by the enemy State'. That is not, of course, necessarily the case. If a combatant in uniform is engaged in a sabotage mission, or indeed in any other mission behind enemy lines, whatever that term means in the context of modern warfare, then upon capture by the enemy, such a person will have combatant status and immunity, and thus will not be liable to prosecution for his or her lawful acts of war. The act of sabotage or the presence of an individual behind enemy lines does not *per se* cause the individual to forfeit combatant status. It is only when sabotage is given a meaning that presupposes, say, that the member of the armed forces is acting while out of uniform or that he or she is otherwise behaving in a manner that deprives him or her of combatant status that the stated proposition becomes correct. It is recommended that this passage be amended to make the correct position clear.

After noting in paragraph 4.17.1 the various meanings that have been applied to the words 'spy' and 'saboteur', paragraph 4.17.1.1 gives their meaning for the purposes of the *Manual*. The *Manual* uses 'spying and sabotage' as a general category of secretive, hostile activities that, when performed behind enemy lines, deprives a person of combatant privileges. The present authors are not of the view that sabotage has the same status at law as espionage. They consider that there is no inherent illegality under the law of armed conflict associated with sabotage, and that there are significant differences between the two classes of activity, such that they ought to be dealt with individually in the *Manual*. Perhaps this interpretation should be put at the beginning of the section, as to do so would arguably render some of the introduction unnecessary, or less confusing. The reference to 'spying, sabotage and similar acts behind enemy lines' is legitimate. The relevant acts may indeed go wider than spying and sabotage, but care is required here. We do not, for example, wish to see journalists classed as unprivileged belligerents because of loose drafting.

Paragraph 4.17.2 adopts, in slightly adjusted form, the Hague Regulations 1907, Article 29 definition of a spy. The *Manual*'s version is 'a person can only be considered a spy when, (1) acting clandestinely or under false pretenses, (2) in the zone of operations of a belligerent, (3) he or she obtains or endeavours to obtain information, (4) with the intention of communicating it to the hostile party'. These elements are then considered in turn.

Paragraph 4.17.2.1 correctly interprets 'acting clandestinely or under false pretences' as 'deliberately concealing or misrepresenting one's identity and conduct', such as a member of the armed forces wearing a disguise so that the enemy will fail to identify him or her as a member of the opposing armed force. As the paragraph explains, members of the armed forces wearing their normal uniforms do not fulfil this criterion. The paragraph includes, however, the following sentence: 'In addition, observers on military reconnaissance aircraft have not been regarded as acting clandestinely or under false pretenses.' There are several points to be made. The first is that if the aircraft is a military aircraft, it will bear the military and nationality marks of the State operating it, and this will preclude any suggestion that the persons in it are acting clandestinely etc. Second, the authorities cited in support of the *Manual* text include Article 29(2) of the Hague Regulations, which concerns itself with carrying despatches and maintaining communications, not reconnaissance. Third, the suggestion attributed to Winthrop that merely observing the enemy with a view to gaining intelligence as to his or her movements does not constitute spying is correct if – and, it is suggested, only if – no clandestine behaviour or false pretence is involved.

Paragraph 4.17.2.2 interprets the zone of operations of a belligerent as including areas that support the war effort. An equally acceptable formulation would be areas that are within the control of the belligerent. The important concluding sentence of the paragraph notes correctly that a person who, from outside that zone, collects information that is within it is not acting as a spy for the purposes of these international law provisions. A person who attempts to obtain information may be punished as a spy even though he or she does not succeed in obtaining the information or in transmitting it to the enemy, but the intent must have been to transmit the information to the hostile party.[32]

Paragraph 4.17.3 explains that persons other than spies acting secretively or on false pretences and with a hostile purpose behind enemy lines have been treated as spies. Some valuable authorities are cited in the footnotes. Perhaps the most useful is an extract from the 1958 *UK Manual* which explains that whether persons dropped or landed behind the lines of the belligerent to commit acts of destruction or terrorism, i.e. saboteurs, are to be treated as spies

[32] This is correctly noted in *DoD Manual*, paragraphs 4.17.2.3 and 4.17.2.4.

depends on whether they are caught in disguise or not; the point is made that if they are caught in their own uniform, they must be treated as PWs.[33] Paragraph 4.17.3 notes that acts other than sabotage that assist one side's war effort and that are committed behind enemy lines have been punished as 'war treason', 'secretly entering the lines' and as 'activities hostile to the security of the State'. The authorities cited in the associated footnotes suggest that an element of secretiveness or false pretence, not mentioned in the main text, would also be required. The view, correctly adopted in paragraph 4.17.3, is that a belligerent's presence in the territory controlled by an opposing State, with a hostile purpose and while acting clandestinely or on false pretences, suffices for that person to be treated as a spy under the law of war.

However, as paragraph 4.17.4 correctly observes, both spying and sabotage – and, one might add, other similar acts committed behind enemy lines – are not *per se* prohibited under the law of war and are not, accordingly, war crimes. The paragraph should then distinguish sabotage of military objectives from sabotage of civilian objects, on the basis that the latter would certainly constitute war crimes, whether executed openly, clandestinely or on false pretences. Most sensibly, paragraph 4.17.4 draws attention to the prohibition of perfidy, and notes that commanders and persons engaged in such activities must take special care not to kill, wound or, in the case of States party to API, capture by resort to perfidy.[34]

Paragraph 4.17.5 notes again that, because of the inherent failure to distinguish themselves, combatants who act as spies, saboteurs or otherwise engage in hostile, secretive activities behind enemy lines forfeit their entitlement to combatant privileges. Paragraph 4.17.5.1, relying on Hague Regulations, Article 31, notes that a spy who, after rejoining the army to which he or she belongs, is subsequently captured by the enemy, incurs no responsibility – or, the *Manual* tells us, liability – for his or her previous acts of espionage. It would perhaps be helpful if Article 31's requirement that such persons be treated as PWs were to be repeated explicitly in the paragraph. Somewhat obviously, and arguably unnecessarily, the paragraph points out that persons who never had combatant status do not benefit by regaining a combatant status that they never had. Paragraph 4.17.5.2 then explains that where there is doubt as to the entitlement to PW status of a person who has committed a belligerent act, the person has the right to have his or her status determined by a competent tribunal and to be treated as a PW in the meantime.[35]

[33] 1958 *UK Manual*, paragraph 331.

[34] Consider Hague Regulations 1907, Article 23(b) and API, Article 37(1).

[35] GPW, Article 5(2).

PRIVATE PERSONS WHO ENGAGE IN HOSTILITIES

The *Manual* justifies the reference to 'private persons', as opposed to 'civilians', on three grounds. The first, essentially, is that the former reflects 'long-standing explanations of the principle of distinction', essentially meaning Articles 22 and 23 of the Lieber Code. One might comment that discussion of these issues has progressed somewhat since the middle of the nineteenth century. The second is 'because private persons who engage in hostilities are liable to treatment in one or more respects as combatants'. This is again a consequence of the US's reluctance to view combatant as a status, as opposed to as a reflection of what an individual is doing, and it leads to the rather unsatisfactory argument that because some civilians do some things that some combatants do, we therefore cannot describe such persons as civilians. However, the criterion accurately reflects the US view, and therein lies its relevance and legitimacy in the *Manual*. The third is that non-military personnel belonging to a State, such as persons authorised to accompany the armed forces, raise issues that merit special consideration – as opposed to the case of a private person who decides to engage in hostilities. The discussion in the present book relating to section 4.15 of the *Manual* argued that, while there are limited distinctions in the legal treatment of 'persons authorised', they do not justify special categorisation of such persons, and this will be especially the case for States party to API.

Revealingly, the next portion of the paragraph makes the somewhat mixed-up point that '[w]hether a particular person is liable as a consequence of his or her conduct to treatment as a combatant (e.g., being made the object of attack, internment, or prosecution for acts of unprivileged belligerency) must be assessed with reference to the specific legal rule at issue rather than based on the use of a conclusory label, such as "enemy combatant"'. The person would not be treated as a combatant in the sense of having the legal right to participate, but in the sense of having taken a direct part in the hostilities. Moreover, if, as the present authors believe, it is indeed the specific legal rule that must be assessed, this rather demonstrates the lack of usefulness of the 'combatant' classification as used e.g. in this part of paragraph 4.18.1.

Paragraph 4.18.2 contends that 'private persons' who engage in hostilities forfeit many of the protections afforded to civilians under the law of war. Particular mention is made of the right to detain such persons in order to address the threat they pose. Paragraph 4.18.3 correctly explains that private persons who engage in hostilities are not entitled to combatant privileges and may be punished after a fair trial. The notion of a 'revolving door of protection', exemplified by the expression 'farmer by day and guerrilla by night', is explicitly –

and, in the present authors' view, correctly – rejected in this paragraph. The paragraph then plausibly suggests that the denial of combatant privileges to private persons who engage in hostilities may be based on their lack of 'State authorisation', but this merely explains why they do not enjoy such privileges. It should be noted that, as observed earlier in this chapter, this is not a reflection of the *jus ad bellum*, but follows from the *jus in bello*, because of the link in the Hague Regulations 1907 between combatant status, membership of the armed forces and status as an organ of the State. While the law of war does not prohibit private persons ('civilians' is really the better term) from directly participating in hostilities, the fact that they can be punished under domestic law for their hostile acts is the real issue here. The points are also made that '[p]rivate persons who engage in hostilities risk undermining the protections afforded the civilian population', that such private persons have generally not been trained in the law of war, that they are not subject to the same disciplinary regime as members of the armed forces and that their participation in hostilities has been associated with the commission of war crimes.

Paragraph 4.18.4 addresses the difficult issue of determining which activities of private persons constitute engaging in hostilities. It is well known that the ICRC and the Asser Institute jointly organised an expert process with the objective of clarifying the notion of direct participation[36] and that, following the failure of the experts participating in that process to reach substantive agreement, the ICRC issued its *Interpretive Guidance*.[37] One would have thought that some mention should have been made of this in the early part of the discussion of these matters in the *Manual*, if only to demonstrate the lack of international consensus and thus to clarify the status and legal basis for what is being put forward.

Paragraph 4.18.4.1 takes the view that being part of a non-State armed group that is engaged in hostilities against a State is a form of engaging in hostilities that renders the person liable to treatment in one or more respects as an unprivileged belligerent. This will often be the case, but the present authors would apply the additional requirement that the individual must have an actual or contingent combat role. Members of such groups who fulfil purely diplomatic or administrative roles and who have no role relating to hostilities or to the command of those engaging in hostilities ought not, solely by virtue of their association with the group, to be classified as engaging in hostilities. The potential difficulty in establishing whether an individual is a member of a

[36] Personal knowledge of both of the present authors, who, as experts, participated in the ICRC/Asser Institute process.

[37] Melzer, *Interpretive Guidance*.

non-State armed group, the likely absence of formal indicia such as uniforms or identity cards and the possible requirement to use functional or circumstantial information are all properly noted in the paragraph.

The *Manual* then discusses persons who, although not members of such groups, 'are functionally part of those organisations'. Noting that such persons may fulfil roles analogous to the support provided to State armed forces by persons authorised to accompany those forces, the *Manual* argues that these individuals 'may be regarded as constructively part of the group, even if they are, in fact, not formal members of the group'.[38] While at first glance the argument is appealing, the problem with this approach is that it would classify such persons as 'engaging in hostilities' essentially on a class/quasi-membership basis, when the persons from whom the analogy is drawn – namely, persons authorised to accompany the armed forces – do not lose protection on a class basis. It would be both simpler and more legally accurate to say that the persons referred to here will lose protection if they engage in hostilities and that whether they do so must be determined by reference to their roles in the activities in which they participate.

As paragraph 4.18.4.2 correctly states, private persons who bear arms against, or attempt to kill or injure, enemy personnel would become liable to be made the object of attack. The reader is, however, rather left with the impression that the discussion here could have been made much clearer if the *Manual* had started by simply explaining that it is engaging in hostilities that has the relevant consequences for private persons, and had then discussed what engaging in hostilities does and respectively does not include. Instead, the final sentence of the paragraph restates what has been covered already, namely that 'spying, sabotage and other hostile activities behind enemy lines would render a person liable to prosecution for such conduct'. It would also make the relevant person liable to be made the object of lawful attack and to be lawfully detained; these are matters that could have been addressed simply as the consequence arising from engaging in hostilities, no matter what the form of that engagement might be.

Paragraph 4.18.5 states that 'under international law private enemy nationals are not generally regarded as being prohibited from engaging in hostilities during international armed conflict'. This is a curious way of putting an essentially correct proposition. The rule, after all, does not just apply to an enemy. It also applies to US personnel. It would therefore be both legally accurate and, arguably, more sensible to refer simply to 'private persons'. The paragraph then notes that 'like other forms of unprivileged belligerency, private

[38] *DoD Manual*, paragraph 4.18.4.1.

engagement in hostility has been described in some contexts as a "war crime" or as a violation of international law or the law of war'. It would perhaps have been more helpful if the US position in this regard had been explicitly stated. At least some of the sources referenced in the associated footnotes[39] do not use the term 'war crime' in its more modern sense. This is, for example, revealed in the concept of 'war criminal to the enemy', indicating a situation in which an individual has committed a breach of enemy domestic law in the context of a war.

The paragraph concludes by noting correctly that private acts of hostility are prohibited in particular contexts. The cited contexts are private expeditions against a foreign State from another State that has friendly relations with it, piracy and terrorism.

Overall, this is a somewhat disappointing section. It could have usefully explained to the reader the US position as to which kinds of activity, particularly in the context of modern methods of warfare, respectively are and are not considered to amount to engagement in hostilities. Alternatively, the factors that members of the armed forces should consider in determining whether an individual is or is not engaging in hostilities could profitably have been addressed. Some indication could have been given of when such engagement is considered to start and when it is deemed to finish, as to the action an individual needs to take in order to demonstrate that he or she has renounced such engagement and so on. The section does not really go into that kind of detail, and that is a matter for some regret.

RIGHTS, DUTIES AND LIABILITIES OF UNPRIVILEGED BELLIGERENTS

Section 4.19 states again the general proposition that unprivileged belligerents lack the distinct privileges afforded to combatants and civilians and are subject to the liabilities of both classes of individual. As the section accurately notes in summary form, they may generally be made the object of attack, must be treated humanely if *hors de combat* and may be punished by the enemy on conviction after a fair trial for their engagement in the hostilities.

Paragraph 4.19.1 acknowledges that unprivileged belligerents are entitled to 'basic guarantees of humane treatment', which the paragraph clarifies to mean 'elementary considerations of humanity', and to certain treaty-based protections, which the associated footnote suggests are limited to Common Article 3 of the Geneva Conventions and Article 5 of GC. US practice is described as affording such persons, as a matter of domestic law or policy, more favourable

[39] *DoD Manual*, footnotes 391 and 392 on page 161.

treatment than is their entitlement under international law, but US practice reportedly recognises that they should not be afforded the distinct privileges of lawful combatants or the protections of peaceful civilians under the law of war.

The reader is given relatively little detail here as to the protections that the US considers unprivileged belligerents should be given. Specifically, which basic guarantees of humane treatment they are entitled to and what elementary considerations of humanity boil down to in practice are not made clear at this stage in the discussion.

Paragraph 4.19.2 accurately explains that although unprivileged belligerents lack the right to participate in hostilities, they must nevertheless comply with the law of armed conflict in their conduct of such hostilities. The paragraph states again that they may be made the object of attack by enemy combatants unless they are *hors de combat*, in which case they must be treated humanely.

Paragraph 4.19.3 states that '[u]nprivileged belligerents are liable to capture and detention, like lawful combatants'. It would be more accurate to point out that unprivileged belligerents are as liable to be captured and detained as lawful combatants,[40] but that the mode of detention is likely to differ.

The requirement that detained unprivileged belligerents be treated humanely is addressed in paragraph 4.19.3.1. The paragraph states that they must as a minimum receive the fundamental guarantees of humane treatment set forth in Common Article 3 to the Geneva Conventions. The paragraph also explains that the United States has supported 'out of a sense of legal obligation' the fundamental guarantees set forth in Article 75 of API 'as minimum standards for the humane treatment of all persons detained during international armed conflict'. The clear inference is that the US still supports those guarantees, but this is not explicitly stated. Equally unstated is whether the US considers that these fundamental guarantees in Article 75 also apply during non-international armed conflict. While the inference to be drawn from the quoted passage is that the US regards Article 75 as customary in its application to international armed conflicts,[41] it would be useful for that aspect to be clarified. Moreover, if the US believes that fundamental safeguards considered customary in relation to international armed conflicts do not apply in relation to non-international armed conflicts, it would be interesting to learn why.

40 The expression 'lawful combatant' is, of course, a contradiction in terms for a State party to API.

41 The inference is based on the reference to a perceived legal obligation relating to a provision by which the US is not treaty-bound.

Paragraph 4.19.3.2 again[42] points out that in cases of doubt whether a person held as an unprivileged belligerent is in fact entitled to PW status or treatment, the person should enjoy PW protections until their status has been determined by a competent tribunal. Paragraph 4.19.3.3 correctly explains that a State may take necessary security measures with regard to unprivileged belligerents. The paragraph notes that the rights of unprivileged belligerents who are protected persons under GC are subject to derogation for security reasons, as to which see the discussion in Chapter X of the *Manual* and Chapter 10 of the present book.[43]

Paragraph 4.19.3.4 mentions that unprivileged belligerents detained to prevent their participation in hostilities must generally be released when hostilities have ended, absent some other justification for their continued detention. DoD practice is stated to be periodically to review the continued detention of all persons who do not have PW status or treatment. Paragraph 4.19.4 reports that unprivileged belligerents lack the combatant's protection from prosecution and may therefore be punished subject to applicable requirements, such as a fair trial. Whenever this is mentioned, it would seem sensible to remind the reader that the combatant's privilege only extends to his or her lawful acts of war in an international armed conflict.

Paragraph 4.19.4.1 starts by noting that spying and other forms of unprivileged belligerency have generally not been regarded as war crimes; they are described as punishable but not prohibited under international law, which is correct provided that the contemplated punishment is pursuant to domestic law. That said, the paragraph notes that spying and unprivileged belligerency have also been described as offences against the law of nations or law of war, indicating differences in the meaning being given to 'war crime' (as briefly discussed earlier in the present chapter) and a different appreciation of the meaning of 'law of war'. The important, well-accepted point comes in the final sentence of the paragraph: 'States may punish unprivileged enemy belligerents after a fair trial.'

CHILDREN

Paragraph 4.20.1.1 quotes the GC, Article 24 stipulation that the parties to the conflict must take all feasible measures to ensure that children under fifteen years old who are orphaned or separated from their families as a result of the war are not left to their own resources and that their maintenance, the exercise of their religion and their education are facilitated in all circumstances.

[42] See also paragraph 4.17.5.2.

[43] Specifically, see section 10.4 and paragraph 10.4.4.

As the *Manual* notes, citing the *GC Commentary*,[44] maintenance for these purposes means feeding, clothing, accommodation, care for their health and, where necessary, medical and hospital treatment. Their education should, where possible, be entrusted to persons of a similar cultural tradition, and inappropriate religious or political propaganda should be excluded.[45] Continuing with quoted extracts from Article 24, the paragraph notes that 'parties to the conflict shall facilitate the reception of such children in a neutral country for the duration of the conflict with the consent of the Protecting Power, if any, and under due safeguards for the observance of the principles stated in the first paragraph of Article 24 of GC'.

The parties to the conflict must endeavour to arrange for all children under twelve to wear identity discs or to be identified by some other means.[46] The required arrangements for the protection of alien children in a belligerent's own country, which will be discussed in paragraph 10.7.1 and Chapter 10, and for the protection of children in occupied territory, which will be discussed in paragraph 11.13 and Chapter 11, are mentioned in summary form in paragraphs 4.20.2 and 4.20.3, respectively.

Paragraph 4.20.4 notes that GC protections afforded to children in the context of internment relate to internment with their parents, special treatment of children during internment and relevant special agreements affecting children. These matters are discussed in more detail respectively in paragraphs 10.10.3, 10.16.2, 10.13.1.2, 10.16.3 and 10.9.6.

Having noted in paragraph 4.20.5 that certain provisions of international law and of US domestic law seek to restrict the recruitment and use of child soldiers in armed conflict, paragraph 4.20.5.1 specifies that US law makes it an offence, under certain circumstances, to recruit, enlist or conscript a person to serve in an armed force or group while that person is under fifteen years old or to use such a person to participate actively in hostilities. Reference is made in an associated footnote to Article 77(2) of API and to the Convention on the Rights of the Child,[47] Article 38(2) to (3), to which the US is not party,[48] but in which similar provision is made.

Paragraph 4.20.5.2 notes that the US is party to the Optional Protocol to the Convention on the Rights of the Child on the involvement of children

[44] J S Pictet (ed.) *Commentary IV on Convention Relative to the Protection of Civilian Persons in Time of War*. International Committee of the Red Cross (1958), 187.

[45] GC, Article 24; *GC Commentary*, page 187.

[46] *DoD Manual*, paragraph 4.20.1.2; GC, Article 24.

[47] Convention on the Rights of the Child, New York, 20 November 1989.

[48] Source https://treaties.un.org/Pages/ViewDetails.aspx?src=IND&mtdsg_no=IV-11&chapter=4&clang=_en, viewed on 17 December 2017.

in armed conflict. That treaty requires the US to take all feasible measures to ensure that members of its armed forces who have not attained the age of eighteen years do not take a direct part in hostilities.[49] The paragraph also notes the obligation to ensure that persons who have not attained the age of eighteen years are not compulsorily recruited into the armed forces, it being noted that the minimum age at which persons may be voluntarily recruited into the US armed forces is seventeen.

Paragraph 4.20.5.3 correctly explains that the rights, duties and liabilities of combatant status apply to children as to others, so there is no age criterion for entitlement to PW status and the issue of direct participation in hostilities is not age-related. The possibility that detained children who have directly participated in hostilities or who have been associated with an armed force may need special consideration is acknowledged, and, to be fair, education is referred to in particular. The obligation seems to be understated here, however, and it would be better to cross-refer here to the numerous specific legal requirements as to particular treatment for children discussed in Chapter X of the *Manual* and in Chapter 10 of this book.

Section 4.20 arguably does not address in sufficiently specific terms the moral dilemma faced by adult soldiers who are confronted by child soldiers fighting for the enemy. Referring to rights, duties and liabilities of combatant status in the abstract rather fails to address the practical issue sufficiently directly, so perhaps an additional piece of text is required on that topic.

MERCENARIES

The customary law position in relation to mercenaries is explained in section 4.21. The section correctly states that, at customary law: it is not a crime to be a mercenary and mercenaries enjoy the same rights, duties and liabilities as other combatants; mercenaries are entitled to PW status if they meet the requisite requirements, such as by being a member of part of the armed forces of a State; mercenaries may be tried and punished for violations of the law of war; States that employ mercenaries are responsible for their conduct; and mercenaries are usually nationals of States not party to the conflict and should not be more severely treated by the enemy State than a national of the opposing party would be treated for a similar act.

[49] Optional Protocol, Article 1. As the *Manual* notes in footnote 443 on page 169, the US made a statement on ratification giving its interpretation of the meaning of 'direct part in hostilities' for the purposes of the Optional Protocol, and the footnote makes the point that the phrase may be interpreted differently in other contexts.

Having usefully set this as the context, paragraph 4.21.1 notes that the US rejects a number of treaty provisions directed at repressing mercenary activity because 'these efforts are not consistent with fundamental principles of the law of war'. The paragraph notes that API denies mercenaries combatant and PW status, a provision that the *Manual* rightly attributes to the wish of a number of States to condemn mercenary groups that had played a role in armed conflicts in sub-Saharan Africa since 1960. However, and again as the paragraph correctly observes, mercenaries are defined very narrowly for the purposes of API, and States party to API are permitted to choose to treat mercenaries as PWs and to accord them combatant privileges. The paragraph then mentions the Convention for the Elimination of Mercenarism in Africa, adopted in 1977, and the Mercenaries Convention,[50] noting that the US is party to neither treaty.

API PROVISIONS ON CIVIL DEFENSE PERSONNEL

In brief terms, section 4.22 notes that Articles 61 to 67 of API deal with the performance of certain humanitarian tasks intended to benefit the civilian population, i.e. civil defence. The section reports the US position that civilian civil defence organisations and their personnel should be respected and protected as civilians and be permitted to perform their civil defence tasks subject to imperative military necessity. Unspecified 'military operational problems' are stated to apply to the API provisions, which, the *Manual* states, are understood not to preclude an attack on an otherwise lawful military objective. Ignoring the tautology associated with the term 'lawful military objective', the section is making it clear that so far as the US is concerned, the protection to which civilian civil defence personnel are entitled is limited to that accorded to civilians in general. This is self-evidently not the case for States that are party to API. It might have been useful if the nature of the 'military operational problems' referred to in the section had been explained a little more.

LAW ENFORCEMENT OFFICERS

Section 4.23 points out that members of police forces generally receive the rights, duties and liabilities of civilian status,[51] but recognises that if

[50] International Convention against the Recruitment, Use, Financing and Training of Mercenaries, New York, 4 December 1989.

[51] Paragraph 4.23.1 correctly points out that routine domestic law enforcement does not constitute 'taking a direct part in hostilities' such as would deprive someone of their protection from

States choose to use police officers as part of the armed forces, the officers receive the rights, duties and liabilities of combatant status by virtue of their membership in the armed forces. Members of law enforcement agencies may also be authorised to accompany the armed forces. Paragraph 4.23.2 suggests that such persons 'have the legal status of persons authorized to accompany the armed forces', or, as the present authors see it, are civilians who would have PW status if captured. Finally, paragraph 4.23.3 properly notes that police officers may have an enhanced role during non-international armed conflicts because the State may treat all participation by enemy personnel in such conflicts as criminal.

JOURNALISTS

Section 4.24 correctly explains that journalists are generally civilians but may be members of the armed forces, persons authorised to accompany the armed forces or unprivileged belligerents. If they are members of the armed forces, they have the same status as other members of the armed forces.[52]

Paragraph 4.24.2 starts with an accurate statement of the law, namely '[i]n general, independent journalists and other media representatives are regarded as civilians'. As footnotes to the paragraph point out, this is reflected in Article 79(1) of API. The sentence continues, 'i.e. journalism does not constitute taking a direct part in hostilities such that a person would be deprived of protection from being made the object of attack'. It would perhaps be better to state that journalism *per se* does not necessarily constitute taking a direct part in hostilities, adding that whether a particular journalistic act amounts to direct participation will depend on the nature of the act and the attendant circumstances. After all, a journalist who surreptitiously obtains information as to matters of military significance from, and in the territory of, one party to the conflict and then broadcasts it to another party is at risk of an accusation of espionage, or at least of gathering tactical military intelligence, a kind of activity widely recognised as also constituting direct participation.

Paragraph 4.24.2.1 correctly explains that if journalists authorised to accompany the armed forces, sometimes called 'war correspondents', are captured during an international armed conflict, they have PW status by virtue of GPW,

being made the object of attack, but members of the armed forces used in police roles are combatants; *DoD Manual*, paragraph 4.23.2.

[52] *DoD Manual*, paragraph 4.24.1.

Article 4A(4). They must be issued with identification cards in order to be able to establish their entitlement to PW status if captured.

Self-evidently, journalists who enter an area of military operations assume a significant risk of injury or death arising from an enemy attack or other dangers. Having made that point, paragraph 4.24.3.1 therefore suggests that they should seek to distinguish themselves from military forces but points out, as already noted, that relaying information might in some circumstances amount to direct participation. The paragraph then potentially confuses readers by referring to '[c]ivilian journalists and journalists authorised to accompany the armed forces'. The latter will be civilians just as much as the former. The underlying point of the sentence, however – that journalists should not participate in the fighting between belligerents in that or in any other way if they wish to retain protection from being made the object of attack – is of course correct, and if journalists engage in hostilities against a State, they may be punished by it after a fair trial.

Paragraph 4.24.4 notes the apparent similarity between reporting on operations and collecting intelligence or spying, and that a journalist who acts as a spy may be subjected to security measures and punished if captured. The paragraph therefore sensibly suggests that journalists should act openly and with the permission of relevant authorities, and that the presentation of identification documents, such as the identification card issued to authorised war correspondents, may help them to avoid being mistaken for spies.

Clearly, as paragraph 4.24.5 properly points out, States may need to take security measures, including censorship, to avoid the revelation of sensitive information to the enemy. The paragraph makes the valid and important point that journalists have no special right to enter a State's territory without its consent or to access areas where military operations are taking place without the consent of the State conducting those operations.

DELEGATES OR REPRESENTATIVES OF THE PROTECTING POWERS

Paragraph 4.25.1 explains that the Protecting Powers may appoint, subject to the approval of the State where they are to perform their duties, delegates from among their nationals or those of other neutral States to carry out duties under the GPW and GC. The parties to the conflict must as far as possible facilitate the tasks of the delegates and representatives of the Protecting Powers, who must not exceed their duties under the Conventions and who must take account of the imperative necessities of security of the State wherein they carry out their duties.[53] A belligerent may impose legitimate security restrictions on their activities in its territory or facilities as an exceptional and temporary measure when rendered necessary by imperative military necessities.[54]

ICRC AND OTHER IMPARTIAL HUMANITARIAN ORGANIZATIONS

Section 4.26 explains correctly that the ICRC and other humanitarian organisations may, subject to the consent of the parties to the conflict concerned, provide humanitarian aid and seek to ensure the protection of war victims, and in some cases may assume the humanitarian functions of the Protecting Powers. Paragraph 4.26.1 starts with the following not particularly illuminating sentence: 'To be an "impartial humanitarian organization" under the 1949 Geneva Conventions, a humanitarian organization must be impartial.' One rather wonders about the usefulness of such statements of the obvious. Slightly more usefully, the paragraph goes on to contrast non-impartial humanitarian organisations that have an allegiance to a party to the conflict, such as national Red Cross societies.

Paragraph 4.26.2 notes the requirement for State consent to humanitarian activities of the ICRC or other impartial humanitarian organisations and correctly bases this requirement on the sovereign right to control access and on the right of a belligerent to control access to territory it controls or to its military operations. States may consent to impartial humanitarian organisations having access, and such organisations must operate within the terms of that consent;[55] such terms may reflect security concerns.[56] The paragraph then suggests that the requirement to protect PWs from public curiosity might be a justification for limiting access of impartial humanitarian organisations to PWs. This seems to be a somewhat far-fetched suggestion. If the activities of an impartial humanitarian organisation were to facilitate such exposure, its impartiality and its humanitarian credentials would both be called into serious question.

There is a drafting error that renders paragraph 4.26.2.2 difficult to understand. It might be preferable simply to quote the relevant language of the Amended Mines Protocol.[57]

53 *DoD Manual*, paragraph 4.25.2, quoting GPW, Article 8 and GC, Article 9.

54 GWS and GWS-Sea, Article 8; *DoD Manual*, paragraph 4.25.3.

55 *DoD Manual*, paragraphs 4.26.2 and 4.26.2.1.

56 *DoD Manual*, footnote 499 on page 177 usefully illustrates some reasons why such security concerns may legitimately arise.

57 Amended Protocol on Prohibitions or Restrictions on the Use of Mines, Booby-Traps and Other Devices (1996).

It is good to see the special status of the ICRC among impartial humanitarian organisations being clearly, properly and fulsomely recognised, and the unparalleled value of its humanitarian work being properly acknowledged, in paragraph 4.26.3. The breadth of the tasks that the ICRC undertakes is appropriately summarised, and the present authors wish to associate themselves fully with these sentiments. However, given the main intended focus of Chapter IV of the *Manual*, one wonders whether this section of the chapter might address a little more the legal status of the ICRC delegates and representatives as they perform their various tasks and the responsibilities of the parties to the conflict in their dealings with them.

DETERMINING THE STATUS OF DETAINEES IN CASES OF DOUBT

Paragraph 4.27.1 notes the importance of identification cards in establishing the identity of detainees during international armed conflicts. Parties to GPW must provide them to persons under their jurisdiction who are liable to become PWs,[58] while parties to GWS must provide identification cards to retained personnel denoting their status. In each case, the person concerned may not be deprived of the card. Duplicates, electronic or otherwise, should be kept by States of the cards that they issue.[59] Most helpfully, and citing the *GPW Commentary*,[60] the paragraph points out that such cards may be lost, damaged or stolen, so the inability to produce an identity card does not necessarily mean that a person lacks a particular status.

Paragraph 4.27.2, after noting two of the many kinds of circumstance that may give rise to doubt as to the status of a detained person, states again the GPW, Article 5 rule that during an international armed conflict where doubt exists as to whether a person who has committed a belligerent act and who has fallen into the hands of the enemy is entitled to PW status, such a person shall enjoy the protection of the GPW until his or her status has been determined by a competent tribunal. Paragraph 4.27.3 accurately explains that, while sometimes courts have made the determination,[61] and while satisfying the 'competent tribunal' requirement generally involves the Detaining Power convening an administrative board, GPW, Article 5 gives substantial discretion as to the composition and procedures of an Article 5 tribunal. Where no doubt as to status exists, no tribunal determination is required.

58 GPW, Article 17(3). 59 GWS, Article 40; GPW, Article 17.

60 J S Pictet (ed.) *Commentary III on Geneva Convention Relative to the Treatment of Prisoners of War*. International Committee of the Red Cross (1960), 64–5.

61 *DoD Manual*, footnote 518 on page 180 gives examples of cases in which a court made the determination.

Paragraph 4.27.4 makes the point that although Article 5 of GPW is only concerned with a person's entitlement to PW status or treatment, other status questions may be appropriate for an administrative process, such as entitlement to retained personnel or civilian status. DoD practice as to the use of Article 5 tribunals for such purposes is then noted.

5*

The Conduct of Hostilities

Chapter V, on the Conduct of Hostilities, is appropriately one of the lengthier chapters in the *Manual*, and is certainly one of the most important parts of the text. It is something of a statement of the obvious that the way in which the fight is conducted is central to the progress of the war and is likely to be determinative of its outcome. The proper emphasis that the *Manual* gives to the law on these matters is therefore reflected in the detail with which the provisions are considered in the present chapter.

Paragraph 5.1.1 addresses terminology, focusing in particular on 'means of warfare' and 'methods of warfare'. There seems to be insufficient emphasis on attack in relation to the *Manual*'s discussion of means. Perhaps the authors could have achieved a more specific interpretation that incorporates this aspect if they had adopted the definition in the AMW *Manual*,[1] namely: '"Means of warfare" mean weapons, weapon systems or platforms employed for the purposes of attack.'[2] Equally, a clearer understanding of 'methods of warfare' might be forthcoming if, again, the AMW *Manual* definition were to be employed, namely: '"Methods of warfare" mean attacks and other activities designed to adversely affect the enemy's military operations or military capacity, as distinct from the means of warfare used during military operations, such as weapons. In military terms, methods of warfare consist of the various general categories of operations, such as bombing, as well as the specific tactics used for attack, such as high altitude bombing.'[3] Such an approach has the

* The first sections of the present chapter, up to and including the section addressing 'human shields', are to be published as a discrete chapter in M Newton (Ed), *The United States Department of Defense Law of War Manual: Commentary and Critique*, CUP.

[1] *HPCR Manual on International Law Applicable to Air and Missile Warfare*, Program on Humanitarian Policy and Conflict Research at Harvard University (2010).

[2] AMW *Manual*, rule 1(t). [3] AMW *Manual*, rule 1(v).

advantage of highlighting the distinction between the two expressions in a clear way.

OVERVIEW OF THE RULES FOR THE PROTECTION OF CIVILIANS

It is section 5.3 that gives an overview of the rules as to the protection of civilians. Footnote 13 is an interesting example of something that one observes in numerous parts of the *Manual*, namely the use of previous correspondence[4] or statements from US officials[5] in support of stated legal rules. Some such correspondence or statements will be evidence of single national (i.e. US) State practice[6] or of the US interpretation of the meaning of a rule, and they are therefore of considerable utility in a military manual, the purpose of which, after all, is to set out the relevant State's understanding of the law that binds it. However, they are not, of course, evidence of the existence of a rule as such. The reader is left with the impression that sometimes the cited correspondence and single national statements are being used as the basis for the existence of the particular rule of law, which would not be a correct approach.

Footnote 13 refers to the prime responsibility of the party to the conflict that controls civilians and civilian objects for their protection. It is curious that, rather than refer to Article 58 of API,[7] to which at the time of writing 174 States are bound,[8] reference instead is made to internal US correspondence dating from 1972. Article 58, the general propositions of which are widely accepted as having customary law status,[9] would seem to be a more persuasive indicator of the protection requirement at law than internal single national correspondence.

The text accompanying footnote 22 in part addresses a somewhat tricky issue, namely the distinction between the law of targeting rules as to 'attacks'

4 See, for example, *DoD Manual*, footnote 13 to Chapter V.

5 See, for example, *DoD Manual*, footnotes 15 and 89 to Chapter V.

6 This will, for example, frequently be the case where the reference is to the Final Report on the Persian Gulf War, which is a reference to 'Conduct of the Persian Gulf War, Final Report to Congress', issued by the US DoD in 1992; consider, for example, *DoD Manual*, footnotes 14 and 75 to Chapter V.

7 API, when used here and hereafter, will refer to the Protocol Additional to the Geneva Conventions of 12 August 1949 and Relating to the Protection of Victims of International Armed Conflicts, Geneva, 8 June 1977.

8 www.icrc.org, viewed on 17 December 2017.

9 See, for example, AMW *Manual*, Section H; *Tallinn Manual on the International Law Applicable to Cyber Warfare*, 2013 (*Tallinn Manual*), rule 59; ICRC Customary Law Study, rules 22–24.

and those rules, reflected in Articles 48, 51 and 57 of API, that relate to military operations. More will be said on the general way in which the *Manual* addresses that distinction in later paragraphs of this chapter. At this stage, it is worthy of note that footnote 22 is lengthy and cites mainly US practice. To establish the status in international law of the specific proposition being advanced, namely that it is legitimate temporarily to detain civilians for reasons of mission accomplishment, self-defence or their own safety, a proposition which the present authors are not seeking to dispute, it would have been preferable to cite authorities of a more international nature.

Taking paragraphs 5.3.2 and 5.3.2.1 together, one can deduce a US position as to which military operations against civilians are prohibited during international armed conflict. Paragraph 5.3.2 makes it clear that civilians must not be made the object of attack. The first sentence of paragraph 5.3.2.1 asserts that the 'principle that military operations must not be directed against civilians does not prohibit military operations short of violence that are militarily necessary'. So, it is being made clear here that, in the opinion of the *Manual*'s authors, the prohibited military operations against civilians are characterised by violence. Given that the use of violence against the enemy, whether in offence or defence, is the customary law definition of an attack,[10] it would seem that the effect of this US position is to limit the protection of civilians to protection from attack. Certainly, the *Manual* does not give a list of operations other than attack that may not be directed at civilians. The problem here lies in the distinction referred to in the previous paragraph. If the military operations that those customary rules in Articles 48,[11], 51[12] and 57[13] regulate are limited to attacks, why was the word 'attack' not used in those provisions, given that it is specifically employed in relation to other detailed rules in Articles 49–58 API? In an era of new military technologies, when increased options are being developed for offensive operations that lie at the boundaries of what might be seen as 'violence', one might legitimately question whether limiting prohibited military operations to attacks remains acceptable.

[10] API, Article 49(1); *San Remo Manual*, rule 13b (omitting reference to the adverse party); *AMW Manual*, rule 1e (making a similar omission to the *San Remo Manual*).

[11] Article 48 of API requires that the parties to the conflict 'shall at all times distinguish between the civilian population and combatants and between civilian objects and military objectives and accordingly shall direct their operations only against military objectives'.

[12] So far as is relevant to the point being made here, Article 51 of API provides that the 'civilian population and individual civilians shall enjoy general protection against dangers arising from military operations'.

[13] Article 57(1) of API provides that '[i]n the conduct of military operations, constant care shall be taken to spare the civilian population, civilians and civilian objects'.

Paragraph 5.3.3.2 discusses what precautions to protect civilians are to be regarded as 'feasible' and, thus, required. The paragraph states: 'The standard for what precautions must be taken is one of due regard or diligence, not an absolute requirement to do everything possible.' UK Prime Minister Neville Chamberlain's statement of 21 June 1938 is cited in a footnote in support of this formulation. Interestingly, in footnote 32, Michael J Matheson's 1987 article in the *American University Journal of International Law and Policy* is cited as follows: '[w]e support the principle that all practicable precautions, taking into account military and humanitarian considerations, be taken in the conduct of military operations to minimize incidental death, injury, and damage to civilians and civilian objects . . . ' This is the formulation that seems to approximate closely to a requirement to 'do everything possible'; after all, that which is practicable is also that which is possible, and if something is not possible it is also not practicable. The Matheson position was being put forward in 1987 as being the US position as to the relationship between customary law and the Additional Protocols of 1977, and one wonders therefore whether the US interpretation has in the intervening years become more restrictive. If it has not, revision of this paragraph of the *Manual* text would seem to be necessary.

If the US interpretation has indeed become more restrictive, one would also expect to see a clear explanation as to why this is the case. Such an explanation ought, it is suggested, to note and explain the revised interpretation by reference to novel technologies associated with offensive operations, referred to previously.

The position becomes potentially opaque if one reads further in paragraph 5.3.3.2. Having in the first sentence said that the standard is not an absolute one to do everything possible, the *Manual* then asserts: '[f]easible precautions are those that are practicable or practically possible, taking into account all circumstances ruling at the time, including humanitarian and military considerations.' There would at first glance seem to be something of an inherent conflict between this statement and the earlier statement in paragraph 5.3.3.2. However, it is a correct statement of the law to say that the obligation is not to do everything that is theoretically possible, but to do that which is contextually possible, and the context for these purposes consists of the surrounding military and humanitarian considerations. Examples of these are noted later in the paragraph.

As an example, the *Manual* asserts that 'if a commander determines that taking a precaution would result in operational risk (i.e. a risk of failing to accomplish the mission) or an increased risk of harm to their own forces, then the precaution would not be feasible and would not be required'. As noted in the previous paragraph, the decision as to whether a precaution is practicable is reached 'taking into account' military and humanitarian considerations. This suggests that both such classes of consideration must be taken into account and does not suggest that one trumps the other. One cannot therefore help wondering whether the example has been expressed in rather absolute terms, when a somewhat more nuanced explanation might have been in order. If, for example, the humanitarian consequences of failing to take a precaution were to be dire, and the increase in operational risk or in the chance of harm to one's own forces were to be relatively small, it would seem inappropriate to conclude that just because there is some such increase, however trivial, the precaution is thereby automatically rendered impracticable and thus is not required. That would seem to play into the hands of those who suggest that some interpretations of the law of targeting devalue civilian life.[14] The annotation in support of the example, footnote 39, again cites a US official statement. Such citations are of course entirely legitimate as a way of clarifying the stated US position. However, in a manual of this sort, and in the context of this part of the discussion, one might have expected a disclosure of the basis in international law of the proffered interpretation.

One cannot therefore but agree with the statement in the final sentence of the paragraph that 'military commanders must make reasonable efforts to reduce the risk of harm to civilians and civilian objects', or with the view expressed immediately beforehand that what is reasonable will, of necessity, be a contextual issue.

Paragraph 5.3.3.4 draws attention to the API, Article 57(1) obligation to take constant care to spare the civilian population, civilians and civilian objects. This is a rule that is widely recognised as having customary law status.[15] It is therefore disappointing that it is described merely as a rule that States party to API have accepted, and that no indication is given as to whether the US considers itself to be bound by the rule or believes the rule to have customary law status. While acknowledging, as the paragraph observes, that States may interpret the rule differently, it would have been useful to learn here how the US interprets it.

[14] Note, for example, *UK Manual*, paragraph 5.32.2.e, where it is stated that any commander selecting a target will have to pay regard to a number of factors, which may include 'the risks to his own forces necessitated by target verification'. In the associated footnote 202, on page 82, it is observed that '[t]raditionally commanders have accepted some risk in identifying targets by using, for example, artillery spotters, forward air controllers, and intelligence gatherers operating in enemy-held territory'.

[15] See, for example, the effect of *San Remo Manual*, paragraph 46; *AMW Manual*, rule 30; *Tallinn Manual*, rule 52; ICRC Customary Law Study, rule 15. References in military manuals of States that are party to API are not relevant, of course, to the customary status of the rule, because they will reflect the treaty obligations of the relevant State.

ASSESSING INFORMATION UNDER THE LAW OF WAR

Section 5.4 makes the important point that decisions in war must be made in good faith on the basis of all available information interpreted in good faith. The legal obligation, as reflected in a statement made by the UK on ratification of API, is to make decisions on the basis of all *reasonably* available information,[16] and it is suggested that the word 'reasonably' should be appropriately inserted in the text. Absent reference to that word, there is the danger that readers will deduce, incorrectly, that there is no obligation to obtain, where necessary, further information, and that it is sufficient to consider only the information that happens to be available. Some of the factors that are liable to arise in war and that may limit the availability of information or the ability to process it accurately are properly referred to. The section deals with the matter in an admirably practical way, noting, for example, that the circumstances of armed conflict may make an accurate determination of facts difficult, that the enemy may be actively seeking to deceive and that some uncertainty is inevitable. So, when the section notes that it may be difficult to determine whether a person is a combatant, a civilian or a directly participating civilian, whether an object is making an effective contribution to military action or what is the direct military advantage to be derived from an attack, that observation is correct as far as it goes. To deduce from it that it would be lawful to attack a target in ignorance of whether it is a lawful target would not, however, be right.[17] In that regard, perhaps some clarification of what the notion, emphasised in the text, of good faith actually requires would have been helpful. It would not, of course, be right to imply, nor for the *Manual*'s reader to deduce, that in a situation where there is little or no information on which to conclude that a person or object is a lawful target, the obligations of the law are in any sense dispensed with.

It is noted that the jurisprudence cited in support is from domestic, US courts.[18] It would have been interesting to see international court decisions being referred to in these assessments of international law obligations. The point is properly made that it is the decision maker's assessment of the

[16] Statement (c) made by the United Kingdom on ratification of API on 28 January 1998: 'Military commanders and others responsible for planning, deciding upon, or executing attacks necessarily have to reach decisions on the basis of their assessment of the information from all sources which is reasonably available to them at the relevant time.'

[17] Consider, for example, the obligation in API, Article 57(2)(a)(i) to 'do everything feasible to verify that the objectives to be attacked are neither civilians nor civilian objects and are not subject to special protection . . .' This would seem to follow logically from the widely accepted and customary constant care obligation.

[18] See *DoD Manual*, footnotes 50 and 53 to Chapter V.

situation at the relevant time that is to be considered, and not information that may only have become available later. Here, it is noteworthy that the stated positions of other States are cited in support. Perhaps that approach could profitably have been adopted in relation to some of the propositions discussed earlier in this chapter.

RULES ON CONDUCTING ASSAULTS, BOMBARDMENTS AND OTHER ATTACKS

Section 5.5 starts with a useful clarification of the applicable terminology, in which the important distinction is made between persons and objects being made the object or purpose of an attack and injury or damage being caused to such persons or objects as an incidental consequence of an attack directed at some other person or object. Having cleared up this point, the *Manual* notes that '[p]arties to a conflict must conduct attacks in accordance with the principles of distinction and proportionality',[19] and then lists in summary form rules that must be observed. At the risk of being pedantic, and as noted in Chapter 2, the proportionality principle is one of the core principles underlying the law of armed conflict and requires that 'the expected losses resulting from a military action should not be excessive in relation to the anticipated military advantage',[20] an altogether more general notion than the proportionality *rule* as reflected in API, Articles 51(5)(b) and 57.[21]

Having already addressed in section 5.4 the requirement for commanders to make decisions on the basis of the information available at the time, the *Manual* returns to that matter in paragraph 5.5.3. In the second sentence of the latter provision, the point is made that 'the commander must, on the basis of available information, determine in good faith, that a target is a military objective before authorizing an attack'. Clearly, the ambiguity we noted earlier in relation to section 5.4 must be interpreted in the light of this later, legally accurate statement. Indeed, it would have been appropriate, and perhaps helpful, if the sentence under review had made it clear that the obligation to make this determination applies not just to commanders but to all persons who decide upon attacks.[22]

19 *DoD Manual*, para 5.5.2. 20 *UK Manual*, 21 and para 2.6 as amended.

21 Article 51(5)(b) of API gives as an example of an indiscriminate, and thus unlawful, attack, 'an attack which may be expected to cause incidental loss of civilian life, injury to civilians, damage to civilian objects, or a combination thereof, which would be excessive in relation to the concrete and direct military advantage anticipated'.

22 This aspect of Article 57(2) of API would seem to be customary, and thus binding on all States.

In the second part of paragraph 5.5.3, it is stated that in making judgments required by the law in relation to attacks, 'persons may rely on information obtained from other sources, including human intelligence or other sources of information', and that 'in a long distance attack, a commander may rely on information obtained from aerial reconnaissance and intelligence units in determining whether to conduct an attack'. The use here of the word 'may' has the potential to mislead the reader. The obligation at law is quite simple. Commanders, planners and other decision makers are obliged to consider all reasonably available information.[23] They will then act on the basis of their interpretation of that information. Thus, while it is strictly correct to say that they 'may' rely on particular classes of information, it would perhaps be preferable to explain to commanders and decision makers the twin aspects of considering all available information and of acting on their interpretation of it.

Paragraph 5.5.3.1 should be considered with some care. It argues that '[a]lthough doing so would exceed the requirements of the law of war, applying heightened standards of identification may be a policy choice to reduce the risk of incidental harm in conducting an attack'. As a general proposition, it would be correct to point out that commanders may always require, as a matter of policy, that action above that required by the law be taken to enhance the protection to be afforded to protected persons and objects. The problem is that the wording chosen in paragraph 5.5.3.1 might be understood as asserting that the heightened standards are not required by the law of war. Widely accepted law requires, as we have noted, that all available information be considered in making attack decisions. It also requires that constant care be taken, and that all feasible (i.e. practically possible) steps be taken to verify that the object of attack is a lawful target and that the planned attack, if undertaken, will not breach targeting law (e.g. the proportionality rule). Perhaps paragraph 5.5.3.1 is simply in the wrong place, in that if it were to appear after the points mentioned here have been explained, any ambiguity as to its intended meaning would cease to exist.

Footnote 75 cites as a supporting authority a White House Fact Sheet of 2013 about US Policy Standards on the use of force in counter-terrorism operations outside areas of active hostilities. The strict relevance of such a source is debateable given that uses of force outside armed conflict will be governed

[23] This proposition is reflected in statement (c) made by the United Kingdom on ratification of API on 28 January 1998, but is essentially a widely accepted reflection of the obligation of an attacker to take constant care to spare civilians and civilian objects, as noted in API, Article 57(1).

not by the law of war but by applicable domestic and human rights law. Later in the same footnote, an extract from the Report on the Persian Gulf War is cited. In that extract, instructions were noted to the effect that if a pilot could not positively identify the target or could not be confident that the weapon would guide properly, he or she could not deliver that weapon. Again, it is to be doubted that this is indicative of the application of rules above what the law of war requires in terms of constant care, the taking of all practically possible precautions and the consideration of all available information. After all, a pilot who cannot be confident that a weapon is going to guide properly but who nevertheless fires that weapon is taking an obvious risk that the attack he or she is about to launch will be indiscriminate and thus unlawful. It is difficult to accept that such conduct could be seen as consistent with any sensible interpretation of the principle of distinction.

The final authority cited in footnote 75 is an extract from rules of engagement issued in 1971 during the Vietnam War. The textual extract has been duplicated for reasons which are unclear. The comment made in the last paragraph would also apply to this cited passage in the footnote, unless it is being suggested that the stated requirement goes beyond the requirements of the law as it stood in 1971, but such a point has not been argued in the footnote entry. Perhaps the intended point here would emerge more clearly if the respects in which positive identification exceeds the feasibility requirements of applicable law were to be explained, so that the reader could understand how the cited rules of engagement impose more exacting obligations.

On a point of minor detail, the extract from Article 52(3) of API set forth in the first part of paragraph 5.5.3.2 should refer to 'military action', not 'military actions'. Subject to that minor comment, the paragraph, which addresses the doubt rules in Articles 52(3) and 50(1) of the same treaty, explains the basis for the known US objections to these rules persuasively and well. Paragraph 5.5.4 correctly notes that the failure by the enemy to separate or distinguish does not relieve the attacker of the obligation to discriminate in attack. In particular, the second part of the paragraph helpfully notes that while, confronted by such enemy failure, the attacker must continue to seek to discriminate, his or her practical ability to do so will inevitably be affected by that enemy failure, or by the enemy's illegal activity.[24]

[24] Consider in this regard the API, Article 51(8) requirement that '[a]ny violation of these prohibitions shall not release the Parties to the conflict from their legal obligations with respect to the civilian population and civilians, including the obligation to take the precautionary measures provided for in Article 57'. The prohibitions referred to here include the prohibition of making the civilian population or individual civilians the object of attack and the prohibition of indiscriminate attacks.

The second part of paragraph 5.5.5 talks about the legitimacy of conducting attacks outside the immediate area of hostilities. The broad way in which the paragraph is drafted might, however, lead to misinterpretation. The discussion in this part of the *Manual*, it must be remembered, is centred on *jus in bello* as it applies in international armed conflicts. There is indeed no rule of law that specifically requires that attacks be limited to the location where fighting has previously been taking place. Provided that the object of attack is a lawful target and that other aspects of targeting law are complied with, the attack is likely to be unobjectionable. During a non-international armed conflict, the use of lethal force outside the territory where that conflict is occurring, and without the consent of the relevant sovereign authorities, is of course a highly controversial legal issue. The decision in footnote 89 to refer to a speech about the US President's counterterrorism strategy may seem to contribute to the potential misinterpretation noted earlier in the present paragraph.

Paragraph 5.5.6 correctly asserts the lawfulness of the use of overwhelming force. Section IX of the ICRC's *Interpretive Guidance* famously and incorrectly argued that 'the kind and degree of force which is permissible against persons not entitled to protection against direct attack must not exceed what is actually necessary to accomplish a legitimate military purpose in the prevailing circumstances'.[25] It is therefore useful to see specific State practice to the contrary effect recorded in the paragraph under review. The only matter for regret is that it is internal US correspondence, training course materials and single service US manuals that are cited as the relevant authorities, as opposed to the recognised sources of international law, but then this is a criticism that applies to diverse parts of the *Manual*. It is indeed difficult to see how so many elements of an authoritative treatise on international law can be properly based on so relatively few references to its recognised sources.[26]

After correctly reporting the lawfulness of surprise attacks, attacks on retreating forces and harassing fires in legally unobjectionable terms,[27] the *Manual* turns to what some might regard as the controversial topic of 'attacks on specific individuals'. It is good that that descriptor is used and that the term 'assassination' is avoided, no doubt on the basis that it would have involved inappropriate and irrelevant overtones. The main *Manual* text is commendably brief

[25] Melzer, *Interpretive Guidance*, 82.

[26] The recognised sources of international law comprise 'international conventions, whether general or particular, establishing rules expressly recognized by the contesting states', 'international custom, as evidence of a general practice accepted as law' and 'the general principles of law recognized by civilized nations'; Statute of the International Court of Justice, 1945, Article 38(1)(a) to (c).

[27] *DoD Manual*, paragraphs 5.5.6.1 to 5.5.6.3.

and accurate in asserting that military operations may be undertaken against specific enemy combatants and that the US has often conducted such operations. In footnote 102, arguments that such targeted operations during armed conflict are not lawful are reported and correctly rejected.

Paragraph 5.5.7 repeats the well-established rules on the denial of quarter and explains them accurately. Curiously, a sentence is added at the end of the paragraph asserting that this rule also applies in non-international armed conflicts. That is a sentence that has not appeared in relation to the previous rules, and it would not be right to imagine that none of those previous rules applies in non-international armed conflicts. The sudden appearance of the sentence in this paragraph might therefore cause misunderstanding.

The *Manual* addresses the wearing of uniform by combatants in paragraphs 5.5.8 and 5.5.8.1. Paragraphs 5.5.8 and 5.5.8.2 correctly state that the customary law position as to the obligation of combatants to distinguish themselves goes somewhat wider than the corresponding obligation in Article 44(3) of API, as it is not limited to when they are conducting attacks or in military operations preparatory to an attack. It also briefly refers to the prohibition of treacherous killing and to certain other matters. In footnote 114, an example taken from the writings of J M Spaight of an airman fighting without uniform is cited in support.[28] Of course, if the airman was at the time flying a properly marked military aircraft, as is assumed to have been the case, it is the required nationality markings and military markings of the aircraft that will have satisfied the requirements of the principle of distinction, and the presence or absence of the airman's uniform would only become relevant in the exceptional circumstance that for some reason the airman continued the fight outside and separate from his military aircraft.

In the second part of paragraph 5.5.8.1, it is stated that '[m]ilitary personnel not in uniform may resist an attack, so long as they are not wearing the enemy's uniform and do not kill or wound treacherously'. The example is then given of military personnel not in uniform who resist an attack and who do not purposefully seek to conceal their status as combatants, noting that they commit no violation of the law of war and remain entitled to combatant privileges. This would at face value seem to be a most remarkable part of the *Manual*. The present authors have always understood that the second sentence in Article 44(3) of API is a provision to which the US is vehemently opposed and constitutes one of the core reasons why it will not ratify that treaty.[29] Unless,

[28] J M Spaight, *Air Power and War Rights*, 3rd edn. Harlow: Longman Green Co. (1947), 101.

[29] Article 44(3) of API provides: 'In order to promote the protection of the civilian population from the effects of hostilities, combatants are obliged to distinguish themselves from the

as is entirely possible, the present authors are completely misinterpreting the paragraph in the *Manual*, it would rather seem that the *Manual* is according customary law status to a rule that bears a remarkable resemblance to that sentence in API. In that connection, for example, the idea of 'not purposefully seeking to conceal their [combatant] status' would seem to have its parallel in the idea of carrying arms openly.

As a side issue, it is assumed that the term 'attack' is being used here, as elsewhere, in the sense of an act of violence against the adversary, whether in offence or defence.[30] The proposition discussed in the previous paragraph would therefore apply irrespective of whether the violent force were being used in an offensive or a defensive posture.

DISCRIMINATION IN CONDUCTING ATTACKS AND MILITARY OBJECTIVES

Section 5.6 differentiates between the persons and objects that, respectively, may and may not be made the object of attack. After introducing that idea and indicating the kinds of person and object that come into each category, the focus of Section 5.7 narrows to the idea of military objectives, which, for the purposes of the *Manual*, are quite properly interpreted as comprising persons and objects. It is made clear that dual-use objects will be military objectives by virtue of their military use. However, there seems to be a fair degree of repetitiveness or redundancy in the section, and it might have been more helpful for the reader if the definition of military objectives, as that notion applies to objects, had been given before e.g. the dual-use notion was discussed. This would have enabled the reader to appreciate more readily the significance of the military-use aspect of such dual-use objects.

The definition of military objectives, insofar as objects are concerned, is, however, given at paragraph 5.7.3. The paragraph reads as follows: 'Military objectives, in so far as objects are concerned, include "any object which by its nature, location, purpose or use makes an effective contribution to military action and whose total or partial destruction, capture or neutralization,

civilian population while they are engaged in an attack or in a military operation preparatory to an attack. Recognizing, however, that there are situations in armed conflicts where, owing to the nature of the hostilities an armed combatant cannot so distinguish himself, he shall retain his status as a combatant provided that, in such situations, he carries his arms openly: (a) during each military engagement; and (b) during such time as he is visible to the adversary while he is engaged in a military deployment preceding the launching of an attack in which he is to participate. Acts which comply with the requirements of this paragraph shall not be considered as perfidious . . . '

30 API, Article 49(1).

in the circumstances ruling at the time, offers a definite military advantage".' It is somewhat intriguing that in the associated footnote no reference is made to the primary international law source for this formulation, namely API Article 52(2), and that the prime reference is instead drawn from the Amended CCW Mines Protocol, the States party to which number only 104.[31]

Equally intriguingly, later in that footnote an extract from the US UCMJ is cited, in which objects that effectively contribute to the war-fighting or war-sustaining capability of the adverse party are stated to be included within the notion, provided that their total or partial destruction, capture or neutralisation in the prevailing circumstances offers a definite military advantage. The reader may wonder why a definition in the main text that is limited to objects that contribute effectively to military action is being supported in the footnote by a reference that widens the notion by reference to objects that are war-sustaining. The answer to this potential conundrum seems to lie in the use in paragraph 5.7.3 of the word 'include'. Presumably, the *Manual* is telling us that, so far as the US is concerned, the notion of military objective includes objects that satisfy the API definition but goes wider than this, impliedly to include the war-sustaining objects referred to in footnote 144.

This broadening of the military objectives notion may place the cardinal, intransgressible principle of distinction[32] in some peril. As the early part of this section of the *Manual* makes clear, that principle has at its core the idea that there are certain kinds of person and object that it is lawful to attack and certain others that must be protected. If distinguishing between those respective kinds of object is made more difficult, maintaining respect for the underlying principle becomes potentially problematic. While objects that are making a direct contribution to military action can often be differentiated fairly readily from those which are not, the scope of objects that sustain the war effort is very much wider, and the notion of sustainment is itself less precise, thus reducing the sharpness of the distinction between objects that can and respectively cannot be made the object of lawful attack.

The same paragraph of the *Manual* observes that the 'definition of military objective may be viewed as a way of evaluating whether military necessity exists to attack an object'. While there might be an element of circularity in that observation, given that the notion of military utility, if not necessity, is inherent in the cited definition, nevertheless the implicit point is both correct and useful.

[31] www.icrc.org, viewed on 17 December 2017.

[32] ICJ, Advisory Opinion on the Threat or Use of Nuclear Weapons, 1996 ICJ Reports 226–256 at 250.

Paragraph 5.7.4 argues that two types of object are categorically recognised as military objectives; that is, 'the definition of military objective is always considered to be met as a matter of law with regard to these objects'. If the definition of military objective given in the first part of paragraph 5.7.3 is regarded as binding, then the twin tests must apply irrespective of the type of object concerned and irrespective whether it is nature, location, purpose or use that causes the object to become a military objective. It would be accurate to say that the objects listed in paragraphs 5.7.4.1 and 5.7.4.2, such as military bases, vehicles, ships, weapons and supplies, military headquarters, ministries of defence and intelligence facilities, will almost always in the prevailing circumstances satisfy the two tests in the definition and therefore will almost always be military objectives. Indeed, the circumstances may well be such that very little thought is required before concluding that such objects are indeed military objectives and thus liable to be attacked. It is, however, only by making that determination that the requirements of the widely accepted definition in API, Article 52(2) can be satisfied, and a proper interpretation of that article, and thus of the rule that is widely accepted as having customary law status,[33] demands that the twin tests set forth in that article must be applied to all objects being considered for attack. In footnote 47 of the *Manual*, the *UK Manual*, paragraph 5.4.1, is cited in support of the stated US position. It would have been more accurate, however, if the *Manual* had also cited the third sentence of that paragraph of the *UK Manual*, in which the point is explicitly made that '[o]bjects are only military objectives if they come within the [API] definition'. This latter extract from the *UK Manual* reflects what is understood to be the widely accepted interpretation of the law.

It is in this context that the next paragraphs develop the notion of military objective in more detail. Paragraph 5.7.5 correctly points out that there are twin tests implicit in the recognised definition, and significantly refers to objects that 'somehow' directly contribute to military action as satisfying the first of these. At paragraph 5.7.6, the definition of military objective is broken down into its constituent parts. In the discussion of objects that by nature are military objectives, it is suggested that '"nature" can also be understood to refer to objects that may be used for military purposes . . . ' This is not correct. Many ordinarily civilian objects, such as civilian buildings, church towers, civilian cyber networks and civilian automobiles, *may* be used for military purposes.

33 Consider *San Remo Manual*, paragraph 40; *AMW Manual*, rule 1y; *Tallinn Manual*, rule 38. It will be appreciated that the military manuals of States party to API will reflect the treaty obligations of those States and will not therefore assist in determining the customary law status of the definition.

If that actually occurs, they become military objectives by virtue of that use, not by their 'nature'.

The *Manual* then contends that an object becomes a military objective by virtue of 'purpose' through 'its intended or possible use in the future'.[34] In the supporting footnote,[35] extracts from the *Australian*[36] and *UK Manuals* are cited, both of which actually describe 'purpose' in terms of the intended future use of an object, which, in the view of the present authors, is the widely accepted and correct interpretation of the 'purpose' language. No supporting justification is given for the reference in the *Manual*'s text to *possible* future use. Moreover, if one recognises that almost any object or location is capable of being used for military purposes, to say that possible future use renders an object a lawful target clearly has the potential, depending on how the idea is understood, to expand the notion of military objective to such a degree that the principle of distinction risks being deprived of meaning. It would have been more accurate to refer to 'purpose' as intended future use, including future uses that can properly be inferred from an understanding of the developing tactical situation and from the information from all sources that is reasonably available to the decision maker at the relevant time, including information as to the enemy's intentions.

At paragraph 5.7.6.2, the correct point is made that '[m]ilitary action has a broad meaning and is understood to mean the general prosecution of the war'. Tony Rogers is cited in support of this proposition. The legal problem with the US position, as the present authors see it, arises in the next but one sentence, when an effective contribution to war-sustaining capability is considered to suffice for these purposes. Clearly, an indirect contribution to war-sustaining capabilities is liable to be afforded by a wide selection of objects, and, as has been noted, the wider the selection of objects that are capable of being lawfully regarded as military objectives, the less constraining, and thus the less effective in protective terms, the associated principle of distinction. Effective protection of civilians in war presupposes reasonable restrictiveness in this regard. War sustaining, as Yoram Dinstein has opined, goes too far.[37]

However, as reflected in footnote 162, Hays Parks draws attention to State practice that supports the war-sustaining interpretation. There can be no doubt that during World War II, Gulf War I and recent air operations in Iraq and Syria, war-sustaining targets have been attacked not just by the US but

[34] *DoD Manual*, paragraph 5.7.6.1. [35] *DoD Manual*, footnote 157 on page 209.

[36] Australian Defence Force, Australian Defence Doctrine Publication 06.4, *Law of Armed Conflict* (11 May 2006).

[37] Dinstein, *Conduct of Hostilities*, 109; see n. 5 to Chapter 3.

also by other coalition members.[38] One could speculate that the definition of military objective in API, Article 52(2) was something of an aberration and that the customary definition goes – and always went – wider, to encompass war-sustaining objects.[39] Such a view might imply that States party to API are accepting a more restrictive interpretation of the military objective notion that would not, according to that view, be binding on all States. Of course, States that are party to API, that are thus bound by the Article 52(2) definition and that are nevertheless attacking war-sustaining targets in Syria must of necessity have an explanation for their adoption of such a position. Perhaps the approach in this part of the *Manual* will help them to develop such a narrative.

The terms 'capture' and 'neutralisation' are discussed in paragraph 5.7.7.1. As a preliminary matter, it should be noted that the *Manual* fails to exclude prize measures from the concept of 'capture' when discussing that concept in the context of the military objectives definition. It is important to appreciate that capture as prize is lawful even if the captured object does not qualify as a military objective.

In relation to 'capture', the *Manual* suggests that 'the seizure of a city may be a military objective because of its strategic location'. This statement seems to mix up two rather distinct, and different, meanings of 'objective'. In the context of the relevant discussion, 'objective' is being used to describe objects that it would be permissible, *inter alia*, to attack. It is assumed for the purposes of this discussion that the authors of the *Manual* are not seeking to argue for differing interpretations of military objective depending on whether attack, capture or neutralisation is contemplated. The inference that some may draw from the cited part of the text, that the whole of a city may be a military objective and might therefore lawfully be made the object of attack, is, it is assumed and hoped, not intended by the *Manual*'s authors. However, the

38 For recent such events, see, for example, Operation United Resolve website at http://www.defense.gov/News/Special-Reports/0814_Inherent-Resolve, viewed on 23 December 2015; M R Gordon and E Schmitt, US Steps Up Its Attacks against ISIS controlled Oil Fields in Syria, *New York Times*, 12 November 2015, available at http://www.nytimes.com/2015/11/13/us/politics/us-steps-up-its-attacks-on-isis-controlled-oil-fields-in-syria.html?_r=0; F Perraudin, H Siddique and M Safi, Syria Airstrikes: Britain Launches 'Offensive Operation' after Vote to Bomb ISIS Targets: As It Happened, *Guardian*, 3 December 2015, available at http://www.theguardian.com/world/live/2015/dec/03/syria-airstrikes-britain-launches-bombing-against-isis-targets-rolling-report; French Airstrike Hits IS Group Oil Facility in Syria, *France 24*, 9 November 2015, available at http://www.france24.com/en/20151109-france-syria-strike-islamic-state-oil-facility-military.

39 Consider W Hays Parks, *Air War and the Law of War*, 32 *The Air Force Law Review* 1, 141ff. (1990).

idea that seizure is a military objective as that term is used in Article 52(2) or its customary equivalent is also clearly wrong, because seizure is not a physical or other object but an aim, intent or purpose.[40]

The *Manual* then gives helpful and legally accurate explanations of three concepts, namely neutralisation, the vital contextual aspect to the definition and the idea of 'definite military advantage'.[41]

In the succeeding paragraphs, examples are given of objects that may, or that have often been, regarded as military objectives. This would seem to be a better way of expressing such a point, because it properly reflects the contextual nature of the determination that an object is or has become a military objective. However, economic objects associated with war-sustaining industries are included, and this again would seem to be stretching the definition too much. Even those who advocate a war-sustaining approach in the recent literature[42] limit targets justifiable on this basis to 'staples', as opposed to objects whose contribution may be less vital to the continuation of the enemy's war effort.[43] It has been long accepted in the literature that the only method of economic warfare that is permissible in accordance with the law of armed conflict constitutes blockade.[44] To attack targets on the basis of the economic value they have for the opposing party is highly controversial, indeed arguably illegal.[45]

COMBATANTS

Section 5.8 addresses the law of war idea of 'combatants'. Immediately, the difference of approach between the US and States that are party to API becomes evident, as the *Manual* refers to ideas of privileged and unprivileged combatants. Under API, Article 43, members of the armed forces of a party to an international armed conflict, other than medical and religious personnel, are defined as combatants, 'that is to say, they have the right to participate directly in hostilities'.[46] It is therefore clear that combatant status under API confers the combatant's privilege. With such an approach, there can be no such thing as an unprivileged combatant. In the US approach, the term

[40] Note the reference to seizure by an army of occupation in Article 53(2) of the Hague Regulations 1907. Some may interpret such action as a form of capture in the specific circumstances of occupation.

[41] As to the last of these, see *DoD Manual*, paragraph 5.7.7.3.

[42] R Goodman, The Obama Administration and Targeting 'War-Sustaining' Objects in Non-International Armed Conflict, 110 *American Journal of International Law* 663–679 (2016).

[43] Ibid. [44] Dinstein, *Conduct of Hostilities*, 109; see n. 5 to Chapter 3.

[45] Ibid. [46] API, Article 43(2).

'combatant' does not afford status under the law but, rather, describes what an individual is doing, i.e. engaging in combat. It is therefore entirely logical, given that understanding of the meaning of the term, that US practitioners should wish to qualify the notion by the descriptors 'privileged' and 'unprivileged' to reflect that not all persons taking a direct part in the fight have the legally conferred right to do so.

It is noteworthy that the expression that has also frequently been used in the past, namely 'unlawful combatant',[47] is not the expression of choice in the *Manual*. It might be argued that the *Manual*'s use of the term 'unprivileged combatant' brings the US and API positions a step closer together, but the fundamental difference in view remains.

Paragraph 5.8.1 looks at the liability of members of armed forces and of armed groups to be made the object of attack and concludes that all members of both are liable to be attacked irrespective of whether they are taking a direct part in hostilities at the relevant time. The view that members of the armed forces are liable to be attacked at all times during an armed conflict is, of course, not controversial. However, the *Manual*'s stated position in respect of members of armed groups puts the US approach into clear conflict with the ICRC's interpretation that it is only members of organised armed groups that have a continuous combat function who are liable to be attacked at all times.[48] Absent that continuous combat function, the ICRC would limit the liability of such members to attack to the occasions when they are directly participating in the hostilities.[49] The ICRC's interpretation creates, of course, an inherent imbalance between the vulnerability to attack, respectively, of members of the armed forces and members of armed groups. The US approach does not imply such imbalance, and would accordingly seem to be the preferable understanding of the position.

The next sentence of paragraph 5.8.1 suggests that '[t]his [i.e. that members of armed forces and organized armed groups are liable to be made the object of attack regardless of whether they are taking a direct part in hostilities] is because the organization's hostile intent may be imputed to an individual through his or her association with the organization'. 'Hostile intent' is an expression employed in rules of engagement but that is not to be found in relevant treaty or customary provisions of the law of war. Its employment in

47 *The US Commanders' Handbook on the Law of Naval Operations*, NWP 1–14M, Department of the Navy, Department of Homeland Security (July 2007) (NWP 1–14M), paragraph 5.4.1.2 provides as follows: 'Unlawful enemy combatants are persons not entitled to combatant immunity who engage in acts against the United States or its coalition partners in violation of the laws and customs of war during armed conflict.'

48 See Melzer, *Interpretive Guidance*, 33–4.

49 Ibid., 35.

the present paragraph is therefore liable to confuse rather than clarify matters. The armed forces are the manifestation of the enemy's resistance, and it is only by achieving their defeat that such resistance can be overcome. It is on this basis that members of the armed forces are lawful targets at all times during an armed conflict.

In the second part of paragraph 5.8.1, it is accordingly stated that 'combatants may be made the object of attack at all times, regardless of the activities in which they are engaged at the time of attack'. The reader from an API State looking at this and other provisions of the *Manual* relating to combatants in general must recall that the API definition of combatants is not necessarily – indeed, is necessarily not – being referred to here, and will look to the definition in paragraph 5.8.2, which is entitled 'Categories of Persons who are Combatants for the Purpose of Assessing their Liability to Attack'. This is a curious title. It suggests that a person may be a combatant for the stated purpose but not a combatant for other purposes. In the present discussion, that proposition, and the arguable risk that it may confuse, will not be pursued.

In paragraph 5.8.1.1, the US practice in declaring a force hostile is mentioned. For an API State, once a situation of international armed conflict has arisen, the lawful human targets for attack will comprise combatants as defined in Article 43 and directly participating civilians. No declaration is required in that regard.

More to the present point, paragraph 5.8.2 answers the pressing question of who are liable to be lawfully attacked at any time by virtue of being, in the US view, combatants. Combatants are listed as 'members of the armed forces of a state; members of militia and volunteer corps; participants in a *levee en masse*; persons belonging to non-State armed groups; and leaders whose responsibilities include the operational command and control of the armed forces or of a non-State armed group'.

This definition therefore defines the combatant notion by reference to membership of an armed force of some kind, whether State or non-State. It excludes persons who take a direct part in hostilities without being a member of an armed group, but the *Manual* addresses the position of those individuals a little later in the text. One observation should be made, namely that the inclusion of all those who are members of non-State armed groups is likely to prove over-inclusive. Indeed, including them at all in the category of combatants is distinctly problematic. Moreover, some members of non-State armed groups may have functions that are limited to diplomatic or other activities that do not constitute participation in the armed conflict. It could certainly be argued that such individuals should not be included in the combatant classification. Paragraph 5.8.3 suggests that such individuals would be liable to be lawfully attacked, although it could perhaps be argued that they lack the intention of personally taking part in the group's 'hostile intent'.

The first part of paragraph 5.8.3.1 most helpfully lists some direct information that would indicate an individual's formal membership of an armed group. Recognising that in many instances direct information may not be available, the *Manual* lists other information that 'might indicate that a person is a member of a non-State armed group'. The listed indicators would all seem to be both relevant and useful. It may, however, be that in particular cases more than one such indicator may need to be present for a reliable determination of membership to be made, and it might be helpful for the *Manual* to make that point.

The *Manual* then develops a notion of functional membership in an armed group, a concept that is applied to persons who are integrated into the group without necessarily having formal membership but to whom the hostile intent of the group can be imputed. Paragraph 5.8.3 stipulates that such individuals may also be made the object of attack by virtue of this functional membership. There would likely need to be clear information demonstrating the required integration and shared hostile intent, because this really constitutes the line of distinction between combatants, as that term is employed by the *Manual*, and civilians. Clearly, this distinction is of utmost importance. It differentiates between persons who are liable to be attacked at any time and irrespective of what they are actually doing at the time of attack and persons whom all involved in the armed conflict have a legal responsibility to spare. Any determination that an individual who is not a formal member of a group is nevertheless constantly liable to be lawfully attacked must be based on clear information not just that the individual shares the general objectives and perspectives of the group, but that he or she is sufficiently involved in its hostile activities.

After dealing in appropriate terms with how an individual might achieve dissociation from or renunciation of membership of a group,[50] the *Manual* at paragraph 5.8.4 considers when leaders are liable to be made the object of attack. It is of course correct that leaders who are members of the armed forces are liable to be attacked on the basis of their combatant status. Equally, it is right that leaders who take a direct part in the hostilities, whether by virtue of their functional responsibilities or because they become involved e.g. in target approval, are liable to be attacked while so participating. Having noted that the President of the United States, as Commander in Chief of the US armed forces, would be liable to be attacked, the *Manual* then makes a rather

[50] *DoD Manual*, paragraph 5.8.3.3.

broad assertion that the prime minister of a constitutional monarchy would be similarly liable. If a prime minister of a constitutional monarchy is not a member of the armed forces and has no role in relation to the conduct of the hostilities, for example on the basis that all such responsibilities have been passed to the minister of defence, that prime minister will not be liable to lawful attack merely by virtue of his or her position as prime minister. It is the status as a combatant (in the API sense) or the participation of an individual in the hostilities that renders him or her liable to be targeted, and this aspect could be more clearly articulated in this part of the *Manual*'s text.[51]

CIVILIANS TAKING A DIRECT PART IN HOSTILITIES

Section 5.9 then addresses the customary yet controversial topic of direct participation in hostilities. It is noteworthy that the heading to this section in the *Manual* uses the term 'civilians' and not the expression 'private persons' that is employed in section 4.18. Consistency of terminology suggests that a single term should be used in both parts of the *Manual*, and the present authors suggest that that term should be 'civilians'. While it is recognised in the general practice of States that a civilian who directly participates in hostilities loses his or her protection as a civilian while doing so,[52] the States that negotiated the relevant treaty provisions, namely Common Article 3 to the Geneva Conventions, Article 51(3) of API and Article 13(3) of APII, did not adopt commonly agreed language to explain the notion, and an important attempt by international experts to reach agreement on such a meaning was not successful.[53] Moreover, while some elements of the *Interpretive Guidance* published by the

[51] Such an insertion in the *Manual* might make the point that members of a war cabinet, obviously including a prime minister, would be likely to have roles that would amount to direct participation and that would therefore render the relevant individuals liable to be attacked at any time while such participation continues.

[52] Geneva Conventions 1949, Common Article 3, which refers to active participation, and API, Article 51(3), which refers to direct participation. These concepts are generally regarded as being synonymous; see *DoD Manual*, paragraph 5.9.1.1. Note also the statement in the *Manual* that, while the US does not accept that API, Article 51(3) has customary status, it does accept the customary provision on which that paragraph of API is based; *DoD Manual*, paragraph 5.9.1.2 and footnote 218. Quite what is the difference between recognition of the underlying customary principle and acceptance of customary status of the treaty rule is not made clear and is hard to understand.

[53] The ICRC and the Asser Institute co-sponsored a series of annual meetings of experts from 2003 to 2008. The failure of that initiative to achieve consensus among the experts as to a general interpretation of the direct participation notion is within the personal knowledge of the present authors, who participated as experts. At the end of the process, the ICRC, on its own initiative, published the *Interpretive Guidance* to which reference is made in footnote 26.

ICRC are accepted as reflecting customary law, substantial parts of it are not so accepted, *inter alia*, by the US,[54] and indeed the *Interpretive Guidance* has been the subject of controversy in the academic literature.[55] Section 5.9 therefore articulates the US interpretation of a concept that international law has conspicuously failed to explain. Of course, the interpretation offered in the *Manual* is also not necessarily customary in status, recognising as one must that there is unlikely yet to be a sufficient generality of practice or, indeed, of interpretation to justify any particular understanding as having achieved customary status.

Paragraph 5.9.2 makes the important and accurate point that the rule specifically applies to civilians. It also correctly notes that civilians are persons who are not combatants (ignoring, for the time being, the question of non-combatants). An issue arises because, as we have seen, the US definition of combatants in paragraph 5.8.2 includes members of non-State armed groups, whereas, as has been noted, the API, Article 43 definition does not. However, States party to API and States party to APII would consider that members of organised armed groups do not qualify as civilians, at least in relation to a non-international armed conflict.[56] For the US, members of all non-State armed groups are counted as combatants, are therefore persons to whom the direct participation notion does not apply[57] and are, accordingly on that basis, liable to be attacked at all times during an armed conflict. The use of the word 'separate' in line 3 of the second part of paragraph 5.9.2.1 is therefore potentially misleading. All combatants are liable to be attacked at all times, and the relevant persons are classed by the US as combatants.

Paragraph 5.9.3 tackles the difficult task of explaining direct participation in hostilities as such. It does so by making the proper distinction between, on the one hand, taking part in the combat or substantially contributing to a party's ability to conduct or sustain combat operations, both of which would in the US view amount to direct participation, and, on the other hand, providing general support to the war effort, such as by purchasing war bonds. The

54 *DoD Manual*, paragraph 5.9.1.2 and footnote 219.

55 See, for example, the Forum in 42 *New York University Journal of International Law and Politics* 3 (2010).

56 Note that a non-international armed conflict requires the participation of at least one non-State organised armed group. If Common Article 3 to the Geneva Conventions is interpreted as applying to civilians in a non-international armed conflict, this may be understood as referring to all persons who are not members of non-State organised armed groups or of the State's armed forces.

57 This point is made in paragraph 5.9.2.1 of the *Manual*, where it is correctly pointed out that while what may be summarised as the US and API approaches imply differing methodologies, they will often yield the same practical interpretations.

Manual does well to emphasise the importance of the context in which an act is performed in determining whether it does or does not amount to direct participation, and it is most helpful that, later in the paragraph, some considerations that may be relevant in making that determination are suggested, it being implicitly recognised that the offered considerations are illustrative, not an exhaustive list. In paragraph 5.9.3.1, examples are given, again on a non-exhaustive basis, of actions that would be regarded as direct participation. The examples that are chosen would all seem to be non-controversial. In the next paragraph, 5.9.3.2, examples are given, again on a non-controversial basis, of activities that would not amount to direct participation.

In paragraph 5.9.4, the *Manual* appropriately rejects the notion of the revolving door of protection,[58] a concept that is explained and discussed in more detail in paragraph 5.9.4.2, where the position is adopted that civilians who repeatedly perform acts of direct participation do not regain protection during the time intervals between such direct participation acts.[59] As paragraph 5.9.4.1 suggests, it must also be right to hold that a person who has permanently renounced direct participation ceases as a consequence to be liable to be attacked, and the assessment of whether a person has indeed permanently ceased directly to participate must be based on a good faith evaluation, which, one would suggest, must be informed by all the information from all sources that is reasonably available to the decision maker at the relevant time.

PERSONS PLACED HORS DE COMBAT

Section 5.10 explains the legal arrangements concerning persons who are placed *hors de combat*. The provisions of Article 41 of API are cited, and the *Manual* text starts by summarising those who are to be regarded as *hors de combat*. Much of the discussion in this section is not controversial. An ongoing point of some difficulty, however, concerns surrender. Article 41 of API provides that a 'person is *hors de combat* if... He clearly expresses an

58 The idea of the revolving door of protection has its roots in a strict interpretation of the treaty provision that civilians retain protection from attack 'unless and for such time as' they directly participate. If the idea of direct participation is interpreted, in accordance with the Interpretive Guidance approach, as limited to specific acts, it logically follows that during the intervals between these specific acts, an individual regains protected status, hence the revolving door of protection. So far as the ICRC is concerned, the revolving door is not a malfunction of the law; Melzer, *Interpretive Guidance*, 70.

59 The rejection of the revolving door concept is based in part on the imbalance it would imply between the positions of combatants and of directly participating civilians, and on the view that such an interpretation would actually erode the protection of civilians; *DoD Manual*, paragraph 5.9.4.2, final sentence.

intention to surrender'. The *Manual* takes the position that '[f]or an offer to surrender to render a person *hors de combat*, it must be feasible for the opposing party to accept the offer'.[60] The Final Report on the Persian Gulf War, a US DoD document, is cited as the authority for this interpretation. Article 41 of API, however, makes no specific mention of such a feasibility requirement as a condition for *hors de combat* status. According to that text, it is the act of manifesting an intention to surrender that produces that status.

The discussion of these issues at paragraph 5.10.3.3 may at first glance seem to provide ample justification for the feasibility aspect of the *Manual* position.[61] Certainly, a soldier who indicates a willingness to surrender in circumstances, such as those discussed in that paragraph, where it is manifestly impractical to accept that surrender cannot reasonably expect to be taken into custody. However, the observations in the AMW *Manual* are relevant here. That manual comments: 'Enemy personnel who surrender will normally be taken into the custody – and placed under the protection – of the detaining Belligerent Party. However, this is not always feasible. If the military unit, in whose custody the surrendering personnel are, is incapable . . . to escort them to a POW-camp, they must be released without harm. Thus the obligation on the part of the Belligerent Party is not necessarily to detain surrendering enemy personnel, but to desist from further attack on persons complying with the conditions set out in rule 127.'[62] It is suggested that it would have been better if the *DoD Manual* had expressed the legal position in these or similar terms, thereby emphasising that the practical ability to accept surrender and thereafter take the surrendering individuals into custody are not the determinants of *hors de combat* status; rather, surrender is contingent on three cumulative conditions: clearly communicating the intent to surrender, desisting from further hostile acts and not attempting to evade capture. Persons complying with these conditions are *hors de combat* and must not be made the object of attack, whether capturing them is practicable/feasible or not.

Paragraph 5.10.4 correctly outlines the protected status of persons who are rendered unconscious or who are otherwise incapacitated by wounds, sickness or shipwreck, while paragraph 5.10.5 addresses the status of persons parachuting from an aircraft in distress. It is accurately stated that their protected status is analogous to that accorded to combatants who are *hors de combat*.

60 *DoD Manual*, paragraph 5.10.3.3.

61 It is emphasised that what is being discussed here is the US position on the matter, not the correct interpretation of the requirements of API, Article 41 as that article applies to a State that is party to the treaty.

62 AMW *Manual*, Commentary accompanying rule 125, paragraph 5. The conditions in rule 127 are to communicate the intention to surrender in a clear manner to the enemy; not to engage in any further hostile acts; and to make no attempt to evade capture.

However, in the final element of the paragraph, it is argued that paratroopers parachuting from an aircraft in distress outside the context of an airborne assault would be protected from attack as being *hors de combat*. A number of potential difficulties arise with this formulation. It may be impossible for defending forces to determine from which of a group of aircraft paratroopers are emerging, particularly if only one such aircraft is stricken. Similarly, it may be difficult for defenders to determine whether the descending paratroopers are genuinely out of the fight or are intent on continuing the hostilities, and whether, therefore, delaying an attack on them until they have landed and manifested their intent is to forego the only opportunity for successful engagement of them.

Thus, while it may be correct as a matter of strict interpretation of the applicable law that such persons are capable of being *hors de combat*, it would seem that only if they clearly come within the provisions of Article 41 should they be entitled to protection, it being acknowledged, as appears to be the US position, that Article 41 does not necessarily contain an all-embracing definition of the persons who may be classed as *hors de combat*.

FEASIBLE PRECAUTIONS IN CONDUCTING ATTACKS TO REDUCE THE RISK OF HARM TO PROTECTED PERSONS AND OBJECTS

Paragraph 5.11 is an important provision in that it addresses the precautions that an attacker is obliged to undertake. There is a clear link, as the *Manual* acknowledges, between these precautionary obligations and the practical implementation of the discrimination principle.[63] The corresponding provisions in API are to be found in Article 57, so while recognising here, as elsewhere, that the US is not a party to that treaty, the widely accepted provisions of the article will provide a useful baseline for considering the stated US position.

The section starts with a reference to the duty to give an effective advance warning of an attack that may affect the civilian population unless the circumstances do not permit it.[64] It is unfortunate that in the same paragraph, reference is also made to the entirely different warning obligations that arise before any attack of certain medical units, vessels or facilities is permissible. Including reference to these warning requirements in paragraph 5.11.1 may cause confusion, for example, when it is suggested in paragraph 5.11.1.1 that there is no set form for warnings, that they may be general and that they may

[63] *DoD Manual*, footnote 279, citing an extract from a letter from Harold Koh, Legal Adviser, Dept of State, dated 30 December 2009.

[64] *DoD Manual*, paragraph 5.11.1.

be communicated in a variety of ways. While such remarks are correct insofar as they refer to warnings of attacks that may affect civilians, they do not reflect the specific requirements as to warnings before an attack on e.g. medical facilities can legitimately be undertaken.[65]

Paragraph 5.11.1.2 makes the correct point that there is no obligation under Article 57 to give warnings e.g. of attacks that will not affect the civilian population. Interestingly, this paragraph gives no guidance as to the interpretation of the word 'affect'. Specifically, it does not suggest that the notion is limited to attacks that are intended or that may be expected to cause death or injury to civilians.

Paragraphs 5.11.2 to 5.11.4 address some of the general precautionary measures that can be taken with a view to minimising civilian casualties, and include the proper point that international law does not, as such, specify any requirement to use precision guided munitions on any particular occasion.

Paragraph 5.11.5 expresses the US view that the rule in API, Article 57(3) is not a rule of customary law.[66] This would lead one to conclude that, so far as the US is concerned, where a choice is possible between a number of military objectives for the achievement of a similar military advantage, there is no legal obligation to choose the target the attack of which offers the least danger to civilians. The associated footnote[67] cites the *Digest of United States Practice in International Law*, from which it appears that the rejection of customary status of this rule derives from notions of mission accomplishment, allowable risk and the possibility that the decision maker may conclude that making such a determination is not possible. Arguably, if mission accomplishment is going to be rendered impossible, if taking the precaution would involve unacceptable own forces risk or if making such a determination is simply not possible, then either the choice referred to in the rule is impossible or the military advantage anticipated from the attack is no longer similar. In either such circumstance, the rule would not be engaged, so it is difficult to agree that the stated arguments provide a sound basis for the rejection of the rule as it is expressed in API.

[65] Note, for example, Article 13 of API, which is concerned with the discontinuance of protection of civilian medical units and which specifies that protection of such units may cease 'only after a warning has been given setting, whenever appropriate, a reasonable time limit, and after such warning has remained unheeded'; Article 13(1). The nature of the warning will involve pointing out the respects in which the unit is being used outside its humanitarian function to commit acts harmful to the adversary, and will require the cessation of such activities. Thus, the nature, purpose and intended effect of this kind of warning are fundamentally different to those prescribed by Article 57(2)(c) of API.

[66] The text of API, Article 57(3) is given later in the present section.

[67] *DoD Manual*, footnote 303.

So, what do these paragraphs tell us about the rules as to precautions in attack that the US accepts? Footnote 279 cites, seemingly with approval, Article 27 of the Hague Regulations 1907 and, in relation to naval forces, Article 5 of Hague Convention IX of the same year. Correspondence from Harold Koh, Legal Adviser at the Department of State, dated 30 December 2009, is quoted to the effect that the US accepts Article 57(2)(ii) and (4) as 'an accurate statement of the fundamental law of war principle of discrimination'.[68] Paragraphs 5.11.1 to 5.11.4 of the *Manual* stipulate that combatants must take feasible precautions in conducting attacks to reduce the risk of harm to civilians and other protected persons and objects, noting that such feasible precautions may include giving warnings, adjusting the timing of an attack to reduce the risk of incidental harm,[69] selecting certain weapons with a view to reducing the risk of incidental harm while achieving a given or superior military advantage[70] and identifying zones in which military objectives are more likely to be present or civilians are more likely to be absent. However, it should be noted that these are described in terms of possible feasible precautions, it being pointed out that what it is in fact feasible to do by way of precautions will depend on the prevailing circumstances.[71]

It is therefore instructive to note which explicit precautionary duties stipulated by API, Article 57 are not specifically reflected in this section of the *Manual* text[72] as being accepted by the US as mandatory obligations.[73] They are:

68 Article 52(2)(a)(ii) of API, which is the provision to which the erroneous *DoD Manual* reference to Article 57(2)(ii) is seemingly intended to refer, provides that with respect to attacks, the following precautions shall be taken: 'those who plan or decide upon an attack shall . . . (ii) take all feasible precautions in the choice of means and methods of attack with a view to avoiding, and in any event to minimizing, incidental loss of civilian life, injury to civilians and damage to civilian objects;'. Article 57(4) provides that in the conduct of military operations at sea or in the air, 'each Party to the conflict shall, in conformity with its rights and duties under the rules of international law applicable in armed conflict, take all reasonable precautions to avoid losses of civilian lives and damage to civilian objects'.

69 *DoD Manual*, paragraph 5.11.2.

70 *DoD Manual*, paragraph 5.11.3.

71 *DoD Manual*, paragraph 5.11, second sentence.

72 Note, however, footnote 304, which relates to the next section on proportionality. An extract from FM 27–10 addresses some relevant concepts, but in terms which are somewhat different from the corresponding API provisions. The *Manual*'s reader is invited to consider Articles 51(5)(b) and 57(2)(a)(iii), but there is no indication as to whether these rules are considered binding on the US in the stated terms and/or as to whether they are considered to be customary.

73 The point being made here is that these API duties are not explicitly reflected in terms in these paragraphs of the *Manual*. It is a matter of interpretation whether some or all of these explicit obligations of API are regarded as being subsumed within the somewhat more generally expressed rules that the *Manual* sets forth.

a. The requirement that those who plan or decide upon an attack shall 'do everything feasible to verify that the objectives to be attacked are neither civilians nor civilian objects and are not subject to special protection but are military objectives within the meaning of paragraph 2 of Article 52 and that it is not prohibited by the provisions of th[e] Protocol to attack them';[74]
b. The requirement that those who plan or decide upon an attack shall 'refrain from deciding to launch any attack which may be expected to cause incidental loss of civilian life, injury to civilians, damage to civilian objects, or a combination thereof, which would be excessive in relation to the concrete and direct military advantage anticipated';[75]
c. The obligation that 'an attack shall be cancelled or suspended if it becomes apparent that the objective is not a military one or is subject to special protection or that the attack may be expected to cause incidental loss of civilian life, injury to civilians, damage to civilian objects, or a combination thereof, which would be excessive in relation to the concrete and direct military advantage anticipated';[76]
d. The requirement that, '[w]hen a choice is possible between several military objectives for obtaining a similar military advantage, the objective to be selected shall be that the attack on which may be expected to cause the least danger to civilian lives and to civilian objects'.[77]

Undoubtedly, US forces will in practice frequently undertake the precautions listed in elements (a) to (d) of the previous paragraph. In operational terms, there will often be little or no difference in the precautionary steps, therefore, that the US and States party to API respectively take. The significance from the perspective of the *Manual* lies in the arguably limited and general nature of the precautions that the currently discussed paragraphs of the *Manual* regard as being legally required. Such a divergence of legal interpretation therefore has potential, if not necessarily actual, implications for interoperability, for example during coalition operations.

PROPORTIONALITY IN CONDUCTING ATTACKS

Section 5.12 is where the *Manual* addresses the proportionality rule as it applies to targeting law. It does this in the following terms: 'Combatants must refrain from attacks in which the expected loss of life or injury to civilians,

[74] API, Article 57(2)(a)(i). [75] API, Article 57(2)(a)(iii).
[76] API, Article 57(2)(b). [77] API, Article 57(3).

and damage to civilian objects incidental to the attack, would be excessive in relation to the concrete and direct military advantage expected to be gained.'[78] Interestingly, here again there are evident departures from the language that binds the very numerous States that are party to API. Thus, the *Manual* does not explicitly link the proportionality rule to the prohibition of indiscriminate attacks; it only addresses combatants, impliedly omitting application of the rule to civilians who are taking a direct part in the hostilities; it refers to the loss of life, not the loss of civilian life, incidental to the attack, implying that incidental loss of combatant or of directly participating civilian life ought to be considered in the collateral damage aspect of the proportionality evaluation, which cannot of course be correct; and the grammatical construction that is chosen in the *Manual*'s formulation has the effect that only the damage to civilian objects is required to be incidental to the attack, not the death or injury to civilians. It is also noteworthy that the military advantage to be considered must be expected, it being an interesting question worthy of consideration whether the requirement for expectation is, arguably, more exacting than the API reference in Article 51(5)(b) to anticipation.

One really wonders why the API definition, which has always been understood as having generally accepted, customary status, has not been adopted here. From a grammatical perspective, it offers a text that is noticeably clearer than, and thus preferable to, the formulation put forward in the *Manual*.

Paragraph 5.12.1 makes the valid point that the rule only applies where civilians or civilian objects are at risk of harm from an attack, while paragraph 5.12.2 notes that forms of harm that are less than death, injury or damage need not be considered. While that comment may well be correct, more contentious is the observation that temporary losses would be an example of such lesser forms of harm that do not need to be considered. Whether this is accurate as a statement of law will depend on the meaning to be given to 'temporary losses'. A temporary loss of functionality in a computer network that could be expected to cause death, injury or damage to civilians or civilian objects would indeed need to be considered in a proportionality evaluation of a proposed cyber attack. If the intended point here is that temporary loss of service or use that does not in turn occasion death, injury or damage does not have to be considered in the proportionality evaluation, this might usefully be spelt out, it being in the present authors' view a rather less controversial

[78] The corresponding provision of API, namely Article 51(5)(b), provides that 'the following types of attack are to be considered as indiscriminate: ... (b) an attack which may be expected to cause incidental loss of civilian life, injury to civilians, damage to civilian objects, or a combination thereof, which would be excessive in relation to the concrete and direct military advantage anticipated'.

position. Paragraph 5.12.2.1 makes the generally correct point that consequences of an attack that are too remote should not be considered, it being understood that we are talking here about remoteness in causal terms. Ultimately, the proportionality rule requires attackers to consider expected collateral damage, and whether particular damage will be too remote to be expected will depend on the relevant facts.

Paragraph 5.12.2 contends that '[p]ersons or objects harmed through action directly attributable to enemy action, or beyond the control of either party, would be excluded from the attacking party's proportionality analysis'. As is well understood, the API proportionality rule uses expectation as the criterion for distinguishing between collateral consequences that either must, or that do not have to be, considered. One can visualise circumstances in which it is known that if a particular kind of attack is undertaken, the enemy will employ a particular capability or technique in response which can be expected to have a particular effect. To fail to consider that expected effect on the basis that it is attributable to enemy action would appear to be to fail to apply the proportionality rule as that rule is widely articulated and understood. Similarly, circumstances may be beyond the control of either party, such as weather conditions, yet their effect on the expected consequences of an attack may be evident. In such circumstances also, it is surely the case that the expected consequences must be considered in the proportionality evaluation, irrespective of the inability of either party to control the particular circumstance. These interpretative difficulties would be avoided if the *Manual* were to focus on the relevant issue of expectation and to analyse hypothetical scenarios accordingly.

Paragraph 5.12.3 makes the point that harm to military objectives, combatants and directly participating civilians that is incidental to the intended target of the attack is understood not to prohibit an attack under the proportionality rule. This is correct.[79] The paragraph also, however, goes on to suggest that harm to certain persons who may be employed in or on military objectives would also be understood not to prohibit an attack on grounds of proportionality. The examples cited are persons authorised to accompany the armed forces, parlementaires and civilian workers who place themselves in or on the military objective knowing that it is susceptible to attack, such as ammunition factory workers. For a State that is party to API, there is no blanket exclusion from the collateral damage calculus of persons in the stated categories. Rather, Article 51(4) and (5)(b) obliges the attacker to take these and any other classes of person protected from attack into account in considering whether

79 *DoD Manual*, paragraph 5.12.3.1.

the expected collateral damage is indeed excessive. Accordingly, in the case of ammunition factory workers, for example, the expected casualties among the civilian workers in the factory should be considered along with casualties among civilians living in the vicinity of the factory and all other categories of collateral damage,[80] it being appreciated that only in relatively rare cases will the expected casualties among the workers be excessive in relation to what is likely to be the considerable military advantage accruing directly from the planned attack on the ammunition factory.[81] There will be those who would argue that such workers should be reckoned with reduced value in the proportionality assessment because of their, it is assumed voluntary, assumption of risk. Be that as it may, it is generally recognised that they should be considered, whatever the value accorded to them, and that their expected deaths and injuries should not be simply ignored. So, while it is right that such individuals are unlikely to prohibit the proposed attack on proportionality grounds, it would probably be more legally accurate to say that the proportionality rule should be applied, that the relevant persons should be considered when doing so and that, in normal circumstances, the attack is likely to be found not to breach the rule.

Paragraph 5.12.3.3 turns to the legally vexed question of human shields, and starts by correctly noting that the use of civilians to shield military objectives from attack is unlawful. The paragraph goes on to observe, again correctly, that the party using human shields takes responsibility for injury to them, provided that the attacking party takes feasible precautions in attack. This formulation of the position does not, however, fully reflect the position binding on States party to API by virtue of Article 51(7) and (8), in that the treaty provisions, having asserted the illegality of human shielding, then require that attackers comply with their legal obligations with respect to the civilian population and civilians, including the obligation to take precautionary measures, notwithstanding the violations by the opposing party. In this connection, it is perhaps interesting and illustrative of the points made earlier in respect of the sources the *Manual* cites that in footnote 315 reliance is placed, *inter alia*, on materials from an Instructor Training Course, while no mention is made of the arguably infinitely more authoritative provisions of API. It would have been preferable to see a specific explanation of the API position and of why that position is rejected by the US. In the somewhat brief discussion in the second part of the paragraph of the application of the proportionality rule in human shield situations, no distinction is made between voluntary and involuntary human shields. It would have been useful if the US position on the

80 See Dinstein, *Conduct of Hostilities*, 160; see n. 5 to Chapter 3.

81 Ibid.

application of the proportionality rule to these two recognised and distinct kinds of human shield had been set forth.[82]

Paragraph 5.12.4 properly draws attention to the 'excessiveness' aspect of the proportionality rule. Later in the same paragraph, the open-ended, subjective and imprecise nature of the inquiry that the rule requires in cases other than those that are clear-cut is appropriately noted. A rich selection of sources, including well-known and authoritative extracts from the Final Report to the ICTY Prosecutor by the Committee Established to Review the NATO Bombing Campaign against the Federal Republic of Yugoslavia, from the writings of Tony Rogers and of W Hays Parks, is cited.

Paragraph 5.12.5 addresses what it describes as 'concrete and direct military advantage expected to be gained'. The thought that by requiring the military advantage to be expected rather than anticipated, the *Manual* is raising the bar for allowable military advantage was discussed earlier. In the ensuing discussion, the idea of definite military advantage in the military objective definition is linked to the proportionality rule's concept of concrete and direct military advantage, and the interpretation is offered that while the military advantage does not have to be immediate, it cannot be merely speculative or hypothetical. This is a widely accepted and correct interpretation. The military advantage is not limited to tactical gains, may indeed, as the *Manual* proposes and should refer to the attack as a whole, not to isolated or particular parts of it. Here, interestingly, statements by a number of States on ratification of API are referred to in the associated footnote.[83]

Having looked at how the *Manual* deals with the principle of distinction and with some of its most closely related rules, the present discussion now moves on to look at some of the rules that derive from that principle, but that contain specific protections of particular objects or persons, or that in some other respect develop the law and the protections it affords in some way.

ATTACKS ON WORKS, FACILITIES OR INSTALLATIONS CONTAINING DANGEROUS FORCES

Section 5.13 notes that '[c]ertain facilities containing dangerous forces, such as dams, nuclear power plants, or facilities producing weapons of mass destruction, may constitute military objectives', a proposition that is clearly

[82] The AMW *Manual* makes this distinction in paragraph 5 of the Commentary to rule 45. The views of the participating experts as to how voluntary and involuntary human shields should, respectively, be addressed in the application of the proportionality rule are given in paragraphs 6 and 7 of the same Commentary.

[83] DoD *Manual*, footnote 323 to Chapter V.

correct. Such objects are capable of fulfilling the definition of military objective; indeed, almost any object is capable of doing so. The first paragraph of the section goes on to give some examples of reasons why a commander might wish to attack such objects, again in uncontroversial terms. In the next paragraph, the US position is given that the attack of such facilities is lawful provided that it is done in compliance with applicable rules, including those as to discrimination and proportionality.[84] Given that the US is not party to API and that it explicitly and consistently rejects Article 56 of that treaty (discussed later), this is clearly a correct statement of the law. Furthermore, the point is made that in view of the additional potential incidental harm, additional precautions may be appropriate to reduce the risk that the release of the dangerous forces would pose for the civilian population. So, while the US is not party to API and rejects Article 56, the philosophy of that article is apparently accepted by the US on a voluntary basis, whereas a legal duty as set forth in the article is rejected.

Paragraph 5.13.1 gives a generally accurate summary of some aspects of the rule in API, Article 56, and notes the basis of the US rejection of that rule as protecting objects that would be considered legitimate military objectives under customary international law and as deviating from the distinction and proportionality rules. It should be noted that while the *Manual* provision is dealing in general terms with facilities containing dangerous forces, the corresponding Article 56 provision addresses explicitly and exclusively dams, dykes and nuclear electrical generating stations.

FEASIBLE PRECAUTIONS TO REDUCE THE RISK OF HARM TO PROTECTED PERSONS AND OBJECTS BY THE PARTY SUBJECT TO ATTACK

Section 5.14 correctly draws attention to the obligation of parties to the conflict to take feasible precautions to reduce the risk of harm to protected persons and objects from the effects of enemy attacks, and the associated footnote cites the corresponding provisions of Article 58 of API. The section correctly observes that what precautions are feasible will be determined by the context, including operational aspects, and then gives a helpful list of possible precautions. Which of the listed precautions will in fact be feasible will therefore depend on the circumstances, and this may explain why the verb 'may' is used when

[84] It is noteworthy that the rules as to discrimination and proportionality are merely examples of the rules to be complied with, although they would seem to be the most relevant – in addition, of course, to the rules as to precautions in attack.

discussing each of the suggested precautions. Nevertheless, simply to say in paragraph 5.14.1 that it may be appropriate to avoid placing military objectives in or near densely populated areas is not an adequate statement of the law. It would, it is suggested, be more accurate to provide that all practically possible steps should be taken to avoid so locating military objectives. The billeting of troops may, as the second part of the paragraph suggests, be a legitimate exception, and it is indeed unlikely that the rule applies in counter-insurgency operations that fall short of armed conflict, although it is hard to see the relevance of operations falling short of armed conflict in a manual devoted to the law of war.

Paragraph 5.14.2's obligation to remove civilians and civilian objects from the vicinity of military operations is also expressed in rather permissive terms, but the law and possible implementing steps are correctly stated, and the need to keep civilian hospitals away from military objectives is properly emphasised. Paragraph 15.4.3 deals in uncontroversial terms with the establishment by agreement between the parties of locations or zones where civilians or the wounded and sick are protected, including civilian hospital and safety zones and localities, military hospital zones and localities and neutralised zones. Paragraph 5.14.4 suggests the use of distinctive and visible signs to identify protected persons and objects, citing civilian hospitals and civilian air-raid shelters as examples,[85] but making the important point that such marking would not be appropriate where the enemy seeks to make civilians the object of attack. Paragraph 5.14.5 then makes the proper point that the obligations to carry arms openly and to wear a distinctive uniform/emblem help to protect the civilian population from erroneously being made the object of attack. The *Manual* asserts that the obligation of armed forces to distinguish themselves includes, but is not limited to, when they are undertaking attacks, but qualifies this by observing that the obligation to distinguish is not an absolute one, even during combat.[86]

UNDEFENDED CITIES, TOWNS AND VILLAGES

Section 5.15 and paragraph 5.15.1 note the difference in language between the references in Article 25 of the 1907 Hague Regulations and in Hague Convention IX, 1907 to undefended localities and the reference in Article 59,

85 Article 27 of the 1907 Hague Regulations and Article 9 of Hague Convention IX, 1907, are quoted in support of this rule.

86 See the discussion associated with paragraph 5.5.8.1 and note the position set forth in API, Articles 43 and 44.

API to non-defended localities. The *Manual* argues persuasively, on the basis of consistency of terminology across the French texts, that there is no substantive difference between the terms. Similarly, the *Manual* argues, again non-controversially, that the ideas of 'open' and of 'undefended' can also be used interchangeably to describe populated areas that are protected by the law of war from attack.[87]

The conferment of undefended status by agreement between the parties or by unilateral declaration of the party in control of a particular town, city etc. when it is in or near the contact zone between the opposing parties, and the associated detailed requirements, are then discussed. Importantly, the undefended city must be open for immediate occupation by opposing ground troops, so a city behind enemy lines that it would not be feasible for opposing forces to occupy cannot be declared undefended.[88] The section also notes the implied requirement to declare undefended status,[89] the option of a belligerent to refuse to recognise such a declaration if the city etc. is assessed as not satisfying all the requisite conditions,[90] and the fact that such a declaration should be made by the authority with the power to enforce the required conditions.[91] Those conditions are correctly addressed in paragraph 5.15.4, and comprise the evacuation of combatants and movable military equipment, not making hostile use of fixed military facilities and refraining from hostile acts against the occupying force and from activities in support of military operations.[92] Even if all of these conditions are not met, a location can be accorded undefended status by agreement.[93] Following occupation, retention by the place of undefended status will be contingent on the occupier continuing to comply with the relevant conditions.[94]

API, in Articles 59 and 60, distinguishes between non-defended localities and demilitarised zones. The former are declared by the appropriate authorities of a party to the conflict in relation to an inhabited place in or near a zone where armed forces are in contact. The place must be open for occupation by an adverse party and must fulfil conditions set out in Article 59(2) of API. The declaration must be acknowledged by the recipient party, who shall

87 DoD *Manual*, paragraph 5.15.1.2.

88 DoD *Manual*, paragraph 5.15.3.1.

89 DoD *Manual*, paragraph 5.15.3.2.

90 DoD *Manual*, paragraph 5.15.3.3, where the obligation to notify the refusal is given.

91 DoD *Manual*, paragraph 5.15.3.4.

92 Note that supporting authority is primarily drawn from FM 27–10 (Change No. 1 1976) and that the reader is invited to 'consider' the corresponding provisions of API, Article 59, which are quoted.

93 DoD *Manual*, paragraph 5.15.5, where matters to be included in the agreement are suggested.

94 DoD *Manual*, paragraph 5.15.6.

treat the locality as non-defended and refrain from attacking it. Provision is also made, in Article 59(5), for the establishment of non-defended localities by agreement. Article 60, API also provides for the parties to the conflict to agree to establish demilitarised zones[95] and prohibits the extension of military operations to such zones in breach of the terms of such agreements. The *Manual* does not seem to deal in terms with this idea of demilitarised zones, unless the more generalised discussion of establishing undefended places by agreement is intended to reflect the notion.

PROHIBITION ON USING PROTECTED PERSONS AND OBJECTS TO SHIELD, FAVOR OR IMPEDE MILITARY OPERATIONS

Section 5.16, citing the US Code, restates the widely accepted customary rule prohibiting the use of the presence or movement of protected persons or objects[96] to try to make certain points or areas immune from attack, to shield military objectives from attack or otherwise to shield or favour one's own military operations or impede those of the adversary. In paragraph 5.16.1, the *Manual* explains usefully that this rule does not affect the use for military purposes of what otherwise would be a civilian object and does not prohibit 'persons who would otherwise be civilians from participating in hostilities or assuming the risks inherent in supporting military operations'. When considering this wording, it should be recalled that civilians who directly participate in hostilities remain civilians and that they and others who support military operations thereby assume risks, the nature and extent of which will depend on exactly what they do or where they are located.[97]

Paragraph 5.16.2 makes the accurate point that it is the intent to endanger the lives of protected persons that lies at the root of this rule, drawing the proper distinction between such action and the failure to take feasible precautions to separate protected persons and property from the dangers of military operations. It must be right, as the *Manual* argues later in the same paragraph, that this rule does not prohibit either the restriction of movement of protected persons in order to enable military operations to proceed unimpeded or the evacuation of civilians for their own safety or to enable military operations to proceed.

95 API, Article 60.

96 Paragraph 5.16.1 lists protected persons and objects for these purposes, starting the list with the words 'in particular', which indicates that it is not to be regarded as necessarily exhaustive.

97 The risks may include injury or death collateral to an attack on a military objective in which they are located, prosecution for their participation irrespective of their compliance with the law of armed conflict or that they will have no PW status if captured.

Paragraph 5.16.3 acknowledges the customary rule in international and non-international armed conflict forbidding the taking of hostages or the threatening of harm to detainees in order to dissuade an attack. Indeed, one would suggest threatening to harm or otherwise adversely to treat detainees pursuant to other motives would also be prohibited, but this is not indicated in this paragraph of the *Manual* text, which is strange because this point is reflected explicitly in the texts from the US Code that are quoted in the associated footnote.[98]

Paragraph 5.16.4 essentially repeats the point made at paragraph 5.5.4 to the effect that the breach by the adverse party of the prohibition on using protected persons to shield, favour or impede military operations does not relieve the attacker of the obligation to seek to discriminate between lawful and unlawful targets, although such breaches may impede the attacker's ability to discriminate and may increase the risk of harm to protected persons and objects. Footnote 410 usefully illustrates the point by reference to Iraqi conduct during Gulf War I.

SEIZURE AND DESTRUCTION OF ENEMY PROPERTY

Section 5.17 deals with the seizure and destruction of enemy property, and includes an uncontroversial statement of the prohibition of destruction not justified by imperative military necessity.[99] Logically, some associated rules, such as the prohibition of pillage, rules as to the seizure of public and private enemy property and the war crime of causing wanton damage not justified by military necessity are included within this section. A short sentence should be inserted dealing with capture and destruction as prize, to which specific rules of air and naval warfare apply. This would usefully make the point that the discussion in this section is concerned with land warfare. In paragraph 5.17.2.1, it is contended that 'if sufficient military necessity exists to justify attacking an object as reflected by that object meeting the definition of military objective, then imperative military necessity would also exist to justify seizing or destroying that object by measures short of attack', a proposition with which one can readily agree. The *Manual* goes on to contend that objects the seizure or destruction of which is justified by military necessity do not necessarily meet the criteria to be a military objective. Paragraph 5.17.2.2 develops the point, citing e.g. tree-cutting to open a field of fire and seizing transportation to support

[98] *DoD Manual*, footnote 406.

[99] Hague Regulations 1907, Article 23(g). See the *Manual*, paragraph 5.17, first bullet and paragraph 5.17.2.

military operations as examples where objects that are not military objectives may nevertheless be seized or destroyed. Where the destruction of objects to open a field of fire is concerned, such action must be considered part of the wider military operation that renders the field of fire necessary and is an example of the need to assess military advantage by reference to the attack as a whole, not in relation to isolated or particular parts of the attack.[100] Subject to that point, arguably, and depending upon the precise circumstances, trees that shield the enemy's current or future intended movements would thereby become military objectives. Similar considerations apply in the case of battlefield seizures.

Paragraph 5.17.2.3 takes the discussion of what militarily necessary destruction permits a stage further by stating that '[i]t may be imperatively demanded by the necessities of war to seize or destroy enemy property in order to diminish the enemy's ability to conduct *or sustain* operations', such as war-sustaining infrastructure. The example of the destruction by Union forces during the American Civil War of the cotton crop in Confederate states with the purpose of depriving the Confederacy of the ability to fund its military operations is cited in support of this proposition. There is an evident link here with our discussion earlier of the reference to 'war-sustaining' in the US suggested definition of military objective.[101] It is not considered necessary to repeat that discussion here, but it should be noted that there is the potential for misunderstanding because of the view expressed in the *Manual* that objects contributing to the war-sustaining effort are military objectives. In short, there seems to be a considerable overlap between the discussion in the present section and that in sections 5.6 and 5.7. Paragraph 5.17.2.4 makes the proper point, however, that damage to enemy property that is incidental to combat operations and that is reasonably related to defeating the enemy is permitted. In footnote 426, Greenspan's realistic, pragmatic remarks in this regard are usefully cited.

Paragraph 5.17.3 and its subparagraphs then describe the status of property seized on the battlefield, dealing specifically with the liability of any enemy public movable property on the battlefield to seizure as war booty, the liability

[100] Consider UK Statement (i) Made on Ratification of API on 28 January 1998, where this specific point is made.

[101] Note the discussion earlier in this chapter of the military objective definition in relation to sections 5.6 and 5.7 of the *Manual*. In footnote 425, the more recent example of the destruction by coalition forces of narcotics in Afghanistan to deny funding to the Taliban and al Qaeda is cited. The concern remains that to conclude that war-sustaining objects are lawful targets is potentially substantially to extend the scope of lawful objects of attack to such a degree that the practical utility of the cardinal, intransgressible distinction principle is called into question.

of private military property on the battlefield (except for certain equipment for clothing, feeding or personal protection) to seizure if it is susceptible to direct military use and the limitation on seizure of private movable property that is not susceptible to immediate military use. On a point of detail, and at the risk of stating the obvious, the reference in paragraph 5.17.3.1 to arms, ammunition, military papers and military equipment is a reference to examples of items that would be susceptible to immediate military use and that would therefore be liable to seizure. Paragraph 5.17.3.2 makes the important point that property found on the battlefield belongs to the capturing State, and cites the authority of the 1958 *UK Manual*, while going on rightly to spell out that individual personnel who find or capture property acquire thereby no title to it.

Paragraph 5.17.4 repeats the prohibition of pillage, noting that this also applies in non-international armed conflicts. The paragraph defines the term[102] and properly notes that it does not include appropriation justified by military necessity. The link between the effective prevention of pillage and the maintenance of discipline of the fighting force is made clear, and is well supported by an authoritative quote from the 1958 *UK Manual*.

Paragraph 5.17.5 makes the point that feasible precautions should be taken with a view to mitigating the impact of military operations on civilians. It asserts, correctly, that civilians should be treated humanely and with consideration to the extent that the circumstances allow if, for example, their private residence is to be used for military purposes. The way the paragraph is written might imply to some readers that humane treatment and consideration are only required in relation to the use of a private residence and not necessarily in relation to all military operations that might impact on civilians other than in relation to their homes. It would, arguably, be more accurate to make the humane treatment and due consideration requirements of more clearly general applicability. The paragraph ends by citing the 1958 *UK Manual* in support of the proposition that 'there is no obligation to protect abandoned property in the area of active operations'. This may have been an accurate and complete statement of the law in 1958, but it arguably now needs at least some qualification. A reader should not, for instance, interpret it as implying that attacking abandoned civilian objects is permissible,[103] nor as implying that

[102] Pillage is 'the taking of private or public movable property (including enemy military equipment) for private or personal use'; *DoD Manual*, paragraph 5.17.4.1, citing the elements of the crime of pillage under Article 8(2)(b)(xvi) of the Rome Statute of the International Criminal Court, 1998.

[103] API, Article 52(1) prohibits making civilian objects the object of attack and reflects customary law binding all States.

constant care is not required to spare them.[104] If, for example, civilians have been forced to abandon their homes due to the severity and/or proximity of the fighting, the mere fact that the residents are no longer in occupation does not *per se* deprive the buildings of their status as civilian objects[105] and, therefore, of their protection from being made the object of attack. If the purpose of the quoted passage in the *Manual* is merely to indicate that the obligation to protect does not go beyond the provisions cited in this discussion, this should arguably have been made clearer.

PROTECTION OF CULTURAL PROPERTY DURING HOSTILITIES

Section 5.18 addresses the protection to be afforded to cultural objects during hostilities, and starts by correctly noting that '[c]ultural property, the areas immediately surrounding it, and appliances in use for its protection should be safeguarded and protected'. The second substantive paragraph under section 5.18 makes a valid point as to the applicability of the 1954 Convention when US forces are operating in a State which is not party to that treaty. It would, perhaps, have been helpful if this section of the *Manual* had started with a clear statement noting that the United States is a party to that Convention.[106] The comment in section 5.18 that the US regards some of the Convention's provisions as customary remains, of course, relevant, as it will indicate that those are provisions that, in the US view, should be complied with by other States that may not be party to the Convention – and by the US, as a matter of law rather than policy, when operating in a non-party State.

Paragraph 5.18.1 breaks down the definition of cultural property from Article 1 of the 1954 Convention into the three essential categories and traces the emergence of the cultural property notion in the Lieber Code and subsequent texts. Helpfully, the *Manual* then addresses each of the three categories of cultural property under discrete headings. Dealing with the first category, namely 'movable or immovable property of great importance to the cultural heritage of every people', paragraph 5.18.1.2 asserts that 'property must be of great importance to the cultural heritage of every people to qualify as

[104] The constant care rule is to be found in Article 57(1) of API, and again, in the opinion of the present authors, reflects customary law.

[105] The negative nature of the definition of civilian objects in API, Article 52(1) means that all objects that do not qualify as military objectives benefit from the obligations to distinguish at all times (Article 48), to take constant care of (Article 57(1)) and not to direct attacks at (Article 52(1)) such objects.

[106] The US ratified the Convention on 13 March 2009; source www.icrc.org, viewed on 17 December 2017.

cultural property', a statement that might be misunderstood. It would be more accurate to say that movable or immovable property must fulfil that criterion in order to be so classified. Technically, under the 1954 Convention definition, buildings and refuges, referred to in Article 1(b), and centres, referred to in Article 1(c), are defined as cultural property but are not required to satisfy the 'of great importance to the cultural heritage of every people' criterion. The paragraph usefully lists examples of such cultural property, largely taken from Article 1(a) of the Convention.

Paragraphs 5.18.1.3 and 5.18.1.4 discuss the second and third parts of the definition of cultural property, namely buildings, refuges and centres, in legally uncontroversial terms.

In paragraph 5.18.2, the twin obligations to safeguard and to respect cultural property are set forth clearly and their mutually reinforcing nature is suitably emphasised. That the failure of a State to honour its peacetime obligations to safeguard does not relieve another State of its duty to respect is properly noted in paragraph 5.18.2.1. Likewise, paragraph 5.18.3 nicely explains the duty to refrain from any use of cultural property that is likely to expose it to destruction or damage in the event of an armed conflict, and notes the imperative military necessity caveat. However, in paragraph 5.18.3.1, it is suggested that the imperative military necessity waiver in relation to cultural property under Article 4 of the 1954 Convention is analogous to 'the requirement that enemy property may only be seized or destroyed if imperatively required by the necessities of war'. While the language is indeed similar, the present authors take the view that the cultural property waiver should be interpreted as imposing greater restraint on the military use of or on the directing of hostility against cultural property than the degree of restraint applying to the seizure or destruction of enemy property in general.

Paragraph 5.18.4 usefully lists precautions that can be taken to reduce the risk of harm to cultural property. The listed precautions are presented as examples, it being clear that in particular circumstances, other kinds of precaution may be required in order to achieve the protective purpose. Paragraph 5.18.5 is, in a sense, the twin of paragraph 5.18.3, in that the former reflects in legally accurate terms the obligation in Article 4 of the Convention not to undertake acts of hostility against cultural property, its immediate surroundings or appliances in use for its protection, whereas the latter reflects the requirement of the same article not to use such objects, surroundings or appliances for purposes liable to lead to their destruction or damage.

The imperative military necessity waiver is discussed in paragraph 5.18.5.1, making the valuable point that such necessity should not be confused with convenience, nor should it be used to cloak slackness or indifference to preservation of cultural property. The paragraph, by way of example, then states that 'if cultural property is being used by an opposing force for military purposes, then military necessity generally would imperatively require its seizure or destruction'. In the same vein, it is stated that the waiver may apply where cultural property or its surroundings are used to protect military objectives or if a military objective is located near such property. It is important to note that the *Manual* is making it clear that while the application of the waiver may – and, in the first example, will usually – be appropriate, this will not necessarily be the case. It might, perhaps, have been helpful if the *Manual* had included guidance as to when, in the circumstances discussed in paragraph 5.18.5.1, the application of the waiver would not be appropriate. That said, the paragraph does observe that if the waiver is applied and cultural property, its surroundings or appliances for its protection are attacked, the expected harm to them must be considered when the proportionality test is applied, and feasible precautions should be taken to minimise that harm.

Paragraph 5.18.6 discusses the obligation, set forth in Article 4(3) of the Convention, to prohibit, prevent and, if necessary, put a stop to any form of theft, pillage or misappropriation of, and acts of vandalism directed against, cultural property. It also addresses the prohibition on requisitioning movable cultural property situated on the territory of another State party to the Convention. Examples are provided of suitable action to give effect to these obligations. Paragraph 5.18.7 discusses the use of the distinctive cultural property emblem, its status at law as a means of identification and the prohibition of its use for purposes other than those provided for in the Convention. Paragraph 5.18.8 then sets forth the special protection provisions of Articles 8 to 11 of the Convention as supplemented by its Regulations.[107] On a point of detail, it is noted in paragraph 5.18.8.3 that the US has taken the position that the distinctive emblem repeated three times may be used as a means of identifying all cultural property subject to special protection, not just immovable cultural property subject to special protection, as indicated in Article 17(1) of the Convention.[108]

In paragraph 5.18.8.4, the limited permitted circumstances in which immunity of cultural property subject to special protection can be withdrawn in accordance with Article 11 of the Convention are set out. Article 11(2) notes that such immunity shall be withdrawn 'only in exceptional cases of unavoidable military necessity, and only for such time as that necessity continues', and that such necessity can only be established by an officer commanding a

[107] Hague Cultural Property Regulations, 14 May 1954.

[108] But see *DoD Manual*, paragraph 5.18.7.2, where Article 17(1) is accurately reflected.

force equivalent to a division or larger. The *Manual* goes on to state that 'such necessity should not be construed to impose an unreasonable and disproportionate responsibility on the attacker to avoid damage to cultural property. Moreover, all property may be attacked using any lawful and proportionate means if required by military necessity and notwithstanding possible collateral damage to such property.'[109] This position reflects a statement made by the US on ratification of the Convention on 13 March 2009. At face value, it seems to have the effect of depriving cultural property to which Articles 8 to 11 of the Convention apply of its special protection. Indeed, it would seem to imply that cultural property, including that accorded special protection by the Convention, does not even rank as a civilian object: that might be an inference to be drawn from the 'notwithstanding possible collateral damage' language. Military necessity, it could be inferred, is, according to the US, the only determinant of whether attacking specially protected cultural property is legitimate. It is, however, difficult to see how such an approach can be consistent with the object and purpose of the Convention. It would therefore be desirable for the position of the US on this important matter to be made rather clearer.

Paragraph 5.18.9 explains the protection afforded by Articles 12 and 13 of the Convention for the transport of cultural property under special protection and in urgent cases, and addresses the immunity of such cultural property from seizure, capture and prize. It reports the rules as set forth in the Convention, supplemented where appropriate with the relevant provisions of the Regulations. In paragraph 5.18.10, appropriately brief mention is made of the protective provision in Article 53 of API.

SIEGES AND ENCIRCLED AREAS

Citing, *inter alia*, the *UK Manual*,[110] section 5.19 of the *Manual* correctly asserts the lawfulness of besieging enemy forces as a method of warfare and distinguishes this from the naval method of blockade. The *Manual* defines siege as encirclement of enemy forces to induce their surrender by cutting them off from reinforcement, supplies and communications with the outside world.[111] Paragraph 5.19.1.1 correctly points out that 'the right to conduct a siege or encirclement impliedly recognizes the authority of the military commander to exercise control over civilians and other persons in the immediate

[109] *DoD Manual*, paragraph 5.18.8.4. [110] *UK Manual*, paragraph 5.34.1.

[111] It is also stated to be lawful to seek to starve enemy forces into submission. Note that Article 54(1) of API only prohibits starvation of civilians as a method of warfare.

vicinity of military operations' and gives appropriate examples of the form of such control. Paragraph 5.19.2 is problematic. It is entitled 'Removal and Passage of Certain Personnel – Vulnerable Civilians, Diplomatic and Consular Personnel, the Wounded and Sick, and Medical Personnel'. The paragraph starts by asserting the besieging commander's right to prevent all access and communications, but recommends attempts to achieve, on a voluntary basis, local agreements for the removal of certain kinds of vulnerable people and for the passage of specified classes of personnel and equipment.

The *UK Manual* deals with this aspect in what seems to be a more legally accurate way. It recognises that encirclement poses problems for the besieging commander if civilians[112] are located in the besieged area. The *UK Manual* notes that in any bombardment, the normal rules as to precautions in attack,[113] the prohibition of starvation of the civilian population as a method of warfare[114] and the protection of supplies indispensible to the survival of the civilian population[115] all apply, and that there is an obligation to allow essential relief supplies to reach the civilian population.[116] Perhaps it would have been better to start paragraph 5.19.2 of the *Manual* with a brief discussion of these provisions, as this would provide the context for the suggestion that agreements between belligerents be concluded e.g. to allow civilians to leave the area that is besieged, or that is to be besieged.

It is arguable that paragraph 5.19.3 also does not fully deal with the applicable law. It states that commanders *should* make arrangements for the free passage of consignments of medical and hospital stores, objects for religious worship for civilians and essential foodstuffs, clothing and medicine for children under fifteen, expectant mothers and maternity cases. As is noted in the *Manual* at footnote 596, however, Article 23 of GCIV, on which the paragraph in the *Manual* is clearly based, is expressed in mandatory terms, using the verb 'shall'. The paragraph correctly notes, however, that free passage of these items is not required 'unless [the besieging] party is satisfied that there are no serious reasons for fearing' the diversion of the consignments, that control may not be effective or that a definite advantage may accrue to the military efforts or economy of the enemy. Similarly, when addressing the requirement to forward the relief consignments as rapidly as possible, the mandatory 'shall' in Article 23 becomes 'should' in paragraph 5.19.3.1 of the *Manual*.

[112] The *UK Manual* refers explicitly to civilians, but, to the extent that they may not be civilians, one could also refer to the wounded, sick, infirm, aged persons, children and maternity cases.

[113] API, Article 57.

[114] API, Article 54(1).

[115] API, Article 54(2).

[116] GCIV, Article 23; API, Article 70.

Paragraph 5.19.5 refers to the requirement of besieged forces to take feasible precautions to reduce the risk of incidental harm. The paragraph states that they 'should' take such precautions. It is difficult to see how the use of that word is consistent with the generally accepted rule that 'constant care shall be taken' to spare the civilian population, civilians and civilian objects.[117] Arguably, a more mandatory word than 'should' ought to have been used.

STARVATION

Section 5.20 sets forth the customary rule prohibiting starvation of the civilian population as a method of warfare[118] and recognises that the rule applies in non-international armed conflicts. The section asserts the lawfulness of starvation of enemy forces, a concept which it interprets as including directly participating civilians.[119] Paragraph 5.20.2 of the *Manual* prohibits starvation of enemy forces if the incidental harm to civilians would be excessive in relation to the anticipated military advantage. Applying the proportionality and precautions rules set forth in paragraph 5.20.2 would be a legally correct manifestation of the customary obligation to take constant care to spare civilians, it being accepted that 'the law is not violated if military operations are not intended to cause starvation but have that incidental effect'.[120] Moreover, the rule on starvation 'does not apply where [the relevant] objects are for the sole use of members of the enemy armed forces or in direct support of military action'.[121] So a military operation that is aimed at starving enemy armed forces but that has the incidental effect of depriving civilians of food or water is not necessarily thereby rendered unlawful.

Paragraph 5.20.4 reproduces, subject to a couple of minor errors,[122] the Article 54(2) API prohibition of attacking, destroying, removing or rendering useless objects indispensable to the survival of the civilian population. The

[117] API, Article 57(1). [118] The corresponding rule in API is found in Article 54(1).

[119] *DoD Manual*, paragraph 5.20.1. If it is lawful to make directly participating civilians the object of attack while they so participate, logic might suggest that subjecting them to starvation would also be lawful. The API Commentary, paragraph 2098 interprets Article 54(1) as protecting the civilian population, which would imply a distinction between peaceable members of that population and those participating in the fight, so the US interpretation would seem to be reasonable. However, the time dimension to direct participation needs to be borne in mind. If a civilian ceases directly to participate, subjecting that civilian to starvation will cease to be legitimate.

[120] *UK Manual*, paragraph 5.27.2. [121] *UK Manual*, paragraph 5.27.1.

[122] The correct quote reads 'and' irrigation works, and 'to' cause them to move away.

paragraph correctly notes that the prohibition does not apply to attacks for specific purposes other than the denial of sustenance,[123] nor to objects used solely to sustain members of the armed forces[124] or in direct support of military action.[125] Reference is also made to Article 54(5)'s limited exemption for scorched-earth policies. The *Manual*, perhaps reasonably, finds it difficult to conclude that all of these detailed elements reflect customary law, but states that the US has supported, and impliedly continues to support, the principle that the starvation of civilians may not be used as a method of warfare.

OVERVIEW OF GOOD FAITH, PERFIDY AND RUSES

Section 5.21 starts with a clear declaration that absolute good faith with the enemy must be observed as a rule of conduct,[126] acknowledges the apparent indistinctness of the line between what that rule prohibits and permits[127] and gives as examples of the former killing or wounding the enemy by resort to perfidy,[128] misuse of certain signs, fighting in enemy uniform, feigning non-hostile relations to obtain a military advantage and compelling enemy nationals to take part in hostilities against their own side. Ruses, intelligence collection, military information support operations (e.g. propaganda) and some forms of bribery are given as examples of what is permitted under the rule. The inference is that this position is reflective of customary law, but that is not explicitly stated. The *Manual* then gives examples of the adverse consequences that may be expected to follow breach of the obligation of good faith.

TREACHERY OR PERFIDY USED TO KILL OR WOUND

Section 5.22 correctly states the rule prohibiting killing or wounding of an enemy by resort to perfidy, and goes on accurately to describe perfidy as involving acts inviting the confidence of enemy persons[129] that they are

[123] Reflecting statement (l) made by the UK on ratification of API on 28 January 1998.

[124] API, Article 54(3)(a).

[125] API, Article 54(3)(b) and the *Manual* correctly reflects the proviso in this paragraph of the article.

[126] The *UK Manual* links the requirement for good faith to 'non-hostile relations between parties to an armed conflict', requiring that any agreement reached must be scrupulously observed; *UK Manual*, paragraph 10.2.

[127] The *Manual* cites the 1958 *UK Manual*, paragraph 310 to like effect.

[128] Hague Regulations 1907, Article 23(b). For states party to API, capture of an enemy by resort to perfidy is prohibited; API, Article 37(1).

[129] The reference to enemy 'persons' leads one to conclude that, so far as the US is concerned, misleading a computer system, for example by pretending to have protected status under the

entitled to receive, or are obliged to accord, protection under the law of war and with the intention to betray that confidence.[130] The *Manual*, in the present authors' view correctly, distinguishes between perfidy as such,[131] which the law of war does not prohibit, and killing or wounding[132] by resort to perfidy, which are prohibited and which are war crimes.[133] Paragraph 5.22.2.1 notes the API Article 37(1) prohibition of capture by resort to perfidy, but states that the US does not accept this aspect of the rule as reflecting customary law.[134] Examples are then given of acts that would amount to killing or wounding by resort to perfidy.[135]

USE OF ENEMY FLAGS, INSIGNIA AND MILITARY UNIFORMS

Paragraph 5.23.1 and footnote 659 record the US position that the use of enemy flags, insignia and military uniforms is prohibited during combat but not preceding, following or outside of combat.[136] While it is arguable that use of enemy uniforms etc. to kill or injure would amount to the war crime of killing or wounding treacherously,[137] the *Manual* correctly notes that perfidy would not arise if there were no element of feigning of protected status.[138] Paragraph 5.23.1.2 states the position, reflected in State practice, that the use of an enemy uniform where there is no intention to deceive is not prohibited, citing extracts from the 1958 *UK Manual* to the effect that if it becomes necessary to use clothing captured from the enemy, badges should be removed before the clothing is worn, while articles of uniform

law of war, would not amount to perfidy and, thus, would not be prohibited under the law of war.

[130] See API, Article 37(1), which the US accepts as a definition of the synonymous concepts of treachery and perfidy; *DoD Manual*, paragraph 5.22.1.1 and footnote 640.

[131] *DoD Manual*, paragraph 5.22.2.

[132] In the case of a State party to API, capturing by resort to perfidy is also prohibited.

[133] Rome Statute, Article 8(2)(b)(xi).

[134] The US, a State not party to API, therefore does not consider itself bound by the 'capture' aspect of the rule.

[135] *DoD Manual*, paragraph 5.22.3.

[136] Paragraph 5.23.1.3 describes use outside of combat as a ruse and thus as lawful. The use of enemy codes, passwords and counter-signs is rightly described as a ruse; *DoD Manual*, paragraph 5.23.1.5.

[137] Consider, for example, Rome Statute, Article 8(2)(b)(xi).

[138] *DoD Manual*, paragraph 5.23.1.1. API, Article 37(1) defines perfidy as follows: 'It is prohibited to kill, injure or capture an adversary by resort to perfidy. Acts inviting the confidence of an adversary to lead him to believe that he is entitled to, or is obliged to accord, protection under the rules of international law applicable in armed conflict, with intent to betray that confidence, shall constitute perfidy.' Article 37(1) then gives examples of perfidious acts.

distinctive of a particular army should only be used in cases of absolute necessity.[139] Paragraph 5.23.1.4 goes on correctly to assert the lawfulness of the use of enemy uniforms to effect escape or to evade capture, provided that they are not used in combat.[140]

For States party to API, the corresponding, more restrictive provision is in Article 39(2), which is set forth, so far as relevant, at paragraph 5.23.3 of the *Manual* and which, to the extent that it differs from the preceding paragraphs, the US does not accept.

IMPROPER USE OF CERTAIN SIGNS

Section 5.24 addresses the rules that prohibit improper use of certain signs and emblems, including signs, uniforms or emblems of neutral or non-belligerent States, the distinctive emblems of the Geneva Conventions, the markings for PW and civilian internee camps, hospital, safety or neutralised zone markings and the distinctive emblem for cultural property.

RUSES OF WAR AND OTHER LAWFUL DECEPTIONS

Section 5.25 of the *Manual* addresses ruses of war, and paragraph 5.25.1 gives a definition of ruses consistent with that in Article 37(2) of API. In paragraph 5.25.1.2, fighting in the enemy's uniform is correctly categorised as an activity that is not perfidy but that, as it breaches the rule discussed earlier, is also not a ruse. Rather than ascribe the perfidy point to 'enemy military personnel . . . not [being] generally protected by the law of war', it might be better simply to say that protected status under the law of armed conflict is not involved, but this is a trivial drafting point. Paragraph 5.25.2 then lists some examples of activities that would amount to lawful ruses and provides valuable historical practice in support of these examples.

Paragraph 5.25.3 explains that some acts that amount to feigning of protected status under the law of war are not prohibited by that law. The paragraph correctly notes that it is not prohibited to feign incapacitation or death to facilitate escape from the enemy. The paragraph then asserts that it is permissible to feign civilian status to facilitate spying or sabotage. While the

139 DoD *Manual*, footnote 663, citing paragraph 322 and note 1 to that paragraph of the 1958 *UK Manual*.

140 The *Manual* correctly notes that if the persons are not escaping PWs, they are liable, if caught behind enemy lines, to be treated as spies or saboteurs; paragraphs 5.23.1.4 and 5.23.2.

feigning of civilian status to facilitate spying is permissible, all uniformed forces must comply with the law of armed conflict by distinguishing themselves from the civilian population when undertaking sabotage missions.[141] Using an informal ceasefire to withdraw unseen is also cited as a non-prohibited deception. This would indeed not be prohibited absent the unlikely situation that the circumstances in which it was done rendered it a breach of good faith with the enemy.[142]

NON-FORCIBLE MEANS AND METHODS OF WARFARE

Paragraph 5.26 describes propaganda, information gathering and bribery as lawful means and methods of warfare.[143] In principle, they are indeed all lawful in international law terms, and they would all seem to be methods rather than means of warfare.[144] Propaganda is generally lawful under the law of war,[145] and important sources cited in the *Manual* attest to that lawfulness; the *Manual* gives as examples of lawful propaganda encouraging enemy personnel to commit acts that violate their law, encouraging enemy combatants to defect, desert or surrender and encouraging insurrection among the enemy civilian population. Propaganda must not, however, breach the law of war,[146] nor may it incite violations of that law, such as attacks on civilians.[147] Other useful examples of prohibited propaganda are given in this paragraph of the *Manual*.

Paragraph 5.26.2 makes the valid point that obtaining information about the enemy in ways that do not breach specific rules of the law of war, such as the prohibitions of torture or of improper treatment of detainees, is not prohibited. Paragraph 5.26.3 notes the well-established position that while it is lawful to offer rewards for assistance with the conduct of hostilities, putting a price on

141 This will require, in the case of States party to API, that combatants comply with Article 44 when undertaking such missions. In all probability, it is the second sentence of Article 44 that will apply to such a mission. For US personnel, the requirements in Article 1 of the Hague Regulations will apply.

142 *DoD Manual*, paragraph 5.25.3.

143 The reference in paragraph 5.26.1.2 to propaganda as a means of warfare is therefore incorrect.

144 Means of warfare are generally understood to refer to weapons and weapon systems, whereas methods of warfare refer to the kinds of operation undertaken as part of the conduct of the war. See, for example, *AMW Manual*, rules 1(t) and 1(v).

145 *DoD Manual*, paragraph 5.26.1.

146 Propaganda that amounted to a threat to give no quarter would breach this rule, because it is unlawful to threaten denial of quarter.

147 *DoD Manual*, paragraph 5.26.1.3.

the heads of enemy persons or offering a reward for them 'dead or alive' is prohibited.[148]

PROHIBITION AGAINST COMPELLING ENEMY NATIONALS TO TAKE PART IN THE OPERATIONS OF WAR DIRECTED AGAINST THEIR OWN COUNTRY

Section 5.27 explains in uncontroversial terms that it is prohibited in an international armed conflict to compel enemy nationals to take part in hostilities against their own nation even if the relevant individuals were in the belligerent's service before the war began,[149] basing the rule on the prohibition on forcing foreign nationals to commit treason or to violate their allegiance.

[148] Hague Regulations 1907, Article 23; 1958 *UK Manual*, paragraph 116; *UK Manual*, paragraphs 5.14 and 5.14.1. Rewards may be offered for the capture unharmed of enemy personnel and for information e.g. to facilitate lawful attacks.

[149] See also Hague Regulations 1907, Article 23 and *UK Manual*, paragraphs 11.15 and 11.21. In the context of occupation, the *UK Manual* notes that civilians cannot be required to take part in operations against their own country, to assist the war effort of the Occupying Power against their own country, to serve in the Occupying Power's armed or auxiliary forces or to give defence information to the Occupying Power; *UK Manual*, paragraph 11.15. As the *Manual* rightly acknowledges, it is also prohibited to use propaganda to secure voluntary enlistment of protected persons in the Occupying Power's armed or auxiliary forces, whereas States are permitted to persuade persons to betray allegiance to a non-State armed group during a non-international armed conflict; *DoD Manual*, paragraph 5.27.2.

6

Weapons

INTRODUCTION

It is logical that, having discussed the law relating to the conduct of hostilities in Chapter V, the *Manual* should address in the succeeding chapter the law that regulates the tools that are the most closely relevant to that activity, namely those that are employed to undertake attacks, i.e. weapons. Interestingly, the weapons chapter starts with a discussion of weapon reviews and of the practical implementation of weapons law, before explaining to the reader what the rules of that body of law comprise. It is a matter of opinion, and perhaps of personal taste, whether the chapter gets these matters the right way round.

At the outset, the valid point is made that a considerable amount of law, US policy, rules, regulations and orders apply to the various kinds of weapons, not all of which are or can sensibly be reflected in the chapter. The present chapter will, however, proceed on the assumption that Chapter VI of the *Manual* is intended accurately to describe the law of war rules as to weapons that are considered to bind the US, and will evaluate the sections and paragraphs of the text accordingly.[1] Paragraph 6.1.1 seeks to draw the proper distinction between the lawfulness of weapons as such, which the present authors would regard as the weapons law issue, and the discrete problem of whether a particular use of a weapon complies with targeting law, the latter not being an issue that is determinative of the lawfulness of a weapon. While these matters are not explained in the most elegant of terms in this part of the *Manual*, the

[1] It is in this regard a little difficult to know exactly what to make of the comment in the chapeau to section 6.1 to the effect that in giving advice on the lawfulness of a weapon, undue reliance should not be placed on the absence of discussion in Chapter VI as indicating an absence of regulation.

proper point is made that while some weapons are unlawful *per se*, others are the subject of restrictions as to their employment.[2]

DOD POLICY OF REVIEWING THE LEGALITY OF WEAPONS

Section 6.2 notes that 'DoD policy has, for many years, required the legal review of the intended acquisition or procurement of weapons or weapon systems' and makes the point that 'this review includes ensuring that such acquisition or procurement is consistent with the law of war'. DoD Directives going back to 16 October 1974 and mandating the undertaking of these reviews are cited, and examples of Navy, Army and Air Force regulations giving effect to these Directives are listed in a footnote. It is pertinent to note that, ironically given that it is not bound by the explicit treaty obligation,[3] the United States has complied with the implied legal obligation[4] to review new weapons more assiduously, more consistently and for more years than virtually any other State.[5]

Paragraph 6.2.2 suggests that a review of a weapon for consistency with US law of war obligations should consider three questions, namely 'whether the weapon's intended use is calculated to cause superfluous injury', 'whether the weapon is inherently indiscriminate' and whether the weapon is one of a class that has been specifically prohibited. Although it is well known that the US rejects the API, Article 35(3) and 55 rules relating to the protection of the environment, the US does, it is believed, accept an obligation in warfare to have due regard to the natural environment, which in turn implies a requirement at least to consider the expected environmental impact of new weapons. One would therefore expect to see some reference to this aspect in paragraph 6.2.2's list. The paragraph correctly notes, however, that consideration should also be given to whether international law restricts the circumstances in which the

[2] DoD *Manual*, paragraph 6.1.1.

[3] Article 36 of API, reproduced in paragraph 6.2.3 of the *Manual*, requires that '[i]n the study, development, acquisition or adoption of a new weapon, means or method of warfare, a High Contracting Party is under an obligation to determine whether its employment would, in some or all circumstances, be prohibited by th[e] Protocol or by any other rule of international law applicable to the High Contracting Party'.

[4] The obligation can be inferred, *inter alia*, from the requirement in Article 1 of Hague Convention IV of 1907, for States party to issue instructions to their land forces, from the undertaking in Article 1 common to the Geneva Conventions, 1949, to respect and ensure respect for the Conventions and from the general duty to apply in good faith the rules of international law that bind the State.

[5] Indeed, as the *Manual* notes in paragraph 6.2.3, the US system of weapon reviews pre-dates the adoption of the API provision.

relevant weapon may be used, and draws attention to the potential relevance of e.g. training, doctrine and dedicated rules of engagement.

The *Manual* rightly notes that using weapons in accordance with their designed purpose and associated doctrine,[6] and refraining from modifying them without appropriate authorisation, from using personal firearms and ammunition and from using captured weapons other than as a matter of field expediency, all contribute to the practical implementation of weapons law obligations.[7]

PROHIBITED WEAPONS AND LAWFUL WEAPONS

After noting the general rules that weapons calculated to cause superfluous injury and those that are inherently indiscriminate are prohibited,[8] paragraph 6.4.2 lists weapons that are specifically prohibited by treaty or customary international law. Each of the general rules and each of the listed kinds of prohibited weapon is discussed in a subsequent dedicated section of the *Manual*, and this chapter will deal with each of those sections in turn. It suffices for the present purposes to note some interesting omissions from the list in paragraph 6.4.2, such as explosive bullets designed for use against personnel, expanding bullets and cluster munitions.[9] These omissions are rendered the more interesting by section 6.5's assertion that all weapons not described in paragraph 6.4 are lawful for use by US armed forces. As we shall see, the two kinds of bullet are discussed later in the chapter by reference to the two general rules, and they would be classed as prohibited to the extent that they breach either of those general rules. Importantly, the *Manual* points out that the adoption of a Protocol under the CCW prohibiting or restricting the use of a weapon 'does not necessarily reflect the conclusion that the weapon is calculated to cause unnecessary suffering or is inherently indiscriminate'.[10] Paragraph 6.5.1 gives a comprehensive list of weapons the use of which is restricted by international law, and, again, the terms in which the *Manual* describes those restrictions will be discussed by reference to the sections dedicated to them.

[6] At paragraph 6.3.1, the *Manual* makes the rather obvious, but sensible, point that use of certain weapons, whose lawful uses are restricted by international law, must be in accordance with doctrine and policy, because that doctrine and policy will reflect the relevant law.

[7] *DoD Manual*, section 6.3.

[8] *DoD Manual*, paragraph 6.4.1.

[9] The omission of cluster munitions is logical, as the US is not a party to the Cluster Munitions Convention (CMC), 2008, and the provisions of that Convention do not have customary law status. The legal position in relation to explosive and expanding bullets is addressed later in the *Manual* and will be discussed later in this chapter.

[10] *DoD Manual*, paragraph 6.4.3.

Paragraph 6.5.2 asserts that, apart from the general rules mentioned earlier, 'there are no law of war rules specifically prohibiting or restricting' certain listed kinds of weapon 'by the US armed forces'. So, this paragraph purports to list the weapons that are not the subject of *ad hoc* prohibition or restriction that is binding on the US. Interestingly, included in this list are exploding bullets (the US is not party to the 1868 St Petersburg Declaration),[11] expanding bullets (the US is not party to Hague Declaration 3 of 1899 concerning expanding bullets),[12] fragmentation weapons (the US is a party to Protocol I to CCW)[13] and shotguns.[14]

In paragraph 6.5.4.3, it is stated that 'the use of exploding bullets, including use against enemy personnel, is not prohibited'. The *UK Manual*'s formulation of the rule, as we saw earlier, limits the prohibition to 'explosive or incendiary bullets designed solely for use against personnel'. That formulation does not therefore prohibit the use against personnel of explosive bullets not designed exclusively for use against personnel. The US formulation omits reference to design intent. The important point, however, comes in the second part of the *Manual*'s paragraph, namely that, absent a military reason for the additional injury and suffering, a bullet that is designed to

[11] Note the UK view that the 'practice of states indicates that the use of explosive or incendiary bullets designed solely for use against personnel is not permissible under customary law'; *UK Manual*, paragraph 6.10. Such a customary rule would, of course, bind all States, irrespective of whether they are parties to the 1868 Declaration.

[12] The UK states it is prohibited to use in an international armed conflict 'bullets which expand or flatten easily in the human body', basing that prohibition on Hague Declaration 3 of 1899, but links the prohibition to bullets that cause unnecessarily serious injuries. Great Britain is a state party to Hague Declaration 3. 'To the extent that States consider that the use of such weapons, as opposed to full-jacketed ammunition, is militarily necessary for the direct protection of civilians or to seek to ensure the discriminate use of force, there is no customary prohibition on their use in those circumstances in connection with an international or non-international armed conflict'; W H Boothby, *Weapons and the Law of Armed Conflict*, 2nd edn. Oxford: Oxford University Press (2016), 142. The treaty law prohibition in Declaration 3 applies only to international armed conflicts.

[13] Source www.icrc.org, viewed on 17 December 2017; the US ratified Protocol I to the Conventional Weapons Convention on Non-Detectable Fragments on 24 March 1995. The UK takes the view that the superfluous injury principle does not preclude the use of fragmentation weapons, but would ban weapons 'that discharge broken glass, nails and the like'; *UK Manual*, paragraph 6.11.1.

[14] See also *DoD Manual*, paragraph 6.5.4.2. There is indeed no specific rule prohibiting or restricting the use of shotguns. Paragraph 1419 of the API Commentary suggests that 'hunting shotguns are the subject of some controversy, depending on the nature of the ammunition and its effect on a soft target'. The Bundesministerium der Verteidigung Joint Service Regulation (ZDv) 15/2, *Law of Armed Conflict Manual* (May 2013) (*German Manual*), at paragraph 440, essentially provides that shotguns, like other weapons, must be considered by reference to the customary principles. See also Dinstein, *Conduct of Hostilities*, 77; see n. 5 to Chapter 3.

explode in the human body will breach the superfluous injury principle, as a non-exploding bullet would incapacitate an enemy combatant with equal efficiency.[15]

Paragraph 6.5.4 asserts that the law of war does not prohibit the use of bullets that expand or flatten easily in the human body, a view that will surprise many non-US readers. The paragraph contends that such bullets are only prohibited if they are calculated – by whom is not made clear – to cause superfluous injury. Given that the US is not a party to Hague Declaration 3 of 1899, this statement amounts to an assertion that, in the US view, there is no customary rule prohibiting such bullets, a position on which, as we have seen, the UK and doubtless other States would differ.[16] The US position that expanding bullets are only prohibited to the extent that they are calculated to cause superfluous injury is likely to be shared by other States so far as the customary rule applying in non-international armed conflict is concerned, but not yet[17] in relation to the treaty and customary rules applying in international armed conflicts. However, the US interpretation does, as paragraph 6.5.4.5 recognises, reflect the relevant crimes under the Rome Statute of the International Criminal Court and their associated elements, including those reflected in the Kampala amendment relating to non-international armed conflicts.[18]

While the *Manual* correctly observes that there is no specific law of war rule regulating small arms, cannon and other guns, other law of war rules may be rendered relevant e.g. by the way the weapon is designed or adapted, or by virtue of the ammunition it uses; examples are given.[19]

The *Manual* correctly notes that knives, bayonets, swords, lances, tomahawks, serrated weapons and other stabbing and cutting tools are not

15 Note, the ICRC Customary Humanitarian Law Study, rule 78, finds a rule that 'the anti-personnel use of bullets which explode within the human body is prohibited'. The US position is that such use has taken place in conflicts since World War I, e.g. in the form of aerial strafing.

16 The paragraph in the *Manual* refers to past US use of such ammunition in counterterrorism and hostage rescue operations, some of which took place in an armed conflict context. In the context of non-international armed conflict, the customary rule is indeed a manifestation of the superfluous injury principle; if the use of such ammunition is necessary e.g. to achieve a rescue, the additional harm inflicted cannot be regarded as unnecessary.

17 Hostage taking and other situations in which civilians would be at unnecessary risk if normal, high-velocity rounds were used are liable also to arise in international conflicts. If evolving State practice reveals the use of expanding ammunition in such circumstances, this may call into question the terms of the international armed conflict rule.

18 Rome Statute, 1998, Article 8(2)(b)(xix) in relation to international armed conflicts; in relation to non-international armed conflicts, see Article 8(2)(e)(xv), adopted on 10 June 2010 and inserted into the Rome Statute by RC(Res) Advance Version, Annex I dated 16 June 2010.

19 *DoD Manual*, paragraph 6.5.4.1.

specifically prohibited or restricted, but must not be such as to breach the superfluous injury principle.[20] A complex point needs, however, to be made. The superfluous injury principle, as it is being applied in the *Manual* to serrated weapons, only prohibits a weapon that is calculated to[21] cause superfluous injury or unnecessary suffering.[22] The *Manual* expresses the position that '[p]rovided that the design intent of the serrated edge is not to aggravate suffering unnecessarily, ... the serrated edge is not prohibited'.[23] States bound by the API provision are, however, likely to compare 'the nature and scale of the generic military advantage to be anticipated from the weapon in the applications for which it is designed to be used with the pattern of injury and suffering associated with the normal intended use of the weapon'[24] and to assess whether the customary principle is breached on that basis.[25] The *Manual*'s requirement that the actual design purpose of the weapon be to cause the prohibited injury or suffering may have the effect of narrowing the scope of the principle, thus enabling the finding that serrated edge weapons are not, so far as the US is concerned, legally objectionable.[26]

The *Manual* then explains, correctly, that the use of large-calibre guns and cannon against enemy personnel is not unlawful.[27] Also not prohibited is the use of blast munitions[28] or of fragmentation weapons.[29] The *Manual* is right to note that the likelihood that enemy personnel will receive multiple injuries from a fragmentation weapon does not alter the lawfulness of the weapon. Rather than say that the 'fragments or projectiles in such weapons must be detectable by X-rays', it would be more legally accurate to say that

[20] *DoD Manual*, paragraph 6.5.3. Applying barbs, smearing with an inflaming substance or designing the blade with a view to increasing suffering unnecessarily is correctly stated to breach the principle.

[21] Article 23 of the Hague Regulations, 1899, prohibited weapons of a nature to cause the prohibited injury or suffering; Article 23 of the 1907 Hague Regulations expressed the same rule but employed the 'calculated to cause' language. For a discussion of the significance of this language, see W Hays Parks, Conventional Weapons and Weapons Reviews, 8 *Yearbook of International Humanitarian Law* 55 (2005), at 86–7, note 123.

[22] Note that for an API State party, Article 35(2) prohibits weapons that are of a nature to cause the prohibited injury or suffering.

[23] *DoD Manual*, paragraph 6.5.3.1. [24] Boothby, *Weapons and the Law*, 54.

[25] The AMW *Manual* notes that it does not matter whether the weapon is intended to cause superfluous injury or unnecessary suffering, 'it will be equally sufficient if the weapon by nature has that consequence'; *AMW Manual*, Commentary accompanying rule 5(b), paragraph 3.

[26] See API Commentary, paragraph 1419 and ICRC Customary Humanitarian Law Study, volume 1, page 243, listing, *inter alia*, bayonets with a serrated edge and lances with a barbed head as prohibited by the principle. Paragraph 6.6 of the *UK Manual* gives serrated-edge cutting weapons as an example of weapons that breach the principle.

[27] *DoD Manual*, paragraph 6.5.4.7. [28] *DoD Manual*, paragraph 6.5.5.

[29] *DoD Manual*, paragraph 6.5.6.

fragmentation weapons are lawful provided that they comply with relevant law, including Protocol I of the CCW.[30]

The use of depleted uranium to facilitate armour penetration, a topic that has provoked controversy as to the medical impact of the substance,[31] is discussed at paragraph 6.5.7 and in some lengthy associated footnotes. UK parliamentary statements are cited in support of the position that 'States have regarded the use of depleted uranium weapons as consistent with their law of war obligations', a statement that would appear to be accurate.[32] Equally non-controversially, paragraph 6.5.8 notes that there is no law of war prohibition on the use of remotely piloted aircraft.

In paragraph 6.5.9, the *Manual* tackles autonomy, starting with the correct observation that its use in weapon systems is neither specifically prohibited nor restricted by the law of war.[33] Paragraph 6.5.9.1 gives a rather broad interpretation of autonomy. It points out that mines may be seen as rudimentary autonomous weapons because they are designed to explode other than by the decision of the operator, while other weapon systems may have more sophisticated autonomous functions enabling them to select or engage targets automatically after activation. While it is correct to note that autonomy may be applied to particular functions within a weapon system, one rather doubts the usefulness of a discussion of this nature that fails to give clear meaning to the term 'autonomy', not least because such a discussion may raise inappropriate doubts in the minds of some readers as to the lawfulness of mines. However, it is right to point out that some applications of autonomy may enhance law of war compliance, e.g. homing functions that promote discrimination in attack and self-destruction and self-deactivation that enhance civilian protection.

Paragraph 6.5.9 deserves careful thought. The first part of the paragraph notes that the law of war rules on conducting attacks place obligations on persons, not on the weapons they use, and do not require weapons to make legal determinations. The second part of the paragraph then essentially makes the point that it is persons who must ensure the law is complied with. So, for example, a person using a weapon that selects and engages targets autonomously

[30] The point being made here is that a fragmentation weapon is not automatically rendered unlawful if it includes fragments that escape detection. A weapon only breaches the Protocol if the primary effect is to injure using such fragments.

[31] See, for example, A Bleise, P R Danesi and W Burkart, Properties, Use and Health Effects of Depleted Uranium: A General Overview 64 *Journal of Environmental Radioactivity* 93 (2002), 99–100.

[32] The investigations that have taken place into the health effects are reported, and it is stated in footnote 97 that nothing was found.

[33] It is also right to observe that other law of war rules may apply to weapon systems with autonomous features; *DoD Manual*, paragraph 6.5.9.2.

must refrain from using the weapon where its use may be expected to breach the proportionality rule. The *Manual* also notes that the obligation on the weapon user to take feasible precautions may be more significant[34] when the weapon system has more sophisticated autonomous functions.

While the focus on the responsibilities of personnel associated with the use of autonomous weapons is to be welcomed, the discussion arguably does not go into anything like enough detail. The *Manual* ought usefully to have identified the diverse roles in relation to which relevant human responsibilities lie, and it fails to address adequately what, in the present authors' joint view, is the core issue for offensive autonomous weapons: namely, the question whether the weapon system is capable of making the determinations that the law of targeting requires, given that no person is involved in making them. Recognising the somewhat broad concept of autonomy that the *Manual* appears to adopt, these issues seem likely to arise during the legal review of what the *Manual* refers to as 'weapon systems with more sophisticated autonomous functions'. Reference is then made to – but relatively few details are given about – the DoD Directive on Autonomy in Weapon Systems, dated 2012.[35]

Paragraph 6.5.10 comprehensively deals with non-lethal weapons. It correctly notes that they are not addressed as a class by the law of war; that applicable US DoD policy requires that non-lethal weapons that are being acquired be subjected to weapon review;[36] and that there is no obligation to employ non-lethal weapons before using lethal force if the use of the latter is appropriate.[37] Recognising that they do not have zero probability of causing death or permanent injury, the paragraph lists some examples of non-lethal weapon technologies.

WEAPONS CALCULATED TO CAUSE SUPERFLUOUS INJURY

Section 6.6 addresses what is usually referred to as the 'superfluous injury principle'. Paragraph 6.6.1 notes the differing English translations of the identical authoritative French texts of Article 23(e) of the 1899 and 1907 Hague Regulations,[38] whereupon the *Manual* argues that 'calculated to cause superfluous injury' is preferable as being the more accurate translation of the French '*propres à causer des maux superflus*'. For States that are party to API,

34 For example, monitoring the operation of the system or building in a facility for it to deactivate after a period of time.

35 *DoD Manual*, paragraph 6.5.9.4.

36 *DoD Manual*, paragraph 6.5.10.4.

37 *DoD Manual*, paragraph 6.5.10.5.

38 Regulations Respecting the Laws and Customs of War on Land annexed, respectively, to Hague Convention II, 1899 and to Hague Convention IV, 1907. The English translation of the 1899 text prohibits the employment of 'arms, projectiles, or material of a nature to cause superfluous injury'; the English translation of the 1907 text prohibits the employment of 'arms, projectiles, or material calculated to cause unnecessary suffering'.

the debate is somewhat sterile, as Article 35(2) prohibits the employment of 'weapons, projectiles and material and methods of warfare of a nature to cause superfluous injury or unnecessary suffering'. Moreover, it would represent too restrictive an interpretation of the customary rule to limit the prohibition only to those cases in which the designer of the weapon can be shown deliberately to have enhanced the expected injury or suffering beyond that which military necessity requires. A weapon that will inevitably cause superfluous injury when used properly and for its intended purpose should be regarded as breaching the rule irrespective of the intent that its designer may originally have had, however easy or hard that factor might be to establish. If those who espouse the 'calculated to cause' language share that view, the US interpretation is unobjectionable. The *Manual* does not completely resolve the matter.

In paragraph 6.6.2, the link between the rule and the humanity principle is properly shown, but the following statement is also made: 'weapons that are regarded as lawful in peacetime . . . would not be prohibited under the superfluous injury rule.' As we have seen, the *Manual* denies that an explicit rule prohibits expanding ammunition, linking any prohibition to the superfluous injury rule. As the *Manual* notes, however, expanding ammunition is lawfully used in peacetime.[39] The somewhat surprising US view would therefore seem to be that no rule, either *ad hoc* or as a derivative of the superfluous injury rule, prohibits expanding ammunition.

After discussing the military necessity and suffering/injury aspects of the rule in appropriate terms,[40] and having noted the difficulty of assessing and comparing these notions, the *Manual* suggests, probably correctly, that 'a weapon is only prohibited if the suffering is clearly or manifestly disproportionate to the military necessity'.[41] The *Manual* concludes this section by correctly noting that '[w]eapons that have been modified for the purpose of aggravating the harm inflicted on incapacitated persons are . . . prohibited by the superfluous injury rule', and comments that it may be easier to apply the rule to a modified weapon, because the unmodified version provides a point of reference.[42]

INHERENTLY INDISCRIMINATE WEAPONS

The *Manual* correctly links the prohibition of inherently indiscriminate weapons to what it describes as the principles of distinction and

[39] *DoD Manual*, paragraph 6.5.4.4. [40] *DoD Manual*, paragraphs 6.6.3.1 and 6.6.3.2.

[41] *DoD Manual*, paragraph 6.6.3.3, citing Bothe, Partsch & Solf and W Hays Parks. It is right that the practice of other States may tend to show whether a particular weapon is considered to breach the principle, and that the assessment should take into account alternative, lawful weapons; *DoD Manual*, third part of paragraph 6.6.3.3.

[42] *DoD Manual*, paragraph 6.6.4.

proportionality.[43] It has been noted in earlier chapters that in the present context, the reference should be to the proportionality rule, but that point of detail apart, it is correct to say that a weapon that, when used, would necessarily violate these rules is prohibited and that this is an example of where military and humanitarian interests coincide.[44] The test, as explained in the *Manual*, is whether the use of the weapon is expected to be unlawful in all circumstances, taking into account its planned or intended uses and recognising that precautions may be feasible that would mitigate the incidental harm to be expected from the use of the weapon.[45] However, quoting a letter by the DoD General Counsel dated September 1972, the *Manual* contends that 'the principle of proportionality does not prohibit the use of weapons whose destructive force cannot be limited to a specific military objective'. While that statement of law is correct, Article 51(4) of API does prohibit attacks 'which employ a method or means of combat the effects of which cannot be limited as required by th[e] Protocol' and which 'consequently . . . are of a nature to strike military objectives and civilians or civilian objects without distinction'. There is a danger that targeting law will be mixed up in the mind of the reader with weapons law if proportionality is addressed in the context of a weapons law rule.

POISON, POISONED WEAPONS, POISONOUS GASES AND OTHER CHEMICAL WEAPONS

Section 6.8 starts with a clear and accurate statement that the use of poison, poisonous weapons, poisonous gases and chemical weapons is prohibited. It would have been nice to see a statement that the poison prohibition reflects customary law. It is, however, helpful to see, in paragraph 6.8.1, poisons being defined as 'substances that cause death or disability with permanent effects when, in even small quantities, they are ingested, enter the lungs or bloodstream, or touch the skin'.[46] The bases of the long-established prohibition,

43 While the status of distinction as a principle is not in dispute, the present authors interpret the proportionality 'principle' as addressing destruction and injury in general, whereas the proportionality 'rule' is that set forth in Article 51(5)(b) of API.

44 DoD *Manual*, paragraph 6.7.1.

45 DoD *Manual*, paragraph 6.7.2. The *Manual* usefully spells out that weapons that are designed to target or to terrorise the civilian population breach the rule. The *Manual* correctly observes that the use of 'blind' weapons and of uncontrollable weapons, such as communicable diseases, would breach the rule; DoD *Manual*, paragraph 6.7.4.

46 The *Manual* rightly comments that the rule does not apply to weapons designed to injure or cause damage by other means but that generate toxic byproducts, nor to herbicides that are harmless to humans; DoD *Manual*, paragraphs 6.8.1.1 and 6.8.1.2.

namely uncontrollability, the inevitability of death or permanent disability and the perceived treachery associated with their use, are correctly stated.

Curiously, paragraph 6.8.2 does affirm the US view that the prohibition of the use in war of asphyxiating, poisonous or other gases, and all analogous liquids, materials and devices, is a customary law rule – so why, the reader will wonder, is that statement not made in relation to poisons? A rather strange error seems to have been made in the citation in the final two lines of footnote 175, namely the omission of the word 'sole'. The 1899 Hague Declaration 2[47] provided that '[t]he contracting Powers agree to abstain from the use of projectiles the sole object of which is the diffusion of asphyxiating or deleterious gases'. This reference to 'sole object' meant that the use, e.g. in the trenches of the Western Front during World War I, of weapons that combined gas diffusion with some other object did not breach that provision. The *Manual* states that the rule has been understood only to apply to the use of gases designed to kill or injure human beings. It cites in support of this view a memorandum published by the then Judge Advocate General of the US Army in an academic journal in 1971. While the interpretation is unlikely to be controversial, no formal US statement to that effect was made on ratification of the treaty.[48] The assertions in the same paragraph that the rule does not apply to herbicides and riot-control agents and that it is limited to weapons whose prime or even exclusive effect is to poison or asphyxiate[49] are also unlikely to be controversial and were also not reflected in US statements on ratification.[50]

As to chemical weapons, the *Manual* correctly gives the relevant CWC[51] definitions[52] and prohibitions,[53] expresses the respectable US view that they do not encompass chemicals that only harm plants and properly reflects the comprehensive nature of the prohibitions in the Convention that continue to apply even after an adverse party has used such weapons.[54] The uses of chemicals and their precursors that the Convention does not prohibit are discussed correctly at paragraph 6.8.3.4. Unfortunately, these paragraphs fail to disclose whether the US views the prohibitions e.g. on the possession and use of chemical weapons to have customary law status. While official expressions of revulsion as to the use of such weapons in Syria would suggest the US views

[47] Declaration (IV,2) Concerning Asphyxiating Gases, The Hague, 29 July 1899.
[48] Source www.icrc.org, viewed on 17 December 2017. [49] *DoD Manual*, paragraph 6.8.2.
[50] Source www.icrc.org, viewed on 17 December 2017.
[51] Convention on the Prohibition of the Development, Production, Stockpiling and Use of Chemical Weapons, and on their Destruction, Paris (13 January 1993).
[52] *DoD Manual*, paragraph 6.8.3. [53] *DoD Manual*, paragraph 6.8.3.2.
[54] *DoD Manual*, paragraph 6.8.3.2.

these rules as customary, a clear statement to that effect would have been helpful. The *Manual* does make the point, however, that the prohibitions apply in relation to both international and non-international armed conflict. Unfortunately, this chapter of the *Manual* fails to make it clear whether, in the US view, a number of other provisions also apply in non-international armed conflicts, and the reader may infer from the *Manual*'s silence that the US position is that they do not: a position which would put the US at odds with the prevailing view.

BIOLOGICAL WEAPONS

Section 6.9 correctly reflects the prohibition of bacteriological and biological weapons and warfare. Again, the US view on the status of the relevant prohibitions at customary law is unfortunately not stated; neither is there an indication whether, in the US view, the prohibitions apply in non-international armed conflicts. The omission of reference to 'use' in the Convention is correctly noted,[55] but explicit reference should perhaps have been made to the confirmation at the Fourth Review Conference in 1996 that 'use' is effectively prohibited.[56] The notion of toxins is correctly explained, and the prohibitions in Article I of the Biological Weapons Convention[57] are set forth.

CERTAIN ENVIRONMENTAL MODIFICATION TECHNIQUES

The first few paragraphs of section 6.10[58] address the prohibition of the use of environmental modification techniques set forth in the UN Convention.[59] The *Manual* accurately gives the relevant rules, noting that the Convention prohibits the use of the environment as an instrument of war[60] against another State party to the treaty. Paragraph 6.10.3.1 then starts to get to grips with the environmental protection provisions in Articles 35(3) and 55 of API, which the US has consistently rejected as being overly broad and ambiguous and

55 *DoD Manual*, Chapter VI, footnote 200.

56 BWC/CONF.IV/9, Part II, Art. I, paragraphs 4, 15 and Art. VIII, paragraphs 7, 22, 23.

57 Convention on the Prohibition of the Development, Production and Stockpiling of Bacteriological (Biological) and Toxic Weapons and on their Destruction, 1972, ratified by the US on 26 March 1975.

58 *DoD Manual*, paragraphs 6.10 to 6.10.3.

59 United Nations Convention on the Prohibition of Military or Any Other Hostile Use of Environmental Modification Techniques, 2 September 1976 (ENMOD).

60 Environmental modification for peaceful purposes is not prohibited; *DoD Manual*, paragraph 6.10.4 and ENMOD, Article 3(1).

not part of customary law.[61] The substance of these provisions is the prohibition 'to employ methods or means of warfare which are intended, or may be expected, to cause widespread, long-term and severe damage to the natural environment'. The latter provision refers additionally to thereby prejudicing the health or survival of the population. The further US objection is that the use of such weapons is only prohibited if the proportionality rule is thereby also breached.[62]

WEAPONS INJURING BY FRAGMENTS NOT DETECTABLE BY X-RAYS

Section 6.11 correctly explains Protocol I to the CCW prohibiting the use of weapons the primary effect of which is to injure by fragments which in the human body escape detection by X-ray.

LANDMINES, BOOBY-TRAPS AND OTHER DEVICES

The international law addressing landmines, booby-traps and other devices is discussed in section 6.12. It is a complex subject, and the *Manual* sensibly explains at the outset that while none of the three classes of weapon is prohibited as such, certain kinds of such weapons are unlawful, and restrictions apply to others. The relevant terms are defined in generally accurate language. However, while in paragraph 6.12.1.2 the use of the Claymore in trip-wire mode is described as a mine, in paragraph 6.12.1 the use of a hand grenade with a trip-wire mechanism is described as a booby-trap. As the associated footnotes explain, this accurately reflects the declared US position on the matter.[63] If, however, the activation mechanism is identical, there will, in the absence of the stated US position, be little justification for classifying

61 DoD *Manual*, paragraph 6.10.3.1, citing the US Response to the ICRC Customary Humanitarian Law Study. One might suggest that international law, both treaty-based and customary, is replete with examples of broad, ambiguous provisions, to not all of which has the US objected.

62 DoD *Manual*, paragraph 6.10.3.1, final sentence, citing the US Response to the ICRC Customary Humanitarian Law Study. This accurately states the US position. For an API State party, both Articles 35(3)/55 and Article 51(5)(b), as well as other applicable rules, must be complied with for an attack to be lawful. In footnote 219 of this chapter of the *Manual*, a persuasive example is cited of a situation, involving an attack on weapons of mass destruction concealed in a rain forest, in which considerations of proportionality would likely permit the attack to proceed but Articles 35(3)/55 might be expected, unreasonably in the US view, to prohibit it.

63 Note the US statements on ratification of the Amended Mines Protocol on 24 May 1999, statement 6B, that 'a trip-wired hand grenade shall be considered a booby-trap under article 2(4) of the Amended Mines Protocol and shall not be considered a "mine" or an "anti-personnel mine" under Article 2(1) or 2(3) respectively'.

the two kinds of munition differently. If contact with the trip wire is sufficient to cause either kind of munition to detonate, then it is a mine.[64] If more than mere contact is required, and if the definition in Article 2(2) of Protocol II[65] or the definition in Article 2(4) of the Amended Mines Protocol[66] applies, then the munition will be classed as a booby-trap. However, the US position should be interpreted by reference to its statements on ratification.

The discussion of the definition of anti-personnel mines, for the purposes of the Amended Mines Protocol, is not controversial, and states the US position that for incapacitation to come within the definition, it must be permanent, thus excluding a number of non-lethal technologies.[67] After reflecting the treaty provisions relating to mines other than anti-personnel mines and to remotely delivered mines,[68] the chapter gets into the technicalities of the self-destruction, self-neutralisation and self-deactivation requirements under the Amended Mines Protocol, followed by a discussion of booby-traps based on the definition in Article 2(4) of the Amended Mines Protocol and of 'other devices' based on the definition in Article 2(5).[69]

In the succeeding paragraphs, the *Manual* deals in turn with the classes of munition that are specifically prohibited by the Amended Mines Protocol. Paragraph 6.12.4.1 has the subtitle 'Mines, Booby-Traps and Other Devices Calculated to Cause Superfluous Injury'. The associated text then cites Article 3(3) of the Amended Mines Protocol, which prohibits such weapons 'which are designed or of a nature to cause superfluous injury or unnecessary suffering'. The United States made no statement in relation to the Article 3(3) language when it ratified the treaty, and must therefore be taken to accept, in the context of mines, booby-traps and other devices, the position that such weapons whose nature is to cause superfluous injury are prohibited to the

64 As the *Manual* correctly reports, the Amended Mines Protocol defines a mine as 'a munition placed under, on or near the ground or other surface area and designed to be exploded by the presence, proximity or contact of a person or vehicle'.

65 Protocol on Prohibitions or Restrictions on the Use of Mines, Booby-Traps and Other Devices, Geneva, 10 October 1980.

66 The Amended Mines Protocol defines a booby-trap as 'any device or material which is designed, constructed, or adapted to kill or injure, and which functions unexpectedly when a person disturbs or approaches an apparently harmless object or performs an apparently safe act'. The apparently safe act in the trip-wire context would be walking on the path or other relevant place.

67 This accurately applies statement 7 made by the US on ratification of the Amended Mines Protocol on 24 May 1999.

68 *DoD Manual*, paragraphs 6.12.1.4 and 6.12.1.5.

69 The point is made that hand grenades are excluded from this definition by virtue of US statement 6C to that effect, made on ratification of the Amended Mines Protocol, and that trip-wired hand grenades are treated as booby-traps.

United States as a matter of treaty law. It would not be legally correct to argue that because the United States holds a certain understanding of the superfluous injury principle, that it necessarily follows that Article 3(3) must be interpreted coherently with that view in the absence of a statement of understanding on ratification.

Paragraphs 6.12.4.2 and 6.12.4.3 accurately report the prohibition of mines, booby-traps and other devices that are specifically designed to be detonated in the stated manner by commonly available mine detectors and the prohibition of self-deactivating mines with anti-handling devices so designed that the anti-handling device can operate after the mine has ceased to be able to function.[70] Paragraph 6.12.4.4 discusses, also correctly, the prohibition of anti-personnel mines that are not detectable in accordance with provisions in the Technical Annex to the Amended Mines Protocol.[71] The specification as to detectability of the mines is to be found in paragraph 2 of the Technical Annex, and is set forth in paragraph 6.12.4.4 of the *Manual*.

Paragraph 6.12.4.5 explains the prohibition of remotely delivered anti-personnel mines that do not comply with the provisions on self-destruction and self-deactivation set forth in paragraph 3(a) of the Technical Annex. In short, this provision requires that not more than one in 1000 such mines that have been activated shall function as a mine 120 days after emplacement.

As paragraph 6.12.4.6 of the *Manual* accurately notes, it is prohibited to use remotely delivered mines that are not anti-personnel mines unless, to the extent practically possible, they are fitted with an effective self-destruction or self-neutralisation mechanism backed up by a self-deactivation mechanism designed so that the mine no longer functions as a mine when it no longer serves its military purpose.

The requirement in the Technical Annex to the Amended Mines Protocol that all mines be marked with specified information is correctly recorded at paragraph 6.12.4.7. In the next paragraph, Article 7(2)'s prohibition of using booby-traps or other devices in the form of apparently harmless portable objects that are specifically designed to explode is also correctly given. Paragraph 6.12.4.8 goes on to state that '[t]his rule does not prohibit field-level adaptation, or adaptation in advance, of objects for use as booby-traps or other devices that are not designed or constructed for such use'. This reflects US statement 6A made on ratification of the Amended Mines Protocol, and is an interpretation that is therefore justified by that statement. The paragraph goes on, however, to give an example as follows: 'it would not be prohibited

70 Amended Mines Protocol, Article 3(5) and (6) respectively.

71 Amended Mines Protocol, Article 4.

to improvise a booby-trap using a trip-wired hand grenade in the form of an apparently harmless portable object.' It should be noted in this regard that while the US statement permits field-level adaptation of objects, the statement does not explicitly permit the adaptation of portable objects, neither does it explicitly permit the booby trap to take the form of an apparently harmless object. Instead, the US statement talks of objects 'not designed or constructed for such use', a notion which would not necessarily permit a booby-trap to take the form of an apparently harmless object.

Article 7(1) of the Amended Mines Protocol lists specific kinds of booby-trap and of other devices that are prohibited, and this list is accurately produced at paragraph 6.12.4.9 of the *Manual*. Targeting rules applied to the use of the three weapon types are found in Article 3 of the Amended Mines Protocol and are reported in paragraphs 6.12.5.1 to 6.12.5.4. These rules prohibit:

- Directing such munitions, whether in offence or defence, against civilians or civilian objects.[72] A footnote correctly cites the treaty provision. The main *Manual* text does not explain that the rule applies in offence and in defence, nor does it note the prohibition of such action as a reprisal: a prohibition against which the US made no statement and therefore by which it is bound.[73]
- Using such weapons indiscriminately.[74]
- Treating separate and distinct military objectives as if they were a single such objective.[75] The treaty rules also require all feasible precautions to be taken to protect civilians[76] and the giving of effective advance warnings, unless circumstances do not permit, of an emplacement of such weapons that may affect the civilian population.[77] Similarly, with one very minor error in the definition, the Technical Annex provisions on 'recording' are correctly set forth.[78]

The rules for using non-remotely delivered anti-personnel mines respectively that are, and are not, fitted with self-destruction and self-deactivation mechanisms which comply with paragraph 3 of the Technical Annex to the Amended Mines Protocol are reproduced in paragraphs 6.12.6 and 6.12.7. The rules applicable to the use of a very particular kind of non-remotely delivered anti-personnel mine, namely one that propels fragments in a horizontal arc of

72 Amended Mines Protocol, Article 3(7).

73 Source www.icrc.org, viewed on 17 December 2017.

74 Amended Mines Protocol, Article 3(8).

75 Amended Mines Protocol, Article 3(9).

76 Amended Mines Protocol, Article 3(10). These are correctly reproduced, apart from a minor error in the main body of the *Manual* in relation to Article 3(10)(a).

77 Amended Mines Protocol, Article 3(11).

78 The word 'mines' is omitted.

less than 90 degrees, are given in paragraph 6.12.8.[79] Paragraph 6.12.9 then deals with the rules on remotely delivered mines,[80] while paragraph 6.12.10 addresses the restrictions on the use of booby-traps and other devices in populated areas where combat is neither taking place nor appears imminent.[81]

The obligation to try to protect certain groups from the effect of minefields, mined areas, mines, booby-traps and other devices is noted in paragraph 6.12.11,[82] and paragraph 6.12.12 looks at the obligations arising after the end of active hostilities.[83] These are all highly complex, technical provisions of law, and the authors of the *Manual* have wisely adhered closely to the treaty language of the Amended Mines Protocol, taking into account, where relevant, statements made by the US on ratification of the treaty.

The final paragraph of the present section looks at US policy on mines, particularly in relation to anti-personnel mines. The important point to recall is that the US is not a party to the Ottawa Convention.[84] However, its policies are achieving greater – but by no means complete – alignment with the key requirements in the Convention. Paragraph 6.12.13 discusses this US Policy, describing it in the following terms: '(1) not to use anti-personnel landmines outside the Korean Peninsula; (2) not to assist, encourage, or induce anyone outside the Korean Peninsula to engage in activity prohibited by the Ottawa Convention; (3) to undertake to destroy anti-personnel landmine stockpiles not required for the defense of the Republic of Korea; and (4) not to produce or otherwise acquire any anti-personnel munitions that are not compliant with the Ottawa Convention.' In a sense, this policy shows how short-sighted it can be to include a provision, such as Article 19 of the Ottawa Convention, prohibiting reservations, as the US would seemingly have been able to ratify Ottawa had it been possible to reserve in relation to the defence of the Republic of Korea.

Paragraph 6.12.14, which discusses the Ottawa Convention, accurately asserts that its prohibitions have not achieved customary law status.

CLUSTER MUNITIONS

Section 6.13 addresses the law on cluster munitions. It starts with the statement that 'cluster munitions are not specifically prohibited or restricted by the law

79 Amended Mines Protocol, Article 5(6).
80 Amended Mines Protocol, Article 6.
81 Amended Mines Protocol, Article 7(3).
82 Reflecting Amended Mines Protocol, Article 12.
83 Amended Mines Protocol, Article 10.
84 Convention on the Prohibition of the Use, Stockpiling, Production and Transfer of Anti-Personnel Mines and on their Destruction, Oslo, 18 September 1997.

of war', which is of course an accurate statement for a State like the US that is not party to the Cluster Munitions Convention (CMC).[85] Indeed, the point is made, with which the present authors would concur, that cluster munition use is likely actually to reduce incidental harm in certain circumstances.

The humanitarian concern that led ultimately to the negotiation and adoption of the Convention was based on the tendency for considerable numbers of sub-munitions to fail to detonate on impact as intended and, instead, to remain a serious threat on the former battlefield as civilians returned to their homes, settlements, fields and forests after the hostilities ended. It is therefore significant that paragraph 6.13.3 describes a US DoD policy developed to 'minimize the negative humanitarian consequences that can sometimes be associated with cluster munitions'.[86] Under that policy, after 2018, the US will only use cluster munitions whose sub-munitions after arming will result in no more than 1 per cent unexploded ordnance over the range of intended operational environments. Until the end of 2018, use of cluster munitions with greater than the 1 per cent failure rate requires combatant commander approval. The *Manual* then briefly summarises some aspects of the Convention, and quotes the interoperability provisions in Article 21(4).

INCENDIARY WEAPONS

The definition of incendiary weapon in Protocol III to the CCW[87] is lengthy and rather complex. It is therefore good to see paragraph 6.14.1 breaking up that definition into its constituent parts and explaining each of them in a clear and legally accurate way. The important definitional point to emerge is that the incendiary weapon notion focuses on 'pure' incendiaries, as the *Manual* describes them, and does not encompass weapons with incidental incendiary effects, combined effects munitions or weapons which do not produce heat or fire as a result of a chemical reaction of a substance delivered to target.

The important non-definitional point is that incendiary weapons are not prohibited, but are subject to restrictions as to the circumstances in which they can be lawfully used,[88] while it is also not prohibited by the Protocol

85 The US has determined that its national security interests cannot be fully ensured consistently with the terms of the Convention; *DoD Manual*, paragraph 6.13.4.

86 *DoD Manual*, paragraph 6.13.3.

87 Protocol on Prohibitions or Restrictions on the Use of Incendiary Weapons (Protocol III), Geneva (10 October 1980).

88 *DoD Manual*, paragraph 6.14.2.

to use weapons falling outside the definition in Protocol III to cause fire or burning injury.[89] The *Manual*, citing 'shake and bake' missions by US personnel against insurgents in Fallujah, as reported in April 2005,[90] asserts the lawfulness of using white phosphorus as an anti-personnel weapon subject to compliance with the general rules such as discrimination and proportionality. While acknowledging that discrimination and proportionality, along with distinction and precautions, must be complied with, one would rather have thought that the superfluous injury principle ought to have received specific mention. Moreover, the present authors would take a more cautious approach, in which the technical specification, design purpose of the particular weapon and precise intended manner of use of a white phosphorus weapon would need to be examined carefully by reference to the incendiaries definition before any proper conclusion could be reached as to its status under Protocol III. Specifically, if the particular weapon is primarily designed to cause fire or burn injury, and if it does this by means of a chemical reaction, it will be an incendiary weapon for the purposes of Protocol III.

Article 2(1) and (4) prohibit making civilians, civilian objects, forests and other kinds of plant cover the object of attack by incendiaries. In the case of forests and plant cover, the prohibition does not apply when they are used to cover, conceal or camouflage combatants or when they are military objectives. Article 2(2) prohibits air attacks using incendiaries against military objectives located in concentrations of civilians, and Article 2(3) contains a qualified prohibition of attacking a similarly located military objective using non-air-delivered incendiaries. These prohibitions are accurately reported in paragraph 6.14.3 of the *Manual*.

The US reserved against this provision when it ratified Protocol III on 21 January 2009. The *Manual* cites the language of the US reservation,[91] which reserves the US right to use incendiaries against military objectives that are so located 'where it is judged that such use would cause fewer casualties and/or less collateral damage than alternative weapons', adding that all feasible precautions will be taken to limit the incendiary effects to the military objective and to avoid or in any event to minimise collateral damage. The *Manual* gives examples of circumstances to which the reservation would apply, such as attacking enemy biological weapons and minimising the

89 Other relevant weapons law rules would need to be considered, including the distinct possibility, perhaps likelihood, that such a method of warfare would be of a nature to cause superfluous injury or unnecessary suffering.

90 DoD *Manual*, page 384, footnote 365.

91 DoD *Manual*, page 386, footnote 377.

danger to civilians by using heat to destroy the toxins rather than risking spreading them through the use of high-explosive weapons.[92]

LASER WEAPONS

Paragraph 6.15 of the *Manual* correctly records that the use of laser weapons to kill or injure enemy personnel is generally permitted, while employment of laser weapons specifically designed as a combat function to cause permanent blindness to unenhanced vision is prohibited by Protocol IV to the CCW.[93] Article 3 of the Protocol excludes from the Protocol's prohibition blinding as an incidental or collateral effect of the legitimate military employment of laser systems, and paragraph 6.15.1.1 gives appropriate examples of the kinds of laser system that would, in principle, be covered by this exemption. Relevant terms in the Protocol are accurately explained, as is the Article 2 obligation to take all feasible precautions to avoid the incidence of permanent blindness from the employment of laser systems.

With these explanations in mind, paragraph 6.15.2.1 is controversial. It states: '[a]lthough feasible precautions should be taken to avoid blinding, the use of laser systems (that are not prohibited as blinding laser weapons) to blind enemy combatants is not prohibited if avoiding such harm is not feasible, i.e. if such harm is militarily necessary.' The *Manual* then gives an example that 'it would not be prohibited for a soldier to use a non-prohibited laser system to blind an enemy combatant to save the user's life'.[94] In a footnote, it mentions that the delegations could not agree that a soldier should be criminally responsible if 'in an *in extremis* situation, he employs a laser device against an enemy combatant to save the user's life'. While the present authors entirely agree with this quoted assessment by W Hays Parks, the inability of the delegates to agree does not constitute proof of the lawfulness of the suggested course of action. While the action referred to may not be universally seen as a crime, some observers will consider it hard to reconcile with Article 2's obligation to take all feasible precautions to avoid the incidence of blindness. Essentially, the *Manual* is arguing that a precaution is not feasible if it involves sacrificing the life of the user of the weapon. On balance, there may seem to be some

[92] *DoD Manual*, paragraph 6.14.3.2 and footnote 378. The use of incendiaries may also reduce risk to civilians by obviating the need for return attacks against particular kinds of target; ibid., footnote 379.

[93] *DoD Manual*, paragraph 6.15.1 and Protocol on Blinding Laser Weapons, Geneva (13 October 1995) (Protocol IV), Article 1.

[94] *DoD Manual*, paragraph 6.15.2.1.

merit in that approach, although in a combat situation it would seem that all feasible precautions have not been taken if the soldier is only equipped with the laser device.

RIOT CONTROL AGENTS

Section 6.16 of the *Manual* gives the well-recognised prohibition of using riot control agents (RCAs) as a method of warfare and correctly excludes from the RCA notion such items as bean bags, water cannon and rubber bullets. The CWC definition refers to RCAs being chemicals not listed in a schedule to the CWC that can produce in humans irritating or disabling effects that disappear a short time after termination of exposure. As a matter of policy, the US considers that RCAs are not chemical weapons. This is an interpretation that the US did not reflect in a statement when it ratified the Convention on 25 April 1997.[95] It is therefore an interpretation that will only have validity if it is objectively correct.

It is thus hard to see how the mere statement of that US policy in footnote 392 can afford such legal justification. The definition of 'chemical weapon' in Article 1 of the CWC includes 'toxic chemicals . . . except where intended for purposes not prohibited under this Convention'. 'Toxic chemicals' comprise, *inter alia,* any chemical that can cause 'temporary incapacitation' to humans.[96] RCAs are clearly designed to do precisely that. Excluded from the chemical weapon definition are toxic chemicals 'intended for purposes not prohibited under th[e] Convention'.[97] Such non-prohibited purposes include 'law enforcement including domestic riot control purposes'.[98] Accordingly, a statement of policy that RCAs are not chemical weapons does not accord with the legal provisions to which the US is a party. It would have been more accurate to write that RCAs intended only for domestic riot control are not chemical weapons. RCAs intended for purposes prohibited by the Convention are chemical weapons, which, of course, is why they are prohibited as a method of warfare.

Paragraph 6.16.2 then acknowledges the prohibition of using RCAs as a method of warfare, and sets forth the US interpretation that this provision does not prohibit the use of RCAs in war in defensive military modes to save lives. Rioting PWs, human shielding of attacks, combat rescue operations and protection of convoys in rear areas are cited as examples of where use of RCAs

95 Source www.icrc.org, viewed on 17 December 2017. 96 CWC, Article 2(2).
97 CWC, Article 1(1). 98 CWC, Article 2(9)(d).

would be regarded as legitimate in accordance with the US interpretation. This interpretation was not, however, reflected in any statement made by the US on ratification of the CWC. The use of RCAs to facilitate attacks of objectives being protected by the use of human shields would seem to constitute their use as a method of warfare, and thus to be prohibited.[99] A policy interpretation or domestic Executive Order does not alter that apparent conflict between interpretation and legal reality.

HERBICIDES

Paragraph 6.17 notes, correctly, that herbicides that are harmless to humans are not prohibited under the poison/poisoned weapons rule. It relates the US policy renouncing first use of herbicides in armed conflict except to control vegetation inside or around the immediate defensive perimeters of US bases.[100] Paragraph 6.17.2 makes the point that, in the perhaps unlikely event that a herbicide is classed as a toxic chemical under the CWC definition, it would likely be intended for purposes not prohibited under the CWC. In a footnote, attention is drawn to the 7th preambular paragraph to the CWC, which recognises the prohibition of the use of herbicides as a method of warfare; this is odd, considering that a proposal to include such a prohibition in the operative provisions of the CWC proved controversial. Even the ICRC Customary Law Study drafts its rules on herbicides on the basis of other rules such as environmental protection and proportionality. Be all of this as it may, the US has its policy, and that policy is reflected in section 6.17.

NUCLEAR WEAPONS

Section 6.18 takes the understandable, and legally defensible, position that nuclear weapons are not prohibited as such but that the law of war governs any use of them. The US policy is that it would only use such weapons in extreme circumstances to defend the vital interests of itself, its allies or its partners, and that it would not threaten such use against non-nuclear States that are parties to and in compliance with the Nuclear Non-Proliferation Treaty.[101] The position of allies that are party to API and that made the nuclear statement when ratifying that treaty is explained.

99 CWC, Article 1(5).

100 *DoD Manual*, page 392, footnote 401, citing Executive Order 11850, dated 8 April 1975.

101 *DoD Manual*, paragraph 6.18.1.

EXPLOSIVE ORDNANCE

Section 6.19 addresses the dangers posed by explosive remnants of war (ERW), referring extensively to Protocol V to CCW,[102] to which the US is a State party.[103] Paragraphs 5.19.1.1 to 5.19.1.3 take the definitions of the requisite terms from Article 2 of the Protocol. Paragraphs 5.19.2 and 5.19.3 reflect the Article 4(1) obligations in relation to recording and retaining information, respectively, as to usage of explosive ordnance and as to its abandonment. Article 4(1) gives the purpose of such action as 'to facilitate the rapid marking and clearance, removal or destruction of explosive remnants of war, risk education and the provision of relevant information to the party in control of the territory and to civilian populations in that territory'. The *Manual* summarises the purpose as reducing the risks posed by ERW, but records the relevant treaty language in a footnote. To be pedantic, it would be better for the *Manual* to say that recording and retaining the information will enable action to be taken with a view to reducing those risks. The Technical Annex to Protocol V is not legally binding, as it contains voluntary best practice as to how a number of the treaty obligations should be implemented. So, paragraphs 6.19.2 and 6.19.3 set out the best practice in Section 1 of the Technical Annex as it relates to recording and retention of information on use of explosive ordnance and as to the abandonment of such ordnance. Paragraph 6.19.4 addresses the storage of that information, and the release of the information is considered in paragraph 6.20.6, discussed later.

Paragraph 6.19.5 of the *Manual* deals accurately with the generic preventive measures set forth in Section 4 of the Technical Annex, which again have voluntary best-practice status. These measures are grouped into munitions manufacturing management processes, munitions management procedures, training, transfer arrangements and future production.

EXPLOSIVE REMNANTS OF WAR

After accurately giving the Protocol V definition of ERW, section 6.20 summarises the obligations that the Protocol imposes. Paragraph 6.20.3 reproduces, accurately and sometimes verbatim, the feasible precautions that Article 5 requires for the protection of the civilian population, civilians and civilian objects and the guidance given in section 2 of the Technical Annex as to the practical implementation of this obligation.

[102] Protocol on Explosive Remnants of War, Geneva (28 November 2003).

[103] The US ratified Protocol V on 21 January 2009; source www.icrc.org, viewed on 17 December 2017.

Paragraph 6.20.4 sets forth in largely identical language the provisions of Article 6 of the Protocol as to the protection of humanitarian organisations and missions from the effects of ERW. Paragraph 6.20.5 asserts that this obligation is triggered by the end of active hostilities. No authority for that proposition is cited, and none is readily apparent on the face of the Protocol. Indeed, it is likely to be a most useful requirement both during ongoing hostilities and after hostilities have come to an end.[104] However, as reflected later in the same paragraph, the US did make a statement on ratification of the Protocol to the effect that nothing in it prevents arrangements in connection with the settlement of armed conflicts, or assistance connected thereto, that allocate responsibilities for ERW in a way that essentially respects the spirit and purpose of the Protocol.[105]

Paragraph 6.20.6 deals with arrangements for release of information as to ERW, as provided for in Article 4 of the Protocol and in section 1 of its Technical Annex. Most helpfully, the *Manual* deals in turn with the timing of release of information, the recipients of such information and the mechanism and the content, respectively, in relation to unexploded ordnance and abandoned explosive ordnance. The language of the Protocol is followed closely, and the legally binding provisions (in the present context, Article 4) are distinguished from the voluntary best practice in the Technical Annex. Paragraph 6.20.7 deals with the ERW clearance, removal and destruction obligations of States party in relation to territory that is under their control. It follows closely the language of Article 3(2)–(4). The useful point is made that territory under a State's control includes territory over which that State is an Occupying Power.

Paragraph 6.20.8 completes the section by setting forth the responsibilities of States that have used explosive ordnance that has become ERW in territory over which they do not have control. Article 3(1) of the Protocol requires such States to provide assistance where feasible bilaterally or through a mutually agreed third party to facilitate the marking, clearance, removal or destruction of the ERW.

[104] Furthermore, the US made no statement of interpretation to that effect when it ratified the Protocol on 21 January 2009; source www.icrc.org, viewed on 17 December 2017.

[105] For the precise text, see *DoD Manual*, footnote 470 on page 405.

7

Wounded, Sick, Shipwrecked, Dead and the Medical Services

Chapter VII of the *Manual* moves the discussion away from the conduct of hostilities – addressed in Chapter V – and from the tools, namely weapons, used to prosecute the war – the focus of Chapter VI – to look at how the law deals with the people who are generally regarded as victims of warfare. The notion of victim encompasses the wounded, sick, shipwrecked, civilians and the dead. The chapter, however, goes significantly beyond victims by also addressing the law associated with the provision of medical services. It is logical to add this aspect to a victim-centred chapter, not least because the victimhood of a number of the individuals covered in the chapter is attributable to their medical condition. Indeed, the law's protection of those medical services is an important element in its protection of the victims themselves – by protecting medical services, the law protects the facilities, resources and skills on which the wounded and sick depend for their hopes of recovery. Be that as it may, the title of the chapter gives a clear indication of its intended scope.

As will be seen from the following paragraphs, the *Manual* adopts numerous interpretations in the Pictet Commentaries. This is by no means a matter of criticism. To the extent that those Commentaries represent a pragmatic approach that is practicable in the relevant circumstances, adopting them makes perfect sense. It should in parentheses, however, be noted that at the time of writing, the ICRC is in the process of issuing updated Commentaries on the Conventions, so at least to the extent that the new Commentaries differ from the old, the *Manual* fails to address that aspect of contemporary thinking.

INTRODUCTION

Section 7.1 concerns itself with a number of preliminary issues that are central to a proper understanding of the subsequent sections. After defining the scope of the chapter in general terms and signposting related provisions outside the present chapter, paragraph 7.1.1 identifies GWS and GWS-Sea as the instruments that set out the rules that bind the US.[1] As paragraph 7.1.1.1 correctly suggests, the provisions of GWS and GWS-Sea should be interpreted in the light of core principles and the subsequent practice of States. Paragraph 7.1.1.2 lists numerous kinds of special agreement between States that can be the vehicle for facilitating the protection of relevant persons and the provision to make additional agreements on any matter on which they think it suitable to make separate provision.[2] Not all of the listed kinds of special agreement are addressed in the present chapter.

APPLICATION OF THE PROTECTIONS

Basing itself on the Pictet Commentaries,[3] paragraph 7.2.1 contends that GWS would no longer apply to a detained member of the armed forces who had recovered from his or her wounds, although the GPW would continue to apply. As the paragraph correctly notes, GWS-Sea ceases to apply when protected persons reach land and GWS applies until repatriation. Similarly, when retained personnel[4] and the dead are landed, GWS starts to apply.

The prohibition of any renunciation of rights by wounded, sick and shipwrecked, and by medical and religious personnel, is recorded in paragraph 7.2.2. The point is made that even partial renunciation is prohibited and the rationale for the rule (namely, the vulnerable position of protected persons, the difficulty in establishing true voluntariness of any renunciation and the fact that a ban serves best the interests of the majority) is correctly stated. The *Manual* then makes the further important point that the rule does not prohibit the reassignment by a State of its medical personnel away from medical duties.

1 Paragraph 7.1.1 acknowledges that GPW has rules as to wounded and sick persons and GC has relevant rules relating to civilians. The 174 states party to API are also bound by its specifically relevant provisions, namely Articles 8 to 34. The *DoD Manual* discusses the API provisions at section 7.20.

2 The paragraph correctly notes that no special agreement can adversely affect the situation or rights of protected persons and that the agreements shall continue to apply as long as the Conventions do unless the agreements specifically provide otherwise or more favourable measures are applied.

3 *GWS Commentary*, 65. Pictet bases his conclusion on the Convention's general structure, noting that while still wounded or sick, both GWS and GPW will apply. This is a widely accepted interpretation.

4 This is a reference to medical personnel and chaplains who are in the hands of an adverse party to the conflict.

RESPECT FOR AND PROTECTION OF WOUNDED, SICK AND SHIPWRECKED

As paragraph 7.3.1.1 correctly notes, citing the *GWS Commentary*,[5] the Conventions do not define the terms 'wounded' and 'sick', and sensible, good-faith interpretations are therefore required. It is also sensible to import into the notion the *hors de combat* requirement that to retain protection, wounded and sick must refrain from hostile acts and must not attempt to escape. Paragraph 7.3.1.2 adopts the GWS-Sea, Article 12 definition of 'shipwreck', namely 'shipwreck from any cause [including] forced landings at sea by or from aircraft'. The *Manual* then, basing itself again on Pictet, argues that the shipwrecked include those 'stranded on the coast who are also helpless'.[6] While the humanitarian motives underlying such an interpretation are well understood, the fact remains that persons who are on the coast are on land and are therefore no longer 'at sea' as required by Article 12(1) of GWS-Sea. Logic suggests, therefore, that they will only have protected status if, as may well be the case, they come within another category of protection, e.g. *hors de combat*.

Sensibly, persons engaged in amphibious, underwater or airborne attacks are not included, although mishap might cause such persons to become shipwrecked or otherwise to have protected status.[7]

Paragraph 7.3.2 accurately lists the categories of wounded, sick or shipwrecked persons who are protected, respectively, under GWS and GWS-Sea. Article 13 of each of the Conventions is the relevant authority, is expressed in similar terms in each Convention and is, as usual in the *Manual*, reproduced verbatim in a footnote.[8] The paragraph notes that wounded and sick civilians are protected under GC; that aspect is discussed later. Readers of the *Manual* would, however, be assisted by the addition of a sentence or two dealing with the status of the crews and passengers of neutral merchant vessels and of civil aircraft that have become military objectives, a topic on which Article 13 of GWS-Sea is silent.

Article 12(1) of GWS and of GWS-Sea requires that wounded, sick and shipwrecked shall be respected and protected. While adhering to each of the specific stipulations in both Conventions will do much to ensure compliance,

5 *GWS Commentary*, 136.

6 *DoD Manual*, paragraph 7.3.1.2, second section, citing J S Pictet (ed.) *Commentary II on Geneva Convention for the Amelioration of the Condition of Wounded, Sick and Shipwrecked Members of Armed Forces at Sea*. International Committee of the Red Cross (1960), 89 (*GWS-Sea Commentary*).

7 This caveat is acknowledged in NWP 1–14M at paragraph 8.2.3.2, cited in *DoD Manual*, footnote 44 on page 416, but not reflected in the *Manual*'s text.

8 *DoD Manual*, footnote 45 on page 417.

the Conventions do not actually define what 'respect' and 'protect' mean. The *Manual's* interpretation is that they shall not knowingly be attacked, fired upon or unnecessarily interfered with. This interpretation is based on an Appendix to a Chairman of the Joint Chiefs of Staff Memorandum of 1985, relating to API.[9] The *Tallinn Manual 2.0*[10] explains that the obligation to 'respect and protect' involves separate obligations: 'The duty to respect is breached by actions that impede or prevent medical or religious personnel, medical units or medical transports from performing their medical or religious functions, or that otherwise adversely affect the[ir] humanitarian functions . . . ' It refers to the duty to protect as implying 'the taking of positive measures to ensure respect by others'.[11] Somewhat more succinctly, the *UK Manual* states that the 'duty of respect means that the wounded and sick are not to be made the object of attack', while the 'duty of protection imposes positive duties to assist them'.[12]

Paragraph 7.3.3.1 contends that the respect and protect obligations do not extend to incidental damage or casualties due to proximity to military objectives nor to 'justifiable mistake', a concept which is not explained. The former exclusion would seem to represent a rather strict application of the *UK Manual* approach, while the latter raises all sorts of questions.[13]

The second sentence in paragraph 7.3.3.1 then argues: 'Because combatants who are wounded, sick or shipwrecked on the battlefield are deemed to have accepted the risk of death or further injury due to proximity to military operations, they need not be considered as incidental harm in assessing proportionality in conducting attacks.' This observation must be approached with considerable care. If such persons are *hors de combat*, they must not be made the object of attack. While the proportionality rule as given in Articles 51(5)(b) and 57 of API only refers to incidental harm to civilians, there is a powerful argument to be made that the rule should be interpreted as encompassing incidental harm to all persons or objects that are entitled to protection from attack, such as persons *hors de combat*, the wounded, sick or shipwrecked, medical and religious personnel etc. If a person is entitled to protection, and

[9] *DoD Manual*, footnote 56 on page 418.

[10] M N Schmitt (ed.), *Tallinn Manual 2.0 on the International Law Applicable to Cyber Operations*. Cambridge: Cambridge University Press (2017).

[11] *Tallinn Manual 2.0*, paragraphs 5 and 6 of the Commentary to rule 131.

[12] *UK Manual*, paragraph 7.3.1 as amended.

[13] For example: Is justifiable mistake limited to non-negligent acts, i.e. errors of judgment, or does it include simple negligence but not gross negligence, or could it even include certain types of recklessness? What degree of care must be taken to avoid the possibility of the mistake in order for the exclusion to apply?

if it is prohibited to make that person the object of attack, it would seem logically to follow that expected injury to that person should be considered when determining whether the attack is indiscriminate and thus prohibited.

The right to take suitable security measures in relation to the wounded, sick and shipwrecked, their liability to be captured, their right to receive appropriate medical care and their status on capture as PWs are all correctly noted. The right of warships to demand the surrender of wounded and sick aboard hospital ships and other listed craft as set forth in Article 14 of GWS-Sea, subject to the caveats in that article, is included within this paragraph. Maybe it would be better to confine the discussion of this topic to the sections dealing with hospital ships and similar craft. The captor's options on dealing with such prisoners, as reflected in Article 16 of GWS-Sea, are then noted, including the prohibition on former prisoners serving for the duration of the war if they are returned to their own country.

SEARCH, COLLECTION AND AFFIRMATIVE PROTECTION

The obligation to search for and collect the wounded, sick and shipwrecked is discussed in Section 7.4, where the limited application of the GWS-Sea obligation to search and collect 'after each engagement' is contrasted with the corresponding duty on land that applies 'at all times'.[14] Paragraph 7.4.2 then suggests, '[i]f practicable, affirmative measures (including, in some cases, the use of force) must be taken to protect the wounded, sick and shipwrecked'. As we have seen, however, Article 12 of each Convention is mandatory in providing that the wounded, sick and shipwrecked 'shall be . . . protected in all circumstances'. Perhaps it would have been better – and it is appreciated that a certain amount of 'word-smithing' is involved here – simply to say that everything possible, including if necessary the use of force, must be done to protect them. Pictet, cited in the *Manual*, makes the point by commenting – and this must be correct – that there will be times when military operations will make the obligation to search impracticable.[15] Paragraph 6.4.4.1 considers the question of acceptance of risk to self in order to rescue others, noting that personnel performing rescue and recovery missions need not expose themselves to undue risk. Indeed, it makes no sense for rescuers to take unreasonable risks and thus potentially add themselves to the casualty count. The paragraph then suggests that the commander of a naval vessel need not increase the risk to the

[14] GWS, Article 15; GWS-Sea, Article 18.

[15] *DoD Manual*, footnote 78 on page 422, citing *GWS Commentary*, 151. The point is explicitly made in *DoD Manual*, paragraph 6.4.4.2.

vessel from threats in order to rescue shipwrecked enemy personnel. To imply, however, as this passage and the associated footnote do, that no additional risk whatever must be accepted is to go too far. There is some risk associated with any activity in war, and to take such an absolute stance risks undermining the obligation to search for and collect.

Paragraph 7.4.3 discusses practical measures to give effect to this section's obligations, with particular mention of armistices, suspensions of fire and other local arrangements to facilitate evacuations, exchanges, removals and/or transportation of the wounded and sick.

The right of the military authorities to request civilian assistance with the collection and care of the wounded and sick, their obligation to permit the civilian population to undertake such activity, the requirement that the civilian population respect the wounded and sick and refrain from offering them violence and the prohibition of molesting or convicting those who nurse the wounded and sick are provided for in Article 18 of GWS and are reflected in paragraphs 7.4.5.1, 7.4.5.2 and 7.4.5.3 of the *Manual*. The broadly corresponding maritime arrangements in Article 21 of GWS-Sea, reflected in paragraph 7.4.6 of the *Manual*, provide for appeals to neutral merchant vessels, yachts and other craft to take on board and care for the wounded, sick and shipwrecked and collect the dead, grant such vessels special protection and provide that such transport activity shall not render them liable to capture.

HUMANE TREATMENT AND CARE OF ENEMY MILITARY WOUNDED, SICK AND SHIPWRECKED IN THE POWER OF A PARTY TO THE CONFLICT

The treaty obligation is to treat enemy military wounded, sick and shipwrecked humanely,[16] to care for them[17] and not to make any adverse distinction based on sex, race, nationality, religion, political opinions or similar criteria.[18] The *Manual* repeats the prohibition of any attempts upon their lives or violence to their persons, as set forth in Article 12 of GWS and GWS-Sea, and notes the requirement for due consideration for women. So, the wounded, sick and shipwrecked shall not be needlessly left without care,

[16] As paragraph 7.5.1 points out, this obligation of humane treatment is also to be found in GPW, and therefore applies also to the military wounded, sick and shipwrecked.

[17] This is an affirmative obligation to take all possible measures to ensure their adequate care; *DoD Manual*, paragraph 7.5.2.2.

[18] GWS and GWS-Sea, Article 12; *DoD Manual*, section 7.5.

nor shall conditions exposing them to contagion be created deliberately.[19] However, a publication of the Surgeon General of the Army is cited as the authority for the view that commitment of (medical) resources should be decided first on the basis of the mission and the immediate tactical situation and then by medical necessity. Interestingly, paragraph 7.5.2.3 and GWS and GWS-Sea, Article 12 state that 'only urgent medical reasons will justify priority in the order of treatment to be administered', and paragraph 7.5.2.3 goes further by opining that, confronted with friendly and enemy patients, doctors should effectively act according to medical priority. One cannot help thinking that medical personnel would feel more comfortable with the somewhat clearer protection of medical duties afforded by Article 16 of API.

Paragraph 7.5.2.4 argues that wounded, sick, shipwrecked and PWs may be ordered to receive medical treatment, and notes that under Article 11(5) of API, persons who are in the power of an adverse party to the conflict have the right to refuse. The *Manual* states that the US does not accept this API rule, as it could operate in an inhumane way in certain cases.[20] Medical treatment of PWs must be free of charge.[21]

In extreme circumstances, the wounded and sick may be abandoned on the battlefield, and paragraph 7.5.3 correctly addresses the action to be taken – notably the requirement, subject to military considerations, to leave medical personnel and materiel to assist with their care.[22] Oddly, the *Manual* describes this as a 'strong recommendation, rather than an absolute requirement'. The language used in Article 12 is 'shall, as far as military considerations permit'. It follows that, if military considerations do permit such action, it is mandatory, not merely recommended.[23] The *Manual* is right to point out in the same paragraph, however, that another party to the conflict encountering and capturing the abandoned wounded and sick is not relieved of its obligations to respect and care for them by the fact that medical personnel and material have – or, as the case may be, have not – been left with them.[24]

[19] *DoD Manual*, paragraph 7.5.2.1.

[20] In a footnote, refusal of life-saving treatment due to mental incompetence, ignorance or the wish to make a political point are cited as examples of such inhumane outcomes; *DoD Manual*, footnote 106 on pages 426–7. The right of a patient to refuse consent to medical treatment is widely recognised in medical ethics, and, while mental incapacity may avoid that requirement, ignorance should not arise, as any consent must be informed and the motives of the refusing patient ought to be irrelevant.

[21] *DoD Manual*, paragraph 7.5.2.5; GPW, Article 15.

[22] GWS, Article 12.

[23] *GWS Commentary*, 142 is the authority on which the *Manual*'s stated position is based.

[24] This would be because the capturing party must comply with the requirements of Article 12 when the abandoned wounded come under their power.

ACCOUNTABILITY INFORMATION FROM ENEMY WOUNDED, SICK, SHIPWRECKED AND DEAD

This somewhat obscure title, as the opening lines of section 7.6 reveal, is concerned with how enemy captured or dead personnel recovered from the battlefield must be accounted for. Paragraph 7.6.1 accurately reproduces the list of particulars that parties to the conflict are required by Article 16 of GWS to record as soon as possible in relation to each wounded, sick, shipwrecked or dead person of the adverse party falling into their hands. Similar information should be recorded in relation to PWs. The same paragraph goes on to suggest useful sources of information that may help to establish the identity of the dead.

Article 122 of GPW requires each party at the outbreak of an armed conflict to establish an Information Bureau. Paragraph 7.6.2 of the *Manual* details the procedure by which information referred to in the previous paragraph is forwarded through this Bureau to the Power on which the person depends. Article 16 of GWS requires this information to be transmitted as soon as possible.[25] That language may permit of some delay for practical reasons, such as security considerations. To justify delay, however, there would need to be a clear basis for saying that earlier disclosure would imperil the successful performance of military operations.

TREATMENT AND HANDLING OF ENEMY MILITARY DEAD

After explaining why enemy non-civilian personnel who die shortly after capture may be interpreted as being addressed both by GWS/GWS-Sea and by GPW, section 7.7 proposes that the GWS/GWS-Sea rules should be applied by analogy to civilian dead, and notes that GC provides rules as to civilians who die while interned. Paragraph 7.7.1 sets forth the well-established, customary rule requiring the respectful treatment of the military dead; the paragraph explicitly states that disrespectful or degrading treatment of the dead is prohibited. In the associated footnotes,[26] criminal proceedings arising from World War II, citing acts ranging from mutilation of the dead to cannibalism, are given as examples of breaches of this rule that attracted severe

[25] Paragraph 7.6.3 of the *DoD Manual* gives the US process for forwarding the relevant information.

[26] *DoD Manual*, footnote 130 on page 430 traces the rule to the writings of Grotius, and footnotes 131 and 132 on pages 430 and 431 give examples of court proceedings for offences arising from breaches of the rule.

punishment. As the *Manual* correctly asserts, posing for photographs with the dead, leaving a calling card on their bodies and booby-trapping those bodies are also prohibited by the rule.

Paragraph 7.7.2 repeats the GWS, Article 15 prohibition of despoiling the dead, which it explains as unauthorised removal or pillaging of their personal effects. As the paragraph correctly notes, recovered personal property of the dead becomes the property of the recovering State pending its return to next of kin, and individual soldiers have no title to such effects. Paragraph 7.7.2.2 correctly reports the obligations in Article 16 of GWS and Article 19 of GWS-Sea to return found items of value through the Information Bureau. Detailed requirements for handling e.g. identity discs, wills and unidentified items are given in the same paragraph. Death certificates and lists of the dead must be forwarded through the same Information Bureau, as discussed in paragraph 7.7.3.

The provisions of Article 17(1) and (3) of GWS as to proper, honourable burial or cremation, carried out individually so far as circumstances permit, and if possible according to the rites of the religion of the deceased, are reflected in paragraph 7.7.4.2. The important rule that one half of a double identity disc stays with the body is emphasised. Article 17(2) GWS is accurately reflected in paragraph 7.7.4.4's statement that imperative reasons of hygiene or motives based on the religion of the deceased are the only justifications for cremation, in which event the circumstances must be described in detail in the death certificate or on the list of the dead. The requirement for an Official Grave Registration Service, its functions and the exchange through the Information Bureau of lists showing the location and markings of graves are provided for in Article 17(3) and (4) of GWS and are reflected in paragraph 7.7.5 of the *Manual*.

RESPECT AND PROTECTION OF CATEGORIES OF MEDICAL AND RELIGIOUS PERSONNEL

Paragraph 7.8.1 lists the categories of medical and religious personnel whom the *Manual* describes as entitled to respect and protection. Interestingly, the list does not include civilian medical personnel. States party to API will note the inclusion in the Article 8(c) definition of 'medical personnel of a Party to the conflict, whether military or civilian' who are assigned by that party to exclusively medical purposes, as set forth in Article 8(e).

The *Manual*'s interpretation of the terms 'respect' and 'protect' in relation to medical and religious personnel and, earlier, in relation to the wounded, sick and shipwrecked are similar.[27] The *Manual* again takes the position that incidental harm to them is not prohibited, which is correct, but then, controversially, that their assumption of risk through their proximity to the hostilities means they do not need to be considered in the proportionality evaluation. The objection to that approach discussed earlier in relation to paragraph 7.3.3.1 applies with equal force here.[28] They may be searched subject to the same rules as apply to PWs.[29]

The rule that medical and religious personnel may only use force against the adversary in self-defence or defence of their patients is correctly reported in the same paragraph. Examples are given in this paragraph of activities that would deprive the medical or religious persons of their protected status and thus would render them liable to be attacked.[30]

Paragraphs 7.8.4 to 7.8.4.2 restate the basic rule as to the wearing of the distinctive emblem by military medical and religious personnel, staff of voluntary aid societies and staff of recognised aid societies of neutral countries. The obligation to wear the emblem as given in Article 40(1) of GWS is set forth. One cannot help thinking that there should have been some discussion in these paragraphs of how the rule should be interpreted in light of the all too frequent practice in modern conflicts of the adverse party deliberately targeting personnel wearing the distinctive emblem.

CAPTURED MEDICAL AND RELIGIOUS PERSONNEL

Paragraph 7.9.1 correctly teases out the three classes of personnel performing medical and religious duties, grouped according to how they are treated in relation to detention. So, staff of a recognised voluntary aid society of a neutral country and specified personnel in service on a hospital ship are exempt from capture or detention.[31] Then, there are the medical and religious personnel who have the status of retained personnel on capture, i.e. they may be retained only insofar as the state of health, spiritual needs and numbers of PWs require. The *Manual* notes this applies to military medical and religious personnel and authorised staff of voluntary aid societies, and makes the point that such

[27] *DoD Manual*, paragraph 7.8.2. [28] *DoD Manual*, paragraph 7.8.2.1.

[29] *DoD Manual*, paragraph 7.8.2.2. Medical and religious personnel can, subject to what is said in paragraph 7.9.1.1 (see later), be detained, and they lose their protection from being made the object of attack if, outside their normal humanitarian functions, they commit acts harmful to the enemy; *DoD Manual*, paragraph 7.8.3. The *GWS Commentary*'s contention is that this follows logically from the rule in GWS, Article 21.

[30] *DoD Manual*, paragraph 7.8.3. [31] *DoD Manual*, paragraph 7.9.1.1; GWS-Sea, Article 36.

captured persons are not PWs.[32] Paragraph 7.9.1.3 then lists the persons who have PW status on capture, such as auxiliary medical personnel (if they are carrying out their medical duties when they come into contact with the enemy or are captured).

The technical requirements of GWS, Article 40(2) and (3) as to medical identity cards to be carried by medical and religious personnel entitled to retained status on capture are reproduced verbatim in paragraph 7.9.2. The stipulation in GWS, Article 40(4) and GWS-Sea, Article 42(4) that '[i]n no circumstances may the said personnel be deprived of their insignia or identity cards nor of the right to wear the armlet' is repeated in the same paragraph of the *Manual* without further comment. It would be interesting to know whether the US considers this prohibition also binds the military authorities of the personnel concerned.

The duties of retained personnel, namely to carry out medical and religious duties on behalf of PWs, are covered in Article 28(2) of GWS and paragraph 7.9.3 of the *Manual*. It is asserted that refusal to perform these duties may cause them to be deprived of retained personnel status, but no authority for this is cited.[33] While Article 30(1) of GWS stipulates that retained personnel whose retention is not indispensable shall be returned to the party to the conflict to which they belong, the *Manual* notes that such return has been exceptional while hostilities continue.[34] Exceptional or not, the requirement to return in the stated circumstances is explicit, and there would seem to be no basis for arguing that the subsequent practice referred to 'establishes the agreement of the parties [to GWS] as to [Article 30(1)'s] interpretation'.[35]

In paragraph 7.9.5, the *Manual* lists the rights and privileges of retained personnel as: the benefits and protection of GPW; the facilities necessary to provide for medical care of and ministration to PWs; periodic visits to PWs in work detachments or hospitals outside the camp; chaplains' freedom to correspond with ecclesiastical authorities; proposal of PWs for examination by Mixed Medical Commissions; and no compulsion to carry out work other than medical/religious duties.[36] The responsibility of the senior

32 *DoD Manual*, paragraph 7.9.1.2; GWS, Article 28; GPW, Article 33.

33 The *Manual* may, however, be drawing the right inference from GWS, Article 28(c)'s reference to retained personnel in a camp being subject to its internal discipline.

34 *DoD Manual*, paragraph 7.9.4. As paragraphs 7.9.4.1 and 7.9.4.2 note, pending return, they do not have PW status, but benefit from all the provisions of GPW. Selection of persons for return must not be discriminatory, but shall be in order of capture; GWS, Articles 30 and 31.

35 Consider Vienna Convention on the Law of Treaties, Vienna, 23 May 1969, Article 31(3)(b).

36 GWS, Article 28 and GPW, Articles 33 and 35.

medical officer in the camp for the activities of retained medical personnel is noted, as is the rule that none of these provisions relieve the Detaining Power of its responsibilities to care for PWs.[37]

MILITARY MEDICAL UNITS AND FACILITIES

Section 7.10 restates that fixed establishments and mobile medical units of the Medical Service may not be attacked and must at all times be respected and protected.[38] 'Respect' and 'protect' are given similar meanings to those in Section 7.3. Paragraph 7.10.1.1 alludes to the GWS, Article 19(2) requirement to situate medical units and establishments so 'that attacks against military objectives cannot imperil their safety'.[39] The *Manual* then asserts that medical units and facilities situated near military objectives 'are deemed to have accepted the risk of death or further injury due to proximity to military operations' and that 'they need not be considered as incidental harm when considering proportionality'. A location, object or facility may, however, rapidly and unpredictably become a military objective as the tactical battle evolves. Fixed medical establishments, as the label implies, may be difficult to move out of the way of that evolving battle, or away from persons or objects positioned in ignorance of the presence of a fixed medical facility. Simply to assert that a fixed medical establishment or mobile medical unit that finds itself near to an object that satisfies the Article 52(2) API definition of military objective can be simply ignored in the proportionality evaluation of an attack cannot be a correct and complete statement of the law. It is therefore curious that in paragraph 7.10.2.1 there is explicit acknowledgement that practical considerations, such as the effective performance of their medical duties, may dictate that such facilities 'must to some degree be intermingled with military objectives'.[40] At this point, the reader may wonder what the intended message is here. The present authors consider that expected incidental damage to medical facilities and expected incidental casualties among medical and religious personnel, wherever such facilities or personnel are located, must be considered in the proportionality evaluation. They believe that the advice in paragraph 7.10.2.2 achieves broadly the correct balance.

Paragraphs 7.10.1.2 and 7.10.1.3 assert that such facilities are not immune from search and capture, which must be right. In the event of capture, paragraph 7.10.5.1 notes that material of mobile units must be reserved for

37 *DoD Manual*, paragraph 7.9.6.
38 GWS, Article 19(1).
39 The article is cited specifically in paragraph 7.10.2, noting the prohibition on using such facilities for shielding purposes.
40 Consider also paragraph 7.10.3.6 in this regard.

the care of wounded and sick, and that the buildings, materials and stores of fixed medical establishments may not be diverted from their function as long as they are required for the care of the wounded and sick.[41]

Paragraph 7.10.3 reflects accurately the circumstances under Article 21 GWS when fixed establishments and mobile medical units lose their protection, namely when 'used to commit, outside their humanitarian duties, acts harmful to the enemy'. Examples are then given of acts that would be harmful to the enemy, and Article 21's obligation to give due warning before protection ceases is stated verbatim.[42] The same paragraph correctly asserts the right to return fire emanating e.g. from a hospital in self-defence, stipulating that the fire in return must be proportionate.[43] The conditions that do not deprive a medical unit or establishment of protection listed in GWS, Article 22 are restated verbatim in paragraph 7.10.3.3.

Paragraph 7.10.3.4 discusses the appropriate arming of medical units and facilities. Generally speaking, it is the personnel rather than the facility that will be armed, and the paragraph correctly emphasises that the purpose must be for internal security and discipline, to protect medical personnel, patients and medical supplies against unlawful, e.g. criminal attacks and theft. They must not be so armed as to appear to present an offensive threat, nor may they resist enemy troops acting in accordance with the law of war. Paragraph 7.10.3.5 asserts that medical personnel may use their weapons 'to defend themselves or the wounded and sick in their care from unlawful attacks, such as those from unprivileged belligerents or other persons violating the law of war'. A civilian who is directly participating in the hostilities does not violate the law of war by virtue of that participation as such. Such an individual does, however, breach applicable domestic law of the *locus in quo*. His or her use of force would therefore constitute a crime, which would seem to justify the use of force against him by defending medical personnel on that basis, but not as a violator of the law of war.

Medical personnel who continue to use force outside these limitations after due warning may render themselves or the facility they seek to defend liable to be attacked. Paragraph 7.10.4 reproduces verbatim the GWS, Article 42 provisions as to the hoisting of the distinctive flag of the Conventions over medical units and establishments, including the steps needed to make the emblem visible.

[41] This reflects GWS, Article 33 and the *Manual* notes that commanders may make use of them in case of urgent military necessity provided prior arrangements have been made for the care of the wounded and sick being nursed there.

[42] *DoD Manual*, paragraph 7.10.3.2.

[43] *GWS Commentary*, 202 is cited as the authority.

GROUND TRANSPORTS OF THE WOUNDED AND SICK, OR OF MEDICAL EQUIPMENT

Section 7.11 correctly notes that medical transports must be respected and protected[44] unless they are used to commit, outside their humanitarian function, acts harmful to the enemy, and gives examples of such acts. The due warning requirement before protection ceases is also correctly stated. The right of the enemy to capture and use for its own purposes such transports is, as the *Manual* notes, subject to the proviso that the care of the wounded and sick being carried thereon is ensured.[45] There is then a somewhat complex discussion in the second part of paragraph 7.11.2 as to the position over the requisition of civilian personnel and vehicles. That part of the text might benefit from some simplification.

HOSPITAL SHIPS, SICK BAYS IN WARSHIPS AND COASTAL RESCUE CRAFT

Paragraph 7.12.1.1 literally repeats Article 22 GWS-Sea, without, however, explaining the different terms used in that provision.[46] It would certainly have added some value had the authors of the *Manual* made clear that a 'military hospital ship' need not fulfil the requirements of the definition of a 'warship', but that it could also be a naval auxiliary. Since warships and naval auxiliaries are operated by the armed forces, they would both qualify as military hospital ships if they exclusively serve the humanitarian function of assisting the wounded, sick and shipwrecked at sea. Paragraph 7.12.1.4 addresses the issue of the size of hospital ships by reference to Article 26 GWS-Sea. While the latter provision is correctly cited, the *Manual*, again, fails to explain important terms, such as 'tons gross'.

Coastal rescue craft and their fixed coastal installations are correctly dealt with in paragraph 7.12.1.5, in particular insofar as their comparatively weak protection under Article 27 GWS-Sea is explained by the small size and speed of such craft. Unfortunately, the *Manual* fails to clarify the US position regarding rescue vessels that are big and that operate at a considerable distance from the coast. In this context, it is important to note that many maritime search and rescue craft can no longer be considered 'small' and that they might thus

44 GWS, Article 35(1).

45 *DoD Manual*, paragraph 7.11.2; GWS, Article 35; *GWS Commentary*, 282.

46 For an in-depth discussion of the issues raised in this section, see the recent ICRC Commentary on GWS-Sea, which is available at: https://ihl-databases.icrc.org/applic/ihl/ihl.nsf/Treaty.xsp?documentId?2F5AA9B07AB61934C12563CD002D6B25&action=openDocument.

be denied the protection under Article 27 GWS-Sea. A further unresolved issue with regard to the protection of coastal rescue craft is the continuing applicability during an international armed conflict of peacetime instruments, such as the Convention on Maritime Search and Rescue.

Paragraph 7.12.2 correctly identifies the duties and liabilities of hospital ships and coastal rescue craft according to Articles 30 and 31 GWS-Sea, and also addresses the use of secret codes that is prohibited by Article 34 GWS-Sea. The authors of the *Manual* take the arguable position that the prohibition must be interpreted with a view to the technological development in maritime communications and that the use of encryption (common in satellite communications) is not prohibited.

While paragraph 7.12.3 on the identification and paragraph 7.12.4 on the rights and privileges of hospital ships and coastal rescue craft are uncontroversial, paragraph 7.12.6 on the forfeiture of protection should have been more elaborate. The mere repetition of Article 34 GWS-Sea is, in the view of the present authors, insufficient, because it does not provide guidance for those seeking advice. Article 34 GWS-Sea indeed deals with the loss of protection if such vessels are used to commit 'acts harmful to the enemy'. However, hospital ships and coastal rescue craft will also lose their protection against capture (as distinguished from attack) if they do not comply with the conditions of protection listed in Article 30 GWS-Sea. In other words, hospital ships and coastal rescue craft will lose their protection against attack if they are used to commit acts harmful to the enemy and if the procedural safeguards correctly identified in paragraph 7.12.6.1 have been observed. If the activity does not qualify as an 'act harmful to the enemy', but rather as non-compliance with the conditions of protection, hospital ships and coastal rescue craft may not be attacked but they will lose their protection against capture.

Paragraph 7.12.6.2 correctly lists the activities that, according to Article 35 GWS-Sea, do not deprive hospital ships of their protection. The highly contentious issue of arming hospital ships is dealt with in paragraph 7.12.6.3. In the light of Article 35 GWS-Sea, it is uncontroversial that the crew may be equipped with weapons in order to maintain order and to protect the wounded, sick and shipwrecked. It is also arguably lawful to allow hospital ships to be equipped with purely deflective means, such as chaff or flares, in order to protect themselves e.g. against misguided missiles. The present authors do have some sympathy for the US position, according to which 'hospital ships may be armed with defensive weapon systems . . . as a prudent anti-terrorism/force protection (AT/FP) measure to defend against small boat attacks'. Indeed, terrorists, and even the enemy forces, may deliberately choose to attack a hospital ship. Then, the hospital ship would most likely be entitled to exercise its right of self-defence against such unlawful attacks. Nevertheless, the present authors would like to emphasise that weapons on board a hospital ship in excess of what is permissible under Article 35 GWS-Sea will be met with the highest suspicion by the enemy, who may thus no longer be prepared to consider the hospital ship a specially protected vessel under GWS-Sea. It may be added that in view of the considerable difficulties of effectively protecting hospital ships against unlawful attacks by State and non-State actors, some States have decided to abandon hospital ships and to assign some of their warships to serve as 'casualty receiving ships'. Seemingly, those States interpreted GWS-Sea in such a manner that they would be prohibited to equip hospital ships with defensive weapons in excess of what Article 35 GWS-Sea permits.

MILITARY MEDICAL AIRCRAFT

As section 7.14 reports, Article 36 GWS ties the definition of medical aircraft to the exclusive use of the aircraft for the removal of wounded and sick and for the transport of medical personnel and equipment, and ties their right to be respected and not to be attacked to compliance with agreements between the parties as to flying altitudes, times and routes of its flights.[47] The *Manual* acknowledges, however, a general proposition that 'known medical aircraft, when performing their humanitarian functions, must be respected and protected', which rather reflects an API provision that the *Manual* declines directly to cite.[48]

Protection of the medical aircraft is contingent on it being exclusively employed for the stated medical purposes.[49]

It must be right, as paragraph 7.14.2.1 suggests, that there can be no objection either to the conversion of ordinary aircraft into medical use[50] or to the

47 GWS-Sea, Article 39(1); API, Article 8(f), (g) and (j); *AMW Manual*, rule 1(u).

48 API, Article 26(1) states: 'Although in the absence of . . . an agreement, medical aircraft operate at their own risk, they shall nevertheless be respected after they have been recognized as such.' The *Manual* does, however, point out that such an aircraft is not a military objective, and that even if it is flying without an agreement, it should not be deliberately attacked or fired upon if its medical status has been identified. Accordingly, an aircraft flying without an agreement but that seeks to obtain medical aircraft protection should make every effort to identify itself and to inform the enemy of its status and operations; note that in a footnote to this passage, Article 27(2) of API is cited. It must also comply with all instructions, e.g. as to where to land and to submit to search.

49 *DoD Manual*, paragraph 7.14.2; API, Article 8(g).

50 The *Manual* limits this to use as medical aircraft under a special agreement, but the present authors see no objection in principle to the conversion of ordinary aircraft into medical aircraft irrespective of the existence or otherwise of an agreement.

use of what formerly were medical aircraft for other purposes, provided the markings showing medical status are removed. Paragraph 7.14.2.2 makes the important point that medical aircraft are not permitted to undertake combat search and rescue and must not impede enemy military operations.[51]

The obligation to mark medical aircraft with the emblem on their upper, lower and lateral surfaces is stated, and they are prohibited to fly over enemy or enemy-occupied territory.[52]

The provisions of GWS, Articles 36(4) and (5) and 37 as to the obedience of summons to land, involuntary landings in enemy or enemy-occupied territory and over-flight of the territory of a neutral are then repeated virtually verbatim.[53]

DISPLAY OF THE DISTINCTIVE EMBLEM TO FACILITATE IDENTIFICATION

Basic rules as to the use and the indicative purpose[54] of the distinctive emblem are given in the opening lines of section 7.15. The Red Cross, Red Crescent and Red Crystal emblems, along with the withdrawn Red Lion and Sun emblem, are reproduced in paragraph 7.15.1. In paragraph 7.15.1.1, it is emphasised that the Red Cross is not intended to have religious significance.[55] The recognition accorded to the Red Crescent and Red Lion and Sun is acknowledged in paragraph 7.15.1.2, while the adoption by Additional Protocol III[56] of the Red Crystal and its equal status with other emblems are referred to in paragraph 7.15.1.3.

Paragraph 7.15.1.4 notes that APIII accords equal status to the distinctive emblems and 'provides that the medical services and religious personnel of armed forces of parties to APIII may, without prejudice to their current

[51] The paragraph does note that special agreements may provide protection for aircraft engaged in search, rescue and recovery.

[52] *DoD Manual*, paragraphs 7.14.3 and 7.14.4; GWS, Article 36(3); but note Article 27(1) of API, which provides that protected status shall be retained during such flights if the prior agreement of the adverse party's authorities has been obtained.

[53] *DoD Manual*, paragraphs 7.14.5 to 7.14.6.2.

[54] The purpose in displaying the emblem is to facilitate identification of protected status; *DoD Manual*, paragraph 7.15.3.1. The emblem does not *per se* establish the right to protection: that right derives from the units, facilities or personnel meeting the requirements for protected status; *DoD Manual*, paragraph 7.15.3.2. Hence, facilities or personnel recognised as meeting the requirements for protected status must be respected and protected whether they are displaying the emblem or not; *DoD Manual*, paragraph 7.15.3.2.

[55] For the relevant explanation, see footnote 384 on page 471.

[56] Protocol Additional to the Geneva Conventions of 12 August 1949, and Relating to the Adoption of an Additional Distinctive Emblem (Protocol III) (8 December 2005) (APIII).

emblems, make temporary use of any distinctive emblems where this may enhance protection'.[57]

GWS, Article 39's obligation under the direction of the competent military authority to display the emblem on the flags, armlets and all equipment of the medical service is repeated in paragraph 7.15.2, and the *Manual* asserts the right of the military command to order the removal or obscuring of the emblem e.g. to facilitate camouflage. Recognising the unscrupulous activities of some adverse parties in recent conflicts, the *Manual* suggests – rightly, the present authors believe – that removal would also be appropriate if it were assessed that enemy forces were likely to fail to respect the emblem and to seek to attack medical personnel.[58]

Paragraph 7.15.4 correctly explains that unauthorised use of the distinctive emblem, whether in peace or war, is prohibited, and gives examples of particular uses that would be unlawful, e.g. while engaged in attacks or in order to shield, favour or protect one's own military operations. Examples of certain authorised non-military uses of the emblems are also given.[59]

PROTECTION OF CIVILIANS WHO ARE WOUNDED, SICK, INFIRM OR EXPECTANT MOTHERS

Section 7.16 readily acknowledges that wounded, sick and infirm civilians and expectant mothers are entitled to particular protection and respect, as they are vulnerable and do not take part in hostilities.[60] The *Manual* also embraces the GC, Article 16 obligation for all parties to a conflict to facilitate the steps taken to search for, assist and protect those listed in the article. However, the duty only applies so far as military considerations allow. That said, as the *Manual* notes, while the civilian authorities will often be responsible for collecting and bringing in civilian casualties, in practice military authorities may be asked to lead such activities or to be jointly involved with the civilian authorities.[61]

57 APIII, Article 2(4). As the *Manual* notes, Israel has adopted the Red Shield of David as its emblem by way of reservation when ratifying the 1949 Conventions.

58 *DoD Manual*, paragraph 7.15.2.1.

59 Paragraph 7.15.4.1 notes the lawful use by national Red Cross societies and authorised voluntary aid societies within the framework of Article 44(1), GWS. Further detail is given as to lawful use by such societies in times of peace and war. Paragraph 7.15.4.2 records the right of the International Red Cross organisations and their authorised personnel to use the emblem at all times. Subject to national legislation, and with the permission of the national society, ambulances and locations of aid stations exclusively devoted to give free treatment to the wounded or sick may exceptionally use the emblem, as noted in paragraph 7.15.4.3.

60 GC, Article 16.

61 *DoD Manual*, paragraph 7.16.1.

CIVILIAN HOSPITALS AND THEIR PERSONNEL

Section 7.17 correctly records that civilian hospitals organised to give care to the wounded and sick, the infirm and maternity cases may in no circumstances be made the object of attack and shall at all times be respected and protected. Paragraph 7.17.1 rightly notes that loss of protection only occurs if such hospitals are used outside their humanitarian duties to commit acts harmful to the enemy and gives examples of such acts. The requirements to give due warning, naming a reasonable time limit, and that the warning shall have gone unheeded are also correctly noted. The right to take action in self-defence is discussed in similar terms as in respect of military medical units, and is similarly correct. The certification requirements under Article 18(2) of GC and the obligation to mark civilian hospitals with the emblem if so authorised by the State and, to the extent military considerations permit, to make those markings clearly visible are reflected in paragraphs 7.17.2.1 and 7.17.2.2.

Paragraph 7.17.3's recommendation that civilian hospitals be located as far as possible from military objectives follows the wording of Article 18 of GC precisely. Similarly, the 'respect and protect' obligation towards persons regularly and solely engaged in the operation and administration of civilian hospitals found in GC, Article 20 is set forth in the same terms in paragraph 7.17.4.1. The provisions of Article 20 of GC are then followed closely in the remainder of section 7.17.

LAND AND SEA CIVILIAN HOSPITAL CONVOYS

Section 7.18 reproduces the wording of Article 21 of the GC in requiring respect and protection for land and sea civilian hospital convoys, noting that the vehicles do not have to be permanently used for medical purposes, but must be exclusively so used at the relevant times. Loss of protection for such convoys involves the same considerations as apply to civilian hospitals, with the same warning requirement.[62]

CIVILIAN MEDICAL AIRCRAFT

Section 7.19 repeats Article 22 GC's prohibition of attacking aircraft exclusively employed for the removal of wounded and sick civilians, the infirm and

62 *DoD Manual*, paragraph 7.18.1. The authority for this provision is the reference in Article 21 of GC to these convoys, trains or vessels being respected and protected 'in the same manner as the hospitals provided for in article 18' of GC, i.e. civilian hospitals.

maternity cases, or for transporting medical personnel and equipment. They must be respected if flying at heights, at times and on routes specifically agreed between the parties to the conflict.[63] The *Manual* notes that such aircraft may be marked with the distinctive emblem, that flights over enemy or enemy-controlled territory are prohibited unless otherwise agreed and that instructions to land must be obeyed.[64] If, on inspection, such an aircraft is found to have committed acts harmful to the enemy, it loses Convention protection; the aircraft may be seized, and the crew and passengers may be interned.[65]

API PROVISIONS ON THE WOUNDED, SICK AND SHIPWRECKED

Section 7.20 acknowledges that Part II of API addresses the wounded, sick and shipwrecked, but states that such provisions have not been referred to in the foregoing sections of Chapter VII 'because the United States is not a party to API'. While the fact that the US is not party to API precludes the application of treaty-based rules in that instrument as a matter of treaty law, any such rules that have achieved customary law status will as a result apply to the US, so whether that arises in relation to particular rules discussed in paragraphs 7.20.1 to 7.20.3 ought therefore to have been considered, arguably in the sections of the *Manual* to which they relate. Nevertheless, these paragraphs do summarise the Protocol's relevant rules in relatively brief terms.

63 GC, Article 22(1). Indeed, known civilian medical aircraft must be respected and protected if they identify themselves and comply with enemy State directions; *DoD Manual*, paragraph 7.19.1.

64 GC, Article 22(2) to (4).

65 *DoD Manual*, paragraph 7.19.4; *GC Commentary*, page 177.

8

Detention – Overview and Baseline Rules

Chapter VIII represents, in the opinion of the present authors, an honest attempt to provide sufficient protection of detainees by reference to the rules that are recognised therein. The chapter does not make significant reference to the human rights law position in relation to detention. This is consistent with the entirely arguable US position according to which human rights do not apply extra-territorially. Nevertheless, there are certain criticisms of the chapter that can properly be made.

Readers of the *Manual* from States that are subject to the jurisdiction of the European Court of Human Rights will take particular interest in how the *Manual* addresses the law applicable to detention operations, and may feel that its failure to address the human rights aspects represents a failure to address what in contemporary practice for numerous States is the core legal issue. The *Manual*, however, is intended to express the US legal position, and the fact that the human rights dimension to the topic is largely ignored in Chapter VIII illustrates how the perspectives of the US differ from those of States subject to the more immediate enforcement of human rights that, for example, participation in the European Convention on Human Rights involves.

INTRODUCTION

As section 8.1 makes clear, detention operations can arise in a variety of operational circumstances to which diverse legal regimes apply. Law in some form will apply to all such activities, but Chapter VIII's stated aim is to relate what it describes as 'baseline rules' that will apply to the detention of persons during military operations in general. DoD policies and regulations are stated to be authoritative, to fill out the requirements of Common Article 3 and of customary law and to exceed in many cases legal requirements. Indeed, US practice is described as going beyond minimalist legal compliance, consistently with security concerns.[1] So, the *Manual* suggests that the source for the baseline standards discussed in Chapter VIII is Common Article 3, reflecting minimum standards for humane treatment applying to all military operations, customary law, US law and national policy, and that the standards are 'animated' by the humanity principle.[2]

The precise intended focus of Chapter VIII is, however, unclear. In paragraph 8.1.1, the chapter is stated to address detention of persons who have participated in hostilities or who belong to armed groups 'but who are not entitled to POW status or protected person status in international armed conflict'; to detention of persons held for reasons related to a non-international armed conflict; and to 'any other detentions'. So, the reader is left with the distinct impression that the chapter is covering all detentions in all classes of conflict. Occasional references to GPW, to GC, to API, to APII and to later chapters of the *Manual* dealing with e.g. PWs and detained civilians reinforce that impression. It is therefore noteworthy that the suggested rules do not always fully reflect, or even refer to, apparently relevant treaty provisions by which the US is bound as a State party. If the chapter were intended only to address situations that lie outside the GPW and GC scope of application, this should have been explicitly stated. Indeed, on a topic of this importance, and given the profile that the topic of detention has achieved by virtue of controversies associated with recent conflicts, it is a little surprising that the ambiguities and perhaps inaccuracies noted in the present chapter should have remained unaddressed.

Paragraph 8.1.3 looks at the detention of persons who are not PWs and who are not civilians being detained either in the belligerent's own territory or in occupied territory. The use of the term 'belligerent' here implies that an armed conflict is taking place at the time of such detention, so the law of war will apply to both stated circumstances. The paragraph suggests that applicable *ad hoc* legal instruments may include an agreement between the detaining State and a host State[3] or provision in a UN Security Council resolution. The *Manual* then notes that the authority to detain may be found in *ad hoc* legal instruments, either specifically or as an incident of general authorisations, such as an agreement or UN Security Council Resolution authorising

[1] DoD *Manual*, paragraph 8.1.2. [2] DoD *Manual*, paragraphs 8.1.4 and 8.1.4.1.

[3] DoD *Manual*, paragraph 8.1.3.2 suggests that such an agreement might provide for the application of GPW or GC, essentially by analogy and for the purposes of the particular conflict, or that it might prescribe additional requirements in relation to detainee transfers.

the conduct of military operations on the territory of another State; alternatively, it may be based on sovereign authority.[4]

Judgments in the course of recent proceedings before the UK courts have questioned the existence of a legal authority to detain in the context of non-international armed conflicts.[5] It is therefore particularly helpful to see the legal right to detain being robustly asserted in paragraph 8.1.3.1.

Paragraph 8.1.4.2 is expressed in distinctly opaque terms and needs to be examined carefully both for what it is and, more importantly, for what it is not telling the reader. It states that the United States 'will choose out of a sense of legal obligation to treat the principles set forth in article 75 [of API] as applicable to any individual it detains in an international armed conflict, and expect all other nations to adhere to these principles as well'. The paragraph goes on to state that these words, originally taken from a White House Fact Sheet relating to detention of individuals at Guantanamo Bay and dated 7 March 2011, were intended to contribute to the crystallisation of the principles in Article 75 as principles of customary international law in international armed conflict. Two questions emerge. First, does the US consider that the Article 75 principles have now become customary, and if not, why not? It is unfortunate that the *Manual* does not take the opportunity to make this clear. Second, why, if the US is prepared to abide by what it regards as fundamental guarantees in relation to international armed conflicts, is it not prepared to state in this section that similar guarantees apply, again as a matter of customary law, in non-international armed conflicts? Why should guarantees seen as fundamental not also protect detainees taken prisoner in non-international armed conflicts? Such prisoners are, after all, every bit as vulnerable as their international armed conflict equivalents. Moreover, the reference in the quoted text to 'legal obligation' implies a US belief that the rules already have customary law status, given that absent that status, and absent US ratification of API, there would be no legal – as opposed to policy – basis for regarding the rules as binding either on the US or, for that matter, on all other States. So, this is a paragraph that perplexes, and it would be good to see the relevant messages clarified. For the avoidance of any doubt, it is the position of the present authors that the Article 75 principles have so crystallised and that they apply to all States in both international and non-international armed conflicts as a matter of customary law.

4 *DoD Manual*, paragraph 8.1.3.

5 *Serdar Mohammed* v. *Ministry of Defence*, [2014] EWHC 1369 (QB); but see the UK Supreme Court Judgment *Abd Ali Hameed Al-Waheed (Appellant)* v. *Ministry of Defence (Respondent)* and *Serdar Mohammed (Respondent)* v. *Ministry of Defence (Appellant)*, [2017] UKSC 2, pp. 56–7, paragraph 111.

Paragraph 8.1.4.4 notes that there may be good reasons to apply by analogy certain provisions of GPW and GC in circumstances to which they do not directly apply. This is particularly true if the relevant provision gives protection to individuals that would be lacking absent the drawing of the relevant analogy. Regrettably, footnote 19 on page 420 might lead one to the opposite conclusion. There, President G W Bush, in a Memorandum on the Humane Treatment of Taliban and al Qaeda detainees dated 7 February 2002, is cited – one has to assume, with approval – as reaffirming the order 'that the detainees be treated humanely and, to the extent appropriate and consistent with military necessity, in a manner consistent with the principles of Geneva'. This statement merits careful consideration. The requirement for humane treatment is admittedly not being subjected to any caveat and is shown to encompass cruel, inhumane, degrading treatment, violence, torture, rape, enforced prostitution, indecent assault, exposure to public curiosity, biological and medical experiments and adverse distinctions. The cited text indicates, however, that compliance with the unspecified 'principles of Geneva', which presumably includes compliance with numerous rules in the various Conventions, is subject to some notion of military need and may even be departed from if it is considered – by whom is not made clear – that it is appropriate to do so. Again, appropriate for what purpose, convenience, need etc. is not made clear. It is an established tenet of the law of war that military necessity is reflected already in all of its rules and that perceptions as to military necessity are no excuse for departure from them. It is suggested that the *Manual*'s authors should think again about the appropriateness of this footnote.

Paragraph 8.1.4.5 appropriately draws attention to the multi-nation Copenhagen initiative to formulate principles and guidelines on the handling of detainees in international military operations. It is correctly pointed out that the Copenhagen Principles and Guidelines do not constitute a legally binding text and that they are intended to apply to international military operations in respect of non-international armed conflicts and peace operations. However, many of the propositions in the text will have legal status either because of their customary nature or to the extent that they are reflected in treaties binding a particular State.

HUMANE TREATMENT OF DETAINEES

The obligation of humane treatment of detainees is addressed in section 8.2, which groups a number of kinds of treatment as breaches of that headline obligation. The *Manual* notes that the obligation is reflected in international law, national law and national and DoD policy, but in the context of the first of these only cites Common Article 3,[6] avoiding any mention of human rights law obligations. This approach certainly marks a significant difference of legal position, or interpretation, as against European States.

Violence, torture, cruel treatment, murder, mutilation, corporal punishment, outrages upon personal dignity such as humiliating or degrading treatment, rape, enforced prostitution, indecent or sexual assault, insults and exposure to public curiosity, biological or medical experiments and threats to commit inhumane treatment are all described in the *Manual* as examples of inhumane treatment.[7] In each case, the prohibition is simply stated and relevant conventional law is cited in a footnote; perhaps in relation to some of the prohibited activities, a little more guidance as to their interpretation might have been offered. Paragraph 8.2.5, however, correctly interprets the duty to protect detainees as including protection against acts by the population or other detainees. It is noteworthy that the prohibition of making adverse distinctions, recorded in paragraph 8.2.6, cites Article 75(1) of API, although to be fair the reader is only invited to 'consider' that provision.[8] The principal cited authority is Common Article 3.

SECURITY MEASURES

The lawfulness of searching detainees and their property is asserted, rightly, in paragraph 8.3.1, recognising that such searches must respect the dignity and honour of the detainee, must not be indecent and that it may be appropriate to have a witness present to protect both the searcher and the person being searched. The appropriateness of female detainees being searched by females is noted, but curiously no corresponding recommendation is made in relation to the search of male detainees.[9] The lawfulness, under the law of war, of temporarily securing detainees with handcuffs, flex cuffs, blindfolds or other security devices is correctly asserted. However, this is another topic on which a European reader might have expected to see some discussion of the human rights law position, a discussion that is absent from this part of the *Manual*.[10]

6 *DoD Manual*, footnote 25 on page 492.

7 *DoD Manual*, paragraphs 8.2.1 to 8.2.4.

8 *DoD Manual*, footnote 40 on page 494. It is right that non-adverse distinctions and distinctions in favour of the more vulnerable are not prohibited; *DoD Manual*, paragraph 8.2.6, parts 2 and 3.

9 *DoD Manual*, paragraph 8.3.1.1. This probably reflects the rule in Article 97(4) of GC that a woman detainee may be searched only by a woman, which does not address the searching of male detainees.

10 Reference is, however, made by the *Manual* to the Copenhagen Process Principles and Guidelines, paragraph 2.2, which note that sensory deprivation may in some circumstances

Paragraph 8.3.4 deals with the tricky subject of the use of force against detainees. Citing the Copenhagen Principles and Guidelines, the paragraph starts correctly by saying only necessary and proportionate force may be used and that any use of weapons must be preceded by a warning. Non-lethal weapons, including riot control agents, may however be used against rioting detainees,[11] although presumably the warning referred to in the previous sentence must be given. Perhaps more importantly, the *Manual* should make the point that if the rioting is directly connected with the conduct of hostilities, such that the use of a riot control agent could be classed as a method of warfare, such use would be prohibited for that reason.

INTERROGATION

Section 8.4 correctly asserts the lawfulness of interrogation of detainees as such, and notes that they must be accorded humane treatment and must not therefore be subjected to torture, cruelty, degrading treatment or threats or acts of violence. It would have been sensible to refer specifically to GPW, Article 17(4), which provides that '[n]o physical or mental torture, nor any other form of coercion, may be inflicted on prisoners of war to secure from them information of any kind whatever. Prisoners who refuse to answer may not be threatened, insulted, or exposed to unpleasant or disadvantageous treatment of any kind.' Accepting that PWs are but one of the possible classes of detainee, nevertheless the law applicable to them has been considered elsewhere in the chapter, and the problem with the *Manual*'s formulation is that it leaves the reader with the impression that there are kinds of coercion that it would be lawful to apply, impliedly to PWs as well as to other detainees, provided that they fall short of inhumane treatment. That would be a legally inaccurate impression, in the opinion of the present authors.

The unreliability of information obtained by torture is emphasised, and rightly so.[12] Indeed, it is made clear that only interrogation treatment or techniques authorised and listed in the *US Army Field Manual on Intelligence Interrogation* may be used. As is well known, certain interrogation methods have attracted severe criticism to the armed forces of the US, and indeed of other States.[13] It is of vital importance that authorised techniques be limited to

amount to ill treatment if employed as a punishment or to inflict suffering. As to the legitimacy of the hooding of detainees and of applying stress positions to them in connection with interrogation, see the Report of the Baha Mousa Inquiry, available at https://www.gov.uk/government/uploads/system/uploads/attachment_data/file/279190/1452_i.pdf.

[11] *DoD Manual*, paragraph 8.3.4.1. [12] *DoD Manual*, footnote 52 on page 496.

[13] Consider Report of the Baha Mousa Inquiry, n. 10.

those that are indeed legally acceptable, that interrogations be properly supervised and that the policy be properly enforced. An examination of the relevant section of the *Field Manual* lies outside the scope of the present volume, but would be necessary to determine whether the first of these requirements has been met. Perhaps the *Manual* should discuss GPW Article 17(4) and should then explain whether, in the US view, similar rules should apply to the questioning of other detainees and if not, should explain why not. Arguably, it should also explain what limits in fact do apply to the questioning of security detainees. This is, it must be stressed, a matter of legal and reputational importance.

The obligation to provide detainees with adequate food, drinking water and clothing is noted in summary form in section 8.5, but is discussed later in sections 9.13 and 10.13. Likewise, paragraph 8.6.1 notes the obligation to afford safeguards as to detainees' health and hygiene, giving examples of appropriate measures and the obligations to afford detainees protection against the rigors of the climate and to avoid locating them close to the combat zone. Paragraph 8.6.4 states that subject to certain requirements discussed earlier, 'there is no prohibition against the humane detention of persons on ships'. It would be more accurate to link this specifically to the detention of civilians. Where detention of PWs is concerned, the paragraph continues: 'The GPW generally requires that POWs be interned in premises located on land.' Perhaps the *Manual* might usefully make the point somewhat differently by stating that while usually detention should be on land, in compliance with the treaty requirement, in certain unusual circumstances, temporary periods of detention on ships may offer the best available conditions and protection for the detainees and would therefore be permissible as a temporary measure until transfer to detention on land can be arranged in appropriately safe conditions.

Section 8.7 deals with the general rule that women should be detained separately from men, subject to the situation where detained families are being detained together, noting that the segregation topic is addressed specifically in relation to PWs and civilian detainees in later chapters.

MEDICAL CARE

Having noted the general obligation to accord to the wounded and sick the medical care and attention required by their condition, section 8.8 states that medical care should where possible be with the consent of the detainee; '[h]owever, medical actions to preserve the health of the detainee may be justified even where the detainee refuses to provide consent.' States that are party to API should recall Article 11(5), which of course only applies in international armed conflict, and which stipulates that persons who are in the power of the adverse party or who are interned, detained or otherwise deprived of liberty 'have the right to refuse any surgical operation'. However, vaccinations and feeding may, according to the *Manual*, be ordered, in the latter case when the individual undertakes a hunger strike. For a State party to API, this would appear to be correct so long as the feeding method employed does not amount to or involve a surgical operation. As footnote 72 makes clear, forced feeding is subject to certain safeguards; namely, there must be a medical determination that immediate intervention is necessary to prevent death or serious harm, and there must be commanding officer approval or approval by the senior officer responsible for detention operations.

Paragraph 8.8.2 states that detainees may voluntarily give blood or skin for grafting, but properly draws attention in footnote 73 to API, Article 11's particular provisions on the subject.

Section 8.9 notes that procedures for disciplining detainees, discussed later, may be established, and that, applying the Copenhagen Principles and Guidelines, a complaints process that does not involve reprisals against detainees who complain should be set up. The second sentence of paragraph 8.9.1, although taken from the Principles and Guidelines, may not quite state what is, it is suggested, the real point. It might be preferable to say that a properly administered process enables detainees' complaints to be made, investigated and addressed in a timely way, whereas evidence may no longer be available and memories may have faded if complaints are first raised many years after the event.

Section 8.10 properly reflects the applicable law as to contact by detainees with the outside world, through individual or collective relief, correspondence, communication with family and ICRC access, referring to discussion of some of these issues in later chapters concerning PWs and civilian internees.[14] The exercise of these rights is stated to be subject to security measures, practical considerations and other military necessities, a rather wide and somewhat loosely expressed range of possible limitations, not all of which would, it is suggested, satisfy the applicable law. With the exception of video conferencing, electronic social media communication options are not considered in this section, which, given the spectrum of modern communication methods, would seem to be a significant omission.

Section 8.11 discusses detainees' rights in relation to religious practice and noticeably places significant reliance in footnotes on DoD Directives; the treaty authorities cited tend to come from Common Article 3 and APII, which

[14] The section cites APII, Article 5 and Common Article 3.

contain the limited legal provisions of treaty law relating to non-international armed conflicts. It would arguably have been more appropriate to cite the treaty provisions applicable in international armed conflict. So, while APII, Article 5 and API, Article 75(1) are quoted, largely in terms,[15] one wonders why no mention is made here of Article 18 of the Hague Regulations 1907,[16] of Articles 33 to 37 of GPW or of Articles 86 and 93 of GC.

Intellectual, physical and recreational facility requirements are summarised at section 8.12, and Guantanamo camp arrangements are cited in an associated footnote. No mention is made of the requirements in Article 38 of GPW, nor of Article 94 of GC. The topic is, however, discussed in specific sections later in the *Manual*, to which cross-references are made.

In relation to working conditions, section 8.13 again does not seem to be expressing all of the applicable law. It refers to detainees having the benefit of working conditions and safeguards 'similar' to those enjoyed by the domestic population. Article 51 GPW goes further, requiring that working conditions for PWs be suitable especially as regards accommodation, food, clothing and equipment, that such conditions shall not be inferior to those enjoyed by nationals of the Detaining Power; that account be taken of climatic conditions; that national labour protection and worker safety legislation be applied; that training and means of protection be given as accorded to nationals of the Detaining Power; and that labour conditions shall not be rendered more arduous by disciplinary measures.

This section should also have made specific reference to GC, Articles 40 and 95, and to GC, Article 51 in relation to occupied territory. In short, the safeguards in the applicable treaty law by which the US is bound are arguably much more extensive than this somewhat short section would imply. The prohibitions of slavery and of enforced prostitution are, however, noted.

Section 8.14, having correctly stated that detainees must be promptly informed of the grounds for their detention, suggests that a person can, *inter alia*, be interned on the grounds of association with an armed group (what degree or nature of association is not made clear)[17] and, perhaps more

[15] *DoD Manual*, footnote 85 on page 502 explains the detailed arrangements made at the Guantanamo Camp to facilitate Islamic religious observance by the detainees.

[16] 'Prisoners of War shall enjoy complete freedom in the exercise of their religion, including attendance at the services of whatever church they may belong to, on the sole condition that they comply with measures of order and police issued by the military authorities'; Hague Regulations 1907, Article 18.

[17] *DoD Manual*, footnote 93 on page 503 refers to the Chairman's Commentary to the Copenhagen Principles and Guidelines, which, in turn, refer to belonging to an enemy organised armed group, but not to mere association with one.

surprisingly, on the ground that he or she is a witness in law enforcement proceedings. The permitted ground for the detention of a combatant stems from that combatant's status and associated role. Article 42 of GC makes it clear that internment of civilians during an international armed conflict is only permissible if the security of the Detaining Power makes it absolutely necessary or if the person concerned demands internment and if his or her situation renders it necessary. Treaty law does not specify the permitted grounds for detention in non-international armed conflicts. The domestic law of the relevant territory, supplemented by applicable human rights law, will limit the permissible circumstances.

Paragraph 8.14.2 explains that DoD practice has been periodically to review the detention of all persons not granted PW status. That statement ought to have made reference to Article 43 of GC, which refers to civilian detainees and which grants any protected person who has been detained the right to have the detention reconsidered 'as soon as possible by an appropriate court or administrative board designated by the Detaining Power for that purpose'. The article then specifies that if the internment is maintained, that body shall 'periodically, and at least twice yearly' consider the person's case with a view to amending the decision if circumstances permit.[18] So, initial and periodic review of persons protected by GC are mandated by law, not mere exercise of voluntary DoD policy. Such review arrangements are not provided for in the law of war in relation to non-international armed conflicts. Arguably, applicable domestic and human rights law will determine whether and, if so, with what frequency and according to what arrangements such reviews should take place. So, the nature of the conflict and the status of the person concerned will determine what review arrangements are called for, and the paragraph should arguably have made that clear. The authority conducting the review of security detainees in a non-international armed conflict may indeed be 'the military commander', as the *Manual* suggests, or more likely an official with suitable training. The cited extract from the Chairman's Commentary to the Copenhagen Process gives good guidance as to the factors that will influence the frequency of detention reviews. It would have been helpful to include in paragraph 8.14.2 a reference to the suggested 6 months' period, as this gives at least some practical guidance to those seeking to make appropriate arrangements.

Paragraph 8.14.3 correctly sets forth the law pertaining to release of persons who have been detained, and refers to some important practical aspects of

[18] The article also requires, subject to certain conditions, that the court or board's decision be notified to the Protecting Powers.

proper and orderly release. Paragraph 8.14.4 deals very briefly with transfer of detainees. It mentions a US policy of not transferring where it is 'more likely than not' that the detainee would be tortured in the receiving State. One cannot help thinking that the paragraph should have drawn the reader's attention to GPW, Article 12(2) and (3) and the obligations of the transferring State to satisfy itself of the ability and willingness of the transferee State to apply the Convention and to take corrective measures in the event the transferee fails in that regard. Similarly, mention should have been made of Article 45 of GC, in particular paragraph (4)'s absolute prohibition of transfer 'to a country where he or she may have reason to fear persecution for his or her political opinions or religious beliefs'. The reference, cited earlier, to 'more likely than not' does not therefore accurately state the position in relations to PWs and interned civilians in international armed conflicts. Moreover, it would be difficult to understand why these clear non-refoulement obligations in international armed conflicts should have no parallel in customary non-international armed conflict law.

Section 8.15 notes the obligation to register detainees within a reasonable time and the requirement to maintain an inventory of their possessions.

CRIMINAL PROCEDURE AND PUNISHMENT

Section 8.16 starts with the basic rule in Common Article 3(d) of the Geneva Conventions. That rule limits itself, however, to the passing of sentences and the carrying out of executions. Article 75(4) of API, which the US accepts and which is otherwise widely accepted as customary law in international and non-international armed conflicts, states that '[n]o sentence may be passed and no penalty may be executed on a person found guilty of a penal offence related to the armed conflict except pursuant to a conviction pronounced by an impartial and regularly constituted court respecting the generally recognised principles of regular judicial procedure'. Article 75(4) then lists ten examples of such principles. The Article 75 reference to penalties being executed seems to go wider than the rule in the *Manual*. Further, the *DoD Manual* rule does not require the court to be impartial, which may be an important shortcoming in some circumstances.

The *Manual* then lists some fundamental guarantees by way of examples. The requirement for individual criminal responsibility is accurately stated and well explained.[19] It cites the requirement that the act be a criminal offence at

[19] *DoD Manual*, paragraph 8.16.2.1, reflecting API, Article 75(4)(b).

the time of its commission and states the prohibition of duplicitous proceedings in terms taken from API.[20] Limitations provided for in APII, Article 6(4) on the imposition of the death penalty are repeated in paragraph 8.16.2.4. API, Article 75(4)(a)'s language is repeated as to the right of the accused person to particulars of the alleged offence and to means of defence.[21] Paragraphs 8.16.3.1 to 8.16.3.6 restate verbatim the principles in Article 75(4)(d) to (g), (i) and (j), respectively.

CONCLUDING REMARKS

This is a chapter that may benefit from some revision. It would be helpful if its intended scope could be defined more precisely. Perhaps it is in the wrong position, in the sense that it might be preferable to start with the discussions of the specific rights that the law accords to PWs and civilian detainees in international armed conflicts and to follow them with a succeeding chapter that specifically considers the rights of detainees to whom the preceding chapters do not apply.

[20] *DoD Manual*, paragraphs 8.16.2.2 and 8.16.2.3, reflecting API, Article 75(4)(c) and (h).
[21] The word 'notice' in the *Manual*'s text is clearly a misprint and should read 'offence'.

9

Prisoners of War

INTRODUCTION

The law applicable to PWs is of great importance. Experience associated with the Vietnam War caused PW treatment to be a sensitive issue in the United States. Events arising from more recent conflicts have done nothing to diminish this sensitivity.

Chapter IX of the *Manual* starts with some observations as to the evolution of the law relating to PWs. The 1929 Geneva Convention and GPW are of course the most important texts on the subject, and API addresses combatant and PW status in Articles 43 to 47.

Turning to the substance of the chapter, paragraph 9.1.2.1, although it would benefit from minor rephrasing in a couple of respects, makes the essentially accurate point that 'prisoner of war' is a term of art defined and used in GPW. Paragraph 9.1.2.2 lists the numerous topics on which agreements may be concluded between the parties, adopting the language of Article 6 of GPW. The essential point is that no such special agreement may adversely affect the situation or rights of PWs under GPW. Paragraph 9.1.3 draws the reader's attention to DoD policies and regulations on the treatment of PWs, which, the *Manual* asserts, exceed the requirements of GPW, US statutes and Executive orders in many cases.

GENERAL PRINCIPLES APPLICABLE TO THE TREATMENT OF PWs

Section 9.2 suggests some general principles as the basis for the rules governing the treatment of PWs. These are that their detention is non-punitive in character; that PWs are in the hands of the enemy Power, not of the military unit or individuals who captured them, and that that Power is responsible for their treatment; that PWs retain responsibilities to the Power on which they depend, while being obliged to obey the laws, regulations and orders of the Detaining Power; that humane treatment of PWs is a fundamental principle; and that PWs should be treated as the Detaining Power would wish its own personnel in enemy hands to be treated.[1]

ENTITLEMENT TO PW STATUS

Section 9.3 distinguishes between the entitlement of some classes of individual to PW status and the according of protection to other persons who are not so entitled. The first group to be considered is those entitled, in the US view, to PW status when in the hands of the adverse party. The list in paragraph 9.3.2 is expressed in non-exhaustive but summarised terms and comprises the six categories of person listed in Article 4A of GPW. A State that is party to API is bound by the understandings of armed forces and of combatants set forth in Article 43 of that treaty. Persons who are combatants under those definitions must be accorded PW status by an API State on capture. Thus, while there will be differences of understanding as to PW status on capture as between e.g. the US and API States party, in the majority of cases, similar determinations will be reached. Nevertheless, and given the frequency with which the US is involved in alliance and coalition operations with States party to API, one would have thought that these differences of interpretation ought to have been at least mentioned in this paragraph of the *Manual*.

Paragraph 9.3.2.1 correctly asserts that spies, saboteurs, persons engaged in similar missions behind enemy lines and nationals of the Detaining Power or of its co-belligerents are not entitled to PW status on capture. Paragraph 9.3.2.2 suggests that certain other classes of individual are not necessarily excluded from PW status on capture. Mercenaries appear in this list; however, for a State party to API, mercenaries coming within the definition in Article 47(2) of that treaty 'shall not have the right to be a combatant or a prisoner of war'.[2] Again, one would have thought that some reference at least should have been made to this provision that binds the overwhelming majority of States. Next are persons alleged to have committed war crimes. It would perhaps be more accurate to say that an allegation that a prisoner has committed war crimes is irrelevant to PW status.[3] Finally, the list includes persons whose capture has not been acknowledged by the Power to which they belong. Again, it would

[1] *DoD Manual*, paragraphs 9.2.1 to 9.2.5. [2] API, Article 47(1).

[3] This interpretation is certainly consistent with API, Articles 44(1) and (2) and 45, and there is no known provision of the law of armed conflict that would have the effect that an accusation of commission of a war crime deprives a detained person of PW status.

have been more accurate to say that such failure to acknowledge is irrelevant to the PW status of the affected individual on capture by the enemy. The 'not necessarily excluded' language in the paragraph chapeau leaves their suggested status altogether too open in the opinion of the present authors.

GPW then lists, in Article 4B, two additional classes of detained person who, although not PWs, are to be treated as PWs, namely persons who belong or belonged to the armed forces of the occupied country, if the Occupying Power considers internment necessary because of such allegiance, and persons listed in Article 4 who have been received by and are required to be interned by neutral or non-belligerent Powers. Paragraph 9.3.3 reflects this rule accurately. Paragraph 9.3.4.1 usefully notes that Article 4A of GPW is concerned with persons 'who have fallen into the power of the enemy', a notion that does not extend to individuals who, of their own choice, have defected to the enemy and have joined the enemy armed forces. While undoubtedly such persons place themselves thereby in the power of what was formerly their adverse party, they cannot be said to have 'fallen' into its power and do not have PW status there. Capture by armed forces, civilian police or local civilian defence organisations can place a person in the power of the enemy, and as noted in Article 4B(2) of GPW, persons interned by neutrals are entitled to PW treatment. The *Manual* goes on to suggest that members of a peace operation detained by a State party to the conflict should receive PW treatment by analogy.[4]

Paragraphs 9.3.5 and 9.3.6 restate the Article 5 GPW provisions as to the duration of GPW protection and as to the determination of PW status in situations of doubt. It might have been useful here to state what arrangements the United States applies by way of a 'competent tribunal' to resolve cases of doubt as to PW status. Paragraph 9.3.7 then restates the Article 7 GPW rule that PWs may not renounce their rights under the GPW, noting the vulnerable position PWs are in, that establishing the voluntary nature of a renunciation would be difficult and that the absolute prohibition serves the interests of the majority. The paragraph notes that the rule only protects those who have fallen into the power of the enemy, and would not apply to an individual defecting to the

[4] *DoD Manual*, paragraphs 9.3.4.2 and 9.3.4.3. However, if United Nations personnel, as defined in Article 1, are captured or detained in the course of the performance of their duties, they shall not be interrogated and shall be promptly released and returned to the UN or other appropriate authorities. Pending release, they must be treated in accordance with applicable human rights law and the Geneva Conventions; Convention on the Safety of United Nations and Associated Personnel, New York, 9 December 1994, Article 8. Arguably, this provision should have been mentioned, at least in a footnote, to ensure that the reader is not left with the impression that the detention of peacekeepers in breach of Article 8 is legitimate.

enemy side before capture. This accurately states the position, in the sense that a person who only purports to defect to the enemy side after capture will clearly come within the rule, and will thus be prevented from renouncing his or her PW rights.

NATIONAL-LEVEL GPW IMPLEMENTATION

Section 9.4 starts, in paragraph 9.4.1, with a valuable list of five bodies or entities that parties to an international armed conflict are required by GPW to establish, all of which are considered in later paragraphs of the *Manual*.[5] In logical fashion, paragraph 9.4.2 then lists certain legal or policy matters relating to PWs that must be notified to the opposing belligerent or to the Protecting Power. These are the policy on parole, the offences that carry the death penalty, the location and marking of PW camps, the requirements for the validity of wills, titles and ranks of persons entitled to PW treatment and the ranks of persons entitled to retained personnel treatment. All of these matters are dealt with more specifically elsewhere in the *Manual*.[6] Paragraph 9.4.2.6 then deals with the obligation of the Detaining Power to inform PWs and the Power on which they depend of how the GPW requirements as to correspondence and relief shipments will be implemented.[7]

Paragraph 9.4.3 notes the GPW, Article 17 requirement for each party to the conflict to issue to each person under its jurisdiction liable to become a PW an identity card, and quotes the details that such a card is required to contain. The paragraph observes the US practice of issuing all members of the US armed forces with what it calls 'identification cards', but it should be recalled that entitlement to PW status on capture also extends to the persons mentioned in Article 4A(4) and (5) of GPW, and if, in the circumstances, such persons are also liable to be taken prisoner, they should also be issued with an identity card.

HUMANE TREATMENT AND BASIC PROTECTIONS FOR PWs

Section 9.5 restates the principle that PWs must be treated at all times humanely and with respect for their persons and honour. Paragraph 9.5.2.2 and the opening sentences of section 9.5 specify the requirement to protect

[5] See *DoD Manual*, paragraphs 18.15.1.1, 9.31.2, 9.31.3, 9.36.5 and 9.34.4.

[6] See *DoD Manual*, paragraphs 9.11.2 and 9.39.1.3, 9.28.6, 9.11.4.2 and 3, 9.21.2.1, 9.22.4.1 and 7.9.5.7, respectively.

[7] This it does using the language in GPW, Article 69.

them against violence (including from the civilian population and from other PWs), intimidation, insults and public curiosity. Paragraph 9.5.2.1, citing and reflecting language from the 1958 *UK Manual*, repeats the absolute prohibition of killing PWs e.g. on grounds of self-preservation or because their presence is impeding the force's movement and notwithstanding the military advantage that might accrue therefrom. The paragraph correctly states that older sources of law that permitted commanders in dire circumstances to deny quarter do not reflect the current law. It would perhaps have been better if the *Manual* had gone on to note that killing of PWs is widely recognised as a grave breach of GPW and thus as a war crime.[8]

Paragraph 9.5.2.3 notes the obligation not to send a PW to, or detain him or her in, areas exposed to the fire of the combat zone, as provided for in GPW, Article 23(1). In the next paragraph, 9.5.2.4, the prohibition of physical mutilation and of medical, scientific and biological experiments is stated in similar terms to the third sentence of Article 13(1) GPW. The words 'in particular' appear in that sentence of the article to show that it is particularising the humane treatment and associated rule in the first two sentences of the article. These words make little sense as used in the *Manual*, as the paragraph 9.5.2.4 rule has, for unclear reasons, been somewhat isolated from its legal context. The paragraph does, however, make the proper distinction between the conduct of biological experiments and the application of novel treatments justified on medical grounds and undertaken for therapeutic purposes. Article 11 of API supports the view that PWs can lawfully give blood for transfusion or skin for grafting, but applies a number of conditions that must be satisfied. While the relevant parts of Article 11 are correctly quoted in a footnote, not all of API's conditions are reflected in the version of the rule given in the *Manual*'s main text. So, for example, while the requirement that the donation be voluntary is noted, the API requirement that generally accepted medical standards and controls must be applied is given in the *Manual* text in rather more optional language than in API by use of the word 'should', and the prohibition in API, Article 11(3) of coercion and inducement is omitted.

Paragraph 9.5.3 correctly states the Article 13 GPW obligation to protect PWs against acts of violence, intimidation, insults and public curiosity. It points out the wise US policy prohibiting photographing of detainees other than for authorised purposes, and in a footnote[9] gives examples of some clear breaches of these rules during past conflicts. The prohibition on

8 Consider GPW, Article 130; Statute of the International Criminal Tribunal for the Former Yugoslavia, 1993, Article 2(a); Statute of the International Criminal Tribunal for Rwanda, Article 4a.

9 *DoD Manual*, footnote 115 on page 527.

making adverse distinctions based on race, nationality, religious belief, political opinions or similar criteria is stated in paragraph 9.5.5 in terms that follow the wording of Article 16 GPW. The *Manual*, basing itself on the use in the rule of the word 'adverse', suggests that non-adverse distinctions would not be prohibited. The additional point should, perhaps, have been made that a distinction that is favourable to one individual or group, is likely, as a result, to be adverse to those who are not similarly advantaged. Much will inevitably depend on the particular facts. The example referred to of assembling prisoners in national, language etc. groups would generally satisfy the rule, as nobody is being either advantaged or disadvantaged. The need for the Detaining Power to make distinctions based on other attributes is properly noted. So, for example, and as paragraph 9.5.6 explains, women PWs must be treated with the regard due to their sex, and the GPW makes reference to separate dormitories and bathing facilities and to separate punitive confinement facilities supervised by women, and the *Manual*, properly going beyond the GPW, contends that women PWs should be under the immediate supervision of women.[10]

SECURITY MEASURES WITH RESPECT TO PWs

The right to search PWs for security, intelligence and administrative reasons is asserted again in paragraph 9.6.1. Examples are given of legitimate objects of such searches, and the obligation to maintain the dignity and honour of PWs as far as possible during such searches is properly emphasised. The advisability of appointing a witness to observe such searches for the protection of both searcher and PW is noted. Paragraph 9.6.1 suggests it is appropriate, when possible, for female PWs to be searched by female personnel. However, other provisions of the Convention stipulating the provision of separate conveniences for women PWs,[11] separate dormitories for them[12] and the requirement that female PWs under sentence be confined in separate quarters under the supervision of women[13] all would suggest that the search of a female PW must be virtually always undertaken by a woman, absent the most unusual and urgent of circumstances.

Paragraph 9.6.2 suggests that when this is necessary for security reasons – for example, to prevent escape or destruction of documents – PWs may be secured temporarily with handcuffs, flexi cuffs, blindfolds or other security devices. Such action would only, in the opinion of the present authors, be

10 Note, for example, GPW, Articles 14(2), 25(4), 29(2) and 97(4).
11 GPW, Article 29(2).
12 GPW, Article 25(4).
13 GPW, Article 108(2).

legitimate as an exceptional measure, such as in the immediate aftermath of capture, and is subject to the requirements to treat them humanely, to evacuate them as soon as possible to camps far enough from the combat zone to be out of danger and to do everything suitable to secure their safety.[14]

Paragraph 9.6.3 suggests that articles in the possession of PWs can be removed and searched for security and intelligence purposes, but that certain items must be returned as soon as possible. This paragraph does not seem to be correct. Article 18(1) of GPW makes it clear that '[a]ll effects and articles of personal use' except certain military equipment and documents 'shall remain in the possession of prisoners of war, likewise their metal helmets and gas masks and like articles used for personal protection'. They must also retain effects and articles used for their clothing or feeding, even if military in nature. Furthermore, they should never be without their identity documents.[15] Perhaps the preferable course would be simply to delete the paragraph, not least because it conflicts with paragraph 9.7.1, which correctly states the law, without indicating to the reader which of the two is to have precedence. Paragraph 9.7.4.1 correctly states that unexplained large sums of money found in the possession of PWs lead to the inference that the money is enemy government property or has been looted or stolen. US personnel reading that paragraph are likely to want to know what action should therefore be taken.

Paragraph 9.7.6 suggests that as a matter of best practice, things other than items of value and money withdrawn from PWs should be recorded with appropriate details to facilitate their return at a suitable time. This must be correct.

INTERROGATION OF PWs

As section 9.8 makes properly clear, the law of war does not prohibit interrogation of PWs, but imposes conditions and limitations. All interrogation must therefore comply with the humane treatment principle: there must be no violence, intimidation, insults, physical or mental torture, or any form of coercion to secure any kind of information from PWs. Article 17(4), (6) and (1) of GPW is stated, supplemented by three examples of prohibited treatment. It is correctly noted that, while a PW is required, when questioned on

[14] GPW, Articles 19 and 20. Consider also the Report of the Baha Mousa Inquiry, available at https://www.gov.uk/government/uploads/system/uploads/attachment_data/file/279190/1452_i.pdf.

[15] GPW, Article 18(2).

the matter, to state his or her surname, first names, rank, date of birth and army, regimental, personal or serial number or equivalent information, no form of coercion may be applied to compel the provision of even this information, other than restriction of privileges in accordance with Article 17(2). Nevertheless, the importance of the information in enabling the Detaining Power to fulfil obligations under GPW is properly stated.[16] Paragraph 9.8.4.1 then draws attention to the obligation to hand to the medical service PWs whose physical or mental condition renders them unable to state their identity.

EVACUATION FROM COMBAT AREAS

Section 9.9 deals with the requirements to evacuate PWs as soon as possible after capture, not to expose them to unnecessary danger, to delay evacuation only where wounds or sickness would render evacuation more risky than staying where they are, to effect the evacuation in conditions similar to those applying to changes of station of their own forces, to supply sufficient food, potable water, clothing and medical attention and to take suitable precautions to ensure their safety. These matters are covered in largely identical terms to Articles 19 and 20 of GPW, and the lawfulness of applying security measures such as handcuffs, flexi cuffs and blindfolding during evacuation is asserted.[17]

Paragraph 9.9.3 deals with the release of persons entitled to PW protection who fall into the possession of an adverse party to the conflict under unusual conditions of combat that prevent their evacuation. The paragraph states that such persons may be released subject to feasible precautions being taken to secure their safety. The associated footnote invites consideration of Article 41(3) of API, which requires release in the stated circumstances. The footnote, however, draws attention *inter alia* to paragraph 8.32.1, which correctly notes that the obligation to release does not apply where safe evacuation is only temporarily rendered impossible and, in agreement with paragraph 9.9.3.2, that there is a continuing obligation to do everything feasible to ensure the safety of PWs while they are in the custody of the Detaining Power.[18] So, if the PWs are released, the *Manual* tells us that the obligation is to 'take reasonable steps under the circumstances to help ensure the POWs' safety and survival', but, for example, a long-range reconnaissance patrol need not render itself militarily ineffective by handing over all its supplies to

[16] *DoD Manual*, paragraph 9.8.4. [17] *DoD Manual*, paragraph 9.9.2.
[18] *DoD Manual*, footnote 174 on page 535.

prisoners it has taken. This would seem to be a practicable and legally correct position. The *Manual* concludes this section with a useful statement of best practice as to taking feasible measures to record the names, serial numbers and unit affiliations of those captured, as well as brief particulars of the capture and release.[19]

TRANSIT OR SCREENING FACILITIES

Section 9.10 correctly notes that PWs may be sent to transit or screening facilities before going to a PW camp and that they 'are to be enabled to' send capture cards therefrom, i.e. that they have the right to do so. Citing Pictet, but adjusting his language, the *Manual* refers to such facilities often being established within a zone of military operations, in order to house PWs captured during fighting in that zone, and notes that due to proximity to the fighting, such facilities cannot always meet all requirements of the GPW, although they must provide reasonable protection from the effects of combat, basic sanitation, food and water. Article 24 GPW, as noted in paragraph 9.10.3, requires that transit or screening camps 'of a permanent kind' be fitted out under similar conditions to PW camps and that 'the prisoners therein shall have the same treatment as in other camps'. It is suggested that the section should remind the reader of Article 19(1) and (3), should emphasise that the facilities being referred to in paragraph 9.10.2 must be of a temporary nature and should avoid the current inference that transit camps in combat zones are routine arrangements as opposed to being limited to circumstances of necessity, as Pictet suggests.

Paragraph 9.10.4 correctly observes that PWs may temporarily be detained on board ships 'if operational or humanitarian needs dictate, pending a reasonable opportunity to transfer them to a shore facility' and acknowledges the general rule that they may be interned only in premises located on land.[20] The best interests of PWs would not be served by an absolute prohibition of all detention afloat where better protection e.g. from a severe climate or from combat can be provided on board ship.

GENERAL CONDITIONS IN PW CAMPS – LOCATION, SAFETY, HYGIENE AND LIVING CONDITIONS

Paragraphs 9.11.1 and 9.11.2 reproduce verbatim and in full Article 21 of GPW, where the right to intern PWs, the limited circumstances when they may be

[19] *DoD Manual*, paragraph 9.9.3.3.

[20] GPW, Article 22(1); *DoD Manual*, paragraph 9.10.4.

closely confined and the legal position as to the release of prisoners on parole or promise are set forth.[21] Paragraph 9.11.3 also restates the Article 22(1) GPW rule, identifying the underlying intent as to secure a relatively healthy, safe environment for PWs and arguing, persuasively, that ships can be used to transport or screen PWs. The paragraph suggests that detention aboard ship for PWs 'captured at sea or pending' the establishment of suitable land facilities is nonetheless consistent with the GPW. The present authors would suggest that the 'or' in the cited text should be replaced with 'and', meaning that detention at sea is only consistent with GPW for persons captured at sea pending the establishment of suitable land-based facilities.

PWs should not be detained in penitentiaries unless justified in their own interests;[22] while their detention is, as the *Manual* correctly notes, not punitive, a penitentiary may offer the most satisfactory option. For security, safety or military reasons, PWs may lawfully be detained outside the theatre of operations.[23] The *Manual* identifies the following measures to be taken to promote the safety of PWs: locating camps away from the combat zone; notifying the location of PW camps through the Protecting Powers; marking, subject to military considerations, such camps with 'PW', 'PG' or other agreed markings so as to be clearly visible from the air; providing air-raid shelters and other protection against hazards of war similar to that available to the civilian population; and implementing fire precautions.[24]

Paragraph 9.11.5 accurately brings together the general obligations of GPW, Articles 22(1) and 29(1) for the Detaining Power to intern PWs in premises offering guarantees of hygiene and healthfulness; where the area is unhealthy or the climate is injurious, to move them to a more favourable climate; and to take all necessary sanitary measures to ensure the cleanliness and healthfulness of camps and to prevent epidemics.[25] The role of PWs in assisting with the maintenance of hygiene is properly noted.

The requirements of Article 29(2) and (3) as to the provision and maintenance of hygienic and clean conveniences (i.e. latrines), as to bath, shower and laundry facilities and as to the availability of sufficient water and soap are reproduced in paragraphs 9.11.5.2 and 9.11.5.3. Paragraph 9.11.6 repeats the GPW, Article 25 requirements that the quartering arrangements for PWs, including as to dormitories, bedding, general installations and blankets, shall

[21] Paragraph 9.11.2 explains that US service personnel are prohibited from accepting parole or special favours from the enemy.

[22] DoD *Manual*, paragraph 9.11.3.2; GPW, 22(1).

[23] DoD *Manual*, paragraph 9.11.3.3.

[24] DoD *Manual*, paragraph 9.11.4; GPW, Articles 19(1), 23(3) and (4), 23(2) and 25(3).

[25] For example, by eradicating vermin and quarantining PWs suffering from infectious diseases.

be at least as favourable as those applying to the Detaining Power's own forces billeted in the same area, and that the premises be damp-free and adequately heated and lit.

Paragraph 9.11.6.1 states the Article 25(4) requirement that women PWs be provided separate dormitories.

SEGREGATION OF PWs

Section 9.12 starts the discussion of the segregation of PWs by reminding the reader of the prohibition of discrimination previously discussed at paragraph 9.5.5. The GPW, Article 22(3) obligation to assemble PWs in camps or compounds according to nationality, language and customs is correctly quoted, as is the Convention's proviso that PWs must not be separated from other PWs of the armed forces with which they were serving at the time of capture, except with their consent. As paragraph 9.12.1.1 acknowledges, there may be other reasons for the legitimate segregation of PWs, such as maintaining order, imposing punishment or for medical reasons. So, for example, as the *Manual* notes, where there is a major schism within the PW group, segregation on the basis of political opinion may be vital to ensuring the security of some prisoners.[26]

FOOD, WATER, TOBACCO AND CLOTHING FOR PWs

Paragraphs 9.13.1 to 9.13.3 largely reproduce the requirements of GPW, Article 26 as to the provision of an adequate quantity, quality and variety of food rations to maintain the health and weight of PWs and to prevent nutritional deficiencies. That additional necessary rations must be given to working PWs whose labour requires it; that account must be taken of the habitual diet of the prisoners; that sufficient drinking water must be supplied; that PWs must be associated as far as possible with the preparation of their meals; and that collective disciplinary measures affecting food are prohibited are all correctly referred to in these paragraphs. Reflecting more modern thinking as to the potential harm of passive inhalation, the *Manual* suggests that the Detaining Power may impose reasonable restrictions on smoking.

Paragraph 9.13.4.1 gives a complete and legally accurate explanation of the law on the provision of uniforms for PWs, noting that enemy uniforms

[26] *DoD Manual*, footnote 238 on page 544. The *Manual* also contemplates the segregation e.g. of deserters and of war crimes suspects.

acquired by the Detaining Power should be made available if suitable for the climate; that, if the Detaining Power's own uniforms are used, removal of insignia may well be appropriate; and that the arrangements made should respect PWs' persons and honour, and should not be humiliating or degrading. Working PWs should receive appropriate clothing if the nature of the work so demands.[27]

MEDICAL ATTENTION FOR INTERNED PWs

Section 9.14 makes the legally correct points that GWS applies in addition to the following specific rules and that irrespective of the availability of retained personnel, the Detaining Power is obliged to provide for the medical care of PWs.

Paragraph 9.14.1 notes the GPW, Article 30(1) requirement that each camp shall have an adequate infirmary and appropriate diet and the Article 30(4) statement that '[p]risoners of war may not be prevented from presenting themselves to the medical authorities for examination'. The *Manual* asserts this does not imply the right to be examined daily by a doctor and does not preclude disciplinary punishments if PWs abusively make groundless requests for examination. Pictet observes '[t]he text . . . is sufficiently clear; it is contrary to the Convention to prevent attendance at these examinations, whether by order of the Detaining Power or because of practical difficulties'.[28] If, as the present authors believe, that interpretation is correct, then disciplinary punishments designed to dissuade PWs from requesting medical examinations would indeed seem to be contrary to the letter and intent of the Convention provision. Nevertheless, it must be recognised that the making of persistent and perverse requests with the apparent aim of seeking to disrupt e.g. medical treatment arrangements within the facility will likely require firm, but sensitive and lawful, handling.

Paragraph 9.14.1.3 faithfully reproduces GPW, Article 31's obligation to hold medical examinations of PWs at least once a month, including recording of their weight and supervision of their general state of health. The GPW, Article 30(2) obligation to admit to any appropriate military or civilian medical unit PWs with serious diseases or who need special treatment, an operation or hospital care is reflected in paragraph 9.14.2.1, and the Article 30(3) stated preference that they be treated by medical personnel of the Power on which they depend – indeed, of their nationality – is repeated. The requirement for the Detaining Power, on request, to certify the nature of the

[27] *DoD Manual*, paragraph 9.13.4.2; GPW, Article 27(2). [28] *GPW Commentary*, 212.

illness or injury and the duration and nature of the treatment given is noted,[29] as is the fact that the costs of treatment must be borne by the Detaining Power.[30]

Paragraph 9.14.3 correctly notes the right of PWs to receive individual or collective shipments, which may include medical supplies. One can well imagine the wish of a PW's relatives to address promptly his or her known medical requirements in such a way. It would have been helpful if a footnote reference to GPW, Article 72(1) had been included here.

Paragraph 9.14.4 states that in certain cases of death or serious injury of a PW, an official inquiry shall be conducted by the Detaining Power. It would have been more accurate, and informative, to have noted here that any death or serious injury of a PW suspected to have been caused by another person, and any death where the cause is unknown, must immediately be the subject of an official enquiry by the Detaining Power.[31]

The provisions of GPW, Articles 34 and 37 as to the latitude accorded to PWs for the exercise of their religious duties, as to the requirement for the Detaining Power to provide adequate premises for religious services, as to the retention of chaplains to minister to them and, in default, as to the requirement to appoint at the request of the PWs concerned a minister belonging to their or a similar denomination or a qualified layman, subject to certain approvals and limitations, are set forth in section 9.15.

INTELLECTUAL, PHYSICAL AND RECREATIONAL ACTIVITIES

Section 9.16 restates the GPW, Article 38(1) obligation of the Detaining Power to encourage intellectual, educational and recreational pursuits among PWs and to take the necessary measures to ensure the exercise thereof. The section gives examples of the kinds of relevant equipment. That participation by PWs in such activities must be voluntary is properly emphasised, and the right of the Detaining Power to censor educational and intellectual materials for matter prejudicial to its security is properly noted.[32] The various possible sources for contributions to the activities referred to in this section are noted in the *Manual*'s text, including learning from fellow prisoners.[33]

29 GPW, Article 30(4); *DoD Manual*, paragraph 9.14.2.3.

30 GPW, Article 30(5); *DoD Manual*, paragraph 9.14.2.4.

31 GPW, Article 121(1); see also Article 121(2) and (3).

32 *DoD Manual*, paragraph 9.16.1. As the duration of detention increases, the Detaining Power should also make an effort to grant facilities for PWs to continue their studies or take up new subjects; *DoD Manual*, paragraph 9.16.2.

33 *DoD Manual*, paragraphs 9.16.2 to 9.16.4.

CANTEENS FOR PWs

Section 9.17 deals with the establishment and running of canteens where PWs can obtain foodstuffs, soap, tobacco and ordinary articles for daily use. The provisions of GPW, Article 28 are restated, supplemented by some sensible guidance based on Gulf War I and other relevant operational experience.

FINANCIAL RESOURCES OF PWs

Section 9.18 reproduces verbatim Article 58 of GPW, which, in summary, permits the Detaining Power to determine the sum in cash that PWs may be permitted to retain, requiring that any surplus be placed to their account with any monies deposited by them. If PWs are allowed to purchase items or services outside the camp, payment is made by the PW or by the camp administration charging the PW's account. The GPW, Article 60 obligation of the Detaining Power to grant to all PWs a monthly advance of pay and the scales of such advances according to the PWs' ranks are reflected in paragraph 9.18.3. The point is made, however, that since 1949, advances of pay by Detaining Powers have been infrequent; the power to modify the amount of advances of pay by special agreement is reflected in GPW, Article 60(2) and in paragraph 9.18.3.2 of the *Manual*. Paragraph 9.18.3.3 sets forth Article 60(3)'s provisions as to the limitation of amounts that can be drawn from special accounts pending the reaching of a special agreement between the parties to the conflict. As paragraph 9.18.3.4 accurately reflects, these advances of pay are made on behalf of the Power on which the PWs depend, and a settling up process is envisaged at the end of hostilities.[34] The obligation of the Detaining Power to accept supplementary payments for PWs from the Power on which they depend, provided the same amounts are paid to each PW in a particular category and are placed in their individual accounts as soon as possible, is reflected in GPW, Article 61 and in paragraph 9.18.4 of the *Manual*; such payments do not affect the Detaining Power's obligations.

Paragraph 9.18.5 accurately repeats the detailed arrangements in GPW, Article 63 as to the receipt and transmission of payments respectively by and from PWs, including payments to be made by PWs in their own country. Paragraph 9.18.6 repeats the GPW, Article 64 obligation of the Detaining Power to hold an account for each PW, lists the items in that article and in Article 59 that must be included in that account and gives the Article 65(1) and (2) detailed requirements as to countersignatures of transactions and PW access to account copies. The account arrangements on transfer of PWs between camps or between Detaining Powers and on termination of captivity

[34] GPW, Article 67.

are found in Articles 65(3) and (4) and 66, and are reproduced verbatim in paragraphs 9.18.6.2 to 9.18.6.5. Noteworthy is that responsibility for settling credit balances due to a PW at the end of captivity rests with the Power on which he or she depends,[35] and that is where claims by a PW for valuables etc. impounded under Article 18 GPW but not forthcoming on repatriation should be submitted.[36]

PW LABOR

Section 9.19 deals with the legal arrangements under GPW as to work by PWs. It is symptomatic of an issue that affects the chapter as a whole. Provisions are not sequenced in the same manner as in the Convention. This would not be a basis for criticism were there to be an improved logic associated with the *Manual*'s chosen sequence, but that is not always the case. In the present section, for example, the kinds of work that PWs may be compelled to do is addressed rather later in the section than might have been preferred. Be that as it may, the section starts with the general rule that the Detaining Power may use the labour of physically fit PWs, taking into account age, gender, rank and physical aptitude.[37] Paragraph 9.19.1 then states that '[i]n determining whether labor should be compelled, as well as the appropriate labor assignment for a POW, the POW's age, gender, rank and physical aptitude should be considered'. While this is indeed correct, it should in the view of the present authors have logically appeared in the *Manual* after the Article 49(2) and (3) restrictions on the work to be assigned respectively to non-commissioned officers (NCOs) and to officers, and after the Article 50 restrictions on the work that PWs can lawfully be compelled to do. Paragraphs 9.19.1.1 and 9.19.1.2 correctly state the GPW, Article 49(2) and (3) restriction of NCO PWs to supervisory or other suitable work and of officers to suitable work exclusively on a voluntary basis. Paragraph 9.19.1.3 correctly notes the prohibition of requiring retained personnel and certain other medical personnel to perform work outside their medical or religious duties.

As paragraph 9.19.2.1 notes, no PW may be employed on unhealthy or dangerous labour unless he or she is a volunteer.[38] The removal of landmines and similar devices is correctly cited as an example of dangerous work, and the role of the Protecting Powers or of the ICRC in verifying that the PW is

[35] GPW, Article 66(3).

[36] DoD *Manual*, paragraph 9.18.7; GPW, Article 68(2), first sentence. This, as the *Manual* notes, is subject to the requirements that the Detaining Power replace items required for use by the PWs while in captivity and that the Detaining Power give a written statement to PWs explaining why particular valuables etc. have not been restored to them.

[37] GPW, Article 49(1). [38] GPW, Article 52(1).

a volunteer and that he or she is appropriately skilled in the work is suitably highlighted.[39]

Paragraph 9.19.2.3 correctly notes the kinds of work that PWs may be compelled to do, as provided for in GPW, Article 50, while paragraphs 9.19.3 to 9.19.3.2 discuss GPW, Article 51 regarding working conditions for PWs, their training and the provision of protection suitable to the work they are undertaking. In these respects, and in relation to the limits on the duration of labour as provided for in Article 53 and repeated in paragraph 9.19.3.3, the obligation is that the conditions for PWs shall at least match those applied to workers of the Detaining Power undertaking similar work. The provisions as to working pay, as set forth in Articles 54(1) and 62 of GPW, are correctly restated in paragraph 9.19.4. Interestingly, Article 62(1) sets a quarter of a Swiss franc as the minimum pay for a working day, a sum that has not been increased by agreement since it was fixed in 1949. Somewhat surprisingly, paragraph 9.19.4 makes no comment about the obviously out-dated aspect of this provision.

GPW, Article 55's provisions as to the medical fitness of PWs for work, and the associated obligation of the Detaining Power to have them medically examined at least once per month, are accurately reflected in paragraph 9.19.5. It is noteworthy that while a surgeon or physician may recommend exemption of a PW from work, there is no obligation on the relevant authorities to implement such a recommendation. The requirement to take care of PWs who sustain accidents or contract diseases in consequence of their work and the obligation to give them a medical certificate for submission to the Power on which they depend are found in Article 54(2) of GPW and are correctly repeated in paragraph 9.19.6. The procedure for the handling of claims arising from work accidents or diseases is set forth in GPW, Article 68(1) and in paragraph 9.19.6.1 of the *Manual*. The provisions of Article 56 as to labour detachments, in particular the responsibility of the military authorities and of the relevant camp commander for compliance with GPW in labour detachments, are accurately restated in paragraph 9.19.7, while paragraph 9.19.8 restates the provisions of GPW, Article 57 that the conditions for PWs working for private persons shall accord with GPW requirements and that the Detaining Power, the military authorities and the commander of the relevant camp are responsible for the maintenance, care, treatment and payment of such PWs.

[39] Note footnote 383 on page 563 of the *DoD Manual* as to the voluntary employment of Argentinian PWs on mine clearance on the Falkland Islands/Malvinas. No PW may be employed on duties that would be looked upon as humiliating for a member of the Detaining Power's own forces; *DoD Manual*, paragraph 9.19.2.2; GPW, Article 52(2).

PW CORRESPONDENCE

Paragraph 9.20.1 sets out the right of every PW immediately on capture to send a capture card to his or her family and to the Central Prisoner of War Agency notifying them of his or her capture, address and state of health.[40] The limitations on additional correspondence by PWs, as set forth in Article 71(1), are restated in paragraph 9.20.2.1, where certain other kinds of correspondence are listed that do not come within the stated limits, namely formal requests and complaints, correspondence between PW representatives respectively at a principal camp and at a labour camp and certain correspondence by chaplains and by a senior medical officer at a camp. The point to note is that these rules have not been updated to take account of electronic and digital means of communication. Talk of capture cards seems rather dated these days. The *Manual* does not offer any thoughts in this respect.

Paragraph 9.20.2.3 reproduces the GPW, Article 71(2) right of PWs in particular circumstances to send telegrams. Interestingly and appropriately, in relation to this provision, the *Manual* suggests that more modern methods of communication, such as email, should be considered where appropriate. Paragraphs 9.20.2.4 and 9.20.2.5 restate the Article 71(3) and (4) stipulations that the language of PW correspondence shall generally be the PW's native language and that sacks of PW correspondence shall be sealed, labelled and addressed as provided for. Paragraph 9.20.3, restating Article 72(1) to (3), sets forth the right of PWs to receive by post or other means individual parcels or collective shipments of food, clothing, medical supplies and religious, recreational or educational articles. The Detaining Power remains bound by its GPW obligations, and these shipments can only be limited by the Protecting Power in the PWs' interests. The rules as to composition of consignments in Article 72(4) are restated in paragraphs 9.20.3.1 and 9.20.3.2, noting that, exceptionally, special medication can be sent from family members to a PW. Special agreements may be made between the parties as to the conditions for sending individual parcels and collective relief. Absent such special agreement as to collective relief, rules annexed to the Convention must be applied.[41] Article 73(2) and (3), which makes further provision in respect of such agreements as to collective relief shipments, is reflected in paragraph 9.20.3.4.

Paragraph 9.20.4 restates the GPW, Article 74(1) and (2) exemption of relief shipments for PWs from import, customs and other dues and the exemption of correspondence, relief shipments and remittances of money addressed to PWs or despatched by them from postal dues. Paragraph 9.20.4.3 refers to the

[40] GPW, Article 70. [41] See GPW, annex III.

corresponding exemption from postal charges under Article 17(1) of the Universal Postal Convention, 1989, notes the 5 kg and 10 kg weight limits provided for in that Convention and refers to the '*Service des prisonniers de guerre*' marking to be applied to items exempt from postal charges on this basis. As the *Manual* notes, where relief shipments cannot be sent through the post office for any reason, transportation cost is borne by the Detaining Power in areas under its control and by other States party in their respective territories. Any additional costs are covered by the senders.[42] Paragraph 9.20.5 reflects Article 75(1) of GPW, to the effect that if military operations preclude the arrangements referred to in Articles 70, 71, 72 and 77 of the Convention, the Protecting Powers, the ICRC or another organisation approved by the parties to the conflict may undertake to ensure their conveyance, and other parties to the Convention shall endeavour to supply them with appropriate transport. The paragraph and article list types of correspondence and reports that may also be transported at the same time. The use of alternative means of transport for such purposes is provided for in Article 75(3) and (4), and these arrangements are repeated in paragraph 9.20.5.

Paragraph 9.20.6 deals with the right of the Detaining Power to censor material sent to or by PWs. As the *Manual* correctly states, this right is implicitly recognised in GPW, and the Article 76 requirements as to timeliness in censorship, the protection of consignments from deterioration during examination, the avoidance of delay in delivering consignments to PWs and the need for any prohibition of correspondence to be temporary and as short as possible are set forth in the same paragraph.

PRIVATE LEGAL MATTERS OF PWs

Section 9.21 correctly observes that PWs retain the civil capacity they enjoyed at the time of their capture. As the *Manual* helpfully explains, this means that the law that applied to them before capture will continue to apply, and that therefore, to the degree permitted by their captivity, they can take legal steps they were able to take before capture, such as disposing of property, making wills, giving consent to marriage, voting and executing a power of attorney. Paragraph 9.21.2 then usefully points out the Article 77 obligations of the Detaining Power to 'provide all facilities for the transmission' of relevant documents intended for or dispatched by PWs and to facilitate the preparation and execution of such documents. Paragraph 9.21.2.1 restates the

[42] GPW, Article 74(3) and (4); *DoD Manual*, paragraph 9.20.4.4.

requirement that PWs' wills be drawn up in accordance with the validity requirements of their country of origin, which shall notify these to the Detaining Power. The right of a PW to request that his or her will is transmitted to the Protecting Power, and that a copy be sent to the Central Agency, is also noted.[43]

INTERNAL DISCIPLINE OF PW CAMPS

The GPW, Article 39(1) requirement that every PW camp be placed under the immediate authority of a responsible commissioned officer of the Detaining Power's armed forces is reflected in paragraph 9.22.1. It is correctly stated that that officer has disciplinary powers over PWs, who also remain subject to the law, disciplinary authority and regulations of the Power on which they depend.[44] Paragraph 9.22.3 correctly notes that PWs, with the exception of officers, 'must salute and show to all officers of the Detaining Power the external marks of respect provided for by the regulations applying in their own forces'.[45] The Paragraph then states: 'PoWs need not salute Detaining Power non-commissioned officers' or persons of equivalent status to officers of the Detaining Power. This seems to be a correct interpretation of Article 39(2). Officer PWs must salute Detaining Power officers of higher rank and the Camp Commander, irrespective of his or her rank. Paragraph 9.22.4 correctly observes that officers and PWs of equivalent status must be treated with the regard due to their rank and age,[46] that they may wear their badges of rank, nationality or decorations and that PWs awarded disciplinary punishments may not be deprived of the prerogatives of rank. Promotions in rank notified by the Power on which the PW depends shall be recognised.[47]

The Convention text, special agreements provided for in Article 8, any regulations, orders, notices and publications relating to the conduct of PWs and any order or command addressed to PWs individually must all be in a language which they understand. The detailed rules of Article 41 GPW in this regard are accurately reproduced in paragraph 9.22.5. Paragraph 9.22.6 repeats the characterisation that we have already seen earlier in the *Manual* of the use of force against PWs – especially PWs who are escaping or attempting to escape – as an extreme measure, and again makes the point that

43 GPW, Article 120(1); *DoD Manual*, paragraph 9.21.2.1.

44 *DoD Manual*, paragraph 9.22.2.

45 GPW, Article 39(2).

46 GPW, Article 44(1).

47 *DoD Manual*, paragraph 9.22.4.2; GPW, Article 43(2).

such a use of force 'shall always be preceded by warnings appropriate to the circumstances'.[48]

Paragraph 9.22.6.1 then notes that riot control agents can legitimately be used against rioting PWs. This is a correct reflection of the CWC's exemption for the use of riot control agents for law enforcement purposes from the general prohibition of their use as a method of warfare.[49] There then follows the somewhat cryptic passage: 'If the use of deadly force is warranted and authorized against PoWs, there is no legal requirement to use non-lethal weapons before resort to deadly force.' The statement is correct, but because of its essentially negative construction, this part of the *Manual* does not articulate clearly the circumstances in which the US considers that the use of lethal force against PWs would indeed be justified. That is an omission that might usefully be addressed in any future revision of the *Manual*.

PW REQUESTS, COMPLAINTS AND REPORTS ABOUT CONDITIONS OF CAPTIVITY

Section 9.23 accurately reflects GPW Article 78's right of PWs to make their requests as to the conditions of captivity known to the military authorities in whose power they are and their unrestricted right to draw attention to complaints either direct to the Protecting Powers or through their prisoners' representative. Paragraph 9.23.1.1 usefully points out that such complaints may also properly be made known to the ICRC, which has in the past been able to take appropriate measures, sometimes confidentially, to improve the PWs' situation. Paragraph 9.23.2.1 rightly notes that the Detaining Power may properly review and censor for security reasons such requests and complaints that are sent to the Protecting Power, but asserts that the PWs' right to make these complaints to the Protecting Power must not be restricted. Clearly, there is a proper balance to be struck here. Article 78(3)'s prohibition of punishment of PWs for making unfounded complaints is noted, and the sensible point is made that the making of unfounded complaints may be counter to PWs' interests, as proper matters of concern may as a result not receive appropriate attention. Similar review and censorship may be applied by the Detaining Power to the periodic reports by prisoners' representatives.[50]

48 GPW, Article 42.

49 Convention on the Prohibition of the Development, Production, Stockpiling and Use of Chemical Weapons and on their Destruction, Paris (13 January 1993), Articles I(5) and II(9)(d).

50 GPW, Article 78(4); *DoD Manual*, paragraph 9.23.3.

PW REPRESENTATIVES

Section 9.24 of the *Manual* deals with the appointment and duties of PW representatives. Article 79(5)'s requirement that such representatives have the same nationality, language and customs as the PWs they represent is properly stated. It is also right that, generally speaking, retained personnel should not be appointed as PW representatives, partly because they have their own representatives in relation to professional matters and partly because their different duties might interfere with one another.[51] Article 79 GPW makes detailed procedural provision for the appointment of PW representatives, and these arrangements are discussed in paragraph 9.24.2. On a point of minor detail, paragraph 9.24.3 correctly notes the duties of such representatives as being to represent the PWs before the military authorities, the Protecting Powers, the ICRC and any other organisation that may assist them; however, it cites Article 80 as the relevant provision, instead of Article 79(1). As paragraph 9.24.3.2 notes, PW representatives have duties, in addition to their general duties, in three areas, namely relief activities, relations between PWs and the authorities and verification that GPW guarantees are respected. The duties under each category are listed and will be discussed where relevant below.

In addition to considering the right to appoint – and the role of – PW representatives' assistants, paragraph 9.24.4 accurately records the exemption of PW representatives from work that would make the accomplishment of their duties more difficult and notes that material facilities must be granted them, including a certain freedom of movement necessary for the accomplishment of their duties; that they have a right to visit premises where PWs are detained; and that PWs have a right to consult freely with them.[52] The arrangements as to payment of PW representatives and their assistants, as set forth in GPW, Article 62(3), are restated in paragraph 9.24.4.5. Paragraph 9.24.4.6 reproduces much of GPW, Article 81(4)'s requirement that '[a]ll facilities shall likewise be accorded to the prisoners' representatives for communication by post and telegraph with the detaining authorities, the Protecting Powers', the ICRC, Mixed Medical Commissions and the bodies that give assistance to PWs. It also notes the right of PW representatives of labour detachments to the same communication facilities with PW representatives of the principal camp. These references to modes of communication are of course dated, and unfortunately the *Manual* does not give guidance here as to how these obligations should be interpreted in the present, digital age. As GPW, Article 80(3) provides, and

[51] *DoD Manual*, paragraph 9.24.1. [52] GPW, Article 81(1) to (3).

paragraph 9.24.4.7 recognises, PW representatives are not to be held responsible by reason of their duties for offences committed by PWs.

Paragraph 9.24.5 correctly notes that if a PW representative is dismissed, the reasons must be communicated to the Protecting Power. Also correct is the observation that the GPW does not provide for dismissal by the PWs themselves, although they have the option of not re-electing an individual.[53]

PW ESCAPES

Paragraph 9.25.1 correctly observes that PWs who successfully escape and are subsequently recaptured are not liable to punishment for their previous escape.[54] What constitutes a successful escape is defined in GPW, Article 91(1), and the relevant provisions are accurately restated in paragraph 9.25.1.1.

PWs who are captured after an unsuccessful attempted escape retain PW status and, along with any other PWs who aided and abeted their attempt to escape, are liable only to disciplinary punishment,[55] as correctly noted in paragraphs 9.25.2 and 9.25.3.

Paragraph 9.25.2.1 rightly observes that PWs captured by e.g. civilians must be promptly handed over to the competent military authorities.[56] Such recaptured PWs are, as paragraphs 9.25.2.2 and 9.25.2.3 note, also only liable to disciplinary punishments, even if their act of escape is repeated. The same applies to non-violent acts committed to facilitate escape, such as offences against public property, theft without intent of self-enrichment and the drawing up of false papers and wearing of civilian clothing. The attempted escape is not an aggravating factor if the PW is subject to judicial proceedings for an offence committed during it.[57] Collective punishment of PWs for escapes by other PWs is prohibited. The general prohibition of collective punishments is to be found in Article 87(3) of GPW, and the present authors would suggest that this provision ought to be cited in this paragraph of the *Manual*.

Paragraph 9.25.4 notes the right to subject PWs who have unsuccessfully attempted to escape to special surveillance, provided it does not affect their health, is undergone in a PW camp and does not suppress any GPW safeguards.[58]

53 See GPW, Article 81(6).

54 GPW, Article 91(2). The paragraph draws the interesting parallel with the similar arrangements applying to spies who return successfully to their own lines and are thereafter captured by the enemy.

55 GPW, Article 92(1).

56 GPW, Article 92(2).

57 GPW, Articles 92(1) and 93(1) and (2).

58 GPW, Article 92(3).

If PWs escape or are recaptured, the Detaining Power's PW Information Bureau must inform the Power on which the PWs depend.[59]

GENERAL PRINCIPLES APPLICABLE TO PW DISCIPLINE

The term 'disciplinary measures' refers to punishment by the commander of a PW camp and equates with summary disposal by a commanding officer. 'Judicial proceedings', by contrast, refers to trial and punishment by a court and equates to trial by court-martial.[60] The general principle is that the laws, regulations and orders applying to the armed forces of the Detaining Power apply to PWs, and judicial or disciplinary measures may be taken against PWs if they breach those laws, regulations or orders. Punishments awarded must not be contrary to Chapter III of GPW, and the competent authorities, when deciding between judicial and disciplinary proceedings, must exercise the greatest leniency and adopt disciplinary measures wherever possible.[61] Paragraph 9.26.3 correctly limits proceedings against PWs to military courts except where existing laws of the Detaining Power permit its armed forces to be tried before civil courts for the particular offence. Any court trying a PW must, however, offer the generally recognised essential guarantees of independence and impartiality and the accused's rights and means of defence provided for in GPW, Article 105.[62] These rights also apply if a PW is prosecuted by the Detaining Power for acts committed before capture, and such persons retain GPW benefits even after conviction.[63]

As to punishments, no PW may be punished more than once for the same act or on the same charge,[64] nor may PWs be sentenced to penalties other than those provided for in relation to members of the armed forces of the Detaining Power who have committed the same acts.[65] Certain prohibited forms of punishment are listed in GPW, Article 87(3) and repeated in paragraph 9.26.6. In fixing penalty, the courts and authorities of the Detaining Power must take into account that the PW is not bound to that Power by any duty of allegiance and is not under its authority by his or her own will; they may reduce the penalty below the minimum provided.[66] Moreover, the treatment of PWs when undergoing punishment shall not be more severe than

59 *DoD Manual* paragraph 9.25.5; and, in part, GPW, Article 94.

60 *DoD Manual*, section 9.26.

61 GPW, Articles 82(1) and 83; *DoD Manual*, paragraphs 9.26.1 and 9.26.2.

62 GPW, Article 84.

63 GPW, Article 85; *DoD Manual*, paragraph 9.26.4.

64 GPW, Article 86; *DoD Manual*, paragraph 9.26.5.

65 GPW, Article 87(1); *DoD Manual*, paragraph 9.26.6.

66 GPW, Article 87(2); *DoD Manual*, paragraph 9.26.6.

that applied in respect of the same punishment to the Detaining Power's own armed forces personnel of equivalent rank.[67]

DISCIPLINARY PROCEEDINGS AND PUNISHMENT

Paragraph 9.27.1 notes that only the camp commander or an officer acting for him or to whom he has delegated his powers may award disciplinary punishment.[68] A PW accused of a disciplinary offence may not be kept in confinement unless a member of the Detaining Power's own armed forces accused of a similar offence would also be so kept or if confinement is necessary in the interests of camp order and discipline.[69] Paragraph 9.27.3 explains the rights that an accused PW has before sentence is announced, as set forth in GPW, Article 96(4). Interestingly, no reference is made here to the rights set forth in Article 75 of API. If the US position is that those rights do not apply in the case of disciplinary proceedings against a PW, it would have been useful for the *Manual* to have explained here the reasoning behind such a surprising view. Simply not to mention Article 75 is less than satisfactory.

The list of permitted disciplinary punishments, namely a fine, discontinuance of privileges, fatigues and confinement, is given in paragraph 9.27.5, subject to the limitations provided for in GPW, Article 89. No punishment may continue for longer than 30 days, and periods of confinement pending the hearing must be deducted from the award.[70]

As to the conditions in which PWs serve disciplinary punishment, paragraph 9.27.6 correctly states the requirement for humane treatment, that PWs may not be transferred to penitentiary establishments, that officers shall not be lodged with NCOs or men and that women shall be confined separately from men and under the supervision of women. For some reason, this paragraph omits Article 97(2)'s requirement that '[a]ll premises in which disciplinary

67 GPW, Article 88; *DoD Manual*, paragraph 9.26.7. It is noted in paragraph 9.26.7 that women PWs may not be punished or treated while undergoing punishment more severely than a male or female member of the Detaining Power's armed forces would be for a similar offence; and that, subject to the surveillance following unsuccessful escape attempts discussed earlier, PWs who have served their sentence must not be treated differently from other PWs.

68 GPW, Article 96(2).

69 GPW, Article 95(1); *DoD Manual*, paragraph 9.27.2. Any such confinement must be kept to a minimum – not exceeding fourteen days – and the GPW safeguards applying to confinement under sentence (Articles 97 and 98) must be satisfied; GPW, Article 95(2) and (3); *DoD Manual*, paragraph 9.27.2.

70 The additional detailed provisions in Article 90(3) and (4) as to the serving of sentences are repeated in the same paragraph of the *Manual*.

punishments are undergone shall conform to the sanitary requirements set forth in article 25. A prisoner of war undergoing punishment shall be enabled to keep himself in a state of cleanliness, in conformity with article 29.' Paragraph 9.27.6.2 makes the important point that PWs undergoing punishment retain the protections of GPW, except as necessarily rendered inapplicable by the state of confinement, and may not be deprived of the benefit of Articles 78 and 126.

The GPW, Article 98(2) right of PWs awarded disciplinary punishment to retain rank privileges is stated and explained in paragraph 9.27.6.3. Their medical safeguards, right to exercise and right to have access to the open air, and the GPW obligations in relation to reading, writing, letters and packages provided for in Article 98(3), (4) and (5), are accurately repeated in paragraphs 9.27.6.4, 9.27.6.5 and 9.25.6.6.[71]

JUDICIAL PROCEEDINGS AND PUNISHMENT

Section 9.28 asserts that the following rules apply to judicial proceedings and punishment in addition to the principles already enunciated. Paragraph 9.28.1 prohibits trial or sentencing for an act not prohibited by the law of the Detaining Power, or international law, at the time of the act.[72] Secondly, a PW can only be validly sentenced if the sentence was pronounced by the same courts according to the same procedures as in the case of the Detaining Power's armed forces and if Chapter III of GPW has been complied with.[73] Third, the Protecting Power must be notified of the decision to institute judicial proceedings as soon as possible and at least three weeks before the opening of the trial.[74] Fourth, if no evidence is submitted that the notification was received by the Protecting Power, by the PW and by the prisoner's representative at least three weeks before the trial, the trial must be adjourned.[75]

[71] Paragraph 9.27.7 repeats the stipulation in GPW, Article 115(1) that a PW eligible for repatriation or accommodation in a neutral country may not be held back on the ground that he or she has not undergone his or her punishment.

[72] GPW, Article 99(1); *DoD Manual*, paragraph 9.28.1.

[73] GPW, Article 102; *DoD Manual*, paragraph 9.28.2.

[74] GPW, Article 104(1); *DoD Manual*, paragraph 9.28.3.1.

[75] GPW, Article 104(4); *DoD Manual*, paragraph 9.28.3.1. The same paragraph of the *Manual* restates the GPW Article 104(2) requirements as to the information that the notification must contain. The requirement for rapid investigation so that the PW's trial can take place as soon as possible is stated, and the restrictions on the confinement of the PW pending trial, set forth in GPW, Article 103(1), are restated; *DoD Manual*, paragraphs 9.28.3.2 and 9.28.3.3. Time spent in confinement pending trial must be deducted from the ultimate sentence, and GPW, Articles 97 and 98 apply to confinement pending trial.

Paragraph 9.28.4 notes: the prohibition of coercing a PW to admit the offence of which he or she stands accused;[76] the rights of the accused PW to present his or her own defence and to the assistance of a qualified advocate or counsel;[77] and e.g. the rights of the accused PW to call witnesses and, where he or she deems it necessary, to the services of an interpreter.[78] Further detailed provision as to the appointment of counsel in GPW, Article 105(2) is included in the same paragraph of the *Manual*. Paragraph 9.28.4.3 restates the provisions of Article 105(3) as to the facilities that must be afforded to the advocate or counsel conducting the defence, and paragraph 9.28.4.4 restates Article 105(4)'s provisions as to furnishing the accused PW with particulars of the charge and other documents generally issued to the accused by virtue of the laws in force in the armed forces of the Detaining Power. The right, in normal circumstances, of the Protecting Power to attend the trial is accurately noted.[79]

Rights of appeal or petition against sentence must match those applicable to members of the Detaining Power's armed forces. The PW must be informed of these rights and of the time limits for making such appeals, and the Detaining Power must inform the Protecting Power of the PW's decision as to appeal or petition.[80] As the *Manual* correctly observes, if the PW is finally convicted or if a sentence of death is imposed in the first instance, the Detaining Power must send a detailed report to the Protecting Power, containing the wording of the finding and sentence, a summary report of the investigation and trial and notification of the establishment where the sentence will be served.[81] PWs and the Protecting Powers must be told which offences carry the death sentence under the law of the Detaining Power, and a death sentence cannot be pronounced on a PW unless the attention of the court has been drawn to the fact that the PW is not bound by any duty of allegiance to the Detaining Power and that he or she is in its power in circumstances independent of his or her will.[82]

Paragraphs 9.28.7.1 to 9.28.7.5 repeat in terms the provisions of GPW, Article 108(1) to (3) as to the conditions in which PWs may be required to serve

76 GPW, Article 99(2). 77 GPW, Article 99(3). 78 GPW, Article 105(1).

79 GPW, Article 105(5); *DoD Manual*, paragraph 9.28.4.5. Paragraph 9.28.4.6 deals with the notification to the Protecting Power, to the PW's representative and to the accused PW of the judgment and sentence; GPW, Article 107(1).

80 GPW, Articles 106 and 107(1) in this regard are replicated in *DoD Manual*, paragraph 9.28.5.1.

81 GPW, Article 107(2), restated in *DoD Manual*, paragraph 9.28.5.2.

82 GPW, Article 100(1) and (3); *DoD Manual*, paragraph 9.28.6. A death sentence shall not be executed before six months has elapsed since the receipt by the Protecting Power of the Article 107 report.

sentences. The paragraphs accurately state: the requirements as to health and humanity; the obligations as to separate quarters for women PWs under the supervision of women; and the continuing rights to receive correspondence and parcels, as to regular exercise and as to access to the open air. Penalties must also accord with GPW, Article 87(3).

TRANSFER OF PWs FROM THE PW CAMP

The detailed GPW rules on the transfer of PWs are to be found in Articles 46 and 47, and these articles are reproduced word for word in paragraphs 9.29.1 and 9.29.2 of the *Manual*. Likewise, the procedures for the transfer of PWs from the camp as given in Article 48 are reproduced verbatim in paragraph 9.29.3.

TRANSFER OF PWs TO THE CUSTODY OF ANOTHER DETAINING POWER

Paragraph 9.30.1 repeats the provisions of Article 12 as to the transfer of PWs to another Detaining Power. While such transfers to a Power that is party to the GPW are permitted once the Detaining Power has satisfied itself of the ability and willingness of the transferee to apply GPW, if the transferee fails in this regard, the transferor, on being notified, must take effective measures to correct the situation or must request the return of the PWs, a request that must be complied with. As paragraph 9.30.3 notes, special agreements may be made in this regard, e.g. providing for inspections by the transferring State.

NATIONAL ACCOUNTING OF THE DETENTION OF PWs

Having correctly noted in section 9.31 that a proper accounting for PWs is an important responsibility of the Detaining Power, paragraph 9.31.1 lists the information that GPW, Article 122(2), (4), (5) and (6) requires to be provided – within the shortest possible period – to its Bureau, thence to be forwarded as rapidly as possible to the Powers concerned through the Protecting Powers and the Central Agency.[83] The final element of paragraph 9.31.1 refers to the forwarding of wills, records of death, lists of graves and particulars of interred PWs, in much more permissive terms than Article 120 of GPW indicates. These two sentences in the *Manual* should, it is suggested, be amended to reflect the mandatory terms in which the Convention

[83] See GPW, Article 122(3).

requirements are expressed. Paragraph 9.31.1.1 correctly notes that these provisions involve some items of information that the PW is not obliged to disclose. Paragraph 9.31.2 deals with GPW, Article 122(1) and (2)'s provisions as to the establishment, equipping and basic functioning of National PW Information Bureaux – specifically, the receiving and forwarding of certain information, replying to inquiries relating to PWs and collecting of personal valuables left by PWs, as provided for in GPW, Article 122(2), (3), (7) and (9).

The arrangements in Article 123 of GPW for the establishment of a Central PW Information Agency in a neutral country, the functions of that Agency in collecting all information respecting PWs and transmitting it as rapidly as possible to their country of origin or to the Power on which they depend and the obligation of the parties to the conflict to provide facilities for effecting such transmissions are set forth in paragraph 9.31.3. The fulfilment of this role, and the corresponding role under GC, in past conflicts by the ICRC through its Central Tracing Agency is also noted there. US field practice in this regard is explained in paragraph 9.31.4, while exemptions from certain postal and telegraphic fees for such national and central information agencies are referred to in paragraph 9.31.5.

ROLE OF THE PROTECTING POWER IN GPW

The various functions of the Protecting Power under the GPW are listed under section 9.32. This is a useful way of presenting its duties, and cross-references are helpfully provided to the paragraphs of the *Manual* that deal with each such function. Similarly, in paragraph 9.32.3, the ways in which the GPW contemplates the Protecting Powers actively working to promote the welfare of PWs are listed, again with cross-references to associated paragraphs of the *Manual*.

ACCESS TO PWs BY THE PROTECTING POWERS, ICRC AND RELIEF ORGANIZATIONS

Paragraph 9.33.1 restates verbatim the provisions of Article 126 of GPW as to the full liberty, both as to duration and as to frequency, for representatives or delegates of the Protecting Powers to visit all places where PWs are interned, imprisoned and held to perform labour, and all places of departure, passage and arrival where they are under transfer, as well as to interview PWs and their representatives without witnesses. The paragraph notes in particular the similar rights of access for ICRC delegates. Paragraph 9.33.2 restates, again verbatim, the provisions of GPW, Article 125 as to the granting by the

Detaining Power of access by relief organisations to PWs for the distribution of relief supplies and for related matters.

DEATH OF PWs

Section 9.34 addresses the obligations arising from the death of PWs. Paragraph 9.34.1 reports again the obligation in GPW, Article 120(1) on the death of a PW for the Detaining Power to transmit the will without delay to the Protecting Power, with a certified copy going to the Central Agency. Death certificates in the form annexed to the Convention or certified lists of PWs who have died must be sent as rapidly as possible to the National PW Agency.[84] GPW, Article 120(3)'s requirement for a medical examination to confirm death and to enable a report establishing identity is reflected in paragraph 9.34.3.1. Paragraph 9.34.3.2 records the detaining authorities' obligation under GPW, Article 120(4) to ensure that PWs who have died in captivity are honourably buried, where possible according to the rites of the religion to which they belonged. The obligation in the same part of the article, to ensure that their graves are respected, suitably maintained and marked, is to be found at paragraph 9.34.4, and paragraph 9.34.4.1 sets forth the requirements of Article 120(6) to the effect that particulars of burials and of graves must be recorded with the Graves Registration Service established by the Detaining Power. Lists of graves and particulars of the PWs interred in cemeteries and elsewhere must be transmitted to the Power on which they depend. Responsibility for the graves and for any subsequent moves of the bodies rests with the Power controlling the territory. The stated provisions apply also to ashes, which shall be kept by the Graves Registration Service pending proper disposal in accordance with the home country's wishes. The preference that PWs who depended on the same Power be buried together and the requirements that they be buried individually unless unavoidable circumstances dictate otherwise, that cremation should only occur for imperative reasons of hygiene or in accordance with the religion or wishes of the deceased and that the reasons for cremation be recorded on the death certificate are all correctly stated in paragraphs 9.34.3.2 and 9.34.3.3.[85]

The requirement in GPW, Article 121(1) for an official inquiry by the Detaining Power into any death or serious injury of a PW caused or suspected to have been caused by a sentry, by another PW or by any other person, or

84 GPW, Article 120(2); *DoD Manual*, paragraph 9.34.2. The required details for inclusion in the death certificates and in the certified lists are given in paragraph 9.34.2.

85 GPW, Article 120(5).

where the cause of the death is unknown, is reflected in paragraph 9.34.5, noting also the requirement to notify the Protecting Power. Footnote 838[86] gives useful information as to the practical application of these rules by the UK during the Falklands/Malvinas War and by the US during Gulf War I.

EXCHANGES AND OTHER RELEASE AND REPATRIATION OF PWs DURING HOSTILITIES

The possibility that PWs, other than those whose release is mandatory, are released by agreement between the belligerents and as an act of mutual convenience under what are known as 'cartel agreements' is discussed in paragraph 9.35.1. Such releases and repatriations will not necessarily be on the basis of exchange, but must be with the consent of the affected individuals.[87]

DIRECT REPATRIATION AND ACCOMMODATION IN NEUTRAL COUNTRIES DURING HOSTILITIES

As paragraph 9.36.1 notes, parties to the conflict are obliged to return to their own country seriously wounded and seriously sick PWs after caring for them until they are fit to travel, and provided they consent to be returned.[88] The categories of seriously wounded or seriously sick PWs who are eligible for direct repatriation are listed in GPW, Article 110(1), and the list is repeated verbatim in paragraph 9.36.1.1; paragraph 9.36.2 restates, also verbatim, the two categories of prisoner who may be accommodated in a neutral country in accordance with Article 110(2). Accordingly, the Detaining Power, the Power on which the PWs depend and a mutually agreed neutral Power shall endeavour to reach an agreement to enable PWs to be interned by the neutral until hostilities close.[89] Such an agreement will also be required to fix the status of prisoners accommodated in a neutral country and the conditions that such prisoners must fulfil for repatriation by the neutral. The GPW prescribes the two categories of sick prisoner who should generally be repatriated by the neutral, and these are accurately stated in paragraph 9.36.3.1. Absent agreements of the sort referred to here, the arrangements set forth in the Model

[86] *DoD Manual*, page 625. The taking of statements by the inquiry, especially from PWs, and the prosecution of those found to be responsible are stipulated in GPW Article 121(2) and (3).

[87] *DoD Manual*, paragraph 9.35.2.

[88] GPW, Article 109(1) and (3).

[89] GPW, Article 111; *DoD Manual*, paragraph 9.36.3. The *Manual* suggests that a Detaining Power unable to meet minimum GPW standards would seek to achieve such an agreement. Perhaps 'must' would be a better verb to use here.

Agreement and in the Regulations concerning Mixed Medical Commissions, annexed to GPW, shall be used to settle such cases.[90] While examination by a Mixed Medical Commission may not be necessary for those who are manifestly seriously injured or sick, the Convention does list, and the *Manual* repeats, the categories of individual who may present themselves for such examination.[91] Detailed provisions as to attendance at the examination by physicians of the PW's nationality and as to the costs associated with repatriation or transportation to a neutral country are also included.[92] The important point is then made that '[n]o repatriated person may be employed on active military service'.[93]

RELEASE AND REPATRIATION AFTER HOSTILITIES

In paragraph 9.37.1, the obligation in GPW, Article 118(1) for the release and repatriation of PWs 'without delay after the cessation of active hostilities' is reported and discussed. The point is made that 'it is proper to expect that each party's conduct with respect to the repatriation of POWs will be reasonable and broadly commensurate' with that of the other and that it would not be reasonable to expect a State to release all the PWs it holds without assurance that its own personnel held by the enemy will also be released.[94] This must, however, be subject to the explicit obligation of Article 118(2), cited in full in paragraph 9.37.1, that absent any stipulations in agreements between the parties, each Detaining Power must establish and execute without delay a plan of repatriation conforming with the general obligation in Article 118(1). Citing no lesser an authority than Lauterpacht, paragraph 9.37.2 accurately describes the notion of 'after the cessation of active hostilities' as referring to 'the complete end of the fighting with clearly no probability of resumption of hostilities in the near future'. Paragraph 9.37.3 correctly contends that 'without

90 GPW, Article 110(4); *DoD Manual*, paragraph 9.36.4.

91 GPW, Article 113(1) and (2); *DoD Manual*, paragraphs 9.36.5.1 and 9.36.5.2.

92 GPW Articles 113(3) and 116; *DoD Manual*, paragraphs 9.36.5.3 and 9.36.6.

93 GPW Article 117; *DoD Manual*, paragraph 9.36.7. The *Manual* cites convincing authorities, including the 1958 *UK Manual* and the Commentary to the Convention, to the effect that, although of apparently general application, this prohibition only applies to prisoners repatriated under Articles 109 or 110 GPW. 'Active military service' is, subject to a special agreement to the contrary, taken to mean any direct or indirect involvement in armed operations against the former Detaining Power or its allies, but not medical or strictly administrative duties; *DoD Manual*, paragraph 9.36.7.2.

94 The Eritrea/Ethiopia Claims Commission, Partial Award: Prisoners of War, Eritrea's Claim, 17 (1 July 2003), paragraphs 148 and 149 are cited as the authority for this view.

delay' here does not affect the requirement to ensure that repatriation takes place in a safe and orderly manner, and notes certain factors, such as the ability of countries to receive large numbers of PWs, as increasing the time required to conduct release and repatriation.

PWs WHOM THE DETAINING POWER IS NOT REQUIRED TO REPATRIATE

Deserters do not have to be repatriated. Paragraph 9.38.1 argues that the same applies to persons who have been illegally enrolled in the armed forces of the enemy. It is not clear what precisely is meant by this statement in the *Manual*. Certainly, if a person entitled to PW status has been unlawfully required to serve in the armed forces of his or her enemy, then on the cessation of the hostilities, he or she should in the opinion of the present authors be repatriated to the country on which he or she depends, but only on a voluntary basis. PWs may, however, make an informed, voluntary and personal choice to reject repatriation and seek asylum with the Detaining Power, and this possibility is properly reflected in paragraph 9.37.4.2. As the *Manual* notes in this paragraph, the voluntariness of the decision can be verified in interviews with an impartial intermediary, a neutral State (presumably meaning a representative of a neutral State) or the ICRC.

It is correct, as paragraph 9.37.4.3 asserts, that repatriation cannot be delayed on the grounds that a disciplinary proceeding or punishment is outstanding. Where, however, a pending proceeding is for an indictable offence, the PW may be held until the end of such proceeding and until the completion of the punishment. Likewise, PWs already convicted for an indictable offence may be detained until the end of the punishment.[95]

Paragraph 9.37.6 restates the arrangements as to the apportionment of repatriation costs as set forth in GPW, Article 118(4). The basic rule is that these costs must be equitably apportioned between the Detaining Power and the Power on which the PWs depend. Two specific arrangements that are repeated in the *Manual* apply respectively where the two parties are and are not contiguous.

95 GPW, Article 119(5). As the *Manual* observes, this arrangement is practical because only after the conflict can the majority of – and the principal – offenders be apprehended and tried. The names of PWs affected by this rule shall be communicated between the parties to the conflict, and the persons affected shall remain protected under GPW until eventual repatriation. By agreement between the parties, commissions shall be established to search for dispersed PWs and ensure their repatriation with minimum delay; *DoD Manual*, paragraph 9.37.5.

PROCEDURE ON RELEASE AND REPATRIATION AFTER HOSTILITIES

The conditions of repatriation must be similar to those specified in GPW, Articles 46 to 48, having regard to Articles 118 and 119. So, the conditions must be humane and not less favourable than those applying to the forces of the Detaining Power. Precautions for the health and safety of PWs must include provision of sufficient food, drinking water, clothing, shelter and medical attention. The plan for repatriation must be notified to the PWs,[96] they must be identified and listed before departure and the National PW Information Bureau must be notified in advance.[97]

Paragraph 9.38.3 restates the provisions of GPW, Article 119(2), (3) and (4) as to the return to PWs on repatriation of any items impounded from them and as to the transportation of their personal effects and the arrangements to be made for personal effects that cannot be transported with them. Paragraph 9.38.4 draws attention to the requirements of GPW, Article 66 as to PW account action to be taken on repatriation and notes the Article 67 stipulation that advances of pay and payments made under Articles 63(3) and 68 should be the subject of arrangements between the Powers concerned.

Section 9.39 sets forth and explains the Code of Conduct for US Armed Forces. It is neither necessary nor appropriate to comment here on the content or explanation of that topic given in the *Manual*.

CONCLUDING REMARKS

This chapter of the *Manual* stays rather close to the language of GPW, but includes, particularly in footnotes, considerable material based on the Pictet Commentary and adds some useful reflections based on US operational experience. It would have been helpful to see the US view expressed in relation to provisions of the conventional law that have clearly been overtaken by events, e.g. as to modes of modern communication or as to currency values of pay rates for the work of PWs.

It is noteworthy that the GPW provisions have been restructured and resequenced in such a way that quite a lot of repetition of particular provisions has been required. Sometimes, this is useful, in that the opportunity has been taken helpfully to bring together associated provisions from diverse parts of the Convention, but on other occasions the repetition may prove to be a

[96] To enable them to pack baggage and inform next of kin.

[97] *DoD Manual*, paragraph 9.38.2; see GPW, Article 118(3).

distraction for some readers. Perhaps the repetition could be reduced by placing greater reliance on cross-references.

Frequently, footnotes repeat exactly the language that is to be found in the corresponding paragraph of the main text. One rather wonders what the perceived utility of such a practice might be. It certainly has the effect, arguably unnecessarily, of increasing the overall length of the text, which is already substantial.

The chapter gives little if any indication of which of the reported provisions the US considers reflect customary law. This is, in the opinion of the present authors, an unfortunate omission.

However, these criticisms are relatively minor. In general, this is a well-organised, comprehensive and accurate chapter that addresses an important aspect of the law of war with suitable thoroughness.

10

Civilians in the Hands of a Party to the Conflict

INTRODUCTION

From PWs, attention now shifts to the situation confronting civilians in the hands of a party to the conflict. It is made clear at the outset of Chapter X that the focus is on international armed conflicts, and particularly on the rules that apply both to civilians in the home territory of a belligerent and to those in occupied territory. GC is therefore, as the *Manual* acknowledges, the primary source of relevant law and is, the *Manual* states, interpreted in light of the goal of achieving humane treatment of protected persons and by reference to subsequent practice, both of which are proper bases for interpretation of such a text.

After some notes on terminology in paragraph 10.1.1.1, the value of which is debatable, paragraph 10.1.1.2 lists a number of topics specifically provided for in GC and on which States can conclude special agreements to facilitate the protection of civilians. Bringing such a list together usefully draws attention to the kinds of topic that should be considered for inter-belligerent discussion before or at the commencement of a conflict; no such special agreement may adversely affect the situation of protected persons nor restrict their GC rights,[1] and protected persons will continue to benefit from such special agreements until GC no longer applies, unless express contrary provision is contained in that or a later agreement or more favourable measures are taken by a party to the conflict.[2] Paragraph 10.1.2 then directs the reader to consult DoD policies and regulations on the treatment of internees, as they frequently exceed the requirements of the GC, US statutes and executive orders.

[1] GC, Article 7; *DoD Manual*, paragraph 10.1.1.2.
[2] GC, Article 7(2); *DoD Manual*, paragraph 10.1.1.1.

NATIONAL-LEVEL GC IMPLEMENTATION MEASURES

Section 10.2 helpfully lists the action that must be taken in accordance with GC at the national level to facilitate the protection of protected persons. Such action involves the appointment of a Protecting Power, the establishment of a National Protected Person Information Bureau, the establishment of a Central Information Agency for Protected Persons, the notification to the opposing belligerent of certain laws and policies as to protected persons, the provision of useful information as to the geographical location of places of internment and the notification to detained persons, to the Power to which they owe allegiance and to the Protecting Power of measures taken e.g. as to correspondence, family visits and relief shipments, and of any changes to such measures.

PROTECTED PERSON STATUS

Section 10.3 correctly identifies that GC refers to the notion of 'protected persons' and, citing the *GC Commentary*,[3] that such persons mainly comprise enemy nationals living in the belligerent State and inhabitants of occupied territory. The important point is made that certain baseline protective rules apply to detained persons who are neither protected persons nor PWs. Towards the end of paragraph 10.3.1, it is noted that '[a]lthough the GC addresses the protection of civilians, *protected persons* may include certain unprivileged belligerents'. This is an interesting observation, in that it acknowledges that at least some individuals categorised by the US as unprivileged belligerents nevertheless are entitled to protected person status. The paragraph then asserts that '[c]ertain rights and privileges that protected persons who are unprivileged belligerents receive . . . are subject to derogation for security reasons'. This will be discussed later, in relation to section 10.4.

Paragraph 10.3.2 defines persons protected by the Convention using the language of GC, Article 4(1), noting correctly that the notion of persons in the hands of a party to a conflict of which they are not nationals permits the possible inclusion of stateless persons. Basing itself on the writings of a distinguished assistant Attorney General, paragraph 10.3.2.1 suggests that an element of happenstance or coincidence is implicit in the notion of persons 'finding themselves' in the hands of a party to a conflict of which they are not nationals. In the view of the present authors, the 'find themselves' language, when combined with the preceding words 'in any manner whatsoever', suggests that

3 Page 45.

the circumstances giving rise to the presence of such persons in the relevant location are irrelevant to their protected person status. Citing the same assistant Attorney General, paragraph 10.3.2.2 suggests that '[t]o be entitled to the protections provided under the GC for "protected persons", a person must be located in either (1) occupied territory or (2) the home territory of a Party to the conflict'. Insofar as item (2) is concerned, this is not what Article 4(1) of the Convention states. It provides that being 'in the hands of' a Party to the conflict of which they are not nationals' is the criterion. The present authors would argue that a civilian person who is in the hands of an opposing belligerent outside that belligerent's territory has protected person status under GC. Specifically, a decision by the Detaining Power to hold such persons, detained in connection with an international armed conflict, in a location that is not within the sovereign territory of that Power does not affect the detainees' entitlement to protected status under GC. It is, of course, appreciated and accepted that when the GC *Commentary* was written, the main classes of protected person were indeed those in occupied territory and in the territory of the Detaining Power. That does not affect the protected status of persons in the hands of a belligerent of which they are not nationals otherwise than on its territory, nor does the general applicability of the Convention to such persons affect the accepted fact that particular Convention provisions are stated to apply only to those detained in the territory of the party to the conflict. Such particular provisions do not, however, affect the generality of application of Article 4(1).

Paragraph 10.3.2.3 is right that persons protected under one of the other three Geneva Conventions are not protected persons under GC, and previous hostile or belligerent conduct does not *per se* disentitle a person to GC protected person status.[4] Reference should, however, be made to the discussion of section 10.4.

Paragraph 10.3.3 correctly notes that, by covering the populations of the parties to the conflict in their entirety, Part II of the Convention has a wider scope of application than protected persons as provided for in Article 4. The *Manual* also correctly notes that a State's own nationals who are in its hands are not protected persons and that nationals of a neutral State who find themselves in the territory of a belligerent State or nationals of a co-belligerent State are not regarded as protected persons while their State of nationality has normal diplomatic representation in the State in whose hands they are.[5] The

[4] *DoD Manual*, paragraph 10.3.2.4.

[5] GC, Article 4(2); *DoD Manual*, paragraph 10.3.3.3, and see footnote 46 on page 652 as to the negotiating background to this provision.

paragraph makes the important point that civilian nationals of a neutral State in occupied territory are protected persons.

Paragraph 10.3.4 rightly observes that protected person status commences from the outset of any occupation or conflict mentioned in Article 2 and generally ceases when the GC ceases to apply, namely on the general close of military operations where the territories of the parties to the conflict are concerned, i.e. the final close of all fighting. In the case of occupation, the GC ceases to apply one year after the general close of military operations, but the Occupying Power is bound, for the duration of the occupation, to the extent that such Power exercises the functions of government in such territory, by the provisions of the articles specified in Article 6(3) of GC and correctly restated in paragraph 10.3.4 of the *Manual*. Protected persons whose release, repatriation or re-establishment takes place after the one-year period has expired continue to benefit from GC until that event.[6]

A State's responsibility for the treatment accorded to protected persons by its agents is established by GC, Article 29 and is repeated in paragraph 10.3.5. The following paragraph notes that protected persons may not wholly or partially renounce their rights under GC or under special agreements referred to in GC, Article 7.[7]

DEROGATION FOR SECURITY REASONS

Article 5(1) of GC applies where a protected person in the territory of a party to the conflict 'is definitely suspected of or engaged in activities hostile to the security of the State' and provides that he or she shall not be entitled to claim such GC rights and privileges as, if exercised by him or her, would prejudice that State's security. Article 5(2) addresses protected persons detained in occupied territory as spies, saboteurs or as persons definitely suspected of activity hostile to the security of the Occupying Power. '[S]uch persons shall, in those cases where absolute military security so requires, be regarded as having forfeited rights of communication under [GC].' The requirement to treat such persons with humanity, not to deprive them in case of trial of the rights of a fair and regular trial and to grant them full GC rights and privileges at the earliest date consistent with the security of the State or Occupying Power is set forth in Article 5(3). These provisions are stated accurately in Section 10.4.

[6] GC, Article 6(4); *DoD Manual*, paragraph 10.3.4.

[7] GC, Article 8; *DoD Manual*, paragraph 10.3.6.

Paragraph 10.4.3 argues that where protected persons are located outside occupied territory or the territory of a party to the conflict, but where the circumstances specified in Article 5(1) or (2) apply, 'it would be reasonable for such rights and privileges similarly to be subject to derogation'. It is noteworthy, first, that the possibility of protected persons being outside occupied or belligerent State territory is being explicitly acknowledged here, an acknowledgement that sits uncomfortably with the terms of paragraph 10.3.2.2 discussed earlier. Second, as the somewhat hesitant language of paragraph 10.4.3 implies, there is no explicit GC provision to this effect, meaning that paragraph 10.4.3 is seeking to deprive rights from those to whom the GC would require such rights to be accorded, which is a less than satisfactory approach.

HUMANE TREATMENT AND OTHER BASIC PROTECTIONS FOR PROTECTED PERSONS

Section 10.5 restates in terms the general protections for protected persons prescribed in Article 27(1) of GC. Paragraph 10.5.1 explains these protections in legally correct terms. The prohibition of measures of physical suffering, extermination or other brutality, such as murder, torture, corporal punishment and medical or scientific experiments not necessitated by the medical treatment of a protected person as set forth in Article 32 of GC, is restated in paragraph 10.5.1.1.

Paragraph 10.5.1.2 restates the GC, Article 27(2) special protection of women against any attack on their honour, particularly rape, enforced prostitution, and any form of indecent assault, making the point that this provision is properly interpreted nowadays as also protecting men and children against these offences. Paragraph 10.5.1.3 repeats the GC, Article 28 prohibition of using protected persons to render points or areas immune from military operations, i.e. as human shields, while the GC, Article 34 prohibition of the taking of hostages is noted in paragraph 10.5.1.4.

Paragraph 10.5.2 states that '[i]nternees must at all times be protected against insults and public curiosity'. No GC authority is cited. In fact, the second sentence of GC, Article 27(1) stipulates that protected persons 'shall be protected especially against all acts of violence or threats thereof and against insults and public curiosity'. It is therefore suggested that the paragraph be amended to show that the protection applies to all protected persons, not just internees, and that a footnote be inserted citing the GC provision.

Paragraph 10.5.3.1 correctly notes the GC, Article 31 stipulation that '[n]o physical or moral coercion shall be exercised against protected persons, in particular to obtain information from them or from third parties'. The paragraph goes on, however, to note that the requirements of US law and policy and other requirements would also apply to interrogation of protected persons. This is correct, provided it is understood that any such additional requirements must not amount to or permit physical or moral coercion. It is, however, right for the paragraph to note that this provision does not prohibit the use of lawful force to protect one internee against another or to prevent escape from internment.

Punishment of a protected person for an offence he or she did not commit, collective punishments, intimidation, terrorism, pillage and reprisals against protected persons are all prohibited by Article 33 of GC and by paragraphs 10.5.3.2 to 10.5.4; moreover, the GC, Article 27(3) prohibition on making adverse distinctions based on race, religion or political opinion is restated verbatim in paragraph 10.5.5.[8]

Paragraph 10.5.6 restates in terms the requirements of GC, Article 30 that protected persons be given every facility for applying to the Protecting Powers, the ICRC, national Red Cross/Crescent etc. societies and any other organisation that may assist them; such organisations must in turn be provided all facilities for that purpose. Likewise, the Detaining or Occupying Powers must facilitate visits to protected persons by representatives of other organisations whose object is to give spiritual aid or material relief to such persons. The obligations are spelt out in an associated footnote.[9]

MEASURES OF CONTROL AND SECURITY

Section 10.6 restates the Article 27(4) general permission for a party to the conflict to take such control and security measures in relation to protected persons as may be necessary as a result of the war. Sensible examples are given of the kinds of person to whom such measures might reasonably be applied, and equally sensible suggestions are given as to the kinds of measure that might appropriately be taken, ranging from reporting requirements or a requirement to carry identity cards or particular papers to assigned residence or internment. Section 10.6 starts by considering searches. These are, clearly, measures of control, and will therefore be lawful, as the paragraph makes clear, in accordance with Article 27(4) to the extent that they satisfy the

8 Permitted distinctions for humanitarian reasons are noted by reference to the *GC Commentary*, page 426, as is the absence of a prohibition of favourable distinctions to advance legitimate interests such as the maintenance of order in a place of internment.

9 *DoD Manual*, footnote 87 on page 658. This note includes a useful extract from *GC Commentary*, page 218.

necessity criterion. Any such search must be conducted consistently with the humane treatment requirement, with the dignity and honour of the protected person being protected as far as possible. The advisability of having a witness present during such searches is also usefully mentioned. As paragraph 10.6.1.2 notes, only women may search female internees, whereas it is merely appropriate for female protected persons also to be searched by women.

Without citing an authority for this, paragraph 10.6.1.3 asserts that when necessary for security reasons, protected persons may be temporarily secured with handcuffs, flexi cuffs, blindfolds or other security devices. When such securing ceases to be temporary is not made clear, and which security devices would be regarded as unacceptable for such purposes is also not made clear. It would be sensible to address all three of these shortcomings. Paragraph 10.6.1.4 states that protected persons' property may be removed and searched 'when necessary as a result of the war'. This also seems a rather non-specific basis for what is expressed as a wide-ranging power. The property of protected persons may, of course, take a great number of forms, and the suggested power is not supported here by any cited authority. The paragraph is right that property should be returned as soon as possible absent a lawful reason for its seizure, and in that regard Article 46(2) of the Hague Regulations 1907, which prohibits confiscation of private property, should be borne in mind, subject to Articles 52 and 53(2) thereof.

Paragraph 10.6.2 correctly states that any interrogations of protected persons must be conducted in accordance with the general protections discussed in section 10.5 and paragraph 10.5.3.1. The US law and policy on interrogations, referred to in paragraph 10.6.2.2, must not, of course, contradict protections granted in GC. Paragraph 10.6.3 correctly explains that the most severe measures of control that may be imposed are assigned residence and internment under GC, Articles 42 and 43.[10] Likewise, if the Occupying Power considers it necessary for imperative reasons of security to take safety measures, it may at most subject protected persons to assigned residence or internment.[11]

Paragraph 10.6.4 correctly sets forth the somewhat complex arrangements in Articles 41(2) and 78(3) GC, the purpose of which is to seek to ensure that the support that is provided to protected persons who are subjected to assigned residence is guided by the standards applicable to internment cases. Likewise, protected persons in occupied territory made subject to assigned residence and therefore required to leave their homes enjoy the full protection of GC, Article 39. Paragraph 10.6.5 restates a somewhat obscure provision in Article 44 of GC that when 'applying the measures of control mentioned' in GC, 'the

[10] GC, Article 41(1). [11] GC, Article 78(1).

Detaining Power shall not treat as enemy aliens exclusively on the basis of their nationality *de jure* of an enemy State, refugees who do not, in fact, enjoy the protection of any government'. This, of course, leaves open the possibility of treating them as such on other grounds.[12]

GENERAL TREATMENT OF PROTECTED PERSONS IN A BELLIGERENT'S OWN TERRITORY

Paragraph 10.7.1 repeats verbatim GC, Article 38, which stipulates that, with the exception of special measures under GC such as measures of control and security, the situation of protected persons shall continue to be regulated in principle by the provisions relating to aliens in time of peace. The paragraph, and the article, then list specific rights that must be granted to them, namely to receive relief sent to them, to receive necessary medical attention and hospital treatment to the same extent as the State's own nationals, to be allowed to practice their religion and to receive spiritual assistance, to be allowed to move from areas particularly exposed to war dangers to the same extent as the State's own nationals and, in the case of children, pregnant women and mothers of young children, to benefit from preferential treatment to the same extent as nationals of the State.[13]

Protected persons who lose their employment as a result of the war must be given the opportunity to find paid employment, which, subject to security considerations and to Article 40,[14] must be an equal opportunity to that enjoyed by nationals of the Power in whose territory they are.[15]

Article 39(2) provides that when control measures are applied to a protected person that result in his or her inability to support him- or herself, particularly when the measures prevent the finding of paid employment on reasonable conditions, the party to the conflict applying those conditions shall provide support to the relevant person and to his or her dependents, a provision repeated in paragraph 10.7.2.1. Moreover, allowances may be received by that person from the home country, from relief societies mentioned in Article 30 or from the Protecting Power.[16]

The restrictions on compulsory work by protected persons in a belligerent's own territory that are set forth in GC, Article 40 are all repeated verbatim in paragraph 10.7.3. The next paragraph, namely paragraph 10.7.4, restates in

[12] See *DoD Manual*, footnote 106 on page 661.
[13] Some of the detail of these provisions has been omitted in the interests of appropriate brevity.
[14] GC, Article 40 addresses the situation when protected persons are compelled to work.
[15] GC, Article 39(1); *DoD Manual*, paragraph 10.7.2.
[16] GC, Article 39(3); *DoD Manual*, paragraph 10.7.2.2.

terms the requirement of Article 46 that restrictive measures as to protected persons and their property be cancelled as soon as possible after the close of hostilities, in the latter case in accordance with the Detaining Power's law. The present authors are unclear why this provision is located at this exact point in the *Manual*.

EXPULSION FROM AREAS WITHIN A BELLIGERENT'S HOME TERRITORY AND DEPARTURE AND TRANSFERS OF PROTECTED PERSONS FROM A BELLIGERENT'S HOME TERRITORY

Paragraph 10.8.1 asserts the right of a belligerent to expel or bar citizens or subjects of the enemy State from areas within its own territory. These areas are specified as seaports, the area surrounding airbases, airports, fortified places, areas of possible attack and actual or contemplated theatres of operation, subject to a requirement of reasonable notice. The paragraph states that Articles 41 to 45 of GC do not apply to this right, basing that contention, footnote 120 on page 664 would suggest, on the point that expelling or barring is not to be equated with the assignment of a specific residence. Arguably, it would have been preferable if the *Manual* had given best-practice guidance suggesting the application of so much of Articles 41 to 45 as the particular circumstances permit.

Paragraph 10.8.2 deals with the departure of protected persons from a belligerent's own territory, and precisely restates the provisions of Articles 35 to 37 of GC, in particular the right of protected persons to leave the territory at the outset of or during a conflict unless their departure is contrary to the national interests of the State. The GC provisions, also repeated in the *Manual*, entitle a protected person who is refused permission to leave to a reconsideration of that refusal. Transfer of protected persons to a Power that is not party to the GC is prohibited. These considerations do not, however, prejudice repatriation or return of protected persons to their country of residence after the close of hostilities.[17] GC, Article 45(4) provides that 'in no circumstances shall a protected person be transferred to a country where he or she may have reason to fear persecution for his or her political opinions or religious beliefs', and this important non-refoulement rule is repeated in paragraph 10.8.3.1. That paragraph continues: '[i]n addition, US policy provides that no detainee shall be transferred to another State if it is more likely than not that the detainee would be tortured in the receiving country.' A number of points should be

[17] GC, Article 45(1) and (2); *DoD Manual*, paragraph 10.8.3. The Detaining Power must satisfy itself of the ability and willingness of the receiving Power to apply the Convention.

made here. First, torture is only one facet of the broader notion used in the Convention, namely persecution. Second, 'more likely than not' is significantly more restrictive in terms of the cases to which it would apply than the 'reason to fear' language in the Convention. Footnote 110 on page 506 of the *Manual* indicates that this US policy is consequent on its participation in the Torture Convention, so the proper interpretation of the language in paragraph 10.8.3.1 seems to be that the US must have additional policy provision specifically reflecting the more extensive obligation in Article 45(4). It would perhaps be useful to refer to that arguably more relevant policy. GC, Article 45(5)'s exemption from the rule for extradition under treaties negotiated before the outbreak of hostilities is then restated.

As GC, Article 45(3) makes clear, if protected persons are transferred, responsibility for GC compliance rests with the Power receiving them while they are in its custody. In the event of failure in that regard, the transferring Power, when notified by the Protecting Power, must take effective measures to correct the situation or request the return of the protected persons: a request that must be complied with.[18]

INTERNMENT

The *Manual*, like GC, starts the Internment section with a requirement that '[t]he parties to the conflict shall not intern protected persons, except in accordance with the provisions of Articles 41, 42, 43, 68 and 78'.[19] Paragraph 10.9.1 draws useful parallels and contrasts between the detention of PWs and the internment of protected persons. The humane treatment requirement, the non-punitive nature of the detention/internment and the Detaining Power's responsibility for treatment of PWs/internees are correctly cited as points of similarity. The requirements for separation of internees from PWs, that internees' internment shall end when the circumstances that necessitated it no longer apply (which may[20] be before the end of the hostilities) and that internees lack certain privileges and immunities to which PWs are entitled are also correctly cited as points of difference between the two classes of individual.

Paragraph 10.9.2 states the general rule in GC, Article 42(1) that internment or assignment of residence in home territory for protected persons shall

[18] *DoD Manual*, paragraph 10.8.3.2 repeats this rule in terms.

[19] GC, Article 79; *DoD Manual*, section 10.9.

[20] The *Manual* notes that the continued internment of some protected persons who have taken an active part in the hostilities may be necessary in order to prevent their participation in the conflict.

only be ordered if the Detaining Power's security makes it absolutely necessary. The requirements and arrangements as to reconsideration of internment or assigned residence and related matters are set forth in Articles 42 and 43 of GC and are restated verbatim in paragraph 10.9.2. Paragraph 10.9.3 notes that the arrangements relating to internment and assignment of residence for protected persons in occupied territory are less elaborate than those applying in home territory, explaining the difference on the basis of practicability concerns. The general rule that '[i]f the Occupying Power considers it necessary, for imperative reasons of security, to take safety measures concerning protected persons, it may, at the most, subject them to assigned residence or to internment' is repeated verbatim in paragraph 10.9.3.1.

The requirements in Article 78(2) that the Occupying Power set up a regular GC-compliant procedure for making decisions on internment and assignment of residence, that there be a right of appeal, that appeals be decided with the least possible delay and that upheld decisions be subject to periodic review, if possible every six months, by a competent body set up by the Occupying Power are restated in the same paragraph. Citing FM 27–10,[21] paragraph 433b and a US Senate Executive Report 84–9 of 27 June 1955, the *Manual* contends that '"Competent bodies" to [undertake these reviews] may be created with advisory functions only, leaving the final decision to a high official of the Government'. As just noted, however, that is not what the Convention stipulates. The Convention requirement is that the review be by a competent body set up by the Occupying Power, not by an official advised by a competent body. Paragraph 10.9.3.2 refers to the provisions of Chapter XI as to the internment of persons being punished for committing minor offences against the Occupying Power. Those provisions will be addressed in Chapter 11 of the present volume.

Paragraph 10.9.4 restates the language of GC, Article 81 as to the obligation of the Detaining Power to provide free of charge for the maintenance of and necessary medical attention for internees and to provide for the support of their dependents who lack adequate means of support or cannot earn a living. Paragraphs 10.9.5 and 10.9.6 reproduce GC, Article 132's requirement for interned persons to be released as soon as the reasons necessitating internment no longer exist, and for the parties to the conflict to try to reach agreements for the release, repatriation, return to places of residence or accommodation in a neutral country of particular 'classes of internees, in particular children,

[21] *US Department of the Army Field Manual: The Law of Land Warfare* (1956), as amended by Change No. 1, dated 15 July 1976.

pregnant women and mothers with infants and young children, wounded and sick, and internees who have been detained for a long time'.

SEGREGATION OF INTERNEES

Paragraph 10.10.1 correctly notes that internees must be accommodated separately from PWs and persons detained for other reasons.[22] The requirement to accommodate internees as far as possible according to nationality, language and customs and the provisions of GC, Article 82, including requirements that internment arrangements be family-sensitive, are accurately set forth and discussed in paragraphs 10.10.2 and 10.10.3.

SAFETY, HYGIENE AND LIVING CONDITIONS IN PLACES OF INTERNMENT

Paragraphs 10.11.1.1 to 10.11.1.3 deal with the safety arrangements that GC, Article 83 requires for internment camps, which include not locating them in areas particularly exposed to dangers of war, giving enemy Powers all useful information as to their geographical location and marking them 'whenever military considerations permit' with the letters 'IC' or in other agreed ways. GC *Commentary*, page 383, is cited to show that the aforementioned caveat reflects that marking is not required 'e.g. if such identification would enable an Enemy Power to instigate a revolt in the camp, provide weapons to the internees, enable escape attempts etc'.[23]

The requirements that sufficient air-raid shelters (in terms of number and structure) be provided in all places of internment exposed to air raids and other hazards of war, that internees be free to enter them as quickly as possible (subject to the stated exception), that any protective measures in favour of the population also apply to internees and that all due precautions be taken against fire are given in GC, Article 88 and restated in paragraph 10.11.1.4 and 10.11.1.5.

Paragraph 10.11.2 restates that part of Article 85(1) which prohibits the location of permanent places of internment in areas that are unhealthy or have an injurious climate. Both provisions require that when an internee is temporarily interned in such an area, he or she shall be removed to a more suitable place of internment as rapidly as the circumstances permit. Hygienic, constantly clean sanitary conveniences (i.e. latrines) must be available day and

[22] GC, Article 84. [23] *DoD Manual*, paragraph 10.11.1.3, second part.

night, and the GC requires that sufficient soap, water and proper facilities be provided for personal cleaning and laundry.[24]

Paragraph 10.11.3 reflects the GC, Article 85(1) obligation for the Detaining Power to do everything possible to ensure that internees are accommodated in buildings or quarters affording every possible health and hygiene safeguard. Protection from dampness, adequate heating and lighting (particularly between dusk and lights out), sufficiently spacious and well-ventilated sleeping quarters, suitable bedding and sufficient blankets are all required, taking into account the climate and the age, sex and state of health of the internees. Female internees who are not interned as part of a family unit must be given separate sleeping quarters and sanitary conveniences.[25]

CANTEENS FOR INTERNEES

Section 10.12 starts with the requirement in GC, Article 87(1) that canteens be installed in every place of internment, except where other suitable facilities are available. The *Manual* suggests local shops as suitable facilities that would exclude the need for canteens, and this may indeed be the case, depending on prices charged, the merchandise available and other factors. Whether, as the *Manual* suggests, the provision of comfort packs free of charge would also obviate the need to establish canteens is likely to depend on what the comfort packs contain and whether internees' needs are addressed by them.

Paragraph 10.12.2, after quoting the second part of Article 87(1), makes the valid point that this provision does not entitle internees to more favourable treatment in relation to purchases from canteens than the local population, with internees also being subject to rationing that is applied to the population generally. Paragraph 10.12.3 deals with canteen management and profits, repeating the provisions of GC, Article 87(2) and (3).

FOOD, WATER, TOBACCO AND CLOTHING FOR INTERNEES

Paragraph 10.13.1 repeats the GC, Article 89 requirements that daily food rations for internees be sufficient in quantity, quality and variety to keep them in good health, that they be given sufficient drinking water, that internees' customary diet be taken into account, that working internees be given additional rations in proportion to the work they do and that expectant and nursing mothers and children under fifteen be given additional food in proportion to

[24] GC, Article 85(3); *DoD Manual*, paragraphs 10.11.2.1 and 10.11.2.2.

[25] GC, Article 85(2) and (4); *DoD Manual*, paragraphs 10.11.3 and 10.11.3.1.

their physiological needs. As paragraph 10.13.3 notes, while Article 89(3) states that internees must be allowed to use tobacco, the arrangements for doing so should be consistent with the maintenance of a healthy environment. Paragraph 10.13.4 reproduces GC, Article 90 as to internees' clothing. Internees who do not have and cannot procure sufficient clothing, taking the climate into account, must receive clothing free of charge from the Detaining Power. Such supplied clothing must not be ignominious nor expose them to ridicule, and workers must receive suitable working outfits, including protective clothing, 'whenever the nature of their work so requires'.

MEDICAL ATTENTION FOR INTERNEES

The general rule is that parties to the conflict who intern protected persons must grant them the medical attention required by their state of health.[26]

Paragraph 10.14.1.2 quotes the GC, Article 91(4) requirement that '[i]nternees may not be prevented from presenting themselves to the medical authorities for examination'. The *Manual* also notes GC, Article 125, which stipulates that internees awarded disciplinary punishment 'shall be allowed, if they so request, to be present at the daily medical inspections. They shall receive the attention which their state of health requires'.[27] Paragraph 10.14.1.2 suggests that internees may be subjected to disciplinary punishment if they abusively (on the basis of a doctor's report) make groundless requests for medical examination. This is an interpretation that is not supported by explicit language in the Convention and that is based on the Commentary.[28] It is, in the opinion of the present authors, difficult to reconcile the unqualified right set forth in GC, Article 125(2) with the idea that disciplinary action might legitimately be taken against those exercising that unqualified right. Article 92's requirement that medical inspections of internees shall be made at least once per month, and its stipulations as to the purpose of such inspections and the matters to be included in them, are repeated verbatim in paragraph 10.14.1.3.[29]

The GC, Article 91(2) obligation to grant maternity cases, internees suffering from serious diseases and those whose condition requires special treatment, a surgical operation or hospital care admission to any institution where adequate care can be given and the related stipulation that that care cannot be inferior to that provided to the general population are repeated in

[26] GC, Article 81(1); *DoD Manual*, section 10.14.

[27] GC, Article 125(2). [28] *GC Commentary*, pages 495–6.

[29] In this regard, see also the first sentence of Article 91(4) of GC.

paragraph 10.14.3.1. The preference that treatment be given by personnel of their own nationality, the requirement for the medical authorities, when requested, to issue internees with certificates as to the illness or injury and as to the treatment given and the stipulation that treatment and associated appliances shall be free of charge to the internee are found in GC, Article 91(3), (4) and (5) and are repeated in paragraphs 10.14.3.2, 10.14.3.3 and 10.14.3.4.

RELIGIOUS EXERCISE BY INTERNEES

The freedom of internees to exercise their religious duties subject to compliance with prescribed disciplinary routines is stated in GC, Article 93(1) and repeated in section 10.15; the Article 86 obligation for the Detaining Power to make suitable premises available to internees for such purposes is reflected in paragraph 10.15.1. Paragraphs 10.15.1 to 10.15.2.1 repeat the provisions of Article 93(2) that interned ministers of religion must be allowed to minister freely to the members of their community, that if they are too few in number the Detaining Power must give them the necessary facilities, including means of transport, and that they must be authorised to visit internees in hospital. Subject to censorship, ministers of religion must also be permitted to correspond with the religious authorities of the country of detention and with 'international religious organizations of their faith'. Article 93(3)'s provision for local religious authorities to appoint ministers with the agreement of the Detaining Power where internees do not have the assistance of ministers of their faith is reflected in paragraph 10.15.3.

INTELLECTUAL, PHYSICAL AND RECREATIONAL ACTIVITIES

Section 10.16 repeats and expands upon GC, Article 94's requirement that the Detaining Power encourage, but not compel, intellectual, educational and recreational pursuits among internees, including sports and games. The treaty obligations to grant all possible facilities for study, to ensure the education of children and young people, to set aside sufficient open spaces in places of internment and to reserve special playgrounds for children and young people are all restated. The *Manual* asserts the lawfulness of censoring educational or intellectual materials for security reasons and is probably correct in that regard. However, refusing to supply internees with anti-democratic political propaganda, which the *Manual* suggests is lawful, is likely to be legally questionable unless it can be shown that the relevant material is likely to be prejudicial to the security of the Detaining Power.

INTERNEE LABOR

As paragraph 10.17.1 points out, the Detaining Power must not employ internees as workers unless the internees themselves desire to be so employed. Moreover, employment is prohibited if (1) it would breach Article 40 or 51[30] if undertaken by a protected person not in internment and (2) it is degrading or humiliating in character.[31]

The provisions of Article 95(4) as to working conditions and wage agreements are reflected in paragraphs 10.17.3 and 10.17.4. Paragraph 10.17.5, replicating Article 96 of GC, deals with labour detachments, noting that they remain part of and dependent on a place of internment and that the competent authorities of the Detaining Power and the commandant of the place of internment are responsible for the observance in them of the GC.

INTERNEES' ARTICLES OF PERSONAL USE

The general rule in Article 97(1), repeated in paragraph 10.18.1, is that internees 'shall be permitted to retain articles of personal use'. Paragraph 10.18.2 argues that internees are not entitled to retain articles that could be used contrary to the interests of the Detaining Power, giving as examples items that pose a risk to security or that might facilitate escape, such as weapons, flares, compasses, maps and cell phones. The present authors consider that this accurately reflects the current law. Articles that are above all of personal or sentimental value may not be taken away, and family or identity documents may only be taken if a receipt is given.[32]

FINANCIAL RESOURCES OF INTERNEES

GC, Article 97(1), reflected in paragraph 10.19.1, prohibits taking monies, cheques, bonds etc. and valuables in the possession of detainees otherwise than in accordance with established procedure, requires the giving of receipts, requires that the amounts taken be paid into accounts provided for in Article 98 and prohibits conversion into another currency unless applicable legislation so requires or the internee consents. Paragraph 10.19.1.1

[30] See the discussion associated with paragraph 10.7.3. [31] GC, Article 95(1).

[32] GC, Article 97(3) and (6); *DoD Manual* paragraphs 10.18.2 and 10.18.3. The latter paragraph notes that internees must at no time be left without identity documents and that if they have none, special documents shall be drawn up and issued to them by the detaining authorities; GC, Article 97(6).

and Article 97(7) permit the retention of pocket money by internees to make purchases. All internees must receive regular allowances sufficient to enable them to purchase goods and articles, and may receive additional allowances from the Power to which they owe allegiance, the Protecting Powers, any organisations that might assist them or their families. Payments from the Power to which they owe allegiance must not be allocated or distributed on the basis of prohibited discrimination.[33] The detailed provisions of GC, Article 98(3) as to internees' accounts are restated in full in paragraphs 10.19.3 to 10.19.3.2. The required arrangements as to the return to internees of their valuables and the settlement of their accounts on release or repatriation and the requirement to give a detailed receipt when articles are withheld by virtue of applicable legislation, set forth in 97(5) of GC, are repeated in paragraph 10.19.3.3.

ADMINISTRATION OF PLACES OF INTERNMENT AND DISCIPLINE

Article 99 of GC requires that places of internment be placed under the authority of a responsible officer of the regular military forces or civil administration of the Detaining Power. He or she must have the GC in his or her possession and is responsible for its application, and the staff controlling internees must be instructed in the GC and in the administrative measures taken to ensure its application. Article 99 requires that the GC be available in a language the internees understand in the place of internment and that regulations, orders, notices and publications be in a language the internees understand.[34]

The disciplinary regime in internment camps must comply with humanitarian principles and must not involve: physical exertion that is dangerous to the health of internees; physical or moral victimisation; identification by tattooing or imprinting of marks on the human body; prolonged standing and roll calls; punishment drill; military drill and manoeuvres; or reduction in food rations.[35]

Paragraph 10.20.4 correctly characterises the use of weapons against internees, especially those escaping or attempting to escape, as an extreme measure always to be preceded by a warning, but qualifies this in paragraph 10.20.4.1 by noting that non-lethal weapons may be used against rioting protected persons or to prevent escape (presumably of internees, although that

[33] GC, Article 98(2); *DoD Manual*, paragraphs 10.19.1.1 and 10.19.2; and see Article 27 of GC.

[34] These provisions are repeated in paragraphs 10.20.1 and 10.20.2 of the *DoD Manual*.

[35] GC, Article 100, repeated in paragraphs 10.20.3 to 10.20.3.2.

is not specified). As non-lethal weapons still constitute weapons, presumably their employment against internees is still seen as an extreme measure that must be preceded by a warning. It is suggested that this should be clarified in paragraph 10.20.4.1. It is right that the use of riot control agents against rioting protected persons as a law enforcement measure would not be prohibited by the CWC. Simply to say that it is not prohibited, as paragraph 10.20.4.1 does, ignores potentially applicable restrictions in domestic law relating to the use of force.

INTERNEE PETITIONS, COMPLAINTS AND REPORTS ABOUT CONDITIONS OF INTERNMENT

The GC, Article 101(1) right of internees to petition the authorities in whose power they are as to conditions of internment and their right to indicate complaints as to conditions of internment to the Internee Committee or the Protecting Power are repeated in paragraph 10.21.1, while the role of ICRC delegates in this regard is noted in paragraph 10.21.1.1. After noting that such complaints must be forwarded unaltered and without delay, and that they must not occasion punishment even if unfounded, the *Manual* asserts that the Detaining Power 'has the right to examine and censor petitions and complaints for security reasons', basing this view on the idea, put forward in the GC *Commentary*, that although censorship is not permitted, 'some supervision by the Detaining Power must be allowed "for security reasons"'.[36] The treaty provision is, however, clear. It prohibits alteration of the complaints. While a review of such complaints that does not involve any delay in their transmission is therefore legitimate, the present authors are satisfied that censorship of them would be a breach of the Convention rule. In paragraph 10.21.1.1, at line 5, there seems to be an erroneous reference to PWs, which is perhaps a typographical error.

The periodic reports by Internee Committees as to the situation in places of internment and the needs of internees may be sent to representatives of the Protecting Powers.[37]

[36] *DoD Manual*, paragraph 10.21.2.1 and footnote 332 on page 691, referring to GC *Commentary*, pages 435–6. While footnote 331 argues that 'matter not constituting either a complaint or report' may lawfully be deleted, it is suggested that care is required here. It would, for example, not be right to delete contextual matter that serves to explain the basis, gravity, context etc. of the matters about which complaint is made, or indeed any matter that is in any way relevant to the topic of complaint.

[37] GC, Article 101(4); *DoD Manual*, paragraph 10.21.3.

INTERNEE COMMITTEES

Articles 102 and 103 of GC, reflected in paragraphs 10.22.1 and 10.22.1.1, make detailed provision as to the mandatory election by internees in every place of internment, and as to the subsequent approval by the detaining authorities, of members of Internee Committees. Their role is representation of the internees before the Detaining and Protecting Powers, the ICRC and any other organisation that may assist them. The duties of these Committees, as prescribed in these articles and elsewhere in the GC, are helpfully brought together in paragraphs 10.22.2 and 10.22.2.2.

Paragraph 10.22.3.1 repeats the GC, Article 104(1) provision that members of Internee Committees may not be required to do other work if it would make the performance of their duties more difficult. As the *Manual* points out, this may seem odd given Article 95(1)'s prohibition of compulsory work for internees, but the *Manual* explains that Article 104(1) is referring to the maintenance (and presumably administrative) duties that internees can be required to undertake in accordance with Article 95(3). Material facilities, including the freedom of movement to perform their duties, such as visiting labour detachments and receiving supplies, must be granted to members of Internee Committees.[38] The rights of communication by post and telegraph provided for in Article 104(3) are repeated verbatim in paragraph 10.22.3.4, where it is noted that censorship can be applied to such communications, provided internees are not disadvantaged by any resulting delay.[39] It would, arguably, have been helpful if the *Manual* had discussed how this rule and the asserted right of censorship might operate in practice in relation to the possible employment of alternative, more modern forms of communication. Here again, the *Manual* satisfies itself with restating the GC provision with the minimum of elaboration.

INTERNEE CORRESPONDENCE AND RELIEF SHIPMENTS

The right of each internee as soon as he or she is interned, or not more than a week thereafter, and in cases of sickness or transfer or hospitalisation, to send to his or her family and to the Central Information Agency an internment card notifying them of his or her internment, address and state of health is provided in GC, Article 106 and stated in terms in paragraph 10.23.1; the cards must be forwarded as rapidly as possible and must not be delayed. Paragraph 10.23.2

[38] GC, Article 104(2); *DoD Manual*, paragraph 10.22.3.3.
[39] *GC Commentary*, page 444 is cited in this regard.

notes that the minimum correspondence that internees shall be permitted to send is two letters and four cards monthly, conforming as closely as possible to the models annexed to the GC at annexes III.II and III.III. Such correspondence must not be delayed or retained for disciplinary reasons.[40] Here again, one would have thought that there ought to have been more consideration given to digital means of communication and some explanation of the US view as to how the present rule should be applied in practice in the digital age. Paragraph 10.23.2.3 refers to telegrams as the rapid means of communication, and the reference to more modern means of communication is cursory and lacking in effective, much needed guidance.

Paragraph 10.23.3 deals, without prejudice to the Detaining Power's obligations, with the internees' right under GC, Article 108(1) to receive individual parcels or collective shipments, which may include foodstuffs, clothing, medical supplies, books and objects of a devotional, educational or recreational character. Article 108(2)'s recognition that military necessity may require the quantity of such shipments to be limited, due notice being given to the relevant organisations, is reflected in the paragraph. Article 108(3) provides that parcels of clothing and foodstuffs may not include books and that medical relief supplies shall as a rule be sent in collective parcels. This, the provisions of Article 109 as to special agreements and regulations concerning receipt and distribution of collective relief shipments and some useful supplementary guidance from *GC Commentary* are all to be found in paragraphs 10.23.3.1 to 10.23.3.4. Paragraph 10.23.4.2 repeats the GC, Article 110(2) exemption of all mail sent to or dispatched by internees from all postal dues. Paragraph 10.23.4.3 gives the exemption from all postal charges, save for surcharges for airmail, provided for in Article 17(2) of the Universal Postal Convention, 1989; notes the 5 kg and 10 kg weight limits; and points out that such items must be marked '*Service des internes civils*', with, if appropriate, a translation. Transport costs for shipments that cannot be sent through the post office are borne by the Detaining Power in all territories under its control and by GC States party in their territories; other transport costs shall be charged to the senders.[41]

'Should military operations prevent the Powers concerned from fulfilling their obligation to ensure the conveyance of the mail and relief shipments provided for in Articles 106, 107, 108 and 113', the Protecting Powers, the ICRC or any other organisation approved by the parties to the conflict 'may undertake the conveyance of such shipments by suitable means'. States party to GC

[40] GC, Article 107(1); *DoD Manual*, paragraphs 10.23.2.1 and 10.23.2.2.
[41] GC, Article 110(3) and (4); *DoD Manual*, paragraph 10.23.4.4.

shall endeavour to provide transport and to allow its circulation, especially by allowing safe conducts. These provisions of GC, Article 111(1) are repeated in paragraph 10.23.5, where the other items that the GC permits such transport to convey are also listed. GC also acknowledges the right of parties to the conflict to arrange other means of transport.[42]

Paragraph 10.23.6, relying on the Final Record of the Diplomatic Conference, correctly states that the Detaining Power has the right to censor all communications sent to or by internees with a view to deleting matter prejudicial to its military security.[43] Likewise, while the examination of consignments for internees is legitimate, it must not be so done as to cause the consignments to deteriorate, it must be done in the presence of the internee or of his or her designated fellow internee and the delivery to internees of individual or collective consignments must not be delayed on the pretext of difficulties over censorship.[44] Article 112(3) and paragraph 10.23.6.2 do, however, permit temporary, short prohibitions of correspondence for military or political reasons.

PRIVATE LEGAL MATTERS OF INTERNEES

As GC, Article 80 and paragraph 10.24.1 provide, '[i]nternees shall retain their full civil capacity and shall exercise such attendant rights as may be compatible with their status'. The Detaining Power must provide all reasonable facilities for transmission to or by internees of wills, powers of attorney, letters of authority or other documents, and must facilitate the execution and authentication of such documents, e.g. by allowing the internee to consult a lawyer.[45] Internees must also be given all facilities to enable them to manage their property, if this is not incompatible with the conditions of internment and applicable law.[46] In the case of court proceedings involving an internee, Article 115 obliges the Detaining Power, if the internee so requests, to inform the court of his or her detention and, within legal limits, to ensure that he or she is not prejudiced in his or her preparation and conduct of his or her case or in any execution of judgment by virtue of his or her internment.[47]

42 GC, Article 111(3).

43 II-A Final Record of the Diplomatic Conference of Geneva of 1949, 839–40.

44 GC, Article 112(1) and (2); *DoD Manual*, paragraphs 10.23.6.1 and 10.23.6.2.

45 GC, Article 113(1) and (2); *DoD Manual*, paragraph 10.24.2. Requirements as to safekeeping of wills in Article 129(1) are restated in paragraph 10.24.2.1.

46 GC, Article 114; *DoD Manual*, paragraph 10.24.3. However, as the *Manual* points out, internees will often delegate their powers, and applicable law may include the Detaining Power's war regulations in relation to enemy property.

47 Repeated in *DoD Manual*, paragraph 10.24.4.

INTERNEES AND VISITS OF FAMILIES AND FRIENDS

Section 10.25 reproduces the Article 116 obligation to allow internees to receive visitors (especially close relatives) regularly and as frequently as possible, as well as to visit their homes in urgent cases, particularly in cases of death or serious illness of relatives.

INTERNEE ESCAPES

On recapture after escaping or attempting to escape, an internee is only liable to disciplinary punishment, even in the case of repeated escapes. The *Manual* correctly notes that unlike PWs, internees are not protected from punishment for successful escapes.[48] Escape or attempted escape is not to be deemed an aggravating circumstance in relation to an offence committed during the escape, and the parties to the conflict must ensure that the competent authorities exercise leniency in deciding between judicial and disciplinary proceedings, especially in relation to acts committed during an escape.[49] As the *Manual* correctly observes, this wording does not presuppose that disciplinary proceedings must be selected in any particular case.

As Article 120(2) provides, and paragraph 10.26.3 repeats, notwithstanding Article 118(3), internees punished for escape or the attempt may be subjected to special surveillance, provided it does not affect their health, is exercised in a place of internment and does not entail abolishing any GC safeguards. Paragraph 10.26.4 deals with the notification responsibilities of the Detaining Power when an internee escapes.

GENERAL PROVISIONS APPLICABLE TO BOTH JUDICIAL AND DISCIPLINARY SANCTIONS REGARDING INTERNEES

It is the law in force in the territory where they are detained that, subject to the provisions of Chapter IX of GC, applies to internees during their internment, and acts that are only punishable if committed by internees shall only attract disciplinary punishment.[50] Internees must not be punished more than once for the same act or on the same count; in sentencing, the court must take into account as far as possible that the defendant is not a national of the Detaining Power; imprisonment in premises without daylight, all forms of cruelty

48 DoD *Manual*, section 10.26 and paragraph 10.26.1. Internees who aid and abet an escape are also only liable to disciplinary punishment; paragraph 10.26.1.1 and see GC, Article 120.

49 DoD *Manual*, paragraphs 10.26.2.1 and 10.26.2.2, correctly repeating GC, Article 121.

50 DoD *Manual*, paragraphs 10.27.1 and 10.27.2, correctly restating GC, Article 117(1) and (2).

and collective punishments are prohibited; and periods of preventive detention shall be deducted from any sentence of confinement that is imposed in judicial or disciplinary proceedings.[51]

DISCIPLINARY PROCEEDINGS AND PUNISHMENT

Paragraph 10.28.1 correctly reproduces GC, Article 123(1) to the effect that apart from courts and higher authorities, disciplinary punishment may only be awarded by the commandant or by the responsible officer or official who replaces him or her and to whom he or she has delegated his or her powers.

Paragraph 10.28.2 restates, with supplementary explanations, Article 122 of GC requiring: that offences against discipline, including escape, be immediately investigated; that recaptured internees be handed over to the competent authorities as soon as possible; that confinement while awaiting trial for disciplinary offences be as short as possible and must not exceed fourteen days; and that the conditions of confinement while awaiting disciplinary trial be no worse than those for confinement under disciplinary sentence. GC, Article 123(2) and (5) requires, *inter alia*, that before any disciplinary punishment is awarded, the accused internee must have precise information of the charges and must be given an opportunity to explain his or her conduct, to defend him- or herself, to call witnesses and to have access to an interpreter. These provisions are accurately restated in paragraphs 10.28.3 and 10.28.4.

Paragraph 10.28.5 accurately deals with the permitted disciplinary punishments as provided for in GC, Article 119. They must not be inhuman, brutal or dangerous to health; the *Manual* correctly suggests that prolonged standing and roll calls, punishment drills, military drills and manoeuvres and reduction in food rations are prohibited punishments. Permitted punishments are a fine of up to 50 per cent of the wages the internee would otherwise receive under Article 95 for up to 30 days, discontinuance of privileges that exceed GC requirements, fatigue duties of up to two hours per day and confinement, all taking into account the age, sex and health of the internee. The punishment must not exceed 30 consecutive days, with confinement awaiting trial being deducted from the sentence of confinement.[52]

[51] *DoD Manual*, paragraphs 10.27.3 to 10.27.4.2, correctly reflecting GC, Articles 117(3) and 118(1), (2) and (4). Once they have served their sentence, such internees should not be treated differently from other internees; *DoD Manual*, paragraph 10.27.5, restating GC, Article 118(3).

[52] GC, Article 122(2). The paragraph restates Article 123(3) and (4)'s requirements that no more than one month expire between disciplinary award and the execution of the sentence, and that at least three days elapse between the execution of any two punishments.

Paragraphs 10.28.6 and 10.28.6.1 require that the conditions in which internees serve disciplinary punishments comport with the requirement for humane treatment. The *Manual* accurately repeats the GC, Article 124 rules; namely, that the transfer of internees to penitentiary establishments to serve disciplinary punishments is prohibited; that premises must conform to sanitary requirements; that adequate bedding must be provided; that internees undergoing punishment must be enabled to keep themselves in a state of cleanliness; and that women internees undergoing disciplinary punishment must be confined in separate quarters under the immediate supervision of women. Paragraphs 10.28.6.2 to 10.28.6.4 correctly repeat the GC, Article 125 rules applicable to internees awarded disciplinary punishment dealing with exercise and access to the open air, daily medical inspections, reading and writing, sending and receiving letters and the provisions of GC, Articles 107 and 143 (addressing the right to make requests and complaints and to have access to the Protecting Power's representatives).

JUDICIAL PROCEEDINGS REGARDING PROTECTED PERSONS IN OCCUPIED TERRITORY OR INTERNEES IN A BELLIGERENT'S HOME TERRITORY

The title to section 10.29 looks unwieldy, but as the section explains, Article 126 of GC applies the penal procedures for protected persons in occupied territories to proceedings against internees in the national territory of the Detaining Power, so it makes sense to deal with both topics together.

Paragraph 10.29.2 deals with pre-trial matters by repeating GC, Article 71(2) and (3). These provisions deal with: giving prompt written notification of the charges and ensuring that they are brought to trial as rapidly as possible; informing the Protecting Power, immediately and at any event at least three weeks before the first hearing, of the proceedings where the death sentence or imprisonment for two years or more is involved; the right of the Protecting Power to obtain information as to the state of the proceedings; the fact that in the absence of evidence that the requirements of GC, Article 71 have been complied with, the trial shall not proceed; and the prescribed particulars to be included in the notification to the Protecting Power.

Paragraphs 10.29.3 and 10.29.3.1 repeat in terms GC, Article 72's provisions as to the accused's right to present evidence in defence, to call witnesses, to be assisted by a qualified advocate of his or her choice (who shall be enabled to visit him or her freely and who shall have the facilities for preparing the defence), to be assisted by an interpreter and to object to the interpreter provided.[53]

The right of representatives of the Protecting Power to attend the proceedings, subject to the exceptional circumstance of a trial *in camera* for security reasons, and the requirement that no sentence be pronounced except after a regular trial are both stated in paragraphs 10.29.3.2 and 10.29.3.3, restating GC, Articles 74(1) and 71(1). Paragraph 10.29.3.4 repeats GC, Article 74(2)'s requirements as to the notification to the Protecting Power of any judgment involving a sentence of death or of imprisonment for two years or more, and the obligation of the court to record other judgments and for this to be open for inspection by representatives of the Protecting Power.

The right of appeal or petition against finding and sentence provided in GC, Article 73 is restated verbatim in paragraph 10.29.4. As to death sentences, GC, Article 75's provisions are restated in full in paragraph 10.29.5, to the effect that persons condemned to death must not be deprived of the right to petition for pardon or reprieve, that at least six months must elapse between notification to the Protecting Power of the sentence or of the order denying pardon or reprieve and the carrying out of the sentence, and that this period may only be reduced in limited circumstances of grave emergency. Paragraph 10.29.6 repeats GC, Article 76's provisions as to the conditions of detained protected persons. These provisions address the separation of such persons from other detainees, food and hygiene, medical attention, the right to receive spiritual assistance, the separate confinement of women, the special treatment due to minors, visits by delegates of the Protecting Power and of the ICRC and the right to receive at least one relief parcel per month.

It is again worthy of note that little or no mention is made of the procedural rights set forth in Article 75 of API, being rights that are widely accepted as having customary law status. While numerous of those rights are reflected in the GC provisions to which reference has already been made, the present authors are of the view that the continuing applicability of these rules could have been reinforced by referring to the corresponding Article 75 provisions.

TRANSFERS OF INTERNEES FROM THE PLACE OF INTERNMENT

Section 10.30 reproduces in terms the GC, Article 127 rules as to the transfer of internees, reordering them into a logical sequence. It starts with the

[53] Note that the paragraphs and the article also deal with the situation in which, failing a choice by the accused, an advocate or counsel is provided by the Protecting Power or, if not, by the Detaining Power.

paragraph 10.30.1 requirement for the Detaining Power to take the interests of internees into account when making decisions as to transfer and not to increase difficulty in repatriating them or returning them to their homes. The paragraph also includes the special rules as to sick, wounded, infirm and maternity cases, namely that they shall not be transferred if the journey would be seriously detrimental to them 'unless their safety imperatively so demands', and as to the removal of internees when the combat zone draws close to a place of internment.

Paragraph 10.30.2 repeats the GC, Article 127(1) requirement that transfers must always be effected humanely, the limitations on the exceptional measure of effecting transfers on foot and the GC, Article 127(2) obligations to take particular precautions, including that the Detaining Power supply internees during transfer with drinking water and food sufficient in quantity, quality and variety to keep them in good health, as well as with necessary clothing, shelter and medical attention.

As to the arrangements for the transfer of internees, paragraph 10.30.3 repeats in terms GC, Article 128's stipulations. The internees must be officially advised of their departure and of their new address, must be given time to pack and to notify next of kin and must be allowed to take their personal effects and correspondence up to not less than 25 kg per internee, and mail and parcels must be forwarded to their new address without delay. There are additional particular arrangements for the transport of community property and as to property internees cannot take with them.

NATIONAL ACCOUNTING FOR PROTECTED PERSONS IN ITS POWER

To facilitate proper accounting for and identification of protected persons in its power, each party to the conflict must within the shortest possible period give to its National Protected Person Information Bureau information as to measures it has taken in respect of protected persons kept in custody for more than two weeks, or who are subject to internment or assigned residence. The information that this Bureau receives and transmits must be such as to make it possible to identify the protected person exactly and to advise his or her next of kin quickly.[54]

[54] GC, Articles 136(2), first sentence and 138(1); *DoD Manual*, paragraph 10.31.1, repeating the required list of information set forth in the second sentence of Article 138(1). The paragraph notes the requirements for the parties to the conflict to notify the Bureau promptly of all changes relating to these protected persons, to give information regularly and at least weekly as to the state of health of internees who are seriously ill or seriously wounded and to forward

Paragraph 10.31.2 reports the GC, Article 136(1) obligation, on the outbreak of an international armed conflict and in all cases of occupation, of parties thereto to establish an official Information Bureau to receive and transmit information relating to protected persons in their power. This Bureau will receive information about protected persons from other departments of the State and shall forward the information as rapidly as possible to the Powers of which the persons are nationals, or where they resided, through the Protecting Powers and through the Central Information Agency for protected persons. As the *Manual* correctly observes, while the Bureau will reply to all enquiries concerning protected persons, it must do so consistently with their protection against insults and public curiosity.[55]

The Bureau has responsibility for collecting all personal valuables left by protected persons who are kept in custody for more than two weeks, or who have been assigned residence or interned. It is responsible for forwarding the valuables to the persons concerned either directly or through the Central Information agency; the obligation and associated detailed requirements, as set forth in GC, Article 139, are accurately stated in paragraph 10.31.2.4. Paragraph 10.31.2.5 brings within this section the important provision in GC, Article 50(4) requiring the setting up of a special section of the Bureau to take all necessary steps to identify children whose identity is in doubt and to record available particulars of their parents or near relatives.

Paragraph 10.31.3 repeats GC, Article 140(1)'s requirement that a Central Information Agency for protected persons be established in a neutral country.[56] It may be the same agency as that provided for in Article 123 of GPW. Its function is to collect from official or private channels all of the information of the kind referred to in Article 136 of GC and to transmit it as rapidly as possible to the countries of origin or of residence of the persons

notices of death, copies of records of death and, as soon as circumstances permit, lists of graves of deceased internees; see GC, Articles 136(2) and 138(2).

55 GC, Articles 136(2) and 137(1) are reflected accurately in *DoD Manual*, paragraph 10.31.2.1; see also paragraph 10.31.2.2. Where transmission of information might be detrimental to the person concerned or his or her relatives, information should nevertheless not be withheld from the Central Information Agency, which on being notified of the relevant circumstances will take appropriate action in accordance with Article 140 (i.e. the Central Agency should not transmit the relevant information to the country of origin or of residence); see GC, Article 140(2).

56 As the *Manual* correctly notes, the functions of this agency have frequently in past conflicts been performed by the ICRC Central Tracing Agency, in relation both to PWs and to protected persons. Paragraph 10.31.4 reports on US practice, which is to the like effect. Paragraph 10.31.5 reflects GC, Article 141's requirement that both the national bureaux and the central agency 'shall enjoy free postage for all mail, likewise the exemptions provided for in article 110' and, as far as possible, exemptions or reduced rates for telegraphic charges.

concerned, except in cases where such transmission may be detrimental to those persons or their relatives.

ROLE OF THE PROTECTING POWER IN GC

Section 10.32 is one of those useful sections which brings together and lists the various functions of an entity that are discussed in the various parts of the Convention and thus under other sections of this chapter of the *Manual*. The section notes that the Protecting Power is an organ for ensuring implementation of the GC, that it transmits information between belligerents, that it monitors compliance with the GC and that it takes an active role in promoting the welfare of protected persons. Paragraph 10.32.1 lists the kinds of information that the Protecting Power helps to transmit between belligerents, while paragraph 10.32.2 lists the kinds of activity that the Protecting Power undertakes to monitor or inspect the Detaining Power's compliance with the GC. Paragraph 10.32.3 states the kinds of activity that the GC contemplates the Protecting Power undertaking to actively work to improve the welfare of protected persons. In the case of each activity, there is a cross reference to its substantive discussion elsewhere in the *Manual*.

ACCESS TO INTERNEES BY PROTECTING POWERS, ICRC AND OTHER RELIEF ORGANIZATIONS

Paragraphs 10.33.1 to 10.33.1.2 reproduce verbatim the provisions of GC, Article 143 granting permission to the delegates or representatives of the Protecting Powers to go to all places where protected persons are, to go to all places occupied by protected persons and to interview protected persons without witnesses personally or through an interpreter. Such visits may only be prohibited exceptionally and temporarily on grounds of imperative military necessity, and there can be no restriction on their duration and frequency. Detailed provision as to the places to be visited, as to participation in such visits by compatriots of the internees, as to the fact that ICRC delegates also enjoy these prerogatives and as to the approval of the appointment of ICRC delegates are included in these paragraphs.

Paragraphs 10.33.2 and 10.33.2.1 accurately reflect the provisions of GC, Article 142. They provide that representatives of religious organisations, relief societies or any other organisations assisting protected persons must receive from the Detaining Powers, subject to security measures deemed necessary or other reasonable need, all facilities for visiting protected persons and distributing relief supplies and material intended for educational, recreational or religious purposes or for helping organise leisure time. Any limitation the

Detaining Power places on the number of societies and organsations so involved must not hinder the supply of effective and adequate relief to all protected persons.

DEATH OF INTERNEES

Noting the obligation of the Detaining Power to receive wills for safe keeping, paragraph 10.34.1 restates the GC, Article 129(1) obligation in the event of the death of an internee to transmit his or her will without delay to the person he or she previously designated. Paragraph 10.34.2 restates the GC, Article 129(2) and (3) requirements for certification of death to be undertaken by a doctor, for a death certificate to be made out showing the cause of death and the conditions in which it occurred and for an official record of the death to be made in accordance with local procedures, a copy being transmitted without delay to the Protecting Power and to the Central Agency referred to in Article 140. The obligation of the detaining authorities to ensure honorable burial, if possible according to the rites of the religion to which the internee belonged and in individual graves, unless the unavoidable circumstances require collective burial, is found in GC, Article 130(1) and repeated in paragraph 10.34.3. Paragraph 10.34.3.1 records the provisions of GC, Article 130(2) that cremation is only permissible for imperative reasons of hygiene, on account of the deceased's religion or in accordance with the deceased's express wishes. The fact of cremation and the reasons must be noted on the death certificate, and the ashes must be kept by the detaining authorities for delivery as soon as possible to the next of kin, at their request.

GC, Article 130(1) and (6) and paragraph 10.34.4 require that graves are respected, properly maintained and marked so they can always be recognised, and that lists of graves be passed to the Power on which the internees depended through the Article 136 Information Bureaux as soon as possible, and no later than the end of hostilities.

Where the death or serious injury of an internee is caused, or suspected to have been caused, by a sentry, another internee or some other person, or where the cause of a death is unknown, there must be an immediate official inquiry by the Detaining Power, with a communication to the Protecting Power. Witnesses' evidence must be taken, and a report must be forwarded to the Protecting Power. Where the inquiry indicates the guilt of one or more persons, the Detaining Power must take the necessary steps to prosecute the persons involved.[57]

[57] GC, Article 13, restated in *DoD Manual*, paragraph 10.34.5.

RELEASE, RETURN, REPATRIATION OF INTERNEES AFTER THE CLOSE OF HOSTILITIES

After noting the GC, Article 133(1) provision that internment shall cease as soon as possible after the close of hostilities, paragraph 10.35.1 makes the valid point that this does not preclude internment thereafter, for example during occupation.[58] Internees in the territory of a party to the conflict against whom penal proceedings are pending for offences not exclusively capable of disciplinary punishment can be detained until the close of the proceedings and, if the circumstances require, until the completion of the penalty.[59]

On the close of hostilities or of occupation, the parties to the GC shall try to ensure the return of all internees to their last place of residence or to facilitate their repatriation,[60] but internees 'who resist repatriation need not be forcibly repatriated'.[61] The present authors take the view that this may understate the position. There are likely to be circumstances in which any attempt at forcible repatriation would be wrongful, such that it would be better for the *Manual* to require that, in cases where an internee resists repatriation, appropriate arrangements be made with a view to his or her relocation out of internment in circumstances consistent with his or her continued safety and security.

Paragraphs 10.35.4 and 10.35.5 deal with the establishment by agreement between the Powers concerned of committees to search for dispersed internees[62] and the allocation of costs associated with internee repatriation arrangements.[63]

CONCLUDING REMARKS

As the preceding discussion demonstrates, Chapter X quotes the language of GC extensively, relying for clarification purposes mostly on the GC *Commentary* and sometimes on the Final Record of the Diplomatic Conference of Geneva. The chapter is therefore reliably grounded in the core legal provisions that address the status of protected persons, and more narrowly of internees, during international armed conflicts. As was the case in relation

58 This view is based on page 844 of II-A Final Record of the Diplomatic Conference of Geneva 1949, quoted in *DoD Manual*, footnote 630 on page 732.

59 GC, Article 133(2) and *DoD Manual*, paragraph 10.35.1.2. This also applies to internees previously sentenced to a penalty depriving them of liberty.

60 GC, Article 134, restated in *DoD Manual*, paragraph 10.35.2.

61 *DoD Manual*, paragraph 10.35.2, based on GC *Commentary*, page 519.

62 Reflecting GC, Article 133(3).

63 Reproducing verbatim GC, Article 135.

to Chapter IX, there are few if any assertions as to the customary nature of any of the cited rules. Perhaps the *Manual*'s authors consider that the universal ratification of the Convention on which the chapter is built renders such assertions nugatory. If that is the case, it might have been useful for them to make that clear.

While reference is made in the opening chapters of the *Manual* to the different human rights law positions confronted by certain States with which the US frequently operates, either in alliance or in coalition, many readers will be surprised by the paucity of human rights law references in a chapter addressing a subject that has generated so much relevant human rights-based jurisprudence, particularly in recent years. While the *Manual*'s authors may adhere to the understandable – although not necessarily contemporarily widely held – view that the present *Manual* is about the law of war and that human rights law therefore has no relevance, simply to ignore human rights law might be viewed as taking that position rather too far.

As has been noted a couple of times in the present discussion, the *Manual* also fails to mention Article 75 of API on occasions when one would have thought it appropriate to do so. As that article is arguably the most modern and widely ratified expression of the rights to which it refers, this omission is in the view of the present authors a significant error.

All of this having been said, within the confines that have been noted, the chapter does address all activities associated with protected persons and internees under GC. The collecting together of listed provisions, e.g. in respect of National Bureaux and Protecting Powers, is most useful, and the insights, where given, of the US position are valuable.

11

Military Occupation

INTRODUCTION

The military occupation of Iraq following the coalition invasion of 2003 and the experience gained therefrom have clearly informed the text of Chapter XI. There are frequent, and in the view of the present authors most useful, footnoted references to the actions of the Coalition Provisional Authority, which frequently illustrate the practical application of a particular rule. Equally, there are informative references to other occupation experience, such as that following World War II. As a result, this is a most authoritative chapter that seems destined to advance understanding of the intricacies of occupation law in a most helpful way.

The chapter wastes little time in getting to grips with the controversies associated with military occupation. In the second paragraph of section 11.1, it describes military occupation as 'a temporary measure for administering territory under the control of invading forces'. Such a description, while consistent with traditional understandings of belligerent occupation,[1] seems to suggest that where the belligerent remains in administrative and military control for a period that can no longer properly be described as 'temporary', the situation no longer amounts to military occupation, which of course begs the question as to what such a situation does indeed consist of at law. This interpretation might, in the eyes of some readers, be reinforced by the use of the present participle 'invading'. While there will often come a time when an invasion is no longer continuing but when a state of occupation nevertheless continues, the longer the period after the completion of the invasion, the more likely it may

[1] The *UK Manual* defines occupation in traditional terms, namely: 'Territory is considered to be occupied when it is actually placed under the authority of external military forces. Occupation extends only to territory where that authority has been established and can in fact be exercised'; *UK Manual*, paragraph 11.2; Hague Regulations 1907, Article 42.

be that the continuing control ceases to have the character, and perhaps legitimacy, of occupation as the *Manual* interprets that term. That said, it must be remembered that the military occupation of West Berlin by the Allied Powers that exercised military authority there continued from 1945 until 1990.

The same sentence in the *Manual* correctly notes that occupation 'involves a complicated, trilateral set of legal relations between the Occupying Power, the temporarily ousted sovereign authority, and the inhabitants of occupied territory'. The temporary nature of this state of affairs is thus being emphasised, which will cause some readers to wonder how the US would characterise some longer-term situations of this kind that currently exist and that were preceded by invasion.

The *Manual* sensibly uses the terms 'military occupation', 'belligerent occupation' and 'occupation' as all referring to situations governed by the law of belligerent occupation. Having correctly observed that law of war rules that are not specific to occupation are capable of applying during periods of occupation, the *Manual* points out that the fact of occupation triggers the application of additional specific rules. It is probably right, as paragraph 11.1.2.2 states, that Articles 47 to 78 of GC and the Hague Cultural Property Convention[2] should be regarded as supplementing Articles 42 to 56 of the Hague Regulations 1907, Article 42 of which is indeed widely accepted as being customary in nature.

It should be noted that in paragraph 11.1.2.3, there is a misinterpretation of Common Article 2. The ICRC Commentary[3] takes the correct stance that a situation of military occupation constitutes an international armed conflict in the sense of Common Article 2(1). Common Article 2(2) aims to address cases of occupation established without hostilities and fills a gap left by Common Article 2(1). Common Article 2(2) was inserted with a view to the occupation of Denmark by Germany, which was established without prior hostilities because the Danish government had decided not to offer resistance.

Paragraph 11.1.2.5 addresses the situation in which, acting under the UN Charter, the UN Security Council establishes authorities or limitations that interact with occupation law. The paragraph suggests that in cases of conflict with treaty or customary law obligations, obligations provided – by which is presumably meant 'imposed' – by the Security Council may prevail. The present authors are of the view that for this outcome to arise, the conflict in

[2] As paragraph 11.1.2.4 accurately notes, the Hague Cultural Property Convention applies to situations of total or partial occupation of a State party's territory by virtue of Article 18 of the Convention.

[3] GC Commentary – J S Pictet (ed.), *Commentary IV on Convention Relative to the Protection of Civilian Persons in Time of War*. International Committee of the Red Cross (1958), 22.

legal provisions would need to be direct, the language in the Security Council resolution would need to be unambiguous and the relevant customary law rule would need not be a rule *erga omnes*. The paragraph does not point out that the Security Council can also absolve the Occupying Power from exercising authority by its armed forces. Accordingly, when the UN Security Council adopted the relevant resolutions, the Coalition Provisional Authority in Iraq was a lawful Occupying Power.

Paragraph 11.1.2.6 sets forth the US view that the International Covenant on Civil and Political Rights 'does not create obligations for an Occupying Power with respect to occupied territory because . . . obligations under the ICCPR only extend to persons within its territory and subject to its jurisdiction'. This position is based on the US position declared in 1950 and helpfully quoted in the *Manual*.[4] Without referring to the words '*lex specialis*', that principle is appropriately cited in the same paragraph as favouring precedence for occupation law in situations of occupation. Sensibly, attention is then drawn to the differing interpretations of the applicability of human rights law that other States may hold; perhaps it would have been useful to point out here that this difference of interpretation may well be attributable to the participation by those States in other human rights treaty regimes.

The final part of paragraph 11.1.2.6 states that '[s]ubject to the Occupying Power's authority to change local laws', an occupied State's domestic laws that have been enacted pursuant to its human rights obligations or that meet its human rights treaty requirements 'may continue to apply during an occupation'. One would have thought that domestic law fulfilling such criteria ought, as a general proposition, to continue to apply during occupation and that the *Manual* should say so. One can, however, envisage a situation in which the human rights requirements by which an Occupying Power is bound, say by treaty rules, are more exacting than those applying under the domestic law of the occupied territory, in which case – if, for example, the Occupying Power is a State party to the European Convention on Human Rights – the Occupying Power would be bound to amend the domestic law to reflect its more exacting obligations, as the population of the occupied territory would likely be regarded as falling within its jurisdiction for the purposes of that Convention.

It is useful that early in Chapter XI, in paragraph 11.1.3, the *Manual* specifies circumstances that do not amount to occupation but in which it might be useful to apply rules of the law of occupation. Thus, it is correct to note in paragraph 11.1.3.1 that mere presence of the enemy armed forces does not

[4] Footnote 23 on page 740.

constitute military occupation, although US guidance seeks to apply the law of occupation in such situations to the extent possible.[5] The law of military occupation also does not apply to the liberation of friendly territory. Where the territory of a friendly State is liberated, a civil affairs agreement may be established between the States involved or a provisional and interim military government may be set up and rules of the law of occupation applied by analogy.[6]

It would have been helpful to include somewhere within this section a reference to the continuing applicability of occupation law, notwithstanding a purported annexation of the relevant territory. The prevailing view following relatively recent Russian action in relation to Crimea certainly seems to be that occupation law continues to apply. On a discrete but somewhat related matter, this section also does not distinguish occupation from siege, encirclement or effective control of the borders outside the affected State's territory, such as that applied, for example, after the Israeli Defence Force had left Gaza.

The law of belligerent occupation usually has no application to non-international armed conflicts, because there is no hostile Power that is occupying territory. As soon as a hostile Power becomes involved, the armed conflict becomes international in character.[7] However, paragraph 11.1.3.3 contemplates the potential application of occupation law when a non-State party to the conflict is recognised as a belligerent and a non-international armed conflict might take place in the context of, or alongside, belligerent occupation.

Paragraph 11.1.3.4 and its associated footnotes make the point that before the adoption of GC, the rules as to occupation in the Hague Regulations 1907 did not apply when hostilities had completely ceased, basing this view on the evident presupposition that a hostile relationship must exist between the invading force's State and the State of the occupied territory. Interesting documents are cited in this regard. The *Manual* notes, however, that the GC continues to apply in occupied territory until one year after the close of military operations and that the Occupying Power remains bound by certain GC provisions for the duration of the occupation to the extent that it exercises the functions of government in the territory; protected persons remain protected by the GC, if they remain in the custody of the Detaining Power after the end of occupation, until their release, repatriation or re-establishment.

5 See 1956 FM 27–10 (Change No 1 of 1976), paragraph 352, cited at *DoD Manual*, footnote 29 on page 741.

6 *DoD Manual*, paragraph 11.1.3.2.

7 See *DoD Manual*, paragraph 11.1.3.3.

Having made these points, the *Manual* suggests that the law of occupation may appropriately be adhered to, or applied by analogy, in post-conflict situations even if it is not applicable as a matter of law.

WHEN MILITARY OCCUPATION LAW APPLIES

Paragraph 11.2.1 observes that '[m]ilitary occupation in a question of fact', by which it presumably means that whether a state of military occupation exists is a question of fact. The legal consequences of occupation do indeed, as the paragraph suggests, illustrate how the law of war can be construed as both permissive and restrictive in nature. The *Manual* rightly points out that the fact of occupation is the basis on which the Occupying Power exercises its authority over the occupied territory, thus precluding a State from claiming the authority of military government over an enemy territory without actually controlling that territory.

Sometimes, it is useful to state explicitly the seemingly obvious. Thus, it is useful for the *Manual* to assert that 'a State that does not in fact occupy an area does not incur the obligations of an occupying power' and that, irrespective of the rights and wrongs of the invasion, once an occupation in fact exists, the rights and obligations of the Occupying Power and of the population in relation to one another apply.

Paragraph 11.2.2 expresses the notion of occupation correctly by reference to Article 42 of the Hague Regulations, namely that territory is considered occupied when actually placed under the authority of the hostile forces, and rightly characterises this as a customary rule. It is therefore correct to say that occupation must be actual and effective, that organised resistance must have been overcome, that the Occupying Power must have taken measures to establish its authority but that the nature of the military units establishing and maintaining the occupation are irrelevant. While military forces must control the most important places, they do not, indeed, have to be ubiquitous. The *Manual* makes the important point, however, that air superiority alone is not sufficient to establish an effective occupation.[8] Moreover, the presence within an area declared occupied of a defended locality still controlled by enemy forces does not invalidate the occupation of the area, provided that the continued resistance in the defended locality does not preclude control by the Occupying Power of the territory that is occupied. The 1958 *UK Manual* is cited in support of this proposition, but that manual adds a proviso 'that such place

[8] *DoD Manual*, paragraph 11.2.2.1, part 3.

or defended zone is surrounded and effectively cut off from the rest of the occupied district'.[9]

It is probably right of the *DoD Manual* to suggest that intermittent insurgent attacks and temporary seizures of territory by resistance forces will not invalidate the occupation – unless, the present authors observe, the seizures are frequent and involve substantial portions of the occupied territory, and the occupation as a result ceases to be effective.[10]

Core to the notion of occupation is the suspension of the territorial State's authority and the substitution of the Occupying Power's authority. Paragraph 11.2.2.2 notes the kinds of step that the occupier may take to establish its authority, such as establishing its own governmental authority and issuing regulations for the temporary government of the territory. Paragraph 11.2.2.3 notes that a situation of hostility must exist between the Occupying Power and the State whose territory is being occupied, but that the occupation need not have been met with armed resistance.[11] Interestingly, the paragraph simply restates the law, but does not refer to the establishment in Iraq of the Coalition Provisional Authority, which did not qualify as a 'hostile army'. Propositions already discussed in paragraphs 11.1.3.2 and 11.1.3.4 are then, arguably unnecessarily, repeated in paragraph 11.2.2.3. Having noted in paragraph 11.2.3 that occupation only extends to territory where military authority has been established and can be exercised, the point is repeated that occupation might apply to only a part of a State's territory.[12] Paragraph 11.2.2.2, final part and paragraph 11.2.4, considered together, explain that while a declaration of occupation is not an explicit condition for the establishment of a valid occupation, 'due to the special relations established between the civilian population of the occupied territory and the Occupying Power, the fact of military occupation and the territory over which it extends should be made known to the citizens of the occupied territory, and to other States', a proposition with which one can only agree.[13]

9 See also *UK Manual*, paragraph 11.3.2, last sentence.

10 But consider the passage from *United States* v. *List et al* (The Hostage Case) XI Trials of War Criminals before the NMT, 1243, cited at *DoD Manual*, footnote 61 on page 746.

11 Common Article 2 to the Geneva Conventions, 1949.

12 This point is first made in paragraph 11.1.2.3.

13 As paragraph 11.2.4 correctly notes, a proclamation of occupation can be used to fix when occupation starts and to advise the inhabitants of occupied territory of the rules with which they must comply and of changes in the law, including penal law. *DoD Manual*, footnotes 75 and 76 on pages 749 and 750 give important historical accounts of the steps taken in connection with the establishment of occupations associated with past conflicts up to and including the 2003 Iraq War, citing opinions of the US Office of the Legal Counsel, US case law and the 1958 *UK Manual*.

END OF OCCUPATION AND DURATION OF GC OBLIGATIONS

Section 11.3 again illustrates a feature of the *DoD Manual* that is, frankly, irritating. The section starts with the undoubtedly correct, if somewhat self-evident, observation that: 'The status of belligerent occupation ends when the conditions for its application are no longer met.' Three lines later, at the start of paragraph 11.3.1, we have a virtually identical sentence. This and similar forms of repetition have the effect of significantly increasing the length of the text and of rendering it at times somewhat unwieldy. Likewise, paragraph 11.3.1 repeats the point made already in paragraph 11.2.2.3 that belligerent occupation ends when a hostile relationship no longer exists between the State of the territory being occupied and the Occupying Power. When, at the beginning of the first substantive paragraph on page 751, one sees exactly the same observation being made for the third time, one is left with the impression that this is a chapter that has not been adequately proofread in advance of publication.

Wading through the surplus verbiage, some useful points are made. First, popular uprising, expulsion or withdrawal of the Occupying Power such as to prevent it from enforcing (perhaps 'exercising' would be a better word) its authority over the occupied territory will terminate occupation. Second, if a new independent government is established in the occupied territory that consents to the continued presence there of previously occupying forces, such a situation will no longer constitute occupation, although perhaps a caveat should be added that the critical issue will be whether the new government is in reality exercising authority in the territory, i.e. whether there has been an effective transfer of that authority from the Occupying Power to the new government. Third, if a peace treaty legitimately transfers sovereignty of the territory to the Occupying Power, the situation of occupation will cease to exist – although the paragraph correctly notes the prohibition under the law of occupation of the annexation of occupied territory.

Paragraph 11.3.2 repeats that the GC ceases to apply one year after the general close of military operations, but that the Occupying Power remains bound for the duration of the occupation and to the extent that it exercises the functions of government in the territory by the provisions of the Convention listed in GC, Article 6(3). Attention is properly drawn to API, Article 3(b), which provides that for States party to API, the application of the Conventions and of the Protocol shall, in the case of occupied territory, end 'on the termination of the occupation'. The related points are also repeated, namely that GC protected persons who remain in the custody of the Occupying Power after the end of occupation retain GC protection until their release, repatriation or re-establishment and that after the end of occupation, it may be appropriate to continue to apply certain law of occupation rules by analogy, even if they do not apply as a matter of law.

LEGAL POSITION OF THE OCCUPYING POWER

Paragraph 11.4.1 bases itself *inter alia* on paragraph 358 of FM 27–10, which does not clarify which entity qualifies as an Occupying Power in a situation where multinational forces have established an occupation regime. Given the multinational character of numerous military operations, this omission is not a matter of purely academic concern. Paragraph 11.4.1 points out that the right to govern enemy territory during occupation is an incident of war and that by the fact of occupation, the occupier is conferred some of the rights of sovereignty, the exercise of which derives from the established power of the occupant and the need, indispensable to the inhabitants and the occupying force, to maintain law and order. Maybe, and this is a minor point, it would have been preferable if the FM 27–10 paragraph 358 observation that occupation 'does not transfer the sovereignty to the occupant' had also been included in its relevant place in this paragraph, thereby putting the reference to some of the rights of sovereignty into context.

Paragraph 11.4.2 correctly notes that '[b]ecause sovereignty is not vested in the Occupying Power, the fact of occupation does not authorize the Occupying Power to take certain actions', such as annexing occupied territory, creating a new State or compelling the inhabitants to become its nationals or to swear allegiance to it. The paragraph also notes the authorities that suggest that there are limitations on the ability of the Occupying Power to alter institutions of government permanently or to change the constitution of the country.[14] In the view of the present authors, these limitations apply as a matter of law and the *Manual* should be somewhat more definitive in addressing this point, particularly in view of the recent annexation action in relation to the Crimea.

DUTY OF THE OCCUPYING POWER TO ENSURE PUBLIC ORDER AND SAFETY

The language of Article 43 of the Hague Regulations 1907 as to the Occupying Power's obligation to take all measures available to it to restore and ensure

[14] Paragraph 11.11 of the 2004 *UK Manual* states: 'Since sovereignty does not pass to the occupying power, that power may not change the constitution and domestic laws of the occupied territory nor set aside the rights of the inhabitants except to the extent permitted under the law of armed conflict.' The *DoD Manual* also refers to other authorities on the matter.

public order and safety while respecting, unless absolutely prevented, the laws in force in the country is restated in section 11.5 and is described as reflecting customary law. This relatively isolated reference to customary law causes one to wonder whether the US recognises the other legal propositions discussed in Chapter XI as being customary. Impliedly it does not, which is troubling. Paragraph 11.5.1 develops the theme by noting that the Occupying Power may enact provisions to ensure the orderly government of the territory but may not arbitrarily suspend, repeal or change the municipal law applicable there.[15]

PROTECTION OF THE POPULATION OF AN OCCUPIED TERRITORY

Paragraph 11.6.1 correctly states the general protections to which protected persons in occupied territories are entitled as set forth in GC, Article 27(1), but, curiously, without directly referencing that provision. The paragraph correctly points out that the protections in Articles 27 to 34 apply to protected persons in occupied territories, and then mentions as examples some of those protections. Paragraph 11.6.2 notes some additional protections specifically for civilian populations in occupied territories. Both sets of protections are discussed later in the chapter. The prohibition in Article 45 of the Hague Regulations to compel the inhabitants of occupied territory to swear allegiance to the hostile State is repeated in paragraph 11.6.2.1, while paragraph 11.6.2.2 prohibits the infliction of general punishments against the population on account of the acts of individuals for which they cannot be held jointly and severally liable.[16]

The paragraph then restates verbatim GC, Article 47's prohibition of depriving protected persons in occupied territory of the benefits of the Convention by any change in the institutions or government of the territory as a result of the occupation, by any agreement between the authorities of the occupied territories and the Occupying Power or by annexation of the whole or part of the occupied territory. So, as the *Manual* explains, subject to limited forfeiture of communication rights for security reasons, protected persons may not be deprived of their GC rights, whether by their own purported renunciation of those rights, by special agreements under GC, Article 7 or by purported annexation of the occupied territory.

[15] *DoD Manual*, paragraphs 11.5.1 and 11.5.2. The *Manual* notes the view that the duty to respect the laws in force, unless absolutely prevented from doing so, does not extend to local administrative laws.

[16] Hague Regulations 1907, Articles 45 and 50.

Paragraph 11.6.4 argues that citizens of neutral States resident in occupied territory 'are generally treated the same as other residents of occupied territory'. While, as residents of occupied territory, they will be subject to the regulations introduced by the Occupying Power in the same way as other residents, their position vis-à-vis the Occupying Power will be fundamentally different in that they will have access to the services afforded by the diplomatic representatives of their (neutral) government. The present authors consider that this aspect should be mentioned in paragraph 11.6.4.

AUTHORITY OF THE OCCUPYING POWER OVER INHABITANTS

Paragraph 11.7.1, citing FM 27–10, paragraph 432, suggests that it is the duty of the inhabitants of occupied territory 'to carry on their ordinary peaceful pursuits, to behave in an absolutely peaceful manner, to take no part whatever in the hostilities carried on, to refrain from all injurious acts toward the forces or in respect of their operations, and to render strict obedience to the orders of the occupant'. It would be hard to find in contemporary occupation law a positive requirement that the inhabitants continue with their private pursuits, whatever they might be, and it is accordingly suggested that this element should be omitted. The remaining requirements are, however, clearly correct. Specifically, it is right that obedience necessary for the security of the occupying forces, for the maintenance of law and order and for proper administration of the territory can be demanded and enforced by the occupant from the inhabitants, subject to international law. This duty of obedience does not affect the allegiance owed by the inhabitants to their State of nationality, as the *Manual* rightly points out.

Measures taken to enforce obedience must be lawful. Collective punishments, torture and reprisals are therefore prohibited, as paragraph 11.7.1.1 notes.

Paragraph 11.7.2 rightly states that the Occupying Power may regulate and censor all forms of media, entertainment, correspondence and communication for security purposes. Accordingly, it explains that newspapers that pose a threat to security may be banned, and that other newspapers and media may be regulated to fulfil the Occupying Power's obligation to restore public order. Here, as in certain other relevant parts of the *Manual*, there is no reference to modern media, nor to modern means of digital communication, with the consequence that the *Manual* does not give here guidance as to the particular and important issues that censorship and regulation of such modern media are likely to generate.

Paragraph 11.7.3 correctly reports the right of the Occupying Power to seize and regulate the operation of all forms of public and private land, sea and air transportation in occupied territory – but one would have expected the authority cited in support of that rule to have been Article 53 of the Hague Regulations 1907, rather than a paragraph in FM 27–10. Paragraph 11.7.4 refers to the imposition of safety measures on protected persons, a topic that is dealt with in Chapter X of the *Manual* and Chapter 10 of the present volume.

ADMINISTRATION OF OCCUPIED TERRITORY

While the occupant becomes the paramount authority in occupied territory, it is open to it to permit the country's government to perform some or all of their functions, provided that the occupant remains in firm possession of the territory and continues to be the paramount authority. This is correctly stated in paragraphs 11.8.1 and 11.8.2, while paragraph 11.8.3 makes the important and equally correct point that the Occupying Power cannot circumvent the restrictions placed on its actions by employing a puppet government, whether central or local. The acts it induces remain its acts.

It is clear that the Occupying Power is responsible for how its agents treat protected persons, irrespective of possible individual responsibility. This would, as paragraph 11.8.4 correctly suggests, also apply to the actions of locally recruited agents who are nationals of the occupied State. Paragraph 11.8.5 explains that military and civilian members of the force of occupation and of the administration and persons accompanying them are exempt from local laws and are not subject to the jurisdiction of local civil or criminal courts unless a competent official of the Occupying Power provides otherwise. The paragraph notes the importance of the Occupying Power ensuring that a system of law applies to such persons and that courts or tribunals are set up to deal with civil and criminal cases concerning such persons. The present authors suggest, however, that while military personnel of the Occupying Power will be subject to their military code (in the case of the US, the UCMJ), ensuring that all civilians, including contractors' employees, are similarly subjected to a system of law and of courts may prove rather more challenging. That said, the final sentence of the paragraph notes the use of the Military Extraterritorial Jurisdiction Act in addition to the UCMJ in recent practice.

LOCAL LAW AND LEGISLATION

The substance and administration of the municipal and penal law of the occupied territory generally remain in force unless altered by the Occupying

Power.[17] Again, the Occupying Power and its personnel are not bound by the municipal law applying in the occupied territory.[18] Repeating, as previously noted in section 11.5, the duty of the Occupying Power to respect, unless absolutely prevented, the laws in force in the country, paragraph 11.9.2 makes the useful point that this obligation prohibits the Occupying Power from arbitrarily suspending, repealing or changing that law; the Occupying Power must use its power in that regard in good faith, and not in order to oppress the population. The paragraph then quotes the Occupying Power's right under GC, Article 64(2) to subject the population of the occupied territory to provisions essential to enabling it to comply with GC, to maintain orderly government and to maintain the security of the Occupying Power, the members and property of the occupying forces or administration and the establishments and lines of communication they use.

Paragraph 11.9.2.1 arguably does not take us much beyond their ordinary meanings when considering the distinction between the terms 'suspension', 'change', 'repeal' and 'enactment', in relation to municipal laws. Paragraph 11.9.2.2 proposes useful lists of examples of laws that may, depending on the circumstances, be suspended, changed, repealed or enacted by the Occupying Power, for example laws as to serious offences that threaten public order, as to possession or sale of firearms by civilians, as to the protection of the Occupying Power's forces or administration, as to political processes, as to the supply of food or other essential supplies and the prevention of hoarding, as to the administration of the law and as to the Occupying Power's obligations under the GC.[19]

Paragraph 11.9.3 asserts, as appears to be correct, that the Occupying Power must inform the population of alterations, suspensions or repeals of existing laws and of the enactment of new ones – a provision that goes beyond the penal law requirements in GC, Article 65. Useful practical guidance is then given that a decree must be published towards the beginning of the occupation clarifying the applicable laws and orders and the associated punishments in the event of non-compliance.

ORDINARY COURTS IN OCCUPIED TERRITORY

A perusal of the footnotes to the texts in section 11.10 leads the reader to anticipate that much of the section is duplicated in section 11.11. Be that as it may,

[17] Note, for example, GC, Article 64(1).

[18] *DoD Manual*, paragraph 11.9.1 and paragraph 11.8.5.

[19] This final category might, for example, include legislation to help provide for child welfare, labour, food, hygiene and public health.

section 11.10, based in part on relatively recent experience with the Coalition Provisional Authority in Iraq, correctly notes that, in general, the courts and tribunals of the occupied territory should continue to operate subject to the direction of the Occupying Power and that such courts and tribunals should only be suspended if the judges and magistrates are unable or unwilling to officiate,[20] if they are corrupt or unfairly constituted[21] or if they have collapsed due to the hostilities.[22]

Paragraph 11.10.2 restates the Article 23(h), Hague Regulations 1907 provision that it is prohibited to declare 'abolished, suspended, or inadmissible in a Court of law the rights and actions of the nationals of the hostile party'. The US and English cases that interpret this provision as applying only to occupied territory are cited and quoted in an associated footnote, and are persuasive. It must also be right, as the *Manual*, supported by quoted authorities, suggests, that the rule has been interpreted as preventing a military commander from arbitrarily annulling the results of civil proceedings between private parties. The present authors suggest, however, that the rule goes rather wider than this and precludes such declarations in relation to the broad spectrum of human, property and other rights whether these have been reflected in a court judgment or not. Perhaps this should be made clear in the *Manual* entry.

CRIMINAL LAW IN OCCUPIED TERRITORY

The rule, discussed in paragraph 11.9.1, that the municipal laws must generally continue to apply in occupied territory, also applies to the penal laws,[23] which may, however, be repealed or suspended[24] where they constitute a threat to the security of the Occupying Power or where they are an obstacle to the application of GC.[25] As the *Manual* states, subject to this and the need to

[20] See *DoD Manual*, paragraph 11.10.1.1.

[21] As to the establishment of committees to consider the suitability of judges and prosecutors, see *DoD Manual*, paragraph 11.10.1.2.

[22] In such circumstances, the Occupying Power may reform local courts and/or use its own properly constituted, non-political military courts to administer local laws.

[23] *DoD Manual*, paragraph 11.11.1. In commendable attention to detail, the *Manual* explains that 'penal laws' comprise all laws and similar measures intended to repress offences; paragraph 11.11.1.1.

[24] The *Manual* suggests that this can be achieved by a simple order, by requiring that the relevant law may only be enforced with the Occupying Power's approval or by subjecting the population to additional provisions that are inconsistent with the relevant law; paragraph 11.11.1.3.

[25] As *DoD Manual*, footnote 193 on page 770 notes, by citing the *GC Commentary* at page 335, this relates in particular to provisions that adversely affect racial or religious minorities.

ensure effective administration of justice, the courts of the occupied territory shall continue to administer local and national penal laws. Courts may be reformed, or new ones established, as part of the Occupying Power's duty to maintain public order, and the Occupying Power may impose additional penal provisions[26] necessary to fulfil its GC obligations, to maintain orderly government and to ensure its security, the security of the members and property of its forces and administration and the establishments and lines of communication it and they use.[27] GC, Article 66 provides that in case of a breach of the penal provisions referred to in the previous sentence, the 'Occupying Power may hand over the accused to its properly constituted, non-political military courts', provided they sit in the occupied country, where the courts of appeal shall also preferably sit.[28]

GC, Article 68(1)'s provisions limiting sentencing to proportionate periods of internment or simple imprisonment for certain non-serious offences only intended to harm the Occupying Power are restated in paragraph 11.11.4. Lesser punishments are, as the paragraph points out, not addressed by the rule. Article 68(2) of GC limits the circumstances in which the Occupying Power may include the death penalty in the provisions it promulgates under Articles 64 and 65 of GC. That penalty may only be applied for offences of espionage, serious sabotage against the Occupying Power's military installations and intentional offences causing death, provided that such offences carried the death penalty before the occupation under the law of the occupied territory.[29]

Paragraph 11.11.7 restates the GC, Article 70(1) provision prohibiting arrest, prosecution or conviction by the Occupying Power of protected persons for

[26] These must not come into force until published in the language of the inhabitants and must not be retroactive; *DoD Manual*, paragraph 11.11.2.1.

[27] *DoD Manual*, paragraph 11.11.2; GC, Article 64(2).

[28] This is correctly reflected in *DoD Manual*, paragraph 11.11.3, which notes the obligations as to the judicial guarantees that such courts must afford and the requirements as to judicial proceedings against protected persons in occupied territory that must be complied with. As to US practice, see paragraph 11.11.3.1. The additional required safeguards applying to the proceedings and sentencing by such courts are given in paragraph 11.11.3.2, based on Article 67 of GC and on relevant elements of the *GC Commentary*.

[29] Restated in *DoD Manual*, paragraph 11.11.5. The paragraph notes the reservation made by the US on ratification of the Convention on 2 August 1955 that it reserves the right to impose the death penalty in accordance with Article 68(2) without regard to whether the offences referred to there are punishable by death under the law of the occupied territory at the time the occupation begins. The paragraph also points out that the attention of the Court should, before a death sentence is pronounced, be drawn to the fact that the protected person does not owe the Occupying Power allegiance, and that such a sentence must not be pronounced on a person under the age of eighteen years.

acts committed or opinions expressed before, or during breaks in, the occupation, other than war crimes. There are also restrictions on the arrest, prosecution, conviction or deportation of nationals of the Occupying Power who sought refuge in the territory of the occupied State. These restrictions in GC, Article 70(2) are restated accurately in paragraph 11.11.7.2 of the *Manual*. As the *Manual* correctly notes, this is an exception to the rule that a State's own nationals are excluded from the GC's protections. Accused and convicted persons fall to be handed over with the relevant records to the authorities of the liberated country at the close of occupation, as paragraph 11.11.8 accurately states, and retain protected person status pending that transfer.[30]

MOVEMENT OF PERSONS IN OCCUPIED TERRITORY

Paragraph 11.12.1 correctly asserts the right of the Occupying Power to control who may move within, enter or leave occupied territory and links this right to the power normally held by the State whose authority has been usurped. This applies to representatives of non-governmental organisations, intergovernmental organisations and foreign States. The right to forbid changes of residence, internal movement or visits to certain areas and the right to require protected persons to carry identification cards is also correctly set forth in the paragraph. Paragraph 11.12.2 notes the GC, Article 48 right of '[p]rotected persons who are not nationals of the Power whose territory is occupied' to 'avail themselves of the right to leave the territory' subject to Article 35, with decisions to be made in accordance with the procedure under that article. Article 35 asserts the right of protected persons who desire to do so to depart 'unless their departure is contrary to the national interests of the State' and addresses the deciding of such applications and requests for the reconsideration of refusals. It should, however, be borne in mind that 'protected persons' for the purposes of Article 48 do not include nationals of the Power whose territory is occupied, persons protected by any of the other Conventions or nationals of neutral or co-belligerent States that have diplomatic relations with the Occupying Power. It might have been sensible for the *Manual* to point this out and to explain the limited classes of individual to whom the provision would actually apply.

Paragraph 11.12.3 repeats the GC, Article 49(1) prohibition of individual or mass forcible transfers and deportations of protected persons, noting this to be a grave breach of the Convention. Paragraph 11.12.3.1 then repeats Article 49(2) of GC to the effect that the Occupying Power may evacuate fully or partially

30 See GC, Article 77.

a particular area if the safety of the population or imperative military reasons so demand. Such evacuations may only take protected persons outside occupied territory if such displacement cannot be avoided for material reasons, and such persons must be returned to their homes as soon as hostilities in the area in question have ceased. The safeguards that Article 49(3) of GC prescribes for such transfers are repeated in paragraph 11.12.3.1. Paragraph 11.12.3.2 makes the correct point that persons who do not receive protected person status under GC do not benefit from the transfer prohibition referred to here and that the Protecting Powers must be notified as soon as any such transfers or evacuations take place.[31] The *Manual* describes these as 'forcible transfers'. The present authors consider 'compulsory transfers' a better term to use.[32] Paragraph 11.12.4 then restates the GC, Article 49(5) prohibition of detaining protected persons in areas particularly exposed to the dangers of war unless the security of the population or imperative military reasons so demand, and paragraph 11.12.5, repeating Article 49(6) of GC, states that the Occupying Power must not transfer or deport parts of its own civilian population into occupied territory.

PROTECTION OF CHILDREN IN OCCUPIED TERRITORY

Section 11.13 suggests that the term 'children' may be understood generally to refer to children under the age of fifteen years. Reference is, however, made to a substantial extract from the GC *Commentary* which argues for a somewhat flexible approach to the interpretation of the term, referring to the degree of development of the mental and physical faculties of the persons concerned, and suggests the application of the provisions until the persons have achieved their majority. These suggestions are persuasive and suggest that a more flexible approach should indeed be adopted in the main text of Section 11.13 to the definition of 'children'.[33]

After repeating the GC, Article 50(1) obligation of the Occupying Power to facilitate the proper working of all institutions devoted to the care and education of children, paragraph 11.13.1 makes the point, based on the GC *Commentary*, that this is an affirmative duty to support such institutions when the responsible authorities of the country fail to do so.[34] GC, Article 50(3)

31 *DoD Manual*, paragraph 11.12.3.3.

32 The present authors do, however, agree with paragraph 11.12.3.4's observation that voluntary transfers, for example of persons who have in the past been persecuted by the authorities of the occupied State, are permissible; footnote 248 on page 779 gives some valuable insights into the drafting history of this aspect of Article 45 of GC.

33 See GC *Commentary*, page 285, cited in *DoD Manual*, footnote 251 on page 780.

34 GC *Commentary*, page 286.

stipulates, and paragraph 11.3.1 reflects, the responsibilities of the Occupying Power where local institutions are inadequate to cope with the maintenance and education of children who are orphaned or separated from their parents as a result of the war and who cannot be adequately cared for by a near relative or friend. The full requirement is given in the associated footnote.

Paragraphs 11.13.2 and 11.13.3 note the Occupying Power's duty to take all necessary steps to identify and register the parentage of children, further note that it may not change their personal status nor recruit them into formations or organisations subordinate to it and draw attention to the role of the National Protected Person Information Bureau, as to which see GC, Article 136. Paragraph 11.13.4 then notes that the Occupying Power may not hinder the application of certain preferential measures that may have been adopted before the occupation in respect of children, expectant mothers and mothers of children under seven years.[35]

FOOD AND MEDICAL SUPPLIES FOR THE CIVILIAN POPULATION

Paragraph 11.14.1 restates the GC, Article 55(1) obligation of the Occupying Power to ensure as far as possible the food and medical supplies for the population, bringing in necessary foodstuffs, medical stores and other articles if resources in the occupied territory are inadequate. The reference to 'other articles' is sensibly interpreted as extending to all urgently required goods essential to the life of the territory. Article 55(2) provides that the Occupying Power may only requisition foodstuffs and medical supplies in occupied territory for use by occupation forces and administration personnel, and only if the requirements of the civilian population have been taken into account, paying, subject to other international conventions, fair value for the requisitioned goods.[36]

Subject to restrictions necessitated by imperative military requirements, under GC, Article 55(3), restated in paragraph 11.14.3, the Protecting Power has the right to verify the state of food and medical supplies in occupied territories.

PUBLIC HEALTH AND HYGIENE

Paragraph 11.15.1 restates the GC Article 56(1) duty of the Occupying Power to the fullest extent of the means available to it to ensure and maintain medical and hospital establishments and services, public health and hygiene in the

[35] Restating GC, Article 50(5). [36] Restated in *DoD Manual*, paragraph 11.14.2.

occupied territories. Cooperation of national and local authorities is contemplated, and emphasis is placed on adopting and applying prophylactic and preventive measures to combat the spread of contagious diseases and epidemics. Drawing on GC *Commentary*, the paragraph notes that prime responsibility rests with national and local authorities, but that where they are unable to provide adequately, the Occupying Power has the duty described in Article 56(1). The requirement to allow medical personnel of all categories to carry out their duties is also restated in the *Manual*.

Paragraph 11.15.3 recognises the GC, Article 56(2) position that if new hospitals not operated by organs of the occupied State are set up in occupied territory, the Occupying Power must, if necessary, grant them, their personnel and their transports recognition under Articles 18, 20 and 21 of GC, thus entitling them to display their right to protection. The obligation, when the Occupying Power is introducing public health and hygiene measures, to take into account the moral and ethical susceptibilities of the population and the limitations imposed by GC on the requisitioning of civilian hospitals by the Occupying Power are set forth in paragraphs 11.15.4 and 11.15.5 and follow, with slight adjustment of wording, the provisions of GC, Articles 56(3) and 57(1). The final part of paragraph 11.15.5, however, states: 'If the requisition of medical supplies is required for the occupying force, they must take the needs of the civilian population into account and resupply the materials as soon as possible.' The cited authority is GC *Commentary*, page 318. This does not seem to take into account GC, Article 57(2), which states clearly: 'The materials and stores of civilian hospitals cannot be requisitioned as long as they are necessary for the needs of the civilian population.' It is suggested that this is the text that should be restated in terms by the *Manual* in place of the cited text.

SPIRITUAL ASSISTANCE

Section 11.16 restates verbatim GC, Article 58's requirement for the Occupying Power to permit ministers of religion to give spiritual assistance to members of their community and to accept consignments of books and articles required for religious needs. Unsurprisingly, given recent experience, a proper distinction is drawn in the *Manual* between religious assistance and activities that are a pretext for political agitation.

RELIEF EFFORTS AND CONSIGNMENTS

GC, Article 59's provisions as to relief supplies and consignments are repeated in terms in paragraph 11.17.1. If any part of the population in occupied territory is inadequately supplied, the Occupying Power must agree to schemes which may be undertaken by States or impartial humanitarian organisations (e.g. the ICRC) and which shall consist in particular of food, medical and clothing supplies. GC, Article 59 and paragraph 11.17.1 specify the obligation of all States to grant free passage to these consignments and the rights to inspect the consignments, to prescribe times and routes for their passage and to be reasonably satisfied that they are for the needy population and not for the benefit of the Occupying Power. Moreover, as paragraph 11.17.1.1 restates, Article 60 of GC prohibits the Occupying Power diverting relief supplies, other than in urgent necessity in the interests of the population of the occupied territory and with the consent of the Protecting Power. Distribution of collective relief consignments must be with the cooperation of and under the supervision of the Protecting Power, a duty that may by agreement be delegated to a neutral State or the ICRC, or to another impartial humanitarian body; rapid distribution must be facilitated by the Occupying Power.[37] The provisions of Article 61(2) and (3) exempting such consignments from charges, taxes and customs duties in occupied territory and requiring States party to endeavour to permit the transit and transport of the consignments free of charge are repeated in paragraph 11.17.1.3. Shipments addressed to particular persons must be allowed to pass, subject to 'imperative reasons of security'.[38] Importantly, relief consignments do not relieve the Occupying Power of its responsibilities under GC, Articles 55, 56 and 59, and this is recognised in paragraph 11.17.3.

Paragraph 11.17.4 restates verbatim the GC, Article 63 provisions dealing with the right of national Red Cross societies and other relief societies to pursue their activities and prohibiting the Occupying Power demanding changes in their personnel or structure that would prejudice those activities. As the *Manual* notes, similar provisions apply in favour of 'special organisations of a non-military character' that ensure 'the living conditions of the civilian population by the maintenance of the essential public utility services'.

37 GC, Article 61(1) and (2); *DoD Manual*, paragraph 11.17.1.2.

38 GC, Article 62; *DoD Manual*, paragraph 11.17.2. The *Manual* contends that if the volume of individual consignments precludes security screening, this would be a lawful basis for forbidding entry. In the view of the present authors, a sensible approach is required here. It would not be lawful for the Occupying Power to allocate manifestly inadequate resources to the security screening task and then to reject consignments on the basis of their volume. The reasons of security must be imperative, which would seem to presuppose the allocation of appropriate resources to the task.

ENEMY PROPERTY DURING OCCUPATION

After citing the general prohibition of pillage in paragraph 11.18.1, paragraph 11.18.2 correctly restates the related general rule that enemy property may not be seized or destroyed unless imperatively demanded by the necessities of war. The application of that general rule to occupied territory, set forth in Article 53 of GC, is then quoted verbatim. Paragraph 11.18.2.1 notes that whether military necessity does indeed require particular destruction is a judgment for the relevant military commander, acting in good faith, and cites an extract from the GC *Commentary* in which the fear is expressed that bad faith might render the safeguard valueless.[39]

Paragraph 11.18.2.2 touches on requisitions, but that topic is also dealt with in later paragraphs. The thing of note here is the statement that 'in the case of private property, an Occupying Power should, where possible, requisition the property', implying that where this is not possible, they may simply seize private property without requisitioning it. Such an implied interpretation would seem to be contrary to Article 53 of the Hague Regulations 1907. The phrase 'direct military use' in this paragraph is also incorrect, in the opinion of the present authors. Any requisitions in occupied territory will only be lawful to the extent that they are required for the purposes of the occupation, and this is an important limitation that should be made clear in the *Manual*. Paragraph 11.18.2.3 then deals with the title to, or ownership of, captured property and property in occupied territory. Confusion is caused by suddenly referring to battlefield capture in a chapter dealing with occupation. This paragraph would benefit from revision to achieve a somewhat clearer explanation of the law.

The qualified prohibition of seizing or destroying submarine cables connecting occupied territory with neutral States as given in Article 54 of the Hague Regulations is repeated in paragraph 11.18.2.4. The interpretation given in the paragraph, and based on a cited extract from the travaux, is that the prohibition only applies to action taken on land, not in the open sea. One might suggest, contrary to the *Manual*'s position, that the words in the treaty should, in accordance with Vienna Convention interpretation principles, be given their ordinary meaning, which would imply no such exclusion from the rule.

Paragraph 11.18.3 asserts the right of the Occupying Power to control public or private property in order to prevent its use by of for the benefit of hostile forces or in a way that is harmful to the Occupying Power. Article 53

[39] GC *Commentary*, page 302.

of the Hague Regulations is concerned with limiting the Occupying Power's right of seizure. Rights of control, including, for example, the freezing of bank accounts, do not imply a taking possession by the occupant[40] and will be lawful to the extent that they are necessary for maintaining the security of the occupying force or administration or for the maintenance of the safety and security of the population. Paragraph 11.18.4 then states: 'The rules for the treatment of enemy property may depend on whether the property is public or private.' This is a rather strange formulation. The word 'may' should, of course, be deleted.

Paragraph 11.18.4.1 makes the proper point that in distinguishing between public and private property, beneficial ownership is the criterion and the holding of the funds in a publicly owned bank will not be determinative. One would have thought that the paragraph could more usefully address the situation where certain activities, such as utilities, that previously were publicly operated have been transferred to private ownership. The *Manual* should make it clear that if such property is not 'strictly the property of the State', it should be classed as private property.

Paragraph 11.18.4.2 considers property of mixed public/private ownership. Citing FM 27–10, the *Manual* argues that cogent evidence of public character is such a complete or partial assumption by the State of the risk associated with holding or managing the property that the State would be subjected to a substantial portion of the loss were the property to be appropriated for use by the Occupying Power. 'Should property that is ostensibly private be subjected to a large measure of governmental control and management, or perform functions that are essentially public, these facts would tend to indicate that the property should be regarded in practice as public.' The present authors disagree. Article 53 of the Hague Regulations refers to property 'belonging to the State'. 'Belonging to' is concerned with ownership, and whether property is owned by the State or not is going to be a question of fact. The Occupying Power must take steps to distinguish between property that is, and respectively that is not, owned by the State, and must exercise its rights under occupation law accordingly and in good faith. So, for example, property that is private may indeed be employed to perform functions that some observers may regard as

[40] Indeed, the paragraph specifically excludes confiscation of private property and repeats the prohibition in paragraph 11.18.6.1, which explains that the prohibition applies not just to outright taking but also to oppressive conduct or exploitative behaviour that has the effect of depriving the owner of the use of his or her property without his consent or lawful authority. The prohibition does not apply to contributions, requisitions or the lawful imposition of penalties.

public in nature. Those functions do not affect the fact that the property is privately owned and should, for occupation law purposes, be subject to the corresponding safeguards. However, the paragraph rightly suggests that if property is jointly owned by the State and by private interests, those private interests should be compensated to the extent of their ownership.[41]

Paragraph 11.18.4.3 explains that property of unknown ownership should be treated as public property until its ownership is ascertained. As the *UK Manual* points out, however, the destruction or non-availability of records may make it difficult to establish ownership.[42]

Military land and buildings of the sort referred to in paragraph 11.18.5.1 are, as the *UK Manual* at paragraph 11.85 agrees, at the disposal of the Occupying Power until the end of the conflict. The *DoD Manual* notes that the Occupying Power may only destroy or damage them if it deems that necessary to military operations, citing FM 27–10 again as the authority. Article 53 of GC, however, addresses the point explicitly, giving absolute military necessity as the criterion. It is suggested that the GC should be cited and that the text be suitably amended.

Paragraph 11.18.5.2 correctly notes the Occupying Power's role as administrator and usufructuary in relation to non-military public property of the occupied territory and that destruction is only permissible if rendered absolutely necessary by military operations. The limitations that the administrator and usufructuary roles imply are then helpfully explained, although it might have been useful to point out that e.g. timber cutting or mining activities should not exceed what is usual or necessary.

Paragraph 11.18.5.3 correctly lists the classes of movable property belonging to the occupied State of which the occupying army may take possession, namely cash, funds, realisable securities, depots of arms, means of transport, stores and supplies and movable property that may be used for military operations. The *Manual* rightly notes that a large proportion of State property is capable of being used for military purposes, but State movable property not capable of such use may not be appropriated and private property may not be confiscated.[43]

The Occupying Power may seize private movable property susceptible to military use provided a receipt is given or a suitable record is made to enable compensation to be settled and restoration of the property to be made at the end of the war. This is correctly reflected in the same paragraph and in

41 *UK Manual*, paragraph 11.90 reaches a similar conclusion.
42 *UK Manual*, paragraph 11.90.
43 *DoD Manual*, paragraph 11.18.6; Hague Regulations, Article 46(2).

paragraph 11.18.6.2, where a list of the kinds of item that are capable of being 'susceptible to military use' is given. Care is required with lists of this sort. While this list may help to illustrate what the relevant term means, it is the susceptibility of a particular item to military use that matters, as opposed to whether the item appears to the reader to come within one of the listed categories. This is a point that could usefully be emphasised in the *Manual*. This paragraph and paragraph 11.18.7 then note the right of the Occupying Power to requisition movable enemy private property for the needs of the army of occupation. Paragraph 11.18.7 restates the Hague Regulations, Article 52 stipulation that such requisitions must be proportionate and must not require the civilian population to take part in military operations against its own country.

As paragraph 11.18.6.3 notes, private immovable property may not be seized but may be requisitioned. The provisions of the Hague Regulations, Article 56 protecting municipal, religious, charitable and cultural property against damage, seizure or destruction and requiring legal proceedings in the event of a breach are restated in paragraph 11.18.6.4. The explanation of municipal property as consisting of the communal property of a parish, town or province accords with the explanation in the *UK Manual*.[44] The paragraph observes that because it is to be treated as private property, the property listed in Article 56 of the Hague Regulations is subject to requisitions, to contributions and to 'certain other purposes'. What those other purposes might be should be made clear, and the legal justification therefor should be stated. It should also be pointed out in paragraph 11.18.6.4 that any such requisitions or contributions will be subject to the limitations in Article 52 of the Hague Regulations, which are discussed in the next paragraph.

As paragraph 11.18.7.1 suggests, it is preferable if requisitions are arranged through local authorities, recognising, as the paragraph does, that if that is not possible, they may be made direct by military detachments. The payment arrangements prescribed in Article 52(3) of the Hague Regulations are repeated, and the right to use coercive measures that are necessary to secure the articles concerned is noted.

PROTECTION OF CULTURAL PROPERTY DURING OCCUPATION

The opening paragraph of section 11.19 draws attention to the applicability in occupation of the general rules as to the protection of cultural property in Chapter V. Paragraph 11.19.1 quotes verbatim Article 5(1) of the Hague Cultural Property Convention 1954 (Hague Convention), requiring that any State

[44] *UK Manual*, paragraph 11.87.

party in occupation of territory of another State party must as far as possible support the competent national authorities of the occupied State in safeguarding and preserving its cultural property. The paragraph then repeats, again verbatim, Hague Convention, Article 5(2)'s obligation for the Occupying Power, in close cooperation with national authorities, to take the most necessary preservation action in relation to cultural property that has been damaged by military operations. Paragraph 11.19.2 refers to the Hague Convention, Article 5(3) obligation of a government considered by a resistance movement to be its legitimate government to draw the group's attention to its obligation to comply with the Convention. Arguably, this should be discussed in Chapter V of the *Manual*, as opposed to the chapter on occupation.

Paragraphs 11.19.3 and 11.19.4 note the Occupying Power's obligation to appoint a special representative for cultural property in the occupied territory, its competence to apply for such cultural property to be entered on the International Register of Cultural Property under Special Protection and the prohibition of the requisitioning of movable cultural property located in the territory of another State party to the Convention.[45] It would be sensible, in relation to the last of these provisions, to cite the applicable authority, namely Article 4(3) of the 1954 Convention. The paragraph goes on to deal with the detailed arrangements prescribed in the Hague Cultural Property Regulations as to the transport of damaged cultural property to a refuge in occupied territory.[46]

LABOR OF PROTECTED PERSONS IN OCCUPIED TERRITORY

Section 11.20 starts by listing the kinds of labour that protected persons may not be compelled to undertake.

Paragraph 11.20.1.1 restates the GC, Article 51(1) prohibition of the Occupying Power compelling protected persons to serve in its armed or auxiliary forces or using pressure or propaganda to secure voluntary enlistment. As the *Manual* notes, such compulsory enlistment amounts to a grave breach of the Convention and is likely to involve compelling the inhabitants of occupied territory to swear allegiance to the hostile State, which is also explicitly prohibited.[47]

Paragraphs 11.20.1.2 and 11.20.1.3 repeat the GC, Article 51(2) and 51(4) provisions that the Occupying Power may not compel protected persons to employ

45 Hague Cultural Property Regulations, Articles 2 and 13; Hague Convention 1954, Article 4(3).
46 *DoD Manual*, paragraph 11.19.4; Hague Cultural Property Regulations, Article 19.
47 Hague Regulations, Article 45.

forcible means to ensure the security of the installations where they are performing compulsory labour and that the requisitioning of labour must not lead to a mobilisation of workers in an organisation of a military or semi-military character. Paragraph 11.20.1.4 correctly notes that Article 44 of the Hague Regulations 1907 forbids a belligerent 'to force the inhabitants of territory occupied by it to furnish information about the army of the other belligerent, or about its means of defense'. Article 51(2) also provides that protected persons may not be compelled to undertake any work which would involve them in the obligation of taking part in military operations, and this is repeated accurately in paragraph 11.20.1.5. As the *Manual* rightly notes, this is a broad prohibition that applies to military operations in general, not specifically to operations against the protected person's own country, and that has the partial purpose of prohibiting the forcing of protected persons to engage in activities that would forfeit their protection as civilians. The *Manual* then gives as examples of 'military operations against their own country' the construction of fortifications, entrenchments and military airfields and the transport of supplies or ammunition in the zone of operations.

Paragraph 11.20.2 repeats the GC, Article 51(2) rule that protected persons may only be compelled to work if they are over eighteen years old and may only do work that is necessary for the army of occupation, for public utility services or for the feeding, sheltering, clothing, transportation or health of the population of the occupied country. As the *Manual* rightly points out, protected persons can only be compelled to do such work provided that doing so is consistent with other prohibitions. Paragraph 11.20.2.1 gives examples of the kinds of service that may lawfully be requisitioned, and paragraph 11.20.2.2 states, correctly, that police, prison guards, firefighters and others whose services are essential to good order in occupied territory may be compelled by the Occupying Power to continue to provide those services in furtherance of the Occupying Power's obligation to maintain public order. The *Manual* is right to note that such officials may not be required to participate in military operations or other measures aimed at countering legitimate belligerent acts against the Occupying Power, but may lawfully be required to counter criminal activities, including criminal activities against the Occupying Power. Paragraph 11.20.3 then repeats the required safeguards for workers performing requisitioned work as set forth in GC, Article 51(3), requiring that the work be carried out only in occupied territory, that the persons concerned, where possible, be kept in their usual place of employment, that fair wages be paid, that the work be proportionate to the physical and mental capacities of the worker and that employment legislation and safeguards be applicable.

Paragraph 11.20.4 notes that there is no prohibition of work that is done voluntarily by protected persons, but that no pressure of propaganda may be used to secure voluntary enlistment in the armed or auxiliary forces of the Occupying Power. No provision, contractual or otherwise, can impair the right of a worker who is a protected person to seek the Protecting Power's intervention, and measures aimed at creating unemployment or restricting the opportunities for workers in occupied territory with a view to inducing them to work for the Occupying Power are prohibited.[48]

JUDGES AND OTHER PUBLIC OFFICIALS

Paragraph 11.21.1 repeats and explains GC, Article 54's prohibition of the Occupying Power changing the status of, applying sanctions to or taking measures of coercion or discrimination against public officials or judges in occupied territory if they abstain from fulfilling their functions for reasons of conscience. As the *Manual* explains, the rule is subject to GC, Article 51(2), so public officials can be compelled to work to meet the needs of the occupation army, public utility and certain police services. Equally, public officials can be removed from their posts.[49]

Paragraph 11.21.2 recalls that the Occupying Power may not compel protected persons to swear allegiance to it, but asserts that public officials who remain in post in occupied territory may be required to swear to perform their duties conscientiously and not to act to its prejudice. The reader may be concerned that the second part of the suggested oath might conflict with the general rule noted at the beginning of this paragraph. It should be recalled that 'allegiance' means 'loyalty or commitment to a superior or to a group or cause'.[50] To ensure that the general rule is not breached by the terms of such an oath, it would be sensible to include language making it clear that the official is not swearing loyalty to the Occupying Power as such, nor to the cause that it espouses, but is undertaking properly to perform his or her duties as a public official, and the paragraph in the *Manual* would benefit from amendment to make this clear. Incidentally, the form of oath cited in footnote 409 on page 807 would satisfy this suggested formulation. It is correct, as the *Manual* states, that public officials must obey the Occupying Power's legitimate orders.

PUBLIC FINANCES AND TAXES

Paragraph 11.22.1 correctly states that if, in occupied territory, the Occupying Power collects taxes, dues and tolls imposed for the benefit of the State, it

[48] *DoD Manual*, paragraphs 11.20.5.1 and 11.20.5.2, restating GC, Article 52.

[49] GC, Article 54(2).

[50] *Concise Oxford English Dictionary* (2006), page 34.

must do so as far as possible in accordance with the rules in force and must defray the administration costs of the occupied territory to the same extent as the country's government was bound to do. Where local taxes are concerned, the Occupying Power can supervise their expenditure to prevent their hostile use.[51]

Paragraph 11.22.1.2 cites extensive authorities in support of the contention that '[u]nless required to do so by considerations of public order and safety, the Occupying Power must not create new taxes. Additional revenue may be raised in some other form, such as monetary contributions or customs duties.' The first part of this cited text is consistent with the 'as far as possible' language in the Hague Regulations, Article 48, which makes it clear that the requirement to comply with existing rules of assessment is not absolute. The maintenance of public order and safety might render variation of the rules of assessment necessary. The second part is consistent with the Hague Regulations, Article 49, provided that the money so raised may only be used 'for the needs of the army or of the administration of the territory in question'. It is suggested that this caveat should be added to the cited text.

Paragraph 11.22.1.3 contends that any surplus of tax revenue over expenditure may be used for the purposes of the Occupying Power. The *UK Manual*, by contrast, opines that '[f]unds raised must not be used for the enrichment of the occupying power',[52] and the present authors consider that the *UK Manual*'s position is more coherent with the relevant treaty provisions. Paragraph 11.22.1.3 is, however, right to note that the Occupying Power is entitled to allocate tax revenues to the cost of maintaining order in the occupied territory and to the benefit of its population. This derives from the general rule that such taxation should be applied to the cost of administering the territory. Having correctly noted in paragraph 11.22.1.4 that the Occupying Power and its personnel are generally exempt from local taxes, paragraph 11.22.1.5 points out that the power to collect taxes is limited to persons and property in occupied territory. That the Occupying Power is not responsible for collecting local social welfare taxes, including from its own employees, is noted in paragraph 11.22.1.6.

The limitation of the levying of contributions to costs associated with the occupation army and administration is noted in paragraph 11.22.2,[53] and paragraph 11.22.2.1 lists items of expenditure that contributions may not be used to defray. The procedure for levying contributions, as provided for in the Hague Regulations, Article 51, is then explained in paragraph 11.22.2.2.

[51] DoD *Manual*, paragraph 11.22.1.1 and footnote 416 on page 808.

[52] *UK Manual*, paragraph 11.31.

[53] Hague Regulations, Article 49.

Paragraph 11.22.2.3 points out that the Occupying Power may seek contributions from the population in the form of forced loans, which differ from regular contributions only in the obligation to repay but which, significantly, are subject to the limitations applying to contributions in general. Paragraph 11.22.3 notes the Occupying Power's right to collect customs duties consistently with the rules relating to the collection of existing taxes and its right to exact new duties as a form of contribution, but only consistently with the conditions limiting contributions. It should be noted that relief shipments for PWs and internees and consignments for occupied territory are exempt from customs duties and that the Occupying Power may suspend customs duties or exempt certain goods.[54]

Having acknowledged a contrary view among some jurists, paragraph 11.22.4.1, relying on Article 53(1) of the Hague Regulations, states the US position that the Occupying Power may collect debts owed to the sovereign provided they may truly be regarded as realisable securities that are strictly the property of the State. The Occupying Power is not obliged to pay the debts of the occupied territory and may prevent payments from the occupied territory to a hostile belligerent.[55] Paragraph 11.22.4.3 states that new debt may not generally be incurred by the Occupying Power on behalf of the occupied territory, save that which is immediately necessary under a fair and reasonable transaction for the welfare of the inhabitants. Paragraph 11.22.4 deals with the possible consolidating or refinancing of the public debt of the occupied territory by the Occupying Power.

The discretion of the Occupying Power to leave local currency in circulation, to issue its own currency or special currency in the occupied territory and to regulate exchange rates is noted in paragraph 11.22.5 – well supported, as is usual in this chapter, with rich practice set forth in the footnotes. The point is well made that such exchange rate regulation must not be the means to deprive protected persons of private property, nor to enrich the Occupying Power.

OTHER ECONOMIC REGULATION OF OCCUPIED TERRITORY

Having asserted the right of the Occupying Power to regulate commercial activity in the occupied territory, e.g. in the military interests of the Occupying Power, in order to satisfy the inhabitants' needs or due to law of war obligations, paragraph 11.23.1 gives examples such as commercial regulations to

54 *DoD Manual*, paragraphs 11.22.3.1 and 11.22.3.2.

55 *DoD Manual*, paragraphs 11.22.4.1 and 11.22.4.2.

prohibit the illegal traffic in and looting of cultural property. Paragraph 11.23.2 limits the burdens that may be placed on the local economy to those required to meet the costs of the occupation, and those costs must be such as the local economy can reasonably be expected to bear, i.e. proportionate to the resources of the occupied territory.[56]

Paragraph 11.23.3 discusses the extensive measures of control that the Occupying Power can exercise in relation to private businesses in occupied territory. These include compelling the business to continue in operation if necessary to serve the needs of the population or of the occupation, granting subsidies out of available government revenues in the occupied territory in order to increase production, closing down businesses detrimental to the interests of the Occupying Power or of the population and assuming control of the business if it is necessary for military purposes or for the needs of the population. In addition, external trade may be regulated or suspended, exchange controls may be instituted, certain assets may be frozen and flows of funds between the occupied territory and other countries may be regulated or stopped, but no such action may have the purpose of enriching the Occupying Power or of circumventing other occupation law rules. The maintenance of order, stability and security and the prevention of an exodus of funds from the occupied territory are likely to be the main reasons for such action.[57] Similarly, price controls may be necessary in order to keep prices at a reasonable maximum level.

CONCLUDING REMARKS

It is immediately apparent that Chapter XI of the *Manual*, as noted at the commencement of the present chapter, has been enriched by the relatively recent experience gained during the military occupation of Iraq by coalition forces following the 2003 invasion of that country. The extensive and numerous cites from Coalition Provisional Authority orders and regulations are supplemented by useful references to instruments and action associated with military occupations dating from the last century and before. Extracts from FM 27–10, from the GC *Commentary* and from other authoritative sources frequently form the basis for the positions taken in the *Manual*, often with minimal or no amendment.

56 This must be a correct adaptation of the Hague Regulations, Article 52(1) restriction on the levying of contributions.

57 DoD *Manual*, paragraph 11.23.5.

Where points deserving comment have been identified, comment has been made. However, this is an authoritative text that will take understanding of the law of military occupation materially forward and that is, in the view of the present authors, one of the most important elements in the *Manual* as a whole.

12

Non-Hostile Relations between Belligerents

INTRODUCTION

Chapter XII, as the title makes clear, deals with non-hostile interaction between belligerent parties to an armed conflict. As a preliminary point, one might have expected such a chapter to appear rather later in the chapter sequence, but the present authors do not consider this to be a major point of criticism. Section 12.1, relying on no lesser an authority than Dr Francis Lieber, explains the general rule that during international armed conflict, even without any special proclamation, all intercourse between the territories occupied by the belligerent forces, including communication, transportation and commerce, ceases.[1] The importance of not supporting the enemy's war effort and of speaking with one voice in communications with the enemy is noted as justifying this traditional rule renouncing such intercourse, and provisions under war powers and domestic legislation criminalising communications with the enemy are noted in this context. As the *Manual* points out, exceptions to the rule tend to require authority at governmental or the highest military levels. Paragraph 12.1.1.1 explains that the laws of neutrality and of military occupation limit the right of a belligerent to control communications between territory it controls and territory controlled by the enemy, and that protected persons must be permitted to leave a belligerent's home territory or occupied territory unless such departure is contrary to the interests of the State.

As paragraph 12.1.2 stipulates, despite the traditional 'no intercourse' rule, non-hostile relations between belligerents may be necessary to facilitate humanitarian activities and the restoration of peace. In the former category are communications to conclude and implement special agreements

[1] Lieber Code, Article 86.

associated with: the protection of the wounded, sick, shipwrecked and medical personnel, including armistices and local arrangements; agreements to effect direct repatriation or transfer to neutral countries of seriously wounded and sick PWs; and agreements to establish areas where the wounded and sick are protected. Such communications may also be required to obtain consent necessary for the appointment of Protecting Powers, to establish safe conduct arrangements and to apply during non-international armed conflicts rules that would normally only apply during international armed conflicts.[2]

Non-hostile relations may also be an important factor in restoring peace, e.g. through ceasefires or local armistices, in concluding armistices that are a prelude to a peace treaty, in achieving the permanent cessation of hostilities through a peace treaty and in arranging information sharing and measures to protect civilians from the effects of minefields, mined areas, mines, booby-traps and other devices. They may also contribute to the provision of certain assistance as to the marking, clearance, removal and destruction of explosive remnants of war where the user of the ordnance does not control the relevant territory.[3] These are appropriate examples to illustrate the kinds of circumstance that will usefully give rise to communications between belligerents, but the circumstances of a particular conflict will determine when such communication is actually necessary.

PRINCIPLE OF GOOD FAITH IN NON-HOSTILE RELATIONS

Section 12.2 makes the correct point that absolute good faith is required in non-hostile relations between belligerents,[4] spelling this out as an obligation faithfully to adhere to compacts with the enemy (such as truces and capitulations), never to take an advantage not intended by the adversary and not to misuse the means of such communication, e.g. the flag of truce. Military operations may nevertheless be continued while negotiations take place, and offers to negotiate may legitimately be ignored or refused.

METHODS OF COMMUNICATION BETWEEN BELLIGERENTS

Section 12.3 correctly explains that belligerents may communicate with one another by a variety of methods, and lists as examples the use of telecommunications, displaying a flag of truce and sending parlementaires during conferences between belligerent representatives in an agreed neutral zone, whether

[2] *DoD Manual*, paragraph 12.1.2.1. [3] *DoD Manual*, paragraph 12.1.2.2.
[4] Note also *UK Manual*, paragraph 10.2.

through another State as a Protecting Power, through the United Nations or indirectly through the ICRC or another impartial humanitarian organisation. These are stated merely to be examples, and it seems likely that during future conflicts, modern communications media are likely also to be used, including emails, social media, mass media and the like. Perhaps this aspect could have been given greater emphasis.

THE WHITE FLAG OF TRUCE TO INITIATE NEGOTIATIONS

Paragraph 12.4.1 correctly explains that the white flag, when used by military forces, 'indicates a desire to communicate with the enemy' and has no other meaning in the law of war.[5] The proposed communication may be with a view to seeking to achieve an armistice, or the showing of the white flag may indicate that an individual combatant or party of combatants wishes to surrender. Adopting similar language to the *UK Manual*,[6] the paragraph talks here of a 'small party' of combatants, but white flags might equally, one would suggest, be used with this intent by a very large group of combatants. The *Manual* is right to explain that although the white flag has been used to facilitate surrender, its use does not necessarily indicate such an intent, and other enemy forces in the area may not have such an intent. Paragraph 12.4.2 explains accurately that the party displaying the white flag bears the burden of communicating to the adversary its intent to engage in non-hostile relations. The paragraph then suggests: 'To indicate that the hoisting of the white flag is authorized by its commander, the appearance of the flag should be accompanied or followed promptly by a complete cessation of fire from that side.' The assumption must be that the word 'its' in the cited text refers to the party or individual hoisting the flag, as opposed to the flag itself. This might usefully be made clear. Moreover, the quoted sentence should not be misunderstood as suggesting that an intent to surrender can only validly be signified by means of a white flag if the commander of the troops displaying the flag approves their action in doing so. The paragraph rightly suggests that the commander hoisting the flag of truce should promptly send a parlementaire to communicate the commander's intent, but, again, it would be better to express the sentence in terms of 'If the display of the flag of truce has been approved by a commander' to avoid creating the mistaken impression referred to previously.

[5] Note also *UK Manual*, paragraph 10.5. Some commentators argue that the white flag indicates an intent to surrender, but the present authors agree with the position as expressed here in the *Manual*.

[6] *UK Manual*, paragraph 10.5.1, final sentence.

Paragraph 12.4.2.1 rightly notes that making improper use of the flag of truce is prohibited. It gives as examples: feigning an intent to surrender when no such intent exists; a party that is sending a parlementaire failing to halt and cease fire while the parlementaire is approaching or being received by the other party; using the flag of truce, while engaging in attacks, to shield, favour or protect one's own military operations or otherwise to impede enemy military operations; and using the flag surreptitiously to obtain military information or to obtain time to facilitate a withdrawal, to secure reinforcements, to resupply or to conduct other operations.

Paragraph 12.4.3 correctly explains that a 'party is not required to cease firing or other military operations when a white flag is raised by the other side'. It is also right, as the paragraph suggests, that it must be determined with reasonable certainty that the flag is being shown with the authority of the relevant commander before basing important action on such an assumption. Fire must not, indeed, be directed intentionally on the person actually carrying the white flag or on persons near him or her unless those persons manifest a clear hostile intent. There is, however, an important caveat that is missing in paragraph 12.4.3. Paragraph 12.4.1 notes that hoisting the white flag may signify that the individual combatant or group of combatants wishes to surrender. A person who clearly expresses an intention to surrender, who abstains from any hostile act and who does not attempt to escape is *hors de combat*. So, paragraph 12.4.3 should make the explicit point that if the circumstances are such that the person or group hoisting a white flag is clearly intending to surrender, fire should no longer be directed at that individual or group unless continued hostile acts from their vicinity make that impracticable. The need for caution, however, as explained in the final two sentences of paragraph 10.5.2 of the *UK Manual*, is clear,[7] and might perhaps be given greater emphasis in the *DoD Manual* text.

RULES FOR PARLEMENTAIRES

Paragraph 12.5.1 correctly summarises the role of a parlementaire, namely to communicate and/or conduct negotiations on behalf of one belligerent commander with an opposing belligerent commander within the lines of the latter. Paragraph 12.5.1.1 mixes up somewhat the quote from Article 32 of the Hague

[7] The *UK Manual* refers to the case of a British officer killed at Goose Green during the Falklands/Malvinas War of 1982 when moving towards a white flag. 'The shots were not fired by those displaying the white flag, but by others in the vicinity'; *UK Manual*, footnote 10 on page 260.

Regulations, but paragraph 12.5.1.2 correctly notes the requirement that the parlementaire carry a written instrument signed by the commander of his or her forces demonstrating his or her authorisation to negotiate. Paragraph 12.5.1.3, again mirroring the view in the *UK Manual*, reports the reference in Article 32 to the parlementaire being accompanied by a trumpeter, bugler or drummer as well as the flag-bearer and interpreter, but suggests that in modern warfare, the parlementaire's party is more likely to include a driver and communications personnel.[8]

Paragraph 12.5.2 explains that a commander is not bound to accept a parlementaire;[9] he or she may, for example, refuse to do so for reasons of military necessity. He or she may not, however, declare in advance that he or she will not receive parlementaires, except as a reprisal for misuse of the flag of truce.[10] The paragraph then notes that the receiving commander may prescribe the formalities and conditions on which the parlementaire will be received and the hour and place at which he or she must appear. Other details that may be prescribed include the number of persons who may accompany the parlementaire, the method of transport to be used and the frequency of meetings, if more than one.

Paragraph 12.5.3 notes the risk of death or injury to those displaying a white flag during combat, a somewhat obvious factual statement which does not affect the prohibition of targeting the flag of truce. The same paragraph correctly notes that it is for the parlementaire to take appropriate measures to communicate his or her status to the enemy, commenting that the parlementaire's party should move slowly and deliberately so as not to be inadvertently attacked. Specifically, the parlementaire must obey all orders and instructions while within enemy lines.

The right of the parlementaire and of members of his or her party to inviolability and the right of the receiving commander to take necessary steps to prevent the envoy taking advantage of his or her mission are both reflected in paragraphs 12.5.4 and 12.5.4.1. Paragraph 12.5.4.2 cites Hague Regulations, Article 34 to the effect that the parlementaire loses inviolability if it is clearly shown that he or she has taken advantage of his or her privileged position to commit or provoke an act of treachery, such as sabotage or gathering information about the adversary while under the adversary's protection.[11]

[8] See also *UK Manual*, footnote 5 on page 259.

[9] He or she may not, however, refuse to accept unconditional surrender, nor declare that he or she will so refuse.

[10] See *UK Manual*, paragraph 10.8, where a similar position is expressed.

[11] As the *Manual* correctly states, it is not an act of treachery for the parlementaire later to report what he or she observed in plain sight. The *Manual* cites the 1958 *UK Manual*, paragraph 408 and J M Spaight, *War Rights on Land*. London: Macmillan (1911), 219.

The circumstances giving rise to the right to detain a parlementaire are fully explained, such detention being only for so long as the circumstances imperatively require, with information as to the detention of the parlementaire and as to any other action taken against him or her or a member of his or her party being passed to their commander.

Paragraph 12.5.5 discusses some measures that might be agreed to facilitate negotiations that it is anticipated will be lengthy, such as setting aside a neutralised area for their conduct and agreeing that no combat activity will take place in or over the area, that forces will be detailed to maintain the area's security and that the area will be designated in maps exchanged between representatives of the belligerents and will be marked in suggested ways to ensure that it will not be attacked.

MILITARY PASSPORTS, SAFE-CONDUCTS AND SAFEGUARDS

Some aspects of the discussion in the opening text of section 12.16 and in paragraph 12.16.1 are not entirely clear, unlike the corresponding discussion, for example, in paragraphs 10.33 to 10.35.1 of the *UK Manual*. A military passport is a document issued by a commander to a person or persons permitting them unmolested movement within the territory of troops under his or her command. Paragraph 12.6.2 of the *DoD Manual* specifies that the person or persons named in the passport must be 'residing or sojourning within' such territory.[12] It may specify routes through the lines and other conditions and limitations, and may be a means of regulating commerce and travel in the area controlled by the commander's forces.

Similar documents issued to persons residing or traveling outside occupied areas but who wish to enter and remain within or pass through such areas are called 'safe conducts'. Similar documents may be issued to permit the passage of designated goods to or from such areas, to enable otherwise forbidden trade[13] or to allow access of diplomatic agents of neutral governments accredited to the opposing party to the conflict.[14] In an international armed conflict, licenses to trade may be issued by the supreme authority of the State controlling territory to relax prohibitions on trading with the enemy.[15]

[12] To 'sojourn' is to stay temporarily; *Concise Oxford English Dictionary* (2006), page 1370.

[13] *DoD Manual*, paragraph 12.6.3.

[14] *DoD Manual*, paragraph 12.6.3.1, which explains that the final category of pass would normally be issued by national-level authorities.

[15] *DoD Manual*, paragraph 12.6.3.2. The paragraph distinguishes between a general licence that 'generally or partially relaxes the exercise of the rights of war in regard to trade' in relation

Safeguards are defined in paragraph 12.6.4. While that definition could perhaps be expressed more simply, paragraph 12.6.4.1 correctly refers to the protected status of personnel forming a safeguard and to the custom of returning them, with their equipment and arms, to their own armed forces when the locality is occupied by enemy armed forces and when military exigencies permit. The second element of paragraph 12.6.4 clearly explains that safeguards are only regulated by the law of war when they are the result of arrangements between the belligerents. The paragraph explains as follows: 'The effect of a safeguard is to pledge the honor of the nation that the person or property will be respected by its armed forces.'[16] The *Manual* stresses the seriousness of performing any act that violates the protection of safeguards.[17]

Citing the 1958 *UK Manual*, paragraph 12.6.5 points out that passports and safe conducts can be revoked by the issuing commander or his or her superior 'for good reasons of military expediency' but that the holder must be allowed to withdraw in safety. The privilege may also be withdrawn if the holder commits a wrongful act or exceeds the terms of the passport or safe conduct.

CARTELS

The broader meaning of 'cartel', as given in section 12.7, would seem to comport with modern understanding, namely a 'convention concluded between belligerents for the purpose of arranging or regulating certain kinds of non-hostile intercourse that would otherwise be prohibited by reason of the existence of the armed conflict'. Both parties must observe the cartel's provisions scrupulously, and the cartel is voidable if it is proved that it has been intentionally violated. Quite what the word 'definite' adds to the notion of proof in section 12.7 is not clear. By insisting that the violation must relate to an 'important particular', the *DoD Manual* is restricting the circumstances that can lead to legitimate voidance of a cartel. Paragraph 10.38 of the *UK Manual* contends that such agreements are voidable on proof of breach of their terms by the other party, which is clearly the correct explanation.

CAPITULATIONS – NEGOTIATED INSTRUMENTS OF SURRENDER

Paragraph 12.8.1 defines a capitulation as an 'agreement (sometimes with certain conditions) entered into between commanders of belligerent forces for

to a community or individuals and a special licence given to individuals for a particular voyage or journey, to import or export particular goods. Paragraph 12.6.3.3 helpfully lists the safe conducts by agreement that are contemplated in the 1949 Conventions.

16 Footnote 102 on page 838 gives useful historical examples of the operation of this rule.

17 *DoD Manual*, paragraph 12.6.4.3.

the surrender of a body of forces, a fortress, or other defended locality, or of a district of the theatre of operations', a definition matching, with only minor adjustment, that given in the *UK Manual*.[18] The paragraph makes the point that a *surrender* of military forces might be arranged at national level without the involvement of commanders, with a *capitulation* being agreed between opposing military forces in implementation of a national-level surrender.

So, a capitulation surrenders the capitulating unit, whereas an armistice suspends the fighting between opposing forces.[19] A capitulation is a surrender pursuant to an agreement, whereas a surrender may be unconditional, and may or may not involve the negotiation of a capitulation agreement. If it does, the agreement will specify no conditions for the surrender, but may, as paragraph 12.8.1.2 notes, stipulate the manner in which the surrender is to be implemented. The presumed authority of a commander under the law of war to conclude capitulation agreements is referred to in paragraph 12.8.2. This authority is limited to the forces under his or her command, and there is generally no authority to cede places subject to his or her command, to surrender sovereignty over territory or to agree other political terms. Terms in a capitulation agreement that exceed the authority of the agreeing commander can be repudiated by the relevant State.[20] The fact that a commander has exceeded his or her authority does not invalidate the capitulation, but may result in the punishment of the relevant commander; brief reference is made to the position under the Code of Conduct for US armed forces and under the UCMJ.

As paragraph 12.8.3 explains, 'conditions involving unnecessary disgrace or ignominy should not be insisted upon' in the capitulation agreement, which may permit the capitulating forces to surrender with their colours displayed, or otherwise allow them some measure of respect. The point is made that treating the adversary honourably may diminish the associated psychological stigma and incentivise capitulations, rather than fighting on without hope of success. The advisability of reducing a capitulation agreement to writing and of detailing there, in precise terms, the conditions to be observed on either side is noted in paragraph 12.8.4. Paragraph 12.8.5 effectively makes the somewhat obvious point that a capitulation agreement in which there are no conditions amounts to an unconditional surrender. Usefully, however, the paragraph details the duties of the capitulating force: it must cease all operations; must maintain the military status quo as at the time the capitulation becomes effective; and must abstain from all destruction and damage of its facilities and equipment, save to the extent permitted by the capitulation agreement. The

[18] *UK Manual*, paragraph 10.29. [19] *DoD Manual*, paragraph 12.8.1.1.

[20] 1958 *UK Manual*, paragraph 467; *DoD Manual*, paragraph 12.8.2, final section.

capturing party may capture as war booty or destroy the weapons, ammunition and military equipment of the capitulating party.

CAPITULATIONS – SUBJECTS USUALLY ADDRESSED

Section 12.9 addresses the topics usually covered in a capitulation agreement.

The agreement may specify: the force or territory that is surrendered; the time when the surrender is to take effect; if relevant, provisions as to the withdrawal of defenders from a place and the the entry there of capturing forces; exactly which forces, including detached forces, are surrendering; and the movements and administration of surrendered forces after surrender.

As paragraph 12.9.2 recognises, surrendering armed forces personnel in an international armed conflict will be PWs on capture, and associated medical and religious personnel will have retained personnel status on capture. The paragraph suggests that if the victor is unable to guard, evacuate and maintain large numbers of PWs or to occupy the relevant area, it may be justified in allowing them to remain in position, to withdraw or to disperse after being disarmed and after giving their parole, if they are willing to do so and are so permitted by the law that binds them. Significantly, this paragraph fails to draw the reader's attention to paragraphs 9.9.3, 9.9.3.2 and 8.32.1 of the *Manual*. This is an important omission, as those paragraphs, taken together, point out that in the kind of situation contemplated by paragraph 12.9.2, the obligation is to 'take reasonable steps under the circumstances to help ensure the POWs' safety and survival'. This would seem to be a practicable and legally correct position that ought to be reflected here. Best practice, as suggested in the earlier paragraphs, is to take feasible measures to record the names, serial numbers and unit affiliations of those captured and brief particulars of the capture and release. The authors of the *Manual* are accordingly invited to include suitable cross-references and perhaps an explicit reminder of the obligation to take reasonable steps.

Paragraph 12.9.2.1 notes that such agreements normally include the requirement that the orders of the victorious commander must be scrupulously carried out by the surrendered forces, with those failing to comply being liable to punishment. Paragraph 12.9.2.2 explains that such agreements normally also include provisions governing the disposition of enemy arms, equipment and other property in the hands of the surrendered force, and paragraph 12.9.2.3 repeats that although the act of capitulation generally has the effect of prohibiting acts of destruction by surrendered forces, the capitulation agreement may specifically prohibit the destruction of classes of object listed in the paragraph. The capitulation agreement may also address the disposition of detainees held by the surrendered forces and the provision of facilities and information as to minefields and other defensive measures and as to the civil administration of the area concerned.[21]

CAPITULATIONS – VIOLATIONS AND DENUNCIATION

Violation of the capitulation agreement by the capitulating commander or his or her higher authority may justify denunciation of the capitulation agreement by the opposing commander and a resumption of the hostilities. If the capitulation was obtained through a breach of faith, similar action may follow. Denunciation is not permissible if one of the parties was induced to capitulate by an act that does not breach the law of war, such as a ruse, or by what the 1958 *UK Manual* describes as 'incapacity or feebleness' on the part of one of the parties.[22]

Paragraph 12.10.2 asserts that the deliberate violation of a capitulation agreement by individuals amounts to a war crime, citing the *Scuttled U-Boats Case* in support.[23] It distinguishes this from an unwitting violation, for example by personnel returning from patrol and unaware of the agreement, where the action of the relevant unwitting individuals would not constitute such a crime. The *UK Manual* finds violation of an armistice amounts to a war crime, basing that view on the same case.[24] While it is clear that breaches of armistices (discussed in the next section) and violations of capitulation agreements are both war crimes, the basis differs between the two classes of agreement. A deliberate breach by an individual of an armistice is as such a war crime.[25] A breach of a capitulation agreement is likely to be a war crime, not *per se* but, rather, because the breach will almost certainly involve a perfidious act.[26] Article 41 of the Hague Regulations stipulates that a violation of the terms of an armistice by private individuals 'only entitles the injured party to demand the punishment of the offenders or, if necessary, compensation for the losses sustained'. There is no reference here to a war crime having been committed,

[21] *DoD Manual*, paragraphs 12.9.3 to 12.9.5.

[22] 1958 *UK Manual*, 484. The *DoD Manual*, paragraph 12.10.1 suggests that a mistake of fact by a party does not entitle it to denounce, and that is probably also correct.

[23] *Scuttled U-Boats Case (Trial of Grumpelt)* (1945) 1 WCR 55.

[24] The agreement of relevance in the *Scuttled U-Boats Case* is dated 4 May 1945. The general armistice was agreed on 8 May 1945.

[25] *UK Manual*, paragraph 16.28.

[26] *UK Manual*, paragraph 10.28. Note that the consequences of the perfidious act fall outside those required by API, Article 37(1), but the war crime is nevertheless committed – in part, it would seem, because of the importance of any breach of the obligation of good faith in dealings with the enemy.

and the inference is that punishment would be by the offender's own force, probably on a breach of orders charge. It is practice since 1907, including the *Scuttled U-Boats Case*, that leads to the conclusion that deliberate armistice breach by individuals constitutes a war crime. Given that, on capitulation, the surrendering forces become PWs, violations of the agreement by them do not deprive them of PW status and may be tried either by the capturing State or by their own State after repatriation.[27]

ARMISTICES AND OTHER CEASE-FIRE AGREEMENTS

Section 12.10 starts with an accurate definition of an armistice as a cessation of active hostilities for the period agreed upon, i.e. military operations are suspended by agreement. A unilateral suspension of hostilities is not therefore an armistice. Moreover, as military operations are only suspended to the extent agreed upon by the parties, a state of war may continue notwithstanding the agreement of an armistice,[28] although, as the *Manual* notes, armistices may be intended as a prelude to peace negotiations or may remain in force for a long time.

Paragraph 12.11.2 distinguishes between general and local armistices in similar terms to Article 37 of the Hague Regulations, suggesting that the former suspend military operations everywhere. As the *DoD Manual* correctly observes, armistice agreements must be concluded by authorities competent to agree to and enforce their terms, and 'if an armistice contains political terms, it must be made under authorization of the governments concerned or subject to approval by them'. Paragraph 12.11.2.1, and the *UK Manual* at paragraph 10.18, make the additional pertinent point that since general armistices are generally of a combined military and political nature and usually, but not always, precede negotiations for peace, they are normally negotiated by senior officials and are subject to approval by each State.

Paragraph 12.11.2.2 correctly defines a local or partial armistice as a suspension of operations between certain portions of the belligerent forces or within a specified area, distinguishing this from a suspension of arms on the

[27] *DoD Manual*, paragraphs 12.10.2.1 and 12.10.2.2.

[28] *DoD Manual*, paragraphs 12.11.1 to 12.11.1.2. Note, however, Yoram Dinstein's view that the Korean Armistice agreement terminated the Korean War, and his associated position that a general armistice agreement no longer has the meaning laid down in the Hague Regulations; Y Dinstein, *War, Aggression and Self Defence*, 5th edn. Cambridge: Cambridge University Press (2011), 41ff.

basis that the local armistice involves large numbers of forces, a greater geographical area and broader interests than local military requirements. Paragraph 12.11.2.3 characterises a suspension of arms as a form of local armistice arranged for local military purposes, such as burial of the dead, collection of the wounded, exchange of detainees or to enable a commander to communicate with his or her superiors or government. Commanders are presumed to have authority to negotiate such suspensions of arms – or suspensions of fire or ceasefires, as the *UK Manual* calls them – in relation to forces and areas under their control.[29] Paragraph 12.11.4.2 repeats the second sentence of Article 36 of the Hague Regulations, to the effect that, if the duration of the armistice is not defined, operations may be resumed at any time provided the enemy is warned within the time agreed upon in accordance with the terms of the armistice. If the armistice is for a specific period, resumption of hostilities after the expiry of that period does not require prior notice.

Offensive military operations constitute a serious violation of an armistice, as paragraph 12.11.4.3 correctly explains, but belligerents may continue to gather intelligence on which they may legitimately rely after the armistice ends. The *Manual* correctly notes that, in a similar vein, and unless the armistice agreement provides otherwise, the belligerents are permitted during an armistice: to move forces within their own lines; to receive reinforcements; to construct new fortifications, installations and bases; to build and repair transportation and communication facilities; to seek information about the enemy; to bring up supplies and equipment; and generally to prepare for resuming hostilities.[30] As paragraph 12.11.4.6 notes, while an armistice does not, without specific provision to such effect, entitle a besieged area to receive food, water and other supplies, the negotiations may provide the opportunity to conclude other local agreements on a variety of possible topics mentioned in the paragraph.

ARMISTICES – SUBJECTS USUALLY ADDRESSED

As section 12.12 explains, an armistice agreement will usually address numerous topics, such as the armistice's start date, time (including time zone), duration and scope. The advisability of giving time for notifications to be received before the armistice becomes effective is noted, and if the armistice is to be of indefinite duration, the terms and manner of giving notice that it is to be ended and the length of notice required before hostilities can resume should

[29] *UK Manual*, paragraph 10.15. [30] *DoD Manual*, paragraph 12.11.4.5.

be stated. Paragraph 12.12.2 suggests the agreement should specify the extent to which military activities are prohibited. It would arguably be clearer simply to say that the agreement should specify exactly which military activities are prohibited, recognising that offensive operations are generally understood to be prohibited during an armistice.

Paragraph 12.12.3 repeats the rather obscure language of Article 32 of the Hague Regulations. What exactly 'intercourse with the inhabitants of one belligerent State and those of the other' means is unlikely to be immediately clear to a modern reader. The paragraph therefore helps considerably by explaining that, absent specific agreement, 'a belligerent retains the right to control all communications or movement of members of the civilian population between its lines and enemy lines'.[31] The agreement may also stipulate the responsibilities of each party for civil administration of areas it controls and of areas the control of which is shared. The paragraph refers to 'neutral areas', but it is clear that the word 'neutral' here is not being given the meaning normally understood under the law of war, so to avoid any confusion it is suggested that an alternative term should be found.

The armistice agreement may also provide for humanitarian activities and for the release or exchange of PWs, retained personnel and civilian internees.[32]

Paragraph 12.12.5 notes the possibility that an armistice agreement will specify mechanisms for its implementation. Such mechanisms might include a restricted-entry zone, designed to minimise the risk of unintentional confrontation by opposing forces; entry would be confined to parlementaires, and to others pursuant to special agreements or for particular reasons, such as the collection of the wounded or the burial of the dead. The present authors prefer the Dayton Agreement term 'Separation Zone' to describe such an arrangement,[33] rather than the term 'neutral'. Equally, a commission comprising representatives of the opposing parties, neutral States and local authorities might be established to supervise the implementation of the armistice.[34] The footnotes associated with these paragraphs give valuable historical examples of the application of the various arrangements. As the *Manual* points out, signals, maps and other imagery is also likely to have a role to play, for example in showing the disposition of the opposing forces.

31 *DoD Manual*, paragraph 12.12.3, second part.

32 *DoD Manual*, paragraphs 12.12.4 and 12.12.4.1.

33 Dayton Accords, Annex 1A, art IV (OHR Doc 14/12/95), referred to in *DoD Manual*, footnote 200 on page 855.

34 *DoD Manual*, paragraph 12.12.5.2.

ARMISTICES – VIOLATIONS AND DENUNCIATION

Serious violations of an armistice by one of its parties give the opposing party the right to denounce the agreement and, in cases of urgency, to resume hostilities immediately.[35] The *Manual* gives as examples of serious breaches of an armistice the conducting of attacks against the enemy, a deliberate advance or construction of works beyond the agreed line, the seizure of any point outside the lines and the withdrawal of forces from an unfavourable position commanded (presumably meaning 'controlled') by the enemy.[36] If there is no urgent necessity, there should always be a delay between denunciation and the resumption of hostilities. Paragraph 12.13.1.2 then has the following sentence: 'This delay allows the denunciation to act as warning and to ensure that the party recommencing hostilities does not rely on the other party's compliance with the armistice as a way of facilitating its offensive military operations'. Apart from the omission of the indefinite article before 'warning', this sentence is hard to understand. After all, it is the opposing party that has breached the agreement, so how the party recommencing hostilities can be relying on that party's compliance is difficult to comprehend. Nevertheless, it is correct to conclude, as the second part of paragraph 12.13.1.2 does, that it would be dishonourable and perfidious during the currency of an armistice to resume hostilities without warning, whether or not there has been a formal denunciation, unless there is convincing proof of intentional and serious violations of its terms by the other party.

The paragraph goes on to discuss cases of urgency, taking the line – correctly, in the present authors' view – that if delay seems likely to give the violator a substantial advantage of any kind, the opposing party is free to resume hostilities without warning and with or without a formal denunciation. The *Manual* then adds that 'the law of war does not prohibit armed forces that reasonably believe an adversary is committing armistice violations from taking necessary and proportionate action in self-defense immediately in response'. The present authors take issue with this analysis. The action taken in response will be lawful action in resumption of the hostilities, because a state of war (or, in modern parlance, of armed conflict) continues to exist notwithstanding the agreement of an armistice, and notions of armed attack and self-defence as reflected in Article 51 of the UN Charter are not relevant to the circumstances being considered. After all, if the violation rises to the level of an armed attack,

[35] *DoD Manual*, paragraph 12.13.1; Hague Regulations, Article 40.

[36] *DoD Manual*, paragraph 12.13.1.1.

it will likely justify the opposing party to resume hostilities without warning, and probably without a formal denunciation.

Paragraph 12.13.1.3 restates Article 41 of the Hague Regulations to the effect that if a belligerent faces serious violations of an armistice, consent of co-belligerents is not required before it resumes hostilities. If the violations are by private individuals acting on their own initiative, the injured party can demand their punishment or, if necessary, compensation. Arguably, compensation would fall to be considered under Article 3 of Hague Convention IV, so while the distinction between necessity and the circumstances so demanding may be minimal, the latter would more accurately describe the relevant criterion.

Paragraph 12.13.2.2 states that violations of an armistice by individuals are war crimes, an issue that has already been discussed in relation to paragraph 12.10.2. Paragraph 12.13.2.2 makes the valid point that such violations by individuals do not justify denunciation of the armistice unless 'they are proved to have been committed with the knowledge and actual or tacit consent of their own government or commander'; consent may be inferred from a persistent failure to punish the offenders. Such violations do not justify depriving a person who otherwise qualifies for it of PW status.[37]

UN SECURITY COUNCIL CEASE-FIRES

Finally, section 12.14 draws attention to the authority of the UN Security Council to call upon or demand that hostilities cease and that members of the UN conclude ceasefire or armistice agreements. In addition, the Security Council may establish a ceasefire to be interpreted in accordance with the international law applicable to armistices.

37 *DoD Manual*, paragraph 12.13.2.3.

13

Naval Warfare

Chapter XIII leaves the reader with an ambivalent impression. On the one hand, it is apparently characterised by a desire comprehensively to address various facets of the international legal framework applicable to naval warfare, including the law of the sea. On the other, important aspects are not addressed or are dealt with only marginally. The latter seems to be due to a hesitation to provide an affirmative position on issues that are not expressly regulated in the long-standing agreements on naval warfare and to avoid any reference to the *San Remo Manual*,[1] despite the fact that it continues to be recognised as a restatement of customary international law.[2] Although the treaties on which the chapter is based are evidently considered by the authors as still binding or as reflective of customary law, some of the rules in the chapter depart from conventional standards without further explanation. Another disturbing pattern is the lack of a coherent structure and of a clear focus on the law of naval warfare applicable in the relations between the belligerents. Although neutrality is dealt with in Chapter XIV, there are again and again references to 'neutral States', 'neutral merchant vessels' and 'neutral aircraft'. Moreover, the chapter does not sufficiently distinguish between targeting law and prize law. While it is conceded that in some instances the two bodies of law overlap – such as when a merchant vessel refuses to comply with a lawful belligerent order or renders active resistance to visit, search and capture – prize measures do not require the relevant vessel or aircraft to qualify as a lawful target. In sum, there is some room for improvement and clarification. The following

[1] Louise Doswald-Beck (ed.), *San Remo Manual on International Law Applicable to Armed Conflicts at Sea*, Cambridge: Cambridge University Press (1995).

[2] *Inter alia*, the *Canadian* and *UK Manuals* have adopted many of the rules of the *San Remo Manual*. It must, however, be accepted that the *San Remo Manual* is more than twenty years old and therefore in need of an update.

comments may not be misunderstood as a condemnatory criticism. They are merely designed to provide some assistance for further updates.

LAW OF THE SEA

Section 13.1 is not what its heading seems to suggest, i.e. an introduction, but it is part of an overview of the peacetime law of the sea and its applicability in times of armed conflict. It is worth mentioning that, in sections 13.1 and 13.2, ten out of the chapter's forty pages are devoted to those issues. Of course, the division of the oceans under the contemporary law of the sea had to be addressed because it defines the regions where belligerents are entitled to exercise belligerent rights at sea.[3] However, it would have sufficed to provide a general, less detailed overview, because the status of neutral waters and the rights belligerents enjoy in those sea areas are dealt with in the chapter on neutrality.

The considerable space – 25 per cent of the chapter – devoted to the law of the sea is surprising. Many of the statements are not necessarily relevant for the law of naval warfare. Of course, it is important to stress that, according to the US position, the 1982 UN Convention on the Law of the Sea (UNCLOS)[4] is reflective of customary law insofar as the division of the oceans and the freedoms of navigation and overflight are concerned, and that the respective provisions provide guidance as to the determination of the region of operations during an armed conflict. However, paragraph 13.1.1 should have explained by explicit reference to Articles 87(1) and 58(2) UNCLOS, that UNCLOS has preserved the right of all States to use the world's oceans for military purposes, including the conduct of hostilities in times of international armed conflict. While this also holds true for the right of individual or collective self-defence, this is not necessarily relevant for the law of naval warfare. The *jus ad bellum* should always be strictly distinguished from the *jus in bello*.[5] The reference in paragraph 13.1.2 to the Agreement on the Implementation of Part XI UNCLOS[6] is certainly redundant. The regime established by that agreement is not necessarily recognised as customary in nature. But even if one were to consider the deep-seabed mining regime as reflective of customary law, it

[3] *German Manual*, paragraphs 1011–16; *UK Manual*, paragraphs 13.7–13.23; *Canadian Manual*, paragraphs 801–4; *San Remo Manual*, paragraphs 14–37. See also C J Colombos, *The International Law of the Sea*, 6th rev. edn. London: Prentice Hall (1967), 528–46.

[4] UN Doc. A/CONF.62/121 of 10 December 1982, 1833 UNTS 396.

[5] See, *inter alia*, C Greenwood, Self-Defence and the Conduct of International Armed Conflict, in Y Dinstein (ed.) *International Law at a Time of Perplexity. Essays in Honour of Shabtai Rosenne*. Dordrecht: Springer (1989), 273–88.

[6] Agreement Relating to the Implementation of Part XI of the United Nations Convention on the Law of the Sea, UN Doc. A/RES/48/263 of 17 August 1994.

would have but a minor impact on the conduct of hostilities at sea, by merely obliging the parties to the conflict to pay due regard to the activities carried out in the 'area'. The latter aspect is not addressed at all. Instead, the respective paragraph merely explains the general US position vis-à-vis the Implementation Agreement, which does not provide any guidance to naval commanders in times of armed conflict.

The overview of the various sea areas and the respective rights and duties of coastal States in section 13.2 is a correct restatement of the law of the sea as it stands today.[7] As already mentioned, it is, however, in most parts redundant in the context of the present chapter, which should have been limited to a general exclusion of neutral waters.

Paragraph 13.2.2.4 recognises the right of belligerent States to restrict in their territorial sea innocent passage by neutral vessels. This is without doubt a correct restatement of the current law of naval warfare. The right to temporarily suspend, in parts of the territorial sea, the right of innocent passage is already recognised in times of peace,[8] and therefore, *a fortiori*, applies in times of armed conflict. Thus, any reference to maritime zones as the means by which such restrictions are established and enforced should have been omitted. Moreover, instead of dealing with the closure of neutral waters, the section should have addressed the rights of transit passage and of archipelagic sea-lane passage in international straits and archipelagic waters belonging to the belligerents.[9] The general recognition of a belligerent's right to restrict or suspend innocent passage in its territorial sea or archipelagic waters is acceptable but incomplete without reference to those special passage rights, which continue to apply in times of international armed conflict.[10]

Paragraph 13.2.3 correctly affirms the status of international waters and the right of belligerents to exercise belligerent rights, including the conduct of hostilities, in all sea areas outside neutral waters, which are limited by the due regard principle only.[11] It would have been helpful had the prohibition of marine scientific research been explicitly addressed in paragraph 13.2.3.1. While surveillance and intelligence gathering is permissible in the EEZ of neutral States, such activities are limited not merely by the due regard principle but also by the generally recognised prohibition of conducting marine scientific research.[12]

[7] See also J Kraska, *Maritime Power and the Law of the Sea*. Oxford: Oxford University Press (2012), 95ff.

[8] See Article 25(3) UNCLOS.

[9] See *San Remo Manual*, paragraph 27.

[10] *San Remo Manual*, paragraph 27.

[11] *San Remo Manual*, paragraphs 34–37.

[12] For a distinction between permissible marine data collection and prohibited unauthorised marine scientific research, see G Walker (gen. ed.), *Definitions for the Law of the Sea*. Leiden: Brill (2012), 241ff.

The law of the sea, because of its continuing importance in times of armed conflict, could not have been avoided altogether in this chapter. Unfortunately, however, the obligations of belligerents, particularly with regard to transit passage and archipelagic sea lanes passage, have not been comprehensively identified. Instead, sections 13.1 and 13.2 deal with aspects of the law of the sea that are irrelevant for the law of naval warfare as applicable between the belligerents and should thus have been dealt with in the chapter on neutrality alone – or not at all, because they are limited to times of peace. Much of the space that could be saved by streamlining the two sections could then be used for a more comprehensive reflection of the law governing hostilities at sea.

OVERVIEW OF RULES FOR NAVAL ENGAGEMENTS

Already, the wording of the heading of section 13.3 is difficult to understand, and it is even more difficult to understand if one takes account of the different matters dealt with in the section, i.e. areas of naval warfare, classification of vessels, vessels entitled to conduct attacks, shipwrecked persons and surrender by enemy vessels. Some of these matters should have been dealt with in separate sections. Other matters are missing, such as the principal limitation of the law of naval warfare to international armed conflicts, the applicability of the basic principles of the law of armed conflict and its emanations, the protection of the marine environment[13] and the difference between hostilities and prize measures.[14] It is unfortunate that the *Manual*'s drafters have lost an opportunity of clarifying the general legal framework applicable to naval operations in times of armed conflict, thus leaving commanders with questions rather than answers.

FUNDAMENTALS OF THE LAW OF NAVAL WARFARE

The introductory sentence of section 13.3 is insufficient insofar as it merely states that 'in general, the rules for conducting attacks, such as bombardments, by naval forces are the same as those for land or air forces'. First, this holds

[13] *San Remo Manual*, paragraphs 11 and 44.

[14] Prize measures or 'measures short of attack' are: interception, visit, search, diversion and capture. They are directed against enemy and neutral merchant vessels and civil aircraft that do not qualify as lawful military objectives. Therefore, military manuals often deal with prize measures in separate chapters or sections. See *UK Manual*, paragraphs 13.84–13.112; *Canadian Manual*, paragraphs 858–75; *San Remo Manual*, paragraphs 112–58. See also AMW *Manual*, section U, rules 134–46.

true only for attacks directed against targets on land. Article 49(3) API, which can be considered as reflective of customary law,[15] clarifies that Articles 48 to 67 API 'apply to any land, air or sea warfare which may affect the civilian population, individual civilians or civilian objects on land. They further apply to all attacks from the sea or from the air against objectives on land.' However, the provision also expressly preserves 'the rules of international law applicable in armed conflict at sea or in the air'. Accordingly, Articles 48 to 67 API do not apply to sea-to-sea, sea-to-air, air-to-sea or air-to-air engagements during an international armed conflict. The fact that the US has not become a party to the API is without prejudice to the correctness of the latter finding. Therefore, an important characteristic of the law of naval warfare has not been taken account of. It should have been made clear that the basic principles of the law of armed conflict, in particular the principle of distinction, apply to naval attacks even if they are not directed against targets on land or they do not affect the civilian population, individual civilians or civilian objects on land. If the principle of distinction is recognised as applying to naval engagements, naval attacks other than those directed against targets on land must also be strictly limited to objects qualifying as lawful targets (by nature, use or purpose).[16] In that context, it should have been stressed that in naval warfare, measures will mostly be taken against objects (platforms), because they are the primary concern, and that in rare cases only will attacks be directed against individuals. Without such clarification, commanders might be induced to seek for guidance in the *Manual*'s chapters on land warfare, which are not necessarily suitable for the genuine characteristics of naval operations.

Another important aspect relates to the obligation to take precautions in attack.[17] In Chapter XIII, precautions are merely addressed in the context of naval mines. The general reference to the rules applicable to land and air forces could be understood as a recognition of the standard of 'feasibility' to apply to all naval engagements, because bombardments are but an example. It is important to bear in mind that even the parties to API are not bound by the standard of 'all feasible precautions' when it comes to naval engagements that are not directed against targets on land. Article 57(4) API provides: 'In the conduct of military operations at sea or in the air, each Party to the conflict shall, in conformity with its rights and duties under the rules of international law applicable in armed conflicts, take all reasonable precautions to avoid losses

[15] Insofar as the limitations applicable to land warfare do not apply to naval warfare.

[16] *San Remo Manual*, paragraphs 39–41.

[17] *UK Manual*, paragraph 13.32; *Canadian Manual*, paragraph 825; *German Manual*, paragraph 1021; *San Remo Manual*, paragraph 46.

of civilian lives and damage to civilian objects.' This provision has given rise to a contentious debate about its exact meaning.[18] It is, however, safe to conclude that Article 57(2) and (4) API does not apply to operations excluded by Article 49(3) API. Accordingly, the standard of 'reasonableness' applies only to naval operations that may affect the civilian population, individual civilians or civilian objects on land. The standard of reasonableness thus applicable is certainly less strict than the standard of feasibility. This begs the question as to the precautionary standard applying to naval operations that are neither directed against targets on land nor affect civilians or civilian objects on land. According to the *San Remo Manual*, belligerents are obliged to take all feasible precautions in attack.[19] This may be a correct statement of the law, but its correctness could be doubted in view of the different standard recognised in Article 57(4) API. In any event, the lack of a clarification of the standard that must be observed in the context of precautions in attack is a fundamental defect of Chapter XIII.

OTHER ASPECTS DEALT WITH IN SECTION 13.3

The area of naval warfare has been correctly identified in paragraph 13.3.1 by the exclusion of neutral waters from the region of naval operations during an international armed conflict. Still, it is somewhat disturbing that the paragraph merely refers to attacks, because the exclusion of naval operations from neutral territory applies equally to prize measures.[20]

Apart from the fact that the matter should have been dealt with in the chapter on neutrality, the second sentence of paragraph 13.3.1 is not correctly phrased. If neutral territory or neutral waters are abused by the enemy then the neutral State is under an obligation to terminate the violation of its neutral status. If the neutral State is either unwilling or unable to so do, the aggrieved belligerent is entitled to take all necessary measures to terminate the violation in lieu of the neutral State.[21] This is, as rightly stated in footnote 57, rather a measure of self-help than a conduct of hostilities in neutral territory, which are and remain prohibited.

[18] For a discussion and further references, see C Pilloud and J Pictet, Article 57 AP I, in: *Commentary on the Additional Protocol of 8 June 1977 to the Geneva Conventions of 12 August 1949*. Geneva: International Committee of the Red Cross (1987), 687ff.

[19] *San Remo Manual*, paragraph 46.

[20] See, *inter alia*, 1907 Hague Convention XIII (Article 2 of the Convention (XIII) Concerning the Rights and Duties of Neutral Powers in Naval War, The Hague, 18 October 1907, 2 AJIL Suppl. 202–16 (1908). See also *German Manual*, paragraph 1017.

[21] R W Tucker, *The Law of War and Neutrality at Sea*. Washington, DC: US Naval War College (1957), 261ff.; *San Remo Manual*, paragraph 22.

The classification of enemy vessels in paragraph 13.3.2 is correct and, in view of the clarifications following in the next sections, sufficient. However, with a view to enemy warships and auxiliaries, it should have been made clear that they constitute booty of war rather than being liable to capture. Although this is clearly stated in paragraph 13.4.3, the constant use of the term 'capture' may be misunderstood as meaning 'capture as prize'. This could have been avoided had the differences between hostilities and prize measures been identified in the introductory paragraph of section 13.3.

Moreover, there should have been an additional paragraph dealing with the determination of enemy character of merchant vessels. According to the *San Remo Manual*, enemy character can be determined by the flag, registration, ownership, charter or other criteria.[22] This is of high practical relevance, because enemy merchant vessels are liable to capture during the entire duration of an international armed conflict.[23] If only the flag provided conclusive evidence of enemy character, many vessels flying so-called 'flags of convenience' would not qualify as enemy merchant vessels.

Paragraph 13.3.3 rightly limits the right to conduct attacks at sea during an international armed conflict to warships and military aircraft.[24] This limitation, however, also applies with regard to the exercise of prize measures.[25] This section should have provided a brief explanation by reference to the abolition of privateering under the 1856 Paris Declaration.[26] Since naval operations are conducted in high-seas areas, the exercise of belligerent rights by vessels other than warships could be perceived by neutral warships as constituting either piracy or privateering, both of which are prohibited under long-standing rules of international law.

Problematic is the unqualified statement as to the right of 'all vessels', i.e. enemy auxiliary vessels and merchant vessels, to 'defend themselves (including resisting attacks by enemy forces)'. The problem is due to the use of the verb 'defend', which may be understood as referring to the inherent right of self-defence against unlawful attacks. Enemy merchant vessels are, however, liable to attack, if by use they make an effective contribution to the enemy's military action,[27] and they are liable to capture as prize even if they do not qualify as lawful military objectives. Hence, measures taken against them are presumed to be lawful. It is, however, important to bear in mind that enemy

22 *San Remo Manual*, paragraphs 112–17.

23 Colombos, *International Law of the Sea*, 548ff.; Tucker, *Law of War*, 74ff.

24 *German Manual*, paragraph 1019; Tucker, *Law of War*, 38; *AMW Manual*, rule 17.

25 *German Manual*, paragraph 1019; Tucker, *Law of War*, 38; *AMW Manual*, rule 17.

26 Declaration Respecting Maritime Law, Paris, 16 April 1856, 1 AJIL Suppl. 89–90 (1907).

27 *San Remo Manual*, paragraph 60.

merchant vessels are not obliged to comply with the enemy's orders. Therefore, the concept of direct participation in hostilities does not apply to enemy merchant vessels engaging in attacks or rendering resistance against capture.[28] Although they thus become lawful targets, the masters and the crews may not be prosecuted under the domestic criminal law of the captor State. This is different in the case of neutral merchant vessels, because they are under a clear obligation to comply with legitimate belligerent orders.[29]

It is true that the law of non-international armed conflict does not limit the exercise of belligerent rights to warships, as defined under international law.[30] The mention of treaties in paragraph 13.3.3.1, to which the United States is not a party, is misleading because no treaty addresses the issue. Apart from that, it should at least have been made abundantly clear that the law of naval warfare is, in principle (and not only with a view to the use of warships proper), not applicable in non-international armed conflicts. The mere note that 'acts of hostilities by insurgents on the high seas may be regarded as piracy' is correct but not necessarily helpful.

At first glance, it is a bit surprising that paragraph 13.3.4 deals with shipwrecked persons, without also dealing with the wounded and sick. However, protected persons are dealt with in Chapter V. Therefore, and for the purposes of Chapter XIII, it would have been sufficient merely to clarify the concept of 'shipwreck' as also applying to forced landings at sea.

Equally, the paragraph on the obligation under Article 18(1) GWS-Sea to search, after each engagement, for the wounded, sick, shipwrecked and dead seems to be adequate. In view of the fact that GWS-Sea is binding upon the US, it is, however, hard to understand why paragraph 13.3.4 introduces the standard of 'military exigencies' in addition to the standard of 'possibility' recognised in Article 18(1) GWS-Sea. If a warship is in a position to search for and rescue protected persons and if it has the capacity of taking them on board without exposing itself to unreasonable danger, the obligation according to Article 18(1) GWS-Sea comes into operation.[31] Considerations of military exigencies other than those already covered by 'possibility' do not justify non-compliance with the obligation.

[28] For the famous case of Captain Fryatt, who was sentenced by a German court because he had tried to ram a German submarine, see Colombos, *International Law of the Sea*, 526ff. As to the applicability of the concept of 'direct participation in hostilities' to masters of enemy merchant vessels in naval warfare, see W Heintschel von Heinegg, The Development of the Law of Naval Warfare from the Nineteenth to the Twenty-First Century – Some Select Issues, 17 *Yearbook of International Humanitarian Law* 69–93 (2014), at 85ff.

[29] Tucker, *Law of War*, 332ff.

[30] W Heintschel von Heinegg, Methods and Means of Naval Warfare in Non-International Armed Conflicts, 42 *Israel Yearbook on Human Rights* 55–81 (2012), at 66ff.

[31] *GWS-Sea Commentary*, 161; Heintschel von Heinegg, Development of the Law, 82.

The section widely reflects the traditional ways by which warships can offer surrender. It is, however, far from settled whether a submarine can genuinely surrender by merely surfacing. Therefore, the text in footnote 75 should at least in part have been included into the operative text of paragraph 13.3.5. Moreover, the section fails to address surrender by other means. Although the list is not exclusive, which is indicated by the use of the words 'may include', the section should have mentioned that the traditional ways of surrendering vessels are not operable in an electronic battlefield, in which visual contacts are rather the exception than the rule.

Another contentious issue is the limitation of *hors de combat* status to situations 'in which it is feasible to accept such surrender'. While it is conceded that this will not necessarily prove as problematic as in land warfare, it may result in wrongful attacks against vessels that have surrendered on the spurious basis that those in control of the warship to which the surrender has been offered do not consider themselves to be in a position to take control over the surrendering vessel and/or to capture its crew.

ENEMY WARSHIPS

Section 13.4 starts with the correct classification of enemy warships and auxiliaries as liable to attack and capture within the region of naval warfare. Again, it could have been made clearer that their liability to capture does not relate to capture as prize.

The definition of warships in paragraph 13.4.1 is correct insofar as it reflects the definition provided by treaty and customary law.[32] It would have been helpful had it been accompanied by a short statement as to the irrelevance of whether the ships are armed or not. Unfortunately, the section fails to address unmanned maritime systems. Such systems have been defined as 'self-propelled or remotely-navigated craft that are normally recoverable and designed to perform certain functions at sea by operating on the surface, semi-submerged or undersea' and which are 'either remotely operated, remotely controlled, or perform some or all of their functions independently from a human controller or operator'.[33] According to NWP 1–14M, unmanned maritime systems are considered sovereign immune craft that are almost entirely assimilated to warships.[34] Still, the question remains whether they may be employed in the exercise of belligerent rights during an international

[32] See Article 29 UNCLOS. See also Tucker, *Law of War*, 39ff.; Colombos, *International Law of the Sea*, 515ff.

[33] See the forthcoming *Oslo Manual on Select Problems of the Law of Armed Conflict*, rule 43(b).

[34] NWP 1–14M, paragraphs 2.3.4ff.

armed conflict at sea. Of course, if they are remotely controlled by a platform qualifying as a warship under the definition, one may argue that they share the legal status of the controlling platform. Then, their use for the exercise of belligerent rights would be in compliance with the traditional law of naval warfare. However, modern unmanned maritime systems are increasingly autonomous and cannot be remotely controlled because the characteristics of sea water prevent a continuous contact by radio or other signals. If such autonomous or semi-autonomous unmanned maritime systems cannot be considered warships, the legality of their use for the purpose of exercising belligerent rights in high-seas areas could be denied and neutral States could claim the right to prevent their operation. Hence, a clarification of their status would have been helpful.

The statement as to the privileges and immunities enjoyed by warships is as such correct but not helpful with regard to enemy warships. In the relations between the belligerents, the sovereign immunity of warships is irrelevant. It only matters as between belligerents and neutral States.[35]

The classification of enemy warships as military objectives in paragraph 13.4.2 is correct, but should have been explained by reference to their nature. Accordingly, even unarmed warships qualify as lawful targets everywhere outside neutral territory and neutral waters.[36]

Equally correct is the classification in paragraph 13.4.3 of enemy warships as booty of war if they are captured.[37] Their assimilation to public movable (enemy) property is, however, inconclusive insofar as it seems to refer to the law of land warfare. The concept of booty in naval warfare is a standalone rule, which has been reaffirmed by modern State practice.[38]

ENEMY MERCHANT VESSELS

While Section 13.5 correctly summarises the measures belligerents may take against enemy merchant vessels, it fails to clearly distinguish between attacks on the one hand and prize measures, including destruction under prize law, on the other. As already mentioned, the two bodies of law do in parts overlap. Still, it is important to deal with prize measures in the context of

[35] During an international armed conflict, neutral States continue to be obliged to respect the sovereign immunity belligerent warships enjoy under Articles 32 and 95 UNCLOS and customary international law.

[36] Tucker, *Law of War*, 39; *UK Manual*, paragraph 13.44; German *Manual*, paragraph 1024.

[37] See also Y Dinstein, Booty in Warfare, in: *Max Planck Encyclopedia of Public International Law*, MN 10.

[38] Dinstein, 'Booty in Warfare'.

enemy merchant vessels only, if they do not qualify as lawful military objectives. Only then are belligerents obliged to comply with the provisions of the 1936 London Protocol on Submarine Warfare.[39]

One defect of paragraph 13.5.1 is the lack of rules on the determination of enemy character by either flag or registration, ownership, charter or other criteria.[40] The mere reference to 'other means' only makes sense if the neutral flag is only *prima facie* evidence of the neutral character of a merchant vessel.[41]

Merchant vessels that have been captured indeed qualify as prize (paragraph 13.5.1.1), which must be adjudicated upon by a prize court. However, adjudication on captured enemy merchant vessels is not limited to the completion of transfer of title, but may also be necessary for the final determination of enemy character.

Under prize law, the destruction of captured enemy merchant vessels is permissible as an exceptional measure only.[42] Paragraph 13.5.1.3 seems to apply a more liberal standard by accepting the destruction under prize law 'when military circumstances preclude sending or taking in such vessel . . . for adjudication'. This, however, almost literally repeats the wording of the *San Remo Manual*[43] and should, therefore, not give rise to grave concerns, although it would have been desirable had the exceptional character been explicitly emphasised. What is worrying is the deviation from the clear wording of the 1936 Submarine Protocol. According to that Protocol, 'a warship, whether surface vessel or submarine, may not sink or render incapable of navigation a merchant vessel without having first placed passengers, crew and ship's papers in a place of safety'. According to paragraph 13.5.1.3, the obligation to 'provide for the safety of passengers and crew' is limited by 'all possible measures'. The obligation to also save the ship's documents is equally not absolute, because the use of the word 'should' suggests that there may be exceptions. It should be noted that the International Military Tribunal in Nuremberg, in its judgment on Admiral Dönitz, held that the 'Protocol is explicit. If the commander cannot rescue, then under its terms he cannot sink a merchant vessel and should allow it to pass unharmed before its periscope.'[44] The Tribunal was not willing to accept any exceptions, such as 'military circumstances'. This

39 Therefore, the International Military Tribunal in Nuremberg was 'not prepared to hold Dönitz guilty for his conduct of submarine warfare against British armed merchant ships'; International Military Tribunal (Nuremberg), Judgment of 1 October 1946, 129.

40 *San Remo Manual*, paragraphs 112–17.

41 *San Remo Manual*, paragraph 113.

42 *San Remo Manual*, paragraphs 139, 151.

43 *San Remo Manual*, paragraphs 139, 151.

44 International Military Tribunal (Nuremberg), Judgment of 1 October 1946, 509.

continues to be the contemporary legal standard, because destruction as prize only applies to enemy merchant vessels not qualifying as lawful military objectives by either use or purpose. Hence, the sinking of an enemy merchant vessel without having first placed passengers, crew and documents in a place of safety for the sole reason that capture and sending the vessel into port is impossible or unfeasible because of military considerations will most probably be considered a war crime. This will continue to hold true even if the destruction is, as provided for in paragraph 13.5.1.3, 'promptly reported to higher command'. Moreover, the destruction has to be adjudicated upon by a prize court.

Finally, the destruction of neutral prizes does not necessarily bring with it 'a more serious responsibility'. We will return to that aspect in Chapter 15.

The actions by which enemy merchant vessels may become lawful military objectives by use are correctly identified insofar as they conform with the respective provisions of the *San Remo Manual*.[45] It may be recalled that persistent refusal to obey an order to stop and active resistance to visit, search and capture are the exceptions that have been recognised in the 1936 London Submarine Protocol.

There are, however, three important differences that may give rise to concerns.

The first relates to enemy merchant vessels that are 'armed with systems or weapons beyond that required for self-defense against terrorist, piracy, or like acts'. The US has long since taken the position that the arming of hospital ships in situations where they may be exposed to illegal attack by terrorists or pirates is in accordance with the law of naval warfare.[46] The rule on the arming of enemy merchant vessels seems to be guided by the same logic. Indeed, it is difficult to deny enemy merchant vessels the right to effectively defend themselves against such attacks. Therefore, the problem created by the rule is rather the deviation from the San Remo standards than the recognition of a continuing right of self-defence against terrorists or pirates. According to the *San Remo Manual*, enemy merchant vessels qualify as lawful military objectives if they are 'armed to an extent that they could inflict damage to a warship', and the manual expressly excludes 'light individual weapons for the defence of personnel, e.g., against pirates, and purely deflective systems such as "chaff"'.[47] Heavy weapons, such as 50 cal. guns, that the US considers lawful for hospital ships[48] will always be looked upon either with considerable suspicion or as sufficient to inflict damage on a warship. States other than the US will most probably treat them as lawful targets if they are armed with other than light weapons.

[45] *San Remo Manual*, paragraph 60.
[46] See NWP 1–14M, paragraph 8.6.3.
[47] *San Remo Manual*, paragraph 60(f).
[48] NWP 1–14M, paragraph 8.6.3.

The second difference is the reference to the 1936 London Protocol in the context of any other integration into the enemy's war-fighting/war-sustaining effort. If an enemy merchant vessel qualifies as a lawful military objective, the rules of the London Protocol do not apply. Hence, it may be attacked without having first placed the passengers, crew and documents in a place of safety. This is expressly stated in the subsequent part of paragraph 13.5.2, which begs the question why the reference to the London Protocol has been included at all. The clarification regarding the non-applicability of the London Protocol limitations to enemy merchant vessels that are lawful military objectives could be understood as limiting that category to vessels destroyed as prize. But this would also mean that enemy merchant vessels otherwise making an effective contribution to the enemy's war-fighting effort could only be attacked under the conditions prescribed by the Protocol. That would be a limitation of the well-established belligerent right of attacking enemy merchant vessels that otherwise make an effective contribution to the enemy's military action ('war-fighting effort'), which has no basis in the law of naval warfare.[49] In sum, the fact that compliance with the Protocol's requirements would 'subject the warship to imminent danger or would otherwise preclude mission accomplishment' is irrelevant. It may be added, for reasons of completeness only, that deviating from the London Protocol will never be justified by considerations of mission accomplishment.

The third difference is the inclusion of enemy merchant vessels contributing to the enemy's war-sustaining (as distinguished from war-fighting) effort. Considering the burning of cotton fields during the American Civil War, which was justified because of the high importance of cotton sales for the enemy's revenues and thus for its war-sustaining effort, an acknowledgement of that category would mean that vessels engaged in the transport of important enemy export goods, such as oil or gas, would qualify as lawful targets, because the revenues they provided would enable the enemy to continue its war effort. It may be recalled that the sinking of oil tankers during the 1980–88 Iran–Iraq War was generally condemned as unlawful even though both parties could have relied on the war-sustaining criterion.[50] Therefore, States other than the US have never considered a contribution to the enemy's war-sustaining effort sufficient to render enemy (or neutral) merchant vessels liable to attack.[51] The

49 See the International Military Tribunal's (Nuremberg) judgment of Admiral Dönitz. See also *San Remo Manual*, paragraph 60(g).

50 See, *inter alia*, the UNSC resolutions condemning attacks against neutral tankers, UN Doc. S/RES/540 of 31 October 1983; UN Doc. S/RES/582 of 24 February 1986; UN Doc. S/RES/598 of 20 July 1987.

51 See, *inter alia*, *UK Manual*, paragraphs 13.41, 13.47; *Canadian Manual*, paragraphs 834, 835; German *Manual*, paragraph 1029.

only method of naval warfare which enables a belligerent to interfere with the enemy's exports is and remains a naval blockade.[52]

Paragraph 13.5.2.1, dealing with civilian passenger vessels qualifying as lawful targets, rightly emphasises the requirement of a prior assessment of excessive collateral damage. It should also have stressed that in the case of attacks against passenger vessels, the attacker is under an increased obligation to take all (feasible/reasonable) precautions. The reference in footnote 94 to collateral damage assessments in land warfare would have been redundant had the chapter identified the basic principles of the law of armed conflict applicable to naval warfare. The sinking of the *Lusitania* is a precedent proving that the principle of proportionality applies to naval attacks against lawful targets.

Paragraph 13.5.3 correctly identifies the status of the officers and crews of enemy merchant vessels, who, according to Article 4A(5) GPW, enjoy PW status if they are detained. The section fails to address the exception expressly provided for in that article, applying to those crew members who 'benefit by more favourable treatment under other provisions of international law'. Seemingly, the US is unwilling to accept that exception, which is considered as preserving Article 6 of the 1907 Hague Convention XI.[53] Although passengers of enemy merchant vessels, whether enemy or neutral nationals, are not entitled to PW status, it is probably correct to recognise a belligerent right of detaining them. Unfortunately, the paragraph addresses the legal basis for such detention only with regard to nationals of neutral States who are on board captured enemy merchant vessels having 'participated in acts of hostility or resistance against the captor, or are otherwise in the service of the enemy'. Moreover, it would have been helpful had the 'certain fundamental guarantees of humane treatment' been specified. That could have been accomplished by a mere reference to Article 75 API, which the US seems to be willing to accept as reflecting customary law.

ENEMY VESSELS EXEMPT FROM CAPTURE OR DESTRUCTION

In the introductory sentence of Section 13.6, it is correctly stated that certain classes of enemy vessels are exempt from capture or destruction.

[52] W Heintschel von Heinegg, Blockade, in: *Max Planck Encyclopedia of Public International Law*, MN 27.

[53] Convention (XI) Relative to Certain restrictions with Regard to the Exercise of the Right of Capture in Naval War, The Hague, 18 October 1907, 2 AJIL Suppl. 167–74 (1908). Article 6 provides: 'The captain, officers, and members of the crew, when nationals of the enemy State, are not made prisoners of war, on condition that they make a formal promise in writing, not to undertake, while hostilities last, any service connected with the operations of the war.'

Unfortunately, the text fails to clarify that the rules of the law of naval warfare, in particular the 1907 Hague Convention XI (which is not mentioned), that provide for that exemption are designed to protect those vessels against capture and destruction under prize law. The respective rules are without prejudice to the belligerent right of attacking them if they make an effective contribution to the enemy's military action. Moreover, the section fails to clarify that non-compliance with the conditions of exemption does not necessarily render such vessels liable to attack.

Finally, it is doubtful whether warships are always prohibited from disguising themselves as vessels exempt from capture. While this certainly holds true for feigning the status of a hospital ship, there is no rule prohibiting the feigning of a fishing vessel, provided that the true nature of the vessel is revealed prior to its use to undertake an attack.

It is a correct restatement of the law that such vessels may neither take part in the hostilities nor assist the enemy's military effort. Such activities would make them lawful targets and thus liable to be attacked. Therefore, the more important clarification of their duties is contained in the introductory sentence of section 13.6, according to which exemption from capture requires that they 'are innocently and solely employed in the activities that enjoy exemption', and in the second paragraph of paragraph 13.6.1, which identifies further duties incumbent on exempt vessels. While it is agreed that they are required to immediately identify themselves upon demand and that non-compliance would render them liable to capture, it is highly questionable whether that would also justify their destruction under prize law. A refusal to provide immediate identification may not be assimilated with refusing an order to stop or actively resisting visit, search or capture, which would make them a lawful target.[54] It is important to add that loss of protection against capture is subject to rather strict requirements, in particular insofar as hospital ships are concerned.[55]

The list of classes of exempt vessels in paragraph 13.6.2 is based on the 1907 Hague Convention XI and on customary law.[56] However, not all vessels potentially exempt from capture have been included, such as coastal rescue craft and vessels engaged in transporting cultural property under special

[54] See *San Remo Manual*, paragraph 52(c), according to which 'the circumstances of non-compliance [must be] sufficiently grave that the vessel has become, or may be reasonable assumed to be, a military objective.'

[55] *San Remo Manual*, paragraph 51.

[56] German *Manual*, paragraph 1040; *UK Manual*, paragraph 13.33; *Canadian Manual*, paragraph 828; *San Remo Manual*, paragraph 47.

protection.[57] Although coastal rescue craft, which are dealt with in section 7.12, are protected against capture only insofar as 'operational requirements permit',[58] they should not have been excluded. The fact that vessels designed or adapted to respond to pollution incidents have not been included suggests an unwillingness to recognise their exemption as having customary status. It may be added that the US DoD seems to understand the concept of cartel vessels (paragraph 13.6.2.1) rather narrowly, by limiting their function to the exchange of PWs and by distinguishing them from vessels granted safe conduct (paragraph 13.6.2.4). Both categories require an agreement between the parties to the conflict. Since the term 'cartel' stands for 'agreement', both should have been included into the category of cartel vessels.

As regards hospital ships, paragraph 13.6.2.2 is limited to their uncontested right to communicate via satellites, i.e. by using encryption, and their contested right to be armed with defensive weapons.[59] The US has, when considered necessary, armed its hospital ships with two 50 cal. guns. Interestingly, as far as is known, no government has filed a protest against that practice. Hence, the US may rely on the subsequent practice of States party to GWS-Sea having endorsed the – limited – arming of hospital ships.

Unfortunately, paragraph 13.6.2.2 does not address the difficult distinction between non-compliance with the conditions for protection[60] and 'acts harmful to the enemy'.[61] It is important to emphasise that the former may deprive a hospital ship of its protection against capture but would not render it liable to attack. 'Acts harmful to the enemy', if of sufficient gravity and if certain safeguards have been observed, may render a hospital ship liable to attack.[62]

SUBMARINE WARFARE

Submarines are bound by the same principles and rules of the law of armed conflict as those applicable to surface warships.[63] This is rightly stated in paragraph 13.7.1. Unfortunately, there is again a reference to the destruction of merchant vessels as prize under the 1936 London Protocol. The use of the phrase 'in general' seems to suggest that in certain situations, submarines may sink a merchant vessel without having first placed passengers, crew and the ship's documents in a place of safety. As already emphasised, there are no other

[57] Article 27 GWS-Sea; *San Remo Manual*, paragraph 47(b) and (d).

[58] Article 27 GWS-Sea. [59] See Heintschel von Heinegg, *Development of the Law*, 75ff.

[60] Article 30 GWS-Sea. [61] Article 34(1) GWS-Sea.

[62] *San Remo Manual*, paragraphs 49–51.

[63] 1936 London Submarine Protocol; *San Remo Manual*, paragraph 45.

justifications for deviating from the London Protocol than those expressly provided.

Equally worrying is paragraph 13.7.2, which suggests that the rules equally applicable to surface warships and submarines 'may apply differently in the context of submarine warfare because of the different circumstances of submarine warfare as compared to surface warfare'. Of course, it is true that submarines will often not be in a position to search for and rescue shipwrecked and wounded after an engagement, as provided for in Article 18(1) GWS-Sea. Either they would expose themselves to an intolerable risk by surfacing or they would simply not have the necessary space available to accommodate and adequately treat rescued persons. This has been acknowledged in Article 18(1) GWS-Sea, according to which compliance with the obligation is subject to whether a search and rescue operation is possible. It may be added that passing the location of the protected persons to a surface unit or a shore facility may not be a feasible option because, by doing so, the submarine could become detectable. The problem with paragraph 13.7.2 is the fact that the latter aspect is dealt with as but one example of a different application of the law of naval warfare. This may be misunderstood as a recognition of yet other relaxations from the law applicable to submarines, which are hard to identify without further examples being provided.

BELLIGERENT CONTROL OF THE IMMEDIATE AREA OF NAVAL OPERATIONS

The right of belligerents to control the immediate area of naval operations is, according to the position taken here, customary in character.[64] Therefore, section 13.8. may seem to be an adequate restatement of the law. This, however, only holds true for the definition of the area covered by the concept and for the prohibitions of barring access to and egress from neutral territory and of closing an international strait. The identification of the concept's purposes and of the ensuing belligerent rights may not necessarily correctly reflect the existing state of the law. First, paragraph 13.8.1 merges different belligerent interests that should have been dealt with separately. While it is correct to hold that the concept aims at 'proper battle space management', it is not necessarily a force protection device or designed to contribute to self-defence. Recognised force protection measures, such as warning zones and defence bubbles, are designed to prevent a self-defence situation from materialising. Second, proportionate force protection measures are recognised under both peacetime

[64] *San Remo Manual*, paragraph 108.

and wartime rules, but they may not result in excluding foreign shipping and aviation from the entire area within which hostilities are taking place or belligerent State forces are actually operating. Other vessels navigating within the immediate vicinity of naval operations will, however, operate at their own risk. Third, the concept thus merges aspects of force protection, self-defence and battle space management, which makes it more than difficult to clearly distinguish the concept from other methods, such as zones, that are dealt with in the following section.

According to paragraph 13.8.2, one possible belligerent right connected with the concept is the control of the communication of neutral merchant vessels and aircraft that are within the area and that 'might otherwise endanger or jeopardize those operations'. It would have been helpful had the control measures been specified. Be that as it may. It is conceded that, within the immediate vicinity of naval operations, belligerents are entitled to prohibit or restrict the use of means of communication on board neutral merchant vessels and aircraft if that is necessary for mission accomplishment. Non-compliance with such orders may justify the capture of a neutral merchant vessel or aircraft[65] but will render the vessel liable to attack only if they have become integrated into or have assisted the enemy's intelligence system. Of course, the paragraph is cautiously phrased ('may . . . assume and risk'). Still, it is not necessarily helpful, because the transmission of militarily relevant information is dealt with separately. The terminology should also be reconsidered. Neutral merchant vessels and aircraft engaging in an activity rendering them liable to attack do not assume enemy character, they merely become lawful military objectives by use. Moreover, non-compliance by neutral merchant vessels and aircraft or other activities rendering them liable to capture or attack are not 'inconsistent with the neutral State's duties of abstention and impartiality'. The obligations of neutral States in naval war are laid down in the 1907 Hague Convention XIII. Neutral States are not obliged to prevent the vessels flying their flag or registered aircraft from engaging in unneutral service or activities rendering them liable to capture or attack. The neutral-flag State or State of registry is merely obliged to tolerate the measures belligerents take in response to such activities. Certainly, the activities of neutral merchant vessels or aircraft cannot be attributed to the respective neutral State.

Finally, the claim that distress communications can be prohibited if the 'success of the operation' is jeopardised is problematic in the light of the obligation to render assistance to all who are in distress at sea, which applies equally in times of peace and in times of war.

[65] *San Remo Manual*, paragraph 146(e).

MARITIME AND AIRSPACE ZONES – EXCLUSION, WAR, OPERATIONAL, WARNING AND SAFETY

Zones, in particular exclusion zones and no-fly zones, are today recognised methods of naval and air warfare.[66] Warning and safety zones are equally recognised as lawful methods of force protection or of protecting certain installations against undue interference or dangers. The latter may be established in times of war and peace. It is, therefore, appropriate to deal with all these zones in a law of war manual. However, the various zones differ considerably and should have been dealt with in separate sections. Exclusion zones and no-fly zones serve different purposes than warning or safety zones and are limited to times of armed conflict. In view of the illegal practice during the two World Wars, the concept of 'war zones' should have been omitted altogether.[67]

Section 13.9 seems to suggest that by establishing any of the zones dealt with in the section, a belligerent may gain additional rights vis-à-vis vessels and aircraft entering that zone. This is a most problematic statement. Any measure taken against foreign vessels within a zone, whether diversion, capture or attack, cannot be justified by the mere presence of a vessel (or, one might add, aircraft) within the zone. This holds equally true for warning, safety and exclusion zones.[68]

Finally, the barring of belligerent access to neutral waters is a lawful measure aimed at preserving and protecting the respective State's neutral status and should not be considered as falling under the concept of zones under the law of naval warfare. The reference in footnote 128 to the 1937 Nyon Arrangement is misleading. The Nyon Arrangement[69] was aimed at protecting merchant vessels against attacks by unknown submarines during the Spanish Civil War. The States party to the arrangement did not establish any of the zones addressed in section 13.9, but merely divided the Mediterranean into operational areas or, rather, areas of responsibility, in which certain parties were to take measures against submarines suspected of engaging in illegal attacks.

The legal basis for the establishment of some 'zones' may indeed be the sovereignty of the State in question. This holds true for 'zones' that are limited to the territory, including the territorial sea, and/or the national airspace of

66 *San Remo Manual*, paragraphs 105, 106; *AMW Manual*, rules 105–110.

67 See, *inter alia*, W Heintschel von Heinegg, War Zones, in: *Max Planck Encyclopedia of Public International Law*, MN 10ff.

68 *San Remo Manual*, paragraph 105; *AMW Manual*, rule 105.

69 Nyon Arrangement of 14 September 1937, 181 LNTS 137–40. See also the Geneva Agreement Supplementary to the Nyon Arrangement of 17 September 1937, 181 LNTS 151–2.

the State establishing the 'zone'. It may likewise apply to safety zones around certain installations outside the territorial sea. However, such 'zones' should not be considered as zones under the law of (naval or air) warfare. Any State, whether belligerent or neutral, may bar access to its territory and to its national airspace. Safety zones around marine installations are recognised under the law of the sea and delimit the extent of the coastal State's jurisdiction.[70]

Hence, the only zones that merit specific rules in a law of war manual are either no-fly zones established in enemy national airspace or zones established outside belligerent territory. Such zones, according to paragraph 13.9.1, may find their legal basis in a belligerent's '(1) right to interdict contraband; (2) right to control the immediate area of operations; or (3) right of blockade' and, additionally, in a UN Security Council resolution under Chapter VII of the UN Charter. Apart from the latter, the legal bases identified do not correctly reflect the current state of the law of naval warfare. The immediate vicinity of naval operations has already been dealt with in section 13.8 and must be strictly distinguished from the zones addressed in section 13.9. As regards the belligerent right of contraband control, there is no requirement for a legal basis additional to prize law. If a belligerent decides to limit the exercise of the right of contraband control to a predefined sea area, this may not be mistaken as a zone. It merely is a form of self-restriction, which is always permissible. Finally, blockades must also be strictly distinguished from zones. Zones, including warning zones, are two- or three-dimensional areas regularly defined by coordinates. The belligerent having established them is concerned with everything occurring within those areas. The main feature of a blockade is the blockade line (or 'curtain' in the case of an aerial blockade), which vessels and aircraft may not cross if they wish to avoid capture by the blockading force.[71] By establishing an effective blockade, a belligerent is entitled to capture all vessels or aircraft breaching or attempting to breach it. This is a standalone concept under the law of naval and air warfare that must not be confused with maritime or airspace zones.

In view of the foregoing, paragraph 13.9.1 fails to recognise that warning and safety zones are recognised methods for force protection and for the protection of certain objects at sea. Their legal basis is not self-defence, because such zones are designed to prevent a self-defence situation from materialising, but customary international law.[72] Other zones, particularly exclusion and no-fly zones, are methods of warfare that must be distinguished from warning

[70] See Article 60(4) UNCLOS.

[71] See, *inter alia*, Heintschel von Heinegg, Blocakde, MN 3.

[72] AMW *Manual*, rule 106(b).

and safety zones and from the immediate vicinity of naval operations. Their legal basis is, again, customary international law, not prize law or the law of blockade.[73]

Paragraph 13.9.2 deals with war, operational, warning and safety zones. All these 'zones' are considered to serve the same purpose, namely warning vessels or aircraft. This is a correct restatement of the law insofar as warning and safety zones are concerned, but doubtful as regards war and operational zones. Such concepts should be avoided altogether, because they confuse the already complicated matter of zones and do not add any operational value.

The purposes warning and safety zones may legitimately serve have been correctly identified in the second part of paragraph 13.9.2. Still, force protection and assistance in the defence of a particular area are two distinct concepts.

Paragraph 13.9.2 rightly emphasises that the establishment of warning or safety zones 'does not relieve the proclaiming belligerent State of its obligation under the law of war to refrain from attacking vessels and aircraft that do not constitute military objectives'. Indeed, mere presence within any zone cannot be considered an activity directly contributing to the enemy's military action and rendering a vessel or aircraft liable to attack.[74]

Disturbingly, paragraph 13.9.2 seems to recognise a belligerent right of considering, in the described situation, a vessel or aircraft present within the zone as having acquired enemy character and, thus, qualifying as a military objective. This statement as it stands is not correct. As already stated, warning and safety zones are protective methods designed to prevent a self-defence situation from materialising. Hence, the mere presence of a vessel or aircraft will never suffice to render it liable to attack, even if most other vessels and aircraft have already left the area. Only if the vessel or aircraft, in addition to its presence, engages in an activity that a reasonable commander would characterise as a hostile act or hostile intent will a proportionate use of force be lawful. In this context, the purpose of the zones dealt with in this section plays an important role, i.e. protection of forces, objects or areas. Hence, a use of force is to be strictly limited to measures necessary to respond to a given threat that is imminent.

As already stated, there is no need for an additional method of warfare if a belligerent State decides to control or prevent the transport of contraband. Hence, the 'zones to counter enemy logistics' dealt with in paragraph 13.9.3 are not zones proper but merely a form of self-restriction whereby a belligerent declares that the rights of visit, search and capture under prize law will not be

[73] See, *inter alia*, Heintschel von Heinegg, Blocakde, MN 4ff.

[74] *San Remo Manual*, paragraph 105; AMW *Manual*, rule 105.

exercised in sea areas (or airspace) not covered by the 'zone'. Moreover, it is unnecessary to introduce yet another concept, i.e. countering enemy logistics. This is not a legal concept and, again, rather confuses than clarifies the issues at stake.

The limitations recognised in the second part of paragraph 13.9.3 – prohibitions of starving the civilian population and of putting unreasonable burden on neutral trade in goods not constituting contraband – are in accordance with the law, although they are equally applicable to other methods of naval warfare.

Paragraph 13.9.4 deals with the zones that undoubtedly qualify as methods of naval warfare, i.e. with exclusion zones. Such zones should, however, be distinguished from the suspension of innocent passage and from the closure of the enemy's territorial sea. In those sea areas, belligerents are not bound by the restrictions applicable in times of peace and are therefore free to bar access by neutral vessels and aircraft. In contrast, exclusion zones are established in sea areas beyond the outer limit of the territorial sea, including, if necessary, the international airspace above those sea areas.[75] For that very reason, 'their extent, location, and duration ... and the measures imposed should not exceed what is required by military necessity'.[76] The establishment of an exclusion zone interferes with the rights of neutral vessels and aircraft and is recognised as an exceptional measure only.[77]

According to paragraph 13.9.4, exclusion zones may be established to 'prohibit the entry of vessels or aircraft without authorization'. This seems to be a correct statement, which is, however, not sufficiently clear in view of the obviously intended link to paragraph 13.9.1, which identifies the possible legal bases for zones. Seemingly, exclusion zones that cannot be based on any of the authorities identified in paragraph 13.9.1 will be unlawful. This cannot have been the intention of the *Manual*'s drafters. Rather, paragraph 13.9.4 seems to recognise an independent belligerent right of establishing exclusion zones outside belligerent territory. It would, therefore, have been helpful had the drafters relied on the *San Remo Manual* and other military manuals, including the *AMW Manual*.[78]

Finally, the limitations applicable to exclusion zones – provision of safe passage and no barring of access to and egress from neutral territory – are correctly identified.

75 See *AMW Manual*, rules 107 and 108.

76 Note that according to the *San Remo Manual*, paragraph 106(b), they shall not 'exceed what is strictly required by military necessity and the principle of proportionality'.

77 *San Remo Manual*, paragraph 106.

78 *San Remo Manual*, paragraphs 105ff.; *AMW Manual*, rules 105ff.

The same holds true for the procedure applicable to the declaration and notification of exclusion and other zones dealt with in paragraph 13.9.5. Notice to Mariners (NOTMARs) and Notice to Airmen (NOTAMs) are among the most appropriate and effective means of making neutral vessels and aircraft aware of the establishment of any of the zones dealt with in section 13.9. It may be added that in some instances the use of NOTAMs and NOTMARs may not be sufficient, in particular when a sea area covered by the zone in question is used by small fishing and trade vessels that are not linked to the respective communications centres.

BLOCKADE

The definition in section 13.10 of blockade as a belligerent operation directed against coastal areas belonging to, occupied by or under the control of an enemy State correctly reflects customary international law.[79] It could have been amended by a short statement as to the location of the blockade line (or curtain) outside the territorial sea, because suspension of innocent passage in the enemy's territorial sea may not necessarily qualify as a blockade proper.

The purpose of a blockade may indeed, as reported in paragraph 13.10.1, be 'to deprive the enemy of supplies'. This, however, is but one of the legitimate aims pursued by the establishment of a blockade. For instance, a blockade is the only method of naval warfare directed against enemy exports; alternatively, it may be a preparatory step for a landing operation.

It is true that the blockading power may take measures on the high seas to enforce the blockade, which requires a breach or attempted breach of the blockade by neutral vessels or aircraft. The primary enforcement measure is capture. Visit and search of neutral vessels or aircraft may be a method for verifying the intentions of a suspect vehicle, but those measures can be taken independently from a blockade.

For a blockade to be legal, it must conform with a number of requirements that are dealt with in paragraph 13.10.2, which uses the rather uncommon term 'criteria'. A blockade may be declared by a belligerent State or by the commander of the blockading force. It would probably have been helpful to distinguish here between 'strategic' and 'local' blockades. The establishment of a blockade may also be authorised by a UN Security Council resolution based on Article 42 UN Charter. It is misleading to describe a blockade as a

[79] Heintschel von Heinegg, Blockade, MN 1. See also Articles 1–21 of the 1909 London Declaration.

use of force 'for the purposes of the United Nations Charter' only, because this is also the case in customary international law.

The requirements of notification and the effectiveness of a blockade are, in principle, correctly identified in paragraphs 13.10.2.2 and 13.10.2.3.[80] However, effectiveness is not dependent on whether 'ingress or egress of the blockaded area' is dangerous but rather on whether there is a sufficient probability that vessels or aircraft trying to breach the blockade will be captured. Therefore, the pursuit of a blockade-runner will rather render a blockade ineffective if no sufficient forces remain in the area to prevent its breach. Finally, it should have been made clear here that a naval blockade may be established and enforced by naval mines. This is only marginally referred to in in paragraphs 13.10.3.2 and 13.11.1.

Paragraph 13.10.2.4, on the impartial application of a blockade and the limitations dealt with in paragraph 13.10.2.5, in particular the prohibition of barring access to neutral territory, starving the civilian population and inflicting excessive collateral damage, correctly reflect the law of naval warfare.

The exceptions from the requirement of impartiality by special entry or exit authorisation in paragraph 13.10.3 should also have addressed neutral State vessels and aircraft other than warships and military aircraft, and should have emphasised that, in view of the requirements of impartiality and effectiveness, such special authorisations may be granted in exceptional situations only. The recognition of a principal obligation of the blockading power to allow neutral merchant vessels and aircraft in distress or carrying relief consignments for the civilian population of the blockaded area to cross the blockade line is based on the principle of humanity and is an important clarification of the blockading power's obligations.

In paragraph 13.10.4, it is rightly stated that capture is the primary consequence of a breach or attempted breach of blockade. Unfortunately, breach of blockade is described as 'passage . . . through a blockade without special entry or exit authorization'. Instead, it should be defined as the crossing of the blockade line (or curtain). The determination of an attempted breach of blockade is described as dependent on the 'intention of evading the blockade'. This is not necessarily incorrect, but it is not helpful either. What matters are the objective circumstances of a given situation. For instance, the loitering of a vessel near the blockade line may be considered an attempt to breach the blockade.

It is correct that a vessel or aircraft egressing from the blockaded area may be captured until its journey is completed. This, however, is the consequence of

[80] See also *San Remo Manual*, paragraphs 93ff.; *AMW Manual*, rule 148.

the prior breach of the blockade, not of an attempted breach. The completion of the journey depends on whether the vessel or aircraft has arrived in the territorial sea or national airspace of a neutral State.

The third part of paragraph 13.10.4.1 is a restatement of the doctrine of 'continuous voyage'. Although it has long been a contentious issue whether the doctrine applies to blockade,[81] it is arguable that it does.

As correctly stated in paragraph 13.10.4.2, a blockade may only be enforced against vessels and aircraft that have positive or constructive knowledge of the establishment of the blockade.

NAVAL MINES

Section 13.11 rightly starts with the correct statement that naval mines are lawful means of naval warfare. This is an important clarification, because of early endeavors to ban naval mines[82] and a general misperception of their dangerousness. The primary purpose of the rules on naval mining is correctly identified as mitigating the risk naval mines may pose to neutral vessels.

The reminder that 'different rules apply to landmines' is equally important, but should have been amended by a distinction between naval mines and beach-interdiction mines or explosive devices attached to the hulls of enemy ships or other objects qualifying as lawful military objectives. Since the only treaty regulating naval mines is the 1907 Hague Convention VIII, a definition that covers submarine automatic contact mines and modern mines should have been provided. For instance, in the NATO Glossary, the term 'naval mine' is defined as 'an explosive device laid in the water with the intention of damaging or sinking ships or of deterring shipping from entering an area. The term does not include devices attached to the bottoms of ships or to harbour installations by personnel operating underwater.'[83]

Paragraph 13.11.1 correctly identifies the various uses of naval mines and the distinction between armed and controlled mines. A short reference to the technology used in modern naval mines would have been helpful. Modern

[81] Article 19 of the 1909 London Declaration provides: 'Whatever may be the ulterior destination of a vessel or of her cargo, she can not be captured for breach of blockade, if, at the moment, she is on her way to a non-blockaded port.' See also the references in Heintschel von Heinegg, Blockade, MN 44.

[82] At the Second Hague Peace Conference in 1907, the United Kingdom, in particular, tried to have naval mines banned.

[83] NATO, Glossary of Terms and Definitions, NATO Doc. AAP-6(2014), Brussels (29 April 2014), 2-M-6.

mines do not explode on physical contact, but react to acoustic or electromagnetic signatures or pressure, and they are thus highly discriminating weapons. Accordingly, a modern mine may pose no risk to neutral and innocent shipping even though it is armed.

Paragraph 13.11.2 deals with peacetime mining in various sea areas. This is not surprising, because mine laying is a time-consuming task that can probably no longer be effectively accomplished after the outbreak of an international armed conflict. Of course, a State may decide to lay naval mines in peacetime for other reasons, in particular if the mine laying is necessary for the protection of national defence and security interests.

Peacetime mining is to be judged upon in the light of the law of the sea and the *jus ad bellum*. Accordingly, naval mines may not be laid in foreign sea areas subject to the sovereignty of the coastal State, i.e. internal waters, territorial sea and archipelagic waters (= national waters). If a State decides to lay mines in its own national waters, the distinction between armed and controlled mines becomes relevant. Paragraph 13.11.2.1 prohibits the laying of armed mines in international straits and archipelagic sea lanes. If mines are laid in the territorial sea or archipelagic waters, the right of innocent passage must be suspended and other States must be appropriately notified 'of the existence and location of such mines'. Armed mines must be 'removed or rendered harmless as soon as the security threat that prompted their emplacement has terminated'. These restrictions do not apply to controlled mines. This is a correct statement as to the applicable international law, which should have been amended by also exempting highly sophisticated modern naval mines that pose no threat to innocent shipping.

Paragraph 13.11.2.2 on the peacetime mining of international waters, i.e. of sea areas beyond the outer limit of the territorial sea of any State, is equally useful, because the laying of armed mines is considered lawful only 'under the most demanding requirements of individual or collective self-defense' and if their location has been notified and there is an on-scene presence. Although the laying of controlled mines is not equally limited, paragraph 13.11.2.2 does not provide carte blanche. Rather, the laying of such mines is prohibited if it 'unreasonably interferes with other lawful uses of the oceans'. The factors that might indicate a reasonable or unreasonable interference provide appropriate guidance.

Paragraph 13.11.3 deals with naval mining during armed conflict, and emphasises both the legality of naval mines and the restrictions provided for by the law of naval warfare. Surprisingly, it immediately addresses the laying of naval mines by neutral States, which should be dealt with in the chapter on neutrality. Moreover, it merely mentions automatic contact mines and, in footnote 194, Article 4 of the 1907 Hague Convention VIII. This begs the question whether the right of neutral States to bar access to their territorial sea and internal waters by using naval mines is indeed limited to automatic contact mines or whether it would not equally apply to modern mines. According to the position taken in the *Manual*, the respective technology is without prejudice to the right of neutral States to bar belligerent access to their national waters.

In principle, the obligations incumbent on the mine-laying belligerent have been correctly identified. This certainly holds true for the surveillance of minefields (paragraph 13.11.3.3), the recording of minefield locations (paragraph 13.11.3.4), geographical prohibitions/restrictions (paragraph 13.11.3.5) and the prohibition of mining for the sole purpose of intercepting commercial shipping (paragraph 13.11.3.6). There are, however, some statements that cannot remain unaddressed. While paragraph 13.11.3.1 recognises the standard of feasibility for the precautions that have to be taken, the laying of anchored automatic contact mines is subject to 'every possible precaution'. Although the latter is the standard provided for in Article 3(1) of the 1907 Hague Convention VIII, it is hard to understand why automatic contact mines, which are far more dangerous to innocent shipping than modern mines, are not equally subject to the obligation to take all (feasible) precautions. In paragraph 13.11.3.2, the obligation to notify the location of armed mines is subject to 'military exigencies', which is the standard of Article 3(2) of Hague Convention VIII. In this context, it is important to note that, according to the *San Remo Manual*, armed mines that cannot be directed against vessels qualifying as military objectives must always be notified.[84] It is, therefore, doubtful whether the more liberal standard agreed upon in 1907 is still valid. Hence, the second part of paragraph 13.11.3.2 may also no longer correctly reflect the law as it stands today. The obligation to provide for the neutralisation of mines after loss of control over them is correctly summarised in paragraph 13.11.3.7, which is, however, too focused on automatic contact mines and the respective provisions of Article 1(1) and (2) of Hague Convention VIII. While the loss of control over automatic contact mines can be established rather easily, some guidance as to the loss of control over other naval mines would have been useful. Finally, the obligations to remove the naval mines laid or to inform the former enemy of their location are again limited to automatic contact mines and to the States party to Hague Convention VIII. According

[84] *San Remo Manual*, paragraph 83.

to the position taken in the *San Remo Manual*, those obligations apply to all types of mine and to all belligerents that have laid naval mines *qua* customary law.[85]

TORPEDOES

Section 13.12 on torpedoes is based on Article 1 of the 1907 Hague Convention VIII, and thus correctly reflects the applicable law.[86] In view of the advancements of modern weapons technology, it is sometimes difficult to distinguish between mines and torpedoes. Therefore, the section could have been amended by a short paragraph addressing that issue. The 'notes on terminology' in paragraph 13.12.1 regarding the original meaning of the term 'torpedo' are not misplaced, but they are not relevant either, because the 1907 Hague Convention VIII clearly distinguishes between mines and torpedoes.

DECEPTION BY NAVAL FORCES, INCLUDING THE USE OF ENEMY OR NEUTRAL FLAGS

As rightly stated in section 13.13, the law of naval warfare is less restrictive with regard to permissible ruses than the law of land warfare. This point is explained in the first two parts of paragraph 13.13.1 by the well-known traditional rules. Although 'disguised electronic signatures' are among the activities permissible under the law of naval warfare, the section does not reflect contemporary naval operations. In an electronic battlespace, visual identification of vessels or aircraft is rather the exception than the rule. Therefore, the paragraph should have dealt with electronic deception in greater depth.

The feigning of the status of vessels exempt from capture is indeed prohibited. The summary in the last paragraph should have been amended by coastal rescue craft, vessels protected by the UN flag and vessels engaged in transporting cultural property under special protection.[87]

Surprisingly, the prohibition of perfidy is only briefly mentioned in the introductory sentence of the section. Perfidious activities, such as feigning surrender or distress (e.g. by sending a distress signal),[88] constitute grave breaches of the law of naval warfare if they are undertaken to 'kill, injure or capture an adversary'.[89]

[85] *San Remo Manual*, paragraph 90. [86] *San Remo Manual*, paragraph 79.
[87] *San Remo Manual*, paragraph 110(a), (d) and (g).
[88] *San Remo Manual*, paragraph 111 (b). [89] Article 37(1) API.

CONCLUDING REMARKS

Chapter XIII is an honest effort to summarise the law of naval warfare. Unfortunately, it is characterised by an obvious reluctance to contribute to a clarification of the contemporary law in the area. It is, of course, correct to address the long-standing agreements, in particular the various 1907 Hague Conventions that continue to apply to naval operations during an international armed conflict. However, technology having advanced considerably, the chapter should have provided more guidance as to whether and to what extent the traditional rules can be applied to modern naval weapons. As it stands today, there is a considerable risk that naval commanders may not pay regard to the chapter at all because they consider it of historical interest only.

14

Air and Space Warfare

INTRODUCTION

The United States is arguably the premier State involved in the development and practice of operations in airspace and outer space. The reader might therefore expect that the international law that applies to these two rather discrete yet vitally important aspects of the conduct of modern military operations would be dealt with at some considerable length, and perhaps in distinct chapters, in the *Manual*. In both respects, the reader will be disappointed. What follows is a discussion of what the *Manual* does say on these twin subjects. In the short conclusion, some of the obvious aspects that appear to have received insufficient emphasis are mentioned.

Paragraph 14.1.1 addresses at length the somewhat limited relevance of the Chicago Convention 1944,[1] pointing out that it does not restrict State action in war and generally does not affect State aircraft.[2] This is a legally accurate statement that is likely to confuse the casual reader, who has to wait until section 14.3 before receiving a substantive explanation of what 'State aircraft' comprise. The paragraph rightly notes that the prime focus of the Convention is civil aviation but that it does contain provisions dealing with the requirements governing the entry of State aircraft into foreign airspace and with the obligation to have due regard to the safety of navigation of civil aircraft. Paragraph 14.1.1.1 sensibly draws attention to Article 89 of the Convention and its stipulation that '[i]n case of war, the provisions of this Convention shall not affect the freedom of action of any of the contracting States affected, whether as belligerents or as neutrals'. Citing this provision as an example of the *lex specialis* principle, without applying that Latin term, the paragraph correctly

[1] Convention on International Civil Aviation, Chicago, IL (7 December 1944).

[2] As to the declared US position on these matters, see *DoD Manual*, footnote 12 on page 901.

explains that a State's rights under the laws of war and of neutrality would prevail if they were to conflict with obligations under the Convention.

Paragraph 14.1.1.1 then states that the provisions of the Chicago Convention 1944 'may be relevant during armed conflict insofar as they articulate restrictions that continue to apply to civil aircraft'. Two comments can be made, namely that the word 'may' should become 'will' and, even then, that the sentence is expressing a somewhat circular and self-evident truth. The rather narrow example that is given is that neutral aircraft must still seek permission from a foreign neutral State before carrying munitions or implements of war through that neutral State's airspace. In the view of the present authors, it would be preferable to make a more general point here, namely that the existence of a state of international armed conflict does not in principle and subject to the terms of particular provisions affect the applicability of the Convention to neutrals or as between them.

State aircraft are not permitted to enter the airspace of another State without that State's consent;[3] this, as the *Manual* correctly observes, will continue to apply to neutral State aircraft entering a belligerent's airspace during armed conflict. While the formulation of the point could be clearer, the *Manual* also points out that while a belligerent military aircraft may only enter neutral airspace with the neutral's consent, by doing so it may breach the neutrality of that State. Indeed, it might be more accurate to say that neutrality will be breached unless there are unusual circumstances, for example that the intruding aircraft is an aircraft in distress.

The sentence accompanied by footnote 16 could be more clearly written. It is evidently seeking to explain that consent is not required if a military aircraft is entering foreign neutral airspace to take self-help action when the neutral State is unable or unwilling to prevent or terminate violations of its neutrality.

Paragraph 14.1.1.4 deals with the Chicago Convention 1944 obligation for States party, 'when issuing regulations for their state aircraft . . . [to] have due regard for the safety of navigation of civil aircraft'. On the assumption that the due regard obligation continues to apply during armed conflict – an assumption with which the present authors agree – the *Manual* argues that the degree of care that will be due in particular circumstances will depend on military necessity; this is also correct. By way of example, the *Manual* suggests that 'the use of force against enemy civil aircraft that constitute military objectives and thus may be made the object of attack under the law of war would not be prohibited'. It would be more legally accurate to add that such a use of force would not be prohibited provided that the rules of the law of war as to

[3] *DoD Manual*, paragraph 14.1.1.3; Chicago Convention 1944, Article 3(c).

distinction, discrimination, proportionality and precautions were fully complied with.

The second section of paragraph 14.1.1.4 recognises the practical need in modern complex airspace situations during armed conflict for military aircraft movements to be carefully coordinated with national civil aviation authorities, and accurately explains why such coordination is important. Usefully, the US policy that 'in the event of combat operations during armed conflict, aircraft commanders, consistent with military necessity, [must] take measures to minimize hazards to civil air or surface traffic'[4] is stated.

The 1899, 1907 and 1923 unsuccessful attempts to conclude law relating to air operations in armed conflict and the US position in relation to relevant treaties are briefly mentioned in paragraph 14.1.2. The reader might legitimately have expected a statement as to whether the US DoD considers the 1923 Hague Draft Rules to be reflective of customary law. The inference seems to be that it does not. Moreover, one would have expected there to be some reference here to the *HPCR Manual on International Law Applicable to Air and Missile Warfare*, which was published in 2010 and is referred to in this book as the *AMW Manual*.

LEGAL BOUNDARIES OF AIRSPACE

As section 14.2 acknowledges, there are various reasons why the classification of airspace matters. Paragraph 14.2.1 correctly explains that the lateral classification of airspace depends on the classification of the land or waters over which it sits. Accordingly, national airspace is that airspace over a State's land territory, internal waters, territorial seas and archipelagic sea lanes and is subject to the national sovereignty of that State, whereas international airspace is not subject to the sovereignty of any State. Arguably, it would have been more logical to address these matters of sovereignty in relation to national airspace before the discussion as to intrusions by military aircraft to which reference was made earlier.

The special rules applying to air passage through international straits and archipelagic sea lanes are discussed in Chapter XV, and paragraph 14.2.1 recalls, as discussed in Chapter XIII, that aircraft do not have the rights of innocent passage over territorial seas that are enjoyed by ships. Mention should have been made in the main text of the rights of transit passage and

4 *DoD Manual*, footnote 21 on page 903, citing DoD Instruction 4540.01, Use of International Airspace by US Military Aircraft and for Missile/Projectile Firings (dated 28 March 2007), paragraph 4.2.3.

of archipelagic sea lane passage that continue to apply to belligerent military aircraft in times of armed conflict. A neutral State may not prohibit the exercise of these rights. The same holds true for the airspace above belligerent international straits and archipelagic sea lanes.

Paragraph 14.2.1.1 repeats that States have sovereignty over national airspace, merely adding that it is complete and exclusive sovereignty. The paragraph explains that this means that States have sovereignty in the airspace over the land and waters over which they also have sovereignty, listing national airspace as including: the airspace over a State's land territory, including its internal waters; the airspace over its territorial sea; and the airspace over its archipelagic sea. As this explanation shows, there is a significant amount of unnecessary repetition in these paragraphs of the *Manual*, the effects of which are to render the discussion somewhat unwieldy and further to reduce the detail in which the air and space topics are addressed in Chapter XIV.

Paragraph 14.2.1.2 then correctly notes that all airspace that is not subject to national sovereignty is international airspace, including airspace over the contiguous zone of a State, airspace over a State's exclusive economic zone and airspace over the high seas.

As paragraph 14.2.2 points out, a State's sovereignty over its airspace does not extend to outer space. Acknowledging the generally accepted view that orbiting objects are in outer space, the paragraph gives the US view that 'there is no legal or practical need to delimit or otherwise define a specific boundary between airspace and outer space'.[5] This may seem strange given that national sovereignty is capable of applying to the one but not to the other. While the physics of the matter does not permit of a precise definition, the adoption of the formulation put forward in the *UK Manual*, in the *Australian Manual* and in the *United States Air Force Publication*,[6] all cited in the footnote to the *DoD Manual* text on the matter,[7] would avoid giving a precise definition but would provide the casual reader with a clearer understanding.

Paragraph 14.2.3 correctly explains: that all areas of airspace are allocated to flight information regions; that within such a region, a flight information service and an alert service are provided by the national air traffic control

[5] The *Manual* cites K Hodgkins, US Advisor to the United Nations, Legal Subcommittee (LSC) of the United Nations Committee on the Peaceful Uses of Outer Space (COPUOS) 719th Meeting (8 April 2005); for full explanations of the US position and the quoted positions of certain other States, see footnotes 40 and 41 on pages 905 and 906 of the *Manual*.

[6] Department of the Air Force, *Air Force Operations and The Law*, 85, 3rd edn. The Judge Advocate General's School (2014). See also AMW *Manual*, rule 1(a) and its associated Commentary.

[7] Footnote 40 on page 905.

service responsible for that region; that these services provide a basic level of air traffic service and information to aviators necessary for the safe and efficient conduct of flights; and that each region normally encompasses substantial areas of international airspace and does not necessarily reflect international or national airspace borders.

Paragraph 14.2.3 states the US position, which is believed to be widely shared, that flight information region rules do not apply to State aircraft, including military aircraft, and that military aircraft have freedom of navigation in international airspace without the consent of or notice to coastal State authorities. Arguably, a brief reference in the main text of the *Manual* here to the due regard obligation noted in paragraph 14.1.1.4 would be useful.

Paragraph 14.2.4 describes an air defence identification zone (ADIZ) as 'an area of airspace over land or water in which the ready identification, location and control of aircraft may be required in the interests of national security' and confirms that the US has established ADIZs. While the discussion of ADIZs is, as will be shown later, generally correct, one wonders whether it is really necessary to deal with them at such length in a law of war manual. Paragraph 14.2.4.1 explains the legal basis for a State creating such zones as its 'right to establish conditions and procedures for entry into its national airspace', citing NWP 1–14M and a 1976 Air Force pamphlet in support.[8] The present authors see no basis for disputing the right of any State, as a security measure or, indeed, in order to ensure the general safety of air navigation, to oblige an aircraft that is in the vicinity of and on a course to enter its national airspace to identify itself. The same paragraph makes the point that establishing such a zone does not constitute a sovereignty claim in relation to international airspace and that the establishment of any such zone must therefore respect the rights of other States to use international airspace. The final part of the paragraph states, not quite in these terms, that the US does not recognise the right of a State to apply its ADIZ regulations to an aircraft, State or civil, if there is no intent that the aircraft will enter the State's airspace. Whether such an intent is or is not present will presumably, in the case of an aircraft that is failing to communicate with the relevant authorities, be a matter on which an inference will have to be drawn based on the surrounding circumstances.

Paragraph 14.2.4.2 correctly notes that a failure of an aircraft entering an ADIZ to identify itself does not entitle the declaring State to use force against it, that it may give rise to an interception and that a persistent failure to comply with instructions may be evidence that it poses a threat. The paragraph adds

[8] NWP 1–14M, paragraph 2.7.2.3 and 1976 Air Force Pamphlet 110–31 paragraph 2–1g are cited in *DoD Manual*, footnote 47 on pages 907 and 908.

that the establishment of such a zone does not relieve the declaring State of its obligations under applicable international law. This is correct. As an example, the *Manual* refers to 'its obligation to refrain from attacks against civil aircraft under peacetime international law'. That is not, however, an unqualified obligation, given the terms of Article 3bis of the Chicago Convention 1944,[9] but this part of Chapter XIV does not seem to go into that level of detail. Under peacetime international law, all uses of force, including against military aircraft, are prohibited unless Article 51 or Chapter VII of the UN Charter permits otherwise. It is therefore suggested that the example be amended to refer to 'its obligation under Article 2(4) of the UN Charter to refrain from the use of unlawful force'.

AIRCRAFT STATUS

Paragraph 14.3.1 correctly identifies aircraft used in military, customs and police services as State aircraft for the purposes of the Chicago Convention 1944 and suggests that aircraft operated by a government for sovereign, non-commercial purposes can be similarly classified. The paragraph then reports the US position that aircraft contracted by the US DoD are not State aircraft unless the US Government has designated them as such. Paragraph 14.3.1 contends that there are important implications of the designation of an aircraft as a State aircraft, such as enemy State aircraft being liable to seizure as war booty and neutral State aircraft not being liable to search, seizure or diversion. Dealing with the first point, the 1923 Hague Draft Rules, as the AMW *Manual* explains, 'distinguish between (Art. 4) "public non-military aircraft employed for customs or police purposes" and (Art. 5) "public non-military aircraft other than those employed for customs or police purposes"' and note that 'the latter are "treated on the same footing as private aircraft"'. Article 32 of the Hague Draft Rules makes it clear that '[e]nemy public aircraft, other than those treated on the same footing as private aircraft, shall be subject to confiscation without prize proceedings'. The AMW *Manual* explains that this approach remains valid,[10] so it is not legitimate to characterise all State aircraft as being liable to seizure as war booty; it is suggested that amendment is required. The reference to neutral State aircraft not being liable to search, seizure or diversion is consistent with Article 51 of the Hague Draft Rules so far as neutral public non-military aircraft are concerned. It is suggested that the language of Article 51 might usefully be adopted in the *Manual*'s text and

9 Article 3bis(a), second sentence.

10 AMW *Manual*, paragraph 4 of the Commentary to rule 1(cc).

that the proper reference to Article 51 should be cited in the corresponding footnote.

It should be noted that the Chicago Convention 1944 does not define State aircraft by reference to their designation. State aircraft are defined in Article 3(b) of the Convention as '[a]ircraft used in military, customs and police services'. State aircraft status is therefore linked to the service in which an aircraft is actually used.

Paragraph 14.3.2 correctly points out that State aircraft have the nationality of the State that operates them while civil aircraft have the nationality of the State where they are registered, citing, in relation to the latter provision, Article 17 of the Chicago Convention 1944. Paragraph 14.3.3 considers military aircraft, noting that the US is not a party to any treaty requiring particular qualifications before an aircraft can become a military aircraft, with the result that so far as the US is concerned, military aircraft are those aircraft that are so designated by the State that operates them. It should be noted that the Hague Draft Rules of Aerial Warfare, never adopted in treaty form, did nevertheless prescribe certain requirements for military aircraft status. Moreover, the AMW *Manual*, reflecting what its experts agreed is customary law on the matter, finds that: 'Military aircraft means any aircraft (i) operated by the armed forces of a State, (ii) bearing the military markings of that State, (iii) commanded by a member of the armed forces, and (iv) controlled, manned or programmed by a crew subject to regular armed forces discipline'.[11] While paragraph 14.3.3 acknowledges that in general, military aircraft will have the first three of these features, it is suggested that some reference should have been made to these authoritative statements of law and to whether the US accepts them as accurately reflecting customary law – and if not, why not. This is significant because the four criteria must, in collective expert opinion, be satisfied for an aircraft to be permitted to undertake belligerent acts. An aircraft designated by the US as military but that does not satisfy the criteria would have no such right.[12]

Paragraph 14.3.3.1 acknowledges, first, that only military aircraft are entitled to engage in attacks in armed conflict. It would, as observed in the previous paragraph, actually be more accurate to state that only military aircraft are entitled to exercise belligerent rights.[13] Second, as the paragraph also observes, enemy military aircraft will also generally be liable to be attacked as military

[11] AMW *Manual*, rule 1(x) and paragraph 1 of the associated Commentary.
[12] Consider also UNCLOS, Article 101, under which an aircraft not complying with these requirements may be considered a pirate aircraft if it engages in acts of violence against another aircraft or ship.
[13] AMW *Manual*, paragraph 2 of the Commentary to rule 17(a).

objectives, unless they have surrendered or are medical aircraft. Third, belligerent military aircraft may not enter neutral airspace and are customarily accorded privileges and immunities by friendly foreign States.

Paragraph 14.3.3.2 states: 'Markings may help distinguish friend from foe and help preclude misidentification of aircraft as neutral or as civil.' The referenced extract from the writings of J M Spaight suggests that the quoted sentence should actually be talking about precluding the misidentification of neutral or civil aircraft as being military aircraft with the consequence that an erroneous attack occurs. The suggestion that in some circumstances the use of such markings may be superfluous is disputed by the present authors. Markings are a requirement for military aircraft status. It would be more accurate to say that in certain forms of aerial combat, such as beyond-visual-range air-to-air engagements, markings may have limited practical effect. That the crew of a military aircraft may include civilian members, as stated in paragraph 14.3.3.3, is correct, but such civilian members must be subject to regular armed forces discipline.[14]

STATUS OF AIRCREW ON MILITARY AIRCRAFT

As paragraph 14.4.1 correctly explains, members of the armed forces who are members of the crew of a military aircraft have the status of combatant, and thus the combatant's privileges.[15] Military aircrew must wear military flying clothing distinctive to their armed force to comply with the combatant requirement to distinguish themselves from the civilian population.[16] Paragraph 14.4.2 then refers to '[c]ivilian members of military aircrew'. It is assumed that what is meant by this is 'civilian persons who are members of the crew of a military aircraft'; it is suggested that this revised wording be substituted. Such persons do indeed fall into the category of persons authorised to accompany the armed forces under Article 4A(4) of GPW, and the paragraph makes the somewhat self-evident point that other civilians may also fall into the same category if they have received the required authorisation.

[14] Consider, for example, the UK Armed Forces Act 2006, 2006 c. 52, Schedule 15, Part 1, Paragraph 1.

[15] The right to participate in hostilities, immunity from prosecution for lawful acts of war and PW status if captured.

[16] See *DoD Manual*, paragraph 14.4.1.1, where the need to wear such uniform is linked to the possibility that members of the crew may become separated from their aircraft. However, the requirement arguably also applies to military personnel remotely piloting or controlling unmanned air platforms.

Paragraph 14.4.2 notes the GPW implications of authorisation, and adds that 'they have legal immunity from the enemy's domestic law for providing authorized support services to the armed forces'. This statement is at best ambiguous. To be clear, the entitlement of these particular kinds of civilian to PW status on capture does not mean that they have the combatant's privilege. So, while a military aircraft has belligerent rights, and while civilian persons may be members of the crew of such aircraft, it does not follow that those civilians have the right to take a direct part in hostilities. If they do so, they are liable for the domestic law offences they commit.

Paragraph 14.4.3 deals with the law as it applies to downed aircrew. It starts by noting that in general, aircrew parachuting from an aircraft in distress are treated as if they were *hors de combat* and must not be made the object of attack. Article 42(1) of API is not cited as an authority on the point, with annotation being limited to a cross-reference to Chapter V. If they engage in hostile acts or attempt to evade capture, either during their descent or on reaching the ground, paragraph 14.4.3.1 correctly explains that parachuting aircrew forfeit their protection from attack. Paragraph 14.4.3.2 accurately states that aircrew downed at sea are classed as shipwrecked, that they must not be made the object of attack and that there are obligations to search for and collect them. Citing paragraph 12.70.1 of the *UK Manual*, paragraph 14.4.3.3 then notes that rescuing downed aircrew to prevent their capture by the enemy is a combat activity that enemy military forces may lawfully oppose and that medical personnel, ships and aircraft engaged in rescuing downed aircrew must not impede or interfere with enemy attempts to capture downed aircrew lest they forfeit their protection from being made the object of attack.

The same paragraph in the *DoD Manual* then puts forward the US understanding that 'the prohibition against the use of riot control agents as a method of warfare [does not] prohibit the use of riot control agents to rescue downed aircrew in certain circumstances'. The US made no statement in this regard when it ratified the CWC,[17] and the implication of paragraph 14.4.3.3 must be that the US would not regard it as legitimate to use RCAs in connection with the rescue of downed aircrew to prevent their capture by the enemy. It would, it is suggested, be helpful for the *Manual* to make this interpretation clear in the present paragraph and to confirm that this view is based on such rescues in such circumstances constituting a combat activity, with the result that the associated use of RCAs would constitute a method of warfare that is prohibited by the CWC.

17 On 25 April 1997; source www.icrc.org.

Paragraph 14.4.3.4 correctly notes the right of escaping downed aircrew to use enemy uniforms and civilian clothes to evade capture, pointing out the risk that they will be treated as spies. If captured during an international armed conflict, downed aircrew are entitled to PW status irrespective of attempts to escape or to attack enemy forces. If downed aircrew land in neutral territory, they are liable to internment by the neutral State, as paragraph 14.4.3.5 correctly states.

MEASURES SHORT OF ATTACK – INTERCEPTION, DIVERSION AND CAPTURE

Paragraph 14.5.1 discusses interception, whether to within visual range or to within the range of weapon systems, and notes that interception of civil aircraft that are not military objectives must be undertaken with due regard for their safety. The purposes of interception operations are noted as including: warning a civil aircraft to refrain from entering an area of active hostilities; helping to identify whether an aircraft is a military objective; the belligerent right of visit and search, e.g. when enforcing a blockade; forcing an aircraft to divert and land at a specific airfield for search and capture; and gaining a position from which to attack an aircraft. The *Manual* correctly observes that, as a general rule, interception may not take place in neutral airspace, including during passage through international straits or neutral archipelagic sea lanes.[18]

Where diversion of aircraft is concerned, paragraph 14.5.2 notes that this may take place outside neutral airspace as part of the belligerent right of visit and search. If there are reasonable grounds to suspect that a civil aircraft, its cargo or its personnel are liable to capture, the aircraft may be directed to proceed for visit and search to a belligerent airfield that is reasonably accessible and suitable for the aircraft concerned. If no such airfield is available, it may be diverted from its declared destination. Neutral military aircraft and neutral civil aircraft accompanied by neutral military aircraft of the same nationality are exempt from the belligerent right of diversion for visit and search.

The assertion at the end of the first part of paragraph 14.5.2 that interference with neutral civil aircraft must be justified by military necessity is not correct. If there are reasonable grounds for suspicion that such an aircraft is engaged in contraband carriage, it may be forced to land even in the absence of reasons of military necessity. The final part of paragraph 14.5.2 also fails to point out

[18] *DoD Manual*, paragraphs 14.4.1.1 and 14.5.1.2.

that there are kinds of enemy aircraft that are exempt from measures short of attack.

Paragraph 14.5.2.1 explains that an enemy civil aircraft that persistently fails to comply with military instructions becomes a military objective subject to attack. The present authors consider that this is likely to be correct, but that the attendant circumstances will matter. Moreover, to be a military objective and thus liable to lawful attack, an object must satisfy the Article 52(2) API definition, so it will be a question of fact in the circumstances whether the aircraft is indeed making an effective contribution to military action and whether attacking it offers a definite military advantage. It is in this respect significant that the *AMW Manual*, in rule 27(d), lists refusal to comply with such orders as a circumstance that may, as opposed to will, render such an aircraft a military objective. Even if it does become a military objective, it may only be attacked if the distinction and discrimination principles and the proportionality and precautions rules have been complied with.

The second part of paragraph 14.5.2.1 suggests that a simple failure of an aircraft to comply with military instructions may render it a military objective. Again, the relevant circumstances will be determinative, and all feasible precautions must be taken in order to determine whether it is in fact a military objective.

Enemy civil aircraft and goods on board are, as paragraph 14.5.3 states, liable to capture outside neutral airspace. The liability of enemy public aircraft to confiscation was discussed earlier in relation to paragraph 14.3.1, and corresponding amendment will be required also in paragraph 14.5.3.

BELLIGERENT CONTROL OF AVIATION IN THE IMMEDIATE VICINITY OF HOSTILITIES

Section 14.6 draws a distinction between the right of belligerents to establish zones during an armed conflict and the right of a belligerent State to prohibit, or to establish special restrictions upon, flight activities in the immediate vicinity of military operations in order to prevent such activities jeopardising military operations. It bases this on the right of the belligerent State to maintain the security of its own forces and its right to conduct hostilities without the interference of neutrals. The final sentence of the section then states: 'However, belligerent control of aviation in the immediate vicinity of hostilities may be applicable in the national airspace of belligerents.' It is not readily evident what, if anything, this sentence is adding to what has already been made clear in the first sentence of the section, so deletion might be advisable. Clearly, belligerent control of civil aircraft movements in the vicinity of hostilities should also be directed at maintaining the safety and security of civil aviation.

AIRSPACE ZONES

Section 14.7 notes that airspace zones may be established during armed conflict to prohibit aircraft from entering or flying within designated areas, including areas of international airspace, e.g. to reduce the risk of inadvertent attack of civil or neutral aircraft or to control the scope of the conflict. The topic of zones is discussed in paragraph 14.2.4 and in Chapter XIII of the *Manual* and Chapter 13 of the present book.

ATTACKS AGAINST MILITARY OBJECTIVES IN THE AIR

After making the important point that the general rules on attacks also apply to attacking military objectives in the air, section 14.8 cross-references the special rules on medical aircraft, discussed in Chapter VII. It then states that the rules as to surrender and *hors de combat* apply to those on board enemy aircraft. As a somewhat pedantic point of clarity, it should perhaps be made clear that the rules apply to persons fulfilling the relevant criteria who are, or were, located on enemy military aircraft.

Sensibly, paragraph 14.8.2 makes the point that it may be practically difficult to determine whether persons on board an enemy military aircraft are *hors de combat* and to accept their surrender. It should, in this regard, be recalled that Article 41(1) of API, which is authoritative on the point, limits protection from attack to a person 'who is recognized or who, in the circumstances, should be recognized to be *hors de combat*'. The paragraph continues: 'if surrender is offered in good faith and circumstances do not preclude enforcement, then surrender must be accepted.' This, as was noted in relation to the corresponding discussion in Chapter V, does not correctly reflect the applicable law. While good faith is essential in all non-hostile communications between belligerents, the relevant legal issues are whether an intent to surrender has been clearly expressed and whether the person concerned should be recognised as being *hors de combat*. If it has, if in the circumstances he or she should, if he or she performs no hostile act and if he or she makes no attempt to escape, then he or she must not be made the object of attack. The ability to enforce, by which presumably is meant the ability to detain the surrendering personnel and their equipment, is not the relevant issue.

The concern is that this sentence in paragraph 14.8.2 may create an unfortunate and legally incorrect impression in the minds of some readers that if detention of persons clearly expressing an intent to surrender is not immediately practical in the circumstances, then the persons concerned may nevertheless be attacked. It is suggested that the paragraph be amended to exclude such a possible misunderstanding.

The next sentence states that persons who are conducting attacks against enemy military aircraft must assess in good faith and on the basis of available information whether surrender is being offered in good faith and can feasibly be accepted. For obvious reasons, this sentence requires similar adjustments to those discussed in the previous paragraph. Moreover, if the persons in control of the enemy military aircraft do not clearly express an intention to surrender and should not otherwise be recognised as *hors de combat*, the persons conducting attacks may and should, absent any other lawful impediment, prosecute their attack. Military aircraft, whether disabled or otherwise, can still pose a grave danger to persons and objects of the adverse party.

As paragraph 14.8.2.1 explains, there are likely to be considerable difficulties in determining whether persons on board a military aircraft are *hors de combat*. Uncertainty as to whether the aircraft has been disabled and no longer poses a threat and difficulty in knowing whether an adversary is attempting to surrender are noted as examples. Perhaps, rather than referring to the aircraft no longer posing a threat, it would have been better to refer to the difficulty in knowing the status of the persons on board, e.g. as being unconscious, incapacitated by wounds or otherwise incapable of defending themselves, as these are circumstances that would cause them to be classed as *hors de combat*.

Having noted some acts sometimes cited as indications of an aircrew's desire to surrender, the paragraph concludes, rightly in the view of the present authors, that 'absent an explicit message . . . an intention to surrender cannot be presumed from the conduct of the aircraft'.

Paragraph 14.8.2.2 makes the point that in many circumstances it may not be possible to accept the surrender of enemy aircraft, e.g. when the engagement is over enemy territory, which is of course correct. One cannot help thinking, however, that it would have been better if the *Manual* had cited rules 128 to 130 of the *AMW Manual* on this topic. Rule 129 explains that a 'Belligerent Party may insist on the surrender by an enemy military aircraft being effected in a prescribed mode, reasonable in the circumstances. Failure to follow any such instructions may render the aircraft and the aircrews liable to attack.' Most relevantly, rule 130 explains: 'Aircrews of military aircraft wishing to surrender may, in certain circumstances, have to parachute from the aircraft in order to communicate their intentions.' In short, once the intention to surrender has been clearly expressed, individuals who comply with the remaining requirements of Article 41 of API are *hors de combat* and must not be made the object of attack. It is the circumstances that will determine whether the intention has been clearly expressed, bearing in mind that a pilot who in air-to-air combat remains in his or her aircraft cannot be said to have laid down his or her arms or no longer to have means of defence. To make the issue even clearer, it would be useful for the *Manual* to point out that an indication of a wish to surrender is not synonymous with the clear expression of that intent.

Paragraph 14.8.3 notes that civil aircraft may become military objectives and thus liable to be attacked outside neutral territory. To be pedantic, the paragraph might usefully add 'or neutral airspace'. Paragraph 14.8.3.1 points out that in peacetime, customary law requires States to refrain from the use of weapons against civil aircraft in flight, subject to the rights and obligations of States in the UN Charter, including the inherent right of self-defence. Persuasive authorities are cited in support of the customary nature of this rule.[19] Somewhat irritatingly, paragraph 14.8.3.2 simply repeats the contents of paragraph 14.8.3. The paragraph then suggests that enemy civil aircraft lose their protection from being attacked 'if they acquire the character of enemy military aircraft by' taking direct part in the hostilities or acting as a naval or military auxiliary. Perhaps the problem with this sentence is the term 'acquire the character of'. To be a military aircraft, the platform in question must comply with the definition in AMW, rule 1(x) to which reference was made earlier. A civil aircraft will not do so, and its employment in the hostilities or use in an auxiliary role does not change that. It would be better for the *Manual* to refer to civil aircraft being used for military purposes, and to use the two situations as an explanation of such military use.

The paragraph then addresses the additional circumstances that cause an enemy civil aircraft to forfeit protection from attack, namely persistent refusal to comply with instructions from intercepting military aircraft, flying under convoy of enemy warships or military aircraft, being armed beyond the requirements of self-defence against piracy, terrorism etc., being incorporated into or assisting the enemy's military intelligence system or otherwise being integrated into the enemy's war-fighting or war-sustaining effort. In the opinion of the present authors, it would have been better if the *Manual* had followed the approach in rule 27 of the *AMW Manual* by stating that certain listed activities may render a civil aircraft a military objective, thereby tying the liability to be attacked to the fact that the relevant aircraft has become a military objective. Taking the *Manual*'s cited examples in turn, the refusal to comply with instructions does not have to be persistent, so that word should be deleted. The presumption is that civil aircraft flying under convoy or escorted

[19] See *DoD Manual*, footnote 120 on page 918.

by military aircraft will refuse to comply with instructions, but that presumption is rebuttable, and the circumstances may make it clear that the escorted aircraft will indeed so comply.[20] The final element accurately reflects the US 'war-sustaining' approach to the definition of military objectives, discussed in Chapter V of the *Manual* and in Chapter 5 of this book, but it should be noted that the customary position, as reflected in rule 27(e) of the AMW *Manual*, refers to otherwise making an effective contribution to military action, and this should therefore be reflected in the *Manual*'s text.

Paragraph 14.8.3.3 notes that any attack of a civilian passenger aircraft that has become a military objective must comply with other applicable rules relating to attack, quoting the proportionality rule in this regard. This very limited observation does not, in the view of the present authors, give this topic the prominence that its importance warrants. One would have thought that a great deal more could and should have been written on the subject, such as giving explicit guidance on the factors to be considered and as to the practical application in such circumstances of the precautionary rules.

AIR ATTACKS AGAINST MILITARY OBJECTIVES ON THE GROUND

Paragraph 14.9.1 correctly states that the aerial bombardment of towns, villages, dwellings or buildings that are undefended is prohibited and that this prohibition applies to attack from the air. This prohibition is discussed in Chapter 5 of this book and further consideration is not required here. Paragraph 14.9.2 correctly explains that the selection of the weapon suitable for conducting an aerial bombardment is primarily a military judgment. The paragraph ought, however, to have pointed out that legal considerations may limit the options that can legitimately be considered when making that military judgment, and that much will inevitably depend on the circumstances relevant to the particular attack. The paragraph then correctly notes, in somewhat circular terms, that there is no general law of war obligation to use precision-guided munitions. It follows this up with the comment that commanders have the general obligation to take feasible precautions in attack to reduce the risk of harm to the civilian population, noting correctly that weapon selection may be among those feasible precautions.

Paragraph 14.9.3 deals with the protection of enemy ground forces who are *hors de combat*. The paragraph correctly states that when aircrew or aircraft operators assess that enemy combatants are *hors de combat*, they must refrain from making them the object of attack. That statement is true as far as it

[20] AMW *Manual*, paragraph 2 of the Commentary accompanying rule 27(d).

goes, but it does not, arguably, go far enough. As was pointed out earlier, this protective obligation also favours those who should be recognised to be *hors de combat*. This involves an obligation for planners, attack decision makers and those conducting attacks to consider all available information and to do everything feasible to determine whether the persons concerned are indeed *hors de combat*. It is suggested that this aspect should be added to the relevant text.

Paragraph 14.9.3 suggests that for a person to be *hors de combat*, their surrender must be genuine, clear and unconditional, and given under circumstances where it is feasible for the opposing party to accept it. These matters have already been discussed earlier in the present chapter, and it suffices to note that Article 41 of API makes no reference to genuineness, and that in the haste and the sometimes fraught circumstances that tend to accompany surrenders, those receiving the surrender are likely to be ill-equipped to determine whether it is 'genuine'. The applicable law tends to focus on the actions required of, and prohibited to, surrendering personnel, not on what may or may not have been passing through their minds at the relevant time. The 'clear and unconditional' aspect mentioned in the *Manual* is reflected in the requirement clearly to express the intent to surrender. Article 41 – and, it is submitted, the underlying customary law – includes no requirement as to the feasibility of accepting that surrender.[21]

The final section of the paragraph is right to observe, as was explained earlier in this chapter, that in order to facilitate surrender, it may be appropriate in some circumstances to communicate steps the enemy units should take to show clearly their intent to surrender. Failure to undertake such action will suggest that no such intent exists, or that there is no such continuing intent.

The difficulties confronting aircrew attempting to determine whether persons on the ground are dead, injured, taking cover etc., and those confronting persons on the ground seeking to communicate that they are incapacitated or wish to surrender, are properly mentioned in paragraph 14.9.3.1.

Paragraph 14.9.3.2 addresses the vexed question of the feasibility of air units accepting the surrender of ground forces. The US view is again stated that for a surrender communication to place a person *hors de combat*, 'the person must make the surrender under circumstances where it is feasible for the opposing

[21] Paragraph 5 of the Commentary to rule 125 of the AMW *Manual* puts it rather well: 'Thus, the obligation on the part of the Belligerent Party is not necessarily to detain surrendering enemy personnel, but to desist from further attack on persons complying with the conditions'; that is, persons who are communicating the intention to surrender in a clear manner, not engaging in any further hostile acts and making no attempt to evade capture; AMW *Manual*, rule 127.

party to accept the surrender'. This observation is not accepted by the present authors as being a correct reflection of the law. The contention in the *Manual* that it must be possible for the opposing party to take the person into custody suggests that in the US view, surrender is not possible as a matter of law in certain circumstances. The correct legal position is that it is always open to a combatant under the law of war to communicate an intention to surrender and to take whatever action may be required in order to bring that intent to fruition.

INTERNATIONAL LAW AND WARFARE IN OUTER SPACE

Paragraph 14.10.1 correctly points out that differing legal regimes apply respectively to airspace and outer space, observing that no State has sovereignty over outer space and that space systems of all nations have rights of passage through outer space without interference. Paragraph 14.10.2.1 correctly notes that the Outer Space Treaty[22] does not exclude military space vehicles from its provisions and that it provides for State responsibility for the activities of non-governmental entities in outer space.[23] Other treaties addressing outer space are listed, and the point is made that some of their provisions may not be applicable as between belligerents during an international armed conflict. Unfortunately, no list is offered of the provisions that in the US view would, or respectively would not, be so applicable.

Paragraph 14.10.2.2 notes the provision in Article III of the Outer Space Treaty that requires States party to carry on their activities in the exploration and use of outer space in accordance with international law, including the UN Charter, 'in the interest of maintaining international peace and security and promoting international cooperation and understanding'. Of course, as the paragraph points out, as notions of sovereignty do not apply in outer space, the international law that prescribes conditions for national claims to it also does not apply. The *Manual* correctly suggests that 'the application of the law of war to activities in outer space is the same as its application to activities in other environments'.

Having drawn attention to the ban on nuclear weapon test explosions in outer space, as provided for in the Limited Test Ban Treaty,[24] paragraph 14.10.3.1 quotes the undertaking by States party to the Outer Space Treaty not

[22] Treaty on Principles Governing the Activities of States in the Exploration and Use of Outer Space, including the Moon and Other Celestial Bodies, 27 January 1967, 610 UNTS 205.

[23] See Outer Space Treaty, Article VI.

[24] Treaty Banning Nuclear Weapon Tests in the Atmosphere, Outer Space and Under Water, 5 August 1963, 480 UNTS 43, Article 1.

to 'place in orbit around the Earth any objects carrying nuclear weapons or any other kinds of weapons of mass destruction, install such weapons on celestial bodies, or station such weapons in outer space in any other manner'.[25] The *Manual* accurately notes that the prohibition does not extend to nuclear weapons or weapons of mass destruction that only go into fractional orbit or that engage in suborbital flight, citing intercontinental ballistic missiles as an example. The paragraph then observes that some arms control treaties have prohibited the production, testing or deployment of systems that place such weapons either in full orbit or in a fraction of an orbit, giving a treaty between the US and the USSR of 31 July 1991 (since expired) as an example. The quoted rule does not apply to weapons other than weapons of mass destruction.

As paragraph 14.10.3.2 correctly reports, Article IV of the Outer Space Treaty also prohibits the establishment of military bases, installations and fortifications, the testing of any type of weapons and the conduct of military manoeuvres on the moon and other celestial bodies, but not in outer space as such. The same article also recognises the 'unimpeded right to: (1) the use of military personnel for scientific research or other peaceful purposes on outer space missions, and (2) the use of any equipment or facility necessary for the peaceful exploration of the moon and other celestial bodies'.

Consistently with the Preamble to the Outer Space Treaty, paragraph 14.10.4 gives the US view that outer space should only be used for peaceful purposes, meaning, again in the US view, '"non-aggressive and beneficial" purposes consistent with the Charter of the United Nations and other international law'.[26] The important part of this discussion in the *Manual* lies in the examples of activities that are considered by the US as coming within the 'peaceful purposes' descriptor. So, observation and information gathering from satellites in space are, the *Manual* states, not acts of aggression under the UN Charter and thus would be uses of space for peaceful purposes. Equally, lawful military activities in self-defence, such as missile early warning or, interestingly, use of weapon systems, would be consistent with 'peaceful purposes', in the US view, but activities that violate the UN Charter would not be permissible. The paragraph draws attention to the provision in Article IV of the Outer Space Treaty that restricts the use of the moon and other celestial bodies 'exclusively for peaceful purposes'. The restrictions on the military activities there have already been discussed in relation to paragraph 14.10.3.2.

[25] Outer Space Treaty, Article IV.

[26] As the paragraph comments, this interpretation of 'peaceful purposes' is similar to that given by the US in relation to the Law of the Sea Convention.

Paragraph 14.10.5 refers to Article IX of the Outer Space Treaty's reference to the principle of cooperation and mutual assistance and to the obligation for States party to conduct their activities in outer space with due regard to the corresponding interests of all other States party. Relevant rights include the right for States to have their space systems pass through, and conduct operations in, space without interference. The same article requires a State party to conduct appropriate international consultations before proceeding with activities or experiments planned by it or its nationals that it has reason to believe would cause potentially harmful interference with the activities of other States in the peaceful use of outer space. Conversely, if a State party has reason to believe that a planned outer space activity or experiment of another State party will harmfully interfere with its peaceful activities in outer space, that State has the right to request consultation as to the activity or experiment.

CONCLUDING REMARKS

This chapter deals with its assigned topic somewhat cursorily, even inadequately. There is in the airspace part of the chapter, for example, little or no explicit discussion of what is one of the most important contemporary applications of air power, namely the use of remotely piloted aircraft. There is, likewise, little or no discussion of emerging technologies in this sphere, such as the use of automation in the processing of data from sensors or in target identification, acquisition and prosecution, nor as to the prospective employment of autonomous systems. In the outer space part of the chapter, reference is made to Article III of the Outer Space Treaty, but there is little or inadequate discussion of which specific provisions of international law, e.g. of international weapons and targeting law, would thereby be rendered applicable in the outer space environment, nor of how they should be applied. Although the outer space part of the chapter mentions the Liability, Rescue and Registration Conventions, no explanation is given of their provisions, nor of how they will apply in relation to armed conflict activities in outer space.

These inadequacies are all the more perplexing given the prominence of US activities in each of these environments. One is left with the impression that an opportunity for the US to drive forward legal understanding of these matters is either being lost, or at least is insufficiently grasped.

15

The Law of Neutrality

The law of neutrality is probably the one branch of the law of international armed conflict whose continuing applicability in the twenty-first century is unsettled, or at least highly controversial. Obviously, many States not actively participating in an ongoing international armed conflict no longer consider themselves bound to take an impartial stance vis-à-vis the parties to the conflict, or else they make the applicability of the law of neutrality dependent on conditions that they themselves determine. Some States claim they are bound by the law of neutrality only if there exists a state of war, in particular by virtue of a declaration of war (e.g. France), or if they have made a proclamation in which they declare themselves bound by the law of neutrality (e.g. Sweden). Others consider themselves entitled to openly discriminate between the belligerents by taking a position of 'benevolent' neutrality (e.g. Italy). The divergence of positions may be explained by the fact that during the (few) international armed conflicts of recent decades, the aggrieved belligerents were simply unable militarily or otherwise to respond to, or terminate, violations of the law of neutrality. Probably, neutral States will similarly get away with violations of their duties of abstention and impartiality in future international armed conflicts. If, however, the aggrieved belligerent is willing and able to take responsive measures to terminate violations of neutral obligations, neutral States will have severe difficulties in condemning its responsive actions as violating international law.

The authors of the *DoD Manual* are to be congratulated for having devoted considerable space to the law of neutrality and for having emphasised its continuing validity and applicability in international armed conflicts of a certain duration and intensity. The scope of the chapter, which comprises sixty-five pages, seems to be reflective of the legal, practical and political importance the DoD attaches to that law.

While comment is required on some of the provisions, e.g. the rather vague statements as to its applicability, the chapter is a comprehensive and very detailed restatement of the law of neutrality. Apparently, the US DoD has made a strong commitment to that effect. The provisions of the 1907 Hague Conventions V and XIII,[1] the 1909 London Declaration[2] and the regional 1928 Havana Convention[3] have been almost entirely incorporated, and thus have been recognised as still applicable. This is a laudable approach, because those rules – or at least the essential rules on neutrality – are designed to ensure – and are capable of ensuring – the very object and purpose of the law of neutrality, i.e. the prevention of an escalation of an international armed conflict. There is, however, also a negative aspect. The authors of the chapter have almost slavishly taken the traditional rules as given, and thus sometimes ignore the developments that have occurred since their adoption, which have had a considerable impact on the law in this area. This holds particularly true for the provisions of the 1909 London Declaration on unneutral service. The conduct of neutral merchant vessels considered by the London Declaration as rendering them liable to capture and condemnation will today be considered as rendering them liable to attack as military objectives.

This misperception may be due to the fact that, as in other chapters of the *Manual*, the drafters have not taken into consideration and made use of the *San Remo Manual* or *AMW Manual*.[4] Similarly ignored are the Helsinki Principles on Maritime Neutrality[5] and the provisions of the 1923 Hague Draft Rules of Aerial Warfare,[6] which deal with neutral airspace and neutral aircraft in times of war. This is unfortunate, and does not necessarily serve US interests. Of course, those manuals and draft rules are not binding *per se*, but they are important restatements of the international law applicable to both

[1] Convention (V) Respecting the Rights and Duties of Neutral Powers and Persons in Case of War on Land, The Hague (18 October 1907), 2 AJIL Suppl. 117–27 (1908) and Convention (XIII) Concerning the Rights and Duties of Neutral Powers in Naval War, The Hague (18 October 1907), 2 AJIL Suppl. 202–16 (1908).

[2] The Declaration of London (26 February 1909), printed in J Brown Scott (ed.) *A Collection of Official Papers and Documents Relating to the International Naval Conference Held in London December, 1908–February, 1909*. London: International Naval Conference (1919).

[3] Convention on Maritime Neutrality, Havana (20 February 1928), 135 LNTS 187. Note that, in Chapter XV, the Havana Convention is also referred to as '1928 Pan American Maritime Neutrality Convention'. The authors should use a single title.

[4] *AMW Manual*, section U, rules 134–46.

[5] International Law Association, Helsinki Principles on the Law of Maritime Neutrality, Final Report of the Committee on Maritime Neutrality, International Law Association, Report of the 68th Conference, Taipei (1998).

[6] Reprinted in 17 AJIL Suppl. 245–60 (1923). See also the Commentary on the 1923 Hague Rules in 32 AJIL Suppl. 12–56 (1938).

belligerent and neutral States that have been widely endorsed.[7] Since the two manuals and the Helsinki Principles support many of the provisions identified in Chapter XV, reference to them – which may not be mistaken as a formal endorsement – would have contributed to the *Manual*'s credibility.

INTRODUCTION

Surprisingly, parts of the introduction are phrased very cautiously. In particular, the doubts expressed in the chapeau of the section as to the customary nature of the 1907 Hague Conventions V and XIII are inappropriate because, as already mentioned, the chapter heavily relies on those and other treaties that 'were formulated long ago'. Therefore, there should have been a clear and unambiguous recognition of the continuing validity and applicability of those instruments. The alleged 'implications of more recent treaties', which may prevail over the law of neutrality, can merely be acknowledged insofar as the UN Charter is concerned (which is referred to as but one example). If the DoD believes that other treaties have similar effects to the UN Charter, the authors should have provided at least one more example.

The general description of the law of neutrality in paragraph 15.1.1 is correct. However, one wonders why the authors have identified 'certain rules found in the law of neutrality' as applying to a 'State's duties to prevent a non-State armed group's use of its territory for hostile expeditions against another State'. Those duties, although similar, must be strictly distinguished from those applicable to neutral States in times of an international armed conflict. According to general international law and the principle of sovereignty a State may not 'allow knowingly its territory to be used for acts contrary to the rights of other States'.[8] If the territorial State is either unwilling or unable to comply with that obligation, e.g. by terminating attacks by non-State actors against another State, the victim State is entitled to exercise its right of individual or collective self-defence extraterritorially, i.e. within the territory of the State from which the attacks are launched, provided the measures taken are limited to the non-State armed group. Those rules exclusively belong to the *jus ad bellum* and cannot be regarded as being part of the law of neutrality.

The classification of States in paragraph 15.1.2 is correct insofar as they qualify as either belligerent States or as neutral States. According to both the *San*

7 See *Canadian Manual*, ch. 13; *German Manual*, ch. 12. The *UK Manual* does not address the law of neutrality in a separate chapter, but does discuss it extensively in chs 1, 12 and 13.

8 ICJ, *The Corfu Channel Case* (Merits), *United Kingdom* v. *Albania*, Judgment of 9 April 1949, ICJ Rep. 1949, 4–38, at 22.

Remo Manual and the AMW *Manual*, the term 'neutral State' means 'any State not party to the conflict'.[9] The fact that in the 1949 Geneva Conventions, the term 'non-belligerent Power' is used may not be understood as a recognition of an intermediate status. That term was used as a compromise formulation because the delegates were unwilling to provide statements as to the continuing validity of the law of neutrality. It is, of course, true that the term 'non-belligerent' has been used for States that 'refrain from active participation in hostilities, but that did not adhere to the duties of strict impartiality'. This was, and continues to be, a highly controversial position,[10] as rightly stated at the end of the paragraph. Therefore, a clear recognition or rejection of the concept would have been more than helpful. The fact that the concept of 'qualified neutrality' is recognised in paragraph 15.2.2 is not necessarily sufficient evidence of an endorsement of an intermediate legal status of 'non-belligerency', particularly because different terms have been used. Qualified neutrality is a position a neutral State may undoubtedly take if one party to an international armed conflict has been authoritatively identified by the UN Security Council as the aggressor – a rather rare situation (see later).

The identification of the object and purpose of the law of neutrality in paragraph 15.1.3 is a bit confusing, because the law does not 'permit' States 'to avoid taking sides'. Rather, it obliges neutral States to remain impartial. The true object and purpose, i.e. preventing an escalation of an international armed conflict, is, however, correctly identified in the subsequent two sentences of the paragraph.

Paragraph 15.1.4 is rather disappointing. Seemingly, the continuing validity and applicability of the treaties on neutrality are doubted, although, as already mentioned, the rules of Chapter XV are almost entirely based on those treaties. It is, of course, true that in view of their dates of adoption, they may not always literally apply to 'current factual circumstances'. Still, it is safe to hold that in most respects, those treaties are reflective of customary international law.[11]

[9] *San Remo Manual*, paragraph 13(d); AMW *Manual*, rule 1(aa). See also *Canadian Manual*, paragraph 1302; *German Manual*, paragraph 1201; *UK Manual*, paragraph 13.5(m).

[10] For an analysis of the validity of benevolent neutrality or non-belligerency, see W Heintschel von Heinegg, 'Benevolent' Third States during International Armed Conflicts: The Myth of the Irrelevance of the Law of Neutrality, in: M N Schmitt and J Pejic (eds) *International Law and Armed Conflict: Exploring the Faultlines, Essays in Honour of Yoram Dinstein*. Leiden: Brill (2007), 543–68.

[11] See the references in note 8 of the present chapter. See also the Helsinki Principles; Articles 39ff. of the 1923 Hague Rules of Aerial Warfare; *San Remo Manual*, paragraphs 14ff., 112ff.; AMW *Manual*, sections U (rules 134ff.) and X (rules 165ff.).

APPLICATION OF THE LAW OF NEUTRALITY

The first sentence of the chapeau of section 15.2 may be understood as granting States the right to leave it to their national policies to determine whether and to what extent the law of neutrality is binding upon them. This, however, only holds true for their decision either to actively take part in an international armed conflict or to abstain from such participation. It is a correct statement as to the contemporary international law that the obligations under the UN Charter may significantly modify the rights and duties under the law of neutrality. We will return to that aspect later.

Paragraph 15.2.1 correctly describes the various situations in which the law of neutrality is or is not applicable. As rightly stated in paragraph 15.2.1.1, there is no room for neutral obligations if a State decides to join the armed conflict. The recognition of a state of war or of the existence of an international armed conflict by the belligerents is without prejudice to a State's right to rely on the law of neutrality. Interestingly, recognition of belligerency of a rebel faction in a non-international armed conflict is regarded as a concept that is still valid and that will trigger the applicability of the law of international armed conflict and, therefore, of the law of neutrality.

The limitation in paragraph 15.2.1.2 of the law's applicability to international armed conflicts of a 'certain duration and intensity' is also recognised by other States.[12] It is important to note that the *Manual* does not entirely exclude the applicability of the law of neutrality to international armed conflicts of a limited duration and intensity. Instead, it emphasises the obligation of belligerents to respect the sovereignty of neutral States 'in all international armed conflicts', and thus recognises that the essential rules of the law of neutrality will apply irrespective of the duration and intensity of an international armed conflict. The importance of that recognition, which is also shared by the ICJ,[13] the *San Remo Manual* and the AMW *Manual*,[14] must not be underestimated.

The recognition in paragraph 15.2.1.3 of the application of certain rules in the law of neutrality outside the context of an international armed conflict is, according to the position taken here, based on an erroneous understanding of the *jus ad bellum* on the one hand and the law of neutrality on the other. The obligation to respect the sovereignty of other States and the prohibition to

[12] *German Manual*, paragraph 1202.

[13] ICJ, Legality of the Threat or Use of Nuclear Weapons, Advisory Opinion of 8 July 1996, ICJ Rep. 1996, 226, at 260ff.

[14] *San Remo Manual*, paragraph 13(d); AMW *Manual*, rule 1(aa). See also *Canadian Manual*, paragraph 1303(1).

intervene, on the side of the non-State actor, into a non-international armed conflict are parts of the *jus ad bellum*, not of the law of neutrality.

As already stated, in paragraph 15.2.2, the *Manual* recognises the concept of qualified neutrality, which may not be confused with non-belligerency or benevolent neutrality.[15] While the latter concepts are but poor excuses for a violation of the duties of abstention and impartiality, there is not much room left for a neutral stance if one party to an international armed conflict has been identified as the aggressor. The concept of 'qualified neutrality' would allow a State abstaining from active participation in the hostilities to 'discriminate' in favour of the victim State.[16] However, the practical relevance of the concept is limited to situations in which the UN Security Council has authoritatively identified the aggressor State by a (binding) decision based on Chapter VII of the UN Charter. Without such identification, it is almost impossible to identify the aggressor and the victim of aggression. In the Falklands/Malvinas War (1982) and in the Iran–Iraq War (1980–88), both parties to the respective conflicts claimed to be the victims of aggression and to be exercising their inherent right of self-defence.

The relationship between the law of neutrality and the UN Charter has been correctly described in paragraph 15.2.3, which also reflects customary international law. For instance, the *San Remo Manual* provides: 'Where, in the course of an international armed conflict, the Security Council has taken preventive or enforcement measures under Chapter VII of the Charter, Member States of the United Nations may not rely upon the law of neutrality to justify conduct which would be incompatible with their obligations under the Charter or under decisions of the Security Council.'[17]

Paragraph 15.2.3.1, on the consistency between the law of neutrality and the UN Charter, is, again, based upon an erroneous understanding of the relationship between the two bodies of law, which should be strictly distinguished.[18]

[15] See note 11. See also Colombos, *International Law of the Sea*, 627ff.; E Castrén, *The Present Law of War and Neutrality*. Helsinki: Suomalaisen Seuran Kirjapainon Oy (1954), 448ff.

[16] See also *San Remo Manual*, paragraph 7: 'Notwithstanding any rules in this document or elsewhere on the law of neutrality, where the Security Council, acting in accordance with its powers under Chapter VII of the Charter of the United Nations, has identified one or more parties to an armed conflict as responsible for resorting to force in violation of international law, neutral States: (a) are bound not to lend assistance other than humanitarian assistance to that State; *and* (b) may lend assistance to any State which has been the victim of a breach of the peace or an act of aggression by that State.'

[17] *San Remo Manual*, paragraph 8. For an identical statement, see also *AMW Manual*, rule 165.

[18] The *jus ad bellum* regulates the legality of a State's resort to a use of force, individual or collective self-defence and military enforcement measures under Chapter VII of the UN Charter.

Paragraph 15.2.4 characterises the obligations of States under (regional) systems of collective self-defence as prevailing over the obligations under the law of neutrality. This is not necessarily a correct legal assessment. Rather, membership in a system of collective self-defence, such as NATO, is a political decision in advance on action being contemplated that would preclude neutral status due to the absence of abstention and impartiality. Hence, the obligations under the system do not prevail in a legal sense over neutral obligations.

OVERVIEW OF THE LAW OF NEUTRALITY'S FRAMEWORK OF RECIPROCAL RIGHTS AND DUTIES

It may be doubted whether the overview given in section 15.3 is necessary and adequate in a manual that is designed to provide guidance to political and operational decision makers, because most of the matters dealt with in this section are elaborated upon in subsequent sections. Be that as it may. The summaries of neutral rights in paragraph 15.3.1 and of neutral duties in paragraph 15.3.2 correctly reflect the respective provisions of the 1907 Hague Conventions V and XIII and of the 1928 Havana Convention, as well as customary international law.[19]

Paragraph 15.3.3 is particularly useful in that it perfectly describes the 'correlative or reciprocal nature' of the rights and duties applicable to neutrals and belligerents, which assists those who may not be familiar with the law of neutrality to better understand the nature of that branch of the law of international armed conflict.

REMEDIES FOR VIOLATIONS OF NEUTRALITY LAW

It is rightly held in paragraph 15.4.1 that a violation of the law of neutrality must be distinguished from the termination of the law's applicability. Indeed, a neutral State's violation of its duties of abstention and impartiality must be of such gravity as to justify the conclusion that the neutral State has become a party to the conflict.

If States decide to refrain from a use of force against another State or from directly participating in an ongoing armed conflict, they are complying with their obligations under the UN Charter, not under the law of neutrality.

[19] 1907 Hague Convention V, Articles 1ff.; 1907 Hague Convention XIII, Articles 1ff.; Havana Convention, Articles 3ff.; *San Remo Manual*, paragraphs 14ff.; *AMW Manual*, rules 166ff.; *Canadian Manual*, paragraphs 1304ff.; Colombos, *International Law of the Sea*, 650ff. See also Castrén, *Present Law of War*, 439ff.

According to paragraph 15.4.2, a belligerent is entitled to resort to self-help if a neutral State is either unwilling or unable to 'prevent violations of its neutrality'. The right of the aggrieved belligerent to resort to self-help – or, rather, to enforce the law of neutrality in lieu of the unwilling or unable neutral State – only comes into operation if a violation has in fact occurred. Hence, the neutral State is only obliged to terminate a violation of neutrality. The duty of prevention recognised in Article 8 of the 1907 Hague Convention XIII exclusively applies to the fitting out or arming of belligerent warships and to their departure from neutral territory. Moreover, the right of self-help may be exercised only (1) after prior notification of the violation, (2) if an adequate period of time is given to terminate the violation, (3) if no feasible and timely alternative exists and (4) most importantly, if the gravity of the violation is sufficient to justify the exercise of jurisdiction in foreign territory.[20]

If necessary, a neutral State may terminate a violation of its neutrality by resorting to a use of proportionate force. According to Article 10 of the 1907 Hague Convention V, such responses 'cannot be regarded as hostile acts' and thus are not violations of the duties of abstention and impartiality.[21] This is correctly reflected in paragraph 15.4.3. However, the neutral State's actions in defending its neutrality should not be characterised as a form of self-help, because that is a primary obligation incumbent upon the neutral State.

PROHIBITION ON THE USE OF NEUTRAL TERRITORY AS A BASE OF OPERATIONS

The prohibition of the use of neutral territory as a base of operations is expressly stated in Article 5 of the 1907 Hague Convention XIII and follows from the general inviolability of neutral territory under Article 1 of the 1907 Hague Convention V, which also prohibits other belligerent activities in neutral territory. The examples provided in the chapeau of section 15.5 are illustrative and helpful.

The provisions of section 15.5 are, as already mentioned, almost literally based on the 1907 Hague Conventions V and XIII, which, according to the position taken here, are reflective of customary international law.[22] Even if

[20] *San Remo Manual*, paragraph 22.

[21] See also 1907 Hague Convention XIII, Article 26; 1923 Hague Rules of Aerial Warfare, Article 48; *AMW Manual*, rule 169.

[22] *Canadian Manual*, paragraph 1304; *UK Manual*, paragraphs 13.8ff.; *German Manual*, paragraphs 1205ff.; *San Remo Manual*, paragraphs 15ff.; *AMW Manual*, rules 166ff. See also 1923 Hague Rules of Aerial Warfare, Articles 39ff.; Colombos, *International Law of the Sea*, 650ff.; Castrén, *Present Law of War*, 458ff., 494ff., 587ff.

some doubts remain as to whether the US DoD is prepared to share that classification, section 15.5 is a remarkable and important commitment to those treaties. References are also made to the prohibitions and obligations under Articles 2–5 and 9 of the 1907 Hague Convention V and under Articles 1, 5, 6, 8 and 18 of the 1907 Hague Convention XIII. In the context of the prohibition under Article 3 of the 1907 Hague Convention V concerning the erection and use of 'wireless telegraphy or other apparatus for the purpose of communicating with belligerent forces on land or sea', it would have been helpful had the chapter's authors explained how, in their view, this applies to modern communications technology and whether the exception under Article 8 of the 1907 Hague Convention V applies to communications via cyberspace.[23]

Section 15.5 also makes reference to the exceptions provided for under Articles 6 to 8 of the 1907 Hague Convention V and Article 7 of the 1907 Hague Convention XIII. Article 2 of the 1907 Hague Convention V, which prohibits the movement of troops and of war supplies across neutral territory, has been correctly interpreted as not applying to an authorised passage of the wounded and sick through neutral territory or to the overflight of certain medical aircraft.[24]

NEUTRAL PERSONS

Section 15.6 on neutral nationals is based on Articles 16 to 18 of the 1907 Hague Convention V and on the 1949 GC. Their protected status depends upon whether they refrain from direct participation in the hostilities, as described and limited in Articles 17 and 18 of the 1907 Hague Convention V. The treatment of neutral nationals who are no longer considered protected neutral persons is subject to the limitations identified in paragraph 15.6.2.1.

It would have been helpful had the section been amended to include a short paragraph on individuals with dual citizenship of a neutral State and of the enemy belligerent State. Evidently, dual citizenship was not considered an issue in 1907. Today, however, the number of individuals with dual citizenship has increased considerably.

Paragraph 15.6.3 rightly excludes from the category of protected persons under GC nationals of neutral States which continue to have normal diplomatic relations with the respective belligerent. This correctly reflects Article 4(2) GC.

23 See, *inter alia*, *Tallinn Manual 2.0*, rule 151 and accompanying Commentary.
24 See also *Canadian Manual*, paragraph 1308.

The status of neutral nationals in occupied territory and of neutral nationals having fallen into the hands of the Occupying Power is correctly identified in paragraph 15.6.4. The same holds true for the status of the diplomatic and consular staff (paragraph 15.6.4.2).

NEUTRAL WATERS

Section 15.7 on belligerent uses of neutral waters almost entirely relies on the respective provisions of the 1907 Hague Convention XIII. Accordingly, belligerents are prohibited to use neutral ports and waters 'as a base of naval operations',[25] or to make use of them 'for replenishing or increasing their supplies of war material or their armaments, or for completing their crews'.[26] The exercise of belligerent rights (e.g. conducting hostilities or taking prize measures) in neutral waters is prohibited by Articles 1 and 2 of the 1907 Hague Convention XIII and customary international law.[27] According to Article 25 of that Convention, neutral States are obliged to 'exercise such surveillance as the means at [their] disposal allow to prevent any violation' of their waters and ports. It is important to note that according to the chapeau of section 15.7, the obligations incumbent on neutral States have been identified as being stricter than those under the 1907 Hague Convention XIII. According to the *Manual*, a neutral State is said to have an 'affirmative duty to police its waters to prevent violations of neutrality in its waters'. It may, however, not be left out of consideration that many coastal States, particularly archipelagic States, can hardly be held responsible for something they are incapable of accomplishing. This is particularly so because, according to the *Manual*, any failure by the neutral State to 'detect and expel belligerent forces unlawfully present in its waters' is considered sufficient to bring into operation the aggrieved belligerent's right of self-help. In this context, it may be recalled that measures of self-help are not justified by any failure of a neutral State to terminate a violation of its neutrality.[28]

The definition of 'neutral waters' in paragraph 15.7.1 is reflective of the current state of the law of maritime neutrality, because it includes archipelagic waters and excludes contiguous and exclusive economic zones, which are not

[25] 1907 Hague Convention XIII, Article 5; *San Remo Manual*, paragraph 16(b); *UK Manual*, paragraph 13.9; German *Manual*, paragraph 1215.

[26] 1907 Hague Convention XIII, Article 18; *San Remo Manual*, paragraph 20; *German Manual*, paragraph 1224ff.

[27] *San Remo Manual*, paragraphs 15ff.; *UK Manual*, paragraphs 138ff.; *German Manual*, paragraph 1216.

[28] See *San Remo Manual*, paragraph 22.

covered by the territorial sovereignty of the coastal or archipelagic State.[29] The chapter's authors should have amended that paragraph with a short statement on excessive maritime claims by the neutral State. The mere reference to the maximum breadth of the territorial sea being twelve nautical miles is not sufficient to also cover cases of excessive baselines.[30]

The subsequent paragraphs on the right of neutral coastal States to prohibit or otherwise regulate uses of their ports, roadsteads and waters by belligerent warships or of their prizes (paragraph 15.7.2), on the twenty-four-hour rule (paragraph 15.7.3) and on the passage of belligerent warships through neutral waters (paragraph 15.7.4) reproduce the respective rules of the 1907 Hague Convention[31] and may be considered reflective of customary international law.[32] However, paragraph 15.7.3 should have been amended by two clarifications: (1) the twenty-four-hour rule may not apply in archipelagic waters, whose passage requires more than twenty-four hours; (2) although Article 14(2) of the 1907 Hague Convention XIII on exceptions applying to 'warships devoted exclusively to religious, scientific, or philanthropic purposes' has been correctly reproduced, there should have been a reference to Article 32 GWS-Sea on the stay of hospital ships in neutral ports. Moreover, it would have been helpful had those categories of belligerent warships been specified by concrete examples. The exclusion of warships 'engaged in the collection of scientific data of potential military application' is correct and will most probably result in a strict application of the twenty-four-hour rule and of the other restrictions to all warships engaged in scientific missions, because today it is almost impossible to distinguish between 'pure science' and scientific activities of a potential military value.

Interestingly, paragraph 15.7.4.1 preserves a belligerent right of distress entry for warships damaged by either *force majeure* or enemy action, even though the 1907 Hague Convention XIII does not provide for such an exception. The position taken here suggests that the US accepts as customary the intrinsically humanitarian rules applicable to vessels in distress.[33] The more so, since the right of distress entry is without prejudice to the obligation of the neutral State to intern the vessel and the crew. It may, however, be noted that many coastal

29 *UK Manual*, paragraph 13.7; *German Manual*, paragraph 1214; *San Remo Manual*, paragraph 14.

30 For an assessment of excessive straight baselines, see J A Roach and R W Smith, *Excessive Maritime Claims*, 3rd edn. Leiden: Brill (2012), 72ff.

31 1907 Hague Convention XIII, Articles 9ff.

32 *San Remo Manual*, paragraphs 19–21, 31–33; Castrén, *Present Law of War*, 514ff.; Colombos, *International Law of the Sea*, 650ff.; Helsinki Principles, paragraphs 2.2ff.

33 See also *German Manual*, paragraph 1229; Tucker, *Law of War*, 240.

States do not seem to recognise a right of distress entry either in times of peace or in times of war.

PASSAGE OF BELLIGERENT VESSELS AND AIRCRAFT THROUGH INTERNATIONAL STRAITS AND ARCHIPELAGIC SEA LANES

Section 15.8 is a necessary corollary to section 15.7. While a neutral coastal State is entitled to prohibit, on a non-discriminatory basis, the use of its territorial sea by belligerent warships and prizes[34] (e.g. by a suspension of the right of innocent passage for the duration of the international armed conflict), it is not allowed to suspend, hamper or otherwise impede the rights of transit passage and of archipelagic sea lane passage that continue to apply in times of international armed conflict.[35] Accordingly, it has been rightly emphasised that all ships and aircraft, including neutral vessels carrying contraband, continue to enjoy those special passage rights subject to the limitations identified in paragraphs 15.8.1 and 15.8.2.

SECTIONS 15.9 AND 15.10

Like the previous sections, section 15.9 on the 'additional rules applicable to neutral ports, roadsteads, and internal waters' is based on the respective provisions of the 1907 Hague Convention XIII[36] and on the corresponding rules of customary international law.[37]

Section 15.10 on neutral airspace could not be based on existing treaties (with the exception of the rules applicable to medical aircraft). Since, however, the territorial sovereignty of a neutral State extends to its national airspace, the provisions of section 15.10 can be considered as reflective of customary international law, which protects neutral airspace against belligerent uses, including entry by belligerent military aircraft.[38] Entry into neutral airspace is permissible only above international straits and archipelagic sea lanes and, arguably, by belligerent aircraft in distress. If a neutral State is either unwilling or unable to effectively respond to violations of its national airspace, the aggrieved belligerent is entitled to terminate the violation in lieu

34 See, *inter alia*, Castrén, *Present Law of War*, 494; *San Remo Manual*, paragraph 19.

35 *UK Manual*, paragraphs 13.10ff.; *San Remo Manual*, paragraphs 23–30; Helsinki Principles, paragraph 2.4.

36 1907 Hague Convention XIII, Articles 14 to 25.

37 *German Manual*, paragraphs 1223 ff.; *San Remo Manual*, paragraphs 19–21.

38 See also 1923 Hague Rules, Articles 39ff.

of the neutral State. Again, no limitations applying to measures of 'self-help' are recognised.[39]

RIGHT OF ANGARY

Somewhat surprisingly, section 15.11 recognises the belligerent right of angary. Although the belligerents of the two World Wars made extensive use of that right, most military manuals no longer deal with it. Hence, it would have been more than helpful to provide a definition of the right of angary and to distinguish it from (1) requisition of property in occupied territory and (2) capture and seizure of neutral vessels and cargoes under prize law.[40] Moreover, the legal basis of the right of angary should have been clearly identified. If the legal basis is the territorial sovereignty of the belligerent exercising this right, the scope of applicability will be strictly limited to its territory and national waters. Accordingly, the right of angary could not be exercised in occupied territory, because the mere exercise of jurisdiction would not be sufficient. In this context, it has been rightly held that Articles 52 and 53 of the 1907 Hague Regulations cannot be considered as a recognition of the right of angary but merely as a limited belligerent right of the Occupying Power to requisition private property.[41]

The prohibition in Article 19 of the 1907 Hague Convention V of requisitioning neutral railway material 'except where and to the extent that it is absolutely necessary' may indeed be considered a recognition of the right of angary, as stated in paragraph 15.11.2.

NEUTRAL COMMERCE AND CARRIAGE OF CONTRABAND

At its beginning, the chapeau of section 15.12 provides an important clarification that must also be included in paragraph 13.8.2: the law of neutrality does not prohibit neutral persons from engaging in trade with the enemy, because the duties of abstention and impartiality exclusively apply to neutral States. Accordingly, the rules on neutral commerce and carriage of contraband merely provide belligerents with certain rights of control and of prevention. Outside neutral waters, neutral merchant vessels and civil aircraft must submit to visit and search that provides belligerents the necessary means of

39 See, however, *San Remo Manual*, paragraph 22.

40 For an assessment of the right of angary, see Castrén, *Present Law of War*, 509ff.; W Heintschel von Heinegg, Angary, in: *Max Planck Encyclopedia of Public International Law*.

41 Colombos, *International Law of the Sea*, 571.

verifying whether they in fact have enemy character, are carrying contraband or have engaged in activities rendering them a lawful target. In principle, neutral merchant vessels and civil aircraft may neither be captured nor attacked. If they engage in the carriage of contraband or in some other form of unneutral service, they are liable to capture and – exceptionally – to destruction as prize. These rules are without prejudice to the belligerent right of attacking neutral merchant vessels and civil aircraft that, by use, make an effective contribution to the enemy's military action and, thus, become liable to attack as military objectives.

The rules applicable to neutral commerce and carriage of contraband have been addressed in international treaties only marginally.[42] The only document extensively dealing with the control of neutral commerce, contraband and other prize measures against neutral merchant vessels is the 1909 London Declaration, which never entered into force.[43] That is probably the reason why most of the provisions in section 15.12 refer to national US documents, such as NWP 1–14M.[44] On the other hand, the wording of those provisions is very similar to the rules contained in the 1909 London Declaration, which have also been adopted in the *San Remo Manual* and in the Helsinki Principles.[45] Evidently, the US DoD is prepared to consider them as declaratory of customary law.

The definition of 'contraband' correctly reflects customary international law by limiting contraband to goods destined to the enemy and which are susceptible for use in armed conflict.[46] This definition is, however, considerably modified by the ensuing explanation of the phrase 'susceptible to use in armed conflict'. First, it is said to also apply to enemy exports, which by nature are not 'destined for' enemy or enemy-controlled territory.[47] Second, it includes goods contributing to the enemy's war-sustaining commerce. This is highly problematic because, in view of the rules in Chapter XIII and of paragraph 15.14.2.2 on acquisition of enemy character, 'a contribution to the enemy's war-sustaining effort' could be (mis)understood as rendering neutral merchant vessels and civil aircraft liable to attack as military objectives.[48]

42 See rules 2 and 3 of the Declaration Respecting Maritime Law (16 April 1856), 1 AJIL Suppl. 89–90 (1907).

43 1909 London Declaration, Articles 22 to 54.

44 NWP 1–14M, paragraphs 2.3.4ff.

45 *San Remo Manual*, paragraphs 146ff.; Helsinki Principles, paragraph 5.2.

46 *San Remo Manual*, paragraph 148; *UK Manual*, paragraph 13.5(h).

47 See also Helsinki Principles, paragraph 5.2.5: 'Goods with neutral destination coming from a belligerent port do not constitute contraband.'

48 A highly controversial issue. See the comment on paragraph 13.5.2.

The distinction between absolute and conditional contraband in paragraph 15.12.1.1 may have become obsolete,[49] but it conforms with Articles 22 and 24 of the 1909 London Declaration.[50] The list of 'free goods' in paragraph 15.12.1.2 is acceptable, although the first four categories do not relate to goods of trade, but rather to items specially protected under GWS, GPW and GC because they serve a humanitarian function. It must be conceded, however, that a similar approach has been taken in the *San Remo Manual*.[51]

According to paragraph 15.12.1.3, belligerents seem to have discretion with regard to the publication of contraband lists ('may declare'). This does not correctly reflect the current state of the law. The object and purpose of contraband lists is to inform neutral merchant vessels and civil aircraft that they run the risk of becoming liable to capture if they engage in the transport of particular goods. This provides them the opportunity of either refraining from the carriage of such goods or of taking the risk of being captured. Therefore, belligerents that wish to prevent or interdict the transport of certain goods are obliged to duly publish contraband lists before they resort to capture.[52] Such lists may be 'positive', i.e. by listing the goods considered as contraband, or 'negative', i.e. by listing goods considered 'free goods'.

Paragraph 15.12.2 emphasises the requirement of enemy destination, which seems to contradict the inclusion of export goods in paragraph 15.12.1. Other than in the case of blockade, the doctrine of continuous voyage applies to contraband, which comprises all goods 'ultimately' destined to enemy or enemy-controlled territory.[53] Hence, paragraph 15.2.1 correctly reflects the law. The same holds true for the criteria identified in paragraph 15.12.2.2, according to which destination to enemy territory may be presumed by the responsible naval commander, although the competent prize court might eventually arrive at a contrary conclusion.

Paragraph 15.12.3 rightly recognises the belligerent right of issuing 'navicerts' and 'aircerts' that relieve neutral merchant vessels and civil aircraft from the burden of visit and search or interception.[54] Such certificates, which will only be issued after prior inspection of the cargo, are, of course, without prejudice to the rights of visit, search and capture, particularly if there are reasonable

49 Accordingly, the *San Remo Manual*, the Helsinki Principles and the *UK Manual* no longer distinguish between absolute and conditional contraband.

50 The *German Manual*, paragraph 1239 also distinguishes between absolute and conditional contraband.

51 *San Remo Manual*, paragraph 150.

52 *San Remo Manual*, paragraph 149.

53 See also Helsinki Principles, paragraph 5.2.3.

54 *German Manual*, paragraph 1237; *UK Manual*, paragraph 13.95; *San Remo Manual*, paragraph 122.

grounds for suspicion that the vessel or aircraft is not complying with what has been certified.

The final statement in paragraph 15.12.3, according to which the acceptance of a navicert or aircert by an aircraft or vessel belonging to one belligerent 'may affect how the other belligerent State views the neutrality of that aircraft or vessel', is not necessarily wrong. In order to avoid negative consequences, it should, however, have been amended by adding a sentence clarifying that acceptance of a certificate after prior submission to inspection may not be regarded as 'an act of unneutral service with regard to an opposing belligerent'.[55]

BELLIGERENT RIGHT OF VISIT AND SEARCH OF MERCHANT VESSELS AND CIVIL AIRCRAFT

Section 15.13 on the belligerent right of visit and search of merchant vessels and civil aircraft outside neutral waters and national airspace has been correctly described as serving the purposes enumerated in paragraph 15.13.1.

The same holds true for the list of neutral vessels and aircraft that, according to paragraphs 15.13.2 and 15.13.3, may not be subjected to prize measures because of their sovereign immunity.[56]

The exclusion of neutral merchant vessels under convoy of a neutral warship of the same nationality and the corresponding exclusion of neutral civil aircraft accompanied by neutral military aircraft, provided the other conditions are met, correctly reflects Article 61 of the 1909 London Declaration. Unfortunately, the *DoD Manual* does not recognise the exemption of neutral merchant vessels and civil aircraft accompanied by a neutral warship or military aircraft of a different nationality.[57] Hence, the US Navy may only escort merchant vessels flying the US flag (or civil aircraft bearing US markings), which may require a prior reflagging of the respective vessels. As the reflagging of Kuwait tankers during the Iran–Iraq War has shown, that may prove problematic.[58]

According to paragraph 15.13.3, the right of visit and search may not be exercised within neutral territory, neutral waters or neutral airspace. This

55 *San Remo Manual*, paragraph 123.

56 See also 1923 Hague Rules of Aerial Warfare, Article 51.

57 *UK Manual*, 13.93; *San Remo Manual*, paragraph 120.

58 For an assessment of that practice, see M H Nordquist and M G Wachenfeld, *Legal Aspects of Reflagging Kuwaiti Tankers and Laying of Mines in the Persian Gulf*, 31 *German Yearbook International* 138–64 (1988).

prohibition also applies to neutral international straits and archipelagic sea lanes, which are covered by the neutral State's territorial sovereignty.

Paragraph 15.13.4 on the procedure for visit and search, including if necessary and proportionate the use of force, is a correct statement as to the contemporary law.

ACQUISITION OF ENEMY CHARACTER BY NEUTRAL-FLAGGED MERCHANT VESSELS AND NEUTRAL-MARKED CIVIL AIRCRAFT

According to the provisions of section 15.14, neutral merchant vessels and civil aircraft may acquire the character of enemy warships, military aircraft, merchant vessels or aircraft. The concept of 'acquiring enemy character' is difficult to understand and does not necessarily correctly reflect the contemporary law. Therefore, it should have been limited to those situations in which merchant vessels or civil aircraft that fly the flag or bear the markings of a neutral State in fact have enemy character as a result of registration, ownership, charter or other criteria.[59] Neutral vehicles engaged in any of the activities referred to in section 15.14, including making an effective contribution to the enemy's military action, do not change their neutral character but merely deprive them of their general protection against capture or attack.[60]

Another reason for giving up the concept of 'acquiring enemy character' is the risk of an undue confusion of the law of hostilities and prize law, which occurs in paragraph 15.14.2.2.

While the conditions under which merchant vessels or civil aircraft may be considered to have enemy character are correctly identified in paragraph 15.14.1, paragraph 15.14.2 should have more clearly distinguished between factual enemy character and conduct depriving neutral merchant vessels and civil aircraft of their protection against capture or attack. Paragraph 15.14.2.1 concerning the acquisition of the character of enemy warships or military aircraft is misleading because enemy warships and military aircraft are military objectives by nature, not by the conduct referred to in that paragraph. Moreover, the conduct rendering neutral merchant vessels and civil aircraft liable to attack as military objectives should have been more precisely described and amended by other activities.[61] Paragraph 15.14.2.2 is correct insofar as merchant vessels flying a neutral flag but chartered by the enemy can be considered to in fact have enemy nationality. Resistance to visit and search,

59 *UK Manual*, paragraphs 13.85ff.; *San Remo Manual*, paragraph 117.
60 *UK Manual*, paragraphs 13.47, 13.49; *San Remo Manual*, paragraphs 67, 70.
61 *UK Manual*, paragraphs 13.47, 13.49; *San Remo Manual*, paragraphs 67, 70.

however, will render neutral merchant vessels and civil aircraft liable to attack, because they are no longer protected by the rules of the 1936 London Submarine Protocol and the corresponding customary law.[62] The provisions of the 1909 London Declaration, according to which neutral vessels engaged in unneutral service are liable to condemnation,[63] are no longer declaratory of customary international law. The list of kinds of conduct rendering neutral vehicles liable to capture or attack should have been far more detailed.[64] For instance, neutral merchant vessels travelling in a convoy of enemy warships can be considered as actively resisting visit, search and capture, which will render them liable to attack. As it stands, the list does not provide commanders with guidance they can depend upon.

CAPTURE OF NEUTRAL VESSELS AND AIRCRAFT

The list in paragraph 15.15.1 of activities rendering neutral merchant vessels and civil aircraft liable to capture is correct insofar as they are carrying contraband, breaching or attempting to breach a blockade or presenting irregular or fraudulent papers.[65] However, if they are carrying enemy military personnel, communicating information in the interests of the enemy or avoiding an attempt to establish identity, including visit and search, they become liable to attack rather than merely to capture.[66] Article 63 of the 1909 London Protocol no longer correctly reflects the contemporary law.[67]

Paragraph 15.15.2 on the procedure of capture and condemnation is correct, as are paragraph 15.15.3 on the destruction of neutral prizes[68] and paragraph 15.15.4 on the treatment of persons on board captured merchant vessels or civil aircraft.[69]

SECTIONS 15.16, 15.17 AND 15.18

Section 15.16 on belligerent forces taking refuge in neutral territory, while correctly reflecting the respective provisions of the 1907 Hague Convention V,

62 *UK Manual*, paragraph 13.37(a); *San Remo Manual*, paragraphs 67(a), 70(a). Note that the 1936 London Protocol does not protect merchant vessels 'in case of persistent refusal to stop on being duly summoned, or of active resistance to visit or search'.

63 1909 London Declaration, Articles 45 to 47.

64 For an example, see *UK Manual*, paragraph 13.106.

65 See also 1923 Hague Rules of Aerial Warfare, Article 53.

66 *San Remo Manual*, paragraphs 67 and 70; *UK Manual*, paragraphs 13.47, 13.49.

67 This also holds true for the provisions of Article 53 of the 1923 Hague Rules.

68 See also 1923 Hague Rules of Aerial Warfare, Article 58.

69 1909 London Declaration, Article 47.

should have been amended by a short paragraph distinguishing between 'taking refuge' and gaining authorised entry into neutral territory in accordance with the law of neutrality.

Sections 15.17 on PWs or internees brought to or received by a neutral State is based on the respective provisions of the 1907 Hague Convention V. The same holds true for section 15.18 addressing authorised passage of wounded and sick combatants through neutral territory, which is also based on GWS and GWS-Sea.

CONCLUDING REMARKS

As we have seen, some provisions of Chapter XV require comment. Some of the comments made here might be perceived as reflecting but a different interpretation of the law of neutrality that can be rejected easily. Some, however – particularly on the distinction between prize measures and conduct of hostilities – should not be dismissed without a thorough assessment of their validity and practical utility. It is important to understand that some of the traditional rules the chapter heavily relies upon may no longer correctly reflect the contemporary law of neutrality or be operable in situations of modern warfare.

Nevertheless, Chapter XV is a most detailed and thorough restatement of the law of neutrality. If it is adapted to reflect the preceding comments and the conditions of modern armed conflict, it will continue to serve as a strong piece of evidence as to the current state of the law of neutrality.

16

Cyber Operations

INTRODUCTION

To its considerable credit, the *Manual* includes a chapter setting forth the US position on the conduct of cyber operations during war. It is to be expected that as the technologies, the understanding of those technologies and attitudes towards them develop, Chapter XVI will require revision from time to time. It is to be hoped that the presence of this relatively brief chapter in the *Manual* will inspire other States as they either produce their own military manuals or update their existing texts to similarly set forth their own interpretations of the law on the topic. Such a process would be a most useful element in the literature and would, potentially, reinforce the position of States as leaders in the development in legal understanding of cyber warfare law issues.

Section 16.1 notes how the US policy has been to try to work internationally to clarify how existing international law and norms apply to cyber operations. Most sensibly, the section notes that precisely how the law of war applies to cyber operations is not well settled and that aspects of the law in this area are likely to emerge as new cyber capabilities are developed and as States' views in response to those developments become clear. The US DoD doctrinal position is set forth in paragraph 16.1.1, recognising cyberspace as 'an operational domain in which the armed forces must be able to defend and operate'.

The notion of cyberspace is authoritatively defined in paragraph 16.1.1 as a 'global domain within the information environment consisting of interdependent networks of information technology infrastructures and resident data, including the Internet, telecommunications networks, computer systems, and embedded processors and controllers'.[1] In paragraph 16.1.2, the

[1] This interpretation is taken from Joint Publication 3–12, Cyberspace Operations (5 February 2013), GL-4.

concept of cyberspace[2] operations is explained in a clear and useful way. Cyber operations are described as those operations that involve the employment of cyberspace capabilities, such as computers, software tools and networks, where the primary purpose is to achieve objectives in or through cyberspace. They include operations that 'use computers to disrupt, deny, degrade or destroy information resident in computers and computer networks, or the computers and networks themselves'. They may be preparatory in nature, taking the form e.g. of mapping a network, securing access to key network systems or nodes or carrying out the preliminary emplacement of cyber access tools or malicious code. Equally, they may be a method of acquiring foreign intelligence not necessarily connected with specific military objectives, such as understanding technological developments or gaining information as to an adversary's military capabilities or intent.

Paragraph 16.1.2.2 clarifies matters by giving examples of operations that would not be regarded as cyber operations. Thus, the mere use of computers without the primary purpose of achieving effects through cyberspace would be excluded from the cyber operations notion. Likewise, bombardment of a network hub and jamming of wireless communications would also not be regarded as cyber operations. This is a widely accepted interpretation of the notion.

Paragraph 16.1.3.2 notes the colloquial use of the term 'attack' in the cyber context to refer to many different types of hostile or malicious cyber activity, including website defacement, network intrusion, theft of private information and disruption of Internet services. The point is made that operations described as cyber attacks are not necessarily attacks for the purposes of the rules as to the conduct of hostilities, nor do they necessarily constitute armed attacks for the purposes of the *jus ad bellum*. What paragraph 16.1.3.2 unfortunately does not do is indicate how the term is being used within Chapter XVI. It would assist the reader if that could be clarified at this early stage in the chapter.

APPLICATION OF THE LAW OF WAR TO CYBER OPERATIONS

Section 16.2 starts, sensibly, by suggesting that specific law of war rules may apply to cyber operations even though they were developed before cyber operations became possible. Quite why it is necessary to repeat that suggestion in

[2] As paragraph 16.1.3.1 explains, the terms 'cyber' and 'cyberspace' are used interchangeably in this chapter of the *Manual*.

paragraph 16.2.1 is not clear. Unnecessary repetition of this nature is a feature of parts of the *Manual* and contributes to its very considerable length.

The *Manual* takes the line that the law of war affirmatively anticipates technological innovation and contemplates that its existing rules will apply. Law of war rules may apply to new technologies because the rules are not framed in technological terms. The core deductions in the *Manual* are therefore that 'cyber operations may be subject to a variety of law of war rules depending on the rule and the nature of the cyber operation' and 'if the physical consequences of a cyber attack constitute the kind of physical damage that would be caused by dropping a bomb or firing a missile, that cyber attack would equally be subject to the same rules that apply to attacks using bombs or missiles'.[3] Paragraph 16.2.1 notes the legal complications that cyber operations can pose, because of the various effects they can produce.[4] It then describes information gathering as a method of conducting hostilities. This is an interpretation that the present authors would dispute: the collection of information may certainly be a prelude to the conduct of certain kinds of hostility, but is unlikely in itself to amount to hostilities.

Further clarifying the US position on the application of *jus in bello* to cyber attacks, paragraph 16.2.1 makes the important point that 'cyber operations could be used to create effects that amount to an attack and would be regulated under the rules on conducting attacks'.

Paragraph 16.2.2 helpfully acknowledges that '[w]hen no specific rule applies, the principles of the law of war form the general guide for conduct during war, including conduct during cyber operations'. Perhaps it would be better to acknowledge that the general principles apply at all times in relation to all operations, including cyber operations, and irrespective of the application of specific rules, but that if specific rules exist, they may make additional relevant provision. The paragraph cites the principle of humanity, rightly noting that suffering, injury or destruction that is unnecessary to accomplish a legitimate military purpose must be avoided in cyber operations.

It must, however, be appreciated – and the paragraph does this – that some kinds of cyber operation will not have a clear kinetic parallel in terms of the capability and the effect produced. 'Such operations may have implications that are quite different from those presented by attacks using

3 *DoD Manual*, paragraph 16.2.1.

4 Later in the paragraph, the possibility that a cyber operation might be regarded as the seizure or destruction of enemy property and thus involve consideration of the rules discussed in section 5.17 is contemplated.

traditional weapons, and those different implications may well yield different conclusions.'[5]

CYBER OPERATIONS AND THE JUS AD BELLUM

If the inclusion in the *Manual* of a chapter addressing cyber operations is to be welcomed – and, as already noted, the present authors think that it is – then the decision to discuss *jus ad bellum* issues in that chapter, in section 16.3, is particularly useful.

Paragraph 16.3.1 quotes Article 2(4) of the UN Charter, which requires all Members, and thus all States, to 'refrain in their international relations from the threat or use of force against the territorial integrity or political independence of any state, or in any other manner inconsistent with the Purposes of the United Nations'. Asserting that cyber operations may in certain circumstances constitute a use of force, the paragraph cites as an example cyber operations that cause effects that, if caused by traditional physical means, would be regarded as a use of force. Examples given in the *Manual* are cyber operations that trigger a nuclear plant meltdown, that open a dam above a populated area, causing destruction, or that disable air traffic control services, resulting in aeroplane crashes. These would seem to the present authors to be very grave forms of a use of force which may also be characterised as armed attacks, particularly if, as is implied, significant human casualties are thereby caused.

Using language that could arguably be more clearly expressed, the final part of paragraph 16.3.1 makes the point that action that would otherwise amount to an unlawful use of force contrary to Article 2(4) must have a proper legal basis in order to be justifiable under the *jus ad bellum*.

Paragraph 16.3.2 addresses peacetime intelligence and counterintelligence activities, and starts with a welcome reflection of the conclusion reached by the UN General Assembly-mandated Group of Governmental Experts in its 2013 Report,[6] namely, as the *Manual* puts it, that '[i]nternational law and long-standing international norms are applicable to State behaviour in cyberspace', so that the lawfulness of intelligence and counterintelligence activities must be judged on a case by case basis. The *Manual* adopts the analogy approach,

5 *DoD Manual*, paragraph 16.2.2.

6 Group of Governmental Experts on Developments in the Field of Information and Telecommunications in the Context of International Security, Report A/68/98 (dated 24 June 2013), section III, paragraph 19.

by suggesting that 'to the extent that cyber operations resemble traditional intelligence and counterintelligence activities, such as unauthorized intrusions into computer networks solely to acquire information, then such cyber operations would likely be treated similarly under international law'. The inclusion of the word 'likely' enables the sentence to express the US view without introducing an inappropriate claim to certainty on the point. The final sentence of the paragraph recognises that such activities are subject to 'long-standing and well established considerations', which the reader must assume are reflected in applicable policy, and which, the paragraph notes, include the possibility that such operations could (perhaps 'might' would have been a better word) be interpreted as a hostile act.

Paragraph 16.3.3 draws attention to the inherent right of States to use force in self-defence, in the following terms: 'A State's inherent right of self-defense, recognized in article 51 of the Charter of the United Nations, may be triggered by cyber operations that amount to an armed attack or imminent threat thereof.' It is the use of the word 'may' that causes difficulty. If a cyber operation amounts to an armed attack, the right to use force in self-defence exists. So, if the word 'may' is intended to reflect doubt as to whether a cyber operation that in fact amounts to an armed attack triggers that right, no such doubt exists. If, however, the word 'may' is intended to reflect the controversy over whether acts of violence by non-State actors can amount to an armed attack triggering the self-defence right, the quoted sentence is still inappropriate because if the event is an armed attack, the controversy is irrelevant. The third possibility is that 'may' is intended to convey some uncertainty as to whether cyber operations can in fact amount to an armed attack. If that is the intended meaning, the text should be amended to make that position clearer.

The paragraph then reports the US policy that when warranted, it will respond to hostile acts in cyberspace as it would to any other threat to the country, and draws attention to the requirement to report action taken in self-defence to the UN Security Council.

Paragraph 16.3.3.1 states the evidently long-held view of the US that 'the inherent right of self-defense potentially applies against any illegal use of force', so that any cyber operation constituting an illegal use of force against a State gives rise to that right. In paragraph 191 of the *Nicaragua* judgment,[7] the ICJ distinguished the most grave forms of the use of force as constituting armed attacks triggering the right to use force in self-defence. While it is appreciated that the US does not adopt a similar view, it seems inappropriate

7 Military and Paramilitary Activities In and Against Nicaragua (*Nicaragua* v. *United States*), 1986 ICJ 14 (27 June 1986).

that neither the paragraph in the *DoD Manual* nor the accompanying footnote makes any reference to the contrary view expressed by such an authoritative international body.

As paragraph 16.3.3.2 correctly observes, there is no requirement that the response to a cyber armed attack take the form of cyber action, provided that the necessity and proportionality requirements are met.

Paragraph 16.3.3.3 makes the important point that while cyber operations not amounting to a use of force do not give rise to the right to use force in self-defence, injured States may be justified in taking necessary and appropriate action not amounting to the use of force. Interestingly, acts of retorsion are suggested as examples of the action that might be taken, with no reference having been made at this point to countermeasures, although reference to the latter is made in the accompanying footnote.[8] This is an unfortunate omission, because countermeasures will frequently be the only effective remedy available to an injured State. Such a discussion should also, of course, refer to the requirement of necessity.

Paragraph 16.3.3.4 notes the capacity for adversaries to hide or disguise their activities or identities in cyberspace and the associated issues over attribution. The paragraph asserts, however, the US view that the right to take necessary and proportionate action in self-defence applies whether the attack is attributed to another State or to a non-State actor. While the present authors would generally agree, the important point is that action by way of self-defence will only be legally possible if attribution can be achieved. Decisions as to the invocation of the right of self-defence are generally taken at national level and, paragraph 16.3.3.5 tells us, in the US are usually made by the President, and such action is reportedly reflected in Standing Rules of Engagement for US Forces.[9]

CYBER OPERATIONS AND THE LAW OF NEUTRALITY

The potential for 'bleed-over' effects of a cyber operation to affect States not party to an armed conflict is noted in section 16.4. Paragraph 16.4.1 considers specifically cyber operations that use communications infrastructure in neutral States. The paragraph starts from the position that the law of neutrality has addressed the use of communications infrastructure in neutral States and considers that in certain circumstances, which it does not specify, that law would apply to cyber operations. Pointing out the general rule that neutral territory

[8] *DoD Manual*, footnote 33 on page 1001. [9] *DoD Manual*, paragraph 16.3.3.5.

may not serve as a base of operations for one belligerent against another, the paragraph points to the particular rules that belligerents must not erect on the territory of a neutral State any apparatus for the purpose of communicating with belligerent forces on land or sea and must not use such installations established by them before the armed conflict on neutral State territory for purely military purposes where the installation has not been opened for the service of public messages.[10] Curiously, the relevant authority in Hague Convention V 1907 is not cited in paragraph 16.4.1. The paragraph then takes the position that merely relaying information through neutral communications infrastructure, the facilities of which are made available impartially, would generally not constitute a breach of neutrality.

Paragraph 16.4.1 cites an extract from the Reports to the Conferences of 1899 and 1907 to the effect that this rule was developed because of the perceived impracticability of neutral States censoring or screening publicly available communications infrastructure for belligerent traffic. The conclusion is therefore sensibly reached that 'it would not be prohibited for a belligerent state to route information through cyber infrastructure in a neutral state that is open for the service of public messages, and that neutral state would have no obligation to forbid such traffic'. The paragraph suggests that the rule would 'appear to be applicable' if the information being routed through neutral communications infrastructure may be characterised as a cyber weapon or otherwise could cause destructive effects in the belligerent State. Interestingly, the discussion of this issue takes place in the context of a quoted text from the Department of Defense Cyberspace Policy Report and a published assessment issued by the Office of the General Counsel of the Department of Defense. No reference is made to the prohibition of the movement of munitions of war or supplies across neutral territory as provided in Article 2 of Hague Convention V, nor to the exception provided for in Article 8 of the same Convention.

CYBER OPERATIONS AND JUS IN BELLO

Paragraph 16.5.1 addresses which cyber operations amount to attacks for the purpose of applying the rules as to the conduct of attacks, for example as to distinction and proportionality. By way of example, it is noted that a cyber attack that would destroy enemy computer systems cannot be directed at ostensibly civilian infrastructure such as stock exchanges, banking systems or universities unless they meet the requirements of the military objectives definition. A

[10] 1907 Hague Convention V, Article 3.

somewhat curious sentence then suggests that '[a] cyber operation that would not constitute an attack, but would nonetheless seize or destroy enemy property, would have to be imperatively demanded by the necessities of war'. The legal issues that this kind of approach raises are discussed in relation to paragraph 5.17.2. The sentence rather feeds into the confusion caused by paragraph 16.1.3.2, discussed earlier. For the present purposes, it suffices to note that an attack, as that term is used in this body of international law, presupposes an act of violence, which in turn will require that injury or damage has been inflicted. Thus, cyber operations that destroy enemy property will generally be attacks, but it is right to say that destruction not justified by military necessity may breach the wanton destruction rule, although the insertion of the word 'imperatively' inappropriately narrows the application of the rule. Unfortunately, a clear definition of the term 'attack' in the cyber context has not been given. This is something of a missed opportunity, and it is to be hoped that such a definition will be forthcoming in future amendments of the *Manual*.

Paragraph 16.5.1.1 states the proportionality rule and suggests that in applying it to cyber operations, it may be important to assess the potential effects of a cyber attack on computers that are not military objectives, such as computers of no military significance that are networked to computers that are military objectives. The suggestion that mere inconvenience and economic effects need not be considered in applying the proportionality rule is correct. To argue that temporary loss also need not be considered is potentially more problematic, depending on what exactly is meant by 'temporary loss'. Consider, for example, a distributed denial of service (DDoS) operation that targets a power distribution network with the consequence that the supply of power to a hospital is lost for 48 hours. The operation's effects are temporary in nature, but it is the consequential casualties that will cause such an operation to be classified as an attack. Arguably, therefore, to imply that temporary effects do not need to be considered may result in misunderstanding. In its concluding element, the paragraph notes that even if it is assessed that the proportionality rule will be complied with, feasible precautions must be taken to limit civilian loss of life, injury or damage.

The suggestion in the *Manual* that it may, or even might, be important to consider the stated matters arguably does not go far enough. It will always be necessary for those planning such operations to consider whether these factors are relevant to the particular kind of operation that is being planned, and, if so, to make the required determinations.

Paragraph 16.5.2 aims to state the obvious, namely that a cyber operation that does not amount to an attack is not restricted by the rules that apply to attacks. It would perhaps be more accurate to say that such operations are not restricted by rules that only apply to attacks. The *Manual* suggests that a relevant factor in this regard is whether the operation only causes reversible or temporary effects. Caution is required here, and the reader is reminded of the points made in the discussion of paragraph 16.5.1.1. The paragraph correctly describes cyber operations that generally would not be regarded as being attacks as including: 'defacing a government webpage; a minor, brief disruption of internet services; briefly disrupting, disabling, or interfering with communications; and disseminating propaganda.' The *Manual* takes the position that as they generally would not be attacks, such operations can be directed against civilians and civilian objects, subject to compliance with the military necessity principle.[11] What they would generally be is not, of course, the issue. If they are attacks, such operations must not have as their object civilians or civilian objects. If they are not attacks, then according to the US approach as revealed in the *Manual*, using such operations to engage civilians or civilian objects would be lawful.

The paragraph concludes with the following: 'even if a cyber operation is not an "attack" or does not cause any injury or damage that would need to be considered under the proportionality rule, that cyber operation still should not be conducted in a way that unnecessarily causes inconvenience to civilians or neutral persons.' The first point to make is that this sentence should probably have been crafted in terms of the injury or damage that the operation is expected to cause. The second is that it is assumed that the reference to injury and damage is intended as a reference to injury to civilians or damage to civilian objects. If this assumption is correct, the sentence would be improved by stating so in terms. If, alternatively, that part of the sentence is intended to refer to any injury or damage, including to military objectives, it might be better simply to state that in all cyber operations, inconvenience to civilians and neutrals should to the extent possible be avoided, but such a position is likely to be an expression of policy on the matter.

Paragraph 16.5.3 finds a requirement to take feasible precautions to reduce the risk of incidental harm to the civilian population and to other protected persons and objects. The next sentence slightly develops the point by explaining that parties to the conflict that employ cyber operations should take precautions to minimise the harm of their cyber activities on civilian infrastructure and users. The word 'should' ought to be replaced with 'must'. The requirement to take all feasible precautions is, after all, recognised elsewhere

[11] See the discussion associated with paragraph 5.3.2.1.

in the *Manual* as a legal obligation.[12] The paragraph is right in indicating that the obligation to take precautions applies to all attacks, including those that have been assessed as complying with the proportionality rule. The paragraph then notes, in somewhat curious terms, that the obligation to take feasible precautions against the effects of attacks also applies to a party to the conflict that is not undertaking attacks.

The potential for certain cyber operations that result in non-kinetic or reversible effects to help minimise unnecessary civilian harm is mentioned in paragraph 16.5.3.1. The paragraph correctly notes the possibility that some cyber capabilities would be preferable in policy terms to kinetic weapons because of their reversible effects or because they accomplish military goals without a destructive kinetic effect. The paragraph rightly notes some of the factors that will be considered when deciding whether to use such weapons, namely cost, effectiveness and the possibility that the adversary will devise defences against their further use in the future, observing that cyber weapons will usually not be the only legally permissible option.

The possibility that the law of war prohibitions of the improper use of certain signs apply to cyber operations is considered in paragraph 16.5.3.2. Misuse of communications that initiate non-hostile relations between belligerents and fabrication of a message from the enemy Head of State to the armed forces notifying an armistice or ceasefire are given as examples. While both are indeed capable of being war crimes, e.g. as perfidious behaviour that might occur in cyberspace, neither, at least in the manner described, necessarily involves the use of a sign, so the linkage with the preceding sentence is at best somewhat tenuous. The paragraph then asserts that 'the restriction on the use of enemy flags, insignia and uniforms only applies to concrete visual objects; it does not restrict the use of enemy codes, passwords and counter-signs'. This is an accurate statement of the law, and the *Manual* rightly deduces that it would not be unlawful to disguise network traffic as though it came from enemy computers or to use enemy codes during cyber operations.

Paragraph 16.5.5 rightly points out that it is not prohibited to employ civilian personnel to take a direct part in hostilities, that such civilians forfeit their protection from being made the object of attack and that civilians who are authorised to accompany the armed forces, such as civilian cyber specialists, have the right to PW status if captured.[13]

[12] See *DoD Manual*, paragraph 5.3.3.2 and the discussion of that paragraph in Chapter 5 of this book.

[13] GPW, Article 4A(4).

LEGAL REVIEW OF WEAPONS THAT EMPLOY CYBER CAPABILITIES

Section 16.6 notes that DoD policy requires the legal review of the acquisition of new weapons that employ cyber capabilities with the purpose of ensuring that they are not *per se* prohibited by the law of war. Internal military regulations address which cyber capabilities require legal review. As the section rightly notes, the novelty of a weapon or of its technology does not mean that it is illegal. While the issues requiring analysis in such a weapon review will, indeed, depend on the characteristics of the weapon being assessed, the section rightly points out that a 'legal review of the acquisition or procurement of a weapon that employs cyber capabilities likely would assess whether the weapon is inherently indiscriminate'. Given that the prohibition of indiscriminate weapons is one of the two core principles in the law relating to weapons and given that the rule is recognised in Chapter VI of the *Manual*, it would perhaps have been better to assert that any review of such a weapon must of necessity assess whether it is capable of use in compliance with the indiscriminate weapons rule.[14]

CONCLUDING REMARKS

Many of the footnotes to Chapter XVI are based on statements issued by the US DoD or published by prominent US officials. This is appropriate, as the chapter is discussing emerging issues relating to a developing technology, the international law applicable to which is not clearly settled. However, it would have been helpful if the chapter had made appropriate reference to the *Tallinn Manual*, even where the chapter's authors take a different view. Readers of the *DoD Manual* are likely to be aware of the Tallinn text and would likely welcome guidance on the extent to which they can place reliance upon it.

It is right that the authors of Chapter XVI have set forth the US position in what the present authors regard as commendable detail in the circumstances. Readers should bear in mind the observation at the beginning of the chapter that as the technology, understanding of it and attitudes towards it change, Chapter XVI will need to be revisited in order to ensure that it remains accurate in technological, policy and perhaps legal terms.

[14] This, at least, is the conclusion that the reader would draw from footnote 78 on page 1009.

17

Non-International Armed Conflict

Chapter XVII deals with the law of non-international armed conflict and might be considered comparatively short, because it comprises forty-two pages only. This seems to be because the authors prefer to rely on the few relevant treaty rules rather than to identify customary international law.

Surprisingly, many of the chapter's rules are based upon the 1977 APII, which has not been ratified by the US. Apart from Articles 10 and 13, all operative provisions of APII have been paraphrased or referred to in the footnotes. It is important to note that the only provision of APII that is expressly rejected as not reflecting customary international law is Article 15 on works and installations containing dangerous forces.[1] No such statement has been made on the status of the other provisions of APII, which begs the question whether the authors have implicitly recognised those articles expressly referred to as declaratory of customary international law. Be that as it may. The reference to fifteen out of eighteen operative provisions of APII is not without problems, because the material field of application of the Protocol is considerably limited by Article 1(1) APII. Indeed, many of its provisions can be applied by the non-State party to the conflict only if it in fact exercises control over parts of the territory. Hence, the authors should have provided some clarification on whether and to what extent the obligations under APII can be reasonably applied in non-international armed conflicts not covered by its scope of application. Moreover, some of the chapter's rules should have been explained in greater depth, including by more than two references to the ICRC Commentary on the 1977 Additional Protocols.[2]

It is conceded that it is difficult to determine the customary international law regulating non-international armed conflicts. Nevertheless, such difficulty does not suffice to justify the vagueness characterising some of the chapter's

[1] *DoD Manual*, paragraph 17.7.1. [2] *DoD Manual*, footnotes 129 and 204.

sections. The object of a military manual is to provide guidance as to what the government (or government agency) considers the applicable law to be. The numerous references to other chapters of the *Manual* do not necessarily provide the necessary guidance because (1) it is noted in the introduction that 'in certain cases, the rules applicable in international armed conflict have been applied as a matter of policy'[3] and (2) the chapter's authors repeatedly stress the differences between international and non-international armed conflicts, which seems to suggest that the recognition of certain principles and rules as applying to international armed conflict does not necessarily imply that, in the US view, those same rules and principles apply in non-international armed conflicts.

It may be added that the authors have largely ignored other national manuals,[4] recent research[5] and, in particular, the ICRC Customary Law Study. This study may not correctly reflect the customary international law of non-international armed conflict, but its sheer existence is sufficient reason to take it into consideration, if only explicitly to reject the ICRC's findings. Those seeking guidance from the *Manual* will all too often be confronted with arguments based on the ICRC Study when they should have been provided with an unambiguous statement as to the US position vis-à-vis the rules identified in the study as reflecting customary international law that applies in both international and non-international armed conflicts.

INTRODUCTION

The introductory section provides an overview of the various forms of non-international armed conflict, the differences and commonalities between international and non-international armed conflicts and the basic rules and principles applicable in such conflicts.

The very first paragraph suggests that the chapter is focused on the rules binding State armed forces in their military operations against non-State armed groups. The use of the phrase 'in particular' indicates, however, that the obligations of non-State actors are not excluded. Still, the question arises why the authors have chosen to emphasise the obligations incumbent on State organs. Although paragraph 17.2.4 recognises that non-State armed groups

3 *DoD Manual*, section 17.1, second paragraph.

4 *Canadian Manual*, ch. 17; *German Manual*, ch. 13; *UK Manual*, ch. 15. It may be noted that the only foreign manual referred to – once, in footnote 108 – is the 1958 *UK Manual*, which has been superseded by the 2004 *UK Manual*.

5 See, *inter alia*, S Sivakumaran, *The Law of Non-International Armed Conflict*. Oxford: Oxford University Press (2012).

are bound by the international law of non-international armed conflict, the reader may be left with the impression that the respective obligations differ considerably.

The second paragraph is highly important insofar as it excludes reliance on US practice as evidence of a recognition of a merger of the law of international armed conflict and the law of non-international armed conflict. However, as such, the statement is not very helpful, because it leaves the reader with the nagging question as to which rules of the law of international armed conflict have been applied 'as a matter of policy' only.

Paragraph 17.1.1 provides a basic definition of non-international armed conflict by identifying the requirements of intensity – as distinguished from sporadic acts of violence – and organisation, and by clarifying the various terms used to describe the special features of certain non-international armed conflicts. Unfortunately, neither this paragraph nor paragraph 3.4.2.2, to which reference is made in footnote 3, provides criteria that would assist in distinguishing a non-international armed conflict from sporadic acts of violence. Moreover, it should have been clearly stated that for a non-international armed conflict to come into existence, there must be at least two opposing organised armed groups – one of which may be State armed forces – engaged in protracted armed hostilities. This would have provided an opportunity to distinguish the members of the organised armed groups from civilians and would deal with the requirement of a 'continuous combat function' promoted by the ICRC.[6] Finally, the authors should not have satisfied themselves by merely describing the term 'transnational conflict' as a non-international armed conflict taking place in more than one State. Rather, paragraph 17.1.1.3 should have been based on an interpretation of Common Article 3, according to which the phrase 'occurring in the territory of one of the High Contracting Parties' may be understood as 'occurring in the territory of any High Contracting Party', as distinguished from 'occurring in the territory of a single High Contracting Party'. Then, the authors should have addressed the contested issue of whether such 'transnational conflicts' are limited to neighbouring States or whether there is no requirement of a geographical link.[7] If there is no such requirement, the law of non-international armed conflict may be applicable anywhere members of the respective non-State organised armed group are operating. This seems to be the current US position and should have been expressly addressed.

[6] Melzer, *Interpretive Guidance*, 27ff.

[7] For an in-depth discussion, see ICRC, *Commentary on the First Geneva Convention*. Cambridge: Cambridge University Press (2016), MN 465ff. (ICRC Commentary GCI).

Paragraph 17.1.2 contains an important recognition of the applicability in non-international armed conflicts of the basic principles of the law of international armed conflict. However, the wording is overly cautious and somewhat confusing. The differences between 'certain baseline rules' (paragraph 17.1.2.1) and 'foundational principles of the law of war' (paragraph 17.1.2.2) are as obscure as the specific rules and principles that would qualify. The paragraph should have expressly recognised the applicability of the principles of humanity and distinction and the obligations resulting from that applicability, in particular on the protection of the civilian population and of individual civilians.[8] Neither does paragraph 17.1.2.3 add clarity. The rules of the law of international armed conflict applying to operations against 'unprivileged belligerents' may have much in common with the law of non-international armed conflict. Without an identification of those rules, the reader is, again, left with more questions than answers.

Paragraph 17.1.3 describes some of the differences between the two bodies of law, although it merely provides examples by, *inter alia*, excluding PW status and occupation law from applying in situations of non-international armed conflict. The use of different concepts – 'civil war', 'internal armed conflict' and 'non-international armed conflict' – is not necessarily helpful, because it leaves the impression that the different forms of non-international armed conflict are governed by different rules. Equally unsatisfactory is paragraph 17.1.3.3. While it is true that the restrictions of the law of international armed conflict on the treatment of enemy personnel and on the application of domestic law do not apply in non-international armed conflicts, the question arises as to how the application of the principle of distinction depends upon 'the different circumstances that typically arise in non-international armed conflict'. This statement may be misunderstood as absolving State armed forces from the obligations derived from the principle of distinction, including the obligation to take precautions in attack. Moreover, the 'different circumstances' have been explained marginally only in paragraph 17.1.3, and there is no clarification as to their impact on the principle of distinction or on the other basic rules and principles of the law of armed conflict.

APPLICATION OF INTERNATIONAL LAW TO NON-INTERNATIONAL ARMED CONFLICTS

In the chapeau of section 17.2, the authors correctly hold that the law of international armed conflict may not be extended *in toto* to situations of

[8] See e.g. *German Manual*, paragraph 1307; *UK Manual*, paragraph 15.5.

non-international armed conflict. The fact that the law of non-international armed conflict is less detailed and that 'treaty provisions applicable to international armed conflict have been presumed not to apply to non-international armed conflict' does not, however, necessarily result in an increased 'discretion afforded to States'.

The treaties explicitly or implicitly applying to non-international armed conflict are dealt with in paragraph 17.2.1. As such, this paragraph seems to merely state the obvious. However, even if those treaty rules 'may exceed the requirements of applicable customary international law', the question as to the differences between treaty and customary law remains. It may be recalled that most of the provisions of APII are referred to in this chapter, even though the Protocol is not binding on the US.

The recognition in paragraph 17.2.1.3 of the continuing binding effects of applicable human rights treaties is noteworthy, albeit not helpful because of its lack of specificity. For instance, instead of hinting at the possible impact of the location of an individual on the applicability of the ICCPR, there should have been a clear limitation of the Covenant's applicability to the territory of the States party.[9] The mere characterisation of the 'law of war rules' as *leges speciales* is correct but does not solve the problems arising from a complementary applicability of the two bodies of law.[10]

Paragraph 17.2.2 on the assessment of customary international law applicable to non-international armed conflicts only rudimentarily clarifies the US DoD position. The applicability of the basic principles of the law of armed conflict is recognised in paragraph 17.2.2.1, without, however, explaining to what extent the different circumstances of non-international armed conflicts would justify their modification. The various indicators that could inform an assessment of the applicable customary international law are too generic in nature and should have been avoided in a law of war manual. The reader is provided with a rather basic – indeed, inadequate – methodology of determining something the *Manual* should have determined: i.e. the rules of customary international law applicable in non-international armed conflicts.

9 See Article 2(1) ICCPR, which applies to 'all individuals within [a State's] territory and subject to its jurisdiction'. See also, however, Human Rights Committee, General Comment No. 31, paragraph 10, CCPR/C/21/Rev.1/Add. 1326 (May 2004), according to which a State party to the ICCPR 'must respect and ensure the rights laid down in the Covenant to anyone within the power or effective control of that State, even if not situated within the territory of the State Party'.

10 For an analysis of the relationship between the law of armed conflict and international human rights law, see, *inter alia*, F Hampson, The Relationship between International Humanitarian Law and Human Rights Law from the Perspective of a Human Rights Treaty Body, 90(871) *International Review of the Red Cross* 549–72 (2008).

It is true that the application of humanitarian rules neither affects the legal status of non-State armed groups nor results in their immunity against penal prosecution.[11] However, paragraph 17.2.3 fails to explain why this statement is limited to 'humanitarian rules' and how such rules differ from 'non-humanitarian' rules. It may be added that it has become increasingly difficult to distinguish between rules of a humanitarian nature and rules regulating the conduct of hostilities, because the traditional distinction between Geneva- and Hague-type law has become largely insignificant.[12]

Paragraph 17.2.4 on the binding force of the law on non-State actors is certainly important, but the authors should have omitted the reference to customary and treaty law. The customary or treaty nature of the respective obligations does not explain their binding force on non-State actors. That depends on their substance. Hence, the ongoing debate on whether and why non-State actors can be bound by the international law of non-international armed conflict[13] misses the issue at stake. It is not uncommon that States agree on rules of international law resulting in obligations for non-State actors. For example, States have adopted treaties on the civil liability for oil pollution incidents or on individual criminal responsibility for war crimes, crimes against humanity or genocide. So far, no serious doubts have been raised as to the acceptability of States creating such obligations for non-State actors by means of international law. The law of non-international armed conflict, whether treaty or customary in nature, is designed to regulate the conduct of hostilities by all parties to such conflicts. Hence, the respective rules give ample proof of the consensus of States, according to which non-State actors engaged in hostilities are obliged to comply with those rules, even though they have been neither included in their creation nor invited to consent to their application.

SECTIONS 17.3 AND 17.4

Section 17.3 on special agreements between the parties to a non-international armed conflict correctly reflects the law as it stands; the list of possible matters to be regulated by such agreements provides useful guidance. The same holds true for a State's use of its domestic law in section 17.4.

[11] See also *UK Manual*, paragraph 15.4.1.

[12] See, *inter alia*, S E Nahlik, Droit dit de 'Genève' et droit dit de la 'Haye': Unité ou dualité?, 29 *Annuaire Français de Droit International* 9–17 (1978).

[13] See D Murray, How International Humanitarian Law Treaties Bind Non-State Armed Groups, 20 *Journal of Conflict & Security Law* 101–31 (2015); Sivakumaran, *Law of Non-International Armed Conflict*, 236ff.

PRINCIPLE OF DISTINCTION

The principal recognition of the applicability of the principle of distinction in section 17.5 is probably one of the most important statements made in Chapter XVII, although that applicability is, again, made subject to the characteristics of non-international armed conflict.[14] The authors leave no doubt as to the obligation of all parties to a non-international armed conflict, i.e. including non-State organised armed groups, to conduct attacks in accordance with the principle of distinction (paragraph 17.5.1).[15] It is rightly stressed in paragraph 17.5.1 that failure of non-State forces to distinguish themselves from the civilian population and the difficulties in identifying enemy forces have no impact on the obligation to conduct any attacks in accordance with the principle of distinction. However, two comments must be made. First, the less informed reader should have been provided with a short clarification of the obligation of members of organised armed groups to distinguish themselves from the civilian population. Second, the plain rejection of an obligation to take 'additional protective measures to compensate' for the enemy's failure to distinguish its armed forces from the civilian population probably does not correctly reflect the law, in particular the obligation to take all feasible precautions in attack. If those who plan or decide on an attack are aware of the enemy's failure to distinguish its armed forces from the civilian population, the obligation to take all feasible precautions may require them to take additional measures to determine whether an individual qualifies as a lawful target liable to be attacked or as a protected civilian who may not be made the object of attack.[16]

As regards the 'different support structures' used by non-State organised armed groups, the chapter's authors rightly point to the consequent difficulty of distinguishing between civilian objects and military objectives (paragraph 17.5.1.2). It is, however, problematic that the authors, without any further explanation, suggest that 'denying non-State armed groups such support [i.e. the use of objects] to conduct and sustain their operations' may be justifiable under the law. If objects contribute to the non-States armed group's military action by nature, location, purpose or use, they certainly qualify as military

[14] For the application of the principle of distinction in non-international armed conflict, see ICRC Customary Law Study, rule 7; Sivakumaran, *Law of Non-International Armed Conflict*, 337ff.; *UK Manual*, paragraph 15.5; *German Manual*, paragraph 1307.

[15] ICRC Customary Law Study, rule 7; Sivakumaran, *Law of Non-International Armed Conflict*, 337ff.; *UK Manual*, paragraph 15.5; *German Manual*, paragraph 1307.

[16] As to the obligation to take all feasible precautions in attack, including the verification of lawful targets, see ICRC Customary Law Study, rule 16.

objectives. Therefore, the definition of military objectives should have been expressly recognised in section 17.5. Of course, the *DoD Manual* recognises the US interpretation that includes as military objectives objects that contribute to the enemy's war-sustaining effort, which may, according to the US view, justify attacks on objects that do not directly contribute to the enemy's military action (or war-fighting effort). The attacks in Syria on oil reserves used by the so-called 'Islamic State' to produce revenues by sales on the black market may be considered by some as proving the correctness of the US position, according to which the respective objects might qualify as lawful targets. This, however, should have been made clear by an explicit statement to that effect. It may be added that, according to the position taken here, there is no necessity of extending the list of military objectives to objects contributing to the enemy's war-sustaining effort.[17] In particular, there is no necessity of such an extension with regard to objects used by non-State armed groups during a non-international armed conflict. For instance, the oil in the hands of the 'Islamic State' has been appropriated illegally. The sale of that oil on the black market is equally illegal. The State party to the non-international armed conflict is, therefore, allowed to take all necessary measures, including destruction, to deprive the non-State armed group of the oil or of other illegally appropriated or produced items, such as drugs, irrespective of whether they would qualify as military objectives.[18]

Paragraph 17.5.1.3 on the strategic importance of minimising incidental civilian casualties certainly reflects US practice in Afghanistan and Iraq. This is, however, irrelevant for the purposes of a law of war manual. Rules of engagement are always 'more restrictive than what the law of war requires', whether in an international or a non-international armed conflict. The reasons for the use of certain rules of engagement are manifold and are without prejudice to the applicable international law.

Despite its heading, paragraph 17.5.2 does not really deal with the principle of distinction, but rather with the necessity of providing civilians and the civilian population with increased protection against non-State armed groups' use of civilians as human shields (paragraph 17.5.2.1) and the status of members of law enforcement agencies and of judges handling cases involving members of non-State organised armed groups. It may be that the chapter's authors, in view of its structure, did not have the opportunity to deal with these matters elsewhere. They might, however, consider including in the chapter a

[17] See the comment on paragraph 13.5.2.
[18] See the forthcoming *Oslo Manual on Select Problems of the Law of Armed Conflict*, rule 96.

definition of 'civilians' that distinguishes them from members of organised armed groups.[19] This, again, would provide an opportunity of either rejecting or endorsing the 'continuous combat function' proposed by the ICRC.[20]

RESPECT AND HUMANE TREATMENT OF PERSONS TAKING NO ACTIVE PART IN HOSTILITIES IN NON-INTERNATIONAL ARMED CONFLICT

Although section 17.6 seems to recognise that the civilian population and individual civilians, unless and for such time as they take a direct part in the hostilities, enjoy general protection against direct attacks, it makes reference only to Article 4 (1) APII and not to Article 13 APII. This seems to be due to an accidental omission rather than a deliberate rejection of Article 13 APII. Again, that error could have been avoided by the inclusion of a separate section on civilians (as distinguished from members of organised armed groups) and their general protection under the law of non-international armed conflict.[21]

With the exception of paragraph 17.6.6, the prohibitions listed in paragraphs 17.6.1 to 17.6.7 are based not merely on Common Article 3 but almost literally also on Article 4(1) and (2) APII which, it must be assumed, is recognised by the US DoD as reflective of customary international law. As regards the prohibition of taking of hostages, footnote 102's reference to Article 2 APII should be a reference to Article 4(2)(c) APII. According to paragraph 17.6.6, it is prohibited to 'offer a reward for enemy persons to be turned over dead or alive'. No legal basis other than the law of international armed conflict has been provided. Moreover, the prohibition is said not to apply to 'offering rewards for the apprehension of insurgents or for giving information leading to the apprehension or killing of insurgents in combat'. This statement gives rise to two comments. First, the paragraph fails to explain why the exception is limited to insurgents and why it does not apply to members of all non-State organised armed groups.[22] Second, the killing of an insurgent in combat does not *per se* cause legal difficulty, because the insurgent is a member of a non-State organised armed group and, thus, a lawful target. Hence, information – whether obtained because of an offer of an award or not – leading to the insurgent's apprehension or killing in combat may always be lawfully used.

[19] To that effect, see ICRC Customary Law Study, rules 4 and 5.

[20] See note 7.

[21] See e.g. *German Manual*, paragraph 1308; ICRC Customary Law Study, rules 4 and 5.

[22] See e.g. *Canadian Manual*, paragraph 1713, which does not limit the prohibitions to insurgents.

RULES ON CONDUCTING ATTACKS IN NON-INTERNATIONAL ARMED CONFLICT

Although section 17.7 could have been better structured by more clearly distinguishing between the rules applying to attacks and those relating to prohibited activities, it correctly reflects the customary law applicable to non-international armed conflicts and binding on all parties to such conflicts, including non-State organised armed groups.[23] Unfortunately, there is no reference to Article 13 APII. The rejection of the customary nature of Article 15 APII (paragraph 17.7.1) is based on convincing and valid arguments, because there are good reasons to consider that provision merely to apply to States bound by APII.[24]

Section 17.7 is, however, incomplete without either a separate section or additional paragraphs dealing with those individuals (including civilians) directly participating in the hostilities and with objects that qualify as military objectives, as well as with the details of targeting law. Given that the ICRC has published its *Interpretive Guidance on Direct Participation in Hostilities*,[25] the *Manual* certainly needs to address the distinction between members of non-State organised armed groups and civilians, as well as what, in the US DoD view, constitute the elements of a direct participation in hostilities. As has been demonstrated, the general recognition of the principle of distinction does not as such provide the necessary guidance regarding the rules governing targeting in non-international armed conflict.

SECTIONS 17.8 AND 17.9

Section 17.8 on humanitarian organisations and activities during non-international armed conflicts is rather brief but addresses the important issues at stake, such as the requirement of consent by the State concerned and the prohibition of withholding consent arbitrarily. The only problematic statement made concerns UNESCO offering its services to the parties to the conflict. First, such services are functionally limited by the object and purpose of the 1954 Hague Cultural Property Convention. Second, in a non-international armed conflict, the services must be offered to the State concerned and not to the non-State armed group, whose consent would not provide a legal basis for UNESCO activities. Some clarification as to the status and role of humanitarian organisations in situations in which effective governmental structures no

[23] See, *inter alia*, Sivakumaran, *Law of Non-International Armed Conflict*, 347ff.

[24] For the contrary view, see ICRC Customary Law Study, rule 42. [25] See note 7.

longer exist would have been helpful, because in such situations there is no entity other than the non-State armed group that can provide effective consent to its humanitarian activities.

Section 17.9 on the protection of the civilian population deals not with the general protection against the dangers arising from military operations[26] but rather with the provisions of APII on displacement (paragraph 17.9.1)[27] and on the prohibition of starvation as a method of warfare (paragraph 17.9.2).

Paragraph 17.9.1 quotes verbatim Article 14(1) and (2) APII, amended by the clarification that 'insurgents that control territory must not compel civilians to leave the area under their authority'. Unfortunately, an explanation of this statement is given only in footnote 129, which quotes the ICRC Commentary on the 1977 Additional Protocols. Moreover, the term 'insurgents' is far too narrow and should be replaced by 'non-State party to the conflict'. Paragraph 17.9.1.1 provides two useful examples of reasons that would justify the displacement of the civilian population by the State party to the conflict. Indeed, the protection of the civilian population against non-State armed groups will legitimise forced movements of civilians if there are no other means reasonably available to ensure the protection of the civilian population. 'Reducing the support provided to insurgents from elements of the civilian population' will, as such, however, hardly suffice to justify forced movements. Depriving the non-State armed group of the support provided by civilians (or certain elements of the civilian population) is a legitimate goal, which will, however, only constitute 'imperative military reasons' if the support is (1) substantial and (2) provided by a considerable part of the civilian population. Otherwise, the displacement of the civilian population will continue to be prohibited. The final sentence of paragraph 17.9.1.1, according to which forced movements will not be permissible if the civilians are to be abused as involuntary human shields, states the obvious but correctly reflects the law.

Paragraph 17.9.2 on starvation quotes verbatim Article 14 APII. It is amended by paragraph 17.9.2.1, which rightly excludes from the prohibition the starvation of enemy forces, subject to the prohibition of excessive collateral damage and feasible precautions in attack. This paragraph correctly reflects the law.[28]

[26] See Article 13(1) APII; ICRC Customary Law Study, rule 6; *UK Manual*, paragraph 15.8; *Canadian Manual*, paragraph 1720.

[27] For the prohibition of displacement in non-international armed conflict, see M Jacques, *Armed Conflict and Displacement*. Cambridge: Cambridge University Press (2012), 49ff. See also ICRC Customary Law Study, rules 129ff.; *UK Manual*, paragraph 15.14; *Canadian Manual*, paragraph 1724.

[28] See *UK Manual*, paragraph 15.19; *Canadian Manual*, paragraph 1721.

PROTECTION OF CHILDREN IN NON-INTERNATIONAL ARMED CONFLICT

Section 17.10 on the protection of children literally repeats Article 4(3) APII and is most likely a correct statement of the law.[29] There is, however, no reference to the 2002 Optional Protocol on the Involvement of Children in Armed Conflict, which was ratified by the US on 23 December 2002.

As regards the obligations under Article 4(3) APII, one may wonder whether they apply in their entirety to non-State armed groups. In particular, the obligation of providing children with education will be applicable to a non-State armed group only if it controls sufficient parts of the territory. The obligations under Article 4(3) APII are amended by an important exclusion of the death penalty for children under the age of eighteen and for pregnant women or mothers of young children. With regard to the latter group, the authors should have clarified the term 'young children', which certainly applies to children who are not yet able to feed themselves.

PROTECTION OF CULTURAL PROPERTY IN NON-INTERNATIONAL ARMED CONFLICT

Section 17.11 on the protection of cultural property correctly reflects the law as codified in the 1954 Hague Cultural Property Convention, which, according to its Article 19(1), applies in non-international armed conflicts insofar as the Convention's provisions 'which relate to respect for cultural property' are concerned. Those provisions are summarised in paragraph 17.11.2.[30]

USE OF CAPTURED OR SURRENDERED ENEMY PERSONNEL IN NON-INTERNATIONAL ARMED CONFLICT

Paragraph 17.12.1 correctly identifies the differences between international and non-international armed conflicts as far as the forced employment of captured or surrendered enemy personnel in military operations is concerned. Paragraph 17.12.2 rightly holds that inhumane treatment remains prohibited, whereas a 'combination of threats of criminal punishment and inducements' may be used to gain the cooperation of captured enemy individuals.

29 See, however, *UK Manual*, paragraph 15.39, which suggests that the respective rules are not customary in nature.

30 ICRC Customary Law Study, rules 38–41; *UK Manual*, paragraph 15.18; *Canadian Manual*, paragraph 1723.

WEAPONS IN NON-INTERNATIONAL ARMED CONFLICT

Section 17.13 is probably too brief, although paragraphs 17.13.1 and 17.13.2 correctly list the types of weapon that are either prohibited or whose use is subject to certain restrictions. Instead of merely referring to previous chapters, it should have provided a thorough explanation for the applicability of the respective rules in non-international armed conflict and should have identified the restrictions on the use of the weapons listed in paragraph 17.13.2.[31] This also holds true for the limitation of the restrictions on the use of certain weapons to US armed forces in paragraph 17.13.2, which justifies the conclusion that the chapter's authors are not prepared to consider the restrictions on the use of certain weapons as reflecting customary international law that also binds non-State armed groups. Finally, it would have been useful had the section included a short statement as to the obligation to undertake a weapons review, which may be considered as not being limited to international armed conflicts.[32]

PROTECTION OF THE WOUNDED, SICK, SHIPWRECKED AND DEAD

Section 17.14 is based on Article 7 APII and correctly identifies the obligations regarding the protection of the wounded, sick, shipwrecked and dead. The categories of persons thus protected are listed in paragraph 17.14.1.1. As regards shipwrecked persons, it seems that the section limits that category to persons in distress at sea, which would exclude persons in similar distress in other waters, such as lakes or rivers.[33]

The definition of the obligations to respect and protect in paragraph 17.14.1.2 is not very helpful, because it lacks a clarification of the term 'protection'. The obligation to protect the wounded, sick and shipwrecked includes an affirmative duty to take feasible action to protect them against attacks or undue interference by others. The mitigation of the obligation with regard to protected persons who 'have accepted the risk of harm due to deliberate proximity to military objectives' should have been explained in greater

31 See ICRC Customary Law Study, rules 70ff.

32 For the implied obligation for States not party to API to conduct weapon reviews, see Boothby, *Weapons and the Law*, 342.

33 This is the position of the ICRC with regard to GWS-Sea. See the *Commentary on Convention (II) for the Amelioration of the Condition of the Wounded, Sick and Shipwrecked Members of Armed Forces at Sea*, International Committee of the Red Cross (2017), available at: https://ihl-databases.icrc.org/applic/ihl/ihl.nsf/Treaty.xsp?documentId=2F5AA9B07AB61934C12563CD002D6B25&action=openDocument.

depth. If the parties to the conflict are obliged to do everything feasible to protect the wounded, sick and shipwrecked (as distinguished from the obligation to refrain from attacks and undue interference), then they should be removed from the vicinity of military objectives as soon as possible; expected incidental harm to them would not render an attack unlawful, unless that harm were expected to be excessive in relation to the military advantage anticipated. It is correctly held that the protection of the wounded, sick and shipwrecked 'do[es] not immunize them from search, or other necessary security measures, or capture and detention'. However, such measures must be taken paying due regard to their physical status. The prohibition of booby-trapping the wounded or sick should have been dealt with in a separate section on ruses and perfidy, a topic which unfortunately is not dealt with in the chapter, or in section 17.13.

Paragraph 17.14.2 on humane treatment, medical care and attention is based on Article 7(2) APII. Paragraph 17.14.3 on search, collection and protection is based on Article 8 APII. Both paragraphs correctly reflect the humanitarian obligations aimed at the protection of the wounded, sick, shipwrecked and dead.[34]

MEDICAL AND RELIGIOUS PERSONNEL AND MEDICAL TRANSPORTS

Paragraph 17.15.1 on the protection of medical and religious personnel is based on Article 9(1) APII, which may be considered as reflective of customary international law.[35] Persons qualifying as medical or religious personnel are defined in paragraph 17.15.1.1 as including those who are exclusively engaged in those duties. The term 'exclusively' is explained as also meaning 'permanently'. This is not necessarily correct. While persons who perform both humanitarian and non-protected functions are excluded from the protective scope, there is no reason to likewise exclude persons who exclusively perform protected humanitarian functions for a limited time only. Their protection cannot be separated from the wounded or sick, or from those in need of religious care. Moreover, paragraph 17.15.1.1 should have been amended by a clarification of whether and to what extent members of non-State organised armed groups can qualify as medical or religious personnel.

The meaning of the terms 'respect and protection' is defined in paragraph 17.15.1.2 as in section 17.14. However, the criticism as to those protected persons who 'have accepted the risk of harm' is not valid in the context of

34 See e.g. *UK Manual*, paragraph 15.29; *Canadian Manual*, paragraph 1718; ICRC Customary Law Study, rules 109–11.

35 ICRC Customary Law Study, rules 31 and 32; *UK Manual*, paragraph 15.29.

section 17.15 because the situation of the wounded, sick and shipwrecked differs considerably from the situation of medical and religious personnel.

Paragraph 17.15.2, which is based on Article 11 APII, correctly identifies the rules applying to the protection of medical units and transports.

DISPLAY OF THE DISTINCTIVE EMBLEM

Section 17.16 on the use of the distinctive emblem, including the Red Crystal under APIII, is based on Article 12 APII.[36] Accordingly, paragraph 17.16.1 refers to the 'competent authority concerned'. In that context, it would have been useful had the section clarified whether non-State armed groups can be considered to have such 'competent authorities'. The wording seems to suggest that that is not the case, because the term 'authority' may be understood as applying to governmental institutions only. It is rightly held in paragraph 17.16.1 that for tactical or protective reasons, the distinctive emblem may be concealed or even removed, such as if enemy forces fail to respect the protected persons and objects it identifies. Paragraph 17.16.2 provides some useful examples of prohibited or improper activities involving the use of the distinctive emblem.

DETENTION IN NON-INTERNATIONAL ARMED CONFLICT

At first glance, section 17.17 may be considered too brief, because only three paragraphs are devoted to that subject which is politically sensitive and practically most relevant. However, the detailed rules on detention are extensively dealt with in Chapter VIII of the *Manual*. Therefore, the basic rules identified in section 17.17 should not be considered in isolation.

Section 17.17 rightly distinguishes between detention by State authorities (paragraph 17.17.1) and detention by non-State armed groups (paragraph 17.17.2).

As regards detention executed by State authorities, it is rightly stated in paragraph 17.17.1 that the law of armed conflict does not limit a State's authority to detain but merely prescribes humane treatment for any persons so detained. This reflects Article 5(1) APII, upon which the section is mainly based.[37] The paragraph does not precisely identify the basis of a State's right to detain individuals but merely hints at the State's authority to engage in operations against non-State armed groups under domestic law. This is not incorrect. However,

[36] See also *UK Manual*, paragraph 15.13.

[37] See also ICRC Customary Law Study, rules 118–28.

it should have emphasised that the existence of a non-international armed conflict is without prejudice to a State's right to exercise its jurisdiction to prescribe and to enforce. The 'variety of legal theories under international law' justifying non-punitive detention referred to in paragraph 17.17.1.1 are irrelevant, and any reference to an analogous application of the rules on PWs should have been avoided. The applicability of the law of non-international armed conflict does not prevent the respective government or legislator from providing a domestic legal basis for security or other non-punitive detention, or from enforcing it against members of non-State armed groups, civilians directly participating in hostilities or individuals posing a security threat. A *fortiori*, the same holds true for punitive detention, which is addressed in paragraph 17.17.1.2.

As rightly stated in paragraph 17.17.2, non-State armed groups have no authority to conduct detention operations. Any deprivation of liberty, whether of members of the regular armed forces, of law enforcement officials or of civilians, will properly qualify as a crime under the applicable domestic law.

Paragraph 17.17.3 correctly summarises the obligation to treat detainees humanely and in accordance with further requirements.[38] The reference to Common Article 3 could have been amended by a reference to Article 5 APII.

NON-INTERVENTION AND NEUTRAL DUTIES IN NON-INTERNATIONAL ARMED CONFLICT

Section 17.18 addresses issues not of the *jus in bello*, but of the *jus ad bellum*.

It is prohibited for foreign States to support or to join the armed conflict on the side of non-State armed groups in hostilities against a State. Hence, paragraph 17.18.1 is correctly based on the prohibition of intervention under the UN Charter and on customary international law. In view of the ICJ's Nicaragua Judgment,[39] the prohibition of the use of force could have been referred to as well. As rightly emphasised at the end of paragraph 17.18.1, those *jus ad bellum* prohibitions may not be understood as providing for exceptions in cases of violations of the law of non-international armed conflict by the State party to the conflict.[40] This is re-emphasised by Article 3(2) APII, not Article 2(2) as is erroneously referred to in footnote 210. It may be added that intervention on the side of a non-State armed group will bring into

[38] ICRC Customary Law Study, rules 118–28.

[39] ICJ, *Case Concerning Military and Paramilitary Activities in and against Nicaragua* (*Nicaragua* v. *United States of America*), Merits, Judgment of 27 June 1986, ICJ Rep. 1986, 14, at 118ff.

[40] See also *Canadian Manual*, paragraph 1710.

existence an international armed conflict between the intervening State and the targeted State.[41]

It is, however, incorrect to use in this context the term 'non-belligerent States' and to add references to the law of neutrality. A foreign State may be a belligerent in another armed conflict, but it will still be bound by the prohibitions on intervention and on the use of force vis-à-vis a State party to a non-international armed conflict. As already stated in Chapter 15, the law of neutrality does not apply to situations of non-international armed conflict, although the obligations of abstention and impartiality are similar to those under the prohibition of intervention.

The prohibition of intervening in a non-international armed conflict must also be clearly distinguished from a State's duty of due diligence, i.e. not to 'allow knowingly its territory to be used for acts contrary to the rights of other States'.[42] Whereas the prohibition of intervention only applies to conduct attributable to a State, the duty of due diligence is limited to a State's omission vis-à-vis non-attributable conduct by private individuals or non-State armed groups. It is, however, true that a State's failure to comply with its duty of due diligence may justify an extraterritorial exercise of the right of self-defence by the affected State.

Accordingly, paragraph 17.18.2 correctly reflects the law insofar as it prohibits a State party to a non-international armed conflict to extend the hostilities to the territory of another State, unless that State has given its consent or is unable or unwilling to fulfil its obligation of due diligence. It is, however, questionable whether the lack of consent will also be irrelevant if 'seeking of consent would be likely to undermine materially the effectiveness of the action against the non-State armed group'. As long as the territorial State is willing and able to comply with its duty of due diligence, i.e. to terminate the use of its territory by a non-State armed group, it remains protected by the principle of territorial sovereignty.

In view of the continuing relevance of the principle of sovereignty and the lack of a rule of international law to the contrary, a State party to a non-international armed conflict may ask for military or other assistance by other States. As rightly held in paragraph 17.18.3, those other States will become bound by the law of non-international armed conflict as soon as their armed forces conduct hostilities or other military operations.[43]

41 ICRC Commentary GCI, MN 400.

42 ICJ, *The Corfu Channel Case* (Merits), *United Kingdom* v. *Albania*, Judgment of 9 April 1949, ICJ Rep. 1949, 4–38, at 22.

43 ICRC Commentary GCI, MN 402ff.

Paragraph 17.18.4 on the liability of private individuals for supporting non-State armed groups is a correct reflection of the law insofar as the State party to the non-international armed conflict is entitled to exercise its criminal jurisdiction in accordance with the well-established rules based on the principles of territoriality, active or passive personality and universality. The final paragraph on a possible exercise of criminal jurisdiction by the States in which the respective conduct occurs is equally correct. It should have been made clear, however, that acts of terrorism or piracy must be prosecuted under the applicable treaties or UN Security Council resolutions (or under the ordinary domestic law of the *locus in quo*), and that such acts may not be assimilated too easily with support provided to non-State armed groups. Finally, the paragraph should have been amended to make it clear that in cases other than terrorism or piracy, States are not obliged to prohibit and prosecute private support to non-State armed groups.

CONCLUDING REMARKS

Chapter XVII throws into sharp relief what is arguably one of the most serious failings of the *Manual* as a whole, namely its failure to articulate to the reader the US view as to which rules do, and respectively do not, have customary law status. That omission has been noted in other parts of this book vis-à-vis other chapters of the *Manual*. It is an omission that is rendered all the more poignant by the failure of the United States to participate in a number of the important treaties applying to armed conflict. The result is that the reader of this *Manual* is left wondering whether the US accepts certain rules at all, whether it accepts some rules only as a matter of policy or as a matter of binding law and, in the latter case, whether that acceptance is in recognition of the customary status of the particular rule. The effect of this is that it remains unclear whether certain rules are considered by the US to bind it and its adversaries by virtue of their customary status. It is to be hoped that future revisions of the *Manual* can be used to address this shortcoming.

18

Implementation and Enforcement of the Law of War

Like other national military manuals,[1] the *DoD Manual* contains a chapter on the implementation and enforcement of the law of war, i.e. on the means of preventing and, if necessary, responding to violations of the law of war. The sheer length of the chapter – seventy-nine pages – indicates that its authors have provided a comprehensive overview of the various means or modes for the implementation and enforcement of the law of war according to US domestic law and international law recognised by the US. The chapter deals with the implementation of the law of war in sections 18.2 to 18.9, the means available to States to respond to violations of the law of war by other States in sections 18.10 to 18.18 and individual criminal responsibility in sections 18.19 to 18.23.

The comprehensive nature of Chapter XVIII and the basis on which it explains effective implementation and enforcement of the law of war seem to preclude meaningful criticism, the more so because many of the aspects it deals with involve policy considerations that may not be shared but that must be accepted as reflecting a sovereign policy decision by the US DoD. It must be borne in mind, however, that the endeavour to comprehensively cover all relevant aspects has resulted, partly, in rather descriptive provisions that, although correctly restating the respective rules of US domestic, international treaty and customary law, are not accompanied by the explanations and interpretations that are necessary for the guidance sought by the target audience. The following comments are therefore in order.

INTRODUCTION

The obligations of States to implement and enforce treaties of the law of war are correctly reproduced in paragraph 18.1.2. In view of the ongoing

[1] See *Canadian Manual*, ch. 15; *German Manual*, ch. 15; *UK Manual*, ch. 16.

debate over the exact meaning and nature of the obligations under Common Article 1 of the 1949 Geneva Conventions – to respect and ensure respect for the Conventions in all circumstances – the authors of the *DoD Manual* should not have satisfied themselves with a mere quotation of that article. One may not necessarily share the view the ICRC has articulated in its recent commentaries on GWS and GWS-Sea, according to which the legal duty to ensure respect by other than a State's armed forces comprises both negative and positive obligations.[2] That position has found considerable support from some scholars, but others consider the obligation a mere recommendation.[3] Hence, the question whether and to what extent the US DoD is prepared to share or reject the ICRC's – broad – interpretation of Common Article 1 remains unanswered. This is regrettable, because military commanders should be fully aware of whether they are, according to their government's position, legally (or only morally, or not at all) required to react to violations of the law of war by others, particularly in the context of combined or multinational military operations in which they are participating.[4]

Paragraph 18.1.4 correctly states that the fact that a State's armed forces are part of an international or multinational force or that they are acting through an international organisation does not absolve them from their continued obligation to comply with the law of war. It is similarly correct that international organisations, such as the UN or NATO, are not parties to the 1949 Geneva Conventions and therefore are not bound by those treaties. Still, such international organisations would most probably be bound by the rules and principles of the law of war that have matured into customary international law in respect of conduct of the armed forces that is attributable to them. Hence, the paragraph should have been amended by a statement clarifying that armed forces acting through an international organisation will not be placed at the disposal of the organisation, whose organs will exercise only operational control or operational command, but not full command.[5]

[2] ICRC Commentary GCI, Article 1, MN 153ff., 48ff.

[3] See, *inter alia*, F Kalshoven, The Undertaking to Respect and Ensure Respect in All Circumstances: From Tiny Seed to Ripening Fruit, 2 *Yearbook of International Humanitarian Law* 3–61 (1999), at 59ff.; C Focarelli, Common Article 1 of the 1949 Geneva Conventions: A Soap Bubble, 21 *European Journal of International Law* 125–71 (2010), at 126.

[4] It may be noted that the ICRC holds the position that 'in the event of multinational operations, common Article 1 . . . requires High Contracting Parties to opt out of a specific operation if there is an expectation . . . that it would violate the Conventions'. See ICRC Commentary GCI, MN 161, 51. As regards the alleged positive obligations arising from Common Article 1, the ICRC Commentary GCI, MN 167, 53 stresses that the 'duty to ensure respect . . . is particularly strong in the case of a partner of a joint operation'.

[5] See ILC, Draft Articles on the Responsibility of International Organizations, Article 7, UN Doc. A/66/10.

PRUDENTIAL REASONS SUPPORTING THE IMPLEMENTATION AND ENFORCEMENT OF THE LAW OF WAR

Section 18.2 is important because it provides convincing arguments for why it is prudent and necessary to comply with and to enforce the law of war. All too often, that law is perceived as merely (and unnecessarily) restricting military options, rather than contributing to their success. Moreover, as rightly emphasised in paragraph 18.2.3, compliance with and enforcement of the law of war is crucial for the maintenance of public support and political legitimacy. Therefore, it is important that paragraph 18.2.2 bars any justification of non-compliance by reference to prior violations by the enemy, while at the same time stressing the need for reciprocity. Nevertheless, the section should have emphasised that reciprocity will usually function in situations of international armed conflict only, and it should have addressed in greater depth the problem of ensuring compliance in situations in which the enemy, in non-international armed conflicts most often non-State organised armed groups, deliberately resorts to violations of the law of war as a strategy. Obviously, commanders and soldiers are increasingly frustrated by their continuing obligations of compliance in the face of an enemy that is seemingly advantaged by not complying with the law of war. The mere observation that compliance 'does not depend on whether the enemy complies with that rule' will most probably not be considered particularly helpful.

DUTIES OF INDIVIDUAL MEMBERS OF THE ARMED FORCES

The duties of individual members of the armed forces to comply with the law of war in good faith (paragraph 18.3.1), to refuse to comply with clearly illegal orders (paragraph 18.3.2) and not to understand commands and orders as implicitly authorising violations of the law of war (paragraph 18.3.2.2) are correctly identified. Paragraph 18.3.2.1 should, however, have clarified the concept of 'clearly illegal orders', particularly because it emphasises that there is a presumption that orders have been lawfully issued. An order may be considered as 'clearly illegal' if a reasonable soldier readily and without a deeper knowledge of the law perceives or understands that it requires conduct that contradicts the basic principles of the law of war, in particular the principle of distinction.

SECTIONS 18.4 TO 18.8

Sections 18.4 to 18.8 dealing with the obligations of commanders, the role of judge advocates and legal advisers, dissemination, instructions and inclusion of the law of war in the planning of military operations do not invite any criticism. The only question concerns the distinction between judge advocates and legal advisers, because some members of the JAG Corps may be in doubt as to whether they are, for these purposes, counted in the latter category. Legal advisers, however, are likely to comprise the military or civilian personnel who have been appointed to fulfil the advisory roles being described in the respective paragraphs.

STATES' OBLIGATIONS WITH RESPECT TO VIOLATIONS OF THE LAW OF WAR

Equally unproblematic is Section 18.9, which briefly deals with State responsibility (paragraph 18.9.1, which is to be read in conjunction with section 18.16), grave breaches of the 1949 Geneva Conventions (paragraph 18.9.3), breaches of other treaties (paragraphs 18.9.3 and 18.9.4) and the concept of war crimes (paragraph 18.9.5). In particular, paragraph 18.9.3 provides valuable guidance as to the US position on the grave breaches regime under the 1949 Geneva Conventions, which is rightly considered as reflective of customary international law (paragraph 18.9.3). Seemingly, the US DoD no longer holds the position that the grave breaches regime also applies to violations of Common Article 3 of the 1949 Conventions, because paragraph 18.9.3.2 refers to the decision of the Appeals Chamber of the ICTY in the Tadic Case, according to which the grave breaches provisions only create obligations applicable in international armed conflicts.[6] A closer look reveals, however, that breaches of Common Article 3 remain punishable under US law.[7] Nevertheless, it would have been preferable had there been a clear statement as to the continuing validity under the law of war of the US position regarding the applicability of the grave breaches to violations of Common Article 3.

STATE RESPONSES TO VIOLATIONS OF THE LAW OF WAR BY THE ENEMY

Sections 18.10 to 18.18 deal with methods available to the injured State for responding to violations of the law of war by the enemy. While section 18.10 provides a brief overview, sections 18.11 to 18.18 address the respective methods individually. The sections dealing with protests and demands to the offending

6 See ICTY Appeals Chamber, *Decision on the Defence Motion for Interlocutory Appeal on Jurisdiction* (*Prosecutor* v. *Tadic*), paragraph 71, IT-94-1-AR72 (17 July 1995).

7 Paragraph 18.9.3.2, footnote 94, quoting 18 USC § 2441.

party (18.11), UN Security Council measures (18.12), national investigations (18.13), international mechanisms (18.14), Protecting Powers (18.15) and retorsion (18.17) state the obvious and prompt no significant criticism. Hence, for the present purposes, it suffices to briefly comment upon section 18.16 on State responsibility for violations of the law of war and on section 18.18 on belligerent reprisals.

In section 18.16, the focus is on inter-State agreements settling claims (paragraph 18.16.1), international claims commissions (paragraph 18.16.2) and payment or other compensation *ex gratia* (paragraph 18.16.3); the obligation under Article 3 of the 1907 Hague Convention IV, which is broadly identical with Article 91 of the 1977 API, is dealt with in one sentence. This is surprising insofar as the obligation of States to pay compensations for violations of the law of war has proven to be of considerable practical relevance and is a highly contentious matter.[8] For instance, Germany has been confronted with various claims based on violations of the law of war during World War II[9] and with regard to alleged violations of that law during the conflict in Afghanistan.[10] It is quite probable that other States, including the US, will find themselves in a similar situation. Therefore, section 18.16 should have dealt with the matter in greater depth and with greater caution.

The chapeau of the section starts with a reference to the rules and principles of general international law on the responsibility of States for internationally wrongful acts, then continues to state that that principle 'also applies to the law of war'. This is not necessarily incorrect, but the first two sentences of the chapeau are silent on the relationship between the two legal regimes. According to the position taken here, Article 3 of the 1907 Hague Convention IV is *lex specialis* that prevails over the general rules on State responsibility. Accordingly, there is no obligation under the law of war to make full reparation, but only to pay compensation 'if the case demands'. The latter phrase may be understood as excluding from the scope of Article 3 a general obligation to pay compensation for any breach of the law of war. Only those violations that result in material damage, which must be compensated because natural restoration is impossible, will thus trigger the obligation to

8 Admittedly, other national manuals deal with the matter equally briefly. See *UK Manual*, paragraph 16.15; *Canadian Manual*, paragraph 1506; *German Manual*, paragraph 1529.

9 See, *inter alia*, ICJ, *Jurisdictional Immunities of the State* (*Germany* v. *Italy: Greece intervening*), Judgment of 3 February 2012, ICJ Rep. 99 (2012).

10 For allegations of war crimes in the Kunduz incident, see W Heintschel von Heinegg and P Dreist, The 2009 Kunduz Air Attack: The Decision of the Federal Prosecutor-General on the Dismissal of Criminal Proceedings against Members of the German Armed Forces, 53 *German Yearbook International* 833–66 (2010).

pay compensation.[11] Moreover, section 18.16 also fails to quote the second sentence of Article 3 of the 1907 Hague Convention IV, which reads: 'It [i.e. the belligerent party] shall be responsible for all acts committed by persons forming part of its armed forces.' This sentence should not be misunderstood as merely stating the generally recognised rule on the attribution of the conduct of State organs, i.e. of the members of the armed forces; rather, it is to be understood as extending the obligation under the first sentence to any conduct that has been contrary to given orders and instructions or that was resorted to without any orders having been given. At the same time, the second sentence excludes from the obligation the unlawful conduct of other State organs and of private individuals.

It may be added that paragraph 18.16.4 rightly states that the obligation of States to pay compensation for violations of the law of armed conflict is owed to other States and not to individuals. This sentence should have been moved to that part of the section dealing with the obligation under Article 3 of the 1907 Hague Convention IV. Moreover, it should have been amended by a clarification as to individual claims for compensation based on an alleged violation of human rights law during an international armed conflict. According to the position taken here, the very existence of Article 3 of the 1907 Hague Convention IV, which has been reaffirmed by Article 91 API, excludes any reliance on human rights law, at least insofar as individual claims for compensation are concerned. The two provisions provide ample proof of the unwillingness of States to accept such claims in the context of an international armed conflict regardless of whether they agree with a complementary applicability of human rights law or not.

Section 18.18 on belligerent reprisals does not give rise to criticism. In view of the importance of reprisals, which often are the only effective means of inducing an enemy to cease violating the law of war, it is worthwhile to stress that the chapter's authors have rightly taken a restrictive approach as to the legality and advisability of resorting to belligerent reprisals. Accordingly, belligerent reprisals are considered lawful only if the conditions identified in paragraph 18.18.2 – careful determination of a prior violation of the law of armed conflict by the enemy, exhaustion of other means of securing compliance, decisions on reprisals reserved to the national level (as distinguished from service members and units), proportionality and prior public announcement – are met and if they are taken for the sole purpose of inducing the enemy to return to lawful conduct. The fact that only the prohibitions

[11] For an in-depth analysis, see F Kalshoven, State Responsibility for Warlike Acts of the Armed Forces, 40 *International and Comparative Law Quarterly* 827–58 (1991).

of reprisals under the 1949 Geneva Conventions, and not those under API, are accepted by the *Manual* comes without surprise and, in view of similar statements by States party to API, correctly reflects customary international law.[12] The final paragraph 18.18.4 is of particular value because it enumerates practical considerations that 'may counsel strongly against taking such measures', even if the law allows the injured belligerent to resort to belligerent reprisals.

WAR CRIMES

Sections 18.19 to 18.23 deal with individual criminal responsibility under both US domestic law and the law of war. In principle, these sections correctly reflect the law, and certainly the US position on matters such as the International Criminal Court (paragraph 18.20.3). Accordingly, only a few comments are in order.

According to paragraph 18.19.2, the US is considered to have 'no international law obligation to prosecute an offense as a "war crime" as opposed to an ordinary criminal offense'. At the same time, paragraph 18.22.1 recognises an international obligation of States to punish individuals for violations of the law of war. While these two statements may not necessarily contradict each other, it is still doubtful whether it is admissible to prosecute grave breaches of the 1949 Geneva Conventions merely as ordinary criminal offenses, because the respective national provision and the punishment provided for may not fully reflect the gravity of a grave breach.

According to paragraph 18.21.1, the US is not prepared to accept the prosecution and punishment of war crimes based on the principle of universality. This is somewhat regrettable, particularly with a view to grave breaches of the 1949 Geneva Conventions and to war crimes as defined by criminal international law. Still, it is arguably possible to hold that the universality principle continues to be controversial and, thus, is not yet reflective of customary international law. Then, however, the reference to the prosecution of war crimes committed by enemy nationals against nationals of allies and of co-belligerents and against stateless persons should either be deleted or should be amended by adding an explanation of why such an exercise of criminal jurisdiction, which cannot be justified by either territoriality or the active or

[12] See, *inter alia*, the statements on ratification of API by the Federal Republic of Germany (1607 UNTS 626), the United Kingdom (2020 UNTS 75) and Italy (1425 UNTS 438). See also *UK Manual*, paragraph 16.19.1. For the contrary view, see, however, *Canadian Manual*, paragraph 1507.

passive personality principle, is considered to be in accordance with international law.

Another problematic issue is the reference in paragraph 18.21.2 to the 'international law doctrine *tu quoque*'. First, it is highly doubtful whether a belligerent is precluded by law from claiming a violation of the law of war by the enemy for the mere reason that that belligerent has also violated the same rules.[13] Such claims may be considered 'unfair' or 'unjust', but they are not excluded by the law of war as it stands today. Second, the paragraph explicitly states that the same illegal conduct does not preclude a State from punishing enemy personnel for such violation. This paragraph should be deleted, because it gives rise to misunderstanding rather than contributing to a clarification of the law.

Paragraph 18.22.4 on superior orders correctly restates the law insofar as it literally repeats the statutes of international criminal courts and Principle IV of the International Law Commission's (ILC's) 1950 Principles.[14] Accordingly, acting pursuant to superior orders may relieve an individual of responsibility if 'no moral choice' was in fact possible to that individual. However, this begs the question as to when and under what conditions a moral choice is in fact given. The *Manual* is silent on that question, and provides no clarification. A further problem relates to the criteria that must be fulfilled to consider an order as illegal. Again, the *Manual* is silent. This is unfortunate, because the *Manual* also states that orders that are not apparently illegal may be presumed to be lawful unless the subordinate has specific knowledge to the contrary.

A final brief comment relates to section 18.23. Despite its heading, the section does not deal with 'theories', but merely with conduct that may result in criminal liability or with the different modes of criminal liability. Because of the section's focus on individual criminal responsibility for violations of the law of war, the reference in paragraph 18.23.4.1 to similar modes under the law of State responsibility (regarding aiding and abetting) should be omitted.

CONCLUDING REMARKS

Chapter XVIII on the implementation and enforcement of the law of armed conflict is certainly necessary and valuable insofar as it clarifies the US position on various issues at stake. It is, however, not sufficiently specific with regard to some of the problems concerning certain important legal concepts,

[13] F Kalshoven, *Belligerent Reprisals*, 2nd edn. Leiden: Brill (2005), 364.

[14] ILC, Principles of International Law Recognized in the Charter of the Nürnberg Tribunal and in the Judgment of the Tribunal, YBILC 1950 II, 374.

such as the obligations arising from Common Article 1 of the 1949 Geneva Conventions or the duty to pay compensation for violations of the law of armed conflict. This is unfortunate, because those seeking guidance from the *Manual* are, of course, often going to be confronted with a variety of complaints and claims to which they wish to respond in a manner that is appropriate and that correctly reflects the US position. Therefore, the chapter's authors may wish to consider some of the preceding comments and to provide more specific statements in a further updated version of the *Manual*.

19

Documentary Appendix – Notes on Treaties and Other Relevant Documents

In a somewhat unusual chapter for what is in reality a military manual, Chapter XIX of the *DoD Manual* provides what is described as background information with regard to certain treaties and documents. The second introductory sentence clarifies the purpose of the chapter as follows: 'This Appendix is intended to describe DoD views and practice in relation to those documents as of the date of publication of this manual.' Although referring to an 'appendix', it is evident that Chapter XIX, i.e. a substantive chapter, is in fact the subject of the sentence. Perhaps the original intention was that the text now being reviewed would indeed be an appendix but for some reason it was elevated to become a chapter.

While some readers will inevitably wonder about the usefulness of this chapter, there have, to be fair, been criticisms in the earlier chapters of the present book that the *Manual* is too frequently less than clear, e.g. as to whether particular rules are considered by the US to be binding on it as a matter of customary law. If the reader is expecting to achieve that clarity about all such rules in Chapter XIX, he or she will be disappointed. However, the present authors well understand the dangers in a global Power expressing itself too definitively on important legal matters that may still be controversial or liable to rapid change. Only the reader of the *Manual* can decide whether the right balance has been struck. The present authors are left with the feeling that a little more clarity on these matters might have been possible and desirable.

LISTS OF TREATIES AND OTHER DOCUMENTS

Section 19.2 places each treaty or document into one of five classifications, the nature of which will become clear as this discussion unfolds. The classifications distinguish, *inter alia*, between law of war treaties and arms control treaties. The section correctly explains that law of war treaties generally focus on use of weapons in armed conflict. That is only true, of course, if the treaty is concerned with weapons. GWS, GWS-Sea, GPW, GC and a number of other treaties are not focused on weapons but are most certainly law of war treaties. Be that as it may, the section rightly makes the point that arms control treaties generally focus on restricting development and acquisition of weapons. It then makes the fair point that some law of war treaties may have elements of arms control and some arms control treaties will have elements of law of war about them.

Paragraph 19.2.1 addresses the first classification, namely 'law of war treaties to which the US is a party', and simply lists those treaties, giving the abbreviations used for those treaties in the *Manual*. In the same way, paragraph 19.2.2 lists arms control treaties to which the United States is a party and that are of direct relevance to the law of war. The list comprises the 1925 Geneva Gas Protocol, the 1972 Biological Weapons Convention, the 1976 UN Environmental Modification Convention and the 1993 CWC. The inclusion of the 1925 Geneva Gas Protocol in this list is surprising, given that the treaty limits itself to prohibiting use in war of asphyxiating, poisonous or other gases, all analogous liquids, materials or devices and bacteriological methods of warfare. The treaty makes no reference to possession, production, stockpiling, transfer or, indeed, any other activity associated with such weapons. Accordingly, the treaty should be seen as a law of war treaty, not as an arms control treaty.

An equally interesting omission from the list is Protocol IV to the CCW, the Blinding Lasers Protocol. Article 1 of the Protocol prohibits the employment of a laser weapon specifically designed as one of its combat functions to cause permanent blindness. In addition to this prohibition of use, Article 1 also provides: 'The High Contracting Parties shall not transfer such weapons to any State or non-State entity.' This provision might sensibly be regarded as taking the treaty beyond pure law of war provision and as rendering it an arms control treaty.

Paragraph 19.2.3 gives examples of treaties that have been signed but not ratified by the United States and notes, by reference to Article 18 of the Vienna Convention on the Law of Treaties, the obligation on a State in such circumstances to refrain from acts that would defeat the object and purpose of the treaty until it makes clear its intention not to become party to the treaty. The cited examples are the 1936 London Protocol, the 1969 Vienna Convention on the Law of Treaties, API and APII of 1977, UNCLOS and the 1998 Rome Statute of the International Criminal Court.

Paragraph 19.2.4 gives examples of law of war and arms control treaties that the United States has neither signed nor ratified. The chosen examples are the

1856 Paris Declaration, the 1899 Hague Declaration on Expanding Bullets, the 1907 Hague Conventions VI and VII, the First Protocol to the 1954 Hague Cultural Property Convention, the 1997 Ottawa Convention, the 1999 Second Protocol to the Hague Cultural Property Convention and the 2008 CMC.

Paragraph 19.2.5 contains the last of these lists, namely of treaties and documents that are regarded as being largely of historical interest, a descriptor that accurately fits the texts in the list.

THE LIEBER CODE

At this point, the chapter devotes individual sections to the discussion of particular documents, starting, in section 19.3, with the Lieber Code. That the Lieber Code was prepared by Dr Francis Lieber and was issued to the United States forces as General Order 100, Instructions for the Government of Forces of the United States in the Field on 24 April 1863 is well known. Interesting points made in the section are that the Code was an early example of the law of war being implemented through military instructions or regulations, that the Confederate forces agreed with certain provisions in the Code but disagreed with others and that by applying what were then seen as rules for 'regular war' to the forces of the Confederacy, which the United States did not recognise as a legitimate government or State, the issuing of the Lieber Code was an example of the application of the doctrine of the recognition of belligerency. It is a debateable point whether issuing the Code had that effect. Rather, it would be tangible action taken by the Union side in its specific dealings with the Confederacy that would be capable of having such an effect.

1856 PARIS DECLARATION RESPECTING MARITIME LAW

Section 19.4 argues that the Paris Declaration is an illustration of how a law of war treaty 'may be written with a view towards being able to be accepted and applied by all States'. The associated footnote[1] reproduces an extract from the Declaration expressing the goal of universal ratification or accession to the treaty, which is often to be seen reflected in treaties but which on this occasion is stated in somewhat more fulsome, perhaps optimistic, terms than usual. Arguably, stating that goal is not the same thing as designing the operative part of the treaty in such a way as will make it more likely that the goal will be realised. Section 19.4 does not explain how the operative part of the treaty is thought to have been adapted for that specific purpose.

[1] *DoD Manual*, footnote 67 on page 1139.

1864 GWS

The 1864 Geneva Convention for the Amelioration of the Condition of the Wounded in Armies in the Field is rightly celebrated in section 19.5 for providing for the use of the Red Cross as a distinctive emblem to assist in the identification of medical personnel and in providing for the wounded and sick to be collected and cared for regardless of nationality. Mention could also have been made, for example, of the early formulation of the 'retained personnel' status of medical and religious personnel, which was developed in later Conventions. The full title of the Convention requires correction in both the text and the associated footnote.

1868 ST PETERSBURG DECLARATION

Section 19.6 discusses the 1868 St Petersburg Declaration. This is perhaps a point of detail, but the title is again not accurately stated. Even more mystifying is the fact that in the extract quoting the operative paragraph of the Declaration, there are no fewer than three inaccuracies, and these inaccuracies are repeated in the associated footnote. The general message is correct, but some of the words are not. The section describes the reference in the Declaration's preamble to 'the employment of arms which uselessly aggravate the sufferings of disabled men' as being 'contrary to the laws of humanity' as an early statement of the prohibition against weapons calculated to cause unnecessary suffering. It is recognised that the US prefers the 'calculated to cause' formulation of the rule. However, the language cited from the preamble is rather more supportive of a rule prohibiting weapons, means and methods of warfare *of a nature to cause* unnecessary suffering.[2] The words in the Declaration do not imply the subjective element that is implicit in the reference to 'calculation' in the US formulation. Section 19.6 then correctly notes that the operative part of the Declaration has been overtaken by subsequent general usage of ammunition coming within the Declaration's terms.

1899 AND 1907 HAGUE DECLARATIONS ON WEAPONS

Paragraph 19.7.1 refers to the 1899 Hague Declaration Concerning Expanding Bullets, correctly quoting the operative prohibition of such ammunition and rightly noting the effect of the general participation clause in limiting the application of the treaty to international armed conflicts in which only States

[2] See the discussion in relation to section 6.6 of the *DoD Manual*.

party are involved. The position expressed in paragraph 6.5.4.4 is restated, i.e. that the US is not a party to the treaty and does not regard its provisions as having customary law status in either international or non-international armed conflicts.

Paragraph 19.7.2 addresses the 1899 Hague Declaration Concerning Asphyxiating Gases. The significance of the treaty lies in its limitation to projectiles the *sole* object of which is the diffusion of asphyxiating or deleterious gases. One would have thought that the existence of the word 'sole' in the treaty text, providing as it seems to have done the loophole that led to the dreadful gas attacks in the World War I trenches, would have been the reason for discussing this treaty in Chapter XIX. It is therefore curious that the fateful word is actually omitted from the relevant passage in paragraph 19.7.2. The paragraph correctly notes that the 1925 Geneva Gas Protocol contains a broader prohibition to which the United States is party.

Paragraph 19.7.3 draws attention to the 1899 and 1907 Declarations on the Discharge of Projectiles and Explosives from Balloons, noting that these Declarations were in 1942 regarded as no longer binding, as continues to be the position to this day.

1899 HAGUE CONVENTION II AND 1907 HAGUE CONVENTION IV AND THEIR ANNEXED REGULATIONS

Section 19.8 deals with these two Conventions and the regulations annexed to them, correctly noting that the criteria set forth in Article 1 of the 1899 regulations for militia and volunteer corps to have combatant – and thus, on capture, PW – status are repeated in Article 4A of GPW. As paragraph 19.8.2 observes, the US ratified 1907 Hague Convention IV on 27 November 1909. This means that it is this Convention and its associated regulations that are binding on the US, as opposed to the texts of 1899. Paragraph 19.8.2.1 then states, 'Provisions of Hague IV and Hague IV Regulations have been found to reflect customary international law', and makes particular reference to Article 42, which gives the widely recognised meaning of 'occupation'. The footnote associated with this paragraph cites findings from the Nuremburg War Crime Tribunals that the regulations as a whole reflect customary international law. The problem with the cited language is that it is ambiguous as to whether the Regulations as a whole or only part of them are now regarded by the US as customary. If the US takes the latter view, the *Manual* should have specified which of the rules in the Regulations are, or are not, considered to be customary and should have given reasons why, taking particular care to explain any deviation from the Nuremburg Tribunal approach.

Citing the text of the Martens Clause taken from the Preamble to the 1899 Convention, paragraph 19.8.3 explains that the clause was a compromise 'following difficult and unresolved debates at the 1899 Hague Peace Conference about the status of resistance fighters in occupied territory'. The paragraph makes the useful points that the relevance of the clause is by no means limited to the resistance fighter issue, that it is cited in numerous other contexts and that the clause reflects the idea that when no specific law of war rule applies, its principles form the general guide for conduct during war.[3]

Section 19.9 explains that 1907 Hague Convention X was replaced by GWS-Sea in relation to the parties to the latter document, and paragraph 19.10 points out that the 1922 Washington Treaty on Submarines and Noxious Gases never entered into force because all of the signatory Powers did not ratify it. The language of Article 5 in respect of asphyxiating gases found its way, however, into the 1925 Geneva Gas Protocol.

1923 HAGUE AIR AND RADIO RULES

Section 19.11 explains how the 1922 Washington Conference on the Limitation of Armament adopted a resolution under which the Commission was appointed that in due course produced the Hague draft rules relating to aerial warfare and the use of radio in warfare. The *Manual* states: 'The 1923 Hague Air Rules were not, however, subsequently adopted as a treaty by the United States.' This is a rather odd way of putting it, given that unilateral action by a single State cannot constitute a treaty. The more usual way of explaining the position is simply to say that the 1923 Draft Rules were never adopted by States in treaty form.

The paragraph then states that some of the provisions of the Draft Rules 'may reflect customary international law', citing as an example the permissibility of using tracer, incendiary or explosive projectiles by or against aircraft notwithstanding the St Petersburg Declaration. The problem is the use of the verb 'may'. The reader is left with an unanswered question, namely which specific rules the US considers do reflect customary law. In a manual of this nature, one might reasonably expect this aspect to be made clearer. The purpose of such a manual is, after all, to tell its readers what the US regards the law as being, and the customary status or otherwise of particular rules is an important element of the law. The section rightly notes that the draft

[3] The 1907 text of the clause is reproduced in a footnote to the discussion of paragraph 2.1.2.2 in Chapter 2 of the present book.

rule that suggests that only military personnel may be members of a military aircraft crew is not customary. However, it then argues that 'certain efforts in the [Rules] to limit the effects of attacks also do not reflect customary international law'. Again, it would be more helpful to know which specific rules the US does and does not consider to be customary, and to be told the reasoning for that view, given that a number of the 1923 rules on bombardment would be generally recognised as customary.

1925 GENEVA GAS AND BACTERIOLOGICAL PROTOCOL

Section 19.12 correctly states the scope of application of the 1925 Geneva Gas Protocol, noting that the US ratified the Protocol on 10 April 1975. The section recalls that on ratification, the US made a 'no first use' reservation, indicating that it would cease to be bound by the treaty 'in regard to an enemy state if such state or any of its allies fails to respect the prohibitions laid down in th[e] Protocol'. As the section makes clear, this 'no first use' reservation only permitted the retaliatory use of gases, liquids, materials or devices. It did not refer to, and thus would not excuse any use (retaliatory or otherwise) of, bacteriological methods of warfare. The *Manual* makes the mistake of referring here to 'biological weapons'. The treaty refers explicitly to 'bacteriological methods of warfare', the point being that there are biological substances capable of offensive use that are not bacteriological in nature and the Protocol's prohibition relates only to the narrower class of methods.

1929 GENEVA CONVENTIONS

Section 19.13 mentions the 1929 GWS and GPW, both of which have effectively been superseded by the corresponding 1949 treaties. It is usefully noted that the 1929 GPW was found by the World War II war crimes tribunals to reflect customary law, and that some of the provisions of the 1929 texts informed corresponding provisions adopted in 1949.

1930 LONDON TREATY FOR THE LIMITATION AND REDUCTION OF NAVAL ARMAMENT AND 1936 LONDON PROTOCOL

Section 19.14 draws attention to the 1930 London Treaty on the Limitation and Reduction of Naval Armament, Article 22 and the 1936 London Procès-Verbal Relating to the Rules of Submarine Warfare, which provide that in their action with regard to merchant ships, submarines must conform to the rules of international law to which surface vessels are subject. The US ratified the 1930 treaty on 27 October 1930 and signed the 1936 treaty on 6 November 1936.

1935 ROERICH PACT

Section 19.15 notes the conclusion of the Roerich Pact in Washington on 15 April 1935 and its ratification by the US on 13 July 1935. The Pact concerned itself with the protection of specified kinds of cultural property and of certain associated personnel. The section points out that all States that became party to the Pact are now party to the 1954 Hague Cultural Property Convention. The distinctive emblem of the 1954 Convention should be used in place of the distinctive flag provided for in Article III of the Pact.

1949 GENEVA CONVENTIONS

Section 19.16 recognises the very extensive – it would perhaps be better to say 'universal' – ratification of the four Conventions and acknowledges that the US has viewed many of the protections embodied in them as 'reflecting appropriate US practice in armed conflict regardless of formal treaty obligations'. Is this, one wonders, yet another way of skirting around a clear answer to the question of whether those rules are customary? After all, as was noted in the relevant chapters, that is an assertion that is only relatively rarely made, which might imply to some readers that in the US view there is only fairly sparse customary law in relation to the treatment of the wounded, sick, shipwrecked, PWs and civilians in the hands of an adverse party. Certainly, there is no clear statement being made in this section as to which Convention rules are now seen by the US as being customary.

The section rightly explains the status of the Pictet Commentaries to the Conventions, namely that they often assist with understanding the provisions but that they are not an official interpretation. The *Manual* adds that only participating States are qualified to give an official interpretation. This is probably correct in the light of Article 31 of the Vienna Convention on the Law of Treaties, 1969, to which the US is not party.[4]

Paragraph 19.16.1 usefully explains that the duplication inherent in the common articles of the four Conventions is because each Convention was designed to be effective even if a State only ratified a single one. Thus, as the paragraph correctly points out, the list of persons entitled to PW status under GPW is repeated in GWS and GWS-Sea.

[4] *DoD Manual*, paragraph 19.2.3.

Paragraph 19.16.1.2 quotes the important language of Common Article 2, noting that that language helps to explain when the law of war applies, including in situations of unopposed belligerent occupation. It is right that the 1954 Hague Cultural Property Convention repeats Common Article 2 language and that CCW incorporates such language by reference. The paragraph does not mention, however, that API explicitly defines its scope of application by reference to Common Article 2.[5]

Paragraph 19.16.1.3 describes Common Article 3 to the Conventions. The paragraph suggests that Common Article 3 'reflects a minimum yardstick of humane treatment protections that apply more broadly, including during international armed conflict'. The better view, it is suggested, is that the minimum acceptable level of treatment of persons who are not taking an active part in the hostilities involves more rules, more prescriptive protections, more safeguards and a generally better level of treatment than that specified in the minimal obligations in Common Article 3.

Paragraph 19.16.1.4 states that Article 4 of GPW 'explains which persons are entitled to receive POW status under the GPW' and that the provision is mirrored in GWS and GWS-Sea. To be precise, it is Article 4A that defines those entitled to PW status on capture, and it is GPW Article 4A's provisions that are replicated in GWS and GWS-Sea. That those entitled to GPW protections are not protected under GC is noted. Paragraph 19.16.2 briefly lists three of the areas of protection provided in GWS, which are addressed in more detail in Chapter VII of the *Manual* and in Chapter 7 of this book. It is noted that the Convention replaces those of 1864, 1906 and 1929 'in relations between the parties to the GWS'. The final words may seem to be an unnecessary addition to the sentence, given the universal or virtually universal participation of States in the treaty. The insertion of those words is, however, an accurate reflection of the language of Article 59 of GWS. Paragraph 19.16.3 similarly briefly mentions three topics addressed in GWS-Sea and discussed in more detail in Chapter VII of the *Manual* and Chapter 7 of this book. The *Manual* correctly states that it replaces 1907 Hague Convention X. Paragraph 19.16.4.1 explains that GPW replaces the 1929 Convention 'in relations between the parties to the GPW' and argues that it is complementary with Chapter II of the Hague Regulations of 1899 and 1907. Paragraph 19.16.5.1 lists the broad topics covered by the various parts of GC, all of which are considered in significant depth in Chapter X of the *Manual* and Chapter 10 of this book. It is suggested in paragraph 19.16.5.2 that Articles 22 to 56 of the 1899 or, as the case

5 API, Article 1(3).

may be, of the 1907 Hague Regulations are supplemented by GC, implying that the provisions of the latter apply alongside those of the former. Given the customary status of the rules in the Hague Regulations, this would seem to be the correct interpretation: an interpretation that would also apply to the relationship between GPW and the Hague Regulations discussed earlier in the present paragraph.

1954 HAGUE CULTURAL PROPERTY CONVENTION

Section 19.17 refers briefly to some of the topics addressed in the 1954 Convention and notes that the United States ratified the Convention on 13 March 2009 subject to four statements of understanding. The United States is not a party to either of the two Protocols to the Convention. Paragraph 19.17.1.1 argues that the 1954 Convention is supplementary to the Hague Regulations of 1899 and 1907 and to Hague Convention IX for States that are party to the relevant treaties. This, again, would seem to be correct, in that the provisions in each that are protective of cultural property and by which a State is bound will apply alongside one another. Paragraph 19.17.1.2 argues for a similar supplementary arrangement in relation to the Roerich Pact, subject to the requirement to use the emblem of the 1954 Convention in place of the Roerich Pact flag. This would also seem to be a sensible, practical approach.

VIENNA CONVENTION ON THE LAW OF TREATIES

Section 19.18 reminds the reader that the Vienna Convention on the Law of Treaties, adopted on 23 May 1969, is a treaty to which the US is not party, although it is stated to view many – again, unfortunately unspecified – provisions of the treaty as customary.

BIOLOGICAL WEAPONS CONVENTION

Section 19.19 refers to the Biological Weapons Convention ratified by the United States on 26 March 1975 and reflected in US domestic legislation, the significant provisions of which are reproduced in a footnote.[6]

[6] *DoD Manual*, footnote 196 on page 1159. It should be noted that it was the US decision on 25 October 1969 to renounce biological weapons, together with its decisions to destroy stockpiles and cease the production, use etc. of toxins for war purposes, that was an important factor in initiating the process that led to the Convention. This aspect is not reflected in section 19.19.

ADDITIONAL PROTOCOLS TO THE 1949 GENEVA CONVENTIONS

Section 19.20 suggests that because the two Additional Protocols were negotiated at the same time, they may indicate States' views on the differences between the rules applicable in international and non-international armed conflicts. It is certainly apparent on the face of the respective treaties that only less detailed provision could be agreed in respect of the latter class of conflict. Maybe the *Manual* is right that this means that States believe that fewer rules actually apply in the latter situation. An alternative understanding is that the differences in provision reflect the limits on what the delegations to the 1974 to 1977 Diplomatic Conference could achieve, which may or may not reflect States' views forty years later. Paragraph 19.20.1 is right to suggest that API supplements the Conventions. This is indeed explicitly stated in Article 1(3) of API. The paragraph then notes that the *Manual* references API provisions, some of which are stated to be consistent with DoD practice, but that unless explicitly noted, no determination is made as to whether any API provisions reflect customary law.

Paragraph 19.20.1.1 refers to examples of API provisions that the US has accepted in later treaties. The paragraph mentions the child soldier provisions in the Optional Protocol and the 'definition of military objective in Article 51(2)', which is substantially similar to that in Article 2(6) of the Amended Mines Protocol of CCW. The first comment here is that the military objective definition is in Article 52(2) of API, not in Article 51(2). The second is that the US is known to favour a more expansive interpretation of military objectives that includes war-sustaining objects. Perhaps it would therefore be more accurate to say that the US accepts that all objects that come within the Article 52(2) definition will be military objectives, but that it would include in addition the war-sustaining objects already referred to. Paragraph 19.20.1.2 correctly suggests that the API requirements to make legal advisers available to commanders and to conduct weapon reviews may not be customary but are consistent with long-standing US practice. Paragraph 19.20.1.3 restates that the US supports and promotes as a matter of national policy the fundamental guarantees in Article 75 of API. Perhaps it is the absence of apparent global implementation of these standards that causes the US reasonably to doubt their customary status. The present authors take the view that failure to adhere to those guarantees is frequently condemned, and that therein lies the basis for their customary status.

The US also supports the principle that 'journalism is generally to be regarded as a civilian activity', although not necessarily as a customary rule, nor necessarily as militarily acceptable in all respects. Of course, the provision in Article 79(1) of API that journalists engaged in dangerous professional missions in areas of armed conflict shall be considered as civilians is subject to the proviso that they take no action adversely affecting their status as civilians. This would seem to go a long way to addressing the concerns that are likely to be represented in the *Manual*'s use of the word 'generally'.

The paragraph then notes that there are situations in which the US supports the customary nature of the principle on which an API rule is based, but not the terms in which it is expressed in API. The direct participation in hostilities provision in Article 51(3) is cited as an example, but no preferred wording is offered. Another example given in the paragraph recognises US support for the prohibition of starvation of the civilian population as a method of warfare, but suggests that the 'intricacy of the provisions of API on objects indispensible to the survival of the civilian population make it doubtful that such provisions could be characterized as customary'. Again, which of the 'intricacies' of Article 54(2), (3) and perhaps (5) of API are considered to go beyond customary law and which are not is left unstated.

Paragraph 19.20.1.5 usefully lists the API provisions to which the United States has objected. Many of these objections are well known. The listed topics are: national liberation movements, discussed in paragraph 3.3.4; mercenaries, discussed in paragraph 4.21.1; works and installations containing dangerous forces, discussed in paragraph 5.13.1; the criteria for lawful combatant status, discussed in paragraph 4.6.1.2; the obligation of combatants to distinguish themselves, discussed in paragraph 5.5.8.2; environmental protection, discussed in paragraph 6.10.3.1; the presumptions in favour of civilian status in conducting attacks, discussed in paragraph 5.5.3.2; the prohibition of the use of enemy flags, insignia or uniforms to shield, favour, protect or impede military operations, discussed in paragraph 5.23.3; and reprisals, discussed in paragraph 18.18.3.4.

Paragraph 19.20.2.1 points out that the US is not a party to APII and details the interaction between three administrations and the Senate on the matter. It is clear from the paragraph, and the correspondence quoted in the associated footnotes, that 'reviews have concluded that the provisions of APII are consistent with US practice'. It is also, perhaps, worthy of note that Chapter XVII (Non-International Armed Conflict) seems to acknowledge most provisions of APII. Having set forth the limitations on scope provided in Article 1(1) of APII, paragraph 19.20.2.2 interprets these as meaning that the treaty would only cover conflicts in which 'dissident armed forces or other organized armed groups are organized and disciplined like regular armed forces'. It is a matter of opinion whether this interpretation is potentially overstating the relevant requirement in Article 1(1), namely that there be responsible command. It is by no means clear that responsible command necessarily requires organisation and discipline following the regular armed forces model. It appears from the paragraph that the original presidential proposal when the treaty was submitted to the Senate in 1986 was that APII would be ratified on the understanding that it would be applied to all non-international armed conflicts, not just the limited subset of such conflicts coming within Article 1(1) of the treaty. Interestingly, this would have included Article 1(4) API conflicts of national liberation.[7]

CCW, CCW AMENDED ARTICLE 1 AND CCW PROTOCOLS

Paragraph 9.21.1 correctly identifies a State's notification of its consent to be bound by a Protocol as an essential prerequisite to the entry into force of that Protocol for the State concerned. Likewise, amendments to the Convention or to its Protocols are subject to ratification or acceptance by a State before they enter into force for that State. Moreover, the CCW itself is subject to ratification or acceptance by a State wishing to be bound by it so it only enters into force for a State that deposits its instrument of ratification or other acceptance. So, the paragraph makes the point that ratification or acceptance of an amendment to the Convention or to a Protocol is a prerequisite for the application of that amendment to that State.

The paragraph notes that the US is a party to CCW and to all its existing Protocols, and gives the relevant dates when the US became bound thereby. It also observes that on 21 January 2009, the US ratified the extension of the scope of CCW and its Protocols I, II, III and IV to non-international armed conflicts, indicating that this reflected existing US policy. The effect of the extension of scope is correctly described in paragraph 19.21.1.1.

Article 7(4) of the CCW applies the Convention and the Protocols to which a State is party in the case of an armed conflict of the kind referred to in Article 1(4) of API, i.e. an armed conflict in exercise of the right of self-determination, in two circumstances. The first circumstance, covered by sub-paragraph (a) of Article 7(4), is where the State party to CCW is also a party to API. That clearly does not apply in relation to the US. The second circumstance, given in Article 7(4)(b), deals with the situation where a State party to CCW is not also a party to API, which is of course the US position. Paragraph 19.21.1.2 sets out the provisions of Article 7(4)(b) of CCW and notes the reservation entered by the US on ratifying the Convention on 24 March 1995, stating simply: 'Article 7(4)(b) of the Convention shall not apply with

7 *DoD Manual*, footnote 231 on page 1164.

respect to the United States.' This is, of course, consistent with the fact that the US is not party to API and with the fact that Article 1(4) of API is one of the reasons why the US declines to become a party.

Paragraph 19.21.1.3 makes the reasonable point that the restrictions and prohibitions in the CCW and its Protocols generally have not been based on the premise that they are warranted because the relevant weapons are calculated to cause superfluous injury or are inherently indiscriminate. The paragraph asserts that the CCW and Protocols have been drafted on the basis that they are new contractual – presumably meaning 'conventional' – rules and that they are not a restatement of existing customary international law. This is right as far as it goes. Perhaps the more useful point would have been to highlight the 'which may be deemed' language in the title to the Convention and simply to note that deeming that a weapon may have a particular effect in unspecified circumstances is not the same thing as asserting that it does in fact have that effect with the regularity or inevitability required to breach the relevant principle. Paragraph 19.21.2 gives the ratification date, 24 March 1995, of CCW Protocol I.

Paragraph 19.21.3 points out how, when compared with Protocol II of 1980, the Amended Mines Protocol includes more detailed restrictions, and that it applies in non-international armed conflict. All CCW Protocols potentially apply in non-international armed conflicts; the point that could have been made a little more explicitly in the present paragraph is that the Amended Mines Protocol has always also applied to such conflicts. The paragraph asserts that before becoming party to the Amended Mines Protocol on 24 May 1999, US policy was to observe its requirements to the fullest extent possible.

Where CCW Protocol III on incendiary weapons is concerned, paragraph 19.21.4 notes that the US ratified the Protocol on 24 May 1999, subject to a reservation and an understanding. Likewise, paragraph 19.21.5 observes that Protocol IV on blinding lasers was consistent with DoD policy on such weapons before the adoption of the Protocol, and that the US ratified the Protocol on 21 January 2009. The paragraph reports that US legal reviews, conducted before the adoption of the Protocol, concluded that the use of a laser for the purpose of blinding an enemy combatant would not constitute unnecessary suffering. Yoram Dinstein takes a contrary view, commenting that the reason for the disavowal of this particular weapon is a severe, life-long and irreversible incapacitation which was regarded as constituting superfluous injury or unnecessary suffering because a temporary flash blinding would have been sufficient for military purposes.[8] The present authors would prefer

[8] Dinstein, *Conduct of Hostilities*, 90; see n. 5 to Chapter 3.

Yoram Dinstein's view, always assuming that the military task to be accomplished would be satisfied by temporary blinding, that temporary blinding is in fact an available option and that permanent blinding offers no or insufficient additional military benefit. In the overwhelming majority of circumstances, this will indeed be the case.

The paragraph then asserts that the Protocol's restrictions 'may be characterized as arms control obligations in that these restrictions do not establish that the use of lasers as anti-personnel weapons, including for the purpose of blinding, is prohibited by the rule against weapons calculated to cause unnecessary suffering nor otherwise prohibited by the customary law of war'. While the reference quoted in support in the footnote is the highly authoritative work of William Hays Parks, it is by no means clear to the present authors that the conclusions cited flow necessarily from Hays Parks' expressed views. Protocol IV is indeed an arms control treaty, because its prohibitions in the second sentence of Article 1 take it outside the normal law of war realm of simple prohibitions or restrictions of use. It is not right to conclude, however, that any weapons law treaty that cannot be shown to reflect a pre-existing rule of customary law is as a result to be classed as an arms control treaty. That is simply not the case.[9]

Paragraph 19.21.6 correctly notes that Protocol V to CCW is concerned not with restrictions or prohibitions of the use of weapons, but with 'what must be done with respect to unexploded munitions that threaten civilians and post-conflict reconstruction', addressing itself primarily to pre- and post-conflict action. The US became a party to the Protocol on 21 January 2009.

CHEMICAL WEAPONS CONVENTION

Section 19.22 correctly notes that Article 22 of the CWC prohibits reservations and that the annexes to the Convention must not be the subject of reservations incompatible with the Convention's object and purpose. The latter of the two provisions is odd, because Article 19(c) of the Vienna Convention on the Law of Treaties contains a general prohibition of reservations that are incompatible with the object and purpose of a treaty. However, as we have seen, the US is not a party to the Vienna Convention, and therein perhaps lies part of the explanation for the second part of section 19.22.

9 See A Roberts and R Guelff, *Documents on the Laws of War*, 3rd edn. Oxford: Oxford University Press (2000), 37; D den Dekker, The Effectiveness of International Supervision in Arms Control Law, 9(3) *Journal of Conflict & Security Law* 315 (2004), at 316.

The section then includes a lengthy and most useful explanation of the US position in respect of RCAs and of Executive Order 11850. The interesting observation is that the Senate 'as a condition of its advice and consent to ratification [of the CWC] required that the President certify to Congress that the United States is not restricted by the . . . Convention in its use of riot control agents in certain cases and that Executive Order 11850 would not be modified'. President Clinton so certified on 25 April 1997, and the US ratified the Convention on the same day.[10] The legal position in relation to RCAs is discussed in section 6.16 of the *Manual* and in the corresponding paragraphs of Chapter 6 of this book. The section notes that domestic US legislation was enacted to implement the Convention.

ROME STATUTE

Section 19.23 tackles the Rome Statute of the International Criminal Court. The US signed the Rome Statute on 31 December 2000. However, the section notes that the US has identified 'significant flaws' in the document, and refers for example to the concern that the ICC would claim jurisdiction over persons from States that are not party to the Statute. Another reported concern is that the ICC would not grant US persons accused of war crimes the procedural protections that they are afforded under US domestic law. The section points out that on 6 May 2002, a letter was filed with the UN Secretary-General indicating that the US does not intend to become a party to the Statute, noting correctly that in consequence of the letter, the US has no legal obligations arising from its signature. The State Department policy on these matters is described in the section as 'not to frustrate the object and purpose of the Rome Statute'.

1999 UN SECRETARY GENERAL'S BULLETIN FOR UN FORCES

Section 19.24 addresses the 1999 UN Secretary-General's Bulletin for UN Forces in appropriately brief terms. The purpose of the document is stated to have been to set out the principles and rules of international humanitarian law that apply to UN forces conducting operations under UN command. The section argues that the Bulletin is not legally binding. It would probably have been more accurate to state that the document does not have the status of

[10] Footnotes to the section detail the assurances sought by the Senate and those given by the President; see *DoD Manual*, footnotes 277 and 278 on page 1173.

a source of international law. Nevertheless, it is right to state, as the section does, that the Bulletin has been criticised by States.

2005 ICRC STUDY ON CUSTOMARY INTERNATIONAL HUMANITARIAN LAW

Section 19.25 concerns itself with the 2005 ICRC Customary Law Study report. The section points out that there is 'no list of treaty provisions (or other codification) that the United States has agreed reflects the entirely of the customary international law of war'. One could, of course, comment that by the same token, the US, as is its right, has not chosen, or perhaps has chosen not, to issue such a list or text. The serious US concerns about the methodology of the study are mentioned, and the US's contention that it is not in a position to accept the Study's conclusions without further analysis is reported.

Section 19.26 concludes Chapter XIX by noting briefly that the Third Additional Protocol to the Geneva Conventions was adopted on 8 December 2005 and was ratified by the US on 8 March 2007. The Protocol recognises the Red Crystal as a third distinctive emblem alongside the Red Cross and the Red Crescent.

20

Post-Publication Amendments

The DoD *Law of War Manual* was promulgated on 12 June 2015. The comments in Chapters 1 to 19 of this book have been prepared by reference to the text as originally promulgated. It would, however, be wrong to finish the present text with Chapter 19, simply because at the time of writing two sets of amendments have been published. The purpose of this relatively short chapter is therefore to consider those two sets, to explain briefly what they comprise and to make any comment upon them that seems to be appropriate.

MAY 2016 AMENDMENTS

The first set of amendments was issued by the US DoD on 31 May 2016. The detail of the amendments was set forth in pages appearing at the beginning of the *Manual* in its amended form. The amendments consist of minor changes to the discussion of proportionality in section 2.4, minor revisions of the discussion of the principle of honour in section 2.6, substantial revisions of the discussion of journalists in section 4.24, some minor changes for stylistic consistency, the correction of some typographical and administrative errors and adjustments to punctuation and spacing. The changes for stylistic consistency, corrections of typographical and administrative errors and adjustments of punctuation and spacing will not be considered further.

Proportionality

The wording of paragraph 2.4.1.1 has been amended. The argument is put more clearly that proportionality issues arise where one is justified in acting and that where there is no justification in acting, a proportionality analysis is not necessary to show that the attack is unlawful. The problem is that this paragraph is where, in the view of the present authors, the discussion of the proportionality principle in this chapter starts to become confused with the proportionality rule as it applies in the law of targeting. The proportionality principle does indeed presuppose justification in acting, but once that justification can be shown to exist, the matters to be weighed in that proportionality assessment are not military gain versus civilian loss, but the military purpose that the military action is intended to achieve versus the totality or extent of the damage, injury and loss that is being inflicted, both military and civilian, and both to persons and to objects.

The final sentence of the first part of paragraph 2.4.1.2 has been changed in a way that rather reinforces the same error. The sentence, as amended, talks of an obligation under the proportionality principle to refrain from attacks in which the expected incidental harm would be excessive in relation to the concrete and direct military advantage anticipated, and then refers to feasible precautions to reduce the risk to civilians and other protected persons and objects. This makes it even clearer that what is really being referred to here is the targeting law proportionality rule, not the proportionality principle under the general law of war, and that this discussion is therefore misplaced. The principle is not concerned only with incidental harm, but with all harm, both intended and incidental. Accordingly, the stated purpose of the amendment, namely to 'match the language used in the cross-referenced § 5.12', is itself a mistaken purpose.

The change in the title to paragraph 2.4.2 is unobjectionable. The second part of that paragraph, however, states that 'the principle of proportionality described in a more general sense in this section underlies the affirmative duties to take feasible precautions for the protection of civilians and other protected persons and objects'. It would certainly be right to say that general notions of proportionality underlie these duties and rules. What is incorrect is the contention that the law of war principle of proportionality does this.

The title to section 5.12 has been amended to 'Proportionality – Prohibition on Attacks Expected to Cause Excessive Incidental Harm'. The interesting aspect of this amendment lies in the explanation of its purpose given in the amendment description, namely 'to be more specific to avoid potential confusion with the discussion of the broader principle of proportionality'. As has been explained here and in Chapter 2 of this book, this confusion already arises from the terms in which the principle is discussed in Chapter II. On a more minor matter, the title should, it is suggested, use 'of' in place of 'on'. Consequential amendments are then made to footnotes in which reference is made to this section title.

Honour

Section 2.6, which deals with the principle of honour, is also amended. The amendments consist of minor changes in language, such as inserting the word 'military' before 'forces' and replacing the word 'combatant' with 'military forces'. The stated purpose of these amendments is to 'clarify that the principle of honor helps distinguish military forces from terrorist groups and other unlawful combatants'. The notion of 'unlawful combatant' is, of course, a contradiction in terms for States party to API. Leaving that aspect to one side, it is useful that the *Manual* amendment seeks to emphasise honour as an important feature that marks conventional military forces out from fighters that lack that important ethic.

Paragraph 2.6.1 is amended to make the link between the honour principle and more general warrior traditions of ethical behaviour. The amendment also draws appropriate attention to the US canons of personal conduct, with their emphasis on the importance of honour as a core value. The second part of the paragraph notes that the concept of honour being referred to derives from a variety of cultures and time periods, not just from the behaviour of knights in Europe in the Middle Ages.

Journalists

The amendments of 31 May 2016 included substantial revisions of the section dealing with journalists. Rather than seek to comment on each change of wording, the present section will consider the new wording afresh and as a whole. Section 4.24 makes the correct initial point that, in general, journalists are civilians and are protected as such under the law of war. Noting their vital role in free societies, in the rule of law and in providing information about armed conflict, the section sees the proactive release of accurate information to domestic and international audiences as consistent with the objectives of US military operations. The section emphasises the open and independent nature of this reporting and refers to the embedding of journalists with units during military operations.

In that context, paragraph 4.24.1 repeats that '[i]n general, journalists are protected as civilians'. The sentence continues: 'i.e., engaging in journalism does not constitute taking a direct part in hostilities such that such a person would be deprived of protection from being made the object of attack.' The point that journalism does not *per se* constitute direct participation in hostilities is both valid and worth making. The paragraph rightly notes that journalists are not a class in their own right, that they generally share the rights, duties and liabilities of civilians but that their role does not preclude them otherwise acquiring another status, whether as a person accompanying the armed forces or as a combatant. As has been noted elsewhere, persons accompanying the armed forces do not constitute 'another status'. They are civilians, and therefore in principle have the same protections, e.g. from being made the object of attack, as other civilians, and they lose that protection under the same circumstances as other civilians, namely by taking a direct part in the hostilities.

Journalists authorised to accompany the armed forces, sometimes called 'war correspondents', are addressed in paragraph 4.24.1.1, where their entitlement on capture to PW status and the need for them to be issued with appropriate identification cards are noted. Paragraph 4.24.1.2 correctly makes the point that if members of the armed forces serve as journalists, they will nevertheless remain combatants. The paragraph points out that non-State armed groups 'sometimes use their members for propaganda or other media activities, and such personnel are not precluded from being considered unprivileged belligerents'. This is true, but the point could and perhaps should be made that members of non-State armed groups that have no combat-related role of any kind and that are exclusively engaged in diplomatic or other non-hostile activities ought not, merely by reference to their membership, to be regarded as directly participating. The next sentence is, however, important, because it sets out the position here accurately. It makes the point that engaging in journalism is not a basis for considering a person an unprivileged belligerent, but that a person who is an unprivileged belligerent is not precluded from being so considered because he or she works as a journalist. In other words, it is what the individual actually does or, as the case may be, does not do that renders him or her liable to be made the object of a lawful attack or entitles him or her to protection from attack, not the fact that the individual is a journalist.

Recognising that the factual circumstances of armed conflict often expose journalists to dangers not normally encountered by other civilians, paragraph 4.24.2.1 notes the significant risk that such journalists may be injured or killed incidentally to an enemy attack or from other dangers. The paragraph refers to precautions such as distinguishing journalists from combatants and distinguishing their activities from those of enemy forces so as to avoid the erroneous impression that a journalist is a member of enemy forces. Particular mention is made of the need to avoid any activity that adversely affects their status as civilians if they wish to retain the protection of a civilian. It would be better, and would perhaps make it easier for the journalists themselves to grasp the relevant point, if the paragraph avoided referring to activities that might affect journalists' status as civilians. Their activities, short of becoming a member of the armed forces, will not alter their civilian status. Even though they remain civilians, however, their participation in activities related to the hostilities can affect whether they continue to be entitled to the protection enjoyed by other civilians.

Paragraph 4.24.2.2 reminds the reader of the US DoD policy that open and independent reporting will be the principal means of covering US military operations. The correct point is made that the law of war does not prohibit States from taking security measures to reduce the risk that sensitive military information is disclosed, making the specific point that 'military security ground rules' may be developed for media personnel. The paragraph closes by noting that access by the media to military operations must be consistent with law of war obligations such as the requirement to protect PWs and other detainees from public curiosity.

DECEMBER 2016 AMENDMENTS

In December 2016, an additional set of amendments was published. These amendments altered the numbering of the sections of Chapter V, revised extensively the treatment of proportionality in what are now sections 5.10, 5.11 and 5.12 and made certain other adjustments to other parts of the text. The present section will address the new sections 5.10, 5.11 and 5.12, before turning to the remaining somewhat less major amendments.

Amendments to the Manual's *Treatment of Proportionality*

At the time when the first draft of Chapter 5 was written, the text of Chapter V was that originally published by the US DoD in June 2015, so Chapter 5 bases itself on that original text. The present discussion will therefore start with a consideration of the amended Section 5.10, which refers to an obligation to reduce the risk of harm to civilians and other protected persons and objects. It would be more accurate to refer to an obligation to avoid and in any event to minimise such risks, as reflected in API, Article 57(2)(a)(ii): a provision that is widely accepted, probably customary. The immediately following paragraph restates the proportionality rule correctly, except that it talks of 'expected' military advantage when the reference should be to the military advantage that is 'anticipated'. Expectation is arguably a more limiting criterion than anticipation. It is good that paragraph 5.10.1 notes that feasible precautions must also be taken to reduce the harm to protected military personnel, e.g. those who are *hors de combat*.

Curiously, paragraph 5.10.1.2 suggests that the prohibition on attacks expected to cause excessive incidental harm does not require consideration of military medical personnel, military wounded and sick and military medical facilities. This seems to be an illogical conclusion. Given that each of these categories of personnel and facility must be respected and protected, and indeed that they are entitled to protection, e.g. in the form of warnings, that goes beyond that to which civilians are entitled, it cannot be right that expected injury or, as the case may be, damage to them is simply ignored in applying the proportionality rule. The better view must be that because of their *special* protection, such persons and objects must be considered when an attack is being planned or decided upon. It is, of course, right that the expected damage to a sick bay on a warship would not serve to prohibit an attack on that warship. The mere fact that the expected collateral damage would not be likely to outweigh the anticipated military advantage is not, however, justification for the suggestion that it is not necessary to consider injury or damage that ought, in the present authors' view, to feature in the proportionality evaluation. The paragraph concludes by observing that feasible precautions must be taken to reduce the risk of harm to such persons and objects. Again, it would be more accurate to state that all feasible precautions must be taken to avoid, and at any event to minimise, that risk.[1]

The important role of commanders in the implementation of the proportionality rule is properly emphasised in paragraph 5.10.2. Paragraph 5.10.2.1 develops the point by noting that those 'who are responsible for making the decisions and judgments required by the principle of proportionality are those who have the authority' to make them. It might be more appropriate to observe that those with the authority to make such decisions have the responsibility to do so with appropriate care. That said, the paragraph makes the correct point that aspects of the proportionality judgment, such as anticipated military advantage and the feasibility of taking particular precautions, are matters that are likely to require decisions by those with suitable authority over military operations. The paragraph discusses whether what it describes as the 'principle of proportionality' requires military personnel to take actions such as providing warnings. This is not really the right approach in the view of the present authors. The proportionality rule – not principle – describes a kind of attack that is considered indiscriminate. If proportionality is breached, the attack is indiscriminate, and therefore unlawful. It may be possible, by taking

[1] API, Article 57(2).

certain precautions, to render a planned attack compliant with the proportionality rule. If, however, it is determined that the relevant precautions cannot feasibly be undertaken, that does not give the attacking force the right to undertake an indiscriminate attack. The correct approach in such a circumstance would be to refrain from undertaking the planned attack and to find some other lawful way to achieve the desired military purpose.

Paragraphs 5.10.2.2 and 5.10.2.3 correctly note that the commander's decisions on proportionality must be reasonable, must necessarily involve subjective aspects and must be based on common sense and good faith, with reasonable commanders not necessarily making the same decisions. Paragraph 5.10.2.4 recognises that the duty not to comply with clearly unlawful orders also applies to proportionality violations, explaining correctly that subordinates may not be competent to assess whether proportionality would be breached. Paragraph 5.10.2.5 rightly points out the circumstances in which subordinates have discretion as to the conduct of attacks, and paragraph 5.10.3 points to the military procedures through which the proportionality rule is in practice applied, including rules of engagement, doctrine, standard operating procedures and special instructions.

Paragraph 5.10.4 again makes the fundamental error of treating the rules as to precautions in attack as an element of the proportionality rule. The two are related but distinct. As noted earlier, attacks that breach the proportionality rule are examples of attacks that are indiscriminate and thus prohibited. When the paragraph suggests that 'the available time is a constraint in assessing whether an attack is expected to cause excessive incidental harm', the implication is that when time is pressing, the proportionality rule, and by extension the indiscriminate attacks prohibition, does not apply. Such an implication is legally incorrect. It would, however, be right to say that the pressure of time may affect the precautions that it is feasible for the attacker to take. This issue is addressed explicitly in paragraph 5.10.5, where the *Manual*'s approach is justified on the basis that the proportionality and precautions rules are 'fundamentally connected and mutually reinforcing obligations'. They may well be both of those things, but they are also distinct legal obligations, and seeking to wrap them together in the way the *Manual* does may lead to misunderstanding. Nevertheless, the final sentence of the paragraph notes that feasible precautions must be taken even where excessive incidental harm is not expected, and that even when feasible precautions have been taken, an attack could be prohibited as one expected to cause excessive incidental harm. Of course, if feasible precautions are properly taken, an attack expected to cause excessive incidental harm will not be undertaken, which rather reinforces the point being made here as to the distinctness of the rules.

Proportionality – Feasible Precautions in Planning and Conducting Attacks to Reduce the Risk of Harm to Protected Persons and Objects

In section 5.11, the *Manual* discusses on a non-exclusive basis different kinds of precaution that can be taken to reduce the risk of harm to protected persons and objects. Each precaution is discussed in turn in the ensuing paragraphs. Paragraph 5.11.1 addresses the assessment of risks to civilians, noting that this may involve general assessments not necessarily linked to a particular attack, pre-strike assessments, battle damage assessments and other after-action reviews and investigations. The need to learn from such processes and to apply the lessons learned is sensibly mentioned. The important point is then made that a commander's responsibility should not be assessed on the basis of information that only becomes available after the event.

Paragraph 5.11.2 suggests that identifying and designating zones in which military objectives are more likely to be present or in which civilians, protected persons or objects are more likely to be absent may reduce incidental risks. Similarly, paragraph 5.11.3 refers to the possible adjustment of the timing of attacks. These matters are discussed on the basis that such action 'may be appropriate'. Really, the discussion in the *Manual* should go further and explicitly note that in certain circumstances, an attack can only be conducted in compliance with the proportionality rule and thus will only be lawful if the timing of the attack is adjusted so that the expected civilian injuries and/or damage are no longer excessive. The reader must not be left with the impression that if the timing cannot be adjusted, the proportionality rule somehow no longer applies. This is again a risk associated with the failure to acknowledge and operationalise the discreteness of the proportionality and precautions rules.

Paragraph 5.11.4 notes that commanders may decide to cancel or suspend attacks when new information raises concerns as to expected civilian casualties. Acknowledging, rightly, that subordinates will not have the authority to cancel or suspend simply because they disagree with the commander's proportionality assessment, the paragraph properly explains the need to refer up the command chain new information of that sort that comes to light. The *Manual* also correctly notes that subordinates should be understood to have the authority to make decisions required by the law of war. Unhelpfully, however, the *Manual* restricts this authority by adding the words 'in order to effectuate the commander's intent'. Those words should be deleted, as the precautionary obligations apply to all persons who decide upon attacks, and these individuals must of necessity include those who actually undertake them. Moreover, the rule applies irrespective of the commander's intent.

Paragraph 5.11.5 and its subparagraphs describe the obligation to give warnings, adopting the language of Article 57(2)(c) of API and explaining that language in uncontroversial terms. Paragraph 5.11.6 addresses 'weaponeering', i.e. the selection of appropriate weapons, sizes of weapons, aim points etc. to achieve the desired military purpose while minimising civilian risks. An interesting example is given, namely the use of an incendiary weapon to attack biological weapons, thereby preventing the biological agents from adversely affecting the civilian population. As is discussed in Chapter 6, the US made a declaration on ratification of Protocol III to the CCW that would cover such circumstances. States party to the Protocol that made no such statement would only be permitted to use such weapons against such targets in circumstances that comply with Article 2 of the Protocol. Usefully, the paragraph notes that commanders may legitimately decide not to use precision weapons in order to preserve the capability for use on other occasions. This would not, of course, justify an indiscriminate attack on the occasion in question, a point that might usefully be added at the end of the paragraph.

Paragraph 5.11.7 starts with an odd sentence: 'In planning or conducting an attack, the selection of a military objective may reduce the risk of incidental harm.' This sentence again gets matters the wrong way round. An attack that is not directed at a specific military objective is indiscriminate, and thus unlawful. The implication that attacks may be planned or undertaken with no particular military objective in mind is therefore wrong, and the sentence needs to be changed to remove any such implication, for example by referring to the requirement to select. The paragraph then discusses the situation where a choice exists between different military objectives yielding the same military advantage, acknowledging that where 'all other factors are equal' the object to be selected for attack shall be that the attack on which may be expected to cause the least danger to civilian lives and civilian objects. The *Manual* spells out the US view that the rule does not prevent the commander from attacking multiple military objectives; does not prevent the commander from pursuing every military advantage believed to warrant pursuit; does not apply when the choice of targets involves differing risks and benefits potentially yielding differing military advantage; and does not prevent the commander undertaking an attack of a military objective involving higher risk of incidental harm if the attack on that military objective involves a greater likelihood of achieving the military purpose.

Paragraph 5.11.7.1 takes the view that if Article 57(3) of API is interpreted consistently with the foregoing, it can be regarded as reflecting customary law. The present authors take the view that States party to API would indeed interpret Article 57(3) in that way, and that the US stipulations are essentially wrapped up in the Article 57(3) notion of similarity of military advantage, i.e. that military advantage in that provision is to be interpreted broadly.

Proportionality – Prohibition on Attacks Expected to Cause Excessive Incidental Harm

Section 5.12 describes the proportionality rule in language that differs from Article 51(5)(b) of API, which is difficult to understand given that the latter provision is widely accepted as representing customary law. The failure to refer in the definition explicitly to the possibility that a combination of civilian injury and civilian damage might be excessive is unfortunate, but, given the chosen wording and the reference to this aspect in paragraph 5.12.1, is not critical. As noted earlier, the reference to 'expected' military advantage would seem to require a greater probability associated with the military advantage than the API use of the word 'anticipated' implies. Paragraph 5.12.1.1 probably correctly suggests that injury and death of civilians should be given greater consideration than damage to civilian objects, and that damage to cultural property should receive greater consideration than damage to what is described as 'ordinary property', meaning presumably civilian property in general. The *Manual* correctly states that mere inconvenience or disruption to civilian life need not be considered in the proportionality assessment.[2]

Paragraph 5.12.1.3 discusses respectively foreseeable and remote harms, suggesting that expected harms 'mean such immediate or direct harms foreseeably resulting from the attack'. The correct qualifier of the collateral damage to be considered in the proportionality assessment is 'expected'. Many outcomes may be foreseeable but not expected. It is therefore noteworthy that the *Manual* chooses a formulation that would arguably render the proportionality test more restrictive by requiring that outcomes that do not necessarily meet the API criterion of 'expected' must nevertheless be taken into account on the basis that they are capable of being foreseen. The paragraph then refers to the exclusion of what it describes as 'remote harms' from the test. This part of the discussion unnecessarily complicates matters in the view of the present authors. The word 'expected' as used in the widely accepted formulation of the rule should be interpreted by reference to its normal meaning in the English language.[3] Either an outcome is to be expected or it is not, and, it is suggested, more need not be said. As to the examples discussed in the paragraph, economic loss does not fall to be considered simply because it does not amount

[2] DoD *Manual*, paragraph 5.12.1.2.

[3] Vienna Convention on the Law of Treaties, 1969, Article 31.

to death, injury or damage, so its remoteness or otherwise is irrelevant. The *Manual* is right, however, in noting that the consequences of a possible but unexpected munition malfunction do not generally need to be considered.

Paragraph 5.12.2 correctly explains that the military advantage to be gained must be more than hypothetical or speculative but need not be immediate. Based on statements made by a number of States when ratifying API, paragraph 5.12.2.1 rightly asserts that '[t]he military advantage expected from an attack is intended to refer to the advantage gained from the attack considered as a whole, rather than only from isolated or particular parts of an attack', while military advantage is not limited to tactical gains but may be referable to the overall war strategy. The point is then appropriately illustrated using the example of an attack on a communications relay facility.

As paragraph 5.12.3 correctly observes, the notion of excessiveness at the core of the proportionality test involves comparing unlike quantities and values. Reference is properly made both to the requirement for professional military judgment and to the moral and ethical judgments involved in comparing civilians at risk from the attack with civilians or friendly forces at risk if the attack is not undertaken. The paragraph properly refers to the potentially open-ended nature of the inquiry in other than clear-cut cases, pointing to the possibly subjective and imprecise nature of the answer.

As to paragraph 5.12.3.1, the present authors have some difficulty in seeing the proportionality rule as an expression of the notion of 'economy of force'. The former is a core rule of the law of targeting, while the latter is essentially grounded in military doctrine and probably has a more tangible link with the principle of military necessity.

Paragraph 5.12.3.2 argues that 'incidental harm expected to result from strikes in which additional precautions are feasible, but have not been taken, would be more likely to be considered excessive'. This is rather a doubtful proposition. The better view is that either the expected civilian death, injury and/or damage is excessive or it is not. A failure to take feasible precautions renders it more likely that a case in which it is excessive will not be identified before the attack, but it will not retrospectively affect whether an attack was in fact in breach of the proportionality rule. This is another respect in which this blending together of proportionality and precautions leads to potentially misleading interpretations.

Paragraph 5.12.3.3 deals, generally correctly, with the situation of civilians who work on military facilities, noting that by doing so they assume certain risks. However, the reference in the paragraph to 'those determining whether a planned attack would be excessive' should be replaced with language along the lines of 'those determining whether a planned attack would breach the proportionality rule'. The US has frequently and correctly asserted the lawfulness of applying overwhelming force. The issue is not the excessiveness of an attack but the excessiveness of the expected collateral damage by reference to the anticipated military advantage. At the end of the first part of the paragraph, the suggestion is made that those making such determinations 'may consider all relevant facts and circumstances'. The verb used is wrong. They must consider all relevant facts and circumstances: this is an important error that requires correction.

Paragraph 5.12.3.4 deals with the enemy use of human shields. The paragraph properly draws attention to the obligation of the attacking party, notwithstanding the enemy's use of human shields, to undertake feasible precautions. Reference might usefully have been made to API, Article 51(7) and (8). The paragraph correctly states that civilians not taking a direct part in hostilities and who are being used as human shields must be evaluated by the attacking party as civilians, but again refers to the planned attack being excessive when the issue is whether the proportionality rule would be breached. The possibility is offered in the paragraph that voluntary human shields may be regarded by a commander as taking a direct part in the hostilities. It would have been helpful if the paragraph had offered guidance as to the factors that would justify a commander in coming to such a conclusion.